ENVIRONMENTAL PSYCHOLOGY

ENVIRONMENTAL PSYCHOLOGY

THIRD EDITION

PAUL A. BELL
Colorado State University

JEFFREY D. FISHER
University of Connecticut

ANDREW BAUM
Uniformed Services University
of the Health Sciences

THOMAS C. GREENE
St. Lawrence University

Harcourt Brace Jovanovich College Publishers
Fort Worth   Philadelphia   San Diego
New York   Orlando   Austin   San Antonio
Toronto   Montreal   London   Sydney   Tokyo

Publisher	Ted Buchholz
Aquisitions Editor	Eve Howard
Project Editor	Michael D. Hinshaw
Production Manager	Ken Dunaway
Art & Design Supervisor	Vicki McAlindon Horton
Text Designer	Caliber Design Planning, Inc.
Cover Designer	Vicki McAlindon Horton

Library of Congress Cataloging-in-Publication Data

Environmental psychology / Paul A. Bell . . . [et al.].
    p.   cm.
    Rev. ed. of: Environmental psychology / Jeffrey D. Fisher, Paul A.
Bell, Andrew Baum. 2nd ed. © 1984.
    Includes bibliographical references.
    ISBN 0-03-022809-3
    1. Environmental psychology.   I. Fisher, Jeffrey D., 1949–
II. Fisher, Jeffrey D., 1949–   Environmental psychology.
BF353.E58   1990
155.9—dc20   89-71748CIP

Address for editorial correspondence: Harcourt Brace Jovanovich, Inc., 301 Commerce Street, Suite 3700, Fort Worth, Texas 76102

Address for orders: Harcourt Brace Jovanovich, Inc., 6277 Sea Harbor Drive, Orlando, Florida 32887. 1-800-782-4479, or 1-800-433-0001 (in Florida)

PRINTED IN THE UNITED STATES OF AMERICA

  2 3 4 049 10 9 8 7 6 5 4

Harcourt Brace Jovanovich, Inc.
The Dryden Press
Saunders College Publishing

PREFACE

The physical environment affects each of us in profound ways. It can enrich or detract from our lives. We may experience excitement and stimulation when visiting a city or fatigue from too many hours spent at a computer terminal. We may enjoy relaxation from a trip to a park, or annoyance from sitting in a crowded classroom. For many of us a sunny spring day brings feelings of joy; muggy weather listlessness; and rainy cold the "blues."

Just as the physical environment plays an important role in our behavior, almost everything we do has environmental consequences. If we take a Sunday drive, turn the thermostat up, join a crowd, plant a garden, or flush the toilet—we affect our environment.

The field of environmental psychology deals with the reciprocal relationships between humans and their environment. Environmental psychologists study how, and why, this interrelationship manifests itself, and what can be done to enhance its constructive and decrease its destructive consequences. When the first edition of this text appeared in 1978, environmental psychology was a young science with much promise and more questions than answers. It remains young, and there is still much to be learned, but environmental psychologists have made significant contributions to science and society. From the student's perspective, environmental psychology is relevant to everyday life. Our subject is the world around us and the problems we constantly encounter and often cause. The effects of human–environment interactions are concrete, important, and often very personal.

Although we continue to emphasize a social psychological perspective, in revising this edition we have increasingly drawn upon other disciplines and subdisciplines where relevant. We have attempted to create a scholarly, comprehensive, data- and theory-based work that integrates the field, and demonstrates its connections to other disciplines and society. As with the second edition, our goal was to retain the popular format, but to produce a current and scientifically rigorous revision.

We desired to produce a readable book that would help students analyze environmental phenomena in a scientific manner, and that would allow them to understand the field in relation to their own lives. To these ends, we have made every effort to elaborate on empirical research with relevant examples and intriguing paradoxes. Particularly interesting material has been highlighted within boxes. To aid student involvement, each chapter begins with a hypothetical example, and ends with a list of suggested projects. New for this addition are a glossary and lists of important terms. Each of the chapters has received significant content revisions. In particular, the third edition contains new chapters and significantly expanded coverage of spatial cognition and environmental disasters.

The text begins with an introductory chapter which defines the field and presents a brief overview of environment–behavior research methods. Chapters 2 and 3 emphasize the input, storage, and retrieval of environmental information as part of the interrelated processes of sensation, perception, and cognition. We have retained the popular examination of theoretical models of environment–behavior relationships in Chapter 4. The models introduced in this chapter become recurring themes that organize and focus discussion for the balance of the text. The chapter concludes with one working model that integrates the various theoretical approaches to environmental influences on behavior. The next six chapters detail a number of these environmental influences: Chapter 5 is devoted to noise, both as a content area and as a model of environmental stress; Chapter 6 discusses weather and climate; Chapter 7, hazards, disasters, air and water pollution; Chapter 8, personal space and territoriality; Chapter 9, crowding; and Chapter 10, cities. The final four chapters emphasize the actions of humans as they manipulate, adjust, and sometimes degrade the environment. The first of these, Chapter 11, provides a background of the design process, and Chapters 12 and 13 discuss design and behavior in defined settings such as residential environments, hospitals, learning environments, work environments, and recreation areas. Finally, Chapter 14 discusses intervention strategies for modifying our environmentally destructive behaviors and improving our relationship with the environment.

As was true of the first two editions, this book was conceived as a primary text for undergraduate and graduate courses that focus on environment and behavior (e.g., environmental psychology, social ecology, architectural psychology, ecological psychology, and environmental design courses that stress human elements). It can also be used as an adjunct to other more specialized texts in both basic and more advanced courses. In addition, we view *Environmental Psychology* as a resource manual of empirical theoretical work in the field for practitioners and researchers. Writing this book has taught us a great deal, helped to organize our thoughts, and given us an opportunity to examine our field critically and constructively. We hope that we have conveyed the excitement we feel for the field, and that our readers will share our enthusiasm. As in the past, we invite you to send your comments to us.

ACKNOWLEDGEMENTS

Revising this text has only been possible with the assistance of many individuals. We wish to recognize the dedication of the editorial staff at Holt, Rinehart and Winston who contributed their efforts to the project: acquisitions editor Eve Howard, editorial assistant John Haley, and Karee Galloway, assistant editor. Mike Hinshaw, project editor, and Ken Dunaway, production manager, contributed months of unending effort to get the initial manuscript into final print.

We are also grateful for the ideas and suggestions of our reviewers, Sherry Ahrentzen, Jack Aiello, Carl Hummell, John Keating, Paul Paulus, Jim Rotton, Eric Sundstrom, Ralph Taylor, F. Phillip Van Eyl, Abe Wandersman, George Whitehead, and Evan Zucker.

We again thank Ross Loomis for the use of his material from the first edition.

Some of the individuals who helped with photocopying, library work, mailing, proofreading, and all the "little" things that must be done in various phases of the manuscript preparation include Peggy Brechtel, Elizabeth Brent, Craig Colder, Cheryl Connelly, Virginia Goold, Joseph Hopper, Bonnie Hughes, Birgit Kaufmann, Diane Kimble, Barbara Knight, Lauren Maggi, Joelle Truman, Alicia Tucker, and Carol Valone.

Many of these tasks were accomplished with the assistance of our wives, Patty, Allison, Carrie, and Mela, who also contributed encouragement and tolerance. As with the past editions, we thank our family and friends for their patient understanding when they asked us to do something and we said—once again—that we had to work on "the book"! That is one of the many reasons why we have chosen to dedicate this edition to our significant others.

P. A. B.
J. D. F.
A. B.
T. C. G.

CONTENTS

1

THE WHY, WHAT, AND HOW OF ENVIRONMENTAL PSYCHOLOGY

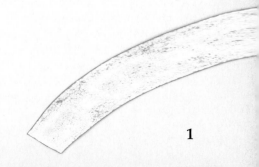

KEY TERMS

accretion measure
archival data
behavior mapping
behavior setting
correlational research
dependent variable
descriptive research
environment
environmental psychology
experiential realism
experimental method
external validity

hodometer
independent variable
informed consent
internal validity
invasion of privacy
observation
random assignment
self-report measures
setting
simulation
unobtrusive measures

WHY STUDY ENVIRONMENTAL PSYCHOLOGY?

Our **environment,** which includes all of our natural and built surroundings, is a delicately balanced system that can easily be bruised or damaged. Whenever we change some part of it, other parts also change, and these other changes may be unintended or even dangerous. Concerns about what we were doing to our environment, having reached unprecedented prominence in the 1960s, have recently resurfaced as some of the consequences of years of neglect have become apparent. The depletion of the ozone layer of the atmosphere, reports of hospital waste washing up on beaches, and discussions of the greenhouse effect and changing climatic conditions reflect these problems. In truth, we have done much to remedy the damage we have done to the environment and have taken steps to prevent some new problems. Yet, the pollution of our air and water, increasing energy use, crowding, noise, toxic accidents, and other environmental

problems continue (see figures 1-1 – 1-5). What more can be done to deal with the situation?

Environmental psychology is a field of study that has evolved to provide some answers to this question. For example, some environmental problems are almost always human-made. Air pollution, a common problem in large cities, is one of these problems, and because human behavior causes it, it is plausible that the best ways to curb or eliminate it will involve modification of behavior. Principles of learning, motivation, perception, attitude formation, and social interaction help explain why we ever engaged in and accepted pollution in the first place. Principles of developmental psychology, social psychology, abnormal psychology, and physiological psychology help explain the deleterious effects of pollution on humans. Furthermore, research on attitude change, behavior modification, social behavior, and personality can suggest some

problem in the earth

Figure 1–1   Among its many unpleasant effects, air pollution can interfere with our enjoyment of scenic vistas. However, visibility across a landscape scene depends not just on pollution levels, but also on such factors as the angle of the sun and the contrast between atmospheric and landscape features.

Figure 1–2   In March, 1979, an accident struck the Three Mile Island nuclear power plant, causing 400,000 gallons of radioactive water to collect in the containment building. More than a year later, unhealthy psychological reactions attributable to the accident were still apparent in some residents of the area. In some ways, these reactions resemble the responses victims have to natural disasters, but in other ways they do not. (Marc A. Schaeffer)

Figure 1-3   Approximately 52 percent of petroleum use in the United States is for transportation. Of that amount, approximately 43 percent is consumed by automobile travel. Although behavioral techniques can be used to increase ridership on mass transit, both private automobile and mass transit forms of commuting are associated with various types of stress reactions. (Courtesy of John L. Rundell, Jr.)

steps that will be necessary to change behavior in order to reduce or eliminate pollution.

Environmental psychologists also study how environments affect people. The design of buildings, once primarily concerned with how they looked, now includes considerations of how they affect people who use them. Principles of crowding, privacy, personal space, and environmental perception, as well as noise, temperature, air circulation, and cost may all be factors in how a building is designed and how well it serves its intended function. College dormitories may now be designed to accommodate the social needs of students as well as more traditional concerns such as cheap housing for large

Figure 1-4   Crowding has been shown to be detrimental to humans in certain situations, but not in others. With animals, the negative effects of high density are much more uniform.

Figure 1–5A   The design of some dormitories and housing projects has been associated with withdrawal in social relationships and may encourage some forms of maladjustment.

Figure 1–5B   Other designs, however, seem to foster healthier forms of human interaction.

numbers and control of noise. Similarly, design of housing projects, racked by major failures 20 years ago, may now include a range of behavioral criteria.

In the process of suggesting possible solutions for environmental problems, psychologists are gaining considerable practical knowledge about relationships between behavior and environment as well as gaining invaluable information about conceptual or theoretical models of human behavior. For this reason, environmental psychology not only is practical but also provides a meaningful focus of traditional psychological disciplines.

The tendency to picture environmental psychology as an applied field is due, in part, to the fact that many of the things environmental psychologists study are chosen because they are problems or opportunities to improve some aspect of our management of our surroundings.

However, research in a number of areas, as well as the development of theories to describe behavior across different situations (see Chapter 4), reflects the fact that environmental psychology is also concerned with building basic knowledge of human behavior and how it interacts with the environment.

In this chapter, we will talk about many different things. First, we must define our field and consider its characteristic approach and basic assumptions. Environmental psychology is distinctive in many ways, and these factors shape the methods that can be used to study environment–behavior relationships.

Hence, we will also discuss methodological issues: How does one go about studying the processes and problems encompassed by environmental psychology? Many obstacles to reliable study of these phenomena are difficult to overcome, and designing and adapting procedures and measures to do so is one of the field's most challenging aspects. Finally, we will discuss some ethical issues associated with the field and preview the content areas to be discussed in the rest of the book.

WHAT IS ENVIRONMENTAL PSYCHOLOGY?

Definitions of Environmental Psychology

The preceding rationale for environmental psychology should convince you that the field offers present-day relevance for the discipline of psychology as well as the exciting possibility of a unique perspective on environmental problems. Yet this rationale does not really *define* "environmental psychology." Like most areas of psychology, it is easier to list what environmental psychologists do than to define the field.

Early definitions of environmental psychology emphasized the relationship between behavior and the physical environment, as in Heimstra and McFarling's (1978) definition of the field as the discipline concerned with relationships between behavior and the physical environment or Proshansky's (1976) characterization of the field as "the attempt to establish empirical and theoretical relationships between the behavior and experience of the person and his built environment" (p. 303). More recent definitions, though somewhat more inclusive, are essentially the same. In the *Handbook of Environmental Psychology*, Stokols and Altman (1987) define the field as "the study of human behavior and well-being in relation to the sociophysical environment" (p. 1). Similarly, Russell and Snodgrass (1987) define environmental psychology as the "branch of psychology concerned with providing a systematic account of the relationship between a person and the environment" (p. 245).

These definitions provide us with a general idea of what environmental psychology is, but are so general that they could conceivably include many other areas of psychology. For example, conceptualizing the field as the study of the relationships between environment and behavior suggests that learning, perception, and sensation (to name but a few possibilities) are a focal part of the field. To be sure, these areas of psychology describe relationships between environmental and behavioral variables. They are not, however, central to what we mean by environmental psychology. In addition, such definitions do not emphasize the bidirectional nature of environment–behavior relationships: Environments affect behavior and behavior affects environments. Limiting definitions to the relationships between behavior and the *built* environment is also unsatisfactory because it omits the non-built environment (e.g., the natural landscape).

Our definitional dilemma should be clear by now: How do we define environmental psychology narrowly enough so that we do not include areas that environmental psychologists would agree are not part of the field, yet broadly enough to include all the topics that environmental psychologists would insist are part of it? One option is to define the field operationally: Environmental psychology is what environmental psychologist do (Proshanky, Ittleson, & Rivlin, 1970). We would then proceed to describe the areas studied by environmental psychologists and the research methods they employ (which we will do in a moment). However, if forced into a corner at pencil-point by students demanding to know what answer to give to the test question, ''Define environmental psychology in 25 words or less,'' we would hazard the following definition, with all its potential shortcomings: **Environmental psychology** is the study of the interrelationship between behavior and experience and the built and natural environment. We will now describe certain characteristics of environmental psychology that make the field unique and further delimit its scope.

Characteristics of Environmental Psychology

The primary distinction between environmental psychology and other fields of psychology is the perspective it takes in studying its subject matter. We shall describe some characteristics of this perspective, drawing on several sources (e.g., Altman, 1976a; Ittleson et al., 1974; Proshansky, 1976b; Wohlwill, 1970). This list of characteristics is by no means exhaustive but

simply reflects the unique perspective of the field.

First and foremost is an emphasis on studying environment–behavior relationships as a unit, rather than separating them into supposedly distinct and self-contained components. Traditional approaches to the study of sensation and perception assume that environmental stimuli are distinct from each other and that the perception (or response to) the stimulus, being distinct from the stimulus itself, can be studied somewhat independently of it. This assumption is the basis of the reductionism characterizing much of American psychology. Environmental psychology looks upon the stimulus and its perception as a unit that contains more than just a stimulus and a response. The stimulus–response perceptual relationship between an urban landscape and an urban inhabitant, for example, depends not just upon the individual stimuli in the landscape. It also depends upon the patterning, complexity, novelty, and movement of the contents of the landscape and upon the past experience of the perceiver (e.g., whether he or she is a long-time resident or a newcomer), his or her ability to impose structure on the landscape, his or her auditory and olfactory associations with the landscape, and his or her personality characteristics. In environmental psychology, *all* these things make up one holistic environmental–perceptual behavior unit. Like Gestalt psychology, which influenced American psychology during the mid-twentieth century, the whole is greater than the simple sum of its parts.

To use another example, to the environmental psychologist an overcrowded dining hall consists not just of separate episodes of people getting in each other's way, but of a physical **setting** containing a high density of people who interact with each other and with the physical setting in very predictable ways, and who experience certain pleasant and unpleasant consequences of these conditions (Figure 1–6). Thus, the environmental setting constrains (limits, influences, and even determines) the behavior that occurs in it. Furthermore, as the

Figure 1–6 To the environmental psychologist, this crowded dining hall consists not just of separate episodes of people getting in each other's way. It is a physical setting containing a high density of people who interact with each other and with the environment in very predictable ways, who experience certain pleasant and unpleasant emotional states, and who anticipate consequences of these conditions.

occupants of this setting move about, they change some aspects of the environment and of their experience of crowding. If the behavior is studied in isolation, separate from these particular environmental conditions, the conclusions derived from the studying process will inevitably be limited. The environment cannot be studied separately from the behavior, and the behavior cannot be studied separately from the environment, without losing valuable information. This does not mean that environmental psychologists never take a close look at a particular environment–behavior relationship in a laboratory setting, but it does mean they assume from the beginning that such dissection of an integral unit cannot tell the whole story.

Another assumption underlying environmental psychology is that environment–behavior relationships are really *inter*relationships: The environment influences and constrains behavior, but behavior also leads to changes in the environment. Consider the issue of energy resources and pollution. The availability of certain energy sources in the environment determines whether certain types of energy-consuming behavior will occur, but that behav-

ior in turn determines the type of pollution that will result. Oil shortages may increase conservation and affect many aspects of one's lifestyle, which in turn may lead to a reliance on other forms of energy, to new forms of pollution, and so on. With continued consumption, energy resources are differentially affected, and this in turn can shift consumption patterns. Note that this example also demonstrates that environment–behavior relationships need to be studied as units in order to see the whole picture.

Environmental psychology also is less likely to draw sharp distinctions between applied and basic research than are other areas in psychology. Other fields of psychology engage in theoretical or basic research as the primary means of understanding behavior. The major goal of such research is to gain knowledge about the subject matter through discovering cause–effect relationships and building theories. If such research also leads to the solution of a practical problem, which it often does, that is well and good, but a practical application is not necessarily a goal of that research. Applied research, on the other hand, is intended from the start to solve a practical problem, and it is valued not for its theoretical relevance but for its specific utility. Theory building may result from applied research, but is not its primary focus.

In contrast, environmental psychology usually undertakes a given piece of research for both applied and theoretical purposes at the same time. That is, almost all research in environmental psychology is *problem-oriented* or intended to be relevant to the solution of some practical issue, and the cause–effect relationships and theoretical material evolve from this focus. Research areas, such as the effects of pollution on behavior, changing environmentally destructive behavior, and the design of environments for efficient human use, are concerned with applications and practical matters, yet much of the factual content and theoretical underpinnings of environmental psychology derive directly from this type of research. The assumption of environmental psychologists that environment–behavior relationships must be studied as a unit within their natural contexts precludes, in a way, the distinction between applied and theoretical research. Once again, this does not mean that environmental psychologists cannot take a practical problem into the laboratory for controlled study, but it does mean that the laboratory research of an environmental psychologist is oriented toward solving real-world problems (Figure 1–7).

Environmental psychology is part of an interdisciplinary field of study of environment and behavior. Environmental perception, with its emphasis on the perception of a whole scene, is relevant to the work of landscape architects, urban planners, builders, and others in related fields. The study of the effects of the physical environment (noise, heat, and space) on behavior is relevant to the interests of industrialists, lawyers, architects, and prison, hospital, and school officials. The design of environments is of concern not only to architects and designers but also to anthropologists, museum curators,

Figure 1–7   The laboratory research of environmental psychologists is oriented toward solving real-world problems. In this photograph, a researcher is studying the effects of noise on concentration and performance.

traffic controllers, and office managers, to name but a few. Moreover, changing environmentally destructive behavior is of concern to everyone who is aware of the dangers of pollution, urban blight, and limited natural resources. Perhaps the need for this type of interdisciplinary perspective is reflected in the growth of related fields, such as urban sociology, social biology, behavioral geography, urban anthropology, and recreation and leisure planning. Throughout this text we will draw on these and other disciplines in order to explain environmental-psychological phenomena.

In summary, environmental psychology is characterized by the following: (1) study of environment–behavior relationships as a unit; (2) study of the interrelationships of environment and behavior; (3) a relative lack of distinction between applied and theoretical research; (4) an interdisciplinary appeal; (5) as we will see, an eclectic methodology. Let us turn now to a description of the methodology of environmental psychology.

Where Did Environmental Psychology Come From?

The scientific study of the relationships between environment and behavior can be traced back to studies in the dawning years of this century (e.g., Gulliver, 1908; Trowbridge, 1913). Nineteenth-century psychologists had begun to study human perception of environmental stimuli such as light, sound, weight, pressure, and so on, and emphasis on learning and the advent of behaviorism led to intensive study of such environmental events as reinforcement schedules and early childhood experience. By the 1940s, a modest amount of research on environment–behavior links had been reported, including early work in behavioral geography, the psychology of cognitive maps of environments, and urban sociology (Moore, 1987). However, these studies did not systematically approach the interaction of environment and behavior in its fullest sense. The studies of how design factors affect the development of social relationships among students reported by Festinger, Schachter, and Back (1950) represent a turning point in the development of systematic study of environment and behavior.

During the 1950s, work in this area slowly increased. Lewin (1951) had conceptualized the environment as a key determinant of behavior, and even though his emphasis was primarily on the social environment, the importance of his theory for environmental psychology is often discussed. Barker and his colleagues compiled extensive systematic research on environment and behavior relationships during this period, examining effects of environments on the behavior of children, comparing behavior in small towns and in schools (Barker & Gump, 1964; Barker & Wright, 1951, 1955). Research on spatial behavior, psychiatric ward design, and other aspects of environment–behavior relationships also developed during this period (e.g., Hall, 1959; Osmond, 1957). Architects and behavioral scientists began what has become a long-standing collaboration in an effort to achieve another objective: designing buildings to facilitate behavioral functions.

Other lines of work have also fed into the present field of environmental psychology. Already noted work by Barker on ecological psychology (see box, p. 15) emphasized the ways in which the entire environment influences the types of behavior that will occur within it, and work by E. T. Hall (1959, 1966) in *proxemics,* or how we use space, as well as the work of researchers interested in the effects of crowding (Calhoun, 1962, 1964) have stimulated volumes of research on these areas of human–environment interaction. Research in environmental psychology in the U.S., Canada, Europe, and Japan began to flourish, and other work in perception and cognition played a significant role in environmental psychology as well. With the advent of concerns over energy use and preservation of the natural environment, more and more researchers are looking into ways of changing our wasteful and destructive practices of interacting with the environment.

By the mid-1970s, these developments led a few psychology

departments to offer formal programs of study in environmental psychology, and many more departments began to offer courses with that title. Textbooks on the subject emerged, journals devoted to the field (such as *Environment and Behavior* and the *Journal of Environmental Psychology*) were started, and organizations such as the Environmental Design Research Association and the Association for the Study of Man–Environment Relations were formed. The American Psychological Association has officially recognized environmental psychology (in conjunction with population psychology) as one of its divisions, and international societies, such as the International Association for the Study of People and Their Surroundings, have become active.

HOW IS RESEARCH IN ENVIRONMENTAL PSYCHOLOGY DONE?

Are environmental psychologists and other psychologists similar or different in the way they view research? As mentioned earlier, two unique qualities of environmental psychology are that it studies environment–behavior relationships as whole units and that it takes a more applied focus than other areas of psychology. These qualities affect environmental psychologists' approaches to research in several ways. Most important is the fact that they tend to conduct research in the actual setting that concerns them and thereby preserve the integrity of that setting (Patterson, 1977; Proshansky, 1972; Winkel, 1987). Thus, they are more inclined to use techniques that take them to field settings rather than to abstract important aspects of reality for study in the laboratory, as is typical of many research psychologists.

Research Methods in Environmental Psychology

Basically, environmental psychologists have the same "arsenal" of research methods as other psychologists; they just use it somewhat differently. What does the arsenal include? It includes experimental methods, correlational methods, and descriptive methods. We will describe each of these techniques, first noting general strengths and weaknesses and then evaluating their appropriateness for research in environmental psychology. It will become apparent that, owing to the different research values held by environmental psychologists, their choice of methods frequently differs from that of other psychologists. The description of their methods is brief and introductory and should give you enough background to understand the methodological issues in the rest of the text.

Experimental Research   Only one methodology allows researchers to identify with certainty the variable that is causing the effects they observe in an experiment. It is called the **experimental method**. In the experimental method, the researcher systematically varies an **independent variable** (e.g., heat) and measures the effect on a **dependent variable** (e.g., performance). Two forms of control are used in experimental research. First, only the independent variable is allowed to differ between experimental conditions, so that all other aspects of the situation are the same for all experimental conditions. When variables other than the ones being studied also vary across different conditions, they are considered confounds. Second, subjects are **randomly assigned** to experimental treatments. This makes it improbable (with a sufficient number of subjects) that differences between treatment conditions are caused by factors other than the independent manipulation (e.g., different personality types). That is, good experiments are high in **internal validity**. Experimental methodologies may be used in both laboratory and field settings, although it is clearly more difficult to manipulate variables and establish controls in the field.

While experimental methodologies have predominated in most areas of psychology, they have not dominated research in environmental psychology to the same extent. Although the fact that they permit causal inference is an advantage, for environmental psychologists the liabilities of experimental methods frequently outweigh their benefits. One problem is that the degree of control required often creates an artificial situation, which destroys the integrity of the setting. This makes findings from these studies less generalizable to the real world; that is, it reduces **external validity**. Further, it frequently is possible to maintain the control necessary for an experiment only over a brief period, which makes most experimental studies short-term. Since many environmentally-caused effects do not manifest themselves over a short term, this is a problem.

However, experimental studies in the laboratory can be useful in studying environmental issues. For example, as we will see in Chapter 5, Glass and Singer (1972) used artificial laboratory conditions to specify some of the psychological aspects of exposure to noise and were able to discover relationships that would

have been difficult if not impossible to find in field studies or nonexperimental investigations. In these studies, subjects in a laboratory were exposed to predictable and unpredictable noise, and some were provided with a sense of control over the noise by virtue of having a way to shut off the noise if they wished. Predictable noise had few negative effects on subjects, while unpredictable noise had several effects. More important, the sense of control attenuated the negative consequences of unpredictable noise. The nature of this phenomenon and the need to isolate individual causes made laboratory experimental study the only feasible way to study these relationships.

An alternate approach to experimental laboratory techniques is to conduct field experiments. By transferring many aspects of experimental science to a field setting, we can increase realism and generalizability and still have enough control over the variables we are studying to be able to derive causal relationships. Subjects are still randomly assigned to conditions, and manipulation of independent variables is done by the experimenter. Field experiments, however, are difficult to set up and often are a little artificial, as conditions must be manipulated in order to study whatever is of interest. Artificiality reduces **experiential realism**.

An example of the value of field experimentation is provided by a study of territoriality conducted by Edney (1975). In general, research on territoriality has been difficult to carry out in the laboratory, because it requires the experimenter to induce feelings of ownership in subjects. Since territoriality already exists in one's home environment, Edney decided to run a field experiment using students' dormitory rooms as the laboratory. He randomly assigned half the subjects to their own room (the ''resident'' condition) and half to the rooms of other students as ''visitors.'' Subjects performed a variety of tasks within this context. The results, reviewed in more detail in Chapter 8, showed that people experience more control when on their home ground than when visiting the territory of another, and perceive their own territory as more pleasant and private. More important for our present purposes is that Edney successfully used a naturalistic setting to observe an environmental phenomenon and to study its effects in a systematic, causal manner. Because subjects were randomly assigned (i.e., to resident and visitor conditions), a degree of control was established over extraneous variables. Experiential realism and external validity were enhanced by the field setting, so this study represents the best of both experimental and field research.

For a variety of reasons, researchers are often unable to do research in the field. The appropriate settings may not be available, the logistics of doing a field study may be too great, or sufficient control may not be attainable. Some researchers have responded by using **simulation** methods, by introducing components of a real environment into an artificial setting. By simulating the essential elements of a naturalist setting in a laboratory, experiential realism and external validity are increased, and some experimental rigor is retained.

Simulation techniques are useful for studying aspects of human–environment behavior other than crowding. One area of environmental psychology, discussed in Chapter 2, is concerned with how people perceive their environment and what factors affect their preference for various settings. Clearly, it would be impractical to study these phenomena by driving subjects around to a variety of places and having them make ratings; yet, at the Berkeley Environmental Simulation Laboratory, people can be "driven through" suburban neighborhoods or urban blocks by means of a large-scale environmental simulator (McKechnie, 1977). One of the elements in the lab consists of a scale replica of the environment placed on a large platform. Suspended overhead is a gantry on which a camera can move in any direction and give the viewer an "eye-level" perspective while moving around the model. With the increased sophistication of computers and computer-aided design systems, sophisticated simulations using computer graphic representations of various environments for research purposes should not be far in the future.

A more conventional means to experimentally view the natural environment is by showing subjects photographic slides of a wide range of settings. In such a simulation, researchers might vary the complexity of urban and rural slides (Herzog & Smith, 1988; Kaplan, 1974; Wohlwill, 1976) that subjects are asked to rate. This would provide information about how complexity affects preference in urban and rural contexts. Overall, slides offer several advantages as a simulation of the real environment: They are easy to present to a small or large group, they are inexpensive to produce and obtain, and they allow a wide variety of scenes to be shown at one time.

Correlational Research   In **correlational research** the experimenter does not or cannot manipulate aspects of the situation and cannot randomly assign subjects to various conditions. In this method, the relationship between *naturally occurring* situational variations and some other variable can be assessed through careful observation of both. Assume that a researcher wants to compare responses to high and low density in a department store (Figure 1–8). By observing the naturally occurring variations in density and shopping behavior, he or she can make a statement about whether changes in one are related to changes in the other. However, since density is not manipulated and the type of control characteristic of experimental studies is not exercised, a causal inference cannot be made. By not being able to randomly assign people to shop at times when density is high and low, one cannot rule out the possibility that the observed relationship between density and shopping behavior may be caused by a third variable; for example, it might be because a different type of person shops during busy and slack hours. Further, without an experiment,

Figure 1–8A & 8B   If we use the correlational method to study the relationship between density of shoppers and shopping behavior, we cannot be certain that density *causes* differences in behavior. To infer cause and effect, we need to use the experimental method.

we know nothing about the *direction* of a relationship between two variables (i.e., we are unsure which variable is the antecedent and which is the consequent). Thus, correlational methods are relatively low in internal validity.

Although correlational methods are clearly inferior to experimental methods in terms of ability to explain the "why" of a reaction to environmental conditions, they offer certain plus factors for the environmental psychologist. First, it is impossible or unethical to manipulate many environmental conditions that are studied, making experimental research out of the question. When this is the case, such as in studies of disasters, correlational research may be the best way to examine relationships between environmental events and behavior. Second, correlational methods permit the experimenter to use the natural, everyday environment as a laboratory. In such research, artificiality is not a problem, and generalizability—or external validity—is greater. What types of correlational research are done by environmental psychologists? Two groups of studies can be identified. One group determines the association between naturally occurring environmental change (e.g., natural disasters) and the behavior of those in the setting. Another group assesses relationships between environmental conditions and archival data (e.g., the relationship between housing density and crime rate).

Descriptive Research   Experimental studies provide causal information, and correlational research tells us if relationships exist between variables. **Descriptive research** simply reports reactions that occur in a particular situation. Since such research is not constrained by a need to infer causality or association and often need not generalize to other settings, it can be quite flexible. The main requirement of descriptive research, as with all research, is that measurements be valid (i.e., they should measure what they profess to measure) and reliable (i.e., they should occur again if repeated). Under these conditions, we can assume the results are an accurate representation of reality.

In general, descriptive techniques are used more frequently in environmental psychology than in other areas of psychology. Their use is prompted to a large extent by the developing state of the field and partly by the phenomena being studied. As Proshansky (1972, p. 455) has stated, the environmental psychologist "must be [concerned at this point] with searching out the dimensions and more specific properties of phenomena involving human behavior in relation to physical settings." Thus, we must often answer such basic questions as, "What are the patterns of space utilization?" before using more sophisticated methodologies to test for underlying causes. In other words, descriptive research may be needed to establish

Barker's Behavior Settings: One
Example of Descriptive Research

Probably the most extensive program of descriptive research ever done by an environmental psychologist was performed by Roger Barker. Barker's research centers around the concept of **behavior settings,** which he describes as public places (e.g., churches) or occasions (e.g., auctions) that evoke their own typical patterns of behavior. Barker feels the behavior setting is the basic "environmental unit" and that research which describes behavior settings in detail "identifies discriminable phenomena external to any individual's behavior" (Barker, 1968, p. 13) that have an important bearing on it.

Fourteen years of such descriptive research were summarized in the book *The Qualities of Community Life* (Barker & Schoggen, 1973). Here, the behavior settings of two towns, "Midwest" (located in the midwestern United States, with a population of 830) and "Yoredale" (located in England with a population of 1310), were detailed. The descriptions are based on the reports of trained observers. Some of their findings are quite interesting and certainly tell us something about the character of the two towns. For example, Midwest had twice as many behavior settings involving public expression of emotions, and the structure of the settings provided children in Midwest with 14 times as much public attention as Yoredale children. Religious behavior settings also were more prominent in Midwest than in Yoredale, as were educational-government settings. However, in Yoredale, more time was spent in behavior settings related to physical health and art. We will describe Barker's behavior setting approach in more detail in Chapter 4.

---

behaviors that occur in a particular setting, so that they can then be studied in other ways. Descriptive research done by environmental psychologists includes studies of people's movements in physical settings, studies of the ways people perceive cities, and studies of how people spend their time in various settings. (For an example of this type of descriptive study, see the preceding box). Two types of descriptive research that are becoming increasingly important are environmental quality assessment and user satisfaction studies, in which environments are evaluated in terms of satisfaction or other characteristics by people who use them. For the most part these studies rely on asking people about their needs, quality of life, and satisfaction. However, there are a number of different measurement techniques that are used in re-search employing experimental, correlational, and descriptive methods.

Data Collection Methods

Many of the ways in which environmental psychologists measure variables that they are studying are common in all areas of psychology. Other methods are more eclectic, borrowing from several fields, and a few measurement strategies are more or less specific to environmental psychology. The important thing to keep in mind when evaluating and choosing different data collection methods is that the assessment of behavior, mood, or response to environmental conditions should be as unobtrusive as possible. Measuring response to a situation should not change the way the setting is perceived. Ideally, subjects should not be aware of what you are measuring or when you are measuring it. This is not always possible and many measurement strategies have evolved.

Self-report measures The most obvious way to measure moods, thoughts, attitudes, and behavior is to ask subjects how they feel, what they are thinking, or what they do or have done. By interviewing subjects, having them answer questionnaires, and using projective techniques, a great deal of important information can be obtained. Thus, if you are interested in the effects of noise on mood, you might ask subjects living in noisy and quiet areas how they feel during noisy periods, all of the time, or in whatever frame of reference you are investigating. The directness of measurement inherent in this technique is a clear advantage, but several problems characterize self-report as well.

First, **self-report measures** require that what you are assessing is something of which subjects are aware. These measures are also influenced by subjects' interpretations, and there are a number of sources of bias here. In the event that you are studying controversial issues, such as the impact of building high-level nuclear waste depositories near communities, self-reports may reflect more than just how people feel or what they think. If you ask people if construction of such a depository would cause them to feel anxious or stressed, their responses could reflect their true feelings or their preferences for construction: People who are opposed to the project might believe that if they say they would feel very anxious and stressed, the construction might not occur. Conversely, people in favor of the project could minimize negative mood to bolster the likelihood of construction. For such a case the responses collected might not reflect mood as much as people's "votes" for or against the project.

Another problem is that people may not interpret questions or response options in the same ways. The ways in which concepts are understood or defined may vary, resulting in misleading answers to questions that the researcher thinks are clear. In crowding studies, for instance, researchers frequently ask subjects if they feel crowded or to rate how crowded they feel. The value of doing this is dependent on all people having similar definitions of crowding. However, Mandel, Baron, and Fisher (1980) found that this is not the case, and that men and women differ in their notions of crowding. When given a choice between two definitions of crowding, one dealing with there being too many people in a setting and the other dealing with there not being enough space, men chose evenly, while women were more likely to choose the definition emphasizing numbers of people. Thus, subjects responding to self-report measures may have different ideas from the experimenter about what questions and answers mean, and may differ from one another in these interpretations as well.

Regardless of these problems, self-report measures are often the only way to collect certain types of data, and as a result, effort has been directed toward minimizing these and other sources of bias. One way to do this is to develop measures that are standardized, or for which norms are available. Standardization of questionnaires or surveys is done by testing them on several different samples to estimate how people respond to them; these norms or estimates of "normal" responding can then be used for comparison to unique samples to which these instruments are administered. Thus, symptom checklists such as the Symptom Checklist 90 (SCL-90) (Derogatis, 1977) were given to several different samples and norms developed so that responses of subjects in a specific study can be compared to how people in different types of groups typically respond. Finding that symptom reports of people living in crowded urban areas approximate those of psychiatric inpatients, while those of uncrowded subjects are more like "normal" nonpatient responses, tells us more than just that crowded people report more symptoms than do people who are not crowded. It also gives us an idea of how intense their discomfort may be and whether it is enough of a problem to require some action.

The most common ways of collecting self-report data are by constructing and administering questionnaires and by interviewing people. Questionnaires are easy to administer and relatively inexpensive to produce and distribute, require little skill to administer, can be given to large numbers of subjects at a time, and can accommodate people's desire for anonymity by not requiring subjects to give their names. However, it requires a great deal of experience and many validation studies to construct a good questionnaire, so many researchers opt to use questionnaires constructed by others. One advantage to this is obvious; the questionnaire has already been used in other studies so we have an idea of how good it is. However, scales such as the Perceived Stress Scale (Cohen, Kamarck, & Mermelstein, 1983) or Moos and Gerst's (1974) University Residence Environment Scale will only be useful if they measure concepts that you are also trying to study.

Interviews are not used as often as are questionnaires, partly because they are more costly and time consuming. Ordinarily, it will take longer for subjects to participate in interviews than to complete questionnaires, and only one subject can be interviewed at a time. As with questionnaires, skill and experience are needed to construct questions and code responses in interviews. However, when using interviews, subjects can be asked to explain inconsistencies in responses or expand on their answers. People may also be more likely to voice honest opinions than when asked to write them down.

Another form of self-report measure is cognitive mapping, which is used to create ''maps of the mind.'' Through a variety of procedures, described in Chapter 3, such images are transposed to paper. Cognitive maps are extremely valuable to researchers as a means of understanding how people code spatial information about their everyday environment. In addition to examining the mapping of city environments,

studies have looked at how college campuses, local neighborhoods, and even nations are perceived. Through the use of these techniques, perceptions of various demographic groups can be measured and compared, and factors that afford qualitatively different perceptions can be identified.

Observational Techniques   A major measurement technique in environmental psychology, probably second in use only to questionnaires, is direct **observation.** In this method, people watch others and report their behavior and interactions in a given setting. This technique can take many forms, ranging from informal observation of an environment, to a recorded narrative of what is seen, or to structured observation in which areas of the setting are preselected and particular behaviors are recorded on special coding forms (see Lofland, 1973). The advantage of observational methods over other techniques is the opportunity to gain first-hand knowledge of the way people behave in natural settings (see box, p. 15).

Unlike self-report measures, which assume subjects are able to express themselves, observational methods measure actions people may not even be aware they are performing. They can also be used with those who are unable to communicate their thoughts, such as young children and the severely mentally retarded. Since they may be used without the subject's knowledge, they minimize responses that are the result of people knowing they are being watched.

Observational methods have a number of disadvantages as well. One is that human error may be made in coding behavior. For example, misidentifying one behavior for another, or being unable to code all the activity because it is occurring too quickly, can damage a study. The researcher using observational methods must also interpret the behaviors that are seen, and his or her interpretation may not be the same as the purpose of the behavior for the people being observed. Observational methods are also time-dependent, which means that the investigator must be present when the behavior under study is taking place. This can often be inconvenient and time consuming, especially for behaviors that are infrequent. Some of these problems can be alleviated through the use of instrumentation (e.g., photographic equipment), but errors in coding and inferences based on them pose problems. However, use of these methods can yield valuable information as seen in the box, page 19.

If you are interested in how people react when the distance between them and others is small, you could ask people how they would react or how much space they would want. A better way to study this is to observe people under varying conditions in which they are close to others, recording whether they move away, how much they look at, talk with, or touch other people, and how far they stand or sit from others (e.g., Caudill & Aiello, 1979; Fagan & Aiello, 1982; Greenbaum & Rosenfeld, 1978). While it is possible that subjects could estimate how far away they might sit or whether they would leave, it is less likely that they could report how much eye contact or touching they might exhibit. Since these behaviors are important aspects of how people use space, an observational study is probably better in this case.

There are times when human observation is not the most productive, economical, or feasible way to collect data. Behavioral events may be sporadic, taxing the attention of the observer and wasting time in long waits with little opportunity to collect data (Lozar, 1974). The area being observed may be too large for one or even several individuals to cover. In these cases, the researcher must either create a device that will do the job or choose from available instruments.

One type of instrumentation that functions quite well as a surrogate observer is photographic equipment. With increasing availability of photographic supplies at reasonable cost, photographs and videotapes are being widely used by researchers. These media preserve records of the environment and events in it for future reference. They may be viewed repeatedly, even for different purposes and different studies.

Davis and Ayers (1975) listed a number of uses for photographs. They may be used to inventory the physical environment, as when Hansen and Altman (1976) used photographic records of dormitory room walls to code the types of posters and the extent to which the walls were covered. Photographic techniques also offer the investigator a means of counting the number of occurrences of a behavior of the people in a given setting. In one study, Preiser (1973) videotaped a large suburban shopping center and later coded the tape to determine the number of persons in particular areas. Photography can be used to identify and investigate selected details of activity, as was done in a

Figure 1–9   Output from a hodometer. This device measures locomotion through areas by using pressure-sensitive foot pads attached to recording devices. (From Srivastava, R., and Peel, T. Human movement as a function of color stimulation, Environmental Research and Development Foundation, 1968. Figure 4, p. 25.)

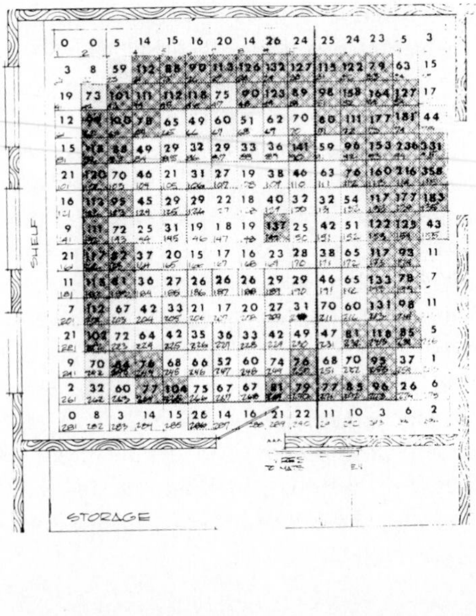

Behavior Mapping: Observing
People in Places

Few techniques are available to observe and record information about a large number of people in a given area. From such a mass of activity, an interpretable measure of behavior must be constructed. One specialized means of accomplishing this task is **behavior mapping**, which is concerned with accurately recording people's actions in a particular space at specific times. In this technique, observers record the behaviors occurring in one or more settings with the use of a preconstructed coding form developed through a series of steps (Ittelson, Rivlin, & Proshansky, 1976). First, the area to be investigated is defined. It may be a large hospital ward, a series of classrooms, or even a single room. The observers initially make narrative observations of the behavior occurring in the setting, either by taking notes or by tape-recording their impressions. From this information,

categories of behavior and interactions are organized and listed on a coding form. Using such forms, the observers code actions that occur in each area of the setting during the period of research.

Behavior mapping can serve a variety of purposes (Ittelson et al., 1976). It may be used to describe behaviors in the setting. In this context, schemes can be developed to code interactions among specified individuals and also to index the type of interaction and where it is taking place. Mapping may also be used to compare behaviors occurring in different situations and settings or behaviors in the same setting at different times of day. It is also a means of learning about the utilization of equipment and facilities (e.g., whether areas are used as intended). Finally, behavior mapping can be employed to predict the use of new facilities.

study by Baxter and Deanovich (1970) who recorded personal space between subjects. Davis and Ayers (1975) investigated pedestrian flow on an airport escalator, and were able to record visual searching by those coming off the escalator, progression into the movement system, and other multiple behavior sequences.

An interesting type of instrumentation created for a specialized purpose (mapping the standing and movement patterns of museum visitors) is the **hodometer** (Bechtel 1970). The device consists of pressure-sensitive pads covering the entire floor of the room, so that every time someone walks on a pad, the counter increases by one. Figure 1–9 shows a grid of a hodometer with the frequency of steps in each box. The darker shade indicates greater use.

Finally, engineers, architects, and designers have developed techniques to measure the full range of ambient conditions, such as the amount of light, noise, temperature, humidity, and air motion (see Rubin & Elder, 1980, for a description of these measures). Some of the methods are inexpensive and easy to learn to use. Since environmental psychologists study the physical setting as well as the behavior occurring within it, ambient conditions are critical measures in studies that must either control for these factors or systematically manipulate them. As an example, Weinstein (1980) measured noise levels on the street of a heavily trafficked urban neighborhood as a means of selecting subjects who lived close enough to the noise to be affected by it.

Task Performance   In some studies the effects of environmental conditions on subjects' abilities to perform is of interest. Some occupational settings may be characterized by high-volume intermittent noise, confinement in isolation, high levels of density, and thermal extremes; it is important to determine how these conditions affect performance. Tasks used to assess environmental effects on performance may deal with manual dexterity and eye–hand coordination, performance on cognitive tasks, or with virtually any other aspect of performance. We will discuss only a few tasks used in environmental research, although a brief search through the literature would reveal many others.

One of the most important aspects of using task performance as a measure of some environmental condition or change is to select a task that requires the kind of skills or effort you want to study. For instance, if you are interested in how some independent variable affects tolerance for frustration, you might want to measure persistence on difficult tasks. This has often been done by using a frustration tolerance task developed by Feather (1961). In this measure, which is also discussed in relation to Glass and Singer's (1972) noise research in Chapter 5, four line drawings are presented on separate pieces of paper. Subjects are given each type of drawing and are told to trace each line without going over any line twice and without lifting the pencil from the sheet. If they make an error, they are to start on a new form. Subjects are also told that if they complete a particular form or give up on it, they should go on to the others. Unknown to them, however, two of the puzzles are not solvable, and constitute the measure for frustration tolerance. All the experimenter has to do to measure persistence is count the number of discarded forms, the amount of time spent on the unsolvable cards, or both.

Other Measures   There are a number of other ways of measuring environments or response to them. **Archival data**, such as police records of crimes in different communities or hospital admissions in these areas can be used to index responses to various environmental characteristics. Physical traces, evidence of specific activities (e.g., cigarette butts in an ashtray as a means of measuring cigarette smoking or wear patterns on a lawn as a measure of traffic patterns) can be used to assess the effects of different settings as well.

For example, littering may be seen as an indication of the perceived quality of a setting and of the perceived degree of personal responsibility for it. A study by Geller, Witmer, and Orebough (1976) varied the antilitter message on the bottom of handbills that were given to shoppers in a grocery. By counting the number of handbills deposited in the proper receptacles (a measure of **accretion**), they were able to show that when shoppers were given the location of trash cans, they were more apt to dispose of the paper properly. Patterson (1978), while studying the issue of fear of crime in the elderly, counted the number of visible markers (signs such as ''No Trespassing,'' barriers such as fences, viewing devices in the doors, and personalized items such as welcome mats) as indications of territoriality. His findings indicated that greater territoriality was related to less expressed fear of crime.

Choosing Measures   With this array of possible measurement strategies, how does one go about selecting the measures for a particular study? Obviously, many factors are involved, including cost, whether we have certain types of instruments, and so on. The most important determinant is the question you are asking: If you are interested in arousal, physiological measures might be used with self-reported mood measures and, perhaps, performance measures. If behavior is the key variable, observation and self-report might be used. There are, however, some issues that are relevant in all studies of environment–behavior relationships.

Many measures are obtrusive—subjects are

aware of them while they are being collected. They are easier to use, but when people are aware of being measured (as well as of *what* is being measured), their responses may be different than they would have been had the measures been disguised. **Unobtrusive measures** are those that can be collected without the subject's being aware of them. Observational measures can be unobtrusive if the observer is not in sight and people are not told about being watched, though this may give rise to ethical concerns. Similarly, use of instruments such as the hodometer can be unobtrusive. Many of these measures, however, have been created for specific study purposes. For example, Bickman and his colleagues (1973) dropped stamped, addressed envelopes in high- and low-density college dormitories and studied helping behavior as a function of density by comparing rates at which letters were found and mailed in the two dorms. Subjects were not aware of being in a study when they found and mailed the letters. Similarly, Cialdini (1977) used littering to predict votes in the 1976 presidential election. To do this, he observed whether people discarded or kept a Ford or Carter communication that had been positioned on their automobile windshield, and predicted that people would vote for the candidate whose communication they kept. Similarly, Webb et al. (1981) proposed assessing the popularity of various environmental settings in museums by measuring the number of nose and hand prints on the display case. For an extensive discussion of other clever and useful unobtrusive measures, see Webb et al. (1966).

The bottom line in doing research in environmental psychology is to apply measurement techniques that address the questions you are asking, that disturb the setting as little as possible, and that allow you to study real people in real environments. Field studies combining self-report, observation, and task performance, such as a study reported by Fleming, Baum, and Weiss (1987), are one way to achieve this. By observing people's behavior in their neighborhoods, gathering extensive self-report data as

well as physiological data bearing on arousal, and by measuring tolerance for frustration on a challenging task, it was possible to document several aspects of living in crowded urban neighborhoods. Integrated studies of laboratory, field, and archival data are also useful in developing a comprehensive picture of the problem under investigation.

Ethical Considerations in Environmental Research

Before continuing our discussion of what environmental psychologists study and how they do so, we should suggest some of the ethical problems and considerations that arise in all environmental research. As you may have noticed, many design and measurement techniques require that the subject be unaware that an investigation is taking place. This frequently improves the validity of research in a number of important ways. Unfortunately, however, it also raises a number of ethical questions.

In 1953, the American Psychological Association (APA) issued a statement on ethics in research, which has been revised since then. Many general texts on social research have devoted entire chapters to ethics (Carlsmith, Ellsworth, & Aronson, 1976; Christenson, 1977; Dooley, 1974), and environmental psychology also addresses this concern. In addition, the United States Department of Health and Human Services has issued directives concerning protection of human subjects when environmental research is being performed under a government grant or contract. Most colleges and universities have review boards to advise the investigator on difficult and ethical issues in research design.

Many ethical considerations appear relevant to environmental research. Two that are especially important are lack of full and **informed consent** by the subject and **invasion of privacy**. We will limit our discussion to these topics, but the interested reader is encouraged to seek out other sources.

Informed Consent One of the APA ethical principles states that whenever possible, subjects should be informed of all aspects of a research project, so they can decide whether or not they wish to participate. The assumption is that a lack of such notification restricts freedom of choice. However, careful consideration suggests that informed consent is not always possible or desirable. For example, the researcher working with the mentally retarded may find it impossible to fully explain a highly technical study. Further, many field studies must be performed unobtrusively, or subjects' knowledge would bias the results to the extent that they are misleading. In considering these problems, Patterson (1974) writes that before unobtrusive field research is undertaken, an assessment has to be made concerning the extent to which human welfare and dignity are in jeopardy, and these concerns must be weighed against the value of the experiment. In effect, the researcher should assure himself or herself that the major issues to be illuminated by the study justify the slight discomfort to subjects who are not offered an opportunity to give consent.

Another issue related to informed consent concerns whether subjects who participate in experiments without their knowledge should be told about the study later. Is it better to leave subjects unaware, so that they will not be upset by the realization of having been in an experiment? Or is it the right of all subjects to receive a full explanation of the purpose and intent of the study? Informing subjects after the experiment has taken place may oversensitize them to the possibility of future research or observation taking place in everyday settings. For some people, the fear of being unwitting participants in research at other times might be quite distressing. On the other hand, there are strong ethical concerns (e.g., the subject's right to know) which the researcher must weigh before withholding such information.

Invasion of Privacy What is the rationale for assuming it is permissible under some conditions to observe people without their knowledge? Obviously, an invasion of privacy is involved in such situations. Since people in public settings realize they are under informal observation by others, most researchers believe formal observation should be no more threatening. However, Davis and Ayres (1975) suggest that if experimental subjects in a public setting become aware of being observed and choose not to participate, the experiment should provide them with an alternative route or area that is not being monitored. While potentially this leads to selection bias in subjects involved in the study, it may importantly protect people's right to privacy.

The assumption that under some conditions researchers have the "right" to observe people requires us to judge when behavior falls in the public domain and when it should be considered private. A comment by Koocher (1977) concerning a study reviewed in Chapter 8, in which people's personal space was invaded in a restroom highlights this issue. Middlemist and his co-workers (1976) assessed the physiological effects of personal space invasion in a men's lavatory by measuring duration and persistence of urination. This was accomplished by stationing an observer with a periscope and a stopwatch out of the sight of the restroom users. Among other things, Koocher commented that the experiment invaded the subjects' privacy, even though it was in a public place, because of the nature of the observation. He also felt there was potential harm for subjects who might have discovered accidentally that they were being observed. In response, Middlemist et al. (1977) stated that the information obtained was available to anyone and that the subjects were involved in an everyday public occurrence. Further, they mentioned that in a pilot study, half of the subjects were later informed that they had been watched and had no objection to the procedure. Obviously, both Koocher and Middlemist et al. may have valid points, and we should realize that sometimes there cannot be absolute ethical guidelines. It is the responsibility of every researcher to consider ethical questions as well as experimental design in conducting behavioral studies.

PREVIEW OF THE CONTENT AREAS OF ENVIRONMENTAL PSYCHOLOGY

Thus far we have described the characteristics of environmental psychology and reviewed briefly the methodological perspective of its practitioners. The remainder of this book is devoted to an examination of the contents of the field, including empirical findings and theoretical perspectives. As indicated in Figure 1–10, we will begin with environmental perception and cognition, examining the ways in which environmental scenes are perceived, how these perceptions are retained and altered by situational factors, and how perceptions lead to favorable or unfavorable evaluations of the environment. Next we will look at ways in which the environment influences behavior, beginning with theoretical perspectives on environment–behavior relationships. We will then see how stress and other reactions to the environment are influenced by such factors as noise, temperature, air quality, disasters, personal space, and crowding. Then we will examine the behavioral relationships involved in defined settings such as cities, residential settings, hospitals, prisons, learning environments, work environments, and recreation areas. In doing so, we will see how knowledge of these environment–behavior relationships can be used in designing environments for maximum human utility. Finally, we will conclude with intervention strategies for modifying environmentally destructive behavior and improving our relationship with the environment.

Figure 1–10   Organization of the book.

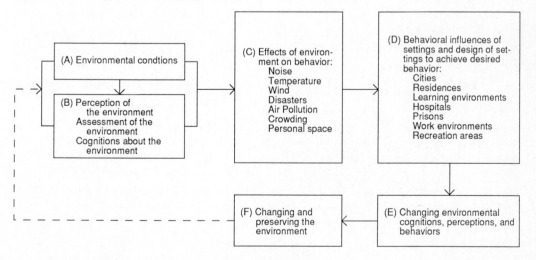

SUMMARY

Environmental psychology is concerned with studying environmental issues by drawing upon the knowledge and techniques of many areas within psychology, and as such it serves as a meaningful focus for these areas. It is easier to describe environmental psychology than to define it, but one reasonable definition is that it is the study of the interrelationship between behavior and the built and natural environments. The distinguishing characteristics of environmental psychology include the following: (1) environment–behavior relationships are integral units; (2) environment–behavior relationships are reciprocal or two-way; (3) the contents and theory of the field are derived primarily from applied research; (4) the field is interdisciplinary in nature; and (5) environmental psychology employs an eclectic methodology.

Methods employed by environmental psychologists include experimentation, from which cause and effect can be inferred; correlation, which is suitable for certain field settings but ambiguous in inferring cause and effect; and description, which is often a necessary first step in new areas of research. Specific research techniques are either obtrusive, in which individuals know they are being studied, or unobtrusive, in which they do not know they are a part of research.

The field of environmental psychology is complex, partly because of the phenomena it studies. Characteristics of its approach are, in a sense, contradictory. Its insistence on the integrity of the person–environment unit means that generalization from study to study is difficult, and that methods must be able to account for behavior without disturbing or changing it. Its focus on problems means that the phenomena of interest will be derived from the real-world expressions of these problems, posing additional challenges. By innovative use of the laboratories, procedure, and measures of other areas of psychology and through development of new approaches to research, environmental psychologists have worked to overcome these and other obstacles.

SUGGESTED PROJECTS

1. How would you define environmental psychology? Would you define it at all? Is there value in defining it? Compare your answers with classmates. What do your definitions (or reasons for nondefinitions) have in common? At the end of this course, see if you change your mind about your answers to this question.

2. Examine psychology journals (see the references at the end of the book, beginning about 1955, for articles relating to environmental psychology). During what year does the field appear to have emerged? When did it really start to grow? Is it tapering off or still growing?

3. Look up an environmental psychology research article listed in the references. What methodology was used? How could the research be done using a different methodology?

4. Make a list of environmental problems you would like to see psychology try to solve. As this course progresses, annotate your list to include the psychological principles and research you think would be applicable to solving the problems you named.

2 ENVIRONMENTAL PERCEPTION AND ASSESSMENT

KEY TERMS

adaptation
adaptation level
affect
affective appraisals
affordances
arousal
attitudes
axial landscapes
coherence
collative stimulus properties
complexity
cue utilization
descriptive landscape assessment
diversive exploration
dominance elements
ecological perception
ecological validity
Environmental Emotional Reaction
  Indices (EERI)
Environmental Quality Index (EQI)
fittingness
functionalism
Gestalt perception
habituation
hedonic tone
incongruity
information processing

invariant functional properties
legibility
lens model
mystery
naturalness
novelty
object perception
perceived control
Perceived Environmental Quality Index
  (PEQI)
perception
physical–perceptual approach
  to landscape assessment
policy capturing
probabilistic functionalism
psychological approach
  to landscape assessment
sensation
specific exploration
surprisingness
systems approach
transactional approach
uncertainty–arousal
valuation
visual air quality
Weber-Fechner function

INTRODUCTION

Consider for a moment two imaginary individuals, one from the metropolitan area of Atlanta, Georgia, the other from the rural region around Fishtail, Montana. What might their reactions be if we brought them together in the modest-size community of

Joplin, Missouri, on a March day with the temperature in the low 60s? The individual from Atlanta might find the day a bit chilly compared to his warmer and more humid climate, while the person from Fishtail might consider it quite warm and pleasant compared to her accustomed cooler weather. The city resident might consider Joplin a rather quiet town with clean air, whereas the rural resident would probably consider it somewhat noisy and polluted.

Let us further suppose that the two take a side trip to the Ozarks, winding through the countryside of small farms and forested glades. One visitor might find the abandoned farm houses and weathered buildings unsightly and incompatible with the landscape. Her companion, however, might think the scene a pleasurable one,

instilling feelings of a rustic, back-to-nature paradise.

What are the psychological factors that result in these two individuals' different perceptions and evaluations? In the present chapter we will begin by looking at how we perceive the environment. We will examine briefly the perception of change and the process of habituation. Finally, we will see how these perceptual processes affect assessments of environmental quality and scenic value.

WHAT IS ENVIRONMENTAL PERCEPTION?

Recall that our definition of environmental psychology emphasized "the interrelationship between behavior and experience and the built and natural environment." As we pointed out, this implies that humans affect the environment and are themselves affected by it. For this interaction to occur, humans must *perceive*. That is, they must somehow be stimulated by sight, sound, smell, or tactile information that offers clues about the world around them (see Figure 2–1). Historically, psychologists have made a distinction between two processes that gather and interpret environmental stimulation (Goldstein, 1989). The term **sensation** has been applied to the relatively straightforward activity of human sensory systems in reacting to simple stimuli such as an individual sound or a flash of light. **Perception,** on the other hand, is a term that is applied to the more complicated processing of the complex, often meaningful stimuli that we encounter in everyday life. Certainly your perception and evaluation of striking architecture, sublime landscapes, or distasteful dumps is founded upon the *sensations* created

by an array of discrete photons of light stimulating individual receptor cells in your eyes. Nevertheless, these environments may not differ much in their purely objective optical qualities such as brightness or color. Your *perceptions* are based upon the organization and meaning that these stimuli have for you. In general, perception is a more active process and one that is more susceptible to differences in an individual's experiences or thoughts. As others (e.g., Goldstein, 1989) have stated, however, the distinction between sensation and perception is often an artificial one, and no firm boundary exists between sensory and perceptual processes.

The study of perception provides a convenient and powerful example of some of the distinctions between traditional approaches to understanding behavior and environmental psychology. One value that has often been shared by traditional psychologists is a desire to carefully control all possible causes of a phenomenon in an effort to simplify understanding. Much of what we know about human percep-

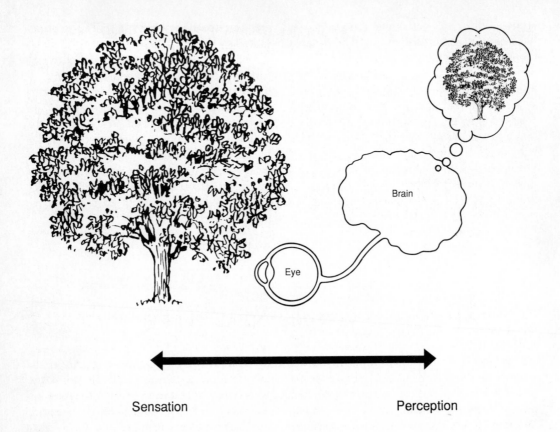

Sensation   Perception

Figure 2–1. The distinction between sensation and perception is often arbitrary. Traditionally, sensation refers to simple biological experiences elicited by environmental stimuli, whereas perception refers to more complex processing or understanding of patterns of stimulation. (Adapted from Goldstein, E. B. (1989). *Sensation and perception*, (Third Edition). Belmont, CA: Wadsworth Publishing Company.)

tion, therefore, is based upon laboratory investigations that constrain the variety and complexity of stimuli. Traditionally, these laboratory investigations have focused on **object perception** (Ittelson, 1970, 1973, 1978; Kaplan & Kaplan, 1982), that is, the patterns of sensation that allow us to scan our memories and to recognize distinct objects with which we have had some prior experience. But the day-to-day challenges of life in the complex environments of the real world are not so simple. We must not only recognize objects, but also locate them in the context of three-dimensional space, to know how far away they are, how fast they are moving, and the importance of these objects to us (Kaplan, 1982). Thus, environmental psychologists recognize that laboratory studies of simple stimuli offer a useful, and in fact necessary foundation, but find their special challenge in the almost overwhelming complexity that characterizes real-world stimuli such as landscapes, buildings, and cities (Figure 2–2).

Perhaps the most thorough discussion of the scope of environmental perception comes from the work of Ittelson (e.g., 1970, 1973, 1976, 1978) and his colleagues. For example, Ittelson (1978) notes that environmental perception includes cognitive (i.e., thinking), affective (emotional), interpretive, and evaluative components, all operating at the same time across

Figure 2–2. Real-world stimuli far exceed the complexity of the laboratory investigations upon which much of our knowledge of perception is based.

Figure 2–3. The sight of a spoiled landscape may be accompanied by anger, fear, or sorrow.

several sensory modalities. As we perceive an environment, the cognitive processes involved might include what we can do in an environment, as well as visual, auditory, and other imagery of the scene. Moreover, we might expect to compare this environment with other places we have experienced or read about. When we say that perception involves reliance on experience and memory, we imply that cognitive processes are involved in perception (e.g., Neisser, 1967). In addition to cognitive processes, our feelings (affect) about the environment influence our perception of it, and our perception of it influences our feelings. When you view the Grand Canyon, for example, you generally do so with feelings of awe and admiration. The sight of a landscape spoiled by garbage, on the other hand, is generally accom-

panied by anger, fear and sorrow (Figure 2–3).

Environmental perception also encompasses the meaning we derive from the environment. Does it remind us of past experiences? Does it suggest ideas? Can we interpret events in the environment in a meaningful way? When we perceive, we actively process information and rely on memory of past stimulation for comparison with newly experienced stimuli.

Finally, environmental perception includes **valuation**, or the determination of good and bad elements. We likely label the dump bad and the Grand Canyon good. The perceived quality of an environment is part of the overall perception. Indeed, the affective and evaluative components of environmental perception are the roots of the attitudes we hold toward the environment.

ENVIRONMENTAL PERCEPTION AS A SYNTHESIS

As we have seen, cognitive, affective, interpretive, and valuative processes are all involved in environmental perception. Although in review-

ing environmental perception we will often discuss aspects of these components separately, our conceptualization of environmental perception considers all of these processes as simultaneous events contributing to the entire experience. Whereas in conventional approaches to perception we discuss how a sensory mechanism detects a single aspect of an object in the environment, in environmental perception we are concerned with a more holistic, encompassing process. That is, the elements of an environment interact with each other and with the personal characteristics of the observer. It is this complex interaction of environmental stimuli and the personality of the perceiver that ultimately forms the experienced environmental unit. This emphasis on studying environment–behavior units rather than separate components is sometimes called a **systems approach**.

Altman and Rogoff (1987) suggest that a systems perspective views perception as composed of separate elements whose patterns of relationships form the whole. Although the patterns of mutual influence are complex, presumably the total system is a construction of these interacting but still separable parts. According to Altman and Rogoff, a **transactional approach** goes one step further and proposes that the system cannot be divided into separate elements or discrete relationships. Rather, the experienced environment is an event in time whose components are so intermeshed that no part is understandable without the simultaneous inclusion of other aspects of the instant. This emphasis on holistic, global responses is similar to the position taken in the first half of this century by the **Gestalt** theory of perception. As you may know, the Gestalt psychologists rejected the notion that an understanding of human perceptual processes could be furthered by reducing these processes into smaller and smaller basic units. Instead, Wertheimer and others concluded that the whole is different from the sum of its component parts (see Chapter 11 for an additional discussion of Gestalt principles). For example, when Wertheimer separately flashed two vertical lines 1 cm apart at intervals of about 50 milliseconds, instead of perceiving two alternating lines,

observers reported a single line which appeared to move from position to position (Goldstein, 1989).

In addition to the cognitive, affective, and valuative components of environmental perception, we can delineate at least three other characteristics of environmental perception, again following the lead of Ittelson. First, related to our statement that we perceive environments as a whole, we can say that the person–environment system is the ultimate unit of study in environmental perception, whether we subscribe to a systems or a transactional world view. The person brings individual goals and values into the perceptual experience, as well as sociocultural influences. The perceptual experience consists of many "significances," or meaningful stimuli or events that reach our awareness. That is, we are most likely to notice those things of significance to us. A name for this perspective from the traditional study of perception is **functionalism**. According to this view (e.g., Kaplan & Kaplan, 1982), our perceptions are molded by the necessity to "get along" with the environment. For example, we compare present sensations with past ones in order to see if the present stimuli signal danger or serve as cues for food or shelter. Often theorists suggest that these functional processes have evolved biologically as part of our species' adaptation to environmental demands.

Environments are rich in stimuli; in fact, the environment contains more information than we can comprehend at once, so we must selectively process it. Right now make a conscious effort to process *all* of the stimulation coming from the environment around you. You may hear the sounds of others, a cough, for example, the turning of pages, or someone shifting positions. Can you feel the pressure of your chair, the temperature of the room, perhaps a draft from a nearby door? You may detect the odor of someone's perfume or the printer's ink on the pages of this book, and you may find yourself distracted by activity outside a window. On reflection, it is quite an accomplishment to make sense out of all of this confusion! Again, we foresee an important role for cognitive processes, specifically, **information processing**. As we will see in Chapter 4, an inability to process important information because of an information overload is one explanation for some of the detrimental effects environments have on us. On the other hand, we actually *seek* certain levels of comprehensible information. Perhaps you agree that this inclination may underlie our attraction to such apparently different environments as exciting amusement parks and informative museums.

Finally, the perceptual process involves actions by us. We bring expectations, experiences, values, and goals to an environment; it provides us with information; and we perceive it through activity. Part of this activity is simple exploration to orient ourselves in an environment (discussed in more detail in Chapter 3); part of it is designed to find strategies for using the environment to meet needs and goals; and part of it is related to establishing confidence and feelings of security within the environment. Since social and cultural factors, such as sex roles, socioeconomic status, and exposure to modern architecture influence what one learns or what one has the opportunity to experience, it stands to reason that factors such as culture influence perception.

A classic example of cultural differences in perception is based upon the fact that certain cultures emphasize rectangular construction, and others employ curvilinear construction, or at least less rigor in erecting vertical and rectilinear walls (Allport, 1955; Allport & Pettigrew, 1957; Segall, Campbell, & Herskovits, 1966). As a result, members of cultures with ''carpentered'' environments see lines on two-dimensional surfaces in a different way than do members of cultures with less carpentered environments. Take the Müller–Lyer illusion depicted in Figure 2–4 as an example. To most of us, the horizontal line at the top appears longer than the one on the bottom, even though both lines actually are the same length.

Apparently, because we live in an environment in which construction is rectangular, we see two-dimensional lines as representing corners in three-dimensional space. The horizontal line at the bottom, however, appears to be closer than the diagonal lines and thus, appears to span less space than the line at the top. Members of African cultures that use rounded construction and pay less attention to rectilinear (straight line) corners tend not to be deceived by this illusion: Their culture and ecology do not require them to perceive intersecting diagonal lines as implying depth (see also Bartley, 1958).

The Lens Model

One theory that seems particularly applicable to environmental perception is the **probabilistic functionalism** of Egon Brunswik (1956), 1959). Brunswik's approach, also known as the **lens model** (see Figure 2–5), envisions the perceptual process as analogous to a lens wherein stimuli from the environment become focused and perceived through our perceptual efforts. For example, suppose that you and a friend are hiking a mountain trail in the wilderness of Montana. Suddenly you notice movement in the bushes to your right! Your perceptual processes become focused on gath-

Figure 2–4.   The Müller-Lyer illusion. To those of us raised in built environments, the line at the top appears longer than the line at the bottom.

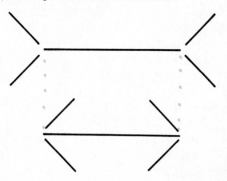

ering information from the environment so that you can identify the stimulus and decide the appropriate behavior. In little more than an instant you decide to carefully back off from what you perceive to be a foraging grizzly. Seconds later your companion laughs, and points to a very small, albeit very loud, chipmunk. How did you make such a mistake? We know that not all stimuli presented by the environment are equally useful in accurate perception. Some of the information presented by the environment may be insufficient, superfluous, or even misleading. The noises coming from the bushes beside the trail provided useful, but not sufficient, information to make an accurate perceptual decision. Noise is one characteristic of animal movements, whether by a chipmunk or a grizzly bear, so it is one useful cue, but perhaps not *as* useful in this instance as knowing the animal's size. Each of the stimuli emanating from the environment might be assigned a weight or probability based upon its usefulness in supporting accurate perception. In Brunswik's terms, these stimuli vary in their ecological validity.

However, two observers might differ in their interpretation of the situation, even when each receives the very same stimulus array. You and your companion might weight the environmental information differently in making a best guess or probabilistic judgment. Perhaps you were just thinking of reports of grizzly bear attacks in nearby Glacier National Park, or perhaps your friend was daydreaming and did not even hear the noises. Thus, not only do certain environmental stimuli differ in their objective usefulness (**ecological validity**), but individuals may weight them more or less appropriately (**cue utilization**) because of past experiences, personality, or other differences. Rather than simply determining the judgments of the average observer, Brunswik's model includes **policy capturing**, a procedure that determines the idiosyncratic patterns of weights assigned by individual judges (Craik & Appleyard, 1980). Subsequent analysis may reveal

Figure 2–5. Brunswik's lens model. Environmental stimuli become focused through our perceptual efforts. Distal cues are based upon objective features of the environment and are of different importance in accurate perception (ecological validity). These cues are in turn weighted and processed differently by individuals (cue utilization) in making perceptual judgments. (Adapted from Brunswik, E., 1965. *Perception and the representative design of psychological experiments.* Berkeley: University of California Press.)

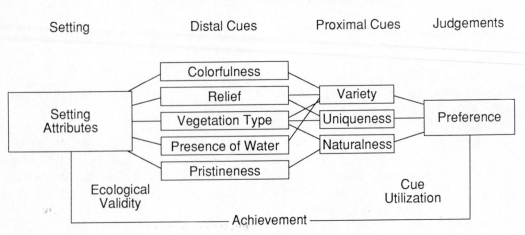

BRUNSWIK'S LENS MODEL

that certain individuals (perhaps possessing common background or personality traits) share similar weighting profiles or policies, a valuable insight that might have been overlooked by traditional averaging techniques.

A concrete example of Brunswik's approach is provided by Stewart's (1987) attempt to develop an observer-based assessment of the visual air quality in Denver, Colorado. Referring once more to Figure 2–5, the environment of interest is a particular scene being viewed and rated by an observer. Certain attributes of this environment can be determined using objective physical measures. *Objective attributes* might include the concentration of particulates and other pollution in the air, the angle of the sun, sky conditions, or humidity. Presumably, these objective characteristics of the environment form the basis for ratings of *subjective attributes* such as the color of the air or the clarity of distant objects, and, in turn, these subjective attributes are weighted by individual observers in reaching their overall judgments of air quality. The researcher could investigate a variety of questions (we will review Stewart's results later in this chapter), including the contribution of various objective physical attributes to judgments of visual air quality, the importance of subjective attributes in making quality judgments, and individual differences in weighting these attributes.

Ecological Perception of the Environment

Our discussion of perception of the environment (particularly from the functional perspective), would not be complete without considering the perspective of J. J. Gibson's **ecological perception**, which in some ways is a bridge between what we have termed conventional perception and the broader concept of environmental perception. According to Gibson (1950, 1966, 1979), it is the ecological properties of environmental stimuli that are important in

perception. In this case, "ecological" implies reciprocal adjustments between individual, social, and physical environments. That is, Gibson does not ask, "What is in the head?" but instead, "What setting is the head in?" Rather than perceiving individual features or cues that we organize into recognizable patterns, we respond to (detect or tune in) meaning that already exists in an ecologically structured environment, readily available to an appropriately attuned organism mobile enough to experience it (see also Heft, 1981).

We have noted that the conventional approach to perception considers perception of the external environment as a function of a variety of interpretive psychological processes, i.e., a stimulus activates a specific nervous system receptor, and the pattern of receptor stimulation is interpreted with the memory of past experiences to get information about the environment. From the conventional perspective, we have to interpret disconnected stimuli in order to construct something meaningful about the environment. Gibson assumes that perception of the environment is more direct and less interpretive than this. That is, perceptual patterns convey much information quite directly—without elaborate processing by higher brain centers. Furthermore, Gibson believes that perception is much more holistic, so that properties of the environment are perceived not as distinct points but rather as meaningful entities. Let us develop the Gibsonian approach to perception a bit further by exploring the concept of affordances.

Perception of Affordances   According to Gibson, we receive much valuable information directly through our perception of the environment. Gibson viewed organisms as actively exploring their environment, encountering objects in a variety of ways. Through this process, we experience the surface of an object, its texture, and angles from different perspectives. This allows us to perceive an object's **invariant functional properties** (i.e., "useful" properties of an object that do not change, such as "hardness"). The invariant functional properties of objects as they are encountered in the course of an organism's active exploration are termed **affordances**. The notion of affordances will become clearer as we look at a few examples. If an object is solid rather than liquid or gaseous, if it is inclined toward the ground at an angle other than 90 degrees, and if at least part of it is higher than the organism, then that object *affords* shelter. If an object is solid and rigid, if it is raised off the ground, if its top surface is fairly horizontal to the ground, then the object affords sitting or sittability. If an object is malleable, can be placed in the mouth whole or in pieces, and is of such biochemical substance as to provide nourishment, then it affords eatability.

Obviously, what affords shelter, sittability, and eatability for a fish does not necessarily do so for a human; what affords these things for a human does not necessarily do so for an elephant. In this sense, affordances are species-specific (although there is, of course, overlap across species). Furthermore, an object affords different things to different species. Whereas a tree affords shelter to a bird and food to certain insects, it affords fuel (among other things) to humans. For this reason, affordances must be viewed from an ecological perspective.

From this perspective, we can see that affordances involve perceptions of the ecologically relevant functions of the environment. To perceive affordances of the environment is to perceive how one can interact with the environment. It is through perception of affordances that an organism can find its niche in the environment. An ecological niche, according to Gibson, is simply a set of affordances that are utilized. In this regard, humans possess a remarkable talent: We can alter an environment so that it affords anything we want, e.g., more expensive shelters, more beautiful scenery, and so on. In doing so, we may change the affordances of that environment with respect to other humans and other organisms. When we dam a river to create a lake, which affords us water and recreation, we may also change the

Figure 2—6. Humans manipulate their environments to change the affordances they provide.

immediate environment so that it affords life support for fish and waterfowl but does not afford life support for groundhogs and bats or for the farmer who lost his or her home or cropland to the lake. Perception of this changed environment, then, depends on the gain and loss of affordances for each organism (Figure 2–6). Certainly, many of the changes we humans have imposed upon our environment for our short-term benefit have had severe long-term consequences for both our species and others. It appears that our skill in manipulating the affordances of our environments is a wonderful, but dangerous thing.

HABITUATION AND THE PERCEPTION OF CHANGE

It is apparent that environmental perception is a very complex and involving process. Because all we know of our world is filtered through perception, perceptual processes underlie much of the balance of this text. In the remainder of the present chapter we will select just a few topics that elaborate on this process and reveal something of the scope of the field. First, let us briefly examine habituation and the perception of change.

Thus far we have talked about perception without regard to time. That is, we have noted some of the principles and properties of environmental perception as if perception is constant from one moment to the next. Once we consider time as a variable in environmental perception, three important phenomena emerge: perception of movement, habituation (adaptation), and perception of change.

Habituation or Adaptation

What happens if a perceivable stimulus does not change across time? The answer involves what is known as **habituation** or **adaptation**: If a stimulus is constant, the response to it typically becomes weaker over time. Many who live near freeways, for example, at first find it difficult to sleep, but after a few nights they become habituated to the noise and have little trouble sleeping. Should they have guests some night, however, the guests are likely to be bothered by the noise (cf. Bryan & Tempest, 1973).

Explanations for adaptation or habituation tend to be either cognitive or physiological (Evans et al., 1982; Glass & Singer, 1972). Sometimes the distinction is made that "habituation" refers to a physiological process and "adaptation" to a cognitive process. Often, however, the two terms are used interchangeably.

Physiological explanations of habituation emphasize the notion that the receptors themselves fire less frequently upon repeated presentation of a stimulus. Cognitive explanations of the phenomenon propose a cognitive reappraisal of the stimulus as less deserving of attention after repeated presentation. The first time you hear a loud noise, you allocate considerable attention to it to find out what it is and to determine whether it is a potential source of threat. Once you know that it is a train, a trash truck, or your neighbor's car, however, you probably evaluate it as nonthreatening to your well-being and thus attend to it less. However, from a cognitive perspective, our example may reflect more of a response bias than a perceptual shift. That is, rather than actually perceiving the noise as less noxious, nearby residents may simply learn to respond to it less intensely or less frequently (e.g., Evans et al., 1982).

Adaptation is not always successful in eliminating unpleasant environmental stimuli, of course. If the stimulus is too unpleasant, it may well continue to be perceived as annoying (e.g., Loo & Ong, 1984). Furthermore, (as we will discuss in more detail in Chapters 4 and 5) even adaptation that appears successful may require the mobilization of the body's physical or cognitive resources and eventually contribute to a general breakdown that may be manifested in stress disorders.

An important factor in adaptation (again, refer to Chapters 4 and 5) is the predictability or regularity of the stimulus. We are more likely to adapt to a constant hum in the background than to the irregular noise of a jackhammer. Bursts of noise that come at regular or predictable intervals are easier to adapt to than unpredictable stimuli, but more difficult to adapt to than constant stimuli. Once we adapt to a stimulus and the stimulus ceases (as in the interval between bursts of noise), our adaptation to the stimulus also dissipates somewhat. When the stimulus recurs, we must adapt again. Furthermore, unpredictable stimuli require that more attention be allocated for evaluation of the stimuli as threatening or nonthreatening. Thus, predictability is an important variable in the adaptation process.

Perception of Change

If we readily adapt to environmental stimulation, will we perceive change in such things as air pollution and urban blight? If we live in an area where air pollution is high, and we adapt to it, how can we perceive changes in the level of pollution? Sommer (1972) suggests that the answer lies in the **Weber–Fechner function** of psychophysics. This function, derived from the research of the late nineteenth century, is based on the amount of increment (increase or decrease) in intensity of a stimulus that is required before a difference is detected between the new and old intensities. Stated simply, this law says that the intensity of a new stimulus required for it to be perceived as different from the present stimulus is proportionate to the present stimulus. To use an economic example, there seems to be more of a difference between one and two dollars than between 1,000,001 and 1,000,002 dollars. It takes only a small increment to detect a difference in very low-intensity stimuli but a much larger increment is needed for high-intensity stimuli. This function (though not as mathematically accurate as more modern psychophysical functions) generally applies to all forms of stimulation, including light, sound, pressure, and smell. Sommer suggests that the law applies not just to individual stimuli in a laboratory but to urban pollution as well. That is, a community with little pollution might become alarmed when clouds of brown smog suddenly appear, but large urban areas with heavy smog should require extremely high levels of additional pollution before becoming alarmed. Similarly, we might expect strip zoning in small communities where careful neighborhood planning exists to be noticeable enough to spur the community to action against such blight. Larger communities where strip zoning is commonplace, however, would probably not care as much when one more fast-food chain appears on the strip.

Sommer proposes that we take advantage of the Weber-Fechner phenomenon in changing detrimental environmental behaviors. Any time we are asked to change our lifestyles to preserve the environment, there is resistance. But what if the change in lifestyle is so small as to go unnoticed? We might be able to make subtle changes that have a great impact on the environment. Requiring that beverages be sold in returnable containers, for example, is not as drastic a measure as banning beverages in all containers. Requiring that recyclable containers be separated from other trash is even a smaller step than banning nonreturnable containers, and so on. In other words, if the perceivable change is small, we will be less resistant to it than if it is large.

Furthermore, change that is rapid (such as movement or burning) is more easily detected than change that is slow (such as growth). There is ecological survival value in knowing that one's environment is changing rapidly. Imagine, for example, the importance of prompt reaction if a forest fire endangers your home. Unfortunately, comparable damage that occurs slowly (as when pollution from cities kills trees), is less noticeable.

ENVIRONMENTAL ASSESSMENT

Environmental assessment broadly encompasses efforts to describe environments or their components (Craik & Feimer, 1987). In the United States, for example, The National Environmental Policy Act of 1969 (NEPA) has been one factor stimulating the development of programs to assess environmental dimensions such as air and water quality. Monitoring these and other characteristics of environments can assist in documenting the effects of historic environmental changes and in predicting the future impacts of proposed projects.

Indices of Environmental Quality

Using sophisticated technology, it is possible to assess pollution levels, noise levels, property deterioration, and other directly measurable aspects of the environment. Such measures can be incorporated into an objective indicator, a physical **Environmental Quality Index (EQI)**. Although these indices themselves are presumably objective physical measures, the term "quality" implies a subjective evaluation. For example, the concentrations of a known chemical toxin considered acceptable by one person or organization may be quite different from that acceptable to another. These differences of opinion reflect contrasting attitudes, the beliefs or feelings that reflect our individual learning and background.

In some instances the goal of assessment is not to determine the presence or level of some physical constituent of environmental quality, but rather the perceived environmental quality as estimated by a human observer. This assessment method does not require sophisticated technology (although it does require careful attention to psychological measurement techniques) and allows for individual differences in environmental perception. Typically some sort of self-report scale asking for subjective assessment of the environmental quality is employed, and results in a **Perceived Environmental Quality Index (PEQI)** (Craik & Zube, 1976). The PEQI is designed to serve a number of assessment purposes. It incorporates a support function for the preparation of environmental impact statements and provides baseline data for evaluating environmental intervention programs. It also facilitates comparison of trends in the same environment over time, comparison of different environments at the same time, and detection of aspects of the environment that observers use in assessing quality. Currently, PEQI's exist for assessing air, water, and noise pollution, residential quality, landscapes, scenic resources, outdoor recreation facilities, transportation systems, and institutional or work environments (Craik & Feimer, 1987; Craik & Zube, 1976). Some of the scales that have been found useful in various PEQIs are depicted in Table 2–1.

Table 2–1. *Examples of Environmental Assessment Instruments (Craik & Feimer, 1987).*

Observer-Based Examples of Environmental Assessment Instruments

College Characteristics Index (Stern, 1963, 1970)
Environmental Descriptor Scales (Kasmar, 1970)
Environmental Q Set (Block, 1971)
Group Dimensions Description Questionnaire (Hemphill, 1956; Pheysey & Payne, 1970)
Landscape Adjective Check List (Craik, 1971)
Organizational Climate Description Scales (George & Bishop, 1971; Halpin & Crofts, 1963)
Regional Q-sort Deck (Craik, 1983)
Social Climate Scales (Moos, 1974, 1975)
University Residence Environment Scale (Gerst & Moos, 1972)
Perceived Neighborhood Quality Scales (Carp & Carp, 1982b)

Technical Environmental Assessment Instruments

Water Quality Index (Coughlin, 1976)
Environmental Noise Measures (U.S. Environmental Protection Agency, 1974)
MITRE Air Quality Index (MAQI) (Thomas, 1972)
Air Quality: Aerosol Light Scattering (Stewart, Middleton, & Ely, 1983)
Indoor Air Monitoring Program (Wallace et al., 1984)
Geomorphological Dimensions of Floodplains (Burton, 1962)
Technical Neighborhood Assessment Indices (Carp & Carp, 1982a)
Behavior Setting Survey (Barker, 1968)
Structural Indices for Work Organizations (Pugh, Hickson, & Hinings, 1969)
Environmental Assessment Technique (Astin & Holland, 1961)

PEQIs provide an estimate of the perceived presence of environmental qualities, but not our feelings or emotional reactions to them (Craik & Feimer, 1987; Ward & Russell, 1981). Instead, **Environmental Emotional Reaction Indices (EERIs)** assess emotional responses such as annoyance or pleasure (e.g., Russell & Lanius, 1984; Russell & Pratt, 1980; Russell, Ward, & Pratt, 1981). Thus, the absolute measured level of sound might be reflected in an EQI, the human perception of this sound in the environment would result in a PEQI, and the emotional reactions engendered by these perceptions would be best characterized by an EERI. These indices may yield very different results. For example, a moderate level of sound might prompt an extremely negative emotional reaction if the respondent wished quiet for study, but high levels might enliven a party (the box on page 39 discusses some of the issues in assessing air quality, just one example of the distinction between different types of environmental assessment).

Affective Appraisals

Just what are these emotional reactions? Russell and Snodgrass (1987) observe that definitions of emotions (often referred to by psychologists as **affect**) are ambiguous. Emotional reactions may be relatively long-term tendencies to feel love toward some individual, or short-term affective states. In the present discussion, we will focus upon **affective appraisals**, which are emotions directed toward something in the environment. How many terms could be used to

Visibility and the Perception of Air Pollution

As we will see in Chapter 7, air pollution has a number of negative effects on human health. One additional concern that has received increased attention (e.g., Stewart, 1987; Stewart et al., 1983) is the need to protect **visual air quality**. In the United States, the National Park Service, the U.S. Forest Service, and others are concerned about the impact of air pollution on the scenic vistas in parks and wilderness areas (Figure 2–7). As part of the amended Clean Air Act of 1977, the U.S. Congress sought to protect and even enhance the visual air quality (defined as the absence of discoloration or human-caused haze) of many pristine areas. The federal land manager is charged with the complex problem of determining whether a given change in visual air quality will have an impact on visitor enjoyment. Since visual air quality is based upon human perceptions and emotional reactions, measures of this phenomenon must be based upon or validated against human responses (Craik, 1983; Stewart et al., 1983). Two critical issues parallel the distinction we have drawn between PEQIs and EERIs. First it is necessary to determine how much of an increase in haze is required to cause a *perceptible* change in the environment. In addition to the concentration and composition of pollution, the detectability of haze is dependent upon factors such as color, whether it is layered in a band (layered

haze does not occur naturally), and the angle of the sun. According to the Clean Air Act legislation, demonstrating that haze is detectable is not enough. It is also necessary to determine whether haze, even if it is detectable, *significantly* changes a visitor's experience. As you might expect, different individuals and different organizations disagree on the definition of "significant."

Figure 2–7.   Layered haze is one manifestation of pollution which is often noticeable to humans. Haze layers are one of the most significant predictors for human estimates of visual air quality.

create an EEQI describing the affective quality of a place? We can think of dozens, perhaps hundreds, but Russell and his colleagues (e.g., Russell & Lanius, 1984) have developed a circular ordering of 40 descriptors of places (see Figure 2–8) that include many commonly used emotional terms. Notice that these adjectives can be represented as a circular array in a space defined by two underlying bipolar dimensions. The horizontal axis ranges from unpleasant to pleasant, and the vertical axis ranges from sleepy to arousing. To pick two examples, the model implies that a serene environment should be pleasant, but somewhat unarousing, whereas a frenzied environment is both arousing and unpleasant.

In the next section we will focus more intently on landscape assessment. As you will see, our interest will shift from a desire to index the relative quality or pleasantness of an area to efforts to explain *why* certain scenes or areas are liked. Vision is the modality through which most humans acquire the bulk of their knowledge about the environment, but we should recognize that other senses may exert powerful influences. For example, some research suggests that olfaction (the sense of smell) exerts particularly powerful influences on emotions (Porteous, 1985), and memory (Engen, 1982).

Figure 2–8. The Russell and Lanius model of the affective quality of places. Emotional reactions to environments can be described by their relative position on unpleasant–pleasant and arousing–not arousing continua. Note that we have few words for emotional neutrality. (Adapted from Russell, J. A., & Lanius, U. F., 1984. Adaptation level and the affective appraisal of environments. *Journal of Environmental Psychology, 4,* 119–135.)

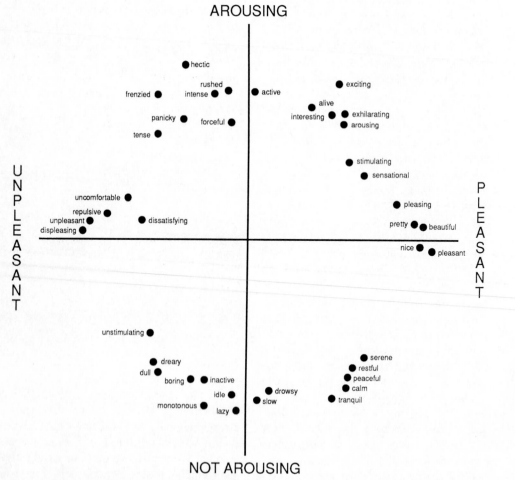

THE SCENIC ENVIRONMENT: LANDSCAPE AESTHETICS AND PREFERENCE

Picture what you consider to be a beautiful landscape. Is your imaginary scene one of snow-capped peaks? A rocky seashore? Perhaps a pastoral scene of rolling hills, covered wooden bridges, and rustic fences? Do you think the scene you are imagining is much like that imagined by people the world over when responding to the same question, or are there differences between individuals? What can we learn about humans as a species from their landscape preferences? Theoretical questions like these have attracted the attention of a number of environmental psychologists and other behavioral scientists (see Kaplan, 1987; Ulrich, 1986; and Zube, Sell, & Taylor, 1982, for reviews).

As Zube et al. (1982) note, another impetus for investigations of landscape aesthetics (more in line with our previous discussion of PEQIs) was provided by governmental legislation of the 1960s and 1970s that required the inventory of scenic resources and the preservation or rehabilitation of these resources. As an example, suppose we are building a new condominium complex in a resort area. Current residents do not want our new project to detract from their vistas, yet prospective occupants want as scenic a view as possible. Furthermore, when our new condos are seen from a distance, we do not want them to detract from the setting as a whole. How do we maximize scenic quality for all involved?

Certainly the importance attached to landscape aesthetics by residents, land managers, and designers suggests that different landscape designs or management practices can affect humans in some important way. Indeed, Ulrich (1979, 1984) reports that viewing natural scenes can lessen the effects of stress.

For our present discussion we will divide research in landscape aesthetics into three categories. First is **descriptive landscape assessment** which evolved from the design tradition of landscape architecture rather than the empirical methods of psychology and related fields. Behavioral scientists have been more prominent contributors to two other general approaches to landscape assessment: the approaches we will label physical–perceptual and psychological. **Physical–perceptual** strategies place emphasis upon the identification of characteristics of the physical environment which can be related statistically to judgments of preference or landscape quality. The **psychological approach**, on the other hand, emphasizes characteristics of the perceivers and their psychological processes or cognitions in influencing aesthetic judgments.

Descriptive Systems of Scenic Preference

Several landscape classification systems rely on expert judgments made by trained professionals, primarily landscape architects. The analysis emphasizes design principles derived from experience and artistic judgment. In particular, vast areas of public lands such as national parks, national forests, and national wilderness areas have been assessed using *descriptive landscape inventory,* an approach derived from the writings of Burton Litton (1972). The basic elements of perception are said to be line, form, color, and texture. Patterns of these **dominance elements** and contrasts created by these patterns are thought to be organized by the viewer's perceptual system, causing a focus of attention on a particular component of a landscape vista. For example, two nearly parallel lines form an

Figure 2–9. In an axial landscape such as this photograph of the Mall in Washington, DC, attention is drawn by converging lines on a focal point, in this instance, the Washington Monument.

axial landscape which focuses one's attention at the distant point at which the lines seem to converge (see Figure 2–9). Similarly, contrasts in lines, forms, colors, or textures are likely to draw attention (Figure 2–10). Note that this description is consistent with the more empirically derived data that emphasize that the human visual processing system is specialized for the detection of contrasts and is particularly "hard-wired" to detect certain simple lines or shapes (e.g., Goldstein, 1989; Heft, 1983; Hubel & Wiesel, 1979), and to seek a focal point or other source of organization (Ulrich, 1979).

Given that these principles help to determine what will receive attention, what determines whether the scene is evaluated as pleasant or unpleasant? In general, it seems that natural landscape components are preferred to those that are the result of human activity. For example, natural scenes in which contrast is high often receive positive evaluations. The contrast of snow-capped mountain peaks with the green valleys at their feet probably heightens their visual appeal. Similarly, many of the scenic areas of the American Southwest are particularly striking because they showcase the brilliant hues of desert sandstones. On the other hand, one would probably wish to minimize contrasts that draw attention to utility lines, mines, and commercial establishments.

As we noted, descriptive landscape assessment depends upon the judgments of experts. The present trend in the landscape assessment literature is to place less emphasis on these expert opinions and instead, to base preference models on the responses of recreationists and other users (Ulrich, 1986). Furthermore, in relying on the artistic (as opposed to empirical) tradition, the descriptive approach may be deficient in terms of reliability and validity (Daniel & Vining, 1983; Ulrich, 1986).

Figure 2–10.   Attention is drawn to contrasts in line, form, color and texture. In this photograph, a dramatic vertical line contrasts with the surrounding landscape of a college campus.

Physical–Perceptual Approaches to Scenic Value

An alternative and more empirical method of determining scenic value is through what we will term the physical–perceptual approach. Here, one (or a group of judges) quantifies the actual physical characteristics of a scene and, through statistical techniques, determines the degree to which these characteristics lead to negative or positive evaluations of scenic quality. In an early study, Shafer, Hamilton, and Schmidt (1969) assessed the preferences of individuals for landscapes in the Adirondack Mountains of New York State and found that preferences were associated with such factors as the area of immediate vegetation multiplied by the area of distant vegetation, vegetation multiplied by the area of water, and so on. In another study, Zube, Pitt, and Anderson (1974) studied scenes of the Connecticut River Valley

and found that scenic quality was related to such components as land-use compatibility, absolute relative relief (i.e., differences in height, such as from valley to mountaintop or canyon rim to the valley floor), height contrast, and density of edges of bodies of water. Other features that have been found to be important include debris in stream beds, width and height of a stream valley, and stream velocity (Pitt, 1976), as well as natural water area, ruggedness, naturalism (Palmer & Zube, 1976) and forest management practices (Daniel & Boster, 1976).

Vining, Daniel, and Schroeder (1984) have extended the same basic model with an eye to providing an understanding of forested residential landscapes. Presumably, identification of manageable characteristics that are likely to be perceived as unsightly (as may be the case in our condominium example) may help to avoid conflicts in areas of high visibility or quality. Similarly, Im (1984) has applied the physical–

Back to Nature

Most authorities agree that natural landscapes are preferred over urban scenes (e.g., Kaplan & Kaplan, 1982; Ulrich, 1986). But what is the definition of **naturalness**? Is natural found only in a true wilderness? Do natural scenes include the pastoral landscapes of farmland? Are urban parks and college campuses perceived as natural? Research in forest environments (Daniel & Boster, 1976; Herzog, 1984) suggests that aesthetic preferences are likely to be higher in managed forests that are thinned to encourage larger diameter trees and that have less downed wood. Indeed, landscapes categorized as ''natural'' encompass many obviously manipulated environments such as golf courses and parks (Ulrich, 1986). Preferred landscapes are likely to possess a focal point or patterning (Ulrich, 1977), smooth, uniform textures (Daniel & Boster, 1976, Ulrich, 1977), and clearly defined depth—all elements that are more likely to be found in a park than a wilderness. In residential settings, R. Kaplan (1985) emphasizes that what is appreciated most is not vast greenbelts or mowed expanses, but rather, a small piece of nature with trees, birds, and perhaps a personal garden. It seems then that liking is not reduced by the presence of human-caused features as long as scenes maintain **fittingness** or harmony between built features and their natural surroundings (Wohlwill & Harris, 1980).

We might also wonder why such scenes are preferred. Wohlwill (1983) noted three possible contributions of natural environments to human well-being. It may be, for example, that people desire contact with the organic world because it exhibits growth and change, or because wilderness or other natural areas act as symbols of our individual value systems or culture. Perhaps the greatest volume of research is devoted to the proposition that nature acts as a refuge from the day-to-day challenges of an increasingly urbanized world. Perhaps nature represents a return to an earlier, even prehistoric time. People do seem to enjoy park-like scenes, and Balling and Falk (1982) note the resemblance between these landscapes and the African savanna where many believe our species evolved. Perhaps our parks, cemeteries, and campuses are constructed approximations of the savanna. But, of course, we don't all have identical landscape preferences. Balling and Falk (1982) suggest that children prefer savanna-like environments, but that these preferences can be modified and become less and less powerful over a lifetime. Perhaps eventually, familiarity with other types of environments, especially those of ''home,'' supersedes childhood preferences for savanna. Lyons (1983) agrees that landscape preferences diverge with age (as well as sex and place of residence), but suggests that the functional–evolutionary perspective of Balling and Falk (1982) underestimates the importance of culture in determining preferences.

Whatever the reason for our affinity for natural elements, there is evidence that natural scenes may possess restorative powers. For example, Ulrich (1979) demonstrated that viewing a series of nature scenes could lessen the effects of the stress induced by a college course examination. A subsequent study (Ulrich, 1984) compared the postsurgical recovery rates for hospitalized patients whose rooms overlooked either a small stand of trees or a brown brick wall. Those with the more natural view had fewer post-surgical complications, faster recovery times, and required fewer painkillers.

. . . .

perceptual approach to study the relationship between landscape characteristics and visual preferences in the enclosed environment of a college campus. In this instance, visual preferences were most positively affected by the slope of the ground and tree canopy or vegetation coverage, whereas the height ratio (described as the height of the landscaped "walls" in a scene) was negatively related to preference.

The physical–perceptual approach is empirically based, and more in keeping with the traditions of behavioral science than art. In general, this research shows both cross-cultural agreement (Zube & Mills, 1976) and consistency within a culture (Anderson, Zube, & MacConnell, 1976; Daniel & Boster, 1976; Wellman & Buhyoff, 1980). Part of the consistency may involve the nature of the judgments made about a scene. In general, judgments of *preferences* for a scene show more variability and individual differences, whereas judgments of *quality* or value seem to be more consistent and have less individual variation (Coughlin & Goldstein, 1970; Craik, 1970a, 1970b; Fines, 1968; Pitt, 1976; Zube, 1973). That is, several individuals may agree that a group of scenes are striking, untarnished, and of high scenic quality; nevertheless, one person may prefer desert landscapes, another mountains, and a third, seascapes. Overall, physical–perceptual approaches do a very respectable job of predicting assessments of scenes (Daniel & Schroeder, 1979; Pitt & Zube, 1979) and have been frequently applied by resource managers, though rarely by designers (Im, 1984).

A shortcoming of the physical–perceptual approach is that the predictors it generates do not always make intuitive or theoretical sense (S. Kaplan, 1975; Ulrich, 1986; Weinstein, 1976). Although this criticism is not terminal (who says reality has to be easily understood?), the predictive equations developed in one setting may only be appropriate for a specific type of landscape. Thus, a more theoretical approach might arrive at more generalizable constructs and thus, predictors which could be more easily applied to a variety of different settings.

The Psychological Approach to Scenic Value

In addition to the descriptive and physical–perceptual approaches, another method of assessing scenic value is through what we will term the *psychological* perspective. Our emphasis has now shifted from quantification of physical features of the environment that might influence aesthetic judgments to an examination of psychological or cognitive processes that underlie aesthetic judgments. This is a shift from content to structure, from the specific elements of a scene (e.g., trees, water) to how they are organized or related to each other. Predictors such as complexity and coherence, for example, are typical of those found in models derived from this approach. Objective, physical measures of complexity or similar psychological predictors in a scene are difficult to obtain, so measures of these factors must be obtained from subjective judgments. In a typical procedure, a panel of judges evaluates scenes on dimensions such as complexity, ambiguity, spaciousness, or uniqueness, and then the same or another panel judges the quality or beauty of the scene. We will present two such schemes, the aesthetic conceptualization of Berlyne, and another approach to environmental preference developed by Kaplan and Kaplan.

Berlyne's Aesthetics: Formalizing Beauty

When we examine the multiplicity of factors that influence the perception and evaluation of the environment, the question invariably arises as to how we make judgments of beauty. Why do we consider a strip mine ugly and a tree-lined boulevard beautiful? Why is the Eiffel Tower thought (by some) to be an attractive landmark but an oil derrick thought (by some) to be an eyesore? The work of Berlyne (1960a, 1972, 1974) on aesthetic judgments in general has been applied to such questions of environmental aesthetics (e.g., Mehrabian & Russell, 1974; Wohlwill, 1976).

Two concepts central to Berlyne's notions of aesthetics are collative stimulus properties and specific exploration versus diversive exploration. **Collative stimulus properties** elicit comparative or investigatory responses. That is, they involve some sort of perceptual conflict that causes us to compare the collative stimulus with other present or past stimuli in order to resolve the conflict. Included among Berlyne's collative properties are **complexity**, or the extent to which a variety of components make up an environment; **novelty**, or the extent to which an environment contains new or previously unnoticed characteristics; **incongruity**, or the extent to which there is a mismatch between our environmental factor and its context; and **surprisingness**, defined as the extent to which our expectations about an environment are disconfirmed.

Berlyne also distinguishes between two types of exploration. **Diversive exploration** occurs when one is understimulated and seeks arousing stimuli in the environment, as when one is "trying to find something to do." **Specific exploration** occurs when one is

aroused by a particular stimulus and investigates it to reduce the uncertainty or satisfy the curiosity associated with the **arousal**. Originally Berlyne formulated his notions of collative properties as adjuncts to his notions of exploration, and showed through considerable research that exploration of a stimulus was a function of its complexity, novelty, incongruity, and surprisingness.

Later work by Berlyne (1974) suggested that aesthetic judgments are related to collative properties and exploration along two dimensions. The first dimension is called "**uncertainty-arousal**." Research suggests that as uncertainty or conflict increases, arousal associated with specific exploration increases. The second factor is called **hedonic tone**. This factor is related in a curvilinear (inverted-U) fashion to uncertainty. As uncertainty increases, hedonic tone (degree of pleasantness) first increases, then decreases. The latter dimension is closely related to diversive exploration. Apparently we are happiest with intermediate levels of stimulation or uncertainty and do not care for excessive stimulation or excessive arousal. Berlyne contended that aesthetic judgments are related to a combination of these two factors, uncertainty-arousal and hedonic tone. Consequently, those environments that are intermediate on the scale of collative properties and thus intermediate in terms of uncertainty, conflict, or arousal should be the environments judged most beautiful. That is, environments that are intermediate in complexity and novelty and surprisingness should be judged as the most beautiful, whereas environments that are extremely high or low in terms of these collative properties should be judged as less beautiful or even ugly.

Although Berlyne's suggestion of a curvilinear relationship between uncertainty and beauty is supported somewhat by research on nonenvironmental stimuli (e.g., paintings, music), Wohlwill (1976) pointed out that data on environmental aesthetics are mixed with respect to corroboration of Berlyne's ideas. The property of complexity appears to offer the strongest support for the validity of Berlyne's position as applied to environmental aesthetics. Schwarz and Werbik (1971), for example, made films of simulated trips along a scale-model street in which complexity was varied by manipulating the distance of houses from the street and the angle of houses to the street. Aesthetic judgments were highest at intermediate levels of complexity. Wohlwill (1976) reported similar results by exposing subjects to slides of human-built environments that varied in terms of complexity: Scenes with intermediate complexity were the most liked. Interestingly, it is difficult to test this hypothesis with natural scenes because they do not have as high a level of complexity as scenes of human-built environments (Kaplan, Kaplan, & Wendt, 1972; Wohlwill, 1976).

With respect to novelty, incongruity, and surprisingness, Wohlwill (1976) reported that a curvilinear relationship between aesthetic judgments and these collative properties in environments is difficult to find. Indeed, current research suggests that a rectilinear (direct or straight line) relationship is more correct: The greater the novelty and surprisingness and the less the incongruity, the more liked the environment. Incongruity in this respect has implications for site location of human-built structures in natural environments. Generally, a mix of human-built and natural elements is seen as incongruous, but if there is a predominance of natural elements, such a scene can still be viewed as aesthetically pleasing. For example, a number of buildings dotting a hillside tends to be less pleasing aesthetically than a single dwelling on the hillside. A final note on Berlyne's aesthetics: Just as we stated that extreme complexity cannot be found in natural environments, current research has not found aesthetic judgments curvilinearly related to the collative properties of novelty, incongruity, and surprisingness, possibly because it has not

employed high enough levels of these properties in the environmental scenes that were used.

The Kaplan and Kaplan Preference Model

Berlyne's work on general aesthetics has important implications for environmental aesthetics. It does not, however, answer all of the questions concerning environmental evaluation. For one thing, Berlyne assumes that identifiable properties in stimuli lead to uniform judgments of beauty or ugliness. Our examination of environmental perception, though, suggested that there are considerable individual differences in perceptions of environments. Presumably, such individual differences should be reflected in evaluations of environments. Moreover, Berlyne assumes that what is beautiful is also preferred. On this basis, once we can identify that which is beautiful, we should be able to predict preferences (i.e., people should prefer what they consider to be beautiful). But how do we explain the fact that some people, if given a choice, would live in upstate New York, others in tropical Florida, others in near-desert regions of Arizona, and others along the coast near San Francisco? And why would some people not care for the swamps of Louisiana and others not care for the plains of Kansas? To answer these questions, we need to turn to research on environmental preference, with a particular focus on the work of Stephen and Rachel Kaplan.

Steven Kaplan (1975, 1987) and Rachel Kaplan (1975) describe the procedures they used in constructing their model of environmental preference. Basically, these researchers collected a large number of slides of various landscapes and asked respondents to classify them according to certain schemes (similar–dissimilar, like–dislike, and so on). Next, the researchers statistically identified the elements in the scenes that led to this classification and evaluation. In this way, they derived several factors that can be used to predict preferences for various types of environments. S. Kaplan

(1982, 1987) describes four factors that appear most important:

1. **Coherence**, or the degree to which a scene "hangs together" or has organization—the more coherence the greater the preference for the scene.
2. **Legibility**, or the degree of distinctiveness that enables the viewer to understand or categorize the contents of a scene—the greater the legibility the greater the preference.
3. **Complexity**, or the number and variety of elements in a scene—the greater the complexity (at least for natural scenes) the greater the preference.
4. **Mystery**, or the degree to which a scene contains hidden information so that one is drawn into the scene to try to find out this information (e.g., a roadway bending out of sight on the horizon)—the more mystery, the greater the preference.

In attempting to summarize these findings, Steven Kaplan (1987) begins with the assumption that aesthetic preferences are not trivial. That is, humans need to make quick and effective predictions about the functional (survival-related) characteristics of a scene. In short, people will generally be attracted to scenes in which they perceive that they will be able to function most effectively. Kaplan suggests that environments may possess characteristics that make them survivable, a position that resembles Gibson's concept of affordances. Just what would such a scene be like? For one thing, it may possess certain contents such as water or abundant food that humans can exploit directly. Certainly humans, like other animals, have a pressing need for food, water, and shelter. But how do humans differ from other species? Perhaps you have already answered our question and are thinking that humans seem to be more intelligent than at least most of the animal kingdom. If so, then perhaps you agree that humans are good at, and even *like,*

Figure 2–11.   A scene from a Japanese garden that is rated as both coherent and pleasant.

processing information (on occasion our students question the proposal that they find processing information *pleasant,* but the popularity of games of knowledge and skill indicates otherwise). This information-processing focus is, of course, a cognitive perspective. If the Kaplans and others are correct, people will be attracted to scenes in which human abilities to process information are stimulated and in which this processing will be successful. In sum, people will like scenes which are *legible,* that is, those that are understandable and make sense. In addition, however, people will also prefer scenes that are not too simple or dull. We like scenes that possess some mystery, that are involving, and invite exploration (see the box on page 49).

The similarity of some of these dimensions (e.g., complexity, coherence) to Berlyne's collative properties is obvious. A distinction be-

Is One Person's Mystery Another Person's Bug-Eyed Monster?

According to the Kaplans' (Kaplan & Kaplan, 1982; S Kaplan, 1987) model of landscape preference, mystery is an element that increases interest and involvement in a scene by providing the promise of further comprehensible information. Typical examples of scenes with high mystery are those featuring paths curving out of sight or in which part of the environment is obscured or shadowed (Gimbett et al., 1985; Kaplan, 1987; Kaplan & Kaplan, 1982). But perhaps you are wondering whether high mystery is *always* a positive predictor of preference. Ulrich (1977) provides an example for thought: Imagine yourself walking alone at night past a dark, curving alley (see Figure 2–12). Would the scene possess mystery? Would the

dark, unknown quality of the scene enhance your preference?

You may not be surprised to learn that Herzog (1987) found that deep, narrow canyons and, especially, urban alleys are exceptions to the general pattern of positive association between preference and mystery. There are several ways to deal with this ambiguity. For example, S. and R. Kaplan (1982) essentially refine their definition of mystery. They suggest that the term is properly applied in instances in which new information is not *forced* upon the perceiver, but is only suggested or implied (see Figure 2–13). They emphasize that the viewer must have the

Figure 2–12.   Although mystery is heightened by hidden information, dangerous scenes are not preferred.

Figure 2–13.   In this instance, the rock formations may intrigue the viewer, inviting him or her to move into the landscape to acquire more information.

ability to control the incoming information by choosing whether or not to move physically into a scene. Having control should reduce or eliminate fear (see Chapters 4 and 5 for more complete discussion of the importance of perceived control in a variety of environmental situations).

Ulrich (1977) took an alternate perspective when he suggested that mystery will be positively related to preference in situations with little risk, but inversely related in threatening situations. A recent study of the relationship between mystery and danger by Herzog and Smith (1988) concluded that danger undermines preference for scenes and mystery enhances it, but that the two variables act independently of each other. In sum, they conclude that the effect of mystery is nearly always positive, but that in some instances danger may be a more salient cue which overwhelms any positive effect of mystery. Finally, Bernaldez et al. (1987) report some interesting differences in the way mysterious elements are evaluated by people of different ages. According to these researchers, whether a scene exhibiting darkness and shadow is perceived primarily as mysterious or risky and dangerous, differs with age. It appears that a childhood fear of darkness and the unknown shifts, and by young adulthood such environments take on a stimulating or artistic quality.

tween the Kaplan model and the Berlyne perspective, however, is that the Kaplan model emphasizes the informational content of a scene in a functional or ecological sense as one basis of preference judgments. For example, coherence and legibility relate to *understanding* or "making sense" out of the environment (being able to comprehend it and what is going on in it). On the other hand, complexity and mystery can be considered aspects of "involvement" with the environment, or the degree to which one is stimulated or motivated to explore and comprehend it. Table 2–2 represents these components in a recent version of the Kaplan model (S. Kaplan, 1987) illustrated by a 2-by-2 matrix. As can be seen, one dimension of this matrix is the "Understanding" vs. "Exploration" distinction. The other dimension revolves around the degree of effort required to process environmental information or the immediacy in time of the components of the environment. That is, coherence and complexity are thought to require less inference or analysis, whereas

Table 2–2. *Organization of the Kaplan and Kaplan model of environmental preference. (Adapted from S. Kaplan, 1987.)*

	Understanding	Exploration
Immediate	Coherence	Complexity
Inferred or Predicted	Legibility	Mystery

legibility and mystery require a more entailed strategy.

In addition to these four factors, Kaplan and Kaplan emphasize the role of familiarity, naturalness (again, refer to the box on page 44), and spaciousness in assessing scenic value. In general, the familiar, especially the "old and genuine" aspects of a scene make it more desirable. As was true of both the descriptive and physical–perceptual approaches, the more "natural" a landscape, the higher its assessed values. Finally, we noted that the Kaplans also acknowledge the importance of spatial organization. In general, the more defined the spaciousness the better. A broad expanse (such as a desert that never seems to end) is not as desirable as one with some suggested boundaries, places of refuge or safety, and definite objects that can be explored (Kaplan & Kaplan, 1982; Ulrich, 1986).

Evaluation of the Psychological Approach
The Berlyne conceptualization of aesthetics and the Kaplan and Kaplan preference model are but two specific examples of what we have termed the psychological approach to assessment. Daniel and Vining (1983), S. Kaplan (1987), Ulrich (1986), and Zube et al. (1982) review other work along these lines. It is encouraging to note that in most cases dimensions such as complexity, coherence, and ambiguity or mystery are found to predict scenic value by a number of researchers using different methodologies. Unfortunately, there is as yet insufficient agreement on how many of these dimensions we need to assess a scene adequately, and the way we combine the dimensions in judging one scene is not always the way we combine them to judge other scenes. That is, complexity may best predict quality in one scene and mystery may best predict quality in another. For a given scene, however, the psychological approach is useful. Once again returning to the example of our condominium developer, we would expect that judgments of complexity, coherence, and so on in our landscape would help predict changes in scenic quality as we make suggested changes in the design and location of the building.

Landscape Values: Suburban America

Each of the landscape assessment approaches we have discussed implies at least a moderate level of stability in judgments of landscape quality or preference. Indeed, the functional approach suggests that the roots of common human aesthetic preferences are deeply embedded in the evolutionary history of our species. Yet we have also noted that perceptions can vary between cultures, and preferences must as well. For example, do you think a student in colonial Boston would view visual aesthetics in the same way you do? We might speak of these different preferences as **attitudes** toward the environment (see box on page 52). In Chapter 13 we will review some of the changes in American attitudes toward the wilderness since Colonial times, but if we restrict ourselves to the end of the twentieth century, do all Americans share a common landscape preference? As you have probably anticipated, the simple answer is, "No, there are both individual and cultural differences in what people find attractive."

Modern American Variation in Landscape Preferences   As we suggested earlier in this chapter, there may be age-related variation in landscape preferences (Balling & Falk, 1982; Bernaldez et al., 1987; Lyons, 1983, Zube et al., 1983). Other researchers (e.g., Duncan, 1973; Hecht, 1975) document cultural differences. For example, Hecht presents a fascinating account of changing landscape styles in Tucson, Arizona. Anglo-American settlers in the late 1800s in Tucson took pride in converting the desert landscape into green lawns much like those of the Eastern towns and villages they had left behind. Perhaps this landscaping served as a symbol of their conquest of the desert, or perhaps they were eager to affirm their Anglo-Americanism by rejecting the dominant Spanish and Mexican architectural influences of street-

Attitudes

What is your attitude toward air pollution, wilderness landscapes, or litter? If you found our question easy to answer, you must have a personal understanding of the term "attitude," yet a formal definition has proven to be elusive. Most theorists would agree that **attitudes** include a relatively stable tendency to evaluate an object or an idea in a positive or negative way, that is, attitudes involve affect or emotion— feelings of pleasantness or unpleasantness, like or dislike for something. Some theorists would add cognitions or a set of beliefs that support, justify, or derive from the affective feelings. Since we have emphasized that environmental perception includes both affective and cognitive components, it is easy to see that environmental perception and environmental attitudes might be closely related. Still other theorists would include in the definition of attitude a set of behaviors or behavioral dispositions consistent with affect and cognitions.

Perhaps because of the theoretical dispute about what exactly an attitude is, many environmental psychologists avoid using the term. In discussing assessment of environments, for example, we chose to speak only of perceived environmental quality as the average affective reaction of evaluators. Nevertheless, when the focus shifts to the affective reactions of an individual or class of individuals in light of their beliefs and learning histories, the term "attitude" is convenient, controversial though it may be. For instance, we will discuss the changing attitudes of Americans toward the North American wilderness (see Chapter 13), and

methods of changing attitudes to prevent damage to the environment (Chapter 14).

Where Do Attitudes Come From?

For many years social psychologists have studied and theorized about the factors involved in attitude formation. For a much more thorough discussion of the area than we can give here, we refer you to any basic textbook in social psychology or to one of the several current reviews (e.g., Chaiken & Stangor, 1987; McGuire, 1985). Basically, attitude formation involves principles of learning: Most attitudes appear to be formed through classical or instrumental conditioning, or through social learning. These processes of attitude formation are not necessarily independent of each other, and all may play a part in the formation and maintenance of a given attitude.

Do Environmental Attitudes Predict Environmental Behavior?

We assume attitudes influence behavior. For example, we assume that if someone thinks that recycling is a good idea, that person will actively engage in recycling efforts. But how strong is the attitude–behavior link? For years, social psychologists have been convinced that on the surface, at least, attitudes are not consistent with behaviors.

An alternative to the direct attitude– behavior link has been proposed by Fishbein and his colleagues (Fishbein & Ajzen, 1975). According to this view, expressed attitudes are influenced by social norms. These norms, together with attitudes, determine behavioral intentions, which in turn predict overt behaviors. For example, it is normative today to express concern over environmental problems, although actual feelings about air or water pollution may not be as strong as the social norm. As a result of our attitude we may say that we *intend* to be environmentally conscious, and presumably, this makes us more likely to behave in environmentally sound ways. Initially, Fishbein and Ajzen (1975) expected that behavior and behavioral intentions would be nearly perfectly correlated. It is now clear that there are a number of variables that affect behavior directly without operating on behavioral intentions (Chaiken & Stangor, 1987). For example, Ajzen (Ajzen, 1978; Ajzen & Madden, 1986) adds a dimension of **perceived control** reflecting the degree to which an individual perceives obstacles that would constrain his or her intended actions. According to Fishbein and Ajzen (1975), a general attitude may not predict a specific behavior; but a multiple-item scale measuring components of an attitude is more likely to predict a *class* of behaviors. A pro-environmentalist may not keep the thermostat at 65°F in the winter, but someone who adheres to several pro-environmental concepts probably does engage in more pro-environmental behaviors (recycling, car pooling, water conservation) than someone who is not concerned with the environment.

A second research approach assumes that some sort of *attitude activation* is necessary before an attitude can direct behavior in a particular situation (Fazio & Zanna, 1981; Fazio et al., 1986). According to this view, the strength of the association between an attitude and a particular attitude object or situation will determine the degree to which that attitude is activated and, thus, exert influence on behavior. This strength will vary depending upon such factors as direct experience with the attitude object and the number of times the attitude has been expressed (Chaiken & Stangor, 1987).

Finally, several researchers believe that attitudes actually *follow from* behavior (Bem, 1971; Festinger, 1957). That is, it may be that if we first change behaviors, attitudes consistent with those behaviors will develop in order to maintain consistency between our behavior and our attitudes as we perceive them or wish them to be perceived by others. Although there is evidence that attitudes do sometimes become more similar to actual behavior, this observation does not always hold true. Just because we are paying for pollution control devices on our cars does not mean that our attitudes toward air pollution are changing (O'Riordan, 1976). It could be, of course, that attitudes both precede behaviors and follow from them.

The nature (if any) and strength of the relationships between environmental attitudes and environmental behaviors are obviously very complex issues. It seems that attitudes are imperfect predictors of behavior, and that they sometimes precede behaviors and sometimes follow them. In the meantime, is it really worth the effort to try to change environmental attitudes in the direction of greater environmental consciousness? Given the consequences of continued environmentally destructive ways, we think the answer is obviously "Yes!" In Chapter 14, we will suggest some of the directions these efforts should take.

side buildings and walled patio gardens. At any rate, with the exception of a few avant-garde Anglos, the non-grass Spanish-Mexican tradition was largely limited to lower-income residences occupied by families of Hispanic descent. Hecht reports an interesting reversal since World War II. For a time each cultural group apparently sought to identify with the other. Higher-priced Anglo subdivisions began to abandon grass lawns in favor of stone and desert shrubs. As they prospered, many Mexican-Americans moved to Eastern-style subdivisions and planted grass lawns. Most recently, more and more Tucsonians have abandoned grass for more native species and landscapes.

How might we account for the fact that in using the same psychological dimensions for evaluating identical environments, individuals often differ in their preferences? One answer lies in the concept of *adaptation level* (Helson, 1964; Wohlwill, 1974; Wohlwill, 1976). Individuals may have different levels of preference for complexity, causing the objectively measurable level of complexity in one scene to be too low for one individual, but too high for another. In other words, experience may lead different individuals to prefer different levels of complexity. Wohlwill refers to an individual's optimum level on any one dimension as his or her **adaptation level,** and deviations from that optimum require adaptive measures (e.g., arousal reduction or sensation seeking).

Russell and Lanius (1984) provide an interesting example of the effects of adaptation on emotional appraisals of landscape scenes. Recall the model of affective appraisal of environments presented earlier in which emotional reactions could be described by a model composed of two independent dimensions, pleasure and arousal (Russell & Snodgrass, 1987). Russell and Lanius (1984) found that exposure to a slide of known emotional appraisal (say, gloomy and unarousing) would be associated with a tendency to evaluate a subsequent target scene in a direction emotionally away from the first stimulus (in our example, toward exciting and less gloomy). Stated simply, adaptation to one landscape is likely to bias affective evaluations of subsequent scenes in a predictable fashion. In Chapter 4 we will see how adaptation level can be used to explain not only individual differences in environmental evaluation but also individual differences in responses to environmental stimulation.

SUMMARY

Whereas the conventional approach to perception examines the way the brain interprets messages from the sensory organs about specific elements in the environment, environmental perception views the perceptual experience as more encompassing, including cognitive, affective, interpretive, and evaluative responses. Moreover, environmental perception is likely to consider the person–environment from a systems or transactional perspective. Environmental perception involves activity on our part, especially in terms of exploring the environment to determine what needs it meets. In addition, exposure to a particular environment may result in adaptation or habituation—the weakening of a response following repeated exposure to a stimulus.

Environmental appraisals may involve the appraisal of physical qualities (EQIs), perceived quality (PEQIs), or emotional reactions prompted by a particular setting (EERIs). Methods of assessing scenic quality can be classified as descriptive, physical–perceptual, or psychological. In many instances (such as in emphasizing the importance of naturalness in scenic evaluations) these three approaches are in agreement, but they differ in both their theoretical underpinnings and in their methodologies. The descriptive approach employs experts to evaluate scenes in terms of dominance elements and contrasts such as in color or form or texture. The physical–perceptual approach quantifies the physical components of a scene and derives a mathematical formula for predicting scenic quality from these physical elements. The psychological approach, on the other hand, uses psychological rather than physical properties of a scene to predict value. Berlyne proposes that aesthetic judgments are a function of collative properties (complexity, novelty, incongruity, and surprisingness) and of diversive and specific exploration. The Kaplan and Kaplan model has identified the dimensions of coherence, legibility, complexity, and mystery as most important in scenic assessment.

SUGGESTED PROJECTS

1. Ask a few friends to provide adjectives to describe several campus environments. Can you place each of the adjectives generated by your friends into the bipolar model of affective reactions suggested by Russell and his colleagues (refer to Figure 2–8)?

2. Look in magazines for various kinds of natural and human-built scenes. What dominance elements are present? What might you do to human-built scenes to make them appear more attractive?

3. Use the same scenes from Number 2 above. Try to rate them in terms of collative properties of Berlyne and mystery as described by the Kaplans. Do the properties relate to your judgments of beauty? Do your classmates agree with your rankings?

3 ENVIRONMENTAL COGNITION

KEY TERMS

action plan
analog representation
augmentation
cognitive map
complexity of spatial layout
degree of visual access
differentiation
distortions
districts
edges
egocentric reference system
environmental cognition
Gouldian maps
hierarchical memory network
inferential structuring
landmarks
legibility
multidimensional scaling

nodes
operationally coordinated and
   hierarchically integrated reference
   system
partially coordinated reference system
paths
place
propositional storage
recognition tasks
semantic network
sequential maps
spatial characteristics
spatial maps
structure matching
survey knowledge
transition
wayfinding
you-are-here maps

INTRODUCTION

Think of yourself as an astronaut in space. Can you picture the clouded globe of the Earth below you? Now try to direct your attention to North America. Many people report that if asked, they can "zoom in" or enlarge a portion of this picture to focus on their region or state. Can you go to an even higher level of magnification and picture your town, your campus, or even your own back yard? Although some people may have actually seen some of these views at one time or another during their lives, probably most have not. It seems that many of us have the ability to create pictures or maps of environments from perspectives that we have never actually witnessed. Think of the room in which you are reading right now. Can you imagine how it would look if you were somehow able to view it from a window in the ceiling? Unless you have ridden in a small plane or balloon, it is unlikely that you have actually seen your back yard from a bird's-eye view, but you may find it possible to create a very realistic picture of it. Humans are not "stuck" in the environment of the present. Even when we are not actively viewing, hearing, or smelling an environment, we can experience it mentally. We acquire facts and opinions about the world around us, and remember emotional reactions to environments from experience. Presumably, we can use this mental representation of the physical environment to make plans, to understand the terrain around us, or to solve problems involving an environmental context—finding a dry cleaning establishment, for example. In general, this ability to imagine and think about the world around us is referred to as **environmental cognition**.

The physiological processes that allow sensation are grounded in observable biological processes and events, but as one begins to account for the effects of past experience and other individual differences in perception, understanding the world as either you or I "see" it will require some understanding of memory. Sensation and perception (see Chapter 2) present us with a "picture" or best guess as to the present state of the environment around us. The specific form of the perceptual input varies. It may be the visual image of a landscape vista, the smells and sounds of a city street, or even the text of this book. Whatever its form, it is the basis of our knowledge or beliefs about the environment. In turn, this knowledge will often provoke affective (emotional) reactions and, presumably, influence human behavior. Historically, social psychologists have used the term *attitude* to describe the interrelationship between beliefs, feelings,

Figure 3–1 An informal model of spatial cognition. Instructions from other humans, printed maps, and memories of past travels help an individual form an action plan for a proposed journey. The success or failure of this plan as it is carried out becomes stored in memory and leads to place associations, future travel plans, and an evolving cognitive map for future reference.

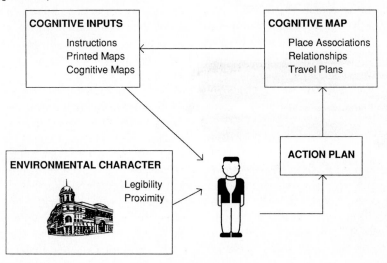

and behavior. In the present chapter we will try to understand how this perceptual information is stored, retrieved, and referenced in our daily interactions with the world around us.

Perhaps you will be surprised to learn that many psychologists have historically shied away from discussing such "cognitive" matters as memory, images, or problem solving. Their reluctance may reflect the historic objection of behaviorists to the study of the "unobservable and unmeasurable" events that occur as we process mental information. Relatively recently, some psychologists have

"rediscovered" these complex operations of memory, thinking, problem solving, and imagery (see Evans, 1980; Golledge, 1987; Neisser, 1967). Many have suggested that the ability to create complex mental images when applied to a large-scale environment may be useful for finding our way from one place to another and back again. Furthermore, this ability may offer insights into the way that we as individuals store, process, and retrieve information about the spatial environment around us, a topic generally discussed as environmental cognition.

AN INFORMAL MODEL OF SPATIAL COGNITION

The ability to capitalize on a rich and varied environment is at least partially dependent upon the human propensity to store geographical information. Humans have long sought to represent this information physically in the form of maps. In fact, the oldest known map is said to date from 2500 B.C. (Beck & Wood, 1976). Useful as maps and charts may be, however, it seems certain that people more typically travel through a familiar environment without these aids. How is this accomplished? Environmental psychologists suggest that all humans carry with them a mental model of their environment, commonly referred to as a **cognitive map**. Simply stated, a cognitive map is a mental framework that holds some representation of the spatial arrangement of the physical environment.

The exact form of these maps is controversial. It does seem clear that cognitive maps are not the same as a cartographer's in either physical form or in content. They are sketchy, incomplete, distorted, simplified, and idiosyncratic (Devlin, 1976; Evans, 1980). We might

think of these maps as composed of three elements: places, the spatial relations between places, and travel plans (Gärling et al., 1984). **Place** refers to the basic spatial unit to which we attach information like name, function, and perceptual characteristics such as affective quality or affordances (see Chapter 2). Depending upon the scale of the particular cognitive map we are consulting, a place may be a room, a building, an entire town, a nation, or, presumably, a planet. In addition, cognitive maps reflect **spatial characteristics**, such as the distance and direction between places and the inclusion of one place within another (your room is inside a building which is itself within the boundaries of a town, and so on). Finally, Gärling et al. (1984) propose the concept of *travel plans* as an important bridge between the mental world of cognitive maps and the navigation and other behaviors that they support.

Whether maps are stored in the mind or on paper, we might ask, "What do maps do for us?" One answer seems to be that they assist in **wayfinding**, the adaptive function that lets us get around in an environment efficiently and which helps us locate valuable items like food, shelter, or meeting places within the environment (Downs & Stea, 1973, 1977; Evans, 1980; Kaplan & Kaplan, 1982).

This leads us to propose an informal model (see Figure 3–1) which will emphasize travel from one place to another as a primary goal of spatial cognition. Before we begin our journey, we will construct an **action plan**, that is, a strategy for moving from one place to another (Gärling et al., 1986; Russell & Ward, 1982). Our plan will need to include some sort of information about the relative locations of places. Without it, we would have to search for locations in a haphazard manner, hitting or missing the desired location in a very inefficient way. In a new environment we may need to depend upon a physical reference such as an atlas or a friendly passerby in order to formulate our travel plan. In the absence of such physical aids or in well-known environments, we will consult the spatial representation in our memory, our cognitive map. Moreover, we can use our cognitive maps to communicate locations to others and to understand others' communications about location to us. Being able to "visualize" the directions someone gives us, and associating the directions with familiar landmarks and paths enhances our wayfinding ability.

Notice that although our figure recognizes a cognitive map as a source of information for the construction of plans, acquisition of the map is itself the result of previous experience in the environment. Thus, although we will begin our discussion with the stored information residing in cognitive maps and then turn to their application in wayfinding, we are really looking at a cyclical system and our starting point is arbitrary.

COGNITIVE MAPS

The topic of cognitive mapping has fascinated not only environmental and cognitive psychol-

ogists, but also researchers in geography, anthropology, and environmental planning and design. Cognitive maps are a very personal representation of the familiar environment that we all experience. Take a few moments to think about the layout of your campus. Try to imagine several vistas and the paths you most frequently take. Now on a clean sheet of paper try to draw a sketch map of the campus showing important features so that a stranger could use your sketch to find his or her way around. This is, of course, your personal cognitive map. You will probably want to refer to it often as you continue reading this chapter.

History of Cognitive Mapping

Investigation of cognitive maps is not really a new idea (cf. Trowbridge, 1913). Modern study of these maps has its most direct roots in the work of E. C. Tolman (1948) who described the way in which rats learn to "map" the environment of an experimental maze. Tolman's basic strategy over a number of experiments was to first train rats to take a particular path in a maze in order to reach a food reward. When the path was later blocked, the rats seemed able to switch to another previously unused path that led toward the goal. In fact, some rats would choose a path never before used and pass up one that had been reinforced if the new path was a more direct route to the goal box (Tolman, Ritchie, & Kalish, 1946). Thus, the rats seemed to have learned not just a series of turns or responses, but also a general idea of where the reward was located in the maze relative to the starting position. In order to describe this place information that his rats had apparently learned, Tolman coined the term "cognitive map."

An Image of the City: Kevin Lynch   At first few investigators were interested in pursuing the study of cognitive maps. Although it would be an exaggeration to say that Tolman's work was forgotten, it was not until the publication of

The Image of the City by the urban planner Kevin Lynch (1960) that there was widespread interest in understanding the formation and use of humans' cognitive maps.

As a planner, Lynch was among the first in his field to try to understand such subjective concerns as people's feelings about the quality of their environment and how their perceptions could be used in environmental design. *The Image of the City* remains *the* classic reference in cognitive mapping, and is still used as a basic text in architecture and urban planning programs (Langdon, 1984). In it, Lynch simultaneously established a field of inquiry, a methodological approach to data collection, and a vocabulary of terms to describe features of cognitive maps that is still widely used. For both historical and pragmatic reasons then, Lynch's approach seems to merit a detailed discussion.

Lynch (1960) reports findings based upon data gathered in Boston, Jersey City, and Los Angeles. Lynch asked his subjects to draw sketch maps of their city, to give detailed descriptions of certain routes such as the path from home to work, and to list the most distinctive and vivid elements of their respective cities. Upon comparing these data, he identified different elements that seemed common across the three different cities (see Figure 3–2).

Figure 3–2   A diagram illustrating all five of the major elements in a mental map. (After Lynch, K., 1960. *The image of the city*. Cambridge, MA: M.I.T. Press.)

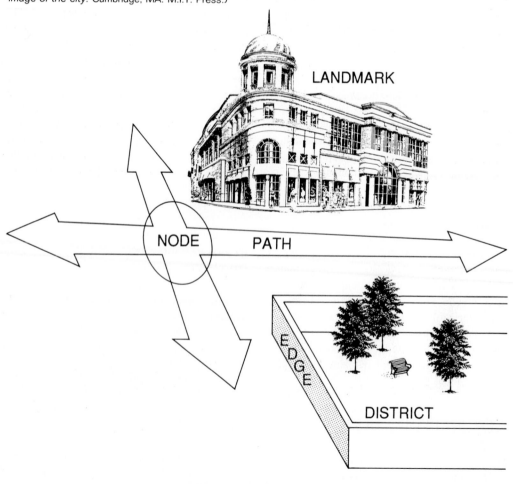

Elements of Cognitive Maps

Return to your sketch map of campus. Are there obvious streets and buildings designated on it? Are there broad areas you could designate as "fraternity row" or "dormitory area" or "athletic complex"? Lynch found that five categories of features could be used to describe and analyze cognitive maps: paths, edges, districts, nodes, and landmarks. **Paths** are shared travel corridors such as streets, walkways, or riverways. **Edges** are limiting or enclosing features that tend to be linear but are not functioning as paths, such as a seashore or wall. Notice that in some instances one person's path (the rail line of a commuter train) may be another person's edge (if the rail line divides a town). **Districts** are larger spaces of the cognitive maps that have some common character such as "Fraternity Row," or the "Chinatown" found in many cities. **Nodes** are major points where behavior is focused, typically associated with the intersections of major paths or places where paths are terminated or broken, such as a downtown square, a traffic circle, or the interchange of two freeways. Finally, **landmarks** are distinctive features that people use for reference points. Usually landmarks are visible from some distance, as in the case of the Washington Monument or a tall building in a city. Can you identify examples of these five categories on your campus map?

Additional Early Observations

The basic elements (paths, landmarks, nodes, edges, districts) outlined by Lynch seem well established (Aragonas & Arredondo, 1985; Evans, 1980), although some have suggested that these elements are most applicable to environments on the scale of cities (for which Lynch developed them) rather than smaller or larger units of analysis. Other early researchers who were inspired by Lynch noticed stylistic differences in people's cognitive maps. Lynch's associate Donald Appleyard (1970), for example, used sketch maps to evaluate the images of residents in a city in eastern Venezuela. The maps seem to fit into one of two categories: those predominantly made up of elements that one might encounter **sequentially** in traveling from one place to another, such as paths, or those that instead emphasize **spatial** organization (a more current term for this type of bird's-eye view is **survey knowledge**) such as landmarks or districts (see Figure 3–3). At least for these city dwellers, Appleyard reported that most maps were sequential, that is, rich in paths

Figure 3–3   Idealized examples of sequential (left) vs. spatial cognitive maps. (After Appleyard, D., 1972. Styles and methods of structuring a city. *Environment and Behavior*, 2, 100–118.)

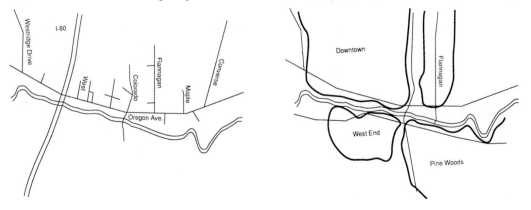

and nodes. This interest in the acquisition of cognitive spatial knowledge and the distinction between sequential and survey knowledge remains very current.

More and more researchers began to discover cognitive mapping in the following two decades, leading to the present variety of research goals and methods all described loosely by the terms "cognitive map" or "spatial cognition."

Current Perspectives

As we said, cognitive mapping has evolved from several scientific disciplines, especially psychology, planning, and geography. This reflects the excitement of interdisciplinary research so characteristic of environmental psychology. At least partly because of differences between these disciplines, however, the general topic of cognitive mapping is actually only a loosely organized literature based upon a variety of methods and research goals.

One might think of an individual's finished cognitive map as representing a personal image of his or her environment. Certainly some features of the physical environment possess characteristics that are likely to cause them to be perceived as more important or distinctive, and thus, more likely to be stored in memory. Planners and geographers have been especially concerned with these physical characteristics (Evans et al., Kaplan & Kaplan, 1973, 1982; 1984; Wohlwill, 1973, 1976). Often the features of greatest concern to these researchers are those that make an environment **legible**, that is, easily learned and remembered. Legibility may be so important that it affects our affective reactions to environment (see Figure 3–4). Indeed, in Chapter 2 we discussed legibility as one important predictor of landscape preference.

In addition to the physical characteristics of a city or rural environment itself, you might expect that different individuals will place varying weights on certain environmental fea-

Figure 3–4   Scenes that allow aerial or long-range perspectives are often rated as highly legible.

tures. For example, you are more likely to know more about the area of a college campus nearest your dorm or along your most frequent path to class. We might expect your map to be somewhat different from a person's living in a different location or from that belonging to a faculty member. Of course, almost all researchers recognize the importance of these individual differences in experience, but this has been particularly important as an area for investigation for psychologists, particularly those with an interest in social or developmental psychology.

Finally, there is the fundamental question of just how these cognitive maps are stored and retrieved from memory. Researchers from several specialty areas, especially cognitive psychology, are fascinated by the general topic of spatial cognition, and this area has generated great excitement (and controversy).

METHODS OF STUDYING COGNITIVE MAPS

Given the variety of disciplines and specialties that have found interest in the general topic of cognitive mapping, you may not be surprised to learn that there are almost as many methodological techniques for gathering and analyzing cognitive maps as there are researchers. This diversity is exciting, but often the source of serious difficulties because data gathered using one method may not be easily compared with data produced by another. In fact, these methodological problems may be among the most serious faced by researchers in the area (Evans, 1980). As we will see, Evans was correct in asserting that methodological studies are sorely needed to compare different procedures for accuracy and utility. The differences that exist prevent the slow accretion of the data base that should form the foundation of future research; certainly these differences will make our review of the field more difficult. Let us begin by describing some of the most common methodological approaches.

Sketch Maps

As you recall, Kevin Lynch (1960) employed several methods in his seminal investigations of people's responses to the spatial environments of Los Angeles, Jersey City, and Boston. His primary method, however, was to ask subjects to draw a sketch map of their city (Figure 3–5). This approach has remained among the most popular, and was responsible for establishing the vocabulary of cognitive mapping terms such as paths, landmarks, districts, nodes, and edges. Sketch maps provide an incredibly rich source of data. They have several liabilities, however, and these seem to become more and more serious as researchers become more sophisticated in their research questions.

One problem concerns the degree to which individual differences in mental maps themselves are uniquely responsible for observed differences in sketch maps. It is quite possible that drawing ability (Blaut & Stea, 1974) or experience with maps (Beck & Wood, 1976; Dart & Pradham, 1967), contaminates the maps produced by subjects, so that those with sophisticated drawing skills will be more able to express their knowledge on paper.

Another problem concerns the scale and the field upon which subjects draw their maps. Classically, subjects are just given a sheet of blank paper and asked to reproduce a particular city, neighborhood, campus, or other spatial environment. In a sense, this method seems unbiased in tapping the resident mental image

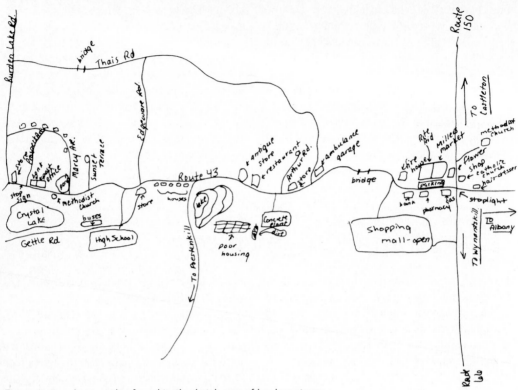

Figure 3–5 An example of a subject's sketch map of her hometown.

of a spatial environment, but the scale and orientation the subject chooses for his or her maps will be idiosyncratic, making comparison across individuals problematic. For example, how can one reasonably compare two maps of a city, one which includes suburbs and outlying areas, another confined to the city proper? Providing subjects with several existing landmarks or an outline of the area's shape (Kozlowski & Bryant, 1977) reduces this variability, but, of course, also introduces artificial constraints on the map by suggesting several reference points, each of which may in fact serve as a nucleus for recalling a series of related places that may or may not have voluntarily appeared. The box on page 67 reviews a different sort of procedure, in which **Gouldian maps** are used to gather information associated with spatial locations rather than being themselves the data of interest.

Recognition Tasks

In his early investigations of residents' images of Boston, Kevin Lynch also asked participants to report whether they recognized photos of landmarks which were interspersed in a collection of pictures of unfamiliar locations. Lynch seems to have included this task as a reliability check for his more familiar sketch map procedure. Stanley Milgram and his associate (Milgram & Jodelet, 1976) revived this approach because it avoids many of the problems inherent in having people with varying abilities draw sketch maps. Unfortunately, the procedure limits our ability to compare the orientations and geographical distances between spatial elements that are often evident both in various mapping techniques and in direct distance estimates as discussed below. In addition, this technique emphasizes **recognition** (the ability

Mapping Reactions to
Remembered Environments:
Gouldian Maps

Peter Gould and Rodney White (1974) present a different approach to mental maps. Whereas the primary focus of the methods presented so far is to reproduce the person's mentally stored image of an environment, Gould's approach recovers not a person's cognitive map, but rather, characteristics or qualities assigned to places within a person's environment which are represented graphically on an accurately drawn map. Various statistical approaches have been employed, but the final result typically provides a realistic map of the study area, upon which are superimposed either the boundaries or shaded areas that may correspond loosely to Lynch's (1960) districts. These shaded areas or region

outlines demonstrate contours of collective assessments of such qualities as areas that are well known, highly preferred, or perhaps, feared. These areas are most like what Lynch (1960) referred to as districts. The maps may be on virtually any scale. For example, Figure 3–6 shows Gould and White's desirability ratings for areas of the U.S. based upon data collected from California residents. Notice the areas of high preference include the West Coast, Colorado, and New England. On the other hand, the deep south and South Dakota receive lower ratings. How would residents of a different location, say the deep south, respond? As you can see from Figure 3–6, people tend to like their regions, even if others in the nation

Figure 3–6   The preference map of the United States as reported by California residents. (Adapted from Alber, Adams, & Gould (1971). **Spatial Organization**. Englewood Cliff, NJ: Prentice-Hall. Reprinted by permission.)

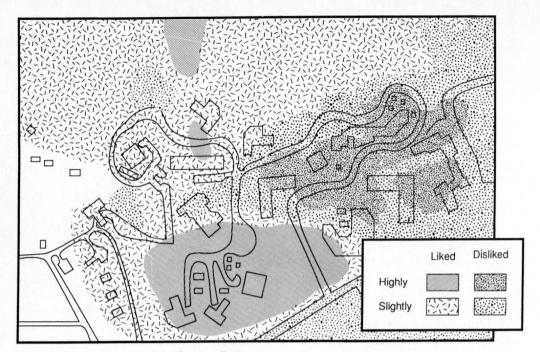

Figure 3–7   Preference contours for a small university campus.

are less favorably impressed. This seems reasonable, if for no other reason than self-selection.

Other researchers have adopted approaches similar to Gould and White's (Greene & Connelly, 1988; Lloyd & Steinke, 1986). One application of this type of mapping technique to the design of a small college campus was reported by Greene and Connelly (1988). All of the college's students, staff, and faculty were mailed campus maps and asked to indicate those areas that were most and least attractive (see Figure 3–7). Computer analysis aggregated all of the individual maps into a large composite showing the areas that were most and least preferred. A consulting design firm then used this visual analysis in creating a campus master plan to maintain the attractive areas and to enhance those judged less attractive.

. . . .

to recognize a place you have seen before) over recall, which asks you to remember and reproduce as much as you can without the assistance of photos to jog your memory. To illustrate, would you typically draw and label the location of your favorite dry cleaner on a sketch map of your hometown? Probably not. Would you recognize the same dry cleaning establishment if you were shown a picture of it? Probably. The distinction between recognition and recall does not necessarily suggest a fatal liability for this or other methods that emphasize recognition. In fact, some (e.g., Passini, 1984) suggest that recognition tasks more closely approximate the way most of us deal with movement within familiar environments (we will return to this issue in our discussion of wayfinding later in this chapter). Still, it should be clear that these recognition tasks are quite different from the standard sketch map technique, and thus, not directly comparable.

Some of the disadvantages of sketch maps have also been dealt with by automating the task of locating places. For example, Baird and his colleagues (Baird, 1979; Baird, Merrill, & Tannenbaum, 1979; Merrill & Baird, 1979) asked subjects to adjust cursers on a computer display to indicate their estimate of the locations of a list of buildings. This method presumably reduces the importance of drawing skills, while still allowing the direct input of a subject's recalled spatial environment. On the other hand, this too is a recognition task. By providing a list of buildings to be placed on the electronic map, these researchers have given clues which may well have helped their subjects avoid overlooking less familiar places in their maps. This may be a promising approach. According to these researchers, direct maps of familiar environments collected in this manner are as objectively accurate as those generated by sophisticated statistical techniques such as multidimensional scaling (discussed below), and furthermore, are subjectively evaluated as preferable to most other methods, both by the people who generated them and by independent assessments by others (Baird, Merrill, & Tannenbaum, 1979).

Distance Estimates and Statistical Map Building

A number of researchers have recently employed several forms of an approach asking people to estimate the distances between locations in a large-scale environment. Certainly these distances seem important both to the accuracy of a person's sketch map and the memories it represents, and to a person's ability to successfully move around in his or her environment. Perhaps the best-known statistical approach is known as **multidimensional scaling**, a statistical procedure based upon the idea of asking subjects to estimate the distances between a number of buildings or other locations in the environment. Given the distance between each point and each of a number of other points, a computer can generate something resembling a map by optimally placing each location so as to most closely account for each component distance estimate.

ERRORS IN COGNITIVE MAPS

Cognitive maps are, of course, rarely perfect representations of the physical environment, but rather are rough conceptualizations. In fact, we can identify several sources of error that frequently occur in them (Downs & Stea, 1973; Evans, 1980; Lee, 1970; Milgram, 1977). First, cognitive maps tend to be incomplete. We often leave out minor paths and details, but we can also omit districts and landmarks. Second, we often **distort** our representation of the environment by placing things too close together, too far apart, or aligning them improperly. In general, de Jonge (1962) suggests that people tend to simplify patterns of paths and space to make them as simple as possible (circles, lines, and right angles rather than quarter-circles and complex curves), in a manner quite similar to the Gestalt principles of good form we will discuss in Chapter 11. More recent investigators have at least partially confirmed de Jonge's hypothesis. Most errors in cognitive maps of cities are made at street intersections. People have a tendency to misestimate the size of intersection angles. Acute intersection angles are often overestimated and obtuse angles are underestimated. We also tend to represent nonparallel paths as being parallel, nonperpendicular paths as being perpendicular, and curved paths as being straight (Appleyard, 1969, 1970; Byrne, 1979; Evans, 1980; Lynch, 1960).

People also have a tendency to overestimate the size of familiar areas in their cognitive maps (see Figure 3–8). For example, Milgram and Jodelet (1976) found that Parisians seem to increase the size of their home neighborhood out of proportion with the rest of Paris.

A third type of error involves **augmentation**, or the addition of features to a map that are not there. Appleyard's Venezuelan study (1970) provides a classic example of these augmentations. A European engineer included a nonex-

istent railroad line in his sketch map because experience led him to predict a rail connection between a steel mill and a mining port. In this instance, the engineer's experience led him to infer a logical, but nonexistent, map component. Notice that this same phenomenon (sometimes referred to as **inferential structuring**) may often lead subjects to make correct assumptions, but these may properly be called augmentations if the person's cognitive map represents features that have never actually been experienced. In these instances in which an actual feature is inferred, the experimenter is unlikely to recognize the augmentation, and will miscode an interesting error as an accurate response.

Altogether, then, our cognitive maps are clearly not always very accurate representations

Figure 3–8   People tend to overestimate the size of familiar areas. A humorous example of the way our cognitive map can be affected by where we live.

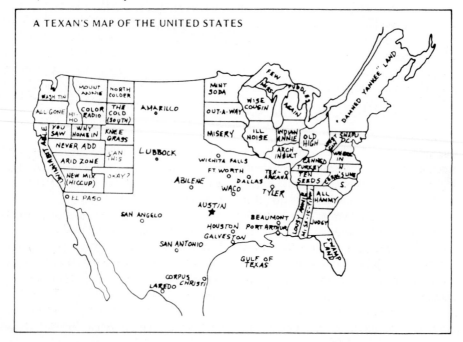

From Downs, R.M. & Stea, D. (1977). **Maps in Minds: Reflections on Cognitive Mapping.** New York: Harper and Row. Reprinted by permission.

of the physical environment. Understanding the sources of these errors may well give us insights into the effect of individual differences in such factors as experience, age, skill, or personality. Furthermore, some researchers are using insights gained from either the errors people make in spatial cognition tasks, or differences in the speeds at which features can be recalled to learn more about the basic processes underlying human memory.

Familiarity and Socioeconomic Class

The types of errors in our maps, as well as the degree of detail in them, vary according to several factors. As you might expect, a number of studies have shown that the more familiar you are with an environment, the more accurate and detailed are your cognitive maps of it (e.g., Appleyard, 1970, 1976; Evans, 1980; Gärling et al., 1982; Hart & Moore, 1973). In general, long-term residents draw richer and more accurate maps (Beck & Wood, 1976). For example, Holahan (1978) found that students drew more complete and detailed maps of the parts of campus they use more frequently. Interestingly, however, Beck found that three- to seven-year residents drew better maps than did natives (those living in the mapped area for more than 15 years) or newcomers (those in residence for fewer than three years). Apparently, natives have a wider exposure to the city, and thus, draw their maps from several points of reference using several coding schemes. Beck hypothesized that this complexity and richness may make a native's map unadaptively rigid. Even familiarity with a particular type of environment can be helpful when you encounter a new situation that has at least some familiar characteristics. For example, Kaplan (1976) found that prior experience with a natural environment increased accuracy in locating such features as distinct pine trees and hills.

Several authors report that familiarity probably explains the frequent observation that people from higher socioeconomic status groups draw more thorough maps than the poor (e.g., Appleyard, 1976; Orleans, 1973). That is, upper- and middle-class individuals probably have more experience with broader areas of a city than lower-class individuals whose mobility is restricted, primarily by the lack of easy access to transportation. In a classic study, Donald Appleyard reported that motorists (generally from the upper class) had the most sophisticated maps of a Venezuelan town, whereas those forced to walk produced less sophisticated sketches. Public transportation users fall somewhere in between (Beck, 1971). In general then, those with more travel experience make better sketch maps (Beck & Wood, 1976). Even more important than just being mobile, those who must attend to the passing environment (drivers, for instance) are more likely to process street names, directions, addresses, and distances. Thus, public transportation users who may well travel great distances but attend only to the passing sequence of stops do not produce the richness or accuracy of the cognitive maps of drivers. In sum, the longer we have experience with an area and the more mobile we are within it, the more thorough our cognitive maps are likely to be.

Perhaps it is only "common sense" that the *quantity* of information stored in memory increases with exposure, and that the opportunity to experience an environment differs by socioeconomic class, age, and perhaps, gender. It is important not to underestimate the value of these observations, however, nor their usefulness for planners and geographers. Nevertheless, perhaps a more interesting area for psychological research centers not on the importance of familiarity and experience in adding to the quantity of stored information, but also *qualitative* changes in cognitive maps (and the memory storage and retrieval processes underlying them). Some early suggestions of such qualitative changes can be found in Appleyard's (1970) study in Venezuela. You will recall that Appleyard distinguished between sequential sketch maps emphasizing paths and nodes and spatial maps featuring a high proportion of landmarks and districts. Appleyard noted that maps were more spatial for long-term residents than for newcomers, and that spatial elements were more prominent in familiar areas of the city. More recent research has systematically investigated this phenomenon. Evans et al. (1981) and Gärling et al. (1981) report that the basic path and node structure appears to be learned first, and then as an individual spends more time in the environment he or she fills in other details such as landmarks. Thus, as an individual becomes more familiar with an environment, his or her cognitive map of it becomes more spatial. Devlin (1976) also supports the primacy effect for path structure in learning new environments, again suggesting that familiarity can lead to more spatially oriented maps.

On the other hand, Heft (1979) reported that adults rely more on landmarks to learn a route through a novel path network the first time they traverse it as compared with later occasions. This would seem to be the reverse of the path–primacy effect. Perhaps elements such as landmarks are used for wayfinding, but are not always represented in sketch maps. In support of this view are several comparisons between adults and children that suggest that one important difference between the maps drawn by people of different ages is that adults are more likely to attend to landmarks that lie at critical points on a route, such as the point at which one has to make a turn, than are children.

Gender Differences

Do males and females differ in their cognitive mapping abilities? Several researchers (e.g., Maccoby & Jacklin, 1974) have reported that males may possess superior visual and spatial skills, at least on paper-and-pencil tasks. If this generalization is true, one might expect males to be superior in their ability to draw complete and accurate cognitive maps. There is also some evidence (Bryant, 1982) that having "a

good sense of direction" is more important to the self-esteem of males than it is for females, so one might expect males to be superior to females for motivational reasons, even if they possess no native superiority.

Perhaps it is surprising that a number of investigators find no such sex differences (e.g., Francescato & Mebane, 1973; Maurer & Baxter, 1972). Others do find some evidence for gender differences in the final product of cognitive mapping exercises, although they conclude that those sex differences that are present are most likely due to differences in familiarity with an area (e.g., Evans, 1980). Appleyard (1976), for example, found men's maps to be slightly more accurate and extensive than women's, but attributed this difference to the higher exposure of men to the city. Even some researchers who have given subjects both cognitive maps and paper-and-pencil tasks have found sex differences on the paper-and-pencil tasks, but not for spatial memory (McNamara, 1986).

More theoretically interesting than simple measures of overall competence in drawing cognitive maps are a limited number of studies that suggest that cognitive maps drawn by women, while as accurate as men's, are *stylistically* different. Again, some hint that differences exist between the maps of males and females which appeared in Appleyard's early investigations, with females appearing to be somewhat more spatially oriented than males. More recently, Pearce (1977) and McGuinness and Sparks (1979) found that females were as accurate overall as males in their maps, but that women tended to emphasize districts and landmarks, whereas males were more likely to emphasize the path structure. In a pair of related experiments, McGuinness and Sparks (1979) found that women included fewer paths between landmarks, included more landmarks, were less accurate in placing buildings with respect to the underlying spatial terrain, but were more accurate than males in the placement of buildings with respect to their distance from one another. Interestingly, the second experiment of the pair demonstrated that females actually did know the locations of many roads and paths that they had not voluntarily included in sketch maps. It seems that women often remember the location of these features, but do not always include them in their maps unless specifically asked to do so. McGuiness and Sparks conclude that whereas females seem to approach the organization of topographical space by grouping landmarks and establishing their distance from one another, males are more likely to begin with a network of roads and paths, which may provide a somewhat more accurate framework. In general, males may begin by setting up an organizational framework of paths and nodes for their sketch maps and then superimpose features such as landmarks and districts on this established framework. On the other hand, women may be more likely to try to establish individual relationships between landscape elements without this organizing framework.

Some other differences have apparently been uncovered. Orleans and Schmidt (1972) found that whereas men typically used base map coordinates when they were provided, women generally ignored these coordinates and used their home as a reference point. In addition, Ward, Newcombe and Overton (1986) have reported that males are more likely to voluntarily give compass directions or distance estimates phrased in measurements such as mileage than are females when asked to give directions based upon a map. Nevertheless, when instructed to phrase their directions using these dimensions, females were as successful as males. Thus females may be as capable of using cardinal directions and mileage estimates as men, but have a stylistic preference not to do so.

In conclusion, females probably are as capable as males in mapping their surroundings, but some stylistic differences await further investigation. The source of these differences is unclear. They may well be explained by differences in experience, familiarity, or the socialization process, but a biological component can not yet be entirely ruled out. Regardless, it is reassuring to know that whatever differences exist, neither males nor females seem to be at a disadvantage in cognitive mapping.

ACQUISITION OF COGNITIVE MAPS

We have noted several instances in which spatial cognition does not match cartographic maps. In general, cognitive maps become more similar to cartographic maps as an environment becomes more familiar (e.g., Evans et al., 1981). The two most common situations in which to observe this process are with children (for whom many environments will be unfamiliar) and with adult newcomers.

Much of the interest among developmental psychologists and others investigating children's spatial cognition is based upon the implication that the changes that occur in these maps reflect not only a change in the amount of information in memory, but a change in the type of information and the way it is used (see Heft & Wohlwill, 1987). For example, differences between children and adults may reflect not just less experience, but a very different approach to problem solving than that employed by adults.

The most influential theory of cognitive development as applied to spatial cognition is the one proposed by Jean Piaget and his colleagues (Piaget & Inhelder, 1967). In one classic study, Piaget asked children to sit in a chair and to view a table on which were placed three model mountains. Three other chairs were placed around the table, upon one of which was seated a doll. From a set of drawings the child was asked to select a view of the scene as it would appear to the doll. Children younger than seven or eight typically chose not the view from the doll's perspective, but the view they themselves saw. Piaget termed this *egocentrism*.

According to Piaget, during the egocentric phase, the child's frame of reference is centered on his or her own activities. Environmental features in the child's spatial image are disconnected and the environment is fragmented. Later, the child's map is oriented around fixed places in the environment that the child has explored, but not necessarily the place he or she now occupies. These known areas are, however, disjointed. Finally, the child's frame of reference assumes the characteristics of a spatial survey map with a more objective representation of the environment. Gary Moore and Roger Hart (Hart & Moore, 1973; Moore, 1979) extended Piaget's findings and proposed that in developing cognitive mapping abilities, children progress through three sequential stages involving progressively more complex frames of reference. First is an undifferentiated **egocentric reference system** in which the image consists of only those elements in the environment that are of great personal significance. Second, children develop a **partially coordinated reference system** in which several clusters of points demonstrate a knowledge of the relationships between landmarks and paths, but for which the clusters are not related to each other. Finally, in an **operationally coordinated and hierarchically integrated reference system** the environmental image is organized into a single spatial reference system.

Although several studies have provided some support for the idea that qualitative changes in cognition occur during childhood (e.g., Acredolo, 1976, 1977), much recent research leads us to temper the conclusions Piaget drew from his three-mountains experiment. For example, children seem better able to ~ke use of aerial photographs (Blaut & Stea,

1974) and maps (Blades & Spencer, 1987) than Piaget would have predicted. The most pronounced changes in children's ability to interpret aerial photographs may occur between kindergarten and grade two (e.g., Blades & Spencer, 1987; Stea & Blaut, 1973).

Much of the data are in general support of the Piagetian observation that preschool children exhibit egocentrism. Somewhat more controversy surrounds whether these findings reflect a truly different way of thinking as Piaget would imply, or a slow increase in the quantity of environmental information and cognitive skills. Much of the research on children's cognitive maps is based upon studies which have employed models to simulate environments. Several authors have suggested that the relatively poor mapping abilities demonstrated by children participating in studies which employ this method may have resulted as much from the artificial methodology of the research as actual mapping deficits (e.g., Cornell & Hay, 1984; Evans, 1980). In general, research done in large-scale environments has found children to be more capable at younger ages than was suggested by the studies employing models or sketch maps (e.g., Cousins et al., 1983).

A related topic being investigated is the accuracy and complexity of cognitive maps. Siegel and White (1975) suggest that children's representations of the spatial environment progress through four sequential developmental stages. First, landmarks are noticed and remembered, followed by paths between landmarks. At the third stage landmarks and paths are organized into clusters, and finally, these clusters and other features are correctly coordinated into an overall framework. Notice that whereas many believe that children first focus on landmarks and then move on to route (path) information as they mature, this trend may not parallel the evolution of adults' cognitive maps. As we have said, as adults become more familiar with an environment most believe their maps develop first from known paths and nodes, with landmarks and districts being added later.

MEMORY AND COGNITIVE MAPS

We have seen some characteristics of sketch maps and other physical representations of human cognition. Notice, however, that cognitive maps themselves have no external physical existence; they reside in our minds. Let us turn now to a very fundamental question: Exactly how is a cognitive map represented in the brain? Psychologists have differing opinions on the matter (Evans, 1980), and investigations of this representational question have sparked sophisticated studies by both environmental and cognitive psychologists. McNamara (1986) presents a way of categorizing several important topics of interest to those who study spatial cognition. Two of the most interesting areas for investigation concern the *form* of the mental representation and the organization or *structure* of a memory or retrieval process (McNamara, 1986).

Form

One characteristic that has received much of the research attention concerns the form of the mental representation of spatial knowledge. One view is that we have an image or mental "picture" of the environment in our memory. This view, termed the **analogical** (meaning the mental map is an analogy of the real world), says that the cognitive map roughly corresponds point for point to the physical environment, almost as if we have a file of slide photographs of the environment stored in the brain (Kosslyn, 1975; Shepard, 1975). Certainly, we often believe that these picture memories exist and direct our activities.

Another view, the **propositional** approach, advocates more of a meaning-based storage of material. That is, the environment is represented as a number of concepts or ideas, each of which is connected to other concepts by testable associations such as color, name, sounds, and

height. When we call on this propositional map we search our memory for various associations, and these are reconstructed and represented as a mental "image" or in a sketch we draw (Pylyshyn, 1973).

Current thinking combines these two approaches and says that cognitive maps contain both propositional and analogical elements (e.g., Evans, 1980; Gärling et al., 1984; Kosslyn, 1980; Kosslyn & Pomerantz, 1977). For example, most information about the environment may be stored in memory through propositions, but we can use this propositional network to very quickly mentally construct an analogical image that has many of the qualities of a photograph. We may then use this image, rather than the propositional network researchers suppose to underlie it, to solve spatial cognition problems.

Structure

Another distinction made by McNamara concerns the *structure* of these relations or associations, and assumes at least some form of hierarchical or propositional network. Some time ago, researchers Collins and Quillian (1969) demonstrated that the retrieval of information from semantic memory (memory for concepts) sometimes acts as if it is based upon a **hierarchical memory network**. That is, information may be stored according to some organizational system that is based upon ordered categories. This is typically presented as a tree diagram illustrating the relationships between concepts as branches like those in Figure 3–9. Presumably, some sort of sequential search of levels in these categories occurs when one is asked to determine relationships between concepts. The exact form of these **semantic networks** is controversial and the subject of a great deal of research in cognitive

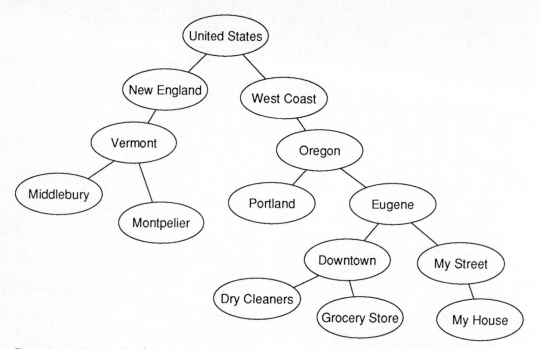

Figure 3-9   An example of a semantic network as it might underlie a cognitive map.

psychology (see Best, 1986, for a readable review).

In an environmental application, a network might also describe the way that spatial information is represented in memory. A networked storage process would be a rather economical system in the memory space it requires. Although theoretically efficient, this storage system might be subject to certain types of errors which would make some memories more difficult or time consuming to retrieve than others. We tend to distort spatial relationships based on our ideas of larger categories within which we place smaller concepts. A study reported by Stevens and Coupe (1978) provides an opportunity to experiment with an interesting example. First draw a map of the United States. Now indicate the locations of San Diego, California, and Reno, Nevada. Do not read further until

you have done so. Finished? Except for those living near the West coast, most people place San Diego west of Reno apparently because they think of California, the *superordinate* category to which San Diego belongs, as being west of Nevada. As you will see upon consulting a U.S. map, San Diego is actually east of Reno! As is often the case, things probably are not so simple. A simple tree diagram is not able to explain all of the phenomena we have observed in cognitive maps. Some propose refinements of the network model (e.g., Collins & Loftus, 1975); others propose quite different memory structures that do not depend upon hierarchical storage (e.g., Smith, Shoben, & Rips, 1974). We will have to leave the complexities of these arguments to cognitive psychologists (see Best, 1986). At the present time, however, versions of the network model (e.g., Gärling, Böök, & Lindberg, 1984; Kaplan & Kaplan, 1982) remain popular within the cognitive mapping literature. Perhaps McNamara's (1986) "partially hierarchical" structure represents the data as well as any. This means that memories may be generally stored according to hierarchical principles, but that there remain some interconnections between areas that cut across this hierarchical structure.

However the exact process occurs, most studies, whether they are lab studies (Allen et al., 1978; Lindberg & Gärling, 1983) or field studies (e.g., Beck & Wood, 1976; Byrne, 1979) indicate that spatial information is acquired quickly and that forgetting is minimal. In general, those with better short-term memory seem to include more elements on their maps, but these are not necessarily more accurately positioned (Beck & Wood, 1976). Finally, it is possible that for spatial memory at least, there may be an upper limit to how much a person can remember (Byrne, 1979; Tversky, 1981).

JUDGMENTS OF COGNITIVE DISTANCE

In addition to studies specifically addressing cognitive maps, recent research on environmental cognition gives us some ideas about the ways our spatial cognitions of the environment are organized. For example, when people are asked to judge whether a pair of states (e.g., Georgia and Mississippi) are closer together than another pair (e.g., Michigan and Iowa), the more similar the distances within the two pairs, the longer it takes to make a decision (Evans & Pezdek, 1980). Moreover, recall of distance between two points on a map is longer the greater the distance on the map (Kosslyn, Ball, & Reiser, 1978). From such evidence we might conclude that cognitive representations of the environment require scanning for judgments to be made about them, and the more information we must scan, the longer it takes to make judgments about spatial relationships.

Other interesting studies also show that cognitive organization influences judgments we make about cognitive maps. For example, judgment of traversed distance, that is distance we have traveled over a given period of time, is in part dependent upon the number of turns we make (Sadalla & Magel, 1980). Students walking a path designated by a line of tape placed on a floor judge a path to be longer the more right angle turns it contains. In addition, the more intersections a path crosses, the longer the path is judged to be (Sadalla & Staplin, 1980b).

Finally, consider a third study (Sadalla & Staplin, 1980a) involving paths marked with tape. One path has intersections marked with proper names that occur frequently in the English language (e.g., Lewis), and another path has intersections marked with relatively unfamiliar names (e.g., Talbot). You are more likely to recognize and remember the familiar names. In addition, these researchers found that you are likely to judge the familiar-named path as being longer, presumably because you have more information about it stored from associations with the familiar names. Thus, when traversing the path mentally to estimate its distance, you must scan more information, so you assume that it is longer. In general, then, the more information we must scan in our memory while making a "mental journey" through an environment, the farther the distance we assume we have traversed.

WAYFINDING

Most of the research we have presented to this point has focused on a rather static, plain-view map of the environment residing in memory (for now, we will lay aside the argument concerning the specific form of this representation). Other authors (e.g., Byrne, 1979; Cornell & Hay, 1984; Gärling, Böök, & Lindberg, 1986; Passini, 1984) are interested in **wayfinding**, the process by which people actually navigate in their environments.

One of the most profoundly troubling experiences we can face is being lost. In such an instance, our human capabilities of information processing and storage have deserted us, and because most of us are dependent upon others and technology, our very survival may be threatened. Being truly lost may be a relatively rare phenomenon, but newcomers commonly experience the stress and anxiety that accompany disorientation in both buildings and natural environments (e.g., Cohen et al., 1986; Hunt, 1984). In some groups, such as the aged, this stress may be particularly serious, even life-threatening (Hunt, 1984; Killian, 1970).

Action Plans and Wayfinding

Gärling et al. (1986) propose one model of wayfinding which may prove useful in organizing our discussion (see Figure 3–10). We will provide a hypothetical example to illustrate the different steps of the model. Imagine that a friend has asked you to drop off some clothes at a dry cleaning establishment. First, a destination is decided upon. Should you take your friend's dry cleaning to your favorite establishment, or to one closer to your friend's home for his or her convenience? Assuming that you decided to choose a dry cleaner near your friend's home, the second step requires the new target destination to be localized; that is, you

must determine the general location of the target environment. If you are unfamiliar with your friend's neighborhood you may need to use a telephone book or some other source to pinpoint the target. Third, a route is chosen between your present location and the dry cleaner, again requiring you to ask directions or to refer to a map if you are unfamiliar with the neighborhood. Finally, you must make a choice of travel mode, depending upon factors such as the distance to the destination and the availability of transportation.

Notice that the model emphasizes an internal psychological process that lets us anticipate or rehearse what will eventually be our actual behavior in moving through the environment. Thus, Gärling et al. have adopted the concept of **action plans** (Russell & Ward, 1982) as links between stored environmental information and wayfinding behavior.

A good cognitive map would be one excellent wayfinding aid, but some authorities doubt whether a person actually needs a detailed map, either mental or on paper, to find a travel goal. For example, Passini (1984) suggests that wayfinding might best be viewed as a sequence of problem solving tasks that require a certain amount of stored environmental information. This may be an easier task than drawing your route on a sketch map for at least two reasons. First, (assuming you have at least *some* experience in the environment in question), you are facing a task of recognition. Instead of recalling a cognitive map, you may only need to *recognize* a particular environmental feature such as a landmark as you encounter it, and to make a correct decision (such as to turn left) when in its presence. Second, wayfinding is in some way self-correcting. If you find yourself suddenly moving into unfamiliar terrain, you may retrace your steps to the point where you erred and try again. Thus errors in wayfinding need not be

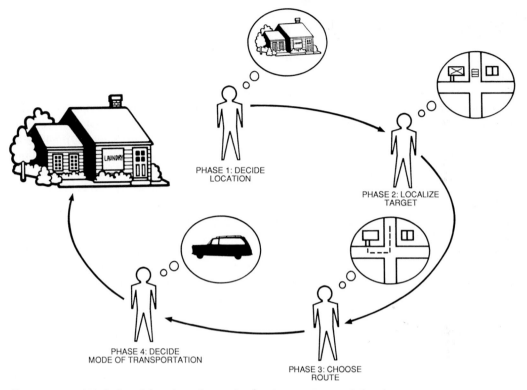

Figure 3–10   Wayfinding: A hypothetical example of a trip to retrieve one's laundry.

PHASE 1: DECIDE
LOCATION

PHASE 2: LOCALIZE
TARGET

PHASE 3: CHOOSE
ROUTE

PHASE 4: DECIDE
MODE OF TRANSPORTATION

cumulative. You may have misjudged the distance or direction from one building to another slightly, but once you do manage to find your way to this key decision point, minor errors earlier in the journey are no longer of any consequence. In general, traditional cognitive maps are less forgiving. You may recall that Byrne (1979) demonstrated that intersections between roads are typically remembered as right angles, even when the actual angle varies from 60 to 90 degrees. Byrne suggests, in fact, that precise information concerning the shape of intersections may be missing from memory entirely. Perhaps, for wayfinding purposes at least, it is sufficient to have a network map which preserves only the connections between steps along a route, but which requires neither knowledge of the distances between choice points or the precise angle at which routes join. On the other hand, it may be that although one

can travel successfully along a predetermined route by recognizing a succession of choice points, a more sophisticated navigation system would allow a person to arrive at the same location via a number of different (perhaps shorter) routes and to find a new location based upon its location with reference to some known landmarks. This more sophisticated type of wayfinding may require the richer spatial understanding characteristic of cognitive maps.

Native or Newcomer: Have I Been Here Before?

Our discussion has led us to suspect that wayfinding may be somewhat different for newcomers than for those who are more familiar with a particular environment (Gärling et al., 1986). Natives have a rich set of environmental associations that are likely to provide not just one, but several routes toward their goal. For those less familiar with an area, wayfinding is obviously more difficult. Information about possible destinations and routes must be obtained from external orientation aides such as maps or a passerby. Of course, some environments are more easily traversed than others, either by accident or (hopefully) by design.

Setting Characteristics that Facilitate Wayfinding

Earlier in this chapter we noted Kevin Lynch's (1960) emphasis on legibility, which largely determines the degree to which an environment facilitates cognitive mapping. Gärling et al. (1986) expand upon this concept and describe three characteristics of physical settings that are likely to affect wayfinding: the degree of differentiation, the degree of visual access, and the complexity of the spatial layout.

Differentiation refers to the degree to which parts of the environment look the same or are distinctive. In general, buildings that are distinctive in shape, easily visible, well maintained, and free-standing are better remembered (Appleyard, 1969; Evans et al., 1982). In the context of interior environments, for example, Evans et al. (1980) demonstrated the effectiveness of color coding in improving wayfinding in a building's interior. Evans et al. (1982) report a variable they label "context," which seems closely related to the distinctiveness created by contrasts in line, form, color, or texture as discussed in descriptive landscape systems (see Chapter 2). In addition to differentiation, the ability to learn a new environment may depend upon the **degree of visual access**. This is the extent to which different parts of the setting can be seen from other vantage points. Of course, Lynch (1960) recognized the importance of visual access in what he termed landmarks. More recently, Evans et al. (1982) speak of

transition, or direct access from a building to the street. Finally, **complexity of the spatial layout** refers to the amount and difficulty of information that must be processed in order to move around in an environment. Too much complexity undermines both navigation and learning. For example, Weisman (1981) found that simple floor plans facilitated wayfinding in campus buildings; in fact, simplicity was even more important than familiarity with the setting in predicting wayfinding difficulties. Taken to an extreme, no amount of familiarity may be able to compensate for extreme architectural complexity (Moeser, 1988). We hasten to distinguish between the complexity of a route or route network, as the term is used here, and the complexity of a particular facade, which should contribute to differentiation as discussed above.

Maps

Recall that Gärling et al. (1986) distinguish between wayfinding in familiar environments and wayfinding for newcomers (see box, page 82). We would expect newcomers to be especially dependent upon signs and maps. Certainly humans often acquire a variety of printed maps and atlases for use as they journey into unfamiliar terrain. It is likely that people learn from maps quite differently than from actually moving through an environment (Thorndyke & Hayes-Roth, 1982). Map learners are privy to a bird's-eye view of the environment, and thus, may acquire what we have called survey knowledge. Thus, a map provides direct access to global relationships of distance and location. On the other hand, spatial learning based upon actual navigation in the environment may be more difficult to obtain, but benefits from the advantages of ecological context and perhaps, more accurate representation of the travel distances for each leg of a journey. Over time, the spatial representations acquired through actual navigation become more like that of survey knowledge. In instances in which the environment is relatively simple, with streets laid out in rectangular grids, navigation may quickly lead to more accurate survey knowledge than that gained from maps (Thorndyke & Hayes-Roth, 1982). On the other hand, for complex environments with many nonperpendicular paths, maps may remain the most efficient method of route learning (Moeser, 1988).

Movies, Slides, and Models: Facilitating Spatial Learning

Although some have expressed concern that even carefully prepared photographic simulations of routes may be inferior to actual walks as wayfinding training aides (Cornell & Hay, 1984), other studies have successfully employed slide photographs as environmental simulations (e.g., Cohen et al., 1986; Hunt, 1984). In fact, in some circumstances day-to-day familiarity may never achieve the level of spatial understanding achieved by subjects given planned instruction (Moeser, 1988). It also follows that if some method could be found to accelerate spatial familiarity, some of the distress associated with relocation could be reduced. Some have focused on the need to assist children in adjusting to new spatial environments. For example, Cohen and his associates (Cohen et al., 1986) investigated the effect of two spatial familiarization experiences on the attitudes of five- and six-year-old kindergarten boys. Two weeks before the start of school some of the boys were given either an on-site tour or a simulated tour accompanied by a scale model of their school. Boys who received either familiarization treatment felt more secure and comfortable several weeks after the start of school than a control group which received no training.

In another study with a quite different population, Hunt (1984) investigated procedures for improving the wayfinding abilities of senior citizen volunteers in an unfamiliar nurs-

ing home. One group of subjects was given a site visit in which they individually received a guided tour through the experimental building. Members of the second experimental group were individually shown photographs of the building ordered in the same sequence as experienced by those on the guided tour. As they viewed the slide photographs, this group could also inspect three-dimensional models of the building's floor plan and exterior. Participants in both treatment conditions were generally superior to a control group on a variety of on-site wayfinding tasks. This result was not surprising; it confirms the usefulness of some prior exposure to an environment, whether simulated or in the form of a tour. More interesting, however, are the differences between the simulation and site visit groups. The groups were similar in their ability to find their way to places along a previously learned route, but members of the simulation group were superior in their ability to find new locations, their ability to identify photographs of building landmarks, and in their understanding of the exterior shape and the spatial configuration of the building. In sum, both groups could learn sequential routes, but the simulation group apparently had a richer and more flexible mental image (presumably because of their exposure to the bird's eye views provided by the scale models).

Of course much of the wayfinding information we acquire comes directly from other people—our friends, acquaintances, or a helpful stranger. Information may include oral instructions, simple sketch maps, or more complex drawings. Interestingly, verbatim instructions (either written or oral) seem superior to more complex or graphic maps that emphasize the overall geography or survey knowledge (Kovach, Surrette, & Aamodt, 1988). Just as not everyone is equally successful in wayfinding, not everyone is equally skilled in *giving* spatial information. Vanetti and Allen (1988) suggest that the ability to give useful route instructions depends upon both spatial skills

You-Are-Here Maps

One problem with maps is that people sometimes have difficulty changing their perspective in translating the map they have learned into a usable navigation plan (Levine, 1982; Thorndyke & Hayes-Roth, 1982). For example, have you ever consulted a **you-are-here map** in a shopping center, museum, or subway terminal? Was the map easy to read and understand, or did you find yourself nearly as confused after reading the map as when you began? Marvin Levine and his associates (Levine, 1982; Levine, Marchon, & Hanley, 1984) have explored the design and placement of these "you-are-here" maps, and have outlined several simple principles that dramatically improve the usefulness of these orientation aides.

Structure Matching

The first problem faced by a you-are-here map user is **structure matching**, that is, the need to pair known points in the environment with their corresponding

Figure 3–11   Structure matching in you-are-here maps. In this map, labels and caricature map symbols allow the user to match the map to the surrounding terrain. (Adapted from Levine, M., 1982. You-are-here maps: Psychological considerations. *Environment and Behavior 14*, 221–237.)

map coordinates. If a person reading the map is unable to accomplish this task, even an accurately drawn map will not be very useful. Technically, Levine argues, two known points on both the map and in the terrain provide the minimum amount of information necessary for a person to relate any object in the environment with its map symbol. A viewer must know not only where he or she is (as would a person viewing Figure 3–11), but also the location of a second pair of points. For example, the figure shows buildings that can be easily identified both on the map and in the environment visible to the visitor. Although in the future this might be accomplished by attaching a sign to building L, we note that the same end might be achieved by using a caricature map symbol that resembles the building as it would be seen from the position of the person reading the map (rather than an aerial or blueprint perspective).

A second way of providing two-point correspondence is to carefully place the map near an asymmetrical feature. This allows the visitor to pinpoint his or her location and that of nearby features. In addition, Levine encourages the use of a bipart you-are-here symbol (also in Figure 3–11). Here both the map the viewer is reading and the position of the visitor are indicated, technically fulfilling the need for two points and allowing the viewer to correctly bring the map and the environment into correspondence.

Orientation

As former Boy or Girl Scouts may know, a map is most easily used if it is placed parallel to the ground and turned so that it is oriented with the terrain. Thus, a goal that is ahead of you on the map is ahead in the terrain, and something to the right on the map is to your right in the environment. In some instances, you-are-here maps in a building can be displayed horizontally so that the map is properly oriented. In most cases, however, practical reasons require the

Figure 3–12   Forward-up equivalence aids in orienting you-are-here maps. (Adapted from Levine, M., 1982. You-are-here maps: Psychological considerations. *Environment and Behavior, 14,* 221–237.

map to be hung vertically on a wall. Although it may not be obvious, correct alignment of these maps may be critical to ensuring that they are easily understood and used by visitors (Levine, Marchon, & Hanley, 1984). These researchers propose that wayfinding maps are best when what is forward on the ground is up on the map (Figure 3–12). This forward–up equivalence also ensures that what is to the right in the terrain is to the right on the map and so forth. Levine et al's. experimental data (1984) show that misalignment of you-are-here maps by 90 degrees or more seriously misleads people, even those who have been alerted to the misalignment!

Unfortunately, the Levine et al. (1984) study also showed that this principle is regularly violated in airports, offices, and other buildings. The severity of the violation may range from being a small inconvenience to shoppers, to potentially life-threatening in the case of fire evacuation maps in an office complex.

- -

and verbal ability. Unless a person knows a spatial layout, he or she is not likely to give useful instructions. On the other hand, if that person is unable to express those instructions clearly, pure spatial knowledge will not be of much use. To examine these ideas, Vanetti and Allen divided subjects into high and low spatial ability and high and low verbal ability groups. Interestingly, there was little difference between the groups in the ability to *follow* route instructions, but those with high spatial ability were more likely to suggest a more efficient route to others.

We might conclude our discussion of wayfinding by noting that people are generally more successful at wayfinding than in cognitive mapping. This observation may be particularly true of children. In spite of the data we reviewed regarding possible deficiencies in children's cognitive maps, particularly their tendency for environmental egocentrism, children beyond kindergarten age seem quite competent at wayfinding. We have already characterized wayfinding as primarily a recognition task and distinguished it from sketch maps that emphasize recall. In addition, many measures of cognitive mapping ability such as sketch maps depend upon skills such as drawing ability that are not so clearly or so often demanded as wayfinding skills in the real world. Finally, perhaps some individuals, particularly children, are intimidated or overwhelmed by the complexity of the task requested by many cognitive map studies, but perform well when faced with an ecologically valid situation.

SUMMARY

Environmental cognition encompasses the general ways of thinking about, recognizing, and organizing the layout of an environment. Cognitive maps are our mental representations of this layout and can be analyzed through a variety of methods. The best known approach to cognitive mapping is that of Kevin Lynch, who emphasized the major elements: paths, landmarks, nodes, edges, and districts.

Cognitive maps are not perfectly accurate representations of the environment; they contain distortions, omissions, and other errors.

These errors often reflect the importance of familiarity with an environment. Current thinking suggests that cognitive maps may be stored as images, as propositions, or both. Propositions, in particular, are often thought of as organized into networks, but the specific form of storage remains controversial.

Action plans serve as the bridge between stored mental images or facts and actual behavior in the environment. The process of using stored spatial information along with maps and other aids is called wayfinding. It seems that wayfinding may involve both recognition of landmarks and other features at choice points, or the recall of a more sophisticated survey or spatial map. Architectural features which make an environment more distinctive or simpler to understand may improve wayfinding. Other attempts to convey spatial information, such as signs and training programs, are likely to improve wayfinding abilities and to reduce the stress of disorientation.

SUGGESTED PROJECTS

1. Ask several friends to draw cognitive maps of your campus. Are the major components similar to each other and to the map you drew while reading this chapter? Do the maps differ by academic major? Are the maps of freshmen or other newcomers different from those who are more familiar with campus?

2. Look for you-are-here maps in your town or on campus. Do any of these maps violate the principles outlined by Levine (1982)? What could be done to improve these maps as wayfinding aids?

3. Make up a short questionnaire to administer to your friends. Ask them to indicate the direction they would travel to get from one to the other of ten pairs of cities. We suggest that you include in your list Reno, Nevada, to San Diego, California; from Oklahoma City, Oklahoma, to Lexington, Kentucky; from Windsor, Ontario, to Albany, New York; from the Atlantic entrance of the Panama Canal to the Pacific entrance; and from London, England, to Minneapolis, Minnesota. Inspect an atlas and construct your own answer key. What kinds of errors did your friends make? Were the pairs of cities we chose particularly difficult? Why or why not?

4 THEORIES OF ENVIRONMENT– BEHAVIOR RELATIONSHIPS

KEY TERMS

adaptation
adaptation level (AL)
adequately staffed
adjustment
adrenal
aftereffects
alarm reaction
ambient stressors
applicants
appraisal
arousal
background stressors
behavioral control
behavior constraint
behavior setting
bivariate theory
capacity
cataclysmic events
catecholamines
challenge appraisal
cognitive control
control models
coping
corticosteroids
curvilinear relationship
daily hassles
decisional control
denial
determinism
diversity
ecological psychology
empirical
empirical laws
en masse behavior pattern
environmental competence
environmental load
environmental press
environmental stress model
epinephrine
equilibrium

extra-individual behavior pattern
galvanic skin response (GSR)
general adaptation syndrome (GAS)
generalizability
harm or loss appraisal
heuristics
homeostatic
hypothesis
intensity
intervening construct
learned helplessness
maintenance minimum
mediating variable
model
nonperformers
norepinephrine
overload
overstaffed
overstimulation
palliative
palmar sweat index
patterning
perceived control
performers
personal stressors
physical milieu
primary appraisal
primary control
psychological reactance
psychological stress
reactance
refractory period
repression—sensitization
REST
reticular formation
retrospective control
screening
secondary appraisal
secondary control
sensory deprivation

social comparison
social support
staffing theory
stage of exhaustion
stage of resistance
standing patterns of behavior
synomorphic
systemic stress

theory
theory of manning
threat appraisal
transactional approach
understaffed
understimulation
Yerkes—Dodson Law

INTRODUCTION

Let us travel back for a moment to a mythical kingdom where there lived an intelligent people ruled by a benevolent royalty. For reasons no one could understand, the kingdom was plagued by periodic winds that could ruin crops, topple peasant homes, and even blow the royal knights off their royal horses. One day a particularly strong wind hit the kingdom, and the royal family decreed that the damage associated with the winds had to stop. They promptly summoned the royal scientist and informed her (forward-looking, nonsexist, mythical kingdoms did exist at that mythical time, you know!) that if she wished to remain on the royal payroll she would have to find a way to keep the wind from wreaking havoc on the kingdom. She began by recording everything that happened when a wind struck. Her most enlightening discovery was that the more the wind bent the chains of the royal drawbridge, the greater the damage observed across the kingdom. "Eureka!" shouted the scientist, "I can stay on the royal payroll!"

She then went to the royal chainmaker and procured 10 three-foot lengths of chain, each made out of a different weight of links. Outside the royal castle she erected a horizontal bar and suspended the chains over it in order of their weight. She now had a way to measure the force of any wind coming through the kingdom. Keeping careful notes, she observed that a wind capable of moving the eight lightest chains would destroy the peasants' huts, any wind that moved the nine lightest chains would knock the royal knights off their horses, and any wind that moved all 10 chains would tear the shutters off the royal dining room. The scientist then arranged for the royal family to hire a royal chainwatcher, who observed the chains and sounded a warning to the royal family and to the peasants whenever the chains indicated a wind strong enough to disrupt their lives was about to hit.

Having thus saved her own royal job, the scientist went on to make more and more scientific observations of the effects of winds of varying forces on the daily lives of the kingdom's inhabitants. Soon she was able to predict from the "chain strength" of the wind not only crop losses but also the disruptive effects of the wind on family life, children walking to school, milk production of the royal dairy herd, and even the pleasantness of the mood of the royal family. Priding herself on the scientific merit of her discoveries, she published her work in the royal scientific journals. When the royal family saw the journal article, "Effects of Wind Chain Force on the Royal Kingdom: A Psychological Stress Theory," they were puzzled as to why psychological stress had anything to do with wind. Summoning the royal scientist, they queried her about the matter. She replied that although physical effects of the wind could be easily observed, in her opinion the psychological reaction to loss of property, inconvenience, and being knocked off one's horse was another important influence of the wind in the kingdom.

The idea of stress in her model was based more on inference than on direct observation, but using the concept of psychological stress had some distinct advantages. Specifically, it helped explain why wind had some of the same effects on people as marital stress, battle fatigue, and the loss of crops through drought. Moreover, incorporating the idea of psychological stress into her model of wind effects helped predict such things as loss of work efficiency and the mood of the royal famly when making important decisions for the kingdom. Finally, the

scientist explained, since much is known about controlling psychological stress, using this knowledge to train the kingdom's inhabitants in more healthy ways of reacting to the wind should help reduce many of the undesirable consequences of exposure to it.

The above tale is intended to illustrate the scientific approach to studying environment–behavior relationships as well as the role of theory in such scientific endeavors. As typically happens in environmental psychology, our mythical scientist first made observations about the effects of wind on behavior, then made theoretical inferences about these effects, and finally used the theoretical notions to explain even more behavioral phenomena. In this chapter we will examine the use and development of those theories in environmental psychology that attempt to explain the influence of environment on behavior. We will begin with a general discussion of the concept and function of theory, then examine some specific psychological theories that have evolved on the nature of environment–behavior relationships, and conclude with our own synthesis of these various orientations.

THE NATURE AND FUNCTION OF THEORY IN ENVIRONMENTAL PSYCHOLOGY

The scientific method is really little more than a specific way of gaining knowledge. Scientists, whether devotees of environmental psychology or any other field, assume there is a great deal of order in the universe that can be discovered with appropriate methodology. Before the applica-

tion of scientific inquiry, however, this universal order is perceived more as chaos or uncertainty than as something systematic. Science (or more specifically the scientific method) is simply a set of procedures for reducing this uncertainty, thereby gaining knowledge of the universal order. It is to these procedures that we owe our progress thus far in environmental psychology. Other approaches to gaining knowledge do exist, of course, such as the methods of religion. In religion, the basis of reducing uncertainity is tradition, faith, revelation, and in many cases, experience. The basis of reducing uncertainty in the scientific approach, on the other hand, is a mathematical prediction of observable events. Once we can predict with near perfection what will happen to phenomenon ''A'' (e.g., crime or violence) when a change occurs in phenomenon ''B'' (e.g., population density), we have taken a giant step toward a scientific understanding of these phenomena.

Suppose, for example, that we want to apply scientific methods to discover the principles involved in getting people to reduce air pollution. We assume that such principles exist (e.g., appealing to conscience, government regulations, administering punishment), and that through scientific inquiry we can not only discover them, but we can also predict how much air pollution will be reduced by applying the principles in varying amounts and combinations. Moreover, the principles should also predict the postive and negative consequences of their application (e.g., cleaner air, better health, potentially reduced profits and productivity of an industry, higher utility bills). Such predictions, however, are rarely perfect. To the extent that our predictions of the phenomena are not perfect, uncertainty remains about the portion of the ordered universe under study. Like the royal scientist, we continue our quest for knowledge.

Thus, scientists assume that events in the universe are related to other events in the universe, and that through scientific inquiry these relationships can be discovered and their consequences predicted. Using scientific methods, environmental psychologists observe fluctuations in some phenomena (e.g., climate changes, inadequate space in an office) and predict their subsequent impacts (e.g., vio-

lence, reduced productivity, efforts to change interior design of space). In psychology, the basic assumption is that behavior is a consequence of the environment, genetics, and intrapsychic (cognitively or emotionally generated) events. Research in psychology, then, is the search for the antecedents of our various behaviors (cf. Franck, 1984).

We should note that the assumption of causation in science involves a philosophical notion of **determinism**. In an absolute sense, a deterministic system implies the opposite of ''free will.'' In a softer interpretation, we can study many interrelated determinants of an outcome, including personal choice (cf. James, 1979; Rotton, 1986). Environmental psychologists are often more concerned with analyzing patterns or shapes of relationships than with a narrower focus on antecedent–consequent dependencies in an environment–behavior system. Altman and Rogoff (1987), for example, note the value of a **transactional approach**, which concentrates on the patterns of relationships rather than on specific causes, although R. Kaplan (1987) cautions that there can be problems of inference in some research which takes a transactional perspective. We should point out that from the perspective of a purist, once we decide that a phenomenon, psychological or otherwise, is indeterminate or is unpredictable, we are really saying that this phenomenon is not within the realm of scientific inquiry, and that we cannot gain knowledge about it through scientific methods.

How do we proceed with scientific research in environmental psychology? Like the royal scientist, we probably start with simple observations. We might observe, for example, that as the concentration of inmates in prisons increases, violence goes up. We have observed two phenomena, prison population density and violence, and we have noted a relationship between the two: As one increases, the other increases (i.e., they are positively correlated). We might then hypothesize, or formulate a hunch, that high population density in prisons leads to increased aggression and violence. (We should caution that actual studies show the effects of prison crowding to be complex, as we discuss in Chapter 9.) The critical step in scientific methodology is the next one—that of testing the hypothesis. All methods of gaining knowledge generate hypotheses. What makes science unique is the method of verifying the hypotheses. Whereas religion may rely on faith, tradition, or individual experience to verify hypotheses, science insists that hypotheses be verified by publicly observable **(empirical)** data. Recall that we described in Chapter 1 several means of acquiring such data. When these observable data do not support the hypothesis, the scientist must either modify the hypothesis or generate an entirely new hypothesis and test it again. If we took the question into the laboratory and found, for example, that putting several individuals into a small room did not increase their level of aggressiveness, we would have to reject the idea that crowding causes aggression and come up with a more complicated hypothesis. For example, maybe it is only under conditions of deprivation (i.e., boredom) that crowding leads to increased aggression. This is a testable proposition (i.e., **hypothesis**). Indeed, as we shall discover in Chapter 9, several investigators have looked at the combined effects of crowding and other variables (such as poverty) on aggression.

This level of scientific research is generally referred to as empirical, meaning observable. Once we have gathered a number of empirical facts, we can proceed to a more abstract and theoretical level. Historically, environmental psychology has followed this course: Once enough empirical facts are known, theories begin to be constructed to explain these facts. Before discussing the general nature of the theory, however, perhaps a word on the distinction between empirical laws, theories, and models is in order. **Empirical laws** are statements of simple observable relationships between phenomena (often expressed in mathematical terms) that can be demonstrated time

and time again. Such things as the law of gravity, the law that magnetic opposites attract, and the law of effect in psychology (i.e., behaviors that lead to pleasurable consequences are likely to be repeated) are easy to demonstrate at an empirical level. Theories usually involve more abstract concepts and relationships than empirical laws and consequently are broader in scope. Theories are not as a rule demonstrable in one empirical setting but are inferred from many empirical relationships. Examples include the theory of evolution, the theory of relativity, and equity theory in psychology (dissatisfaction in a relationship occurs if outcomes are not proportionate to inputs). Finally, a **model** is usually more abstract than an empirical law but is not as complex as a theory. Models are usually based on analogies or metaphors. For example, as was observed in Chapter 3, investigators have assumed that mental maps resemble the ones drawn by cartographers. To take another example, more than one theorist (e.g., Knowles, 1980) has drawn an analogy between the distance that strangers maintain between themselves and others to magnetic or gravitational force fields. A model is often an intermediate step between the demonstration of an empirical law and the formulation of a theory. The distinction can be made that a model is the application of a previously accepted theoretical notion to a new area, but in practice the terms "model" and "theory" are often used interchangeably.

It may be helpful to think of theory as existing at several levels. **Heuristics** are simple principles that facilitate decision-making. For example, the representativeness heuristic says that we decide whether an item fits a category (e.g., whether a sound is meaningless or whether it signals something) based on how representative it is of other items in that category (e.g., whether it resembles other known signals). A model is more elaborate and is based on analogies. A **bivariate theory** simply relates two variables, such as temperature and violence. Well-articulated theories are often quite elaborate and relate multiple concepts to each other. As we shall see, these fully developed theories are not common in environmental psychology.

Basically, a **theory** consists of a set of concepts plus a set of statements relating the concepts to each other. At the theoretical level, we might say that the undesirable effects of high population density in prisons are mediated by the stress associated with high density. That is, high population density leads to stress, and stress in turn may lead to a variety of undesirable consequences, such as increased violence or mental illness. The concept of stress in this example is relatively abstract, in that it is not directly observable but rather is inferred from events that are observable. Such inferred phenomena are often termed **intervening constructs** or **mediating variables**. Empirically, we might infer stress from autonomic arousal (e.g., increased blood pressure, heart rate, or **galvanic skin response**), from verbal and nonverbal signs of anxiety, or from a disintegrated quality of behavior. The distinction between direct observation and abstract inference is one of the main differences between the empirical and theoretical levels of scientific inquiry.

We can identify at least three basic functions of theories. First, theories help us to predict relationships between variables, which implies that we can control what happens to one variable by regulating another variable. For example, if we know that certain conditions of prison crowding lead to violence (i.e., cause violence), we can control the violence to some extent by changing the crowded conditions. If our crowding theory says that stress mediates a relationship between crowding and violence, we might also control violence by controlling stress.

A second function of theories is to summarize large amounts of data. Instead of having to know thousands of pieces of data about the levels of stress and violence under thousands of levels of crowding, if we have a good theory we

can summarize all this information in a few theoretical statements. Such summaries in turn help us predict events that we may not yet have observed at the empirical level.

A third function of theories is the generalization of concepts and relationships to many phenomena, which helps to summarize the knowledge in a particular area. For example, if our theory states that high levels of stress lead to increased levels of violence, this implies that we can generalize the theoretical notion to *any* factor that increases stress, including crowding, noise, poverty, marital discord, and (as our royal scientist suggested) wind. Furthermore, if we can establish that a particular environmental event, such as wild fluctuations in temperature, is stressful, then we can infer from our stress theory that this environmental event will lead to more violence. If empirical evidence does not suggest that a theory generalizes very well, the theory should be modified or rejected in favor of theories that do offer good **generalizability** (Figure 4–1). In one sense, the issue of generalizability is troubling for environmental psychologists, since we like to study environment–behavior relationships in the context where they naturally occur. This proclivity may mean that many relationships observed may

Figure 4–1.   Theory construction.

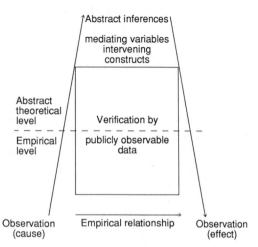

well not exist in any other context. This is just one reason elaborate theories are difficult to generate in environmental psychology (cf. Altman & Rogoff, 1987; R. Kaplan, 1987; Winkel, 1987). Nevertheless, most scientists (including environmental psychologists) would agree that a good theory is high in generalizability.

In addition to these three basic functions, theories are useful in other ways. For one thing, they help to generate additional research by suggesting new relationships between variables. Many scientists assert that the best research is that generated by theories. Another use for theories is in the application of research to practical problems. Solutions to problems are often needed quickly, with little time available for basic research. If theories already exist, they can suggest solutions or at least directions for testing solutions. In a broader sense, theories can help guide policy decisions. Nuclear theory, for example, gives us an idea of the feasibility of widespread use of nuclear generators for electricity as well as an idea of the environmental hazards involved, and thus is useful in establishing public and private policies on nuclear power (cf. van der Pligt, 1985).

Theories in environmental psychology, as in any scientific field, must be constantly evalu-

ated, just as hypotheses must be verified. The basic functions of theories suggest the criteria by which theories should be evaluated. First, a theory is valuable to the extent that it predicts. Given two theories about the same environment–behavior relationship, the one that predicts most accurately most of the time is considered more valuable. Second, good theories do a superior job of summarizing many empirical relationships. Third, a valid theory must be very generalizable. Again, given two theories about the effects of noise on performance, the one that applies to more situations is the more valuable. Fourth, the most useful theories suggest new hypotheses to be tested empirically. In most scientific endeavors, much of the significant research is generated from theories rather than used to construct new theories. Since this research is crucial to our understanding of the phenomena under study, theories that suggest new areas of investigation are highly valued. Because one of the problems often mentioned with environmental psychology is the lack of direction in research, many environmental psychologists await the appearance of theories that will suggest more unifying approaches. We turn now to some of the theories already in use in environmental psychology.

ENVIRONMENT–BEHAVIOR THEORIES: ENERGIZING A GROWING FIELD

As we have just stated, one of the difficulties facing environmental psychology is the lack of a unifying direction in the research of the field. Since one of the functions of good theories is to provide a focus for research, a number of environmental psychologists have made efforts to build models and theories about environment–behavior relationships. Elaborate theo-

ries that meet the criteria of good prediction, summarization, generalization, and research generation are not feasible at this time for at least two reasons. First, the field of environmental psychology is so young that in many cases not enough observations have been made and not enough data have been collected for researchers to be confident about the concepts and relationships (the building blocks of theory) involved. Second, where sufficiently proven concepts and relationships do exist they are so diverse (i.e., they tend to differ from one piece of research to another) that they are difficult to define with the degree of specificity required for a theory (see also Proshansky, 1973).

Since elaborate theoretical systems are not very feasible in environmental psychology at this time, less elaborate theories, each restricted to its own predictive domain, have been developed within the field (cf. Stokols, 1983). Theories or models restricted to environmental perception (e.g., the Kaplan and Kaplan model) have been covered in Chapter 2. In this chapter, we will present a set of theories whose predictive domains are restricted to the effects of environmental conditions on behavior. The empirical data to which these theories are most applicable will be described in subsequent chapters on such topics as noise, weather, air pollution, the city, personal space, and crowding. Specifically, we will examine for now the following six theoretical perspectives, which are probably the most dominant ones in environmental psychology: (1) the arousal approach; (2) the stimulus load approach (overload and underload); (3) the adaptation level approach; (4) the behavior constraint approach; (5) the ecological psychology approach; and (6) the stress approach. Because much of the contribution of these first five approaches (especially the first four) can be incorporated into various aspects of the stress approach, and because stress formulations have been relied upon heavily in environmental psychology, we will elaborate upon environmental stress more than any of the other concepts.

Before elaborating on these various approaches, it will be helpful to keep several points in mind. First, theoretical concepts are not always easy to grasp, and the reader may feel overwhelmed with just one reading of this chapter. Full development and application of the material will become clearer in subsequent chapters. Second, we often rely on more than one theory to explain a given phenomenon. As we will see in the discussion of stress, the mediators of these various conceptual approaches often occur together, and it is sometimes useful to appeal to more than one approach to explain the data. Finally, different theories are useful at different levels of analysis. As we will see, ecological psychology is especially applicable to group behavior, whereas the other approaches are often more useful at the individual level of analysis.

The Arousal Approach

One effect of exposure to environmental stimulation is increased arousal, as measured physiologically by heightened autonomic activity (increased heart rate, blood pressure, respiration rate, adrenaline secretion, etc.) or behaviorally by increased motor activity, or simply as self-reported arousal. From a neurophysiological perspective, **arousal** is a heightening of brain activity by the arousal center of the brain, known as the **reticular formation** (Hebb, 1972). Berlyne (1960a) has characterized arousal as lying on a continuum anchored at one end by sleep and at the other end by excitement or heightened wakeful activity. Since arousal is hypothesized to be a mediator or intervening variable in many types of behavior, a number of environmental psychologists have turned to this concept to explain many of the influences of the environment on behavior.

In fact, you may recall that arousal is one of the dimensions along which any environment can be evaluated (Russell & Snodgrass, 1987). The arousal model makes distinct predictions about the effects on behavior of *lowered* arousal (i.e., toward the "sleep" end of the continuum) as well as *heightened* arousal, and is quite useful in explaining some behavioral effects of such environmental factors as temperature (Bell, 1981), crowding (Evans, 1978; Seta, Paulus, & Schkade, 1976), and noise (Broadbent, 1971; Klein & Beith, 1985). We should emphasize that pleasant as well as unpleasant stimuli heighten arousal. An attractive member of the opposite sex or a thrilling ride at an amusement park can be just as arousing as noxious noise or a crowded elevator.

What happens to behavior when the arousal level of the organism moves from one end of the continuum to the other? As you might expect, several things occur. For one, arousal leads people to seek information about their internal states. That is, we try to interpret the nature of the arousal and the reasons for it. Is the arousal pleasant or unpleasant? Is it due to people around us, to perceived threat, or to some physical aspect of the environment? In part, we interpret the arousal according to the emotions displayed by others around us (Reisenzein, 1983; Schachter & Singer, 1962; Scheier, Carver, & Gibbons, 1979). In addition, the causes to which we attribute the arousal have significant consequences for our behavior. For example, if we attribute the arousal to our own anger, even though it may be due to a factor in the environment, we may become more hostile and aggressive toward others (e.g., Zillmann, 1979). However, attributing the arousal to anger may not be the only reason for increased aggression. According to several theories of aggression (Berkowitz, 1970; Zillmann, 1983), if aggression is the response most likely to occur in a particular situation, then heightened arousal will facilitate aggression. We find, for example, that when noise increases arousal, it may also increase aggression (Geen & McCown, 1984; Geen & O'Neal, 1969). (See also Chapter 5.)

Another reaction we have when we become aroused is to seek the opinion of others. We in part compare our reactions to those of others to see if we are acting appropriately and to see if we are better off or worse off than others (Festinger, 1954; Wills, 1981). This process is known as **social comparison**. We can feel better about our own circumstances if we compare our standing with others who are faring more poorly. Victims of a natural disas-

ter, for example, become very aroused by the circumstances and seek to compare their fate with the fate of others (Hansson, Noulles, & Bellovich, 1982).

Arousal also has important consequences for performance, especially as formulated through the **Yerkes–Dodson Law**. According to this law, performance is maximal at intermediate levels of arousal and gets progressively worse as arousal either falls below or rises above this optimum point. Moreover, the inverted-U relationship between arousal and performance varies as a function of task complexity. For complex tasks, the optimum level of performance occurs at a slightly lower level of arousal than for simple tasks, as depicted in Figure 4–2. This **curvilinear relationship** appears consistent with other findings (see page 46) that humans seek an intermediate level of stimulation—too much or too little is undesirable (Berlyne, 1960a, 1974). From an environment–behavior perspective, we would expect that as environmental stimulation from crowding, noise, air pollution, or any other source increases arousal, performance will either improve or deteriorate, depending on whether the affected person's response is below, at, or above the optimum arousal level for a particular task (see also Broadbent, 1971; Hebb, 1972; Kahneman, 1973). Apparently, low arousal is not conducive to maximum performance, and extremely high arousal prevents us from concentrating on the task at hand.

The arousal approach fares reasonably well as a theoretical base in environmental psychology, although it does have shortcomings. Performance and aggression can be predicted from the effects of the environment on arousal, and the arousal notion does generalize to several environmental factors, most notably noise, heat, and crowding. Unfortunately, arousal can be difficult to measure with a high degree of confidence and generalizability. Some measures used in research include heart rate, blood pressure, respiration rate, blood vessel constric-

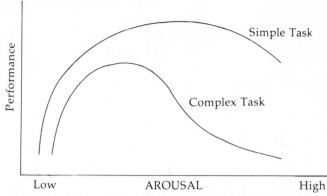

Figure 4—2.   The Yerkes-Dodson Law predicts an optimal level of performance for simple and complex tasks, with arousal below or above the optimum resulting in performance decrements.

tion, **galvanic skin response** (or GSR, meaning electrical conductance of skin due to sweating), **palmar sweat index** (reaction of palm sweat with a chemical), urine secretion, brain wave activity, physical activity level, muscle tension, skin temperature, and self-report scales. Physiological indices of arousal are not always consistent with each other and are often not consistent with self-report, paper-and-pencil measures of arousal (cf. Cacioppo & Petty, 1983; Cervone, 1977; Lacey, 1967). Whereas one measure may indicate increases in arousal in a given situation, other measures may show decreased or unchanged arousal. Which measure to choose in predicting behavior thus becomes a serious problem. Nevertheless, the arousal notion is a useful one and will probably continue to be incorporated into those environment—behavior relationships to which it is applicable.

The Environmental Load Approach

Imagine you are trying to study for three exams you have the following day but your roommate wants to watch television, there is a loud party next door, and two friends come by to entice you to go out for a drink. How can you possibly study for your exams with all this going on? The situation is similar to the circumstances under which the **environmental load** approach explains environment—behavior relationships. This model derives from work on attention and information processing. One consequence of excessive stimulation is that individuals develop "tunnel vision," such that all of their attention is focused on one stimulus to the detriment of other, more peripheral stimuli relevant to the organism's functioning. Cohen (1978) and Milgram (1970) have developed this attention-narrowing process into models that handle much of the data collected about exposure to novel or unwanted environmental stimuli. Rather than explaining the effects of complex environmental stimulation by using only the concept of arousal, Cohen and Milgram suggest that individuals have a limited capacity to process information. When the amount of information from the environment exceeds the individual's capacity to process all that is relevant, information **overload** occurs. The primary coping strategy in response to this overload is to ignore some of the stimulus inputs. It is this ignoring of inputs, according to the environmental load theorists, that accounts for the positive or negative behavioral effects of excessive environmental stimulation, or **overstimulation** (Broadbent, 1958, 1963; Cohen, 1978; Easterbrook, 1959).

A more detailed explanation of the environmental load approach can be found in Cohen's (1978) model, which contains the following four basic assumptions:

1. Humans have a limited capacity to process incoming stimuli and can invest only a limited effort in attending to inputs at any one time.

2. When environmental inputs exceed capacity to attend to them, the normal strategy is to ignore those inputs that are less relevant to the task at hand and to devote more attention to those that are relevant. We often take active steps to prevent less relevant or distracting stimuli from occurring. For example, Ahrentzen and Evans (1984) noted how teachers modify the classroom environment to minimize distractions.

3. When a stimulus occurs that may require some sort of adaptive response (or when an individual thinks such a stimulus will occur), the significance of the stimulus is evaluated by a monitoring process, and a decision is made about which coping responses, if any, to employ. Thus, the more intense or unpredictable or uncontrollable an input, the greater its adaptive significance and the more attention paid to it. Furthermore, the more uncertainty generated by an input about the need for an adaptive response, the more attentional capacity allocated to it.

4. The amount of attention available to a person is not constant and may be temporarily depleted after prolonged demands. After attending to prolonged demands, the total capacity for attention may suffer from an overload. For example, after studying hard for several hours, it is difficult to do anything that demands much attention.

What happens to behavior when an overload occurs? The answer depends on which stimuli are given adequate attention and which are ignored. Generally, stimuli most important to the task at hand are allocated as much attention as needed, and less important stimuli are ignored. If these less important stimuli tend to interfere with the central task, ignoring them will enhance performance. If, however, a task requires a wide range of attention, as when we must do two things at once, performance on less important tasks will deteriorate. In an interesting demonstration of this process, Brown and Poulton (1961) required subjects driving a car either in a residential area (relatively small number of important inputs) or in the parking lot of a crowded shopping center (relatively large number of important inputs) to listen to a series of taped numbers and determine which numbers changed from one sequence to the next. More errors were made on this secondary numbers task when subjects drove in the shopping center, presumably because in the shopping center more attention had to be allocated to important stimuli connected with driving, to the detriment of the less important stimuli of the numbers task.

According to the overload model, once capacity for attention has been depleted owing to prolonged demands, even small demands for attention may cause overloading. Interestingly, once exposure to unpleasant or excessive stimulation has ceased, behavioral aftereffects, such as decreased tolerance for frustration, errors in mental functioning, and less frequent altruistic behavior, may occur (see Chapters 5 and 6 and the box on page 99 for research examples). The overload model attributes these aftereffects to a reduced capacity to attend to relevant cues.

Georg Simmel, a sociologist writing about a century ago, attributed behavioral pathologies in large urban areas to a type of overload (e.g., Simmel, 1957 translation). Milgram (1970) also suggested that the deterioration of social life in large urban areas is caused by the ignoring of peripheral social cues and a reduced capacity to attend to them because of the increased demands of everyday functioning.

The Aftermath of Overload

We have noted that we tend to narrow attention and ignore non-central information when our processing capacity becomes overloaded, so that performance may deteriorate. Interestingly, for some time *after* the overload has apparently stopped, we may suffer from the cost of recovering from the overload. Cohen and Spacapan (1978) reported two studies demonstrating this aftereffect of overload.

First, 80 research subjects viewed a panel of 12 lights, with each light one of three different colors. When a light came on, the subject had to press one of three keys corresponding to the matching color. In a *low load* condition, the time between consecutive illuminations was 0.8 seconds. In the *high load* condition, the time between lights was 0.4 seconds. Thus, in the high load condition subjects had to process more information in a given interval of time. Once they had finished the task, subjects were asked to work on some paper-and-pencil puzzles which were actually impossible to solve. Those who had been in the high load condition spent almost two minutes less than those in the low load condition before giving up on the puzzles. Apparently, the higher load reduced tolerance for the frustration of working on the puzzles.

In a second study, 40 students individually walked through a shopping mall and listed and priced various items in the stores according to a prearranged set of instructions for 26 tasks. All subjects had 30 minutes to complete the sequence of pricing tasks. High load subjects were given twice as many items as low load subjects to list for each task. In addition, half the subjects conducted their mall survey on weekday afternoons (low shopper density) and half on weekend afternoons (high shopper density). The very last pricing task occurred in an isolated hallway. As the subject finished it, an experimenter's assistant (unknown to the subject) standing nearby pretended to lose a contact lens. As the environmental load model would predict, fewer subjects helped look for the lens in the high load than low load condition (17% vs. 57%), and fewer helped in the high than low density condition (also 17% vs. 57%). Thus, even after an apparent overload, there is a negative impact on task performance and social behavior. Cohen and Spacapan also interpreted their results in terms of aftereffects within the context of the environmental stress model, which we discuss beginning on page 114.

Thus, urban ills, such as bystanders ignoring others in distress, may be due in part to an environmental overload in which the hustle and bustle of everyday life in the city requires so much attention that there is very little left over for "peripheral" social concerns. Some city dwellers may be forced to develop an aloof attitude toward others in order to allocate enough time to everyday functioning (see Chapter 10).

The environmental load model stands up to theoretical scrutiny about as well as the arousal model. It does predict some of the behavioral consequences of excessive environmental stimulation. However, there are many difficult-to-determine "if's" incorporated into the model, including whether or not in a given situation an overload occurs, whether a specific task is important, whether ignoring less important stimuli facilitates or impairs performance on a particular task, and whether demand has been sufficiently prolonged to deplete attentional capacity. In terms of generality, the model applies to mental and motor performance and to at least some social behaviors. As far as generating research is concerned, the environmental load model does suggest many possibilities, including evaluating whether or not a given environment is likely to produce an overload, and assessing the extent to which attentional depletion contributes to social and environmental problems.

The Understimulation Approach

The environmental overload approach suggests that many environment–behavior relationships, especially those leading to undesirable behavioral and affective (emotional) consequences, are a function of too much stimulation from too many sources. A number of theorists have suggested, however, that many environment-behavior problems result from *too little* stimulation. **Sensory deprivation** studies (e.g., Zubek, 1969) suggest that depriving individuals of all sensory stimulation can lead to severe anxiety and other psychological anomalies, although some of these effects may be due to suggestibility from laboratory procedures such as the prominent display of a "panic button" and signing liability release forms mentioning the possibility of serious damage (cf. Barabasz & Barabasz, 1985). In fact, there may well be benefits of reduced stimulation (see box on page 101). Nevertheless, other research has documented the deleterious effects of **understimulation** on such processes as the maturational development of the young (e.g., Schultz, 1965). Drawing on these sources, some theorists suggest that the environment should sometimes be made *more* complex and stimulating in order to restore excitement and a sense of

belonging to individuals' perceptions of their environment.

Even limited sensory deprivation can have predictable effects on us. For example, Antarctic isolation has been shown to modify performance on a perception task (Barabasz & Barabasz, 1986). Moreover, the isolation of solitary sailing or from being an air crash survivor in a remote region can generate a "sensed presence" of another individual even when no such person exists (Suedfeld & Mocellin, 1987).

Although cities may have an overstimulating social environment, they may subject inhabitants to an understimulating physical environment. Urbanologist A. E. Parr (1966) has contended that fields, forests, and mountains contain an unending variety of changing patterns of visual stimulation, but that urban areas contain the same patterns repeated on every street. In many tract housing developments in particular, the structures all resemble each other. According to Parr, the giant skyscrapers lining city streets and the interiors of modern windowless structures instill a sense of enclosure rather than a sense of being drawn to the next horizon. Parr and others assert that this lack of stimulation leads to boredom and is in some way responsible for such urban ills as juvenile delinquency and vandalism, and poor education (cf. Heft, 1979).

To better study some of these problems of understimulation, Wohlwill (1966) advocated scaling environments along a number of dimensions of stimulation, including intensity, novelty, complexity, temporal change or variation, surprisingness, and incongruity. As we will see in Chapter 10, the desire for these types of stimulation may explain why people leave cities in great numbers to live in more "natural" environments.

As a theoretical approach by itself, the understimulation angle does help predict some environment–behavior relationships, but it stands in marked contrast to arousal and overload theories that examine the same environments and find too much stimulation. More-

REST: The Benefits of Sensory Deprivation

We have noted that sensory deprivation can have deleterious effects on people. In contrast to such findings, many studies suggest that there are actually benefits to boredom. A procedure called **REST**, or Restricted Environmental Stimulation Technique, or Restricted Environmental Stimulation Therapy (Suedfeld, 1980) involves placing a person in a soundproof, darkened room or into a darkened water tank.

The potential benefits of REST seem to cover many areas. For example, reduced stimulation seems to have favorable outcomes for hyperactive and autistic children (Suedfeld, Schwartz, & Arnold, 1980). Biofeedback seems to have more positive effects when combined with REST (Lloyd & Shurley, 1976; Plotkin, 1978). Hypertension (high blood pressure) can be reduced with REST (Fine & Turner, 1982; Kristeller, Schwartz, & Black, 1982; Suedfeld, Roy, & Landon, 1982), and REST can help some individuals stop smoking (Suedfeld & Baker-Brown, 1986).

How does REST achieve these results? No one knows for sure, but one proposed avenue is that with reduced extraneous stimulation, subjects can better recognize internal states (such as high blood pressure), and thus take more effective self-regulatory steps. Another possibility is that REST disorganizes established mechanisms for maintaining chronic maladaptive patterns, and thus permits new, more adaptive mechanisms to take over.

However it works, REST has become commercially popular in such areas as California. That is, businesses provide REST-type tanks or beds for clients to purchase or rent on a short-term basis. We suspect such ventures will spur more investigations into the value of REST procedures.

over, some researchers claim there are benefits to be derived from deprivation of sensory stimulation (e.g., Suedfeld, 1975). We will reserve further judgment on the understimulation theory until we have examined a theoretical approach that attempts to consolidate the understimulation and overstimulation approaches.

Adaptation Level Theory: Optimal Stimulation

If the research evidence supporting the arousal and overload theories suggests that too much environmental stimulation has deleterious effects on behavior and emotions, and if the evidence supporting the understimulation approach suggests that too little stimulation simi-larly has undesirable effects, it stands to reason that some intermediate level of stimulation would be ideal. This is the approach taken by Wohlwill (1974) in his **adaptation level (AL)** theory of environmental stimulation. Borrowing from Helson's (1964) adaptation level theory of sensation and perception, Wohlwill began with the assumption, for example, that humans dislike crowds, at least on certain occasions, as when trying to make last-minute Christmas purchases or trying to leave a packed football stadium at the end of the game. On the other hand, most of us do not like total social isolation all day either. Wohlwill believed that the same applies for all types of stimulation, including temperature, noise, and even the complexity of roadway scenery. What we usually prefer is an optimal level of stimulation (see also, Zuckerman, 1979).

Categories and Dimensions of Stimulation
At least three categories of environment–behavior relationships should conform to this optimal level hypothesis, according to Wohlwill. These categories are sensory stimulation, social stimulation, and movement. Too much or too little sensory stimulation is undesirable, too much or too little social contact is undesirable, and too much or too little movement is undesirable. (Do you see the similarity between this notion and the Yerkes–Dodson Law described under arousal theory?) These categories in turn vary along at least three dimensions that have optimal levels. The first dimension is **intensity**. As we have noted, too many or too few people around us can be psychologically disturbing. Too little or too much auditory stimulation has the same unwanted effect. We have all experienced the irritation of neighbors making distracting noise while we were trying to listen to a lecture or concert, of loud stereos playing when we are trying to study, and of children screaming when adults are trying to carry on a conversation. On the other hand, if you have ever been in a soundproof chamber for very long, you know that the absence of external sound becomes very unnerving after only five or ten minutes.

Another dimension of environmental stimulation is **diversity**, both across time and at any given moment. Too little diversity in our surroundings produces boredom and the desire to seek arousal and excitement. Too much diversity, as in the typical "strip" of fast-food franchises, gas stations, and glaring neon signs common in many towns and cities, is considered an eyesore. Considerable research (see Wohlwill, 1974) indicates that the perceived attractiveness and the degree of pleasant feelings associated with a human-built scene are maximized at an intermediate level of diversity (see the section on aesthetics in Chapter 2).

The third dimension of stimulation is **patterning**, or the degree to which a perception contains both structure and uncertainty. The total absence of structure that can be coded by our information processing mechanisms, such as diffuse light of a constant intensity or a single tone at a constant volume, is disturbing. By the same token, a very complex pattern that contains no predictable structure is also disturbing. To the extent that a modern built environment is so diverse and complex that we have difficulty imposing a perceptual structure on it, we probably experience that environment as stressful. Urban street patterns are a good example of this dimension. Parallel streets in intersecting grid patterns can be monotonous. On the other hand, complex layouts with no predictable numbering or no easy access to major arteries can cause a headache. An intermediate level of patterning, with gently winding streets and cul-de-sacs, is usually comfortable, yet pleasantly stimulating.

Optimizing Stimulation After assuming the general rule that there are optimal levels of environmental stimulation, Wohlwill introduced a modifier to this rule by further assuming that each person has an optimal level of stimulation, which is based on past experience. Thus, Tibetan tribesmen, who live comfortably at altitudes with so little oxygen that most of us would have difficulty maintaining consciousness, have adapted to a level of oxygen concentration quite different from what most of us would consider ideal. Similarly, those of us who live in cities probably have a higher level of tolerance for crowds and less tolerance for isolation than do most residents of rural areas. After a person raised in a rural area has lived in a city for a few months or years, he or she probably acquires a greater tolerance for crowds than the rural resident who never moves to a city. Wohlwill referred to this shift in optimal stimulation level as **adaptation**, defined as "a quantitative shift in the distribution of judgmental or affective responses along a stimulus continuum, as a function of continued exposure to a stimulus" (1974, p. 134). Adaptation levels not only differ from person to person as a function of experience but may also change with time following exposure to a different level of stimulation. Thus, how one evaluates and reacts to a given environment along a particular dimension is in part determined by how much that environment deviates from one's adaptation level on that dimension. The more an environment deviates from the adaptation level, the more intense the reaction to that environment should be. As you may recall from Chapter 2, there is considerable variation in individual perceptions of what constitutes a "beautiful" or "desirable" environment. Adaptation level theory suggests that the reason for this variation involves individual differences in adaptation level along several relevant dimensions.

Adaptation versus Adjustment Adaptation level theory postulates an interesting environment–behavior relationship in the distinction between adaptation and what Sonnenfeld (1966) calls **adjustment**. Adaptation refers to changing the response to the stimulus, whereas adjustment refers to changing the stimulus itself. Adjustment in this case does not refer to the adjustment–maladjustment continuum conceptualized in clinical psychology (i.e., an internal, psychological state), but rather to a mechanism by which we change the environment. For example, adaptation to hot temperatures would involve gradually getting used to the heat so that we do not sweat as profusely on exposure to it. Adjustment would involve either wearing lighter clothes or installing an air conditioning system so that the temperature stimulus striking our skin is much cooler. For most organisms and for early human societies, adaptation was probably a more realistic option than adjustment. For modern societies with advanced technology, however, adjustment is so clearly a realistic option than we prefer it over adaptation. Witness, for example, one response to the need to adjust thermostats so that heating the indoor environment will use less energy (Figure 4–3). Rather than adapt to temperatures that are only slightly below what we perceive as optimal, we often resort to high-polluting wood stoves or fireplace inserts that will let us maintain the old adaptation level.

Figure 4–3. If we humans were as willing to adapt to the environment as we are to adjust to it, we would accept slightly uncomfortable temperatures rather than adjust the environment by using high-polluting fireplace inserts.

In general, adaptation level theory suggests that when given a choice between adapting and adjusting, people will take the course that causes the least discomfort.

Evaluation of the Optimal Stimulation Approach: Breadth versus Specificity It should be obvious that adaptation level theory incorporates some of the best features of arousal, overload, and understimulation theories. As such, it has rather broad generality, applying to physical and social environments as well as to all forms of sensation and perception. AL theory also suggests that future research might well concentrate on the adaptation process in order to solve many environmental problems. One problem that arises with this theory, however, is that since it allows for so much individual variation in adaptation level, it becomes very difficult to make more general predictions about environmental preference and environment–behavior relationships. This problem typically arises in behavioral science theories. The more specific the elements from which predictions are made, the less general the predictions; the more general the predictors, the less specific the predictions.

Another problem with AL theory is that it is often difficult to identify an "optimal" level of stimulation before we make a prediction. Recall, for example, our discussion of environmental aesthetics in Chapter 2, in which it was proposed that an intermediate level of complexity would lead to optimal judgments of beauty. This prediction often proves incorrect, in part because we have difficulty defining what we mean by an intermediate level of complexity. In order for AL theory to work, we would need to see what conditions maximize judgments of beauty, then define that level of complexity as intermediate. What is really needed is more research which quantifies levels of environmental stimulation. Only then can we know how well AL theory predicts environment–behavior relationships.

The Behavior Constraint Approach

According to the theoretical perspectives we have examined thus far, excessive or undesirable environmental stimulation leads to arousal or a strain on the information-processing capacity. Another potential consequence of such stimulation is loss of **perceived control** over the situation. Have you ever been caught in a severe winter storm or summer heat wave and felt there was nothing you could do about it? Or have you ever been forced to live or work in extremely crowded conditions and felt the situation was so out of hand there was nothing you could do to overcome it? This loss of perceived control over the situation is the first step in what is known as the **behavior constraint** model of environmental stimulation (Proshansky, Ittleson, & Rivlin, 1970; Rodin & Baum, 1978; Stokols, 1978, 1979; Zlutnick & Altman, 1972). So important is the feeling of perceived control that some would classify the behavior constraint model as a subunit of a **"control model"** that is more global. Whatever classification one might prefer, the concepts in the model are extremely important to environmental psychologists.

The term "constraint" here means that something about the environment is limiting or interfering with things we wish to do. According to the behavior constraint model, the constraint can be an actual impairment from the environment or simply our belief that the environment is placing a constraint upon us. What is most important is the cognitive interpretation of the situation as being beyond our control.

Once you perceive that you are losing control over the environment, what happens next? When you perceive that environmental events are constraining or restricting your behavior, you first experience discomfort or negative affect. You also probably try to reassert your control over the situation. This phenomenon is known as **psychological reactance**, or simply **reactance** (Brehm, 1966; Brehm &

. . . .

Environments and the Elderly: Environmental Press and Competence

Adaptation level theory posits that each person has an optimal level of stimulation along several dimensions. A special application of this idea is a model of **environmental press** developed by M. Powell Lawton and Lucille Nahemow to describe environments for the elderly (Lawton, 1975; Lawton & Nahemow, 1973; Nahemow & Lawton, 1973). This model posits that the demands (i.e., press) an environment places on its occupants as well as the competence of the occupants determine the consequences of interacting with the environment. If the impact of the press is within the **environmental competence** of the individual to handle it (i.e., within the adaptation level), positive feelings about the environment occur and the behavior is adaptive. If the press is considerably weaker or stronger than the competence of the individual (i.e., outside the adaptation level), negative feelings and maladaptive behavior occur. Thus, an understimulating nursing home environment or a fast-paced, crime-ridden neighborhood may both be outside the desired adaptation level for press and competence. We will see in Chapter 12 how environments for the elderly can be designed to suit their needs.

. . . .

Brehm, 1981; Wortman & Brehm, 1975). Any time we feel that our freedom of action is being constrained, psychological reactance leads us to try to regain that freedom (cf. Strube & Werner, 1984). If crowding is a threat to our freedom, we react by erecting physical or social barriers to "shut others out." If the weather restricts our freedom, we might stay indoors or else use technological devices (e.g., snow plows, air-conditioned cars) to regain control. According to the behavior constraint model, we do not actually have to experience loss of control for reactance to set in; all we need do is *anticipate* that some environmental factor is about to restrict our freedom. Mere anticipation of crowding, for example, is enough to make us start erecting physical or psychological barriers against others.

What happens if our efforts to reassert control are unsuccessful in regaining freedom of action? The ultimate consequence of loss of control, according to the behavior constraint model, is **learned helplessness** (Garber & Seligman, 1981; Seligman, 1975). That is, if repeated efforts at regaining control result in failure, we might begin to think that our actions have no effect on the situation, so we stop trying to gain control even when, from an objective point of view, our control has been restored. In other words, we "learn" that we are helpless. Students who try to change a class schedule but are rebuffed by the registration office numerous times soon "learn" that they are helpless against bureaucracy. Similarly, if efforts to overcome crowding are unsuccessful, we may abandon our attempts to gain privacy and change our lifestyles accordingly. During a very severe winter there are sometimes reports of individuals "giving up" trying to keep warm when their fuel supplies become depleted, and some people die as a result. While less severe than death, learned helplessness often leads to depression.

The behavior constraint model, then, posits three basic steps: perceived loss of control, reactance, and learned helplessness. The use of this model thus far in environmental psychology has been relatively limited, although com-

. . . .

Perceived Control
and Research Ethics:
A Dilemma

We have noted that perceived control over unpleasant environmental stimulation such as noise reduces the negative consequences of exposure to the stimuli. An interesting problem in this regard has arisen in the area of laboratory research on environmental stressors. Gardner (1978) notes that for years it was possible to demonstrate such effects as reduced proofreading speed and accuracy when laboratory subjects were exposed to uncontrollable noise. Subsequent research, however, has failed to find these detrimental effects. What went wrong? Gardner provides evidence that the "culprit" is a set of research ethics guidelines established by the Federal government and implemented by universities and other research institutions. Among these guidelines is a requirement that subjects be informed of potential risks when participating in experiments, even though the risks are minimal. Moreover, subjects must be told that they are free to terminate the experiment at any time, and must sign an "informed consent" statement disclosing the risks and the termination provision. Gardner provides evidence that such informed consent procedures amount to giving subjects perceived control over the stressor, and thus stress effects are reduced! The situation is then an ethical dilemma: How can one ethically do research on stressful environmental conditions if the ethical procedures in effect eliminate the negative reactions to those conditions? Gardner proposes that where risks are minimal, the need to know about these effects justifies modification of the informed consent procedures. Such a decision would rest with an institutional review board to ensure the safety of subjects. Alternatively, more emphasis may have to be placed on field research involving natural observation. Ultimately, we suspect the ethical dilemma can never be fully resolved (see also, Dill, et al., 1982).

. . . .

ponents are often discussed within the context of the stress or load models. Whether treated within the behavior constraint model or within some other model, it is clear that perceived loss of control has unfortunate consequences for behavior, and that restoring control enhances performance and mental outlook. For example, Glass and Singer (1972) found that telling subjects they could reduce the amount of noxious noise in an experiment by pressing a button reduced or eliminated many of the negative effects of noise, even though subjects did not actually press the button. That is, simply perceiving that they could control the noise reduced the adaptive costs of that stressor.

Perceived control over noise has also been found to reduce its negative effects on aggression (Donnerstein & Wilson, 1976) and helping behavior (Sherrod & Downs, 1974). Moreover, perceived loss of control over air pollution seems to reduce efforts to do anything about the problem (Evans & Jacobs, 1981). Similarly, perceived control over crowding reduces its unpleasant effects (e.g., Langer & Saegert, 1977; Rodin, 1976), and perceived control over crime may motivate us to employ more prevention measures (Miransky & Langer, 1978; Tyler, 1981). Moser and Levy-LeBoyer (1985) showed that loss of perceived control over a malfunctioning phone led to acts of aggression, but the availability of information designed to restore control improved the situation.

Perceived control also has implications for institutional environments. Langer and Rodin (1976), for example, manipulated the amount of control residents of a nursing home had over their daily affairs. For instance, one group was told the staff would take care of them while another group was told they were responsible for themselves. One group was given plants to raise themselves, while the other group was given plants to be cared for by the staff. After three weeks, residents in the high-control group showed greater well-being and enhanced mood and more activity than those in the low-control condition. Even 18 months later the high-control group had more positive outcomes (Rodin & Langer, 1977; see also Lemke & Moos, 1986; Rothbaum, Weisz, & Synder, 1982). Schulz (1976) has also documented positive effects of a perceived control intervention for the institutionalized elderly. After the intervention was terminated, however, those in the high-control condition showed an especially rapid decline (Schulz & Hanusa, 1978), perhaps because a lessened sense of control produced learned helplessness and depression.

Several attempts have been made to elaborate on the types of control we can have over our environment. Averill (1973), for example, distinguishes between categories of : (1) **behavioral control**, in which we have available a behavioral response which can change the threatening environmental event (e.g., turning off a loud noise); (2) **cognitive control**, in which we process information about the threat in such a way that we appraise it as less threatening or understand it better (e.g., deciding there is no danger in working outdoors during a heat wave); and (3) **decisional control**, in which we have a choice among several options (e.g., choosing to live in a quiet rather than a noisy neighborhood). Behavioral control can be manifested either through regulated administration, in which there is control over who administers the threatening event and when they do it, or through stimulus modification, in which the threat can be avoided, terminated, or otherwise modified. Cognitive control can be manifested either through appraisal of the event as less threatening or through information gain about such factors as predictability or consequences. Thompson (1981) has noted that there are some questions about this type of categorization, and adds a category of **retrospective control**, in which we perceive present control over a past aversive event. Weisz, Rothbaum, and Blackburn (1984) distinguish between **primary control**, meaning overt control over existing conditions, and **secondary control**, meaning accommodating to existing realities and becoming satisfied with things the way they are (see also, Thompson, 1981). These authors note that there may be cultural differences in the emphasis placed on primary versus secondary control (cf. Azuma, 1984; Kojima, 1984). Apparently, the amount of control we have is important: Being able to control both onset and termination of a noise results in better adaptation than control over just onset or just termination of the noise (Sherrod et al., 1977). We may also have more control over some areas of our lives (e.g., our bedroom) than over others (e.g., our community; see Paulhus, 1983).

It would be an oversimplification to state that the greater the control we perceive over our environment, the better we are able to adapt to it successfully. In fact, there are some circumstances under which control can lead to increased threat, anxiety, and maladaptive behavior (e.g., Averill, 1973; Folkman, 1984; Thompson, 1981). For example, knowing that you can control a potential flood by building a larger levee may make you worry about the expense and time commitment of the intervention. Or, if your dwelling is built near a toxic waste dump, perceived control through the option of moving away may heighten concern about losing close neighbors and the emotional attachment to your dwelling. Interestingly, sometimes we actually prefer *less* control. For example, there is evidence that some elderly people prefer less personal control over health-related decisions, and wish that others would make these decisions for them (see Rodin, 1986; Woodward & Wallston, 1987).

Just as research has progressed on the perceived control component of the behavior constraint model, so has research on the reactance and learned helplessness components. For our present discussion, the work on learned helplessness seems especially important. For example, Hiroto (1974) found that when subjects were given a chance to terminate an aversive noise, those who had previously been able to control it learned to terminate it. Those who had previously been unable to control the noise, however, responded as if they were helpless, and failed to learn the termination procedure. Similarly, a field study with school children found that those who attended noisy schools near Los Angeles International Airport showed more signs of learned helplesness than those from quieter schools (Cohen et al., 1980, 1981).

Lately, learned helplessness effects have been interpreted in terms of attribution theory (e.g., Abramson, Seligman, & Teasdale, 1978; Miller & Norman, 1979; Peterson & Seligman, 1984; Sweeney, Anderson, & Bailey, 1986; Tennen & Eller, 1977). Attributions are inferences about causes for events or about characteristics of people or events. Although the details of the attribution interpretations of learned helplessness are too extensive for in-depth coverage here, we can make a few general statements. In general, helplessness effects are more likely to occur if we attribute our lack of control over the environment to: (1) stable rather than unstable factors (e.g., to our physical or mental inability to do anything about it rather than to our temporary lack of time to act on it); (2) general rather than specific factors (e.g., attributing pollution to all industry rather than to a specific factory); and (3) internal rather than external locus of control (e.g., attributing our discomfort in a crowd to our own preference for open spaces rather than to the behavior of others in the crowd). In a confirmation of this attributional approach, researchers found that those who attributed negative outcomes to global (general) factors showed helplessness deficits in settings both similar and dissimilar to the setting where an initial negative outcome occurred. Those who attributed the initial negative outcome to specific factors, however, showed helplessness effects only in settings similar to the initial one (Alloy et al., 1984).

Research on reactance, perceived loss of control, and learned helplessness is certain to continue, whether interpreted from the perspective of the behavior constraint model or from some other perspective. The model itself has considerable, though limited, utility. In instances of perceived loss of control, the model is quite useful in predicting some of the consequences. In cases in which there is no reason to infer perceived loss of control, however, other mediators, such as stress, arousal, and overload, are probably necessary to explain environment–behavior relationships. Moreover, the behavior constraint approach places much emphasis on individual reactions, and can minimize the need to look at the entire setting (cf. Stokols, 1979). The conceptualization we will examine next, in contrast, places heavy emphasis on the setting.

Barker's Ecological Psychology

The theoretical perspectives reviewed up to this point have been concerned primarily with the specific effects of the environment on behavior; but, with the exception of the behavior constraint model, they have not been concerned with the effects of behavior on the environment. Yet, as we have noted many times, behavior inevitably influences the environment. The **ecological psychology** approach views environment–behavior relationships as two-way streets or, in other words, as ecological interdependencies.

Barker (1968, 1979, 1987) and his colleagues have been the principal advocates of the ecological approach. The focus of Barker's model is the influence of the **behavior setting** on the behavior of large numbers of people, which is termed the **extra-individual behavior pattern**. The unique aspect of Barker's approach is that the behavior setting is an entity in itself. It is not an arbitrarily defined social scientific concept but actually exists and has a physical structure, although it does change over time (Wicker, 1987). In order to understand just how this behavior setting functions, we will first look at some characteristics of the behavior setting, then see how the setting fits into Barker's theory of undermanning, or theory of staffing.

The Nature of the Behavior Setting A number of behaviors can occur inside a structure with four walls, a ceiling, and a floor; but if we know that the cultural purpose of this structure is to be a classroom, then we know that the behavior of the people in the structure will be quite different than if its purpose is to be a church, a factory, or a hockey arena. The fact that this behavior setting is in a built environment also tells us that the extra-individual behavior will be different from that in the natural environment of a forested wilderness or a desert. This cultural purpose exists because the behavior setting consists of the interdependency between **standing patterns of behavior** and a **physical milieu**. Standing patterns of behavior represent the collective behaviors of the group, rather than just individual behaviors. These behaviors are not unique to the individuals present, but they may be unique to the setting. If the behavior setting is a classroom in a lecture-oriented course, then the standing patterns of behavior would include lecturing, listening, observing, sitting, taking notes, raising hands, and exchanging questions and answers. Since this **en masse behavior pattern** occurs only in an educational behavior setting, ecological psychologists would infer that knowing about the setting helps us predict the behavior that will occur in it. The physical milieu of this behavior setting would include a room, a lectern, chairs, and perhaps a chalkboard and microphone. Once the individuals leave the classroom, the physical milieu still

remains, so the standing behavior patterns are independent of the milieu. Yet they are similar in structure (**synomorphic**) and together create the behavior setting (Figure 4–4). A change in either the standing behavior patterns (as when a club holds a meeting in the classroom) or the physical milieu (such as when the class is held outdoors on the first warm day of spring) changes the behavior setting.

How can we use the behavior setting conceptualization to understand environment–behavior relationships? Perhaps a few examples can best illustrate the utility of this approach (see also, Wicker & Kirmeyer, 1976). One very famous application of ecological psychology is depicted in the box on page 15. In this study Barker and his colleagues (Barker & Schoggen, 1973; Barker & Wright, 1955) compared a small town in Kansas with one in England. Among the findings were that behavior settings under the control of businesses were more common, and the behavior in them lasted longer, in the British setting rather than the American setting. In settings involving voluntary participation, however, Americans spent more time and held more positions of responsibility than did Britons. (The significance of such findings will be more apparent below in the discussion of staffing.) Wicker (1979, 1987) notes that ecological psychology methods are very useful for such diverse goals as documenting community life, assessing the social impact of change, and analyzing the structure of organizations for such factors as efficiency of operation, handling of responsibility, and indications of status. In addition, as Bechtel (1977) notes, ecological psychology can be useful in assessing environmental design. By carefully examining the behavior setting, one can analyze such design features as pathways, or links between settings, and focal points, or places where behavior tends to concentrate. In the lobby of a building, for example, it is important to separate pathways to various elevators, offices, and shops in order to avoid congestion and confusion. An information center in the lobby, though, would be most useful if placed

Figure 4–4. According to Barker's ecological psychology, knowing about the physical setting tells us much about the behaviors that occur there. In the setting shown, what behaviors can you always expect to see?

at a focal point. As another example, open-plan (i.e., no internal walls) designs in schools and offices, although having advantages, often lead to inadequate boundaries between behavior settings, thereby causing interference with the intended functions (e.g., Oldham & Brass, 1979). We will discuss more of these kinds of design implications in Chapter 11, 12, and 13.

Staffing the Setting: How Many Peas Fill a Pod? What happens if a behavior setting such as a classroom or theater has too few or too many inhabitants for maximum functioning efficiency? Do students at small schools, for example, take on more roles of responsibility than students at larger schools? Studies of these questions from the ecological psychology perspective have led to the **theory of manning** (Barker, 1960; Barker & Gump, 1964; Wicker & Kirmeyer, 1976; Wicker, McGrath, & Armstrong, 1972). We should note that although historically the theory uses the term *manning,* we will follow the lead of others in substituting less sex-linked words, such as "staffing," for the word "manning," and use the term **staffing theory**.

In order to understand the understaffing concept, let us first define some terms proposed by Wicker and his colleagues that are related to the concept. The minimum number of inhabitants needed to maintain a behavior setting is defined as the **maintenance minimum**. The maximum number of inhabitants the setting can hold is the **capacity**. The people who meet the membership requirements of the setting and who are trying to become part of it are called **applicants**. **Performers** in a setting carry out the primary tasks, such as the teacher in a classroom, the workers in a factory, or the cast and supporting staff in a play. **Nonperformers**, such as the pupils in a classroom or the audience in a theater, are involved in secondary roles. Maintenance minimum, capacity, and the applicants are different entities for performers and nonperformers. For example, maintenance minimum for performers in a classroom would be the smallest staff (teachers, custodians, secretaries, deans) required to carry out the program. For nonperformers, maintenance minimum would be the smallest number of pupils required to keep the class going. Capacity for performers in a classroom might be determined by social factors (e.g., how many teachers are most effective in one setting) and by physical factors, such as the size of the room, number of lecterns, and so on. For nonperformers, room size is the primary determinant of capacity. Whether your class contains 10 or 1,000 students depends in most cases as much on classroom size as on educational policy. For performers, applicants are the individuals who meet the requirements of the performer role and who seek to perform, as in the number of teachers available to teach a given class. Applicants for nonperformers are those who seek nonperforming roles, as in the number of students trying to get into the class. If students are available but do not seek to get into the class, or if teachers do not want to teach a given class, then they are not considered applicants.

If the number of applicants to a setting (either performers or nonperformers) falls below the maintenance minimum, then some or all of the inhabitants must take on more than their share of roles if the behavior setting is to be maintained. This condition is termed **understaffed**. If the number of applicants exceeds the capacity, the setting is **overstaffed**, and if the number of applicants is between maintenance minimum and capacity, the setting is **adequately staffed**. Wicker (1973) has labeled an adequately staffed setting with a low number of participants as "poorly staffed," and an adequately staffed setting with a high number of participants as "richly staffed." Thus, we can consider a continuum of participation levels from understaffed to poorly staffed to richly staffed to overstaffed.

When conditions of understaffing exist, the consequences for the inhabitants of the setting are many. As stated earlier, inhabitants must take on more specific tasks and roles than would otherwise be the case. As a result, inhabitants have to work harder and at more difficult tasks than they would otherwise, and peak performance on any task is not as great as in an adequately staffed setting. Furthermore, admissions standards to understaffed settings may have to be lowered, and superficial differences

among inhabitants may be largely ignored, whereas in adequately staffed settings these differences are highlighted to fit each person into his or her appropriate role. Each inhabitant in an understaffed setting is more valued, has more responsibility, and interacts more meaningfully with the setting. Since understaffed settings have more opportunities for the experience of failure as well as success (owing to the increase in number of experiences per inhabitant), these settings are likely to result in more feelings of insecurity than adequatley staffed settings. The consequences of understaffing are summarized in Table 4–1.

Overstaffing, on the other hand, results in adaptive mechanisms being brought into play to deal with the huge number of applicants. One obvious solution would be to increase the capacity, probably through enlarging the present physical milieu or moving to a larger one. Another adaptive mechanism would be to control the entrance of clients into the setting, either through stricter entrance requirements or through some sort of funneling process (Figure 4–5). For example, Wicker (1979) describes how ecological psychologists implemented and evaluated a queuing (waiting line) arrangement at Yosemite National Park to alleviate overcrowding and associated disruptive behavior at bus stops. Still another regulatory mechanism would be to limit the amount of time inhabitants can spend in the setting. These three mechanisms are elaborated in Table 4–1.

In general, predictions from staffing theory have been supported by research. For example, in a laboratory study involving too many, too few, or an intermediate number of participants to run a complex racing game, those in understaffed conditions reported more feelings of involvement in the group and having an important role within the group (e.g., Wicker et al., 1976). Studies of large versus small high schools (Baird, 1969; Barker & Gump, 1964) suggest that students in small schools (which are less likely to be overstaffed) are indeed involved in a wider range of activities than students from large schools, and are more likely

Figure 4—5. Funneling is one way to regulate entrance into a potentially overstaffed behavior setting.

to report feelings of satisfaction and of being challenged. Similar results have been reported for colleges as well (Baird, 1969; Berk & Goeble, 1987). Studies of large versus small churches (e.g., Wicker & Kauma, 1974; Wicker, McGrath, & Armstrong, 1972; Wicker & Mehler, 1971; Wicker, 1969) also indicate that members of small churches are likely to be involved in more behavior settings within the church (e.g., choir, committees) and to be involved in more leadership positions; such predictions are based on the assumption that smaller churches are more likely to be understaffed and larger churches overstaffed. Altogether, then, these and other studies suggest that staffing theory is very useful in assessing involvement and satisfaction within a number of environments, from businesses (e.g., Greenberg, 1979; Oxley & Barrera, 1984) to mental institutions (e.g., Srivastava, 1974) to schools and churches.

Barker's approach has its advantages and disadvantages. It necessitates a field observa-

tion methodology (described in Chapter 1), which gives the theory the advantage of using real-world behavior. It certainly insists on preserving the integrity of the person–environment interrelationship. However, it includes the disadvantage of not being able to study many detailed cause-and-effect relationships in the laboratory, though certainly some laboratory research on ecological psychology principles has been and will continue to be conducted (cf. Wicker, 1987; Wicker & Kirmeyer, 1976). Studies of real-world behavior in context lead to difficulties of interpretation without scientific control of variables. For example, the observed effects of large versus small schools or churches could be due to differential group influences such as staffing demands, or to individual differences in the types of people who choose to affiliate with large versus small institutions. We again have a theory that is so broad in its scope that specific predictions about one person's behavior become difficult to make and troublesome to confirm. Since this approach is de-

Table 4–1. *Consequences of Understaffing and Mechanisms for Regulating the Population of a Behavior Setting**

Consequences of Understaffing

Setting occupants typically:

1. Increase effort and/or spend more time to support the setting.
2. Participate in a greater variety of tasks and roles.
3. Participate in more difficult and important tasks.
4. Assume more responsibility in the setting.
5. Perceive themselves and others in terms of task-related characteristics.
6. Become more important to the functioning of the setting.
7. Pay less attention to personality and other non-task related differences between individuals.
8. Lower admissions standards for applicants.
9. Accept lower levels of performance for themselves and others.
10. Feel insecure regarding the success of the setting.
11. Experience success and failure frequently.

Mechanisms for Regulating the Population of a Behavior Setting

1. Regulating access of applicants into the setting:
    by scheduling appointments for entrance;
    by increasinng or decreasing recruiting;
    by raising or lowering admissions standards;
    by asking applicants to wait in holding areas;
    by preventing unauthorized entrances.
2. Regulating the setting's capacity:
    by changing the arrangements or contents of the physical milieu;
    by changing the duration (hours open) of the setting;
    by increasing or decreasing staff (performers) to handle applicants;
    by assigning staff (performers) to different tasks as demands of applicants increase or decrease.
3. Regulating the time applicants or inhabitants can occupy the setting:
    by admitting applicants at different rates;
    by changing the limits on how long people can stay;
    by using a fee structure based on length of stay;
    by establishing priorities for dealing with different classes of applicants;
    by changing the standing patterns of behavior to facilitate the flow of applicants.

* Adapted from Wicker, A. W., & Kirmeyer, S. (1976). From church to laboratory to national park. In S. Wapner, B. Kaplan, & S. Cohen (Eds.), *Experiencing the Environment.* Used by permission of Plenum Publishing.

signed to study group behavior, it does a respectable job of handling group data in the context of a given setting, but it does not handle individual behavior as well as other theories. Finally, ecological theory does generate many valuable research questions, such as what common properties of certain behavior settings result in the same group behavior, what happens when the structure of a behavior setting changes, and what effects one behavior setting has on behavior in another setting.

The Environmental Stress Approach

One theoretical approach, which is widely used in environmental psychology, is to view many elements of the environment, such as noise and heat, as stressors. Stressors, such as job pressures, marital discord, natural disasters, the turmoil of moving to a new location, and urban crowding and noise, are considered to be aversive stimuli that threaten the well-being of the person. Stress is an intervening or mediating variable, defined as the reaction to these stimuli. This "reaction" is assumed to include emotional, behavioral, and physiological components. The physiological component was initially proposed by Selye (1956), and is often called **systemic stress**. The behavioral and emotional components were proposed by Lazarus (1966), and are often called **psychological stress**. Today, environmental psychologists usually combine all of these components into one theory, or the **environmental stress model** (e.g., Baum, Singer, & Baum, 1981; Evans & Cohen, 1987; Lazarus & Folkman, 1984). As we discuss specific stressors (noise, heat, crowding) in subsequent chapters, we will, accordingly, indicate specific physiological and psychological consequences of exposure to these stressors. We should emphasize that physiological and psychological stress reactions are interrelated, and do not occur alone. We will see this point as we elaborate upon the environmental stress conceptualization in this and following chapters. Before proceeding further, we should note that sometimes the term "stress" is restricted to environmental events, and an additional term, "strain," is used to describe the consequence within the organism. However, we will use "stress" to refer to the entire stimulus–response situation, "stressor" to refer to the environmental component alone, and "stress response" to refer to the reaction caused by the environmental component. This response is characterized by emotional changes, behavior directed toward reduction of stress, and physiological changes such as increased

arousal. The process, then, involves all parts of the situation—the threat itself, perceptions of the threat, coping with the threat, and, ultimately, adapting to it.

We will organize our discussion of stress into three basic parts. First, we will consider the *characteristics of stressors* (such as how long they last or how often they occur). Since the degree to which these events actually cause stress is dependent upon how they are interpreted (i.e., whether people notice them and decide that they might be harmful or aversive), we should also discuss the *appraisal of stressors*. Finally, the kinds of *stress responses* that occur (including anxiety, depression, illness, withdrawal, and aggression) will be considered.

Characteristics of Stressors While some environmental events are threatening to almost everyone, and others are threatening to very few, many events can cause a range of problems. In all cases these are *potential* problems—they may or may not occur in a given situation. Nothing is automatic, and no stressor should always be considered threatening. Rather, some events are more likely to be viewed as threats or challenges than others. The probability of an event becoming stressful is determined by a number of factors (Evans & Cohen, 1987), including the characteristics of an event and the way individuals appraise it. We will discuss the characteristics of various stressors here, and reserve our discussion of the appraisal process for later.

There are a number of ways we might classify stressors. Lazarus and Cohen (1977) have described three general categories of environmental stressors. At first they appear to vary along a single dimension—*severity of impact*. However, we shall see that they actually vary along a number of additional dimensions as well.

Cataclysmic events are overwhelming stressors that have several basic characteristics. They are usually sudden, and give little or no warning of their occurrence. They have a powerful impact, elicit a more or less universal response, and usually require a great deal of effort for effective **coping**. Natural disaster, war, or a nuclear accident are all unpredictable and powerful threats that generally affect all of those touched by them. The accidents at Three Mile Island and Chernobyl, the heat waves in the American midwest, the Mount Saint Helens eruption (Adams & Adams, 1984), as well as the more common tornadoes, hurricanes, and other natural disasters (Baker & Chapman, 1962; Baum et al., 1980; Baum, Fleming & Davidson, 1983; Hartsough & Savitsky, 1984; Pennebaker & Newtson, 1983; Sims & Baumann, 1972) can all be considered in this category of stressors.

Because cataclysmic events are usually sudden, the powerful onset of such occurrences may initially evoke a freezing or dazed response by victims (e.g., Moore, 1958). Coping is difficult and may bring no immediate relief. However, the severely threatening period of such an event usually (but not always) ends quickly, and recovery begins. A tornado may strike for only a brief time, and other cataclysmic events may be over in a few days (Baum, Fleming, & Davidson, 1983). When the process is allowed to proceed without a return of the stressor, rebuilding progresses and more or less complete recovery is generally achieved. In the case of Three Mile Island or Love Canal, where rebuilding is not what is needed (nothing was actually destroyed), and the damage already done is less important than the damage that may yet come, recovery may be more difficult.

One important feature of cataclysmic events, which is in some ways beneficial for the coping process, is that they impact on a large number of people. Affiliation with others and comparing feelings and opinions with them have been identified as important styles of coping with such threats (e.g., McGrath, 1970; Schachter, 1959), for **social support** can moderate the effects of stressful conditions (e.g., Cobb, 1976). In other words, having people around to provide support, a source of comparison for one's emotional and behavioral responses, and

other forms of assistance can reduce the negative impact of a stressor. Because people are able to share their distress with others undergoing the same difficulties, some studies have suggested that cohesion results among these individuals (Quarantelli, 1978). Of course, this does not always happen, and residents cannot ''band together'' to fight a stressor indefinitely. When a stressor persists in an apparently unresolvable manner, problems of a different kind can arise.

A second group of stressors may be termed **personal stressors**. These include such events as illness, death of a loved one (e.g., Greene, 1966; Hackett & Weisman, 1964; Lehman, Wortman, & Williams, 1987; Parkes, 1972), or loss of one's job (Dooley, Rook, & Catalano, 1987; Kasl & Cobb, 1970; Kessler, House, & Turner, 1987)—events that are powerful enough to challenge adaptive abilities in the same way as cataclysmic events. Personal stressors generally affect fewer people at any one time than cataclysmic events, and may or may not be expected. Frequently, with personal stressors the point of severest impact occurs early and coping can progress once the worst is over, although this is not always the case. Often the magnitude, duration, and point of severest impact of cataclysmic events and personal stressors such as death and loss of a job are similar. However, the relatively smaller number of people who experience a particular personal stressor at any one time may be significant, because there are fewer others to serve as sources of social support. As we mentioned earlier, this can moderate the effects of negative events. We should also note that a cataclysmic event such as a flood often leads to the loss of a loved one or loss of a job or other personal stressor.

Background stressors are persistent, repetitive, and almost routine. They are considerably less powerful than the stressors discussed above, their effects are more gradual, and they usually are much more chronic. They may be **daily hassles**—stable, low-intensity problems encountered as part of one's routine (Lazarus, et al., 1985; Zika & Chamberlain, 1987). For example, consider the following description of a typical morning provided by a student who lived off-campus and commuted to an urban university:

> I get up and go downstairs for breakfast. There's always a mess down there—my roommates don't clean up and I've got to do it. Anyway, I clean up and eat, get dressed and ready for school. Then I've got to go out and coax my car to start. I usually have to kick it a few times, but sometimes it won't start and I've got to take the bus—which is always late, crowded, and too hot.

Rotton (in press) prefers to divide background stressors into daily hassles (or microstressors) and what Campbell (1983) terms **ambient stressors**, which are "chronic, global conditions of the environment—pollution, noise, residential crowding, traffic congestion—which, in a general sense, represent noxious stimulation, and which, as stressors, place demands upon us to adapt or cope" (p. 360). Whereas daily hassles (losing things, home maintenance) are unique each day and affect a specific individual, ambient stressors such as pollution impact a larger number of people, are chronic and nonurgent, and are difficult to remove through the efforts of one individual. While many background stressors are mundane and of relatively low intensity, some may not even be noticeable, like certain instances of air pollution (e.g., Evans & Jacobs, 1981). Any one or two background stressors may not be sufficient to cause great adaptive difficulty, but when a number occur together they can exact a cost over time, and may be as serious as cataclysmic events or personal stressors. Regular and prolonged exposure to certain low-level background stressors may even require more adaptive responses in the long run than more intense stressors. For example, long-term exposure to noise (Cohen, Glass, & Singer, 1973), neighborhood problems (Harburg et al., 1973; White et al., 1987),

and long-term commuting stress (Singer, Lundberg, & Frankenhaeuser, 1978) can be quite problematic.

With background stressors, it is often difficult to identify a point at which "the worst is over," and it may not be at all clear that things will get better. In fact, things may go from bad to worse. In addition, the benefits for coping of having others who "share in the experience" may not be as great as for other types of stressors. This may be because the intensity of background stressors is frequently so low as to never raise the need for affiliation; or, alternatively, social support may not be appropriate in these situations (cf. Campbell, 1983).

Appraisal Part of the response to an aversive or stressful stimulus is automatic. Selye's (1956) **general adaptation syndrome (GAS)** consists of three stages: (1) the alarm reaction, (2) the stage of resistance, and (3) the stage of exhaustion. Initially, there is an **alarm reaction** to a stressor, whereby autonomic processes (heart rate, adrenaline secretion, and so on) are speeded up. The second stage in the stress process, the **stage of resistance**, also begins with some automatic processes for coping with the stressor. If heat is the stressor, sweating occurs; if extreme cold is the stressor, shivering may occur. When these homeostatic mechanisms do not restore **equilibrium**, signs of exhaustion or depleted reserves will be observed as an organism enters the last of Selye's three stages, the **stage of exhaustion**. The primary indicants of this stage are ulcers, adrenal enlargement, and shrinkage of lymph and other glands that confer resistance to disease.

The concept of stress, however, involves not just a simple automatic stimulus–response relationship, but contains a number of important cognitive components (i.e., involving thought processes) as well. To begin with, not all stressful stimuli are aversive enough in themselves to evoke the automatic alarm and resistance responses. In order for the stress process to begin, there must be cognitive **appraisal** of a stimulus as threatening. To use an environmental example, 90° F (32° C) to a native southerner is not likely to be very stressful in midsummer. To someone living in Barrow, Alaska, however, the mere thought of experiencing 90° F for a few hours a day may well be evaluated as threatening. In other words, the same stimulus that may not be stressful in one situation may be stressful in another—the stimulus has not changed, but the individual's appraisal of it as threatening or nonthreatening has changed. Moreover, cognitive appraisal that an aversive event, such as crowding, is pending is often sufficient to elicit a stress response, even though the physical event itself does not happen (e.g., Baum & Greenberg, 1975).

Lazarus (1966) suggested that this cognitive appraisal is a function of individual psychological factors (intellectual resources, knowledge of past experience, and motivation) and cognitive aspects of the specific stimulus situation (control over the stimulus, predictability of the stimulus, and immediacy or "time until impact" of the stimulus). The more knowledge one has about the beneficial aspects of a source of noise, or the more control one has over the noise (in terms of terminating or avoiding it), the less one is likely to evaluate that stimulus as threatening, and the less stressful the situation is likely to be.

Cognitive appraisal of a situation is more complex than merely assessing its potential threat (see Baum et al., 1982, for a review). Several different types of appraisal are possible. **Harm or loss assessments** focus on damage that has already been done (Lazarus & Launier, 1978). For example, victims of a natural or technological disaster could be expected to make harm/loss evaluations. In contrast, **threat appraisals** are concerned with future dangers. Environmental toxins such as pesticides may evoke perceived threats to one's health, and threat appraisals may precede exposure to them. The ability to anticipate potential difficulties allows us to prevent their occurrence, but may cause us to experience anticipatory stress. It is hard to say which is worse—seeing one's home

destroyed in a hurricane (harm/loss) or not knowing how one will be sheltered from the elements until one can build a new home (threat). As this example suggests, threat and harm/loss appraisals usually go hand-in-hand (Lazarus & Folkman, 1984). **Challenge appraisals** are different from others because they focus not on the harm or potential harm of an event, but on the possibility of overcoming the stressor. Some stressors may be beyond our coping ability, but we all have a range of events for which we are confident of our ability to cope successfully. Stressors that are evaluated as challenges fall within this hypothetical range (Lazarus & Launier, 1978).

A number of factors have been identified that affect our appraisals of environmental stressors. These include the characteristics of the condition in question (e.g., how loud a particular noise is), situational conditions (e.g., whether what we're doing is compatible with or inhibited by the potential stressor), individual differences, and environmental, social, and psychological variables. To cite but one example, the upper-middle class resident of a large city may be less likely to experience difficulty as a result of urban conditions than a poorer resident of the same city. Or, he or she may be better able to avoid the seamy side of the city, and thus less likely ever to be exposed to aversive urban conditions. Attitudes toward the source of stress will also mediate responses; if we believe that a condition will cause no permanent harm, our response will probably be less extreme than if it carries the threat of lasting harm. If our attitudes are strongly in favor of something that may also harm us, we may reappraise threats and make them seem less dangerous. Overall, then, the appraisal of stressors is based on properties of the situation, attitudes toward the stressor or its source, individual differences, and many other factors.

Another moderator of stress appraisals may be social support, the feeling that one is cared about and valued by other people—that he or she belongs to a group (Cobb, 1976). Many have long believed that interpersonal relationships can somehow protect us from many ills (e.g., Cohen & Wills, 1985; Jung, 1984). However, the effects of having or not having social and emotional support have not always been clearly demonstrated (cf. Ganellen & Blaney, 1984; Hendrick, Wells, & Faletti, 1982).

Coping styles or behavior patterns also appear to affect the ways in which events are appraised, as well as which types of coping are invoked. Work on a number of these dimensions, such as **repression-sensitization** (the degree to which people think about a stressor), **screening** (a person's ability to ignore extraneous stimuli or to prioritize demands), and **denial** (the degree to which people ignore or suppress awareness of problems), has indicated that people differing along these dimensions may interpret situations differently (e.g., Bell & Byrne, 1978; Collins, Baum, & Singer, 1983; Janis, 1958; Mehrabian, 1976–77). A study by Baum et al. (1982), for example, suggests that individuals who cope with overload by screening and prioritizing demands are less susceptible to the effects of crowding than people who do not cope in this way.

Perceived control is generally an important mediator of stress, providing a sense of being able to cope effectively, to predict events, and to determine what will happen. Most researchers define perceived control as the belief that one can affect what happens to him or her (Glass & Singer, 1972). Whether the ability to determine outcomes is real or merely perceived, the belief that one has control seems to reduce the negative effects of stress. Much of the evidence for this comes from studies of noise, which we will deal with in Chapter 5.

Another example of how control may affect appraisal comes from the growing literature on cognitive control. Providing subjects with information about a stressor prior to subjects' exposure to it helps them to plan and predict what will happen. Such information increases perceived control and reduces the threat appraisal made when the stressor is experienced. For example, the stress associated with surgery or aversive medical procedures can be reduced by providing patients with accurate expectations of what they will feel (e.g., Johnson, 1973; Johnson & Leventhal, 1974). Other studies have found that accurate expectations about high levels of density reduce crowding stress (Baum, Fisher, & Solomon, 1981; Langer & Saegert, 1977).

Characteristics of the Stress Response
When appraisals are made, responses are determined as well. If an event is interpreted as threatening or harmful, stress responses are more likely. In other words, if an appraisal is "negative" and an event is seen as being dangerous, responses that prepare us to cope will ensue. These stress responses involve the whole body. Physiological changes are part of this response, most reflecting increased arousal. At the same time, emotional, psychological, and behavioral changes may also occur as part of the stress response.

Some responses to environmental stress are virtually indistinguishable from those evoked by direct assault on body tissue by pathogens. Recalling Selye's three-stage process, it appears that stress results in heightened secretion of **corticosteroids** during the alarm reaction, followed by a decline in reactivity (as measured by this secretion) through resistance and exhaustion. Subsequent work has also identified the **catecholamines—epinephrine** and **norepinephrine**—as active in stress. Research has associated emotional distress with these same patterns of arousal (e.g., Konzett, 1975; Schachter & Singer, 1962). Further, challenge, loss of control or predictability, and psychosocial stressors have been linked to increased **adrenal** activity (Frankenhaeuser, 1978; Glass, 1976; Konzett et al., 1971).

Increased catecholamine and corticosteroid secretion is associated with a wide range of other physiological responses, such as changes in heart rate, blood pressure, breathing, muscle potential, inflammation, and other functions. Prolonged or sudden elevation of circulating catecholamines may damage body tissue, and is suggested as a cause of the development of hardening of the arteries and other diseases of the blood vessels (Schneiderman, 1982). Catecholamines also appear to affect cognitive and emotional functioning, and elevated levels of epinephrine or norepinephrine in the blood may affect our mood and behavior (Baum, Grunberg, & Singer, 1982).

These findings may also be viewed as consistent with pioneering work by Cannon (1929, 1931), who suggested that epinephrine has a positive effect on adaptation. Epinephrine provides a biological advantage by arousing the organism, thus enabling it to respond more rapidly to danger. When extremely frightened or enraged, we experience an arousal that may be uncomfortable, but which readies us to act against the thing that scares or angers us. Thus, stress-related increases in catecholamines may facilitate adaptive behavior.

Some studies have shown superior performance on certain tasks following epinephrine infusion (Frankenhaeuser, Jarpe, & Mattell, 1961) and among people with higher catecholamine output in the face of challenge (e.g., Frankenhhaeuser, 1971). On the other hand, arousal has been associated with impaired performance on complex tasks (cf. Evans, 1978). Decreases in problem-solving abilities, increases in general negativity, impatience, irritability, feelings of worthlessness, and emotionality may all accompany a stress response, and emotional disturbances such as anxiety or depression may occur.

Once a stimulus has been evaluated as threatening, other cognitive factors come into play. Recall Selye's notions of the alarm reaction (stage 1) and the automatic coping mechanisms of resistance (stage 2). In the stage of resistance many coping processes are also cognitive, so that the individual must decide on a behavioral coping strategy. According to Lazarus (1966), the coping strategy is a function of individual and situational factors, and may consist of flight, physical or verbal attack, or some sort of compromise. A distinction is often made between **primary appraisal**, which involves assessment of threat, and **secondary appraisal**, which involves assessment of coping strategies. Lack of success in the coping process may increase the tendency to evaluate the situation as threatening. Associated with this cognitive coping process are any number of emotions, including anger and fear. To use another example, the stress reaction to a large crowd in a city might consist of evaluation of the crowd as threatening, physiological arousal, fear, and flight to a less crowded area.

There are many ways of categorizing coping strategies (see Aldwin & Revenson, 1987). Two useful distinctions employed by Lazarus and his colleagues are (1) *direct action* or *problem-focused,* such as information seeking, flight, or attempts to remove or stop the stressor; or (2) **palliative** or *emotion-focused,* such as employing psychological defense mechanisms (denial, intellectualization, etc.), using drugs, meditating, or reassessing the situation as nonthreatening (see also, Roth & Cohen, 1986). To the extent that direct action is not available or practical, palliative strategies become more likely. For example, for residents near the Three Mile Island nuclear disaster, direct action was limited in effectiveness, so palliative measures would be more probable (Baum et al., 1980; Houts et al., 1980). Interestingly, a sense of humor helps cope with most if not all types of stress (Martin & Lefcourt, 1983).

As previously noted, if the coping responses are not adequate for dealing with the stressor, and all coping energies have been expended, the organism will enter the third stage of the GAS, the stage of exhaustion (Figure 4–6). Fortunately, something else usually happens before exhaustion occurs. In most situations, when an aversive stimulus is presented many times, the stress reaction to it becomes weaker and weaker. Psychologically, this process is called **adaptation**. Adaptation to a stressor may occur because neurophysiological sensitivity to the stimulus becomes weaker, because uncertainty about the stressor is reduced, or because the stressor is cognitively appraised as less and

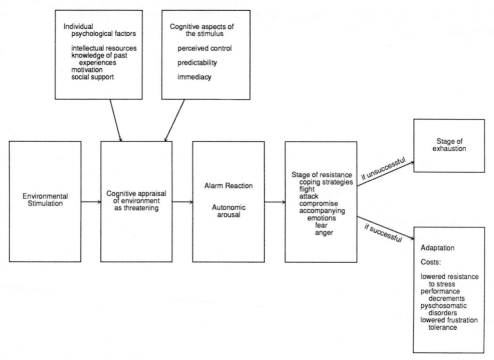

Figure 4–6. The stress model.

less threatening. Visitors to a polluted city, for example, initially may suffer overt physiological symptoms (such as shortness of breath) and may express a great deal of fear about the potential health consequences of exposure to atmospheric pollutants. On successive days in the city, however, these visitors, realizing that they have not died yet, may "lose" the fear of breathing the air (see also Chapter 7).

Adaptation to stress is both beneficial and costly. Almost all events in life, from birth to attending school to driving on freeways at rush hour, involve some degree of stress. Obviously, the individual who has been exposed to stress and has learned to handle it is better able to deal with the next stressful event in life. In this sense, the "teaching" function of stress is beneficial to the organism as long as the stress can be handled—the experience boosts self-confidence and provides skill development (e.g., Aldwin & Stokols, 1988; Martin et al.,

1987). We have seen that environmental stress sometimes improves performance, probably because the arousal associated with stress (if it is not too severe) facilitates performance. Exposure and adaptation to stressful events may also be costly, however. If the total of all stresses at any one time exceeds the capacity of the individual to cope with them, some sort of breakdown, physical or mental, is almost inevitable. Psychosomatic disorders, performance decrements, and lowering of resistance to other stressors are often the costs of adapting to prolonged or excessive stress. Still another cost, one that we have treated previously as a separate theoretical approach, is the resulting cognitive overload: Our information-processing capacity becomes so overloaded by the stressor that we ignore other important stimuli, including other human beings and stimuli relevant to job performance, safety, and health. Some costs of adaptation may occur during exposure to the stressor, including performance decrements and physiological wear and tear. Other costs may occur after the stressor is no longer around. For example, as we will see in Chapter 5, even after an aversive noise has stopped, tolerance for frustration, accuracy of mental functioning, and even altruistic behavior (see box, p. 99) may continue to be impaired (see also, Cohen, 1980).

Cognitive deficits associated with stress may be caused by behavioral strategies that are used for coping with stress—"tuning out" or narrowing one's field of attention (e.g., Cohen, 1978). When under stress, we may be unable to concentrate or unwilling to put effort into a task (e.g., Glass & Singer, 1972). In other ways, our coping response may be specific to the stressor being experienced, reflecting the specific causes of our discomfort. People may respond to crowding caused by too many people by withdrawing and avoiding social contact, whereas their response to crowding caused by limited space might be aggression (e.g., Baum & Koman, 1976). A person might respond to job loss actively if the loss was caused by a lack of effort rather than ability, or may become helpless under certain conditions.

Aftereffects are not specific to certain stressors, but appear to reflect more general effects (Cohen, 1980). Defined as consequences experienced after exposure to a stressor has terminated, these fit in with Selye's (1956) notion of limited adaptative energy. As exposure to stress increases, adaptive reserves are depleted, causing aftereffects and reductions of subsequent coping ability. Evidence for the existence of poststressor effects comes from a number of sources, including research on the effects of noise (e.g., Glass & Singer, 1972; Rotton et al., 1978; Sherrod & Downs, 1974; Sherrod et al., 1977), crowding (Evans, 1979; Sherrod, 1974), and electrical shock (Glass et al., 1973).

Psychological effects that linger or persist may also reflect consequences of adaptation. Calhoun (1967, 1970) has referred to **refractory periods**, which are periods of time during which an organism recovers from a bout with a stressor. If the refractory period is interrupted by another encounter, increased stress-relevant problems are likely.

Assessing the Stress Model   When we evaluate the effectiveness of using stress as a mediator for a theoretical approach in environmental psychology, we find that it does an admirable job with the data in its predictive domain. The stress approach does help predict many of the consequences of environmental deterioration as well as the presence or absence of observable effects of such specific stressors as crowding and extremes of heat and cold. In this respect, the stress approach has a great deal of generality: It applies to many situations and accounts for the combined effects of many environmental and social stressors that are presented at the same time (e.g., Levine, 1988). Perhaps for this reason the stress approach suggests many directions for new research. If we treat a given environmental event as a stressor, then we should be able to predict its effects, with or without the presence of other stressors, from our knowledge of the effects of other stressors. Furthermore, we should be able to use present knowledge about coping with stress to help control reactions to unwanted environmental stressors. On the other hand, one problem with using only the stress approach as a theoretical inroad in environmental psychology is that the identification of stressors is somewhat ambiguous (e.g., Lazarus et al., 1985). For example, suppose we expose individuals to a particular stimulus and get no stress reaction. Should that stimulus be regarded as something other than a stressor, or did those particular individuals just not evaluate it as threatening under the experimental circumstances?

We have stated earlier that some components of the arousal, environmental load, adaptation level, behavior constraint, and ecological approaches fit very well into an environmental stress framework. We have seen, for example, that overload can be viewed as one consequence of coping with stress, and that heightened arousal is a component of stress. Similarly, an optimal level of stimulation (i.e., stimulation at the adaptation level) should result in little evidence of a stress reaction, and multiple constraints on behavior as well as severe overstaffing or understaffing might be expected to lead to considerable signs of stress. In sum, all these theoretical approaches are interrelated and seem in many ways compatible with the stress formulation. We will elaborate upon these compatibilities in following chapters, where we concentrate on specific environmental stressors. Before doing so, it might be instructive to see how we can integrate the major features of all but the ecological psychology approach into one large model.

INTEGRATION AND SUMMARY OF THEORETICAL PERSPECTIVES

It is worth repeating the earlier caution that the above discussion has by no means covered all theories employed by environmental psychologists. Rather, they are simply the most common approaches presently in use, and they are not at all mutually exclusive. Each theory selects one or two mediators inferred from empirical data and attempts to explain a large portion of the data using that mediator. Just because one mediator explains a particular set of data, however, does not mean that other mediators are not operating in the same set of data. It is entirely conceivable, for example, that loud noises produce information overload, stress, arousal, and psychological reactance all at the same time in the same individual. Loss of control, alone, usually increases arousal (Wright, 1984). Furthermore, regardless of which of these mediators is involved (either alone or in combination), any number of coping responses are likely to result, such as flight, erecting barriers or other protective devices, ignoring other humans in need, and directly attempting to stop or reduce the stimulus input at the source. Although one particular mediator may best predict or explain which coping responses will occur in a given situation, other mediators are not necessarily excluded from that or similar situations. It is our position that all of the mediating processes discussed thus far probably occur at some time, given all the possible situations in which environmental stimulation influences behavior. Therefore, we now present an eclectic scheme of environment–behavior relationships as a summary and integration of the theoretical concepts discussed up to this point.

This scheme of theoretical concepts is presented in the flow chart in Figure 4–7. Objective environmental conditions, such as population density, temperature, noise levels, and pollution levels, exist independent of the individual, although individuals can act to change these objective conditions. The scheme includes such individual difference factors as adaptation level, length of exposure, perceived control, and personality, as well as such social factors as liking or hostility for others in the situation. Perception of the objective physical conditions depends on the objective conditions themselves, as well as on the individual difference factors and the perceptual processes discussed in Chapters 2 and 3. If this subjective perception determines that the environment is within an optimal range of stimulation, the result is **homeostatic**, the adjective form of homeostasis, or an equalization of desired and actual input. On the other hand, if the environ-

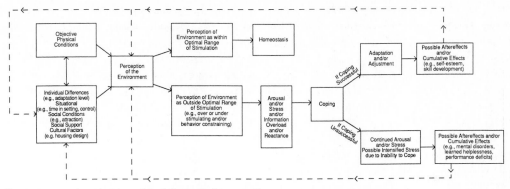

Figure 4—7. An eclectic model of theoretical perspectives.

ment is experienced as outside the optimal range of stimulation, (e.g., understimulation, overstimulation, or stimulating in a behavior-constraining manner), then one or more of the following psychological states results: arousal, stress, information overload, or reactance. The presence of one or more of these states leads to coping strategies. If the attempted coping strategies are successful, adaptation or adjustment occurs, possibly followed by such aftereffects as lowered frustration tolerance, fatigue, and reduced ability to cope with the next immediate stressor. Cumulative aftereffects might include any of these, but would also include increased self-confidence and a degree of learning about coping with future occurrences of undesirable environmental stimulation. Should the coping strategies not be successful, however, arousal and stress will continue, possibly heightened by the individual's awareness that the strategies are failing. Potential aftereffects of such inability to cope include exhaustion, learned helplessness, severe performance decrements, and mental

disorders. Finally, as indicated by the feedback loops, experiences with the environment influence perception of the environment for future encounters and also contribute to individual differences for future experiences.

We present this model not as a completely developed environmental theory, but merely as an attempt to integrate the various mediating concepts that have been applied to environment–behavior relationships. There undoubtedly exist data that do not support one aspect or another of this integration. However, we think this electic approach will help explain many of the environment–behavior relationships to be covered in the next five chapters. In these chapters, we will discuss how the physical environment (disasters, pollution, noise, heat, wind), personal space, and crowding influence specific behaviors. When appropriate, we will point out how the various theoretical notions in this chapter help explain those specific influences.

SUMMARY

Environmental psychology, as a science, seeks to understand cause-and-effect relationships through prediction, and uses publicly observ-

able data to verify these predictions. Once enough predictions are verified, theories are constructed, which consist of a set of concepts and a set of statements relating the concepts to each other. Usually, theories infer that a more or less abstract variable mediates the relationship between one observable variable and another. Good environmental theories should predict and summarize empirical data, should generalize to many situations, and should suggest ideas for research.

The arousal approach to environment–behavior relationships suggests that environmental stimulation leads to increased arousal. According to the Yerkes–Dodson Law, this increased arousal will improve or impair performance, depending on whether the individual's arousal is below or above an optimal level. Other behaviors, such as aggression, also tend to follow this curvilinear relationship with arousal.

The information overload theory proposes that there is a limited capacity to process information and that when excessive stimulation occurs, peripheral inputs are ignored in order to give adequate attention to primary tasks. The result is that responses to these peripheral nonsocial or social stimuli are minimal or nonexistent. The understimulation theory notes that monotonous environmental stimulation leads to boredom and thus to behavioral deficiencies. Wohlwill's approach posits an individual difference variable, or adaptation level (AL), such that stimulation levels above or below this AL will bring discomfort and efforts to reduce or increase the stimulation. The behavior constraint model proposes that perceived loss of control over the environment leads to reactance or efforts to regain freedom of action. If these efforts at reassertion are unsuccessful, learned helplessness may be the result. Barker's ecological psychology model examines environment–behavior interdependencies and focuses on the behavior setting as the unit of study. If the number of applicants to a setting falls below maintenance minimum,

performers and nonperformers in the understaffed setting must take on additional roles in order to maintain the setting.

The stress model of environment–behavior relationships posits that once stimuli have been evaluated as threatening, coping strategies are brought into play. These strategies can be beneficial, as when their use results in learning more efficient ways of coping with stress. However, prolonged exposure to stress can lead to serious aftereffects, including mental disorders, performance decrements, and lowered resistance to stress.

Finally, there is no reason to assume that only one mediator operates in any given environment–behavior situation. An eclectic model is offered that attempts to integrate a number of different theoretical concepts.

SUGGESTED PROJECTS

1. Construct your own model of environment–behavior relationships. How well can you integrate the various theoretical perspectives discussed in this chapter and the previous one?

2. Observe a behavior setting for a week. What behavior patterns are always present? Is the setting understaffed, overstaffed, or adequately staffed?

3. Keep a diary for a week or more of all the events that constrain your behavior. Do you respond with reactance, learned helplessness, or some other behavior?

4. Keep a log of your performance levels in classroom, study, and leisure situations, noting your arousal level and amount of environmental stimulation. Does your performance vary as a function of arousal level, overload, or underload?

NOISE

KEY TERMS

aftereffects
amplitude
annoyance
blood pressure
decibels (dB)
frequency
hearing loss
hertz (Hz)
hypertension
loudness
masking
narrow band

noise
perceived control
permanent threshold shifts
phon
pitch
sone
sound
temporary threshold shifts (TTS)
timbre
tonal quality
white noise
wide band

INTRODUCTION

Of the many environmental stressors, noise is one of the most thoroughly studied. In part, this may be due to its pervasiveness in our society. Noise is the most common complaint people have about their neighborhoods. Consider some of its many sources: traffic, airplanes, construction, sirens, trains, equipment at work, machinery, and, of course, other people. Everywhere we go there is noise, particularly if we live in cities (Figure 5–1). Sometimes we adapt to noise, and may not even be aware of it as we get used to it at a certain level. However, research suggests that noise can harm us in many different ways, and studies have sought to define these consequences, identify factors that make the effects of noise more or less severe, and reduce noise levels or noise-related health problems. Regulations governing noise exposure have been put into effect, reflecting recognition of this important problem.

But, how does noise affect us? Why is it that under some circumstances we can adapt to noise and under others we cannot? Why would trains that noisily pass our home every three hours be easier to get used to than an occasional airplane passing overhead? How can it be that people talking softly but audibly during a movie can be more annoying than the loud sounds of rock music? In this chapter, we will discuss these issues and the kinds of problems that have been associated with noise exposure. Keep in mind as we go through this research that noise is considerably less powerful or overwhelming than are events such as disasters, but that it may be possible that noise can cause more severe and/or long-lasting consequences. How can this be? Could the repetitive or constant nature of noise be responsible for these effects, suggesting that cumulative effects over time can exceed those of very severe, acute events?

Figure 5–1.   An urban street scene. How many sources of noise can you find?

It is also important to remember that noise, for the most part, is a by-product of civilization. There are sources of noise in nature (thunder is one example), but noise rarely occurs as a result of physical changes in the environment. Rather, noise that influences human behavior is usually human-made. Whether this factor is important in the way in which noise affects us is another question that can be explored.

In this chapter, we will first discuss the nature of sound and noise—how we perceive them, how they are measured, and where they come from. The effects of noise on a range of physiological, psychological, and behavioral variables is considered as well, and research on occupational exposure to noise is summarized. As we will see, noise effects on task performance and social behavior have received a great deal of attention. Finally, we discuss some attempts to apply what we know and to evaluate the effects of noise abatement programs.

WHAT IS NOISE?

One question that is immediately apparent is that the meaning of noise is more complex than most people imagine. What is it? How can it best be defined, both conceptually and as an experimental variable? We will consider these issues in this section.

The simplest and most common definition of **noise** is that it is "unwanted sound." You may enjoy listening to your favorite rock group on your stereo, but if the music disturbs your roommate's studying or sleep, then as far as your roommate is concerned the moving sound of the talented musicians is noise. The sound of a garbage truck making pickups early in the morning may be necessary in order to maintain healthy sanitation, and for the early riser this sound may provide a wake-up cue signaling a bright new day. But if you do not wish to be roused so early in the morning, then the motorized contraption is making noise. Loud industrial machinery, jet aircraft, computer line printers, and pneumatic hammers also generate noise, but only if someone finds the sound undesirable. Thus, the concept of noise implies both a significant psychological component

("unwanted") as well as a physical component (it must be perceived by the ear and higher brain).

Perceiving Noise

The measurement of sound is based primarily on its physical component, although the brain's interpretation of the sound is also crucial to the structure of the measuring scale. Physically, **sound** is created by the rapidly changing pressure of air molecules at the eardrum. As these molecules are forced together, positive pressure is created relative to the negative pressure when the molecules pull apart. This alternating pressure can be represented graphically by waves, the peaks of the waves representing positive pressure and the valleys negative pressure (Figure 5–2). These alternating

Figure 5–2. Examples of sound waves. Frequency increases from top to bottom; amplitude increases from left to right.

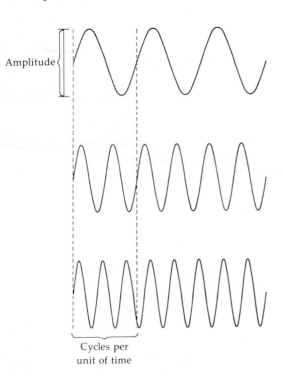
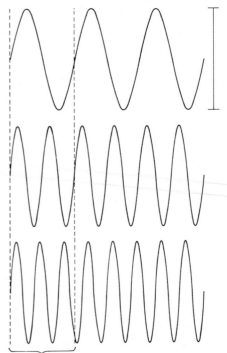

pressures cause the eardrum to vibrate. The eardrum then transmits these vibrations through the structures of the middle and inner ear to the basilar membrane in the cochlea (Figure 5–3A and B). Tiny hair cells in this membrane, which are activated by the noise vibrations, pass along the noise stimulation through the auditory nerve to the temporal lobe of the brain. In the conventional sense, auditory *sensation* consists of the activation of the nervous system by the sound stimulus. *Perception* begins somewhere between the basilar membrane and the temporal lobe of the brain, where a code we have yet to unravel allows the organism to interpret the sound stimulus as high or low in pitch and volume.

Examine the waves depicted in Figure 5–2 once again. Physically, the more times per second the wave motion completes a cycle (from peak to valley), the greater the **frequency** of the sound. Psychologically, frequency is perceived as **pitch**, i.e., highness or lowness. The normal human ear can hear frequencies between 20 and 20,000 cycles per second, or **hertz (Hz)**. However, most sounds we hear are not one frequency but a mixture of frequencies. Psychologically, purity of frequency is known as **timbre** or **tonal quality**. Sound stimuli that consist of a very few frequencies are often called ''**narrow band**,'' whereas stimuli with a wide range of frequencies are called ''**wide band**.'' A very wide range of unpatterned frequencies is called ''**white noise**.''

Besides varying in frequency characteristics, sound waves vary according to height or **amplitude**, experienced psychologically as **loudness**: The greater the amplitude, the louder the sound. The loudness of a sound is related to the amount of energy or pressure in the sound wave. The smallest pressure or threshold that a young adult can detect is about 0.0002 microbars, or dynes per square centimeter, where a dyne is a measure of pressure. At 1000 microbars, the pressure is experienced more as pain than as sound. Since a scale of sound ranging from 0.0002 microbars to 1000 or more

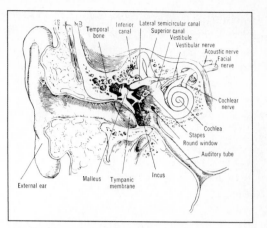

Figure 5–3A. Schematic diagram of human ear, showing important structures associated with perception of sound. (From Gardner, E., 1975. *Fundamentals of neurology*, 6th ed. Philadelphia: Saunders.)

Figure 5–3B. Internal structure of human auditory system. (From Gardner, 1975.)

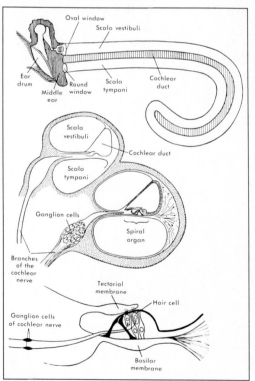

Table 5–1. Decibel Equivalents of Microbars	
Sound Pressure in Microbars	*Equivalent Decibels*
0.0002	0
0.002	20
0.02	40
0.2	60
2.0	80
20.0	100
200.0	120
2000.0	140

microbars would be cumbersome to work with, a scale of sound pressure has been developed that uses **decibels (dB)** as the basic units of sound, where decibels are a logarithmic function of microbars. Table 5–1 gives the corresponding decibel equivalents of the audible range of microbars. Note that an increase of 20 decibels represents a tenfold increase in pressure. Thus, a sound of 80dB is not twice as intense as one of 40dB, it is 10 × 10 or 100 times as intense. Figure 5–4 presents some common sounds associated with various points on the decibel scale.

The decibel scale measures the physical component of sound or noise amplitude. However, this scale does not accurately reflect the perception of loudness. That is, an increase of 20 dB does mean that one sound has 10 times more pressure than another, but it does not mean that the more intense sound will be perceived as 10 times louder. The main reason for this lack of physical-perceptual correspondence is that the human ear is differentially

Figure 5–4. Some common sounds associated with the decibel scale.

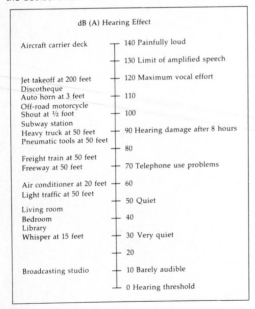

Figure 5–5. Sensitivity of the human ear to different frequencies of sound. (From Turk, A., Turk, J., Wittes, J. T., and Wittes, R. 1974. *Environmental Science.* Philadelphia: Saunders.)

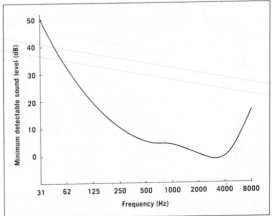

Table 5–2 — Equivalent Decibel, Phon, and Sone Levels for Selected Frequencies*

Frequency	63 Hz			2000 Hz			10,000 Hz		
dB	50	80	90	50	80	90	50	80	90
phon	70	106	115	80	106	114	76	103	111
sone	8	97	180	16	95	172	14	78	140

*Interpolated from Kryter, 1970, after Zwicker, 1960.

sensitive to sounds at different frequencies, as indicated in Figure 5–5. That is, below about 500 Hz and above about 4000 Hz, it takes a more intense sound even to be detected than it does between 500 Hz and 4000 Hz. To find a loudness scale that reflects human perception, we have to turn to *phons* or *sones*.

A **phon** is defined as the level in dB of a 1000 Hz tone when it is judged to be of the same loudness as the sound being tested. That is, to determine the phon level of a given sound, we ask a subject to adjust a 1000 Hz tone until the two sounds appear to be of equal loudness. The dB level of the 1000 Hz tone at the point of apparently equal loudness is then considered the phon level of the sound being tested. A **sone**, on the other hand (Stevens, 1955), is determined by starting with a 1000 Hz tone at 40 dB. The perceived loudness of this tone is defined as one sone. A sound perceived to be twice as loud as this standard tone is defined as two sones, a sound three times as loud is three sones, and so on. Obviously, the relationship between decibels, phons, and sones will depend on the frequencies as well as the intensities of the sounds measured. Table 5–2 depicts equivalent dB, phon, and sone levels for three frequencies. Note that for these frequency and dB levels, an increase of 20 dB (representing a tenfold increase in pressure) represents a two to four-fold increase in perceived loudness. (For a more detailed discussion of sound, see Kryter, 1970.)

Annoyance

Some kinds of noise are more annoying than others. As you might guess, loud noises are often more annoying than quieter noises. However, there is more to it than that. Noise is a disturbing environmental phenomenon because it is, by definition, unwanted. It is this irritating and distracting psychological component that causes noise to be a problem. Kryter (1970) and Glass and Singer (1972) point out that some types of noise are more annoying than others. Three major dimensions influencing the **annoyance** (i.e., irritating) characteristics of noise are: (1) volume; (2) predictability; and (3) perceived control.

How are we affected by noise at different volumes? Above 90 dB, which is the level of noise produced by a heavy truck 50 feet away, noise becomes not only psychologically disturbing but also, after repeated periods of exposure for eight hours or more, physiologically damaging to hearing. Moreover, the louder the noise, the more likely it will interfere with verbal communication, the greater the arousal and stress associated with it, and the more attention one allocates to it.

Unpredictable, irregular noise is also more annoying than predictable, constant noise. A constant unbroken noise (especially if it is not loud) is not disturbing. Once we break it up into periodic "bursts," however, the noise becomes more disturbing; if we then make the bursts of noise aperiodic (i.e., coming at unpredictable or irregular intervals), the disturbing quality becomes even more pronounced. The more unpredictable the noise, the more arousing it is, and the more likely it is to lead to stress (unpredictable noises may be evaluated as more novel or threatening than predictable ones). In addition, more unpredictable noises require greater attention to understand and evaluate them, leaving less total attention available for other activities (e.g., Easterbrook, 1959). Finally, it is easier to adapt to a predictable noise, since the same stimulus is presented over and over again; with unpredictable noise, adaptation is more difficult.

Noise over which we have no **perceived control** is also more disturbing than noise we can control readily. If you have the means to stop or muffle a noise, you are less annoyed by it than if you cannot control it. For example, if you are using a noisy power saw, you can control the noise by stopping the saw. If your neighbor uses the saw next door, however, you have less immediate control over the noise, and so it is more disturbing. From the theoretical perspectives discussed previously, uncontrollable noise is more arousing and stressful, requires more attention allocation, and is more difficult to adapt to than controllable noise. From the behavior constraint approach, lack of control over noise can lead to psychological reactance and attempts to regain freedom of action by trying to assert control. If such efforts are unsuccessful, learned helplessness can result (see Chapter 4), in which a person simply accepts the noise and never tries to control it, even though control may become possible at a later time.

These three noise variables can, of course, occur in any combination. That is, we can have loud, predictable, uncontrollable noise, or quiet, unpredictable, uncontrollable noise, and so on. As we will see in a while, loud, unpredictable, uncontrollable noise has the most deleterious effects on behavior. Although these three factors are probably the most important in determining the effects of noise on behavior, research (Borsky, 1969) suggests that other factors also influence how annoying noise is. Annoyance increases if: (1) one perceives the noise as unnecessary; (2) those who generate the noise are perceived as unconcerned about the welfare of those who are exposed to it; (3) the person hearing the noise believes it is hazardous to health; (4) the person hearing the noise associates it with fear; and (5) the person hearing the noise is dissatisfied with other aspects of his or her environment.

SOURCES OF NOISE

As you might guess, noise can come from almost anywhere. Because it has a subjective component (it must be judged as unwanted), noise can come from anything that makes a sound. And, as you would also expect, the same sound may be unwanted at some times but not unwanted at other times. A dripping faucet passes as a faint whisper against the background sound of a busy afternoon, but at night, when we are trying to sleep, it can be noisy indeed.

In spite of this, there are contexts in which most people complain about noise. These settings are ones in which sound is either so loud that it is considered to be a noise, or is a little softer but more interfering, irregular, or disruptive. We will briefly discuss two of the common settings where noise can be a problem.

Transportation Noise

Noise caused by cars, trucks, trains, planes, and other modes of transportation is of great interest for a number of reasons. First, it is very widespread. Surveys have indicated that automobile noise is the most often mentioned source of urban noise, and that opening of new highways is associated with increases in annoyance among nearby residents (Lawson & Walters, 1974). Reports estimate that up to 11 million Americans are exposed to vehicular noise at or above levels that risk hearing loss (Bolt, Beranek, & Newman, Incorporated, 1976; Galloway et al., 1974). Increases in air traffic have increased noise levels around airports, and studies have shown that about two-thirds of those people living near airports where aircraft noise is a problem report annoyance and unhappiness about the noise (e.g., Burrows & Zamarin, 1972; McLean & Tarnopolsky, 1977). Rail traffic also continues to be a problem. Estimates in New York City alone suggest that a half million residents are exposed to loud (85–100 dB) noise from rapid transit trains (Raloff, 1982). Thus, the pervasiveness of noise generated by transportation systems makes it important to study.

A second characteristic of transportation noise is that it is usually loud. This is clear from the sound levels noted above, as well as from estimates of sound levels near airports (ranging from 75–95 dB). A quick glance at Figure 5–4 also provides evidence of this, as do recent EPA measurements of noise levels in third-floor apartments next to freeways in Los Angeles (90 dB) (Raloff, 1982).

Occupational Noise

Noise exposure in the workplace is a second major problem and has also received a great deal of research interest. It is also very pervasive, and the sound levels in many occupational setttings are loud. More than half of the nation's production workers are exposed to regular noise levels above the point at which hearing loss is likely, and more than 5 million are exposed to levels above the legally permissible ceiling of 90 dB (OSHA, 1981). Construction workers may be exposed to equipment noises of 100 dB, aircraft mechanics to levels ranging from 88–120 dB, and coal miners to continuous levels between 95 and 105 dB (Raloff, 1982).

EFFECTS OF NOISE

Physiological Effects of Noise

Hearing Loss Although very loud sounds (e.g., 150 dB) can rupture the eardrum or destroy other parts of the ear, damage to hearing from excessive noise usually occurs at lower noise levels (90 to 120 dB) because of temporary or permanent damage to the tiny hair cells in the cochlea of the inner ear (Figure 5–3). Such **hearing loss** is measured in terms of a baseline of ''normal'' amplitude thresholds at given frequencies. When a hearing loss occurs

at a given frequency, it requires more than the normal amplitude (in dB) for a person to hear that frequency, i.e., the amplitude threshold is greater. The usual index of hearing loss for a given frequency, then, is the number of decibels above the normal threshold required to reach the new threshold. Such hearing losses are generally identified as one of two types: (1) **temporary threshold shifts (TTS)**, in which the normal threshold returns within 16 hours after exposure to the damaging noise; and (2) noise-induced **permanent threshold shifts (NIPTS)**, which are typically measured a month or more after the cessation of exposure to the damaging noise (Kryter, 1970)

Hearing loss, which affects millions of people, is a serious problem in this country. A 1972 Environmental Protection Agency (EPA) survey estimated that close to three million Americans suffer noise-induced hearing loss. A report by Rosen et al. (1962) compared the extent of the problem in the United States with a much quieter Sudanese culture, and found that 70-year-old Sudanese tribesmen have hearing abilities comparable to those of 20-year-old Americans! To avoid serious hearing loss among industrial workers, the Occupational Safety and Health Administration (OSHA) has established guidelines that allow only eight hours a day of exposure to 90 dB noise, four hours for 95 dB, two hours for 100 dB, and so on. Yet a diesel truck at 50 feet emits noise of 95 dB. Thus individuals living near heavy traffic routes are undoubtedly exposed to noise levels for periods of time exceeding government industrial standards. The potential consequences of such exposure are reflected in the box on page 135.

Absolute levels of noise alone do not determine hearing loss. Recent research, for example, suggests that certain drugs may increase the damaging effects of noise (Miller, 1982). Studies with animals have indicated that administration of an antibiotic in conjunction with exposure to noise can increase the effects of the noise and cause greater hearing loss than would the drug or noise levels alone (Raloff, 1982). Other drugs, including aspirin, may also interact with noise and increase effects on hearing, but evidence remains mixed. At this point it appears that a few drugs can, in combination with noise, cause increased hearing loss, but the magnitude of effect of most is small.

College students and teenagers are frequently exposed to another damaging source of noise—loud rock music. Several studies (e.g., Lebo & Oliphant, 1968) have found that rock groups playing in discotheques are exposed to music from 110 to 120 dB for nonstop periods of up to one and one-half hours. Serious hearing loss can result (the federal industrial limit for 110 dB sound is 30 minutes a day). Other research (EPA, 1972) has studied hearing loss across samples of several age groups, and found frequencies to be 3.8 percent of sixth-graders, 10 percent of ninth- and tenth-graders, and a whopping 61 percent of the 1969 college freshman class.

Physical Health   We have suggested that exposure to high levels of noise leads to increased arousal and stress. We might expect, then, that the incidence of diseases related to stress (hypertension, ulcers, etc.) would increase as one is exposed to higher levels of noise. Research evidence on this relationship is not conclusive. On the one hand, Cohen, Glass, and Phillips (1977) reviewed studies done in this area and concluded that, in general, the evidence for noise as a pathogenic agent is weak. On the other hand, noise has been linked to spontaneous outbreaks of illness related to stress (e.g., Colligan & Murphy, 1982) and to incidence of neurological and gastrointestinal problems (National Academy of Sciences, 1981). Ulcers in particular appear more likely among workers exposed to occupational noise. Doring, Hauf, and Seiberling (1980) have suggested that sound can affect intestinal tissue directly, so it does not even have to be heard to predispose a worker to digestive problems. In addition, at least one study (Ando & Hattori, 1973) has found an association between exposure of expectant mothers to aircraft noise and infant mortality. Finally, survey or correlational studies have found that frequent exposure to noise is associated with reports of acute and chronic illness (Cameron, Robertson, & Zaks, 1972) and with increased consumption of sleeping pills and need to see a physician (Grandjean et al., 1973). The latter studies, however, are not definitive because they do not control for related factors such as housing conditions,

Beyond the Laboratory: Costs in the Classroom

Cohen, Glass, and Singer (1973) theorized that urban noise may impair the educational development of children if it is severe enough. Studying a large high-rise apartment complex situated over a noisy highway in New York City (see Figure 5–6), the investigators found that noise exposure on the lower floors of the complex was more severe than on the upper floors. While carefully controlling for such factors as social class and air pollution, which might also vary with the floors of the building, the researchers found that children on the noisier lower floors had poorer hearing discrimination than children on the upper floors.

Figure 5–6. This is the high-rise apartment building used in the study described here. Note the traffic passing underneath.

Moreover, the hearing problems of children on the lower floors may have influenced their reading ability, for it was found that they had poorer reading performance than children on the upper floors.

In another study, Bronzaft and McCarthy (1975) compared the reading skills of children from two sides of a school building. One side of the building was adjacent to elevated railroad tracks, but the other side was much quieter. It was found that 11 percent of teaching time was lost in classrooms facing the noisy tracks. Not surprisingly, the reading skills of children on the quieter side of the building were superior to those of children on the noisy side (see also Crook & Langdon, 1974).

Research also suggests that aircraft noise has effects on children's performance. Cohen et al. (1986) studied children attending school near the Los Angeles International Airport. Some were in schools in which aircraft noise was very loud (up to 95 dB), while others were in schools where there was considerably less noise. After controlling for the effects of socioeconomic variables and accounting for differences in hearing loss, results of a multimeasure assessment indicated that children attending noisier schools had more difficulty solving complex problems. In addition, Damon (1977) found that children living in housing where traffic noise was high were more likely to miss school.

Can such problems be prevented? The report by Ward and Suedfeld

(1973) suggests that they can. In response to a plan for routing a major highway next to a classroom building, the researchers played tape recordings of traffic at noise levels that simulated those of a real highway. Interference with learning was discovered before construction began, suggesting that we can plan ahead to avoid problems of this kind.

. . . .

income, or education.

It can also be readily demonstrated that exposure to high concentrations of noise (e.g., living near an airport, working in a noisy setting) leads to heightened electrodermal activity, constriction of peripheral blood vessels, higher diastolic and systolic **blood pressure**, and increased catecholamine secretions (e.g., Cohen et al., 1980; Frankenhaeuser & Lundberg, 1977; Glass & Singer, 1972; Knipschild, 1980). Data from school children attending schools near the Los Angeles International Airport have indicated that exposure to noisy conditions at school is associated with elevated blood pressure relative to that observed among children attending quieter schools (Cohen, et al., 1986). In addition, workers exhibit lower blood pressures and lower levels of epinephrine in their urine when they wear hearing protectors that reduce the intensity of noise (Ising & Melchert, 1980). The physiological changes accompanying exposure to noise are also associated with stress reactions and cardiovascular disorders, but few controlled experimental studies have been conducted that indicate a direct link between noise and heart disease.

One recent study provides information about how noise may facilitate the development of **hypertension**. Subjects who were already diagnosed as having moderately high blood pressure were exposed to 105dB noise for 30 minutes, and blood pressure measurements were made during quiet and noisy periods (Eggertsen et al., 1987). During the noise there was a significant increase in systolic and diastolic blood pressure, marked primarily by an increase in peripheral vascular resistance as the force of the heart contractions actually decreased. Thus, stress due to noise exposure was associated with constriction of blood vessels, suggesting a mechanism by which noise may contribute to hypertension. Research suggests that the constriction of blood vessels that is associated with noise exposure does not habituate very well when noise is loud or unexpected (Jansen, 1974). This means that, over time, very loud or unexpected noise continues to affect blood vessels long after subjects have "gotten used to the noise" and other physiological responses have diminished. Responses such as heart rate or skin conductance tend to be modest and to decrease with repeated exposure (Borg, 1981; Glass & Singer, 1972). Most of these studies suggest that noise can cause a variety of physiological changes that may contribute to disease. The links to disease, however, are less well established—all of which is to say that despite reported increases of several stress indicators or measures of cardiovascular function when people are exposed to noise, these studies do not show a relationship between noise and cardiovascular disease.

Any analysis of noise exposure, measured as hearing loss, showed few if any relationships with cardiovascular function or disease among Air Force aircrews (Kent et al., 1986). However, this *correlational* study relies on a strong relationship between hearing loss and noise exposure and cannot address other causes of hearing loss. It is also possible that the self-selection biases in aircrew members might have affected the results. Other studies have examined health problems among industrial workers as a function of exposure to noise. These studies (e.g., Cohen, 1973; Jansen, 1973) typically find that exposure to high noise levels is associated with cardiovascular disorders, allergies, sore throats, and digestive disorders. And, in a completely different setting, Rosen and Olin (1985) suggested that low noise exposure among the Mabaan tribe in the Sudan may be a factor in the low prevalence of heart disease in this group.

Interestingly, younger and less experienced workers appear to suffer more from noise exposure, suggesting that more experienced workers have adapted to the noise. Unfortunately, such industrial studies rarely control for other factors that may account for adverse health effects, such as factory conditions, exposure to pollutants, and stressful work activity, so that conclusions about effects of noise on health must be guarded. Furthermore, some studies (e.g., Finkle & Poppen, 1948; Glorgin, 1971) report no association between industrial noise exposure and many of the disorders we have noted.

Another way of studying the health-impairing effects of noise is to examine how it interacts with other stressors or behaviors. For example, we know that noise increases people's blood pressure and other signs of arousal, as does cigarette smoking. How do the two affect us if we smoke while exposed to noise? Given that smoking is described by many who smoke as an effective coping strategy that calms them down, will it cancel the arousing effects of noise or add to them? A study by Woodson et al., (1986) looked at this question in a sample of women. Forty-eight women who smoked and 12 who did not smoke participated in the study. The smokers were assigned to a smoking group or a sham-smoking group (puffing on unlit cigarettes) in which they did not actually smoke any cigarettes. The nonsmokers were assigned to a sham smoking control group. Subjective distress reported by subjects increased during the noise exposure among smokers who did not actually smoke any cigarettes during the session, but did not increase for those allowed to smoke. The arousing effects of smoking did attenuate some noise-related arousal. Smoking appears to dampen some of the physiological responses to noise, particularly noise-induced

increases in heart rate and vasoconstriction. This may have been partially due to the periodic nature of the noise exposure (noise was not continuous) since studies of continuous stressor exposure and smoking find the opposite effect

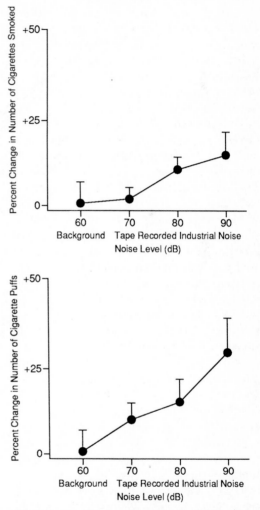

Figure 5−7. The top graph indicates the percent change in the number of cigarettes smoked per session for all subjects at industrial noise levels of 60, 70, 80, or 90 decibels. The bottom graph shows the percent change in the number of cigarette puffs per session. Data points represent the mean percent change values for all subjects, with the mean at the baseline (60 dB) condition set at zero. The vertical lines on each data point represent the standard error of the mean. (Adapted from Cherek, 1985).

or no effect at all (e.g., MacDougall et al., 1983; Suter, et al., 1983).

It is also possible that noise can affect health by changing behaviors that are related to health. If people drink more coffee or alcohol, smoke more cigarettes, or fail to exercise because of noise exposure, then relationships between noise and health might be mediated by these behaviors. A recent study by Cherek (1985) provides some evidence of this by showing that increasing loudness of noise was associated with increased cigarette smoking. As can be seen in Figure 5–7, higher dB levels of noise were associated with higher levels of smoking during an experimental laboratory session as well as with how people smoked. The louder the noise, the more puffs they took when they smoked and the longer the average duration of each puff.

Overall, it is difficult to relate noise *directly* to adverse effects on physical health. More likely, adverse effects of noise exposure on health occur primarily in conjunction with other stressors (such as industrial pollutants, on-the-job tensions, economic pressures, and so on), or are limited to those who are particularly susceptible to certain physiological disorders (Cohen, Glass, & Phillips, 1977).

Noise and Mental Health

We have noted that exposure to high levels of noise leads to the heightened physiological activity typical of stress.

Since stress is a causal factor in mental illness, we might expect noise exposure to be associated with mental disorders (for a review, see Cohen, Glass, & Phillips, 1977: Kryter, 1970). Indeed, industrial surveys typically report that exposure to high-intensity noise is associated with headaches, nausea, instability, argumentativeness, anxiety, sexual impotence, and changes in affect or mood (Cohen et al., 1977; Miller, 1974; Strakhov, 1966). As with surveys on physical health and noise, however, the results of these studies must be interpreted

with caution, since other stresses related to home and work are not fully taken into account. In a relevant experimental study, Ward and Suedfeld (1973) found that exposure to "piped in" traffic noise caused people to experience more tension and uncertainty and led people to talk faster than a group exposed to ambient sound conditions.

An interesting and controversial series of studies has attempted to examine the relationship between airport noise and mental health. In one study (Abey-Wickrama et al., 1969), researchers compared psychiatric admission rates for high and low noise areas around London's Heathrow Airport. Higher admission rates occurred in the noisy area. Chowns (1970) challenged these results because the populations of the two areas may have differed in important ways, although Herridge (1974) and Herridge and Low-Beer (1973) found similar though weaker results with improved survey techniques. (See Figure 5–8.)

As with physical health, we must tentatively conclude that to the extent noise contributes to mental illness, it does so in combination with many other factors that precipitate mental disorders. However, in addition to influencing stress, noise exposure may lead to loss of perceived control and learned helplessness (see Chapter 4), which in turn increase susceptibility to psychological disorders. Cohen et al. (1977) noted that residents of high-noise areas tend to "give up" and not complain about the noise because they perceive their voices will not carry weight with authorities. Together with the social and economic burdens typical of high-noise areas of cities, a sense of hopelessness and helplessness may develop, which can lead to psychological disorders.

Effects of Noise on Performance

Effects During Exposure People report that they make more errors in noisy than in quiet settings, but their beliefs about noise do not always match their performance (Smith &

Figure 5–8. Some research has tried to associate airport noise with mental health problems of residents in the area. Although the findings are controversial, there is limited evidence that psychiatric hospital admissions are unusually heavy for areas surrounding airports.

Stansfield, 1986; Weinstein, 1974). Laboratory research on the influence of noise on performance has shown mixed results. For a detailed review, the reader is referred to Cohen et al. (1986), Glass and Singer (1972), and to Kryter (1970). Briefly, whether noise affects performance adversely, favorably, or not at all depends on the type (e.g., predictable or unpredictable) and intensity of noise, the type of task performed, and the stress tolerance and other personality characteristics of the individual (e.g., Cohen & Weinstein, 1982; Koelega & Brinkman, 1986). In general, data from laboratory research suggest that regular noise in the range of 90 to 110 dB does not adversely affect performance of simple motor or mental tasks. However, noises in this amplitude range that are unpredictable (intermittent at irregular intervals) will interfere with performance on vigilance tasks, memory tasks, and complex tasks in which an individual must perform two

activities simultaneously. On the other hand, Glass and Singer (1972) found that even these performance problems were minimal for individuals who perceived that they had control over the noise (i.e., could stop it if they wished). Other research (Broadbent, 1954) suggests that sudden, loud, unpredictable noises may momentarily distract an individual from a task and thereby cause errors if the task requires much vigilance or concentration. Woodhead (1964) noted that recorded sonic booms cause momentary errors in a task requiring intense concentration.

To some extent the kind of effects that noise has on task performance may be a matter of personality; research has indicated that noise effects on performance may depend in part on personality, as in Auble and Britton's (1958) finding that only subjects who are high in anxiety are adversely affected by noise on certain types of tasks. Other individual differences may be important as well (Vallet, 1987). Age, sex, and other characteristics could be influential. Children do not experience as much disturbed sleep, and younger subjects have been shown to have smaller physiological changes when exposed to noise than do older subjects (Vallet, 1987). However, among younger people, there appear to be sex differences in response, with females exhibiting more sleep disturbance than males (Lukas, 1975). Finally, limited research (e.g., Corcoran, 1962) suggests that the arousal properties of noise may actually facilitate performance for individuals who have been deprived of sleep for a day or more.

Exposure to loud, uncontrollable noise appears to bias retrieval of information from memory, causing more attention or greater recall of negative mood-laden items or memories (Willner & Neiva, 1986). This is not unlike observations of depressed people, who suffer from negative memory biases and seem better able to retrieve unpleasant memories (e.g., Fogarty & Hemsley, 1983). Since exposure to uncontrollable stressors has been shown to lead to symptoms of learned helplessness and helplessness may be associated with depression, all of this seems to fit together. Or does it? Failure on a computer game task, which should also contribute to learned helplessness, did not affect retrieval of negative memories (Isen, et al., 1978). Though the effects of noise in distorting memory observed by Willner and Neiva (1986) were found only when the noise was uncontrollable, it may be that some characteristic of noise is also important in this relationship. The effects of stressors on this sort of memory distortion and bias toward negative recollections represent an important area for future research.

Cognitive impairment by noise among children also has been observed, though it appears that these effects are not universal. For example, Hambrick-Dixon (1986) studied children who attended day-care centers close to noisy elevated subways and far from the subways.

Psychomotor task performance was impaired by experimentally imposed noise in a laboratory setting, but the nature of performance during noise was determined by the noisiness of their day-care center. Children from the noisier centers performed *better* when exposed to noise than when not, while children from quieter centers showed the opposite pattern.

In a series of studies examining the effects of chronic exposure to loud aircraft noise at school, Cohen et al. (1986) compared problem-solving performance of children from noisy and quiet schools near the Los Angeles International Airport. Subjects were given either a solvable or an unsolvable task before performance was assessed, and in one of the samples, subjects were allowed to choose a game to play if they wished. The effects of success or failure among children from noisy or quiet schools on subsequent performance was thus assessed.

Results showed that children attending noisy schools were less likely to solve the solvable task than were students from quieter schools. Regardless of whether they were pretreated with success or failure on the first puzzle, they were less able to solve the second task, and were more likely to give up. These data suggested that students from noisy schools were simply less able to solve cognitive tasks. To some extent this was due to the tendency of children from the noisier schools to give up more quickly. Of those children given a choice during the experimental sessions, children from noisier schools were less likely to make the choice than were children from quieter environments.

These studies also examined school achievement and distractibility among these young students. Over time, the effects of chronic exposure to aircraft noise did not habituate; that is, the effects did not decrease or go away with time. Instead, students seemed to be more distractible the longer they attended school under noisy conditions. School achievement was not affected by noise levels in schools, but was affected by noise levels at home.

How can we explain why noise affects performance only under certain circumstances? To answer this question we can turn to the theoretical approaches discussed in Chapter 4. For example, adaptation level theory predicts variations in performance for different levels of skill, experience, and stimulation for each individual. Furthermore, the Yerkes–Dodson Law and the arousal approach suggest that noise that is arousing will facilitate performance on simple tasks, up to a point. High levels of arousal interfere with performance on complex tasks, and extremely high levels of arousal interfere with performance on simple tasks. Data from research on noise and performance are consistent with this explanation.

The environmental load approach also explains much about the relationship between noise and performance. Unpredictable noise requires more allocation of attention than predictable noise, so it should interfere more with performance. For complex tasks, very much attention is required for optimal performance, and any noise that distracts attention will hurt performance. Finally, the behavior constraint approach explains why lack of perceived control over noise hurts performance: When control is apparently lost, more effort may be given to restoring control than to attending to the task at hand.

Aftereffects   Noise has more than just immediate effects on performance. Glass, Singer, and Friedman (1969) had subjects perform tasks after a 25-minute exposure to 108 dB noise. One task involved attempts to solve puzzles that were actually unsolvable (Figure 5–9). The number of attempts to solve such puzzles served as an index of tolerance for frustration, or persistence. The second task involved proofreading a manuscript, which required considerable vigilance and concentration. Compared to a no-noise control group and groups exposed before the task to either predictable *or* controllable noise, subjects exposed before the task to 108 dB of unpredictable *and* uncontrollable noise showed one-half to one-third as much tolerance of frustration and also made considerably more proofreading errors. Apparently, the **aftereffects** of noise can be as severe as the effects during perception of the noise. In a similar experiment, it was found that aftereffects depend on the amount of perceived control (Sherrod et al., 1977). These researchers gave some subjects control over starting the noise, and still others control over both starting and stopping it. Another group had no control over the noise. Results showed that the greater the perceived control, the more persistent subjects were in working unsolvable puzzles once the noise had stopped.

Such aftereffects can also be explained by the theoretical approaches discussed previously. For example, arousal remains elevated for a time after an arousing stimulus (such as noise) has ceased. Thus, this "carried over" arousal can account for some aftereffects. The environmental load approach also suggests that once an attention-getting noise has stopped, a fatigue effect ensues, and it takes time to reallocate enough attention to perform a mental

Figure 5–9.   Examples of puzzles used by Glass and Singer (1972). Figures must be drawn without crossing a line or lifting the pencil. (Adapted by Glass and Singer from Feather, 1961.)

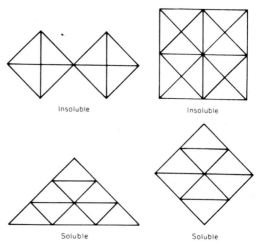

task. If the noise is presented with perceived control, less attention is allocated to it to begin with, so recovery time is less, and the potential for learned helplessness is decreased.

Effects of Noise in Office and Industrial Settings

One of the most serious problems of background noise in commercial and industrial settings is its interference with communication (Mackenzie, 1975; Nemecek & Grandjean, 1973). When a number of distinct auditory signals are presented simultaneously, it is often difficult for the human ear to distinguish or discriminate among them. This phenomenon is known as **masking**, and it accounts for our difficulty in hearing others talk in the presence of loud background noise. The background noise in the Glass and Singer (1972) research was created by combining simultaneously the sounds of a mimeograph machine, a calculator, a typewriter, two people speaking Spanish, and another person speaking Armenian, with the final effect being little discriminability among the various sounds due to masking. Interestingly, it has been found that loud background conversation interferes with performance more than noise that is not distinguishable as conversation (Olszewski, Rotton, & Soler, 1976). Apparently, we try to hear background conversation as communication, so we pay a lot of attention to it. Nonconversational noise, however, requires less attention but does interfere with efforts to communicate.

Difficulty in hearing a communication varies not only according to amplitude and frequency of background noise (the more similar the frequency of the noise and of the communication, the worse the interference), but also according to the distance between communicator and listener. Figure 5–10 demonstrates the combined effects of ambient noise amplitude and interpersonal distance on communication. These "acceptable" levels of background noise are sometimes referred to as "speech interfer-

ence levels" or SIL's (Beranek, 1957). Limited research (e.g., Acton, 1970) indicates that some communicative adaptation to background noise does occur, so that we can learn to communicate effectively in the presence of many types of background noises. Thus, industrial workers accustomed to a noisy environment were found to be more effective in communicating against a loud background noise than were university employees accustomed to a quieter environment. Beranek (1956, 1957) examined self-reports of employees in offices and factories to determine what noise levels they considered acceptable in their work environments. Results correlated quite well with what might be predicted from SIL data, suggesting that 55 to 70 dB is acceptable for executive offices. Many designers and builders use these standards today (Mackenzie, 1975).

Research on the effects of noise on productivity in industrial settings generally finds no direct effect of noise on nonauditory performance (Kryter, 1970). However, several studies have purported to show that noise reduction can boost productivity. Broadbent and Little

Figure 5–10. Relationship between communication effort, noise level, and interpersonal distance. (Adapted from Miller, 1974.)

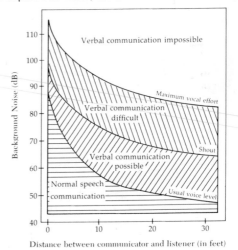

Distance between communicator and listener (in feet)

(1960) found that in a film-producing factory, reduction of ambient noise from 99 dB to 89 dB resulted in fewer errors by workers. Kovrigin and Mikheyev (1965) reported that increasing background noise from 78–80 dB to either 85, 90, or 95 dB reduced the number of letters sorted per hour by postal employees. Kryter (1970) suggests that because such studies are conducted in field settings not subject to strict laboratory control of extraneous variables, the results are inconclusive at best. Reduction of noise, for instance, may boost employee morale, which in turn boosts productivity. In other words, mediating variables, such as morale, fatigue, or communication difficulty, may be more significant than direct effects of noise on performance. Nevertheless, if noise influences productivity even indirectly, industry would certainly want to take such influences into account by designing equipment and working space with noise levels in mind.

Concern over productivity, morale, and detrimental health effects of noise has led many industry and government officials to emphasize noise abatement factors in office and industrial settings (see also Mackenzie, 1975). Among the more common abatement procedures are: use of thick carpeting, suspended and acoustical tile ceilings, sound-absorbing wall materials, heavy draperies, and even plants. Other approaches involve making machines quieter in the first place, such as putting a layer of felt between typewriters and desks, enclosing computer printout equipment with felt or foam-lined covers, and producing equipment with less noisy components. Still another approach is to mask noise with constantly humming ventilating equipment or piped-in music. Whatever the technique, we suspect that an increasing emphasis by labor and management will be placed on reducing noise in working environments.

NOISE AND SOCIAL BEHAVIOR

If noise has stressful, arousing, attention-narrowing, or behavior-constraining properties, exposure to it will be likely to influence interpersonal relationships. We will now look at three specific social relationships—attraction, altruism, and aggression—to determine just what noise can do to social interaction.

Noise and Attraction

One might expect loud, disturbing noise to have a deleterious effect on feelings of liking toward others. That is, noxious stimuli associated with others may lead to less pleasant evaluation of those others. One way to measure attraction, as suggested by research on personal space, is to examine physical distances between ourselves and others; we stand or sit closer to those people we like than to those we dislike. Thus, if interpersonal distance is an indicator of attraction and if noise decreases attraction, we would expect noise to increase interpersonal distancing. In support of this hypothesis, Mathews, Cannon, and Alexander (1974) found that even a noise of 80 dB increased the distance at which individuals felt comfortable with each other. Also, in a correlational study, Appleyard and Lintell (1972) found less informal interaction among neighbors when traffic noise was greater. While this could suggest that noise lowers attraction toward others, additional interpretations are possible.

Other researchers (Bull et al., 1972) have found equivocal results on the relationship

The SST: Why So Loud?

One of the marvels of space-age technology is supersonic flight and the arrival of the supersonic transport (SST) for commercial passengers. The American version of the SST was scuttled for economic and environmental reasons. The British–French Concorde, however, went into production and has been controversial ever since. Among its problems is noise. Engines on an SST must be slim and trim for better flight. As engine diameter decreases and speed increases, jet exhaust noise becomes greater. Typical Concorde noise on a runway is 100 to 120 dB, depending on one's distance from the jet. This is 10 to 20 dB greater than subsonic jets. Research suggests that a single flight of an aircraft 10 dB louder than another produces the same annoyance level as 10 flights of the less noisy aircraft.

Another noise problem with the SST is sonic booms. These thunderclap sounds are produced by any supersonic aircraft. Sound travels at a speed of 334 meters per second (747 miles per hour). The SST moves faster than the noise it produces (since passengers are ahead of the sound, they do not hear it as someone on the ground does). Consequently, the sound waves crowd together, increasing their pressure and causing a sonic boom. The tail of the aircraft leaves a partial vacuum, lowering the pressure as it passes. The result is an increase in pressure followed by a decrease. These pressure changes move away from the jet in the pattern of cones (Figure 5–11), so that anyone on the ground between the two cones hears the boom. If the aircraft is long enough, the positive and negative pressure changes may be heard as two distinct sounds. The boom itself continues from the time the aircraft breaks the sound barrier until it resumes subsonic speeds, but a person on the ground hears it only 0.1 to 0.5 second. Thus, the entire area over which the SST flies at supersonic speeds will experience the sonic boom. For this reason, the SST has been forbidden to fly over the United States at supersonic speeds. (From Turk et al., 1974.)

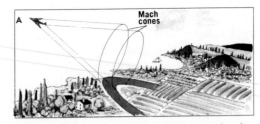

Figure 5–11. Cones representing increased and decreased pressure in a sonic boom. The area where the cones intersect the ground (shaded gray) experiences the sonic boom. (From Turk, A., Turk, J., Wittes, J. T., and Wittes, R., 1974. *Environmental Science*. Philadelphia: Saunders.

between noise and attraction. These researchers found that although exposure to 84 dB of background noise led to less liking in most cases, females actually reported more liking for similar others when exposed to noise. Research by Bell and Barnard (1977) suggests a partial explanation for this unexpected finding. Apparently, males exposed to noxious environmental stimulation momentarily prefer more distant, less affiliative social interaction. Females, on the other hand, may well prefer closer, affiliative social interaction in order to share their uneasiness with others who are experiencing discomfort. Thus, in some circumstances noise may decrease attraction, and in other cases it may increase attraction. Kenrick and Johnson (1979), for example, have shown that among females, exposure to aversive noise may increase attraction toward one who shares the aversive experience with the subject, but decrease attraction toward someone not actually experiencing the noise.

One explanation for some effects of noise on attraction is that noise affects the amount of information that people gather about another person. Theories that suggest that noise causes people to narrow their attention and focus on a smaller part of their environment also suggests that noise causes people to pay attention to fewer characteristics of other people. Thus, noise could cause a distortion in perceptions of other people. Research by Siegel and Steele (1980) suggests that this may be the case, finding that noise led to more extreme and premature judgments about other people but did not cause these judgments to be more negative.

Noise and Human Aggression

Research on the effects of noise on aggression has been much more conclusive than research on noise and attraction. Several theories of aggression (Bandura, 1973; Berkowitz, 1970), predict that under circumstances in which aggression is a dominant response in the behavior hierarchy, increasing an individual's arousal level will also increase the intensity of aggressive behavior. Thus, to the extent that noise increases arousal, it should also increase aggression in individuals already predisposed to aggress.

Geen and O'Neal (1969) sought to test this hypothesis by first showing subjects either a nonviolent sports film or a more violent prizefight film, with the expectation that the violent film would predispose subjects to aggress. Next, subjects were provided with an opportunity to aggress against a confederate "victim" by ostensibly delivering electric shocks to that person. In many studies of aggression, subjects are given the chance to shock a confederate or stooge victim, and the shock level (intensity, duration, or number) they choose is the index of aggression. No shocks are actually administered, although the subject, until the end of the experiment, is led to believe that he or she is actually delivering shocks. During the shock phase of the experiment, Geen and O'Neal exposed half the subjects to the normal noise level of the laboratory and the other half to a two-minute burst of continuous 60 dB white noise (i.e., a broad band of frequencies). It was predicted that the 60 dB noise would increase the level of aggression of subjects exposed to the violent film. Results, as depicted in Figure 5–12, suggested that both the violent film and the added noise increased the number of shocks delivered to the victim. Furthermore, the greatest aggression occurred under the condition that combined the violent film with the arousing noise, as originally predicted.

Additional laboratory research on noise and aggression has been conducted by Donnerstein and Wilson (1976). It will be recalled that Glass and Singer (1972) found unpredictable noise to be more aversive than predictable noise. One would thus expect unpredictable noise to be highly arousing and consequently to lead to heightened aggression, in accordance with the dominant response hypothesis noted above. Donnerstein and Wilson therefore exposed subjects to either 55 dB or 95 dB of unpredictable,

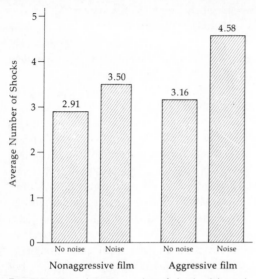

Figure 5–12. Average number of shocks delivered to the victim as a function of noise level and type of film. (Adapted from Geen, and O'Neal, 1969. Copyright © 1969 by the American Psychological Association. Reprinted by permission of the author and publisher.)

one-second noise bursts while they were ostensibly administering electric shocks to a confederate of the experimenter. In addition, half the subjects previously had been either angered or not angered by this victim. As expected, angered subjects delivered more intense shocks than nonangered ones. Furthermore, the 95 dB unpredictable noise increased aggression relative to the 55 dB unpredictable noise only for angered subjects. Apparently, noise made no difference in the intensity of shocks delivered by nonangry subjects.

Following Glass and Singer's findings that controllable noise is less aversive and arousing than uncontrollable noise, we would expect that if subjects were given perceived control over noise, the noise would be less aversive and less likely to facilitate aggression. Donnerstein and Wilson tested this hypothesis by conducting a second experiment to determine the effects of additional noise variables on aggression. As subjects worked on a set of math problems, they were exposed either to no artificial noise, to 95

dB of unpredictable and uncontrollable noise, or to 95 dB of unpredictable noise that they believed they could terminate at any time (i.e., over which they perceived they had control). All noise was terminated when subjects began the shock phase of the experiment, so that only the aftereffects of noise could influence aggression. As in the previous experiment, subjects were either angered or not angered by the victim, in this case immediately after the math task. The results, depicted in Figure 5–13, suggest that more intense shocks were delivered by angry than nonangry subjects, and that unpredictable and uncontrollable noise increased aggression for angry subjects. The 95 dB noise had no effect on aggression, however, when subjects perceived they had control over it.

This finding that noise increased aggressiveness only when people were angry suggests again that the noise served to facilitate aggression caused by anger rather than creating or causing the aggression directly. Konecni et al. (1975) also found this to be the case—noise increased aggressiveness only when subjects had been provoked and made angry.

These experiments suggest, then, that under circumstances in which noise would be expected to increase arousal or a predisposition to aggress (i.e., when subjects were already angry), aggression is increased. However, when the noise does not appreciably increase arousal (as when an individual has control over it) or when the individual is not already predisposed to aggress, noise appears to have little, if any, effect on aggression. Cohen and Spacapan (1984) have argued that noise strengthens or increases aggression but does not provoke it. In order for noise to affect aggressive behavior, the behavior must be present for other reasons.

Noise and Helping

Research suggests that noise influences at least one more social phenomenon—whether or not people help each other. It seems reasonable to assume that aversive noise that makes us

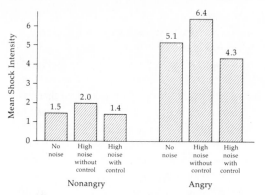

Figure 5–13. Mean intensity of shock delivered by subjects as a function of noise condition and anger arousal. (Adapted from Donnerstein and Wilson, 1976. Copyright © 1976 by the American Psychological Association. Reprinted by permission of the author and publisher.)

irritable or uncomfortable will make us less likely to offer assistance to someone who needs help. Research in social psychology has indicated that people are more likely to help others when they are in a good mood than when they are more negative (e.g., Isen, 1970), and since noise can result in the latter condition, it is likely that helping would also be affected. Another reason for this expected decrease in helping is offered by the environmental load approach discussed in Chapter 4. Since noise reduces the attention paid to less important stimuli, if social cues that someone needs help are less important than cues associated with a more important task, then noise should make us less aware of signs of distress. Cohen and Lezak (1977) demonstrated that the content of slides depicting social situations was less well remembered under noisy than under quiet conditions when subjects were asked to concentrate initially on material other than the slides. Under such conditions, social cues in the slides were relatively unimportant, so noise interfered with attending to these cues.

Consistent with this, two experiments, one conducted in the laboratory and the other in the field, suggest that noise does indeed decrease

frequency of helping (Mathews & Canon, 1975). In the laboratory experiment, subjects were exposed to 48 dB of normal noise, to 65 dB of white noise piped into the laboratory through a hidden speaker, or to 85 dB of white noise from the same speaker. As subjects arrived for the experiment, they were asked in turn to wait in the laboratory for a few minutes with another individual (actually a confederate of the experimenter), who was seated and reading a journal. On the confederate's lap were additional journals, books, and papers. After a few minutes, the experimenter called for the confederate who, upon getting up, "accidentally" dropped the materials right in front of the subject. The dependent measure of helping was whether or not the subject helped the confederate to pick up the spilled materials. Results suggested a definite decrement in helping in the loud noise conditions: 72 percent of the subjects helped in the normal noise condition, 67 percent in the 65 dB condition, and only 37 percent in the 85 dB condition.

The Mathews and Canon field experiment revealed even more interesting results. In this study, a confederate dropped a box of books while getting out of a car. To emphasize his apparent need for aid he wore a cast on his arm in half of the experimental situations. Noise was varied by having another confederate operate a lawnmower nearby. In the low-noise condition, the lawnmower was not running, and background noise from normal sources was measured at 50 dB. In the high-noise condition, the lawnmower was running without a muffler, putting out an 87 dB din. Once again, the dependent measure of helping was how many passing subjects stopped to assist the confederate to pick up the dropped books. As can be seen in Figure 5–14, noise had little effect on helping when the confederate was not wearing a cast. But when the confederate wore a cast (high-need condition), the loud noise reduced the frequency of helping from 80 percent to 15 percent! Apparently, noise led subjects to attend less to cues (i.e., the cast) that indicated that the person needed help.

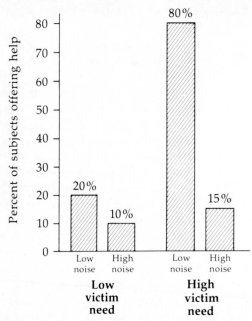

Figure 5–14. Percentages of subjects offering help as a function of noise level and need of victim. (Adapted from Mathews and Canon, 1975. Copyright © 1975 by the American Psychological Association. Reprinted by permission of the author and publisher.)

A series of studies by Page (1977) also provide evidence that noise can reduce the likelihood that people will help each other. In one study, subjects encountered a confederate who, with an armful of books, had dropped a pack of index cards. They were exposed to one of three levels of noise (100 dB, 80 dB, or 50 dB) at the time they saw the confederate drop the cards. Results of this study suggested that people helped most under low levels of noise. However, these results were not strong (see also Bell & Doyle, 1983).

A second study reported by Page (1977) found stronger results. In this one, subjects saw a confederate drop a package while walking past a construction site. When the jackhammers were being used on the site, noise levels were 92 dB; when they were not being used, levels were 72 dB. Thus, depending on the jackhammers, subjects saw a confederate drop a pack-

age during one or another level of noise. People were less likely to help the confederate when noise levels reached 92 dB than they were when it was a relatively quiet 72 dB.

These results suggest that people who experience noise simply may not notice that someone needs help. Page (1977) conducted one more study in which people were approached and directly asked whether or not they could provide change for a quarter. In this context, "narrowing of attention" could not explain any negative effects of noise on helping. However, noise once again decreased the likelihood that people would respond to the request.

The reasons for the suppressing effects of noise on helping behavior are not yet known for sure, but the most likely explanations still appear to be the "narrowing of attention" notion and the "mood" explanation. Nevertheless, each of these has been disconfirmed by at least one study. A study that argues against the idea that noise reduces helping by putting people in bad or irritable moods was reported by Yinon and Bizman (1980). They exposed subjects to one of two noise levels (high or low) while they worked on a task, and then gave them positive or negative feedback on their performance. After this, subjects encountered someone who asked them for help. One might expect the combination of the negative feedback and loud noise to dampen subjects' moods and cause them to refuse to help. This is not, however, what was found. Under the high-noise condition, there were no differences in helping between the positive and negative feedback groups. Only under low noise did the feedback make a difference. Apparently, the loud noise distracted people from focusing on the feedback or provided a reason for the negative feedback. Although it is still possible that mood states were involved, their role in this study does not appear to be crucial.

We have seen thus far that perceived control over noxious noise reduces its impairment of performance and its facilitation of aggression. A study by Sherrod and Downs (1974) similarly demonstrated that perceived control reduces the negative influence of noise on helping behavior. In that study, subjects participated in a proof-reading task while simultaneously monitoring a series of random numbers presented on audio tape. Three conditions were established: (1) a control condition in which the numbers were superimposed on the pleasing sounds of a seashore (e.g., waves striking the beach); (2) a complex noise condition in which the numbers were superimposed over a round of Dixieland jazz and another voice reading prose; and (3) a perceived control condition using the same tape as the complex noise condition but with the subjects told they could terminate the distract-ing noise if they so desired. After 20 minutes in one of these situations, subjects left the laboratory and were approached by an individual asking their assistance in filling out forms for another study. The most help was volunteered by subjects in the seashore sound condition, for whom noise was least noxious. Subjects in the perceived control condition offered more help than subjects in the uncontrollable complex noise condition. Thus, the effects of noise on helping behavior depend on several factors, among which are perceived control of the noise, volume of the noise, and stimulus characteristics of the person needing assistance.

REDUCING NOISE: DOES ANYONE NOTICE?

What happens when noise levels are changed? Noise control procedures have been used in many places to reduce noise in residential areas, but residents' responses to these interventions have not been studied very often. One method that has been used to reduce noise emanating from traffic is to build bypasses so that heavy traffic is routed away from areas in which people live. What effects does this traffic diversion have?

Griffiths and Raw (1987) have argued that changes in noise levels due to such interventions can result in changes in dissatisfaction that are greater than what might be expected on the basis of the resulting noise levels. In other words, if an area is characterized by ambient noise levels of 80 dB and this is reduced to 70 dB by directing traffic away, resulting annoyance or dissatisfaction may be even lower than in a neighborhood characterized by 70 dB noise to begin with. The change may have effects that add to the reduced noise level in producing positive response. Studies have shown that changes in dissatisfaction with traffic and air-craft noise are greater than would be predicted from absolute noise levels when noise is reduced, but it is also possible that these changes can be undervalued (e.g., Griffiths & Raw, 1987; Raw & Griffiths, 1985). This does not appear to be due merely to contrasting conditions, as the increase in satisfaction can persist beyond the change in traffic levels for up to two years (Griffiths & Raw, 1987).

Annoyance does not always decrease when noise reduction interventions are made, but it frequently does change. Research on the effects of acoustic barriers for reducing traffic noise has not shown strong evidence of corresponding reduction of annoyance due to the noise, but studies that consider other methods of noise reduction, such as traffic control and redistribution of noise, may show more substantial changes and, in some cases, evidence of larger changes than would be expected from actual noise reduction (Kastka, 1980; Vallet, 1987).

Bronzaft (1981) has also conducted research on noise reduction in real-world settings. As we noted earlier, she found that students in class-rooms facing elevated subway tracks in New York City had substantially lower reading ability than did students from the same school in classrooms on a quieter side of the building (Bronzaft & McCarthy, 1975), and was able to convince authorities that steps had to be taken to reduce transit noise in these classrooms (Bronzaft, 1985–86). Installation of acoustic ceiling tiles in classrooms and sound-absorbing pads on the tracks reduced noise significantly and was associated with apparent recovery of reading scores; after the intervention, there were no longer any significant differences in reading ability between students from the side of the school facing the tracks and those on the other side (Bronzaft, 1985–86).

CHAPTER SUMMARY

In this chapter, we discussed the nature of noise, where it comes from, and how it affects us. Clearly, noise is a less intense stressor than some that we have examined in other chapters; it is not as overwhelming as disasters nor as momentarily debilitating as many stressors. However, it appears to have many effects. Noise can lead to increased arousal, stress, narrowing of attention, and constraints on behavior. The aversiveness of noise depends on volume, predictability, and perceived control. In combination with other stressors, noise may have adverse effects on physical and mental health. Whether noise hurts or helps performance depends on the type of noise, the complexity of the task, and individual factors such as personality and adaptation level. Noise interferes with verbal communication and may affect productivity. Depending on the situation and the type of noise, noise may increase or decrease attraction, facilitate aggression, or interfere with helping behavior.

Whether noise has these effects, or whether we are even aware of noise is determined by a number of factors. However, its pervasiveness demands careful study, and many interesting and complex issues remain to be explored.

SUGGESTED PROJECTS

1. Get a sound level meter from the psychology, physics, or speech and audiology department (or wherever it might be available). Observe sound levels in places you go every day. Are there different behaviors associated with different sound levels? Now list the places, sound levels, and behaviors you observed and add a note on what the primary source of sound was (e.g., traffic, people talking). Do you see any patterns in these data?

2. Interview people who live in noisy and quiet places. If there are dormitories on campus that are noisier than others due to traffic or some other factor, that might be a good place to start. Ask residents if they are aware of the noise, how much it annoys them, when it is bothersome, and so on. Do peoples' activities, goals, and attitudes about the source of the noise affect their reactions to it?

3. Make a tape recording of an ambiguous sound—one that could be almost anything, or at least could be from one of two or three different sources. Tell some people each of the possible causes. Do the labels you attach to the sound make it more unpleasant or annoying?

6 WEATHER, CLIMATE, AND BEHAVIOR

KEY TERMS

acclimation
acclimatization
air ionization
alveolar walls
ambient temperature
barometric pressure
Beaufort Scale
chill factor
climate
core temperature
curvilinear relationship
decompression sickness
deep body temperature
determinism
effective temperature

ELF-EMF
frostbite
Gaia Hypothesis
greenhouse effect
heat asthenia
heat exhaustion
heat stroke
humidity
hypothalamus
hypothermia
hypoxia
linear relationship
long, hot summer effect
melatonin
negative ions

one atmosphere
ozone
ozone hole
peripheral vasoconstriction
peripheral vasodilation
piloerection
positive ions
possibilism
probabilism

Seasonal Affective Disorder (SAD)
tactile discrimination
Temperature-Humidity Index (THI)
terraforming
thermoreceptors
weather
wind chill
wind speed
wind turbulence

INTRODUCTION

Consider for a moment the following facts:

—Heat wave conditions have been shown to be associated with riots.
—Extremely hot or cold temperatures may be a causal factor in automobile accidents.
—Skyscrapers can increase wind speeds at ground level, causing serious injury to pedestrians.
—Low air pressure environments deprive the body of needed oxygen.
—Members of cultures living in very hot or very cold environments, or at very high altitudes, show physiological adaptations commensurate with the local climate.
—Weather and air pollution are often closely linked. For example, one high-pollution phenomenon is called a *temperature inversion*, in which a layer of cold air lies below a layer of warm air. Usually, the lower cold air is associated with snow on the ground. The upper layer of warm air prevents the pollutants from dispersing.

These examples illustrate a few of the reasons environmental psychologists are interested in the effects of temperature, humidity, wind, and air pressure on behavior. We are all familiar with certain consequences of exposure to these environmental factors. When it gets cold outdoors, we behave in ways that minimize discomfort, such as putting on heavy coats. When the wind blows down the street at 50 miles per hour (80 kph), we behave in ways that will minimize our discomfort from wind exposure, such as not riding a bicycle and walking at an angle to the ground to maintain our balance. When we travel from a cool community to a very hot one, we may restrict our outdoor activity.

Research in the past decade has told us much more about what behavior to expect when people are exposed to abnormal levels of heat, cold, and wind. Such research lets us answer rather detailed questions about specific environment—behavior problems. For example, *how* do high outdoor temperatures affect the level of aggressive and violent behavior in society, as suggested by the popular notion of the **long, hot summer effect** ? Or *how* do weather changes affect mental health and interpersonal relationships? Such questions about the influence of the physical environment on personal and interpersonal behavior are becoming more and more important for at least two reasons. First, humans are constantly exposed to natural changes in the physical environment. Parts of the U.S. typically undergo temperature changes from −20°F to 100°F (−29°C to 38°C) in different seasons. Some cultures exist in hot tropical climates, whereas others thrive in arctic conditions. Do such temperature differences influence behavior? What if climatological changes, which according to many climatologists are becoming more and more extreme, should result in exaggerated cold or hot temperatures? If a long, hot summer effect really does exist, and if climatological changes result in average daily summer temperatures of 110°F in urban centers, are we likely to see disastrous rioting and violence? Whatever the case, it becomes important for us to know the behavioral influence of extreme or even very mild natural changes in the physical environment.

The second major reason we need to know more about the effects of the physical environment on behavior is that we ourselves are making drastic changes in the natural environment, changes that we may be able to correct if they can be shown to have deleterious effects on behavior. For example, if high winds have negative effects on mental health, physical well-being, and behavior, we might want to reevaluate building designs that actually increase wind speeds in pedestrian areas. Another example is the case of modern technology actually heating up our cities. Waste heat from the compressors of air conditioners, heat-absorbing concrete, and air pollutants from burning fossil fuels that trap heat close to the surface (the greenhouse effect—see box, page 156)

are actually heating up cities to levels 10°F (6°C) or more above the temperature of the surrounding countryside. Can we possibly be adding to a long, hot summer effect by the way our daily living habits alter the physical environment?

Whether the source of environmental stimulation is from natural or human causes, the concern of environmental psychologists is the same: What differences in behavior can be expected under different conditions in the physical environment? In previous chapters we have seen how we perceive and process information about the general environment, how we can view environment–behavior relationships from several theoretical perspectives, and how one environmental component, that of noise, influences us. In the present chapter we will examine in detail weather and climate as important types of physical environmental factors, how they affect us, and how these effects can be explained from various theoretical perspectives. Specifically, we will look at the behavioral effects of weather variables—heat, cold, wind, and barometric pressure —as well as at the effects of climate. As we do so, perhaps it would be helpful to keep Figure 4–7 (page 123) in mind as an overall framework. That is, the objective physical environment (e.g., heat, altitude), situational factors, and our perception of the environment as outside an optimal range lead to mediational states (e.g., arousal) and to coping strategies. In the process, health, performance, and social behavior may be affected.

We should mention one caveat before proceeding: Although we will primarily discuss each of the meteorological factors separately (e.g., cold, wind, and low air pressure), in actuality they often occur together, so that it is often difficult to attribute a given behavior change to any one of the factors. We will shortly have more to say on combinations of factors when we discuss climate, as well as at the end of the chapter. In addition, and closely related to the last point, we should briefly note a distinction between weather and climate. Essentially, **weather** refers to relatively rapidly changing or momentary conditions, such as a cold front or a heat wave. **Climate**, on the other hand, refers to average weather conditions or prevailing weather over a long period of time. The distinction is important for environmental psychologists because the measured effects of climate on behavior are often not the same as the measured effects of weather on behavior. For example, climatological precipitation has definite behavioral correlates, but weather measures of precipitation do not predict behavior very well. Also, we can rarely study these variables alone, but rather must control for effects of cultural and social factors that also affect behavior, and it is easier to control for these factors when studying climate than weather. All of these distinctions will become clearer as we first look at formulations about climate and behavior, and then examine how individual weather variables impact behavior.

GEOGRAPHICAL AND CLIMATOLOGICAL DETERMINISM

Much of the literature on the influence of climate on behavior is quite speculative, and not based on sound empirical data. Very early writings on the topic, in fact, are based on nonsystematic observation, and many of the later writings are based on flawed observations. More recent investigations, however, include careful biological measurements that show at least some physiological adaptations associated with climate. Altogether, it is instructive to examine the evidence from both the early and recent literature. In doing so, it is helpful to keep in mind three perspectives which we will cover again in the chapters on architectural influence. Briefly, these perspectives are **determinism**, **possibilism**, and **probabilism** (cf. Rotton, 1986). In terms of climate, *determinism* suggests that climate forcefully causes a range of behaviors, such as heat waves causing crimes. As noted in Chapter 4, environmental psychologists take a broad view of determinism, which means there are many interrelated variables predicting our behavior. Some of the climatological determinists we discuss in this section, however, proposed a more specific determinism of single-factor explanations. *Possibilism* proposes that climate sets physical limits within which behavior may vary, such as modest winds permitting sailing but high winds restricting bicycle riding. *Probabilism* falls somewhat in between these two positions, implying that climate does not absolutely cause specific behaviors, but does influence the chances that some behaviors will occur and others will not. For example, snow decreases the probability that people will drive and increases the probability that people will engage in winter sports. Determinism, possibilism, and probabilism are not necessarily mutually exclusive; they may be differentially applicable to different domains of behavior. For example, climate may influence what type of farming one practices by determining which crops cannot be grown in an area, but making it possible (but

Really Heating it Up:
The Greenhouse Effect,
The Ozone Hole,
And Terraforming

A growing concern that you have probably heard about is the so-called atmospheric greenhouse effect. In a horticultural greenhouse, glass panes help trap heat from the sun: What enters the greenhouse does not easily escape back into the atmosphere. Much of the sun's heat that strikes our planet is transmitted back out from the planet surface into the atmosphere and on into space. Atmospheric conditions regulate the rate at which this heat is lost. Clouds, for example, may prevent some sunlight from hitting the ground, but also tend to trap more heat that would otherwise escape from the ground into the atmosphere. Pollutants (and natural emissions) such as carbon dioxide also tend to trap heat. As we add more carbon dioxide to the atmosphere, we trap more heat. This is the atmospheric **greenhouse effect**: Emissions are thought to warm the planet up. Several factors may moderate the effect, such as the ability of oceans to absorb the heat, and the ability of forests to absorb carbon dioxide. The **Gaia Hypothesis** even says the process is self-regulating by the Earth (e.g., Lovelock, 1988). That is, the heating and cooling fluctuates as vegetation, animal life, oceans, and the atmosphere absorb or release heat and emissions.

The great fear is that we have overdone things: cut forests, increased domestic animal herds and rice paddies (which release large volumes of methane gas), and increased fossil fuel emissions so much that the Earth may become permanently overheated. Over the last century, the Earth's surface may have warmed 1°C or so (1° to 3°F) (e.g., Kerr, 1988a). Over the next 50 to 100 years, we could warm up another 2° to 5°C. What will this do? Melting of even part of the polar icecap will cause coastlines to move many miles inland. Animal habitats will shift by hundreds of miles, and many species will become extinct (e.g., Roberts, 1988).

The **ozone hole** is a related problem to worry about (e.g., Kerr, 1988b). Atmospheric ozone absorbs harmful ultraviolet sunlight, among other things (see box, page 184). It apparently is becoming rapidly depleted over Antarctica and the Arctic in a pattern called the ozone hole. Human use of chlorofluorocarbons is thought to be a major cause of ozone depletion. The ozone-destroying process occurs heavily in stratospheric ice clouds. The greenhouse effect warms the Earth but cools the stratosphere, causing more ice clouds to form and destroying more ozone.

Can anything be done? Reducing harmful emissions is one solution, and in Chapter 14 we will discuss the techniques environmental psychologists advocate for getting us to change our environmentally destructive behavior. Another solution is to use nature. Burning fossil fuels releases 5 billion tons of carbon per year. Some 7 million square kilometers of trees (about the size of Australia) would absorb that much carbon and turn it into wood (e.g., Marland, cited in Booth, 1988). Because of deforestation of areas such as Brazil and Southeast Asia, we would need to plant still more trees, but the idea, considered far-fetched by some, does have its advocates.

Speaking of the far-fetched, another planet might actually benefit from the greenhouse effect (if you consider invasion by humans beneficial). **Terraforming** refers to changing an uninhabitable planet into a habitable one. One proposal to terraform Mars is to add chlorofluorocarbons to its atmosphere. Mars needs to be heated up to be habitable by humans. Since its atmosphere has no ozone, chlorofluorocarbons would not deplete ozone, but rather would trap solar heat in a greenhouse effect. Ice caps would partially melt, releasing water for plant life, which would cycle enough carbon dioxide and oxygen (over hundreds of years) into the atmosphere to make Mars habitable (McKay, as cited in Davis, 1989)!

. . . .

not inevitable) that other crops can be grown in the same area.

It is also appropriate to note that geographical and climatological determinism are closely linked. Indeed, most of the time the two are simply called "geographical determinism." It is often difficult to separate geographic influence from weather influence, since geography plays a major role in weather. Mountains, for example, are usually associated with high altitudes, cooler conditions than surrounding lowlands, wet weather on the side of the mountains facing prevailing atmospheric movements, and dry weather on the side away from oncoming storms. Since the geography and the climate are so closely linked, it is not easy to say whether the weather or the geography is primarily responsible for associated behavior (Figure 6–1).

Early Beliefs about Climate and Behavior

Suspicion that climate determines behavior has been around practically since the beginning of civilization. Sommers and Moos (1976) provide a much more thorough review of early writings than can possibly be covered here. The ancient Greeks, including Hippocrates and Aristotle, believed that weather and climate influenced bodily fluids, which in turn influenced individual disposition. The Roman Vitruvius and the Arab Ibn Khaldun, along with Aristotle, believed that geography and climate made some people more industrious than others, some more spirited, and so on. Not surprisingly, each writer indicated that the prevailing climate in his own region led to superior civilizations! For example, Khaldun believed that moderate climates fostered superior cultures. How, then, could his own civilization on the hot, dry, Arabian peninsula be at an advantage? His answer was that cooling waters of the sea moderated the Arabian climate sufficiently to produce overall favorability (Sommers & Moos, 1976).

Later Climatological Determinism

Sommers and Moos (1976) review the writings of numerous more recent authors, most of whom make equally presumptuous and self-serving observations about climatological influence (see also Glacken, 1967). Some later geographical determinists include such theorists as Carl Ritter, Frederic LePlay, Edmond Demolins, Henry Buckle, and Ellsworth Huntington. Three of these are particularly interesting for the details of their beliefs. Buckle, for one, was the son of a wealthy London merchant and was widely traveled. In *The History of Civilization in England* (1857–1861), he posited that labor conditions and climate were closely intertwined: Cold climates inhibited work and hot

Figure 6–1A & B   Some examples of the connection between geography and climate. (A) The high altitude of the mountain range pulls enough moisture out of the atmosphere to provide extensive forests on the slopes. This moisture does not fall on the relatively dry plains, which require irrigation for any farming. A similar pattern accounts for desert areas of the western United States. (B) Cities, with their concrete canyons and industrial and transportation pollution, create "heat islands" such that they are several degrees warmer than the surrounding countryside.

climates led to lethargy; temperate climates, however, were thought to be invigorating. With fertile soil available, then, temperate climates would lead to heavy production. Moreover, Buckle believed that the advancement of a culture was tied to the creation of a leisure class, which was possible only if some other class produced more than was needed. Thus, temperate climates in regions with fertile soil permitted the necessary overproduction, which permitted the rise of the leisure class, which theoretically, at least, enabled the entire civilization's advancement. The ''proof'' of Buckle's theory came from his ''observations'' of conditions in such diverse regions as Central America, Ireland, Egypt, and India. So inviting was the theory that it was intellectually popular for some time after its writing (Timasheff, 1967). It is also worth summarizing the beliefs of theorist Ellsworth Huntington (1915, 1945), who believed that climatic factors other than temperate conditions were necessary for the growth of major civilizations. The major ingredient was hypothesized to be seasonal change and moving storms. The change could not be too severe, but regular changes should require adaptation, and as ''necessity is the mother of invention,'' the adaptations encouraged creative solutions, which invigorated the civilization. Huntington did indeed collect sociological data on such things as productivity, suicides, and library circulation to support his point of view that geographic bands producing these changing climatic conditions were associated with advancing civilizations (Sommers & Moos, 1976). It should be noted that Huntington believed that many factors besides favorable climate influence the growth of civilizations. Similar to Huntington's ideas about climate adaptation, Markham (1947) suggested that the most important climatic factor for the development of a civilization was living in a cool enough region that technology became necessary in order to keep warm. He noted, for example, that the Romans developed a central

heating system, using pipes to distribute warmth through buildings. How important is this factor? Markham noted that this heating system deteriorated shortly before the decline of Roman civilization.

While appealing in some respects, these geographical and climatological deterministic beliefs have only tenuous empirical evidence, at best, to support them. Climatological experiments on a culture are not practical, so we are left with correlational data—and there are many factors, such as war, natural resources, and technological innovation, which are difficult to measure and assess as possible explanatory variables in climatological studies. In this light, few scientists today would endorse very strong statements of climatological determinism. It is overstepping the cause-and-effect boundaries of methodology to assume that just because a civilization occurs in a given climate, the climate is a prerequisite for that civilization. However, we will see in this chapter that weather and climate do have some direct impact on us.

Current Views and Distinctions

Along with the above caveat on overstating causal relationships, several additional methodological cautions are warranted. Recall that weather refers to short-term variations and climate to average weather over a longer period. Thus, on a given day, a city in the northern U.S. might have a higher temperature than a city in the southern part of the country, but on the average, temperatures in the south are higher. Now consider that more violent crimes occur in the south than elsewhere. Can we conclude that heat has a causal role in these crimes? The problem is that many variables, such as food preferences and ethnic mix, differ between the two regions. With high correlations between so many climatological and sociodemographic variables, we must be very cautious about conclusions (cf. Anderson, 1987; De-

Fronzo, 1984; Rotton, Barry, & Kimble, 1985). In addition, there are seasonal differences in behavior (e.g., automobile buying, television programs, gift purchases) that probably have nothing to do with weather—although the weather certainly varies with these activities. It is the case that more assaults and homicides occur in the U.S. in summer than winter, but the peak time for homicides is December. Thus, we should not conclude that meteorological variables are responsible for seasonal differences in behavior (e.g., Anderson, 1987).

It is also worth noting that biometeorologists in Europe (e.g., Muecher & Ungeheuer, 1961; Tromp, 1980) have focused on the possible effects of "weather phases," or correlated patterns of changes in meteorological conditions (e.g., a storm front). North American researchers, on the other hand, look more at specific variables, such as temperature, precipitation, or barometric pressure. We have organized this chapter primarily around the latter approach for ease of presentation, but we must keep in mind that weather variables such as wind, humidity, and barometric pressure are themselves correlated.

Biological Adaptations to Climate

An area of study with more convincing evidence of climatological influence is that of measuring physiological or other biological factors within a culture that is exposed to extremes of climate. For example, Frisancho (1979) reviews many lines of evidence that people living at high altitudes (such as in Tibet or Peru), in the hot climates of Africa, or in the cold environment of Lapland, may have developed special physiological capabilities for coping with these extremes. Such adaptations may even be genetic, such that ancestors with these adaptive characteristics were more likely to survive the extremes and pass their hereditary characteristics along to the next generation. For example, hearts may be larger and their walls thicker among high-altitude cultures, since hearts need to circulate more oxygen-rich blood at altitudes where oxygen is in relatively lower atmospheric concentration. Some such adaptations may well be acquired (i.e., accruing during one's lifetime) rather than genetic. We will have some more to say about these adaptations as we cover individual weather variables in the remainder of the chapter.

HEAT AND BEHAVIOR

Ambient temperature is a term used to describe the surrounding or atmospheric temperature conditions. In the natural environment, humans experience a range from arctic cold to debilitating tropical heat. As stated previously, temperature is one factor in the physical environment that humans are changing through urbanization and industrialization. Hurt (1975) notes that air conditioners in the downtown area of Houston put out enough waste heat (i.e., heat blown out the window off the "hot" end of the compressor) in eight hours to boil 10 kettles of water the size of the Astrodome! Unfortunately for those who must go outdoors, this heat and heat from additional sources stays in the general area of the city, so that urban centers are typically 10° to 20°F (6° to 12°C) hotter than surrounding agricultural areas. As will be seen in this section and the next, extremes of heat and cold, regardless of the source, can have dramatic effects on people. We will first treat the perception of high and low temperatures together; then we will examine separately the effects of heat and cold on behavior.

Perception of and Physiological Reactions to Ambient Temperatures

Perception of temperature involves physical as well as psychological components. The primary *physical* component is simply the amount of heat in the surrounding environment, typically measured on the Fahrenheit or Celsius scale. One *psychological* component of temperature perception is centered on the internal tempera- ture of the body, known as **core temperature** or **deep body temperature**. Another psycho- logical component involves receptors in the skin (**thermoreceptors**), which apparently are sensitive to changes in ambient temperature. (For a reference on the existence of thermore- ceptors in the skin, see Gardner, 1975). These skin receptors do not transmit nerve impulses based on actual temperatures but on differences in temperature between the skin and the envi- ronment. If the surrounding environment is much hotter than the body, cold will be perceived. This is why you may perceive even mildly warm weather as very hot when your hands are extremely cold from being exposed to winter air.

Since perception of ambient temperature is largely dependent on differences between body and ambient temperatures, the mechanisms controlling body temperature have much to do with the perception of ambient temperature. Body temperature is regulated by the need to keep core temperature close to 98.6°F (37°C). Since death occurs when core temperature rises above 113°F (45°C) or drops below 77°F (25°C), there is definite survival value in maintaining it at a normal level. Without a defensive or adaptive mechanism, the body would overheat when exposed to high ambient temperatures and would "freeze" when ex- posed to cold ambient temperatures. Fortu- nately, a number of such adaptive mechanisms, under the general control of a brain center known as the **hypothalamus**, are available for use whenever core temperature is threatened by adversely hot or cold ambient conditions. When core temperature becomes too hot, the body responds by activating mechanisms designed to lose heat, such as sweating, panting, and **peripheral vasodilation**. The latter process refers to dilation of blood vessels in the extremities, especially those near the surface of the skin, which allows more blood to flow from core areas to surface regions. This blood carries with it the excess core heat, which is removed through air convection or sweating (note that peripheral vasodilation allows more sweat to reach the surface of the skin). In "heat wave" emergencies, the body may increase the supply of water available for evaporation by suppress- ing urine formation and extracting water from body tissues. Such dehydration causes us to become thirsty and to replenish our body's supply of water, which is another process mediated by the hypothalamus. When these adaptive mechanisms fail, a number of physio- logical disorders can result, including heat exhaustion, heat stroke, heat asthenia, and heart attack (see box, page 162). Interestingly, blood pressure may increase upon initial sensation of ambient heat, owing to a "startle" response or alarm reaction (see page 116). Once vasodila- tion begins, blood pressure drops. With heat stroke, blood pressure may rise again, then fall off as coma and death approach. Clearly, measuring blood pressure only once during heat exposure is not a good indication of the overall picture.

Prolonged exposure to moderately high am- bient temperatures need not have disastrous consequences. Individuals who move from cool climates into very warm climates can adapt to the hot environment without too much diffi- culty. This adaptation process is known as **acclimatization**, and it primarily involves changes in physiological adaptive mechanisms. For instance, the body may "learn" to start sweating much sooner after the onset of high ambient temperatures (Lee, 1964). How long does it take to acclimatize when moving from a warm to a cold environment, and vice-versa?

Physiological Disorders Associated with Prolonged Heat Stress

When the body's adaptive mechanisms to heat stress fail to keep core body temperatures close to 98.6° F (37°C), a number of physiological disorders can occur. Among the more common are:

1. **Heat exhaustion**, characterized by faintness and nausea, vomiting, headache, and restlessness. This disorder results from excessive demands on the circulatory system for blood. Water needed for sweating, blood needed near the skin surface for heat loss through convection, and blood needed for normal or increased metabolic functioning place too much strain on the body's capacity to supply blood. Continued loss of salt and water through sweating compounds the problem. Replacement of lost water and salt, together with rest, will both prevent and cure heat exhaustion.

2. **Heat stroke**, characterized by confusion, staggering, headache, delirium, coma, and death. This disorder results from the complete breakdown of the sweating mechanism. Because body heat cannot be lost, the brain overheats. Survival or prevention of brain damage depends on quick action—the most effective being immersion in ice water. When a victim collapses from heat, the continuation of sweating implies heat exhaustion; the absence of sweating implies heat stroke.

3. **Heat asthenia**, characterized by fatigue, headache, mental and physical impairment, irritability, restlessness, insomnia, loss of appetite, and lethargy. Its specific causes are unknown, although one theory implicates the clogging of sweat glands by excessive perspiration. The cure for heat asthenia includes intake of water and change of climate.

4. **Heart attack**, resulting from excessive demands on the cardiovascular system due to increased need for blood by the body's cooling mechanisms. During urban heat wave conditions, most deaths beyond what would normally be expected are caused by heart attacks.

For more information on heat and cold disorders, the reader is referred to Folk (1974).

Tromp (1980) suggests that the answer is no more than 3 to 14 days, depending on an individual's cardiovascular fitness.

Sometimes the distinction is made between acclimatization, meaning adaptation to multiple stresses in an environment (e.g., temperature, wind, humidity) and **acclimation**, meaning adaptation to one specific stressor in an experimental context (see Frisancho, 1979). In our discussion, we will use the term acclimatization, since in most environments we must adapt to more than one element. Frisancho (1979) indicates that acclimatization may occur through developmental changes, through genetic adaptation, or through physiological and behavioral changes following prolonged exposure to heat. The Saharan Touareg, for example, have tall, slender bodies that maximize surface cooling area in proportion to the amount of body tissue that produces heat. Behaviorally, the Touareg avoid heavy exercise during the highest temperatures of the day and wear loose, porous clothing (Beighton, 1971; Frisancho, 1979; Sloan, 1979). Keep in mind, though, that non-native visitors to hot regions can usually acclimatize in a few days. Leithead and Lind (1964) suggest that maximum efficiency in acclimatization occurs with exposure of 100 minutes per day (Figure 6–2).

Physiology of Cold Stress We would like to discuss the range of heat effects before describ-

ing cold effects. However, since the physiology of heat and cold stress is related, it is worth covering cold physiology here. In contrast to overheating, when core temperature becomes too cold, the body reacts by activating mechanisms that generate and retain heat, resulting in increased metabolism, shivering, peripheral vasoconstriction, and piloerection. **Peripheral vasoconstriction** serves just the opposite function of peripheral vasodilation: It keeps core heat inside the body and away from the surface where it is easily lost through convection. This constriction process also makes more blood available to internal organs, which are generating more heat through increased metabolism. **Piloerection** refers to the stiffening of hairs on the skin, usually accompanied by "goose bumps." This skin reaction increases the thick-

Figure 6–2   Acclimatization may occur through genetic changes, developmental changes, physiological changes, or behavioral changes. This desert is normally very hot and dry, but can be cool and wet at times. What would you do to acclimatize to this environment?

Physiological Disorders Associated with Prolonged Cold Stress

If cold exposure persists for long periods of time, two serious consequences can result. One danger is **frostbite,** characterized by the formation of ice crystals in the skin cells. Since the initial reaction of the body to cold stress is constriction of surface blood vessels, freezing of the skin is not uncommon. Another danger of cold exposure arises when the adaptive mechanisms fail to maintain core body temperature. A decline in core temperature is known as **hypothermia**. In the initial stages of hypothermia, cardiovascular activity, including heart rate and blood pressure, is dramatically increased. As core temperature falls between 86°F and 77°F (30° to 25°C), cardiovascular activity falls off and becomes irregular. Below a core temperature of 77°F, death due to heart attack is likely to result. At an intermediate stage of hypothermia, clouding of consciousness and coma may well occur. If the victim has not found shelter by this time, the loss of mental functioning may preclude an effort to seek warmth or assistance. Since inadequate clothing in extremes of cold is most likely to precipitate hypothermia, it is those individuals caught unprepared for cold stress, such as mountain climbers faced with sudden cold winds or shipwreck victims in Arctic waters, who are most likely to suffer the disorder. Removal of wet clothing and provision of warmth are necessary to save the lives of hypothermia victims.

---

ness of a thin layer of insulating air close to the skin, which again helps to minimize heat loss by convection.

Acclimatization to cold environments may take several forms (see also Bell & Greene, 1982). For example, the Alacaluf Indians of Tierra Del Fuego have an elevated metabolism that seems to keep body temperature elevated in the cold environment (Hammel et al., 1960, as cited in LeBlanc, 1975). Bushmen of the Kalahari Desert and Australian Aborigines have another adaptive mechanism for tolerating very low nighttime temperatures. In these populations, shivering does not occur as it would in unacclimatized individuals, but rather core temperature actually drops at night (LeBlanc, 1975). Moreover, LeBlanc (1956) reported reduced shivering in a group of Canadian soldiers who had been moved to a cold climate, and Budd (1973) found a similar pattern for Australians of European heritage on an Antarctic expedition. Exposure to cold increases circulation in the hands for Eskimos (LeBlanc, 1975) and for fishermen on the Gaspé Peninsula of Quebec (LeBlanc, 1962). In sum, several mechanisms are available for acclimatization to cold environments.

Complicating Factors Since perception of ambient temperature depends to some extent on the functioning of the body's thermoregulatory adaptive mechanisms, any environmental factor that interferes with these mechanisms will influence perception of ambient temperature. The primary environmental factors in this regard are humidity and wind. The higher the **humidity** in a hot environment (i.e., the more saturated the air with water vapor), the lower

Table 6–1 *Effective Temperature (°F) at 0 Percent Humidity as a Function of Actual Temperature and Humidity*

Relative Humidity (%)	Thermometer Reading (°F)					
	41°	50°	59°	68°	77°	86°
	Effective Temperature					
00	41	50	59	68	77	86
20	41	50	60	70	81	91
40	40	51	61	72	83	96
60	40	51	62	73	86	102
80	39	52	63	75	90	111
100	39	52	64	79	96	120

the capacity of the air to absorb water vapor from sweat. This is the reason, for example, that conditions of 100°F (38°C) and 60 percent humidity are perceived as more uncomfortable than those of 100°F and 15 percent humidity. Thus, perception of ambient temperature is not a function of temperature alone. Psychologically, the problem of perceptual measurement can be partially solved by taking into account a comfort level that is influenced by both temperature and humidity, thus creating a new ambient environment index. One such index is known as **effective temperature**. A chart showing some effective temperatures is presented in Table 6–1. Other similar indexes exist, such as the **Temperature–Humidity Index**, or **THI** (see Tromp, 1980 for a summary).

Since the amount of air flowing over the skin determines how much sweat is evaporated as well as how much body heat is carried off by convection, **wind speed** must also be taken into account in perceiving ambient temperature. The **chill factor** or **windchill** index does just that. For example, an ambient temperature of 23°F with a wind speed of 15 mph has the same psychological effect as an ambient temperature

Table 6–2 *Wind-Chill Index**

Actual Temperature (°F) at 0 mph	Wind Speed			
	5 mph	15 mph	25 mph	35 mph
	Equivalent Temperature (°F)			
32	29	13	3	−1
23	20	−1	−10	−15
14	10	−13	−24	−29
5	1	−25	−38	−43
−4	−9	−37	−50	−52

*Equivalent temperatures (°F) at 0 mph as a function of actual temperature and wind speed.

of $-1°F$ with no wind. Table 6–2 depicts the broad range of the chill factor index. In very cold temperatures, it becomes extremely important for thermoregulatory survival to take wind-chill into account. Just how critical this factor can be is illustrated by the fact that exposed human skin will freeze in less than one minute at $-40°F$ with a 6 mph (10 kph) wind, at $-20°F$ with a 20 mph (32 kph) wind, and at $0°F$ with a 30 mph (48 kph) wind!

Heat and Performance

Laboratory Settings Laboratory studies of the influence of high ambient temperatures on performance have examined such varied behaviors as reaction time, tracking, and vigilance, as well as memory and mathematical calculations (Bell, Provins, & Hiorns, 1964; Griffiths & Boyce, 1971; Pepler, 1963; Poulton & Kerslake, 1965; Provins, 1966; Provins & Bell, 1970; Wilkinson et al., 1964). In general, temperatures above 90°F (32°C) will impair mental performance after two hours of exposure for unacclimatized subjects. Above this same temperature, moderate physical work will suffer after one hour of exposure. As temperatures increase, shorter exposure times are necessary to show performance decrements (e.g., Poulton, 1970). Interestingly enough, some researchers find that heat has no influence on performance, others find that heat is detrimental to performance, and still others find that heat improves performance. Moreover, some studies suggest that as temperatures rise, performance first improves and then deteriorates, whereas other studies show this pattern for one task but the reverse pattern (i.e., initial decrements followed by improvements) for other tasks (see Bell, 1981, and Sundstrom, 1986, for reviews). Hancock (1986) notes that performance on vigilance tasks is impaired when thermal homeostasis is disturbed, but improved when a new equilibrium state is reached. In general, heat impairs complex mental tasks after prolonged exposure, impairs motor tasks after fairly brief exposure, and may impair or enhance vigilance. Before examining possible explanations for these complex findings, let us first examine heat research from applied settings.

Industrial Settings Industrialists, such as steel manufacturers, are naturally concerned about the effects of blast furnaces and other hot industrial environments on workers who are in these surroundings for eight or more hours a day. Generally, exposure to such industrial heat can cause dehydration, loss of salt, and muscle fatigue, which taken together can reduce endurance and hence impair performance. For example, one study found that productivity of women apparel workers declined as temperatures increased (Link & Pepler, 1970). In order to overcome or avoid such problems, care is generally taken to ensure that workers have an adequate intake of water and salt, are not exposed to intolerably hot conditions for long periods of time, wear protective clothing, and, when new on the job, have adequate time to adapt to working conditions (see Crockford, 1967; Hill, 1967; Sundstrom, 1986).

Classroom Settings Temperature appears to have some effects on classroom performance. Pepler (1972) studied climate-controlled (air-conditioned) and nonclimate-controlled schools near Portland, Oregon. In nonclimate-controlled schools, academic performance showed more variance (i.e., wider distribution of test scores) as temperatures rose. However, at climate-controlled schools, such variability did not occur on the warmest days. Apparently, some students suffer more than others when heat waves hit the classroom! Support for this finding has been reported by Benson and Zieman (1981), who found that heat hurt the classroom performance of some children but actually helped the performance of others (see also Griffiths, 1975) (Figure 6-3).

Military Settings If ambient heat has any deleterious effect on performance, the consequences of moving unacclimatized troops into a

Figure 6–3   Research suggests that many weather variables, including heat and barometric pressure, may influence disruptive behavior and academic performance of children in the classroom. Interestingly, for some children heat has beneficial effects, whereas for others it has detrimental effects.

tropical area (e.g., from New England to Vietnam) could be disastrous. Adam (1967) has reviewed a number of British military studies that generally found that 20 to 25 percent of troops flown into tropical regions from more moderate climates suffered serious deterioration in combat effectiveness within three days and became in effect "heat casualties." Solutions to this problem include allowing several days for acclimatization or expanding the number of troops available to allow for heat casualities.

Interpreting the Data   How can we account for the complexity of the above research findings? Why does heat sometimes hurt performance and sometimes help it? Sundstrom (1986) notes that body temperature, metabolic cost of physical activity, acclimatization, skill level, motivation, and stress (including threat

appraisal) are all factors that make a difference in the impact of heat on performance. Bell (1981, 1982) offers several other suggestions, which require an integration of several theoretical perspectives presented in Chapter 4. First, arousal explains some heat effects. Initially, exposure to heat may cause a brief "startle" response that heightens arousal and hence improves performance (e.g., Poulton, 1976; Poulton & Kerslake, 1965; Provins, 1966). Moreover, Provins (1966) suggests that heat may eventually lead to overarousal, causing performance decrements (cf. Bell, Loomis, & Cervone, 1982), as would be predicted by the Yerkes–Dodson Law (see chapter 4). Eventually, high temperatures would result in physical exhaustion (see box, page 162) as the body can no longer keep core temperature at a safely functioning level, so performance would completely deteriorate. A second mediator of performance, then, is core temperature (see Provins, 1966). A third mediator of performance is attention, as examined in the overload interpretation of environmental stress. As heat stress increases, attention is narrowed toward stimuli central to the task at hand, so that performance on noncentral activities deteriorates (e.g., Bursill, 1958; Pepler, 1963). Bell (1978), for example, found that as heat increased, performance on a secondary task suffered, but performance on a primary task did not. A fourth mediator of heat effects is probably perceived control, as advocated by the behavior constraint model. According to this interpretation, as heat stress increases, individuals feel less and less in control of the environment, and thus performance deteriorates. Greene and Bell (1980), for example, found that subjects in a 95°F (35°C) environment felt more dominated by it than did subjects in more comfortable temperatures (see also Cervone, 1977). Finally, each individual almost certainly has an adaptation level or maximum level of tolerance for heat. Wyndham (1970), for example, has reported considerable variation in acclimatization to heat, with individuals having lower body temperatures being most tolerant of high ambient temperatures (see also Greene & Bell, 1986; Rohles, 1974; Wilkinson, 1974). In sum, arousal, core temperature, attention, perceived control, and adaptation level all probably operate as explanatory mechanisms in understanding the effects of heat stress on task performance.

Heat and Social Behavior

Heat and Attraction Most individuals exposed to high ambient temperatures will report subjectively that they feel uncomfortable and perhaps irritable. We might expect that such negative feelings also will give us an unpleasant disposition toward others. According to one model of attraction (Byrne, 1971), we should expect a decrease in interpersonal attraction

when we are experiencing the unpleasant effects of either debilitating heat or cold. Griffitt (1970) demonstrated precisely this effect by asking subjects to evaluate anonymous strangers who seemed to agree with subjects on either 25 percent or 75 percent of a set of attitudes. Subjects performed this evaluation task under an effective temperature of either 67.5°F (20°C) or 90.6°F (32°C). The results, depicted in Figure 6–4, indicate that high ambient temperatures decreased attraction, regardless of the degree of attitude similarity. Griffitt and Veitch (1971) reported comparable results.

However, research by Bell and Baron (1974, 1976) suggests that heat may have a relatively minor influence on attraction under other circumstances. In two experiments, these re-

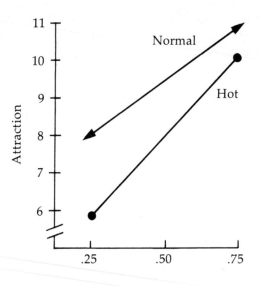

Proportion of similar attitudes

Figure 6–4 Heat decreases attraction between two strangers, regardless of the degree of attitude similarity between the individuals. (From Griffitt, W., 1970. Environmental effects on interpersonal affective behavior: Ambient effective temperature and attraction. *Journal of Personality and Social Psychology, 15,* 240–244. Copyright © 1970 by the American Psychological Association. Reprinted by permission of the author and publisher.)

searchers found that heat did not influence attraction toward another person in the room if that person had recently complimented or insulted a subject. In this situation, the compliment or insult appears to be so overwhelming as to "wipe out" any possible influence of heat (see also Bell, Garnand, & Heath, 1984). Rotton (1983) notes that in the Griffitt studies, subjects were rating hypothetical strangers who were not actually present, whereas in the Bell and Baron studies, subjects rated a real stranger who was actually present in the same room. Perhaps when the stress is not shared with someone actually present, attraction decreases; but when someone is there to share the distress, the decrease may not occur.

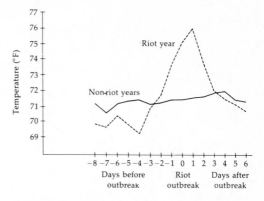

Figure 6–5   Average daily mean temperatures before, during, and after riot outbreak. (From Goranson & King, 1970. Reproduced with permission of the authors.)

Heat and Aggression   During the urban and campus riots of the 1960s, a popular belief arose that riotous acts of violence were in some way precipitated by the unrelenting heat of the summer months. Indeed, this supposed influence of heat on aggression was popularly known as "the long, hot summer effect." It became common for television commentators and newspaper editorial writers to mention fears that, "It's going to be another long, hot summer!" High ambient temperatures became even more suspect when the United States Riot Commission (1968) noted that, of the riots in 1967 on which records were available, all but one began on days when the temperature was at least in the 80s (above 27°C). A more formal study by Goranson and King (1970) strongly suggested, as evidenced in the graph in Figure 6–5, that heat wave or near heat wave conditions were associated with the outbreak of the riots. So strong has the belief in the relationship between climate and violence become that even the *Uniform Crime Reports* of the Federal Bureau of Investigation has listed climate as a variable of importance in explaining the incidence of crimes (FBI, 1981).

Such correlational evidence, however, is not sufficient for inferring a cause-and-effect relationship between high ambient temperatures and aggression. In order to explore the possible existence of such a relationship more closely, Baron and his colleagues initiated a series of laboratory experiments, using as a measure of aggression the willingness of subjects to administer electric shocks to a confederate of the experimenter (Baron, 1972; Baron & Lawton, 1972; Bell & Baron, 1976).

In one experiment, Baron and Bell (1975) arranged for subjects to be either provoked or complimented by a confederate before being given an opportunity to aggress against this individual by means of ostensible electric shock. It was found, as might be anticipated, that subjects in comfortable ambient temperature conditions (73° to 74°F; 23°C) were more aggressive toward an anger-provoking confederate than toward a complimentary confederate. However, subjects in uncomfortably hot conditions (92° to 95°F; 35°C) showed just the opposite behavior: These individuals showed reduced aggression toward the insulting confederate but increased their level of attack against the friendlier one. Why should high temperatures produce a pattern of results opposite to that produced by comfortable ambient temperatures? Further research suggested a possible explanation (Baron & Bell, 1976a; Bell & Baron, 1976).

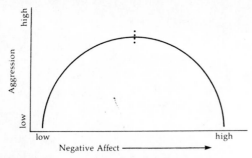

Figure 6–6. Theoretical relationship between negative affect and aggression. Up to a point, uncomfortable conditions facilitate aggression; past that point, more severe conditions decrease aggression. (From Baron, R. A., & Bell, P. A., 1976. Aggression and heat: The influence of ambient temperature, negative affect, and a cooling drink on physical aggression. *Journal of Personality and Social Psychology, 33,* 245–255. Copyright © 1976 by the American Psychological Association. Used by permission.)

According to this explanation, negative affective feelings may be a mediator in the relationship between heat and aggression. This mediating relationship takes the curvilinear form of an inverted U. Up to a critical point, negative affect increases aggressive behavior, but beyond this point, stronger negative feelings actually reduce aggression, since flight behavior or other attempts to minimize discomfort become more important to the individual than aggressive activity (see Figures 6–6; 6–7). This escape tendency is illustrated by Rotton's (1985) finding that on hot days Miami pedestrians walked faster to get to their air-conditioned cars than they did to shop on the streets.

Laboratory tests of the proposition of a **curvilinear relationship** between negative affect and aggression, using heat as one factor influencing affect, have been quite affirmative (Bell & Baron, 1981; Palamarek & Rule, 1979). What these findings suggest with regard to the relationship between high ambient temperatures and aggression is that there is a critical range of uncomfortably high ambient temperatures in which aggression may well be facili-

tated. On the other hand, extremely high ambient temperatures, especially when combined with other sources of irritation or discomfort, may become so debilitating that aggression is no longer facilitated and may well be reduced when individuals prefer to concentrate on escaping the heat. Some research on unpleasant odors (Rotton, et al., 1979) and on cold temperatures (Bell & Baron, 1977) also supports such an inverted-U relationship between negative affect and aggression. But do the field data support the existence of this curvilinear relationship? Three pieces of field evidence provide suggestive support. First, examination of the United States Riot Commission (1968) report of the 1967 urban riots indicates that, although the temperatures on the days the riots broke out were high for the cities involved, they rarely exceeded 100°F (38°C), which is a common high temperature for many cities where riots did not occur. Second, Schwartz (1968) reported evidence that political violence (coups, assassinations, terrorism, guerrilla warfare, and revolts) occurs most often when the season is temperate and less often when the

Figure 6–7 Obtained laboratory relationship between negative affect and aggression. (Adapted from Bell, P. A., & Baron, R. A., 1976. Aggression and heat: The mediating role of negative affect. *Journal of Applied Social Psychology, 6,* 18–30. Copyright 1976 by V. H. Winston & Sons. Used by permission.)

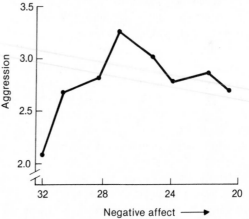

season is the hottest or coolest of a country. Such evidence is certainly not sufficient proof of the curvilinear hypothesis, but it does provide tentative field support for laboratory findings. Third, Baron and Ransberger (1978) examined 102 cases of collective violence between 1967 and 1972. Consistent with the curvilinear hypothesis, they found that the incidence of violence peaked in the mid-80s (29°C), but fell off above or below this point.

Despite all of this evidence in support of the curvilinear hypothesis, considerable research is consistent with a more **linear relationship**— that is, violence continues to increase with temperature, and does not decline at higher temperatures. For example, Bell (1980) found that subjects who were angry at an experimenter evaluated that experimenter more negatively in a hot than in a cool environment. In still another experiment, Baron (1976) found that automobile drivers honked their horns (which can serve as a measure of irritation or hostility) more when temperatures were above 85°F (29°C) than when they were below. For drivers in air-conditioned cars, however, heat did not increase horn-honking. Similar results have been reported by Kenrick and MacFarlane (1986), who studied horn-honking in both moderate and very hot temperatures (well above 100°F, or 38°C) in Phoenix, Arizona: Honking increased linearly with temperatures, and this effect was strongest for those with their automobile windows rolled down. Such results should not be surprising, since the honking was always at a car that did not move when a traffic light turned from red to green. Thus, honking was perceived as instrumental in obtaining relief from the discomfort of the heat, especially for drivers with their windows down (and presumably with no air conditioning): If the stalled car would only move, drivers could get some relief from the heat, and honking might be a way of prompting the driver of the stalled car to get on with it.

Other field research, however, suggests a linear temperature–aggression relationship for

types of violence that would not be particularly instrumental in obtaining relief from the heat. Carlsmith and Anderson (1979), for example, reanalyzed the data of Baron and Ransberger (1978), which originally had suggested that collective violence was more common at moderately uncomfortable temperatures than at comfortable or very uncomfortable temperatures. The new analysis controlled for the fact that moderately uncomfortable days are more common in the first place (such that anything, including baseball wins and losses, would occur more times across the most frequently occurring temperatures), and found that collective violence was more likely at higher temperatures. Speaking of baseball, one study found that batters were more likely to get hit by "errant" pitches on hot than on cool days (Reifman, Larrick, & Fein, 1988)!

Numerous other researchers have found that violent crimes only went up as temperatures increased (e.g., Anderson, 1987; Anderson & Anderson, 1984; Cotton, 1986; Harries & Stadler, 1983, 1985–86; Perry & Simpson, 1987; Rotton, 1986; Stadler & Harries, 1985) (Figure 6–8). How can these studies be reconciled with the laboratory research supporting a curvilinear relationship between temperature and aggression? One possibility is that studies showing only a linear relationship have not examined high enough temperatures: Perhaps only at very high temperatures does violence actually decline. This explanation would seem to be unlikely in light of studies which have employed temperatures well over 100°F (38°C) and still found no decline in violence at these very uncomfortable levels (e.g., Anderson, 1987; Harries & Stadler, 1983). Another possibility is that socioeconomic factors, such as literacy rates and poverty rates, account for some of the differences between studies. This explanation seems to be questionable in light of studies that have controlled for such factors and still found that violence increases linearly with temperature (e.g., Harries & Stadler, 1985–86, 1988; Perry & Simpson, 1987; Rotton, 1986),

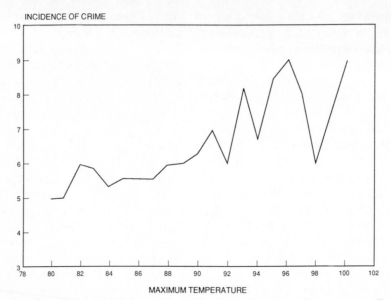

Figure 6–8   Data from Cotton (1986) showing that violent crimes increase with temperature. (From Cotton, J. L., 1986. Ambient temperature and violent crime. *Journal of Applied Social Psychology, 16,* 786–801. Copyright 1986 by V. H. Winston & Sons. Used by permission.)

although socioeconomic status of neighborhood may be important to consider (e.g., Harries & Stadler, 1988; Harries, Stadler, & Zdrokowski, 1984). Controlling for humidity, wind, air pollution, and other atmospheric variables still results in a linear relationship between temperature and violence (Rotton & Frey, 1985). It should be noted that some research fails to find any consistent pattern between climatological variables and violence (e.g., Atlas, 1984), and some research finds a linear or curvilinear relationship of temperature with some forms of violence but not with other forms (e.g., Cotton, 1986; Rotton & Frey, 1985). Quite likely, factors which have been difficult to quantify retroactively in these archival field studies— consumption of alcohol, for instance—have influences on the temperature–aggression relationship that are difficult to assess (cf. Bell & Baron, 1981).

It is important to consider that differences between findings in laboratory research and field research can be attributable to many factors. We have just mentioned that factors such as alcohol consumption are difficult to quantify in field studies, whereas such factors can be controlled in the lab: In the lab studies to date, there has been no alcohol consumption. Moreover, laboratory procedures themselves may introduce artifacts. The box on page 106 notes that informed consent—telling subjects that they will be exposed to heat stress and that they have a right to terminate the experiment at any time—imposes a form of perceived control on the situation. There is surely a very different state of perceived control (or lack thereof) involved in archival field data. The subject's experience in the lab is generally short-term (0.5 to 1.0 hour), whereas exposure to a true heat wave is usually for several days. Lab studies usually involve interactions with strangers, whereas field data involve at least some interaction with acquaintances. Actual murder and aggravated assault cannot be examined in the lab: Only very limited forms of aggression can be scrutinized in this controlled setting.

Thus, although lab studies more often than not find a curvilinear heat–aggression relationship and field studies more often than not find a linear relationship, there are numerous reasons for these differences. Both types of studies do yield valuable information about temperature influences.

One additional explanation of the discrepancies between linear and curvilinear relationships between temperature and violence has been proposed by Bell and Fusco (1986), who reanalyzed the field data originally assembled by Cotton (1986). Cotton had found that temperature and violent crimes in Indianapolis were linearly related: As temperatures went up, so did violent (but not nonviolent) crime. Bell and Fusco (1986) noted that the variability in incidents of violent crime also increased as temperatures increased (Figure 6–8). That is, at a given temperature there would be several days available for measuring incidents of violent crime. For cooler days, there was little difference from one day to the next in the relatively low numbers of violent crimes per day. On hotter days, however, there were much wider differences in the numbers of violent crimes per day: Some would have fairly low numbers of crimes, and some would have relatively high numbers of violent incidents. Recall that the curvilinear hypothesis suggests aggression decreases at higher levels of discomfort because people would rather escape the discomfort than be violent. Perhaps such a tendency at least partly holds for the field studies: On hot days, people have some tendency to avoid violence and escape the heat, but they also have some tendencies (perhaps through the influence of alcohol?) to fight when uncomfortable. Combining these tendencies would lead to results similar to those noted by Bell and Fusco: Some hot days might show increased violence, others not.

We should add that an alternative explanation of the relationship between heat and aggression, which is not inconsistent with the negative affect interpretation, involves the role of the hypothalamus (see page 161) in both thermoregulation and aggression (Boyanowsky et al., 1981–82). According to this interpretation, the hypothalamus works to increase sympathetic nervous system arousal (heart rate, blood pressure, respiration rate) in the presence of some anger-provoking situations, but works to decrease these processes during some phases of heat exposure. The resultant conflict in signals, it is thought, increases irritation and physiological distress, which leads to an increase in aggression. Should this process occur at the intermediate level of negative effect (see Figure 6–6), it would be entirely compatible with the negative affect explanation discussed above. Interestingly, Boyanowsky et al. report that the presence of a thermometer within easy view of research subjects reduces their level of aggression in hot conditions, presumably because it provides an explanation to them for their discomfort that is separate from aggression-provoking anger (see also, Anderson, in press; Bell & Fusco, 1989).

Heat and Helping Behavior   A third type of social behavior that may be affected by high ambient temperatures is that of offering assistance to someone in need of help. Some social psychological research has indicated that when people feel unpleasant, they are not inclined to help others, whereas other research suggests that when people feel bad they do indeed help others in order to feel better (e.g., Cialdini & Kenrick, 1976; Weyant, 1978). Since heat obviously produces discomfort, what might it do to helping behavior?

One study found that after leaving an uncomfortably hot experimental room, subjects were less likely to volunteer their assistance in another experiment than subjects who had been in a more comfortable environment (Page, 1978). Another study (Cunningham, 1979) similarly found that when subjects were asked to help in an interview, willingness to help declined as temperatures rose in summer months, but willingness to help increased when temperatures rose during winter months. Other research, however, has failed to find a relationship between heat and helping. For example, outdoor temperature was found to have no effect on the amount of tips left at an indoor restaurant (Cunningham, 1979). Moreover, neither high nor low temperatures reduced helping when a person: (1) using crutches dropped a book; (2) lost a contact lens; (3) dropped a sack of groceries; or (4) asked for help in a survey (Schneider, Lesko, & Garrett, 1980). Data from Bell and Doyle (1983) also failed to show that heat had any effect on helping, either during or after exposure to the high temperatures. With so little data available, it is difficult (and unwise) to draw firm conclusions about the relationship of heat to helping behavior. It is possible, though, that discomfort increases helping in some cases and decreases it in others, so that these two tendencies may "cancel out" each other in many instances (e.g., Cunningham, Steinberg, & Grev, 1980).

COLD TEMPERATURES AND BEHAVIOR

If the physiological reaction to cold ambient temperatures (i.e., below 68°F, or 20°C) is in many ways the opposite of the reaction to heat, what effects does such exposure have on behavior? The answer is somewhat complex, for several reasons. First, humans rarely have to work or interact in unprotected cold climates. We usually wear protective clothing in uncomfortably cold situations. If we do not, disease or death is not unlikely. Because of the clothing factor, performance outcomes in studies of cold environments are somewhat difficult to interpret. If workers on the Alaskan pipeline wore heavy clothing, their efficiency was not dramatically affected. This does not, however, mean that cold temperatures do not affect performance. A second reason why the relationship between cold temperatures and behavior is complex is that some parts of the body may be cold, while others are not. Whether only the hands are cold, or whether the core temperature is lowered, may make a difference. Finally, in the section on heat we noted that increases of 10° to 15°F (6° to 9°C) above comfort levels (i.e., above about 70°F, or 21°C) often affect performance and other behavior. Comparable temperatures below comfort levels (e.g., 55° to 65°F, or 13° to 18°C) are rarely studied. Instead, research on cold tends to concentrate on behavioral effects of temperatures below 55°F (13°C). With these facts in mind, let us now examine some of the research on cold temperatures and behavior.

Cold Temperatures and Health

We have already mentioned that prolonged exposure to cold can lead to hypothermia and frostbite. Do people living for long periods of time in cold climates experience health effects due to the cold temperatures? The answer appears to be "probably not directly." Eskimos in North America and Lapps in northern Scandinavia do not seem to suffer prolonged disorders associated with cold temperatures. Any noticeable differences from other societies are probably the result of culture. If adequate clothing and shelter are available, cold temperatures are not all that hazardous to health. (For a review of design considerations for adequate shelter in cold climates, see Matus, 1988.)

Mental health also appears not to be directly related to cold temperatures. A study on health at Antarctic stations (Gunderson, 1968) found

Ambient Temperature and Driving: Can Temperature Cause Accidents?

In a review article, Provins (1958) noted that efficiency of driving an automobile may well be affected by ambient temperature. Obviously, cold temperatures that contribute to icy road conditions in turn contribute to accidents. But cold or hot temperatures may also directly affect driving performance in at least four ways:

1. Temperatures below 50°F (10°C) or above 90°F (32°C) reduce grip strength and impair muscle dexterity, which could diminish control over steering, braking, and shifting gears.
2. Temperatures below 50°F (10°C) or above 90°F (32°C) also reduce **tactile discrimination** (sensitivity of touch), which could reduce a driver's "feel" for the road.
3. Temperatures below 55°F (13°C) or above 90°F (32°C) impair vigilance and tracking

performance, possibly making a driver less cognizant of potential hazards and traffic directional or signaling devices.
4. If high or low temperatures produce irritation, drivers may become more aggressive and take more dangerous risks.

When high wind speeds (such as would be experienced by drivers of convertibles or motorcycles) are added, these temperature effects probably become more severe. Perhaps still more frightening is the possibility that increased levels of carbon monoxide and oxidants in the blood of drivers further reduce mental responsiveness (cf. Ury, Perkins, & Goldsmith, 1972). Data are scarce and somewhat inconclusive on the influence of these environmental variables on driving efficiency, but there will certainly be more research in the future exploring this potentially tragic influence.

---

that although residents experience insomnia, anxiety, depression, and irritability, these effects appear more attributable to isolation and work requirements than to climate. To the extent that climate is a factor, concern about it and perceived threat from it are probably more important than temperature itself.

Cold Extremes and Performance

Humans on Arctic expeditions, military maneuvers, and in underwater diving occupations often experience extremes of cold. Research on cold stress and performance (see Fox, 1967;

Poulton, 1970; Provins & Clarke, 1960, for reviews) suggests that even temperatures of 55°F (13°C) can reduce efficiency in reaction time, tracking proficiency, muscular dexterity, and tactile discrimination (sensitivity of touch). As temperatures fall below this level, performance usually deteriorates further. Some evidence (cf. Fox, 1967) suggests that this deterioration is at least partly due to overload and heightened arousal. That is, the body's mechanisms are heavily allocated to maintaining adequate core temperature, so there is not enough energy or attention left for optimum performance on manual and mental tasks. If the hands are exposed, loss of tactile discrimination and stiffening reduce manual dexterity. If the hands do not become cold, lowered core temperature may still hurt performance, though probably not as much. Interestingly, if the hands are kept warm, considerable cooling of the rest of the body can be tolerated without severe performance decrements (e.g., Gaydos, 1958; Gaydos & Dusek, 1958).

Whether less chilling temperatures (55° to 65°F, or 13° to 18°C) actually enhance performance cannot be stated with confidence. However, we might speculate that if the physiological reactions to slightly cooler temperatures increase arousal without overburdening the body's adaptive mechanisms, performance might be slightly enhanced (e.g., Clark & Flaherty, 1963).

Some people appear to be more bothered by cold than others, and performance is less severely affected by cold for some individuals (cf. Fox, 1967). Furthermore, practice on tasks in cold temperatures can improve performance, so some adaptive mechanisms seem to be at work. Adaptation level almost certainly plays a role in temperature–performance relationships in conditions of cold.

Cold Extremes and Social Behavior

Surprisingly little research has been done on the effects of cold ambient temperatures and social behavior. One interesting bit of laboratory evidence does suggest that "low" temperatures around 62°F (16°C) make subjects feel more affectively negative (Bell & Baron, 1977). Consequently, one might expect low ambient temperatures to influence aggression in the same curvilinear fashion as high ambient temperatures in the lab. Bell and Baron (1977) found exactly this result: Moderately negative feelings associated with cold temperatures tended to increase aggression, but more extreme negative feelings associated with cold actually decreased aggression. Although such results are far from conclusive, they are sup-

ported by other research (Bennett et al., 1983) and do suggest that more studies would be valuable in this area (see also Boyanowsky et al., 1981–82). These results do bring to mind "cabin fever," the idea that people forced indoors for prolonged periods during cold weather become agitated and hostile. However, Christensen (1982, 1984) found the idea to be no more than folklore, and Rotton and Frey (1985), studying temperatures as low as 5°F (−16°C), found no increase in family and household disorder associated with cold conditions.

As cited above for heat effects, Cunningham (1979) reported a slight decrease in helping with an interview as temperatures declined in the winter, although Schneider et al., (1980) found no effects of cold temperatures on helping. Informal observation has shown that cold, harsh winters tend to increase helping behavior and to reduce crime rates. Bennett et al., (1983) report supportive evidence for these observations and suggest a cold weather helping norm as one explanation. Others have noted that the severe winter of 1977 resulted in many acts of kindness, such as people rescuing others and sharing food and shelter. In addition, criminal activity during that winter was relatively mild. Attributing such behavior to temperature is speculative, and, as is the case for evidence on heat and helping, there is too little research available to draw any firm conclusions on the relationship of cold temperatures to helping behavior.

Summary of Temperature Effects on Behavior

The body reacts to high and low ambient temperatures by respectively losing or preserving body heat. Associated physiological activity tends to increase arousal, leading to improved performance at low levels of arousal and deteriorated performance at higher levels. Attention, perceived control, and adaptation level also play a role in the relationship of temperature to behavior. Heat has been shown to affect attraction, aggression, and helping behavior in complex ways, depending on other factors. Cold ambient temperatures appear to influence aggression in much the same way as hot temperatures and may increase helping behavior under some circumstances.

WIND AND BEHAVIOR

Anyone familiar with the "Windy City" of Chicago knows how discomforting wind can be when all you want to do is walk along a sidewalk. Few areas of the world can escape this natural phenomenon, although winds tend to be more severe in certain regions. Winds formed in tornadoes and hurricanes can easily reach speeds in excess of 80 mph (129 kph). Parts of the Rocky Mountain states, especially those regions where the mountains meet the plains, experience wind speeds of over 100 mph several times a year. Fortunately, because of the altitude and climate, such Chinook winds are so thin and dry they do little physical damage, but they do cause discomfort and inconvenience (try riding a bicycle in one!). On the other hand, in 1988 wind storms in Chicago blew out 200 windows in the 110-story Sears Tower, moved a refrigerator across a room, and blew furniture, briefcases, and papers onto the streets below (Johnson & Richards, 1988). Such natural winds are not all that humans are exposed to. As indicated in more detail in Chapter 12, tall buildings create uncomfortable and even dangerous winds in the hearts of our major cities (see box, page 413). Because of the influence of buildings on natural wind patterns, these human-made (or human-altered) winds can far exceed natural winds in both **speed** and **turbulence** (gustiness, shifting directions). Some people attribute the Sears Tower winds to wind tunnel effects of nearby skyscrapers. As urban structures are built taller, we can expect even more exposure to these unnatural winds. Thus, we suspect that potential effects of wind on behavior will become a more important topic for future research within environmental psychology.

Perception of Wind

Although the body has specialized receptors for detecting light, sound, odors, and so forth, there are no receptors designed specifically for wind detection. Thus, to detect wind we have to rely on several perceptual systems. If you are actually in a wind, pressure receptors in the skin probably tell you the most about its presence: The stronger the wind, the more pressure on exposed skin. If the wind is particularly cold or hot, moist or dry, temperature receptors in the skin also signal its presence. Muscular effort in resisting the wind is still another clue you can use to detect the force of a wind. The sight of others being blown over or of flags whipping tells you about the force of the wind even if you happen to be in a shelter. Finally, wind makes noise as it brushes past the ears or moves around obstacles, and the intensity and frequency of these sounds give you a clue to the wind's presence and force. One of the earliest and most widely known indexes for evaluating wind is a scale developed by Admiral Sir Francis Beaufort in 1806. The **Beaufort Scale**, depicted in Table 6–3, was originally devised for activities at sea, but it has been adapted to land use over the years. As can be seen from this scale, wind effects range from problems of keeping hair combed to having difficulty walking and even to being knocked off one's feet by gusts of 45

Table 6-3 Beaufort Wind Scale and Related Effects

Beaufort Number	Wind Speed (mph)	Atmospheric and Behavioral Effects
0,1	0-3	Calm, no noticeable wind.
2	4-7	Wind felt on face.
3	8-12	Wind extends light flag; hair is disturbed; clothing flaps.
4	13-18	Dust, dry soil, loose paper raised; hair disarranged.
5	19-24	Force of wind felt on body; drifting snow becomes airborne; limit of agreeable wind on land.
6	25-31	Umbrellas used with difficulty, hair blown straight; walking becomes unsteady; wind noise on ears unpleasant; windborne snow above head height (blizzard).
7	32-38	Inconvenience felt when walking.
8	39-46	Generally impedes progress; great difficulty with balance in gusts.
9	47-54	People blown over by gusts.

Adapted From Penwarden, A. D. Acceptable wind speeds in towns. *Building Science*, 1973, *8*, 259-267. Copyright 1973 by Pergamon Press and A. Penwarden, Building Research Establishment, U.K. 1974. Used by permission.

mph (72 kph) or more. Cases have actually been reported of individuals (especially elderly persons whose agility is less than ideal) being killed by winds that blew them over.

More scientific and precise scales of wind effects on humans have been proposed by Penwarden (1973). Some of these proposed indexes include force of wind on the body (which takes body surface area into account), angle at which one can lean into a wind without falling over, degree of increased metabolic rate from walking into a wind, and body heat loss due to various types of winds. This body heat loss index would of course be influenced by moisture content and temperature of the wind, as indicated in the previous discussion of windchill.

Behavioral Effects of Wind

Very little systematic research has been conducted to date on the specific behavioral effects of wind. A very intriguing series of wind studies, however, has been reported by Poulton et al. (1975). These researchers exposed female subjects to winds of either 9 mph or 20 mph (14.5 or 32.2 kph), with varying degrees of turbulence, in a wind tunnel. Basically, these wind conditions were intended either to be just strong enough to be noticeable and cause slight discomfort or to be extremely uncomfortable and detrimental to performance. Air temperature varied between 65°F and 70°F (18°C and 20°C), with humidity at 70 to 85 percent. Among the findings were that high wind and gustiness (1) significantly deflected subjects from walking a straight path; (2) increased the time required to put on a rain coat from 20 to 26 seconds; (3) increased the time required to tie a headscarf by 30 percent; (4) increased subjects' blinking to 12 to 18 blinks per minute; (5) increased the time required to pick selected words from a list and to find a circled word in a newspaper; (6) caused more water to be spilled when poured into a wine glass; and (7) increased feelings of discomfort and perceived windiness (see also Cohen, Moss, & Zube, 1979). Taken altogether, these results generally suggest that winds influence affective feelings and at least some types of performance. Since some of these effects can be quite disturbing subjectively, we anticipate that many cities will adopt codes to regulate the extent to which new buildings will be allowed to produce annoying winds.

Correlational research has examined interesting behavior patterns associated with winds around the world, such as the Foehn, Bora, Mistral, and Sirocco in Europe, the Sharav and Chamsin in the Near East, the Chinook in Colorado and Wyoming and Santa Ana in California, and the Pomponio in Argentina (Sommers & Moos, 1976). The Foehn and Chinook are warm, dry winds that descend from mountains. It is not uncommon for residents in these regions to attribute depression, nervousness, pain, irritation, and traffic accidents to wind (Sommers & Moos, 1976). In the Near East, some governments even forgive criminal acts that are committed during the periods of disturbing winds. In an empirical study, two researchers (Muecher & Ungeheuer, 1961) measured performance on several tasks. As expected, performance was worse on days of Foehnlike weather than on less stormy days. In addition, they and other researchers (e.g.,

Moos, 1964) have reported that accident rates increase just before or during the approach of the winds. Rim (1975) examined performance of individuals on psychological tests during hot, desert wind (Sharav) periods in Israel, and compared their scores with subjects taking the tests on less turbulent days. The windy days led to higher scores on neuroticism and extraversion, and to lower scores on IQ tests and other measures. Although results are often inconsistent, research in the United States has shown some relationship between windy days and poor classroom behavior (e.g., Dexter, 1904) and between wind speed and mortality rates, felonies, and delinquency (Banzinger & Owens, 1978) (for a review of these studies, the reader is referred to Campbell & Beets, 1981). Whether these effects are directly attributable to wind, to air pressure changes (see below), or even to atmospheric ion changes, is subject to debate (see box, page 180). Also, temperature and other weather changes usually accompany winds, so more than one factor may account for wind effects. Quite probably, these weather conditions increase the stress one experiences, and the heightened stress leads to many of the psychological effects discussed in Chapter 4. Moreover, attention, arousal, and loss of perceived control are likely to mediate many wind effects. Further discussion along these lines is presented in the following section on altitude and barometric pressure.

BAROMETRIC PRESSURE AND ALTITUDE

Many people live at rather high altitudes, such as in the Rocky Mountain region of the United States, the Tibetan Plateau of southern China, the Andes, and the high plains of Ethiopia. Others of us travel to these high places. Still others experience high altitudes in aircraft or

experience below sea-level conditions during underwater dives. At high altitudes we are exposed to a variety of stresses, most notably **hypoxia** or reduced oxygen intake resulting from low air pressure. Other high altitude stresses include increased solar radiation, cold

Air Ionization and Electromagnetic Fields:
Mediators of Weather–Behavior Relationships?

Lightning and other factors may ionize the air. In **air ionization** the molecules in the air partially "split" into positively and negatively charged particles. Moreover, extremely low frequency electromagnetic fields **(ELF-EMF)** are associated with some low altitude weather disturbances. Could it be that these factors play a role in the influence of the weather on behavior? Some researchers think so, at least to some extent. For example, there is evidence that **negative ions** slow brain waves (Assael, Pfeifer, & Sulman, 1974), speed up reaction time (Hawkins & Barker, 1978; Slote, 1961; Wofford, 1966), facilitate other performance tasks (e.g., Baron, 1987a), enhance positive moods (DeSanctis, Halcomb, & Fedoravicius, 1981), moderate aggression (Baron, Russell, & Arms, 1985), and intensify interpersonal attraction (Baron, 1987b). Under some circumstances, however, these effects can be opposite to what others have found (cf. Baron, Russell, & Arms, 1985). **Positive ions** are associated with worsening performance and mental outlook, although some people are more sensitive to ion effects than others (Charry & Hawkinshire, 1981). Interestingly, one interpretation of the disruptive effects of the Sharav wind in Israel (see p. 179) is that this wind generates an excess of positive ions (Sulman et al., 1970).

Research on low frequency electromagnetic fields suggests that such fields may slow reaction time, impair estimation of time (constricting time), and lead to complaints of headaches and lethargy (for reviews, see Beal, 1974; Persinger, Ludwig, & Ossenkopf, 1973). Recent controversial research suggests that when these ELF-EMF are generated by high-power electrical lines, they may be associated with increased frequencies of diseases such as leukemia and cancer (e.g., Savitz & Calle, 1987; Savitz et al., 1988).

Whether or not ions and ELF-EMF account for the effects of weather on behavior is unknown. The effects of ions noted above are primarily from laboratory conditions with higher levels of negative ions than would be found in natural settings (Culver, Rotton, & Kelly, 1988; Kroling, 1985; Reiter, 1985; Rotton, 1987). As with all individual weather variables, more than one factor is operating at a time, so it is difficult to conclude that any one mechanism "causes" the observed behavior or feeling state. It is intriguing to consider the possibility, however, and we are sure that experimentation and speculation will continue in the area.

temperatures, humidity, high velocity winds, reduced nutrition, and strain from negotiating rough terrain (Frisancho, 1979). In underwater environments we also experience problems from high pressures, cold temperatures, and physical exertion. Thus, it is appropriate to examine the physiological and behavioral changes associated with altitude and air pressure differences. (For more detailed reviews, the reader is referred to Frisancho, 1979; Heath & Williams, 1977; Miles, 1967; Pawson & Jest, 1978; and Walder, 1967).

Physiological Effects

Normal atmospheric or **barometric pressure** at sea level is 14.7 pounds per square inch (1.033 kg/cm^2). Lower than normal pressures occur as one rises higher and higher above sea level. Under normal air pressure conditions, oxygen is taken into the body through the **alveolar walls** of the lungs, with the pressure difference between the atmosphere and sides of the walls being just enough to "force" oxygen into the body. In low pressure environments, however, it becomes more difficult for oxygen to pass through the alveolar walls, resulting in reduced oxygen available, or the hypoxia noted above (see also Ernsting, 1963, 1967). Hypoxia has a number of physiological and behavioral consequences; and, it should be mentioned, hypoxia is not limited to high altitude environments, but is also a major problem in carbon monoxide pollution, as discussed in Chapter 7. Most habitable environments are located below 15,000 feet (4,572 m), though at much higher altitudes, two special air pressure problems occur. First, above 30,000 feet (9,144 m), the pressure on the interior (body) side of the lung walls becomes so much greater than the pressure on the atmospheric side that oxygen actually passes from the blood into the atmosphere. Second, above 63,000 feet (19,203 m), air pressure is so low that water in the body at a core temperature of 98.6°F (37°C) will actually vaporize.

As stated above, the hypoxia at high altitudes has a number of physiological ramifications. Frisancho (1979) provides some interesting details. Visitors to high altitude areas are likely to experience deeper, and perhaps more rapid, breathing to help compensate for hypoxia. As a result, more carbon dioxide is removed from the lungs, leading to increased alkalinity of the blood. In addition, resting heart rate increases, though maximum heart rate during exercise decreases. Consequently, total cardiac output is reduced, and enlargement of the heart may occur. Red blood cell count increases, hemoglobin concentration increases, but plasma volume decreases, so total blood volume is largely unaffected. Moreover, retinal blood vessel diameter increases and light sensitivity of the retina decreases. Also, an increased desire for sugar will likely be experienced, although hunger is suppressed and weight loss likely. Hormone production is also affected by high altitudes: Adrenal activity increases and thyroid activity decreases. Testosterone production and sperm production decrease, and menstrual complaints may increase. In sum, initial exposure to high altitudes leads to many physiological changes.

Acclimatization to High Altitudes

Fortunately, most of the physiological changes noted above are short-term responses to high altitudes, and, as Frisancho (1979) elaborates, acclimatization to the environment at these elevations does occur. For example, hemoglobin concentration levels off after six months and testosterone production returns to normal after a week of high altitude exposure. Acclimatization is not without long-term consequences, however. Populations native to high altitude areas do show physiological differences from lowland natives, probably as a result of developmental adaptations. For example, high-altitude natives show larger lung capacity, higher blood pressure in the pulmonary (leading to the lungs) arteries, lower blood pressure for the rest of the body, enlarged areas of the heart, larger chest size, lower weight at birth, slower growth rates, and slower sexual maturation (Frisancho, 1979). Although some of these differences may be attributable to nutrition, genetics, and culture, many of them are almost certainly tied to the hypoxic environment of high elevations.

Behavioral Effects of High Altitudes

Obviously, extreme hypoxia will lead to loss of consciousness and death. Performance impair-

. . . .

A Recycled Cycle: Moon Phases and Behavior

Folklore and commonly held beliefs maintain that many aspects of our behavior are related to phases of the moon. Sexual prowess, menstrual cycles, birth rates, death rates, suicide rates, homicide rates, and hospital admission rates are among the phenomena various people claim are affected by the moon. Often, it is maintained that a full moon increases strange behavior. Surveys of undergraduates indicate that half of them believe people behave strangely when the moon is full (Rotton & Kelly, 1985b). Other beliefs are that the tidal pulls of full and new moons influence human physiology or psychic functioning, or that the moon's perigee (closest distance to the earth) and apogee (farthest distance from the earth) influence us in strange ways. Indeed, the word *lunacy* is derived from a belief in a relationship between the moon and mental illness.

From time to time, research appears that actually gives credence to such beliefs. For example, Blackman and Catalina (1973) found that full moons were associated with an increase in the number of patients visiting a psychiatric emergency room. In another study, Lieber and Sherin (1972) reported a relationship between moon phase and homicide. Rape, robbery and assault, burglary, larceny and theft, auto theft, drunkenness, disorderly conduct, and attacks on family and children have also been linked to a full moon (Tasso & Miller, 1976). At first glance, then, it would appear that science has confirmed the folklore of the ancients (see also Garzino, 1982).

Not so fast! Closer examination of the data indicates that the mysticism of the lunar cycle may be more myth than reality. Campbell and Beets (1978), Campbell (1982), Frey, Rotton, and Barry (1979), Rotton and Kelly (1985a), and Kelly, Rotton, and Culver (1985–86) review the available research on the topic and conclude that no firm relationship exists between any lunar variable and human behavior, although lunar tides do affect some marine organisms (see also Atlas, 1984; Jorgenson, 1981; Lester, 1979; Lester, Brockopp, & Priebe, 1969). For example, studies conducted over a period of three to five years may report a relationship between the full moon and suicide or homicide for only one of the years studied. Researchers who conclude that such a relationship exists are ignoring the fact that it does not exist for the other years, or that these behaviors are actually lower during full moons for another year. Moreover, it is consistently found that crimes increase on weekends. For some periods of the year, lunar phases may coincide with weekends. Data based on only these periods will obviously show a relationship between the moon and crime, but data based on other periods will show the opposite relationship or no relationship at all. In addition, a self-fulfilling prophecy may operate: If police believe crime increases during a full moon, they may become more vigilant at these times and thus arrest more people. Altogether, the evidence reviewed by Campbell and Beets (1978) and by Frey, Rotton, and Barry (1979) suggests that positive links between moon phases and behavior are spurious and are attributable to mere chance probabilities in the data or to variables not considered by individual investigators. Why do these mistaken beliefs persist? Reasons include misconceptions about physical processes (Culver, Rotton, & Kelly, 1988), attitudes acquired from one's peers (Rotton, Kelly, & Elortegui, 1986), and cognitive biases, such as basing conclusions on only a few occurrences. Given the tenacity of beliefs in moon phases causing disruptive behavior, we suspect the lunacy of it all will continue for some time!

. . . .

ment, however, occurs well before this extreme stage. To the extent the body can compensate for hypoxia, high altitudes will not show substantial performance decrements. During strenuous work, however, the capacity of the body to compensate for hypoxia is taxed, and performance decrements are likely to be observed. Task performance can be impaired by altitudes as low as 8,000 feet (2,438m). Learning of a new task can be impaired by rapid decompression to altitudes as low as 5,000 feet (1,524 m). In general, learning of new things is more affected by high altitudes than is recall of previously learned material (Cahoon, 1972; Denison, Ledwith, & Poulton, 1966; McFarland, 1972). We should note that such learning impairments are generally of small magnitude, and people living at high altitudes are certainly capable of learning.

High Air Pressure Effects

Extremely high pressure is experienced primarily under the sea. For each 33 feet (10 m) of depth, the pressure increases by 14.7 pounds per square inch (psi) or by **one atmosphere** (1.033 kg/cm^2). Thus, at 33 feet (10 m), the pressure is 29.4 psi (two atmospheres), at 99 feet (30 m) the pressure is 58.8 psi (four atmospheres), and so on. Hazards encountered at such pressure extremes (see also Miles, 1967; Walder, 1967) include:

1. Increased breathing difficulty caused by reduction of maximum breathing capacity (reduced by 50 percent at a depth of 100 feet (30 m));

2. Oxygen poisoning caused by breathing excess oxygen or oxygen under pressure;

3. Nitrogen poisoning caused by the narcotic effects of breathing nitrogen under extreme pressure. Symptoms include light-headedness and mental instability.

4. **Decompression sickness** caused by nitrogen bubbles forming in body tissues (especially in the circulatory system) when one rapidly changes from a high pressure to a lower pressure environment. The "bends" is one relatively acute form of decompression sickness. Permanent damage to the bones may also result from rapid decompression.

Most of these high pressure problems can be corrected or prevented by breathing the proper mixture of air for the diving depth and by surfacing slowly to permit the gradual release of nitrogen from tissues.

Medical, Emotional, and Behavioral Effects of Air Pressure Changes

Low and high barometric or atmospheric pressures are not only associated with altitude. All of us, in fact, are subjected to often dramatic swings in barometric pressure associated with weather changes. Hurricanes, cyclones, and other "tropical storms," for example, are special types of low pressure weather systems. Clear, sunny skies on the other hand, are generally associated with high pressure. Do these changes in barometric pressure affect our

Sunlight: Its
Many Effects

One weather variable that has significant impact on humans is sunlight. As indicated by Frisancho (1979), thermonuclear reactions within the sun convert millions of tons of hydrogen into millions of tons of helium every second, releasing radiant energy in the process. Approximately eight minutes after it leaves the sun, some of this energy reaches the earth in various wavelengths. Ranging from short to long wavelengths, the energy takes the form of x-rays, ultraviolet rays, visible light, infrared rays, and radiowaves. The wavelengths shorter than visible light are hazardous to life. Fortunately, most of these wavelengths are either absorbed by ozone, blocked by ozone, or "consumed" in the process of making ozone high in the atmosphere. **Ozone** is a form of oxygen in which three atoms are molecularly combined (O_3). As you are probably aware, there has been concern in recent years that several human-generated substances, most notably chlorofluorocarbons in aerosol propellants, destroy the layer of ozone that protects us from harmful solar radiation. When it hits certain atmospheric pollutants, sunlight leads to photochemical smog (see page 218). The solar energy that does reach the surface of the earth can also harm us through sunburn and as a factor in skin cancer. To protect us from some of this danger, the skin produces melanin and other dark pigments to act as a partial shield, a process we know as *tanning* (see Frisancho, 1979). Exposure to excessive midday sun has been implicated in cataracts (Taylor et al., 1988).

Sunlight is not just potentially harmful, of course, but provides us with light, heat, and, through photosynthesis, food. Moreover, sunlight induces the skin to produce Vitamin D.

Behaviorally, increased hours of sunlight have been associated with increased suicide rates and crime rates (see Sommers & Moos, 1976). These effects most probably are not due directly to sunlight, but rather to increased opportunities to encounter social stress (which may lead to depression and suicide) and increased opportunities to engage in criminal activity. There are seasonal trends in suicide rates, with a peak in spring to early summer. Noting seasonal trends, Kevan (1980) concluded from a review of over 80 studies that suicide is not related to meteorological factors.

Interestingly, two experiments by Cunningham (1979) suggest that sunlight not only leads to good moods in people, but is also associated with increased altruistic behavior! In one of these experiments, people in Minneapolis were greeted by an experimenter as they walked outdoors, and were asked to answer a few brief questions. Subjects were more willing to answer the questions the more sunshine was present, regardless of any other weather conditions in both summer and winter. In the second experiment, waitresses in a restaurant were found to receive more tips as a function of the amount of sun shining. This relationship was found even though customers were indoors and were not experiencing direct sunlight at the time of leaving the tip. Moreover, the more sunlight, the more positive the mood of the waitresses. Cunningham interpreted these results in terms of mood: The more pleasant we feel, the more willing we are to be kind to and to

help others (cf. Cialdini & Kenrick, 1976; Weyant, 1978). Apparently, sunlight really does have prosocial benefits!

. . . .

feelings and behavior? According to a number of researchers, the answer is "yes," although the picture is a bit cloudy (pun intended) in that: (1) the data are not always consistent from study to study; and (2) humidity, temperature, and wind variations accompanying pressure changes may account for the observed psychological changes (see also Campbell & Beets, 1977; Moos, 1976).

In general, researchers have observed three types of effects that air pressure changes have on people: increased medical complaints, increased suicide rates, and increased disruptive behavior. With respect to medical complaints, many arthritis victims claim that their condition worsens with changes in weather. Indeed, Hollander and Yeostros (1963) have reported scientific evidence of both increased complaints and medical indications of increased arthritic impairment associated with rising humidity. Moreover, Muecher and Ungeheuer (1961) report an association between general medical complaints and changing weather, especially low pressure or stormy weather.

A number of studies have been conducted over the years to examine the relationship of mental hospital admissions and suicide rates to weather changes. Both of these clinical occurrences show fluctuations with seasons, with the highest rates coinciding with the increased temperatures and daylight hours of spring and summer months (see Campbell & Beets, 1977; Sommers & Moos, 1976). Suicide rates, however, show some specific variation with barometric pressure. In general, suicides increase as barometric pressure falls, and decrease as pressure rises (Digon & Block, 1966; Mills, 1934; Sanborn, Casey, & Niswander, 1970), although not all researchers agree that such a relationship exists (e.g., Digon & Block, 1966; Pokorny,

Davis, & Harberson, 1963). It is entirely likely that weather associations with mental hospital admissions and suicide rates reflect seasonal variations, and that the social contact which goes along with seasonal variations accounts for the behavioral pathologies (e.g., Kevan, 1980).

Finally, several studies have shown that disruptive school behavior and police dispatch calls fluctuate with weather, especially air pressure changes. Even at the turn of the century, one researcher found that low barometric pressure and wind and humidity fluctuations, were associated with poor behavior in the classroom (Dexter, 1904). Similar findings have been reported more recently (e.g., Auliciems, 1972; Brown, 1964; Russell & Bernal, 1977). Also, it has been found that complaints to police and investigative activity increase with low pressure and high temperature, and that accident reports and related investigations increase with stormy weather (Sells & Will, 1971; Will & Sells, 1969).

What do the above findings mean? Are our mental health and behavior helpless victims of barometric and other weather changes? Fortunately, the answer seems to be "probably not." First, the effects of weather changes on most psychological and behavioral indices are small relative to the influence of other factors, such as social conflict. Second, to the extent that weather does affect behavior, it probably does so indirectly, as an added stressor (i.e., as "the straw that broke the camel's back"). For example, increased suicide rates associated with pleasant weather probably reflect increased time available to interact in stressful social situations, and increased opportunities to worry about these social stresses (see Sommers & Moos, 1976). Similarly, weather changes may simply provide something else to worry about

Feeling Down in the Winter:
Seasonal Affective Disorder

We have noted that many human activities, including crime rates and suicide rates, vary with the seasons. For millenia, physicians have observed that depression and mania (a hyperactive state opposite of depression) often come and go with the seasons in some individuals—so much so that at one time depression was thought to be caused by cold and mania by heat (Jackson, 1986). Psychiatrists have recently given the name **Seasonal Affective Disorder**, or **SAD**, to a depressive cycle that varies with the seasons (Rosenthal et al., 1984). SAD usually occurs in women, begins in early adulthood, and the depressive episode typically shows excessive sleep (hypersomnia), fatigue, craving for carbohydrates, and weight gain. Since the most studied pattern is for depression to occur in the winter and a brighter mood (hypomania) to occur in summer, and since the hypersomnia is reminiscent of hibernating animals, the shortening and lengthening of daylight that goes with the seasons has been thought to be a potential causal factor. Indeed, the depression episodes often respond well to intense artificial light

Figure 6–9. Exposure to intense artificial light seems to relieve the symptoms of SAD. (Photo courtesy of The Sunbox Company, Rockville, MD.)

(e.g., Rosenthal et al., 1984; Wehr et al., 1986; Figure 6–9). This pattern has been tied to a substance called **melatonin**, which is involved in hibernation and which declines in concentration in animals exposed to bright light. However, melatonin does not seem to decrease with light therapy in humans (Wehr et al., 1986), and some people have a "reverse" cycle with the depressive episodes occurring in summer months (Wehr, Sack, & Rosenthal, 1987), so the connection of SAD to melatonin and number of daylight hours seems questionable. Although the reasons behind SAD are unclear, it has generated much clinical and research interest, and will certainly continue to do so for years to come.

. . . .

and cope with, adding to the strain on adaptational capacity that has been built up by other stressors. Nevertheless, the additional stresses brought about by the weather must be dealt with, and may have important consequences, especially under times of other duress. (For another viewpoint, see the box on page 186.)

Summary of Air Pressure Effects

Low air pressure is associated with high altitudes and stormy weather conditions. High pressure is found in underwater environments and in fair weather circumstances. At high altitudes, the major stress is hypoxia, or low oxygen intake. Adaptation to hypoxia may have short-term and long-term consequences, including respiratory, cardiovascular, and hormonal changes, as well as performance impairment. High pressure in underwater environments may lead to breathing difficulty, oxygen poisoning, nitrogen poisoning, and decompression sickness, although steps may be taken to avoid these problems. Low pressure associated with weather changes may coincide with increased medical complaints, high suicide rates, and increased disruptive behavior. These observations associated with weather may be due to weather variables other than air pressure, and are likely attributable to additional stress to go along with social stresses and other sources of duress.

INTEGRATING WEATHER AND POLLUTION EFFECTS: A FINAL NOTE

For the most part, we have treated individual weather variables as if their effects on health, mental outlook, and behavior are separate from other factors. We wish to conclude by noting that such singular effects rarely occur in our lives. That is, as noted previously, hot days are often associated with high barometric pressure and calm winds. Stormy days usually involve changes in temperature, wind, humidity, and air pressure. High altitudes not only result in reduced oxygen supply, but in increased exposure to solar radiation. Moreover, low winds and temperature inversions increase the concentration of air pollutants, and high humidity can intensify the effects of photochemical smog (see Chapter 7). Thus, weather and air pollution variables are interrelated, and one can rarely conclude with certainty that a given behavior or health effect is attributable to any one of these factors (cf. Rotton & Frey, 1985).

7 DISASTERS, ENVIRONMENTAL HAZARDS, AND AIR POLLUTION

KEY TERMS

air pollution
air pollution syndrome (APS)
carbon monoxide
cataclysmic events
crisis effect
daily hassles
disaster event
disruption
event duration
levee effect
low point

natural disaster
olfactory membrane
oxides of nitrogen and sulfur
particulates
passive smoking
personal stressors
photochemical smog
post-disaster groups
radon
technological catastrophe

INTRODUCTION

Most of us know what natural disasters are. When hurricanes or tornadoes strike, it is difficult not to notice them. Winds of 100 mph (160 kph) or more, flooding, falling trees, damaged buildings, and, in some cases, death, may occur, and even if the storms are not particularly destructive, they take over the headlines in areas about to be hit or already hit. Earthquakes and other natural disasters are similar; their presence is hard to deny, the threats they pose are intense, and they can kill or maim.

Air pollution, on the other hand, is not always obvious. Sometimes it makes us cough or causes our eyes to water, but for much of the time we are not very aware of it. Yet, pollution can damage our heart and lungs and affect our behavior. However, when asked to rate their risk of dying because of a disaster or because of air pollution, many people say the former is more likely to kill them. However, it would

appear that silent, constant air pollution is more harmful in the long run than are disasters. Their dramatic nature aside, disasters are not necessarily more lethal than less obvious stressors.

Many of the events that occur in the environment are so powerful and intrusive that we cannot avoid them. Others can affect us in subtle ways, often without our even being aware of them. In this chapter we will consider both of these extremes. On the one hand are disasters, events of such fury or threat that one cannot help but be aware of them. On the other hand is air pollution, a problem no less important or potentially hazardous than disasters but which is barely perceived by most of us. We will consider the ways in which these events affect us. Falling somewhere in between, and sharing characteristics of each of these environmental problems, is an increasingly common event—toxic accidents or leaking toxic waste dumps. Thus, in this chapter we will concentrate on the *disturbed* environment.

Air pollution involves "silent" exposure to toxic substances. It is silent because we cannot usually see, feel, or taste it, but air pollution can be dangerous. Somehow, we accept pollution as an inevitable consequence of civilization and technological expansion. Where would we be without our cars, one of the great polluting inventions? However, we are not as charitable about other forms of toxic agents in the environment to which we may be exposed. Accidents such as at Three Mile Island (TMI) and Love Canal have sharpened our awareness of the vast possibility for toxic exposure in our world, and we do not like it. However, this form of exposure to potentially harmful agents is also a by-product of technology, and one could ask, as we did about autos, where would we be without plastics or nuclear power? The issues surrounding toxic exposure will also be considered in this chapter.

In discussing stress in Chapter 4, we noted that Lazarus and Cohen (1977) distinguished between three types of events that cause stress. One type, **daily hassles**, referred to small magnitude events that occur repeatedly—commuting to work, going to class, and so on. Another kind of stressor, termed **personal stressors**, referred to more powerful threats or losses that occur on an individual level, including loss of a loved one, loss of a job, and other personal problems. Still another type of stressor was called **cataclysmic events** to capture the intensity of these events and their potential for widespread devastation and destruction. These sudden, powerful events typically require a great deal of adaptation in order for people to cope, and large numbers of people are affected. They include war, imprisonment, relocation, and natural disaster (Lazarus & Cohen, 1977). As major events with the potential to kill, maim, disrupt, and wipe out communities, disasters are important environmental stressors. However, there are many different kinds of disasters and although some of the characteristics of cataclysmic events are shared by most disasters, other cases are different. In this chapter, we will consider the distinction between natural disasters, caused by natural forces, and human-made catastrophes, due in some way to our actions or modification of the environment. We will consider natural events in the first sections of this chapter. As we do so, keep in mind that many natural disasters—wind storms and droughts, for example—are closely related to the weather phenomena we described in the previous chapter.

NATURAL DISASTERS

Natural disasters are relatively infrequent events, but their dramatic qualities make them memorable and seem more frequent. Few of us will experience more than a few such events in our lives, and then only if we live in areas where they are likely. Earthquakes in California, hurricanes along the Gulf Coast and the Atlantic Seaboard, tornadoes in the southeast and midwest, tsunamis in Hawaii—these are all instances of powerful natural events that tend to occur in certain areas of our country. Defining these events is an important place to begin our discussion of natural disasters (Figure 7–1, A & B).

What Are Natural Disasters?

Natural disasters can be difficult to define. The "natural" part is easy: Natural disasters are caused by natural forces and are not under human control. They are uncontrollable, the product of the physical forces that govern the earth and atmosphere, and people must learn to deal with them when they strike. Defining disaster, on the other hand, is a little trickier. We could simply list all of the events associated with disaster—hurricanes, tornadoes, earthquakes, tsunamis, and the like—but this may not be satisfactory because these storms or

Figure 7–1 A & B Tornadoes are potentially destructive natural events. When one strikes a human community and causes great devastation, we call it a natural disaster. Is this a sufficient definition of a natural disaster?

events do not always cause damage. Typically, one of these **disaster events** must cause damage or death before it is considered a disaster. How should we define or quantify damage? Should it be viewed on the individual level as death, injury, or loss? Is there a cutoff, a certain amount of damage above which an event is a disaster and below which it is not? Or, should responses by victims (for example, if they panic) be used to index disasters? Definitional issues have posed problems for researchers interested in disaster and extreme stress.

In our society, the emphasis seems to be on effects. For example, the Federal Emergency Management Agency (FEMA), the governmental unit responsible for helping disaster victims, offered the following definition in 1984:

> A major disaster is defined . . . as any hurricane, tornado, storm, flood, high water, wind-driven water, tidal wave, tsunami, earthquake, volcanic erruption, landslide, mudslide, snowstorm, drought, fire, explosion, or other catastrophe . . . which, in the determination of the President, causes damage of sufficient severity and magnitude to warrant major disaster assistance (p. 1).

Thus, the nature of the event (if it is one of these disaster events) and the extent of damage are used to officially designate disasters. This definition is used to determine whether and if emergency aid and relief work are to be given and thus focuses on issues related to such action. It shares the same biases as most of us. Disasters are destructive. A tornado in a desolate desert where no one lives and no one may even be around to see it is not a disaster, but the same tornado loose in downtown Birmingham is.

Quarantelli (1985) has argued that physical indices of damage and destruction are not sufficient to define disasters. The magnitude of impact of a disaster event may be better viewed in terms of **disruption**—the degree to which individual, group, and organizational function-

ing is disturbed. It is possible for natural events like earthquakes to be destructive but not disruptive, though the two are frequently related. More importantly, it is possible to have little visible destruction with great disruption. Thus, storms that cause great disruption by the threats they pose might be considered to be disasters even if they wind up doing little damage. The advantage of using this kind of definition is that disruption can be measured and provides an important outcome estimate by telling us how much disorganization or interruption of normal life occurs. Thus, earthquakes in desolate areas can cause destruction but may cause little disruption among the few people living there. Conversely, disasters such as blizzards may cause little physical disfigurement but a great deal of disruption.

This approach suggests that disaster events—those occurrences that can cause disasters—must disrupt victimized communities in order to be considered a disaster. This does not make disasters any easier to measure, but does allow a number of events, such as the blizzard noted above, to be included as disasters. Measuring disruption is fine, but the same problems of how much must occur or where the cutoff for distinguishing between disasters and nondisasters may be arises as soon as we try to apply this definition. Thus, we can define **natural disasters** as events caused by natural forces that disrupt the communities that they strike (see Figure 7–2 A & B). There are a number of characteristics of these events that distinguish some natural disasters from others, but for now, we will settle on this definition.

Our definition of natural disasters thus includes extreme weather of any kind (heat, cold, hurricanes, tornadoes, blizzards, ice storms, wind storms, monsoons, etc.). Earthquakes and volcanic eruptions, mudslides and avalanches are also natural disasters, but may be affected by human alteration of the earth. Underground bomb testing, for example, could cause many of these events under certain conditions. We also include floods in our definition, even

Figure 7–2 A & B   Destructiveness of a natural event is not the only factor in determining a disaster. Some cause people to be evacuated and can cause great disruption and need.

though these are often caused by a combination of natural events (e.g., rain) and actions taken by people (e.g., improper use of riverbanks). Some floods are almost entirely caused by humans, as in the case of dam failure. These would be more appropriately considered as **technological catastrophes** or mishaps. Other cataclysmic events that are human-made, including mine disasters, air crashes, nuclear accidents, toxic waste contamination, and the like may also be considered technological mishaps.

Research on natural disasters is difficult to conduct for a number of reasons. To start with, these events are almost always studied *after they have already occurred*. As a result, we cannot get information about people before they were exposed to the disaster and, therefore, cannot demonstrate changes in mood and behavior. A second problem is the choice of an appropriate control group. With whom shall we compare our findings about victims of a storm or earthquake? Finally, choosing measures is difficult, because research must often be conducted in recently devastated, often chaotic conditions far from the researcher's laboratory. Obtaining samples of subjects is also problematic, because recruitment for a study often must be done quickly. Many times, one cannot sample randomly and must resort to quasirandom sampling (e.g., selecting every third person on a given street). This may cause the sample to be nonrepresentative of the entire area affected by the mishap and can limit the degree to which we can make general statements about our findings. Despite these methodological problems, research has identified several important characteristics of disasters and has begun to document effects of these events on victims.

Characteristics of Natural Disasters

Partly because of these measurement problems, our understanding of natural disasters is not complete. However, a great many studies of these events have been done, and we have learned a great deal about them. We are now familiar with the basic properties of cataclysmic events such as natural disasters. Because they are *sudden,* they are usually *unpredictable*. We may have some warning—living near a fault tells you that there may be an earthquake there—but it does not tell you when it will occur.

Similarly, living in a "tornado alley" may mean that tornadoes are likely but does not pinpoint the time or place of an individual twister. Weather alerts often provide warning of imminent tornadoes, but do not specify exactly where the funnel will touch down. These reports can provide adequate warning of some storms and floods, but often do not. Natural disasters are generally not well predicted and are typically viewed as *uncontrollable*.

The *destructive* power of a natural disaster is sometimes enormous and usually substantial. In other words, they usually do damage and sometimes wreak havoc. The sheer magnitude of some disasters makes them unique among stressors. Anyone who has ever lived through a fierce hurricane or tornado can attest to this. Natural disasters are usually *acute,* as they often last only seconds or minutes and rarely persist for more than a few days. Heat waves and cold spells may persist longer, but most storms, quakes, and other mishaps are over quickly. Once the crisis has passed, coping can proceed, and rebuilding and recovery can be achieved. Usually, this coping requires a great deal of effort.

Of these characteristics of disasters, which are most important in determining how people will react? There is no easy way to answer this question, particularly because not all disasters share all of these features. Some may be sudden, some more drawn out. Some may cause destruction, others may not. Is it possible to identify characteristics that will allow us to predict whether a disaster will have major effects? **Event duration**—how long the disaster event affects people or how long it is physically present—is one important variable (e.g., Bolin, 1985; Davidson & Baum, 1986). Consider the possible effects of varying speeds with which disasters strike and subside: Some, like tornadoes, strike quickly and disappear almost as quickly as they appeared. Others are slower to develop and take longer to recede, as in the case of many floods. Which is worse? Baum, Fleming, and Davidson (1983) introduced the idea of a **low point** to try to address this question. The point at which a disaster no longer poses any direct threat, at which "the worst is over" and recovery may proceed, is called the low point. Some disasters have very clearly defined low points. When a tornado strikes, it does its damage and leaves. From this point on, the trend is toward improvement of conditions as recovery efforts restore community services, rescue victims, rebuild homes, and so on. However, other disasters may have low points that are not easily seen, dragging out the duration of the disaster. Earthquakes may be followed by tremors that may obscure the fact that the major damage has already occurred, and longer disasters, such as the crippling droughts of 1987 and 1988, may never seem to "hit bottom," as things just keep getting worse. Clearly, the duration and intensity of disasters are important, and the low point may provide a way of looking at them that taps into several aspects of these stressors.

Another characteristic of a disaster situation that appears to affect whether it has severe consequences is whether people had adequate *warning* of the storm, quake, or other disturbance. Fritz and Marks (1954) suggested that a lack of warning can increase the consequences of a disaster. However, being warned of a disaster does not ensure minimization of consequences, as the effectiveness of the warning system, the preparedness of a community, and other factors affect usefulness of alerting news. This was shown in a study of response to warnings of a flash flood (Drabek & Stephenson, 1971). The effectiveness of repeated warnings in getting people to evacuate was undermined by several factors. First, when families were separated at the time of the warning, they showed more concern about finding each other than with evacuation. Unless a direct order to evacuate was given, people first sought confirmation of the danger and the need to leave. Further, though the news media actually notified the most people, it was the least effective in producing appropriate responses.

One can easily think of instances in which warnings and evacuations cause problems all by themselves. Say you are living in a coastal area and a hurricane warning is issued. All people living in a particular area are advised to leave their homes and move to higher ground for the storm. Clearly, some people will ignore these warnings, but many will heed them. Without adequate planning, roads may become jammed and people may not know where to go. Some people panic as they are stuck in traffic, others become belligerent because evacuation is taking so long, and still others may worry about their unprotected homes. Even if the hurricane turns and heads back out to sea, sparing the community, it has caused a great deal of disruption because people responded to warnings but the plans for evacuation were not clearly drawn.

Natural disasters, then, have a number of important characteristics. They are sudden, powerful, and uncontrollable, cause destruction and/or disruption, are usually relatively brief in duration, have low points, and sometimes may be predicted. How perception of these characteristic features contributes to the ways in which disasters affect people is the topic of the next sections (Figure 7–3).

Perception of Natural Hazards

At the beginning of this chapter we discussed the fact that people might not be able to discern accurately how much risk is posed by various hazards. To some extent this is due to the dramatic nature of some hazards. Natural disasters are more dramatic than other hazards such as air pollution, and this may lead some people to assume they are riskier and more hazardous.

Figure 7–3   Earthquakes are sudden, powerful, and uncontrollable events that can cause destruction and disruption of daily life. When they do, they are usually considered disasters.

Which factors influence whether individuals are aware of the potential consequences of becoming hazard victims? We will discuss several factors that researchers have found to be important in hazard perception (for more detailed reviews of factors involved in the perception of hazards, the reader should see Burton & Kates, 1964; Burton, Kates, & White, 1968; Kates, 1976; Saarinen, 1969). Among these factors are the crisis effect, the levee effect, and adaptation.

The **crisis effect** refers to the fact that awareness of or attention to a disaster is greatest during and immediately following its occurrence, but greatly dissipates between disasters. Flood warnings, for example, may be largely ignored until there is a flood. Once the flood

occurs, there may be a rush to study the problem, together with the implementation of some public works program. Efforts to prevent the next disaster, however, frequently disappear after this initial rush of activity. The same principle holds for droughts: We tend to take strong water conservation measures only when the drought arrives. We do not practice stringent measures between droughts, and we do not limit population in areas that are drought-prone so that there is more water available in time of drought.

While this may operate at a societal level, the consequences of the crisis effect are also important for the individual. A good example of this is how we responded to the oil shortages of the 1970s. After waiting in long lines for gasoline, people became very conservation-minded, bought small economy cars, and so on. Now, years later, we have an oil glut, and though at a societal level some conservation efforts persist (e.g., more mileage-conscious drivers in smaller, more fuel-efficient cars), as individuals we have largely forgotten about the problem. The next round of shortages may change that.

The **levee effect** pertains to the fact that once measures are taken to prevent a disaster, people tend to settle in and around the protective mechanism. Levees are built to keep floodwaters where they belong and out of populated areas. After a levee is built, however, houses and factories are constructed on what was once considered to be a dangerous floodplain. People seem to be lulled into thinking the levee will protect them from all future floods. Unfortunately, levees are built with projected figures for floodwaters in mind, and projections often go wrong. Many communities along the Mississippi River are testimony to this fact. The levee effect also applies to such preventive measures as breakwaters along coasts and reservoirs in drought-prone areas: Once they are built, people flock to settle nearby.

A third factor involved in hazard perception is *adaptation*. Just as we adapt or habituate to a noise or odor, so, too, do we adapt to threats of disaster. Apparently, we can hear so much about a hazard that it no longer frightens us. Large populations in earthquake-prone regions of the world such as California, Iran, Japan, and parts of China attest to this adaptation phenomenon. Floods, mine disasters, and hurricanes follow the same principle: People in the area "learn to live with it." In learning to live with it, they generally discount the possibility that they themselves might become victims (e.g., Kates, 1976).

Several variables appear to influence adaptation to potential hazards. For one thing, when the hazard is closely related to the well-being or resource use of a community, the inhabitants are more aware of the danger. Individuals whose businesses depend on coastal tourist industries, for example, may take more precautions against hurricane damage than residents whose well-being does not depend on the tourist industry. Farmers are much more aware of the drought hazards than are nonfarmers in the area. Ski resort operators are probably also more likely to be aware of drought hazards, and people with lung diseases are more sensitive to air pollution than those with healthy lungs. Thus, if one's well-being is closely related to the resource that poses a hazard, one is less likely to adapt in perceiving the hazard.

Personality variables may also affect how we perceive hazards, or at least what we do once they are perceived. Sims and Baumann (1972) noted that although the heaviest concentration of tornadoes is in the Midwest, most tornado-related deaths occur in the South. After eliminating natural explanations for this phenomenon, such as stronger storms or higher concentrations of population in the South, the researchers suggested that there might be regional differences in subjective perception of danger and, thus, less preparation for disaster by southerners. The researchers found that such differences related to the personality dimension of internal–external locus of control. "Internals" believe they are in control of their own fate whereas "externals" believe outside forces, such as powerful persons, government, God, or fate control their destinies (Rotter, 1966). In interviewing residents of Illinois and Alabama, Sims and Baumann found that the Illinois residents felt luck had far less to do with their fate than Alabama residents did. Furthermore, Illinois residents appeared to take more precautions when storms approached, such as listening for weather bulletins and warning neighbors, whereas Alabama residents paid less attention to the need to listen to radio or TV bulletins. Apparently then, personality plays some major role in determining humans' perceptions of their control over hazards.

In another study of flood victims in Carman, Manitoba, Canada, it was found that another personality characteristic was associated with efforts to minimize flood damage, such as through elevating houses, installing sump pumps, and purchasing insurance (Simpson-Housley, et al., 1982). Individuals of this personality type are known as "repressers" and tend to deal with threat by denying the existence of the threat and not verbalizing uneasy feelings about a potential danger. Although intuitively it seems odd that such individuals would be the ones to take more precautions against disaster, perhaps by doing so they feel they are in a better position to deny or avoid disaster if damage does occur in an area. Whatever the case, it does appear that personality plays a role in determining humans' perception of their control over hazards (see also Hanson, Vitek, & Hanson, 1979; Jackson, 1981; Payne & Pigram, 1981; Shippee, Burroughs, & Wakefield, 1980).

Effects of Natural Disasters

Research has produced varying findings about how disasters affect behavior and mental health. Some studies suggest that disasters result in profound disturbance and stress that may lead to continuing emotional problems, whereas other studies suggest that psychological effects are acute and dissipate rapidly after the danger has passed. Although conclusions based on studies of disasters are limited by many methodological problems, one can generally conclude that *chronic stress or psychiatric impairment due to natural disasters is rare* and may be limited to those victims with prior histories of psychological problems (e.g., Kardiner, et al., 1945). During the actual precipitating event (i.e., the storm or earthquake that causes the disaster) behavior may be dramatically affected, but the negative effects that many of us expect to appear once the danger has passed are far less common than many people think. In fact, some studies have found that overall effects of disaster may be positive, because of increased social cohesiveness as victims band together in local groups and help others cope.

Obviously, the rational response to an oncoming disaster is to run and hide—to take shelter and other precautions to adequately protect life and property. However, we do not always have enough warning to do that, and even when warnings are issued, protective behavior is not always the first thing people do. Some want to be spectators. Along the east coast of the U.S., when hurricanes are approaching, people go out to "see" them hit. Hurricane parties are not uncommon in areas where these storms strike. However, not everyone wants to watch the raw power of nature at its most destructive, and response to natural disasters ranges from well-planned emergency behavior to random, nonproductive activity (Figure 7–4).

One thing people do not do very often is panic in the face of a natural disaster (e.g., Quarantelli & Dynes, 1972). The immediate response by some is withdrawal, and many people at first appear to be stunned after a disaster has struck. Menniger (1952) reported that these responses included apathy, disbelief, grief, and a desire to talk about the experience with others. Some negative behavior has been noted. For example, after the earthquake that destroyed large parts of Managua, Nicaragua, in 1972, looting was widespread, even while some survivors made efforts to rescue others, put out fires, and so on (Kates et al., 1973). Studies have also shown more positive response to disaster. For example, Bowman (1964) observed the behavior of mental patients after a massive earthquake near Anchorage, Alaska, on Good Friday, 1964. The patients' initial response was positive: wanting to help with problems that arose. They showed "a stimulation of all personnel, a feeling of unity, a desire to be helpful, and a degree of cooperation which I only wish it were possible to have at all times" (p. 314).

Disasters disrupt organizations and communities as well as families and individuals, and the functions once performed by larger groups may be done by small groups of victims. One of the most serious problems in disasters is coor-

Figure 7-4 Nature can cause many disasters, but some, such as aircraft disasters, often are human-caused.

dination of various relief efforts. Despite the need for coordination in successful disaster management, large organizations are often hesitant to assume responsibility. This reluctance can promote the emergence of cohesive local groups who must assume responsibility for things not being done by formal organizations. A lapse of authority also contributes to the development of these groups. Positive social response during or immediately after a disaster event also appears to be influenced by the needs of the community. When destruction is so vast that rescue teams and official relief efforts cannot cover all needs, locally based groups may fill the void (Figure 7-5).

Most of the effects of disaster that we have considered so far are more or less immediate reactions—how people feel and what they do

as a disaster strikes and just after it has passed. Other researchers have been interested primarily in the lasting effects of disaster beyond the impact and recovery periods. Most studies of these effects of disasters have used psychiatric interviews of selected groups of survivors. As a result, most findings are expressed as frequency of certain psychiatric problems, and for the most part, anxiety, depression, and other stress-related emotional disturbances have been found among victims of floods, tornadoes, hurricanes, and other natural disasters (Logue, Hanson, & Struening, 1979; Milne, 1977; Moore, 1958; Penick, Powell, & Sieck, 1976; Taylor & Quarantelli, 1976). These effects have been found to last as long as a year, but often do not last nearly that long. Further, they are not nearly as widespread among victims as one

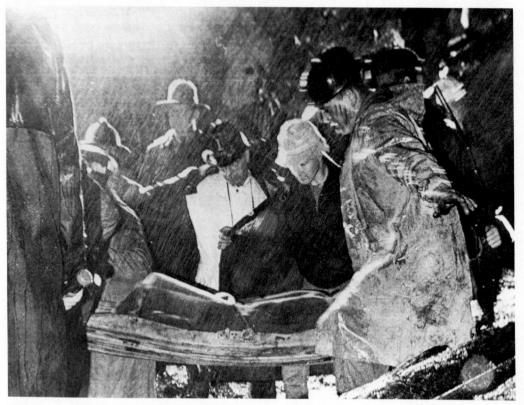

Figure 7–5 Rescue groups and other local groups may emerge in the face of disaster, as is common following coal mine disasters.

might expect. Studies rarely show more than 25 to 30 percent of victims suffering psychological effects months after a disaster, and it appears that people who lost most in the disaster are those who continue to suffer (e.g., Parker, 1977). In other words, it may be more accurate to conclude that the loss of a home or a loved one in a disaster leads to psychological problems than to say that natural disasters cause lasting problems.

This conclusion is consistent with research by Erikson (1976) who suggested that many of the symptoms of disaster survivors arise from the destruction of the community. Disorientation and ''lack of connection'' are common symptoms among disaster survivors when the community has been torn. Older people may emphasize the loss of items that symbolize their lifetimes—a tree or a garden, for example. Children take their cues from their parents (Crawshaw, 1963) and respond to their parents' fear or lack of it. When they are exposed directly to environmental disruption, they react strongly to scenes of death and mutilation (Newman, 1976). They may also regress to earlier stages of behavior.

As we noted earlier, stress formulations as well as other theories or approaches to the study of environmental events can be used to understand the phenomena we will describe in this chapter. Destruction of a community can involve *behavioral constraint*, as options for activity are reduced and behavioral freedom is limited. People may be forced to leave their homes and move to large shelters where behavior must conform to emergency rules. Water and power service may be disrupted, further limiting what people can do, and plans are unavoidably changed by the sudden impact of the event. When our behavior is constrained, we may react negatively to the loss of freedom, feel bad, and act in ways to re-establish our freedom. Continuous constraints on our behavior that cannot be removed may eventually cause us to experience helplessness. Fortunately, once the emergency is past, constraints are reduced—people may return to their homes and normal services are restored. However, for those who are made homeless or that have lost a family member or close friend, constraints and their negative effects may continue. Rebuilding or relocating is necessitated, and choices of activities are further limited by losses and the need to cope with them.

In communities that have lost many people in a disaster, *ecological* perspectives may help to explain the effects of the event. You will recall that *staffing* refers to the number of people in a setting. Over– and understaffing, in which too many or too few people are present in the setting, are viewed as negative states that cause problems. Communities are settings, and there are roles that must be played in them. When a large number of the members of the community suddenly die, the community may become understaffed, and those remaining are forced to assume multiple roles. This can cause strain and, coupled with problems caused directly by specific losses, can help to explain the effects of disaster. However, understaffing can also increase cohesiveness among those left, producing positive effects.

Summary

Natural disasters, then, can affect people in a number of ways. They are clearly stressful, limit freedom and behavioral options, and may cause a shortage of people, leading to the breakdown or disruption of a community. People seem able to cope with disasters, and serious long-term effects of disasters are not extensive. In many ways, these events are similar to disasters caused by human-made parts of the environment. Disasters involving failure of the things we have built, such as dams, bridges, power plants, and mines, also appear to be stressful.

TECHNOLOGICAL CATASTROPHE

To a large extent our dominance of the natural environment and our adaptation to its hazards has been achieved through advances in technology. Improvements in the quality of life, prolongation of life, mastery over disease, and the like are based on a broad technological network we have created. These machines, structures, and other human-created additions to our environment share unparalleled responsibility for supporting our way of life. For the most part, they accomplish this goal and work well under human control. However, this network occasionally fails, and something goes wrong. Hence we have blackouts of major cities, leakage of toxic chemicals from waste dumps, dam failures, and bridge collapses.

Research on human-made disasters shares the same problem as does work on natural disasters. However, many of the characteristics of these catastrophes appear to differ from those of natural disasters, and the effects of being in one may differ as well. We will first consider the characteristics of technological catastrophes, comparing them to natural events, and then discuss their effects.

Characteristics of Technological Catastrophe

What are the differences between these catastrophes and the natural disasters we have already discussed? For one thing, they are *human-made*. They are not the product of natural forces, but rather are caused either by human error or miscalculation, as some part of our extensive technological net fails. *Duration of technological accidents is variable.* They may be acute and very sudden, as in the case of a dam failure or blackout. When a dam fails, the resulting wave of water assumes most of the characteristics of a natural disaster, striking swiftly and continuing on its way. Major power failures can plunge entire cities into darkness in a matter of minutes, but are quickly fixed. These technological mishaps are usually brief, and the worst is soon over. However, other technological catastrophes are more chronic and *may not have clear low points.* The discovery of contamination at Love Canal began a chronic period of distress for area residents, as did the nuclear accident at Three Mile Island. In both of these cases, sources of threat (toxic contamination and radioactive waste) remained for many years, and required long-term coping with these threats. For people affected by these events, the worst was not over quickly, nor was the point at which things began to improve easily identified. A great deal of uncertainty can accompany such events.

Interestingly, technological catastrophes may be more apt to threaten our feelings of control than are natural disasters. This is somewhat paradoxical, since natural disasters are inherently uncontrollable and we never really expect to be able to control their occurrence. Technological catastrophes, on the other hand, are the effects of an occasional loss of control over something we normally control quite well. If this loss of control is intermittent, temporary, and not indicative of an entire collapse, why is it so disquieting?

It is possible that because technological catastrophes are losses of control we are supposed to have, they shake our confidence in our ability to control events in the future. These events are never *supposed* to happen—technological devices are designed never to fail unpredictably, and to warn us when they are worn out. Thus, nuclear power plants are not supposed to have accidents *ever* and toxic waste dumps are not supposed to leak. But these things do happen, and often appear to strike at random. Instead of saying, "No accidents will happen," we may often find ourselves wondering, "Where will the next explosion occur?" "Which plane will crash?" "Which waste dump will leak?" and so on. While the above analysis is somewhat speculative, it provides some feel for the complexities of people's responses to technological catastrophes. These kinds of events can reduce general perceptions of control and lead to stress (Davidson, Baum, & Collins, 1982).

While natural disasters often cause a great deal of destruction, human-made catastrophes are often characterized by a lack of visible destruction. Natural disasters are more familiar to us, occurring at fairly regular rates around the world in almost predictable ways. The chances are that during some seasons in some regions, tornadoes are likely and that at other times, in other areas, hurricanes are likely. Natural disasters also begin very quickly and, to some extent, can be forecast. They are powerful, among the most threatening stressors we know about, and pass fairly quickly. Once they pass, rebuilding and recovery can begin, and once these are complete, a sense of closure may be gained.

Technological disasters are not always destructive. These events are less familiar to us, they seem to occur less often, but are potentially more widespread. Natural disasters are selective in where they occur; hurricanes tend to be coastal, affecting the eastern and southeastern U.S. more than the Great Plains, while the converse is true of tornadoes. Technological accidents are not predictable at all: One cannot forecast the breakdown of something that is never supposed to break down in the same way as one can forecast a storm. The onset of technological catastrophes is usually sudden, with little warning. The speed with which these events unfold often makes them difficult to avoid. As was the case at Buffalo Creek, those in the path of a flood following a dam break have little time to get to safety.

Some technological mishaps, such as factory explosions, train accidents, and mine accidents, have a well-defined low point. In these cases, coping with the disaster may be similar to that of natural disaster recovery. However, it appears that some of the most powerful technological disasters may also be those without a clear low point. For example, situations in which individuals believe that they have been

exposed to toxic chemicals or radiation (e.g., Love Canal and TMI) involve long-term consequences connected with the development of disease many years after exposure. There may be considerable uncertainty about this, and for some technological disasters there is no clear low point from which things will gradually get better. The worst may be over, or it may yet surface. Thus it could be difficult for some persons to return to normal lives after the accident has ended (Figure 7–6).

Another possible difference between natural and human-made disasters is the nature of the post-disaster community response. As we have noted, several studies have found that positive as well as negative effects of disasters are apparent, that social cohesiveness or feelings of social bonds may be stronger afterwards (e.g., Barton, 1969; Cuthbertson & Nigg, 1987; Fritz, 1961). Following natural disasters, these social changes may provide a crucial resource in aiding recovery from loss and disruption.

While these developments do not occur in all areas affected by natural disasters, they are

Figure 7–6 Like other technological mishaps, the accident of Three Mile Island has had long-lasting effects. (Marc A. Schaeffer)

noted often enough to be considered a possible outcome of a natural disaster. But what about human-made disasters? Are the same changes likely after a human-made accident or hazard has occurred? Anecdotal evidence suggests that controversy and conflict among neighbors may be equally likely, leading one to question the post-impact similarities between natural and technological catastrophes.

Cuthbertson and Nigg (1987) studied two human-made disasters to determine whether socially supportive **post-disaster groups** developed in their wake. One involved asbestos contamination at a trailer park, the other spraying of pesticides near residential areas. In both cases, victims included those who were worried about having been exposed to toxic substances (the asbestos and pesticide) and those who thought the exposures were nothing to worry about. Their difference of opinion, common following events involving questionable toxic exposures with long-term, uncertain effects, was the basis for conflict and disagreement among neighbors. Just as at Three Mile Island, where some are strongly opposed to nuclear energy and the TMI plant while others are strongly in favor, those who were worried and those who were not were in conflict. Cuthbertson and Nigg (1987) found evidence of anger, frustration, resentment, helplessness, defensiveness, and a polarization of attitudes about the hazards, and did not find any evidence of the development of supportive, cohesive groups.

While similar in many ways, technological and natural disasters do appear to be different. It is likely that these differences are partially responsible for the greater preponderance of chronic distress among victims of technological accidents that are discussed in the next section.

Effects of Technological Disasters

In many ways, the effects of human-made disasters are similar to those of natural disasters. This is particularly true when technologi-

cal catastrophes are like natural ones in duration, suddenness, and so on. Thus, when Fritz and Marks (1954) studied several human-made accidents, including an air disaster in which a plane plunged into a crowd of air show spectators, they found the same types of responses that have been found in studies of natural disasters. Panic did not often occur, and when it did, it was usually seen as an attempt to escape immediate threat. Less than 10 percent of victims interviewed reported that they felt they were "out of control" during the disaster, and while many were confused and disoriented, others behaved in constructive, "rational" ways.

It is likely that the similarities in response to natural and technological mishaps are fewer when the impact of the technological stressor is longer lasting. When people are told that they have been exposed to toxic chemicals or believe that they have been irradiated, the perceived threat to life and limb may be no less than when a plane is about to crash into a crowd. Clearly, it is less intense, partly because it is longer lasting and usually slower to unfold. Unlike an air crash, where one might have a minute or two at most to decide what to do, people exposed to toxic hazards may have months or years to think about what is happening. Weil and Dunsworth (1958) observed the reacitons of townspeople to a coal mine cave-in at Springhill, Nova Scotia. While rescue efforts were in progress, there was some panic, grief, and anxiety, punctuated by mood swings to euphoria when some miners were rescued, but after rescue efforts had ceased, response appeared more suppressed. Long-term response to technological catastrophes has not been studied as much as has acute response to either type of disaster, and more research is needed.

It has been argued that the consequences of technological catastrophes are more severe, complex, and/or longer-lasting than those caused by natural disasters (Baum, Fleming, & Davidson, 1983; Gleser, Green, & Winget, 1981). Adler (1943) reported on the effects of a

Scapegoats and Disasters

Rumors during and after disasters can develop around who or what was to blame. One pattern is to project blame for disasters onto targets that are not really responsible, rather than to blame those directly involved (Drabek & Quarantelli, 1967). For example, there is a tendency to generalize blame to "big shots" who are in charge of large organizations or who are known to be wealthy and influential. A construction failure in a city is more likely to be blamed on City Hall than on the inspector who worked on that particular project. There is also reluctance to blame the dead following a disaster. A race driver who lost control of his car and died along with several spectators is later regarded as a hero for keeping his car from colliding with other cars on the track.

Drabek and Quarantelli report that one counterproductive outcome of scapegoating is to focus attention on personalities rather than causes. Another is to delay or completely halt changes in municipal codes, disaster planning, and other direct actions designed to prevent or at least control future disasters.

---

human-caused fire at the Coconut Grove night-club in Boston. The fire killed 491 patrons of the club and was characterized by great terror. More than half of the survivors developed psychiatric symptoms such as anxiety, guilt, nightmares, and fear a year after the fire. Interestingly, of those who *did not* develop psychiatric problems, 75 percent had lost consciousness during the fire, most remaining unconscious for more than an hour. Of those who *did* exhibit psychological difficulties, only half lost consciousness, mostly for less than an hour. Remaining conscious through the fire appeared to contribute to emotional distress. Unconsciousness, and therefore less exposure to the terror and horror during the fire, was associated with more positive psychiatric outcomes.

A number of different human-made disasters have been studied, though in many cases there were so few survivors that sample sizes were very small. Leopold and Dillon (1963) reported on a four-year study of victims of a collision between two ships. They found evidence of fairly severe work-related problems and persistent psychiatric distress in more than three-quarters of the survivors. Panic did not occur, but mood disturbances increased over time, and psychosomatic disorders were reported. Henderson and Bostock (1977) interviewed all seven survivors of a shipwreck one or two years afterwards, finding 71 percent with psychological disturbances. Ploeger (1972), in a 10-year study of miners surviving a cave-in, also noted long-term distress. Studies of flooding caused by a dam break at Buffalo Creek have also revealed long-term psychological distress among victims (see box, page 207).

In addition to causing distress, technological catastrophes also involve processes related to the other theoretical orientations discussed in Chapter 4. With few exceptions, technological mishaps lead to behavioral constraint, loss of control, and the problems associated with these states. Evacuation, whether temporary or more permanent, disrupts and limits what we can do. People may find it more difficult to sell their homes if they live near a damaged reactor or hazardous waste site and thus may be limited in their freedom to move. At Buffalo Creek, the destruction of almost everything in the valley also severely limited what people could do, and

The Buffalo Creek Flood

Perhaps the most intensively studied disaster with a human cause is the dam break and flood at Buffalo Creek in West Virginia. On February 26, 1972, a dam constructed by a mining company, which had been dumping coal slag in the creek, gave way and unleashed a wave of millions of gallons of water. The flood washed away houses, automobiles, and everything else in its path, careening off the walls of the valley and killing 125 people. When the wave finally spent its rage and drained into a river at the foot of the valley, it left behind a scene of death and devastation. Five thousand were left homeless, and the valley was disfigured and permanently altered.

The Buffalo Creek flood was clearly due to failure of a human-made device— the dam holding back the creek. As with other technological mishaps, the flood was never supposed to happen. As a result, it was even less predictable than the storms that had swollen the creek behind the dam. And, as we have suggested, this disaster, partly because of its human origins, appears to have had more chronic effects on the victims than ordinary floods or natural disasters. While many of the specific effects are similar to those observed in studies of natural disaster, they seem to have had more lasting consequences.

Research at Buffalo Creek has identified a number of problems occurring as late as two years after the flood. Among these are:

1. *Anxiety.* Fears about the disaster and about the changes in life style that came in its aftermath were common (Gleser, Green & Winget, 1981; Lifton & Olson, 1976; Titchener & Knapp, 1976).

2. *Withdrawal or numbness.* Almost all researchers at Buffalo Creek noted apathy and blunted emotion after the flood (Erikson, 1976; Lifton & Olson, 1976; Rangell, 1976).

3. *Depression.* Many survivors lost everything they had worked a lifetime for and became sad and subdued (Kilijanek & Drabek, 1979; Titchener & Kapp, 1976).

4. *Stress-related physical symptoms.* Almost all somatic or bodily symptoms, including gastrointestinal distress, aches and pains, and so on, were increased (Titchener & Kapp, 1976).

5. *Unfocused anger.* Survivors found themselves angry and upset. When disasters are human-made, the rage tends to be worse. This is due, in part, to the fact that although there was a culpable agent, identification of a specific person to blame was difficult (Gleser, Green & Winget, 1981; Hargreaves, 1980; Lifton & Olson, 1976).

6. *Regression.* Children often regressed to earlier stages of behavior (Newman, 1976; Titchener & Kapp, 1976).

7. *Nightmares.* Dreams about dying in the disaster and about dead relatives occurred frequently. Sleep disturbances were common as well (Gleser, Green, & Winget, 1981; Newman, 1976).

Titchener and Kapp (1976) noted that traumatic neurosis was evident in more than 80 percent of the sample they studied. Anxiety, depression, character and lifestyle changes, and maladjustments and developmental problems in children occurred in more than 90 percent of the cases. Anxiety, grief, despair, sleep disturbances, disorganization, problems with temper control, obsessions and phobias about survival guilt, a sense of loss, and rage were some of the symptoms. Lifton and Olson (1976) listed several characteristics of the flood at Buffalo Creek that intensified the reactions to it: the suddenness, the human-cause factor, the isolation of the area, and the destruction of the community. Survivors were aware of the symptoms. They were surprised at how long they had survived and afraid that recovery was impossible (Lifton & Olson, 1976).

There are many reasons why the Buffalo Creek flood appears to have caused more extensive longer-lasting psychological distress than do most floods. The human cause is but one of these, focusing anger on the mining company and affecting the ways in which the disaster was experienced. In addition, the flood was unusually severe, washing away an entire community and causing immense destruction. Recovery was inhibited by delays in removing debris, and it was weeks before homeless survivors were provided with a temporary home. Trailers, brought in to house victims, were not assigned so as to allow friends and family to live together, further disrupting the sense of community that had characterized the valley. All of these factors are likely contributors to the enduring effects of this disaster.

. . . .

required almost complete attention to a circumscribed set of recovery options. People could, for example, rebuild their homes and places of business, move to a "safer" nearby area, or "call it quits" and leave altogether. Very few realistic options may be available following such an event.

Staffing levels may become important when a community loses many members, but for some technological catastrophes this is not the case. At TMI, the number of people living in the community has not been drastically reduced, while in the Buffalo Creek flood, many people died. Staffing theory will provide useful predictions primarily when losses have occurred.

The Three Mile Island Accident   Research at Three Mile Island (TMI) illustrates the kinds of effects that can occur over a long period of time following a technological catastrophe. In March 1979, an accident occurred in Unit 2 at the TMI nuclear power station. Through a number of equipment failures and human errors (see Chapter 13), the core of the reactor was exposed, generating tremendous temperatures. The fuel and equipment inside the reactor was damaged, and by the time the reactor was brought back under control, some 400,000 gallons of radioactive water had collected on the floor of the reactor building. In addition, radioactive gases were released and remained trapped in the concrete containment surrounding the reactor.

During the crisis, which lasted several days, there were a number of scares. Some people feared a nuclear explosion, others a meltdown, and still others feared massive radiation releases. Information intended to reduce fears often increased them because it was contradictory or inconsistent with other information that had been released. An evacuation was advised, and this probably contributed to the chaos and fear of the moment (Figure 7–7).

There is little doubt that the accident at TMI caused stress. During the crisis period there was

Figure 7–7   The fear that one has been exposed to radiation or toxic substances appears to be associated with chronic stress. Do you think seeing this sight in your backyard would cause you alarm?

a good probability that threat appraisal would occur; research suggests that most people living near the plant were threatened and concerned about it (Flynn, 1979; Houts et al., 1980). Immediately after the accident, studies found greater psychological and emotional distress among nearby residents than among people living elsewhere (Bromet, 1980; Dohrenwend et al., 1979; Flynn, 1979; Houts et al., 1980).

Despite the fact that the severe threats associated with the accident disappeared relatively quickly, it does not appear that the kind of recovery that characterizes the aftermath of many natural disasters followed at TMI. The potential danger of radiation release remained

long after the reactor was brought under control. The radioactive gas remained trapped in the containment building for more than a year after the accident. For some area residents the potential for exposure from this source remained a threat, due to occasional leaks of small amounts of the gas. Approximately 15 months after the accident, this gas was released in controlled bursts into the atmosphere around the plant. The radioactive water remained in the reactor building and decontamination of the reactor required many years.

Research on the chronic effects of living near TMI is still ongoing, but there is evidence that stress effects persisted among some area residents up to two years after the accident. Bromet (1980), for example, has reported evidence of emotional distress among young mothers living near TMI. A series of studies has also identified stress effects among some TMI area residents 15 to 22 months after the accident (Baum, Fleming, & Davidson, 1983; Gatchel, Schaeffer, & Baum, 1985). More recent studies suggest a persistence of symptoms, of sleep-related difficulties, and of stress up to five years after the accident (Davidson & Baum, 1986; Davidson, Fleming, & Baum, 1987). People living near the damaged TMI reactor reported more bothersome symptoms, were more easily awakened at night, and took longer to fall back to sleep than did control subjects (see Table 7–1. Interestingly, urinary norepinephrine levels were higher both while subjects were awake and asleep among TMI area residents, and while controls showed normal differences between sleeping and waking levels, TMI area subjects did not (Davidson, Fleming, & Baum, 1987). Though the intensity of this chronic stress appears to be moderate, the fact that it has persisted for so long is unusual.

These studies were conducted with relatively few subjects, but they examined behavioral and physiological aspects of stress as well as self-reported measures. Symptom reporting, task performance, and physiological arousal were measured, the latter by obtaining urine samples from subjects. In general, these studies found that some residents of an area within five miles of the TMI plant reported more emotional and psychological distress, more somatic distress, showed greater stress-related task performance problems, and exhibited higher levels of physiological arousal than did control subjects. Though levels of these variables did not indicate severe stress, they did suggest chronic, moderate magnitude difficulties. Control subjects lived near an undamaged nuclear plant, a coal power plant, or near no plant at all, and all of them lived more than 80 miles from TMI.

These studies also reported effects of several variables that we have considered as influencing stress. Not all TMI residents seemed to be stressed. Fleming et al. (1982) found that TMI area residents who reported having little or no social support exhibited greater evidence of stress than did those who had a great deal of support. Differences along coping style dimensions were also found. TMI area residents who were more concerned with palliative coping (managing their emotional response) showed fewer stress symptoms than did TMI subjects who were more concerned with taking direct action and manipulating the problem (Collins, Baum, & Singer, 1983). Finally, the continued uncertainty at TMI appears to have suppressed feelings of personal control among TMI area residents, and those who reported the least confidence in their ability to control their surroundings exhibited more symptoms of stress than did residents who were more confident (Davidson, Baum, & Collins, 1982).

Clearly, not all technological catastrophes are like these. For a number of reasons, each accident or failure has unique aspects to it. These studies illustrate the potential for acute and chronic consequences from technological catastrophes. In many cases (e.g., power blackouts) the problems are far less serious and consequences more transient.

There is another factor that probably contributes to the problem at TMI, but which has not yet been formally discussed. The accident at TMI involved a toxic substance, radiation, and it is likely that toxic hazards or accidents pose serious threat to perceived health and well-being. Since many modern-day technological mishaps involve toxic substances, it is difficult to know how much this factor contributes to the development of chronic stress. However, the widespread occurrence of toxic hazards and the suggestion that such accidents cause serious problems for victims is cause to consider these hazards in the next section.

EFFECTS OF TOXIC EXPOSURE

We know that toxic substances such as radiation, dioxin, and chemical wastes can cause physical health problems, but we are not as well informed about how people respond to known exposure. How do people feel when they believe that they have been exposed to toxic substances and what do they do? Can psychological reactions be understood in terms of beliefs about the toxicity of the substances? What is it about these substances that evokes strong reactions in most of us? Why does exposure to toxic substances as a result of accidents or leaks seem to arouse greater response than toxic exposure that results from air or water pollution?

Consider the case of radiation. Experts argue about what levels of exposure are dangerous (of course, at very high levels of exposure people die, but the consequences of long-term, low-level exposure are debated). The possibility of

Table 7–1 *Persistence of Stress at Three Mile Island Three Years after the Accident*					
Group	*Total number of symptoms reported*	*Being awakened at night (1–7 scale)*	*Time to fall back asleep (minutes)*	*Urinary Norepinephrine (mg/ml)*	
				Awake	*Asleep*
TMI	32	3.7	18.0	31.3	35.9
Control	17	2.5	6.3	18.5	13.8

being exposed to radiation evokes strong emotional responses in many of us, and we tend to view nuclear power plants as more risky than do experts (Slovic, Fischoff, & Lichtenstein, 1981). In part this is due to the dramatic nature of the nuclear accidents that have occurred. The invisible threat posed by radiation and the possibility of being exposed to it without even knowing it add to the threat. Finally, the effects of radiation may take many years before they can be detected. Cancers and birth defects, two possible consequences of exposure to radiation and to many toxic chemicals, take years to develop or become evident. Long after TMI, Chernobyl, or Love Canal, concerns about possible future exposure may be compounded by worry and fear about effects that have already been set in motion (Figure 7–6, 7–7).

The belief that one has been exposed to toxic substances, regardless of whether one has actually been exposed, seems to be sufficient to cause stress reactions. In many cases, the extent of real exposure is unclear, but is generally thought to be low. This was so at TMI where experts indicated that relatively little radiation was released. However, some area residents believe that they were exposed to dangerous levels of radiation, and this may have contributed to chronic stress. The lack of early warning signs of toxicants' effects on health, of clear information about whether one was actually exposed to dangerous levels of the toxic substance, and the severity of the long-term consequences of exposure may contribute to uncertainty and distress. The very *belief* that one has

been exposed to toxic substances may cause long-term uncertainty and stress as well as pose a threat to one's health (Baum, 1987). Like many environmental stressors, however, the extent to which this occurs is determined by a number of situational and psychological factors.

Research has considered two different types of toxic exposure, distinguished by where the exposure occurs. Occupational exposure, as the name suggests, occurs at work. Other types of toxic exposure occur at home or in one's neighborhood. Whether the effects of toxic exposure vary as a function of where it occurs is not known. However, it is clear that exposure to toxic substances in either setting can have substantial effects (Figure 7–8).

Occupational Exposure

One of the sources of toxic exposure that occurs at the worksite is asbestos. Used because of its durability and resistance to heat, asbestos was common in many industries, and it has been estimated that in the past 50 years more than 13 million workers have been exposed to asbestos (Lebovits, Byrne, & Strain, 1986). Some asbestos contamination may be found in schools and old buildings, but for the most part, exposure occurs in occupational settings.

When inhaled, asbestos fibers lodge in the lungs where they may be coated by bodily defenses and left there. These particles can then cause damage to the lungs and cause pulmonary diseases, including lung cancer. Asbestos is a

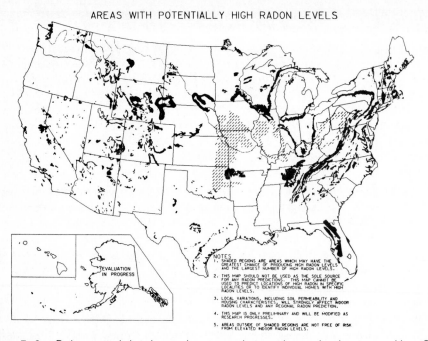

AREAS WITH POTENTIALLY HIGH RADON LEVELS

NOTES
1. SHADED REGIONS ARE AREAS WHICH MAY HAVE THE GREATEST CHANCE OF PRODUCING HIGH RADON LEVELS AND THE LARGEST NUMBER OF HIGH RADON LEVELS.

2. THIS MAP SHOULD NOT BE USED AS THE SOLE SOURCE FOR ANY RADON PREDICTIONS. THIS MAP CANNOT BE USED TO PREDICT LOCATIONS OF HIGH RADON IN SPECIFIC LOCALITES OR TO IDENTIFY INDIVIDUAL HOMES WITH HIGH RADON LEVELS.

3. LOCAL VARIATIONS, INCLUDING SOIL PERMEABILITY AND HOUSING CHARACTERISTICS, WILL STRONGLY AFFECT INDOOR RADON LEVELS AND ANY REGIONAL RADON PREDICTION.

4. THIS MAP IS ONLY PRELIMINARY AND WILL BE MODIFIED AS RESEARCH PROGRESSES.

5. AREAS OUTSIDE OF SHADED REGIONS ARE NOT FREE OF RISK FROM ELEVATED INDOOR RADON LEVELS.

Figure 7–8 Radon, particularly in homes, has emerged as a widespread and serious problem. Occurring naturally, radon is radioactive and thus shares characteristics of many types of hazards.

particularly risky toxicant to people who also smoke cigarettes. Regardless, the diseases and damage caused by asbestos require long periods of time to develop, so that much harm can be done before an individual recognizes that there is anything wrong.

A study of asbestos workers who were first exposed to asbestos at least 20 years before the study provides some insight into reactions to being exposed to this hazard (Lebovits, Byrne, & Strain, 1986). Most had not been aware of the dangers of asbestos when they started working with it, though they had learned of the risks many years earlier than a control group of people who did not work with asbestos. Asbestos workers were also very aware of the consequences of asbestos: Nearly 80 percent of them had known four or more coworkers who had developed asbestos-related illnesses (less than 10 percent of the control subjects knew anyone with such disease). Consequently, asbestos workers reported greater perceived risk

of developing cancer and heart disease than did control subjects (Lebovits, Byrne, & Strain, 1986).

Interestingly, the sample of asbestos workers did not exhibit any more depression, anxiety, or other mental health problems than did control subjects, used mental health services infrequently, and reported comparable perceptions of perceived control as did control group subjects. The asbestos workers also reported that they had not taken preventive precautions, such as wearing masks, visiting their doctor, and so on. A third of them continued to smoke even though they were aware of the special risks of doing so. Apparently denying the risks associated with their occupation and behavior, these workers showed little evidence of distress (Lebovits, Byrne, & Strain, 1986).

Another type of poisoning that often occurs on the job comes from lead exposure. Low-level lead exposure affects the central nervous system and has been associated with anxiety, neuropsychological deficits, and nervous system disorders (e.g., Browder, Joselow, & Louria, 1973; Grandjean, Arnvig, & Beckmann, 1978; Spivey et al., 1979). A recent study by Bromet, Ryan, and Parkinson (1986) found few differences in neuropsychological test scores between a sample of lead-exposed workers and a group of nonexposed control subjects, though they did find that exposed workers were more likely to report conflict in interpersonal relationships. This latter finding is consistent with other findings suggesting that lead poisoning may increase aggression and hostility (Spivey et al., 1979).

Nonoccupational Hazards

Contrary to studies of workers exposed, at least partially with their knowledge and "consent," to hazardous materials, research on toxic exposure in the home and other places suggests that there are a number of consequences of such hazards. The nature of nonoccupational exposures is varied and the dangers many. In addition, people exposed to toxic substances in their homes or neighborhoods appear to show more effects of exposure than do people exposed to hazards at work. For example, Brown and Nixon (1979) studied farmers exposed to polybrominated biphenyls (PBBs) by contaminated feed, and found increased guilt, depressive symptoms, anxiety, and withdrawal. Living near Love Canal and being exposed (or thinking one was exposed) to the toxic waste there appears to have generated fears about developing illnesses while reducing trust in officials responsible for the situation (Gibbs, 1982; Levine, 1982). And, in two studies of two toxic accidents, one involving pesticide exposure and the other toxic smoke from an explosion in a toxic waste facility, (Markowitz & Gutterman, 1986), perceived threat to health was associated with psychological distress.

There are several studies that deal with reactions to living near hazardous toxic waste sites. Love Canal is clearly the most infamous,

and studies of people affected by the situation there suggest some evidence of long-term distress (Levine, 1982). The problems there began when a chemical company dumped thousands of tons of toxic waste in the canal. This land was later sold, and an elementary school was built on the site. A neighborhood of several thousand people grew up around the canal area. About 20 years later, it was discovered that hazardous waste was leaking from the canal, and in 1978 area residents were alerted by state officials (Levine & Stone, 1986). Toxic vapors were detected in some homes, increased miscarriage rates were determined, and offers to move some of the affected residents were announced. The resolution of problems dragged on for years, and the extent of consequences of Love Canal remains to be assessed.

We do know that the Love Canal hazards were stressful for area residents. Of those interviewed in a study reported by Levine and Stone (1986), nearly 90 percent viewed the situation as a problem, and the nature of the problems posed ranged from uncertainty and threat to health, to financial and practical concerns. Residents felt that their health had worsened as a result of living near the canal and reported feelings of lost control and helplessness. Though some positive changes were reported, most evidence suggested a long-term state of distress and worry (Levine & Stone, 1986).

This is consistent with studies of other, less well known toxic waste hazards. Fleming (1985) reported evidence of chronic stress among a group of people living near a toxic waste site rated as one of the 10 most hazardous in the country. Symptoms of trauma were also found among the residents, and the data suggested that the uncertainties surrounding exposure to toxic chemicals were causing people to experience stress (Davidson, Fleming, & Baum, 1986). In another study, this one of people who were using water that had been contaminated by a toxic landfill, chronic stress was once more suggested (Gibbs, 1986). Again, worries and uncertainty about health were prominent, and victims reported high levels of depression, anger, and mistrust.

A relatively "new" hazard that may have severe consequences is **radon,** a colorless, odorless gas that comes from uranium deposits in the ground. It is a naturally-occurring gas, and small exposures are both normal and of little apparent consequence. However, some people's homes have been found to have radon levels far in excess of safe or normal levels, and the health problems that can result from this kind of exposure are extreme. Apparently, radon problems are more widespread than was previously believed, and it has been recommended that everyone test his or her home for radon levels.

Not unexpectedly, people appear to overestimate the risk of radon problems when they do not have dangerous levels in their homes, though when radon is found, risk is underestimated (Sandman, Weinstein, & Klotz, 1987). As with many sources of danger, people's estimates of risk do not correspond to those made by experts. Weinstein's study involved 650 randomly sampled people living in an area in eastern Pennsylvania where some of the highest levels of radon have been measured, called the Reading Prong. Another 140 subjects were sampled in areas of New Jersey where radon had also been found in substantial amounts. Of those surveyed, most knew what radon was but made errors in reporting of health consequences. Most important, the study showed that people experienced uncertainty about their risk for health problems. Some denied the threats posed, using characteristics of radon to excuse not having their homes tested; since radon does not infiltrate all homes on a given street, it is likely that some homes will have high readings while others will not.

The invisible nature of radon makes it like radiation and toxic chemical contamination. Radon does no physical damage and can exist for many years without being detected. However, unlike these other hazards, radon is not human-made but rather is a naturally occurring phenomenon. Thus, it is a natural hazard rather than a technological one, though human factors such as siting and insulation of homes can exacerbate problems (in well-insulated homes, radon may get trapped, and levels may increase due to lack of ventilation; see Chapter 12).

Radon and other toxins that are natural or a by-product of our technology can occur as "silent" hazards for many years. Often, the only way one can detect them is when one starts to experience the symptoms of disease caused by the toxins. However, once people become aware of the possibility of exposure to toxic waste, radiation, radon, and the like, they appear to experience uncertainty, anger, and stress. In many cases, this stress motivates people to take action, either by moving away from the hazard or working to contain it and reduce the threats involved. However, we all live daily with exposure to toxic substances in the air we breathe, and most of us are aware of this fact. Air pollution affords the most widespread possibility of toxic exposure that we know, yet we do not seem to respond to it in the same way as we do to more dramatic toxic hazards.

AIR POLLUTION AND BEHAVIOR

Toxic exposure occurs in many contexts and is not always part of newsworthy events such as a Love Canal. All of us are aware that **air pollution** has become one of the primary environmental problems of the past few decades. Acid rain has become a major issue, as has depletion of the ozone layer of the atmosphere, both threats to our health and well-

Air Pollution:
Then and Now*

Air pollution is not just a modern problem caused by automobiles or factories. Recent evidence uncovered by anthropologists and medical specialists suggests that hundreds of years ago humans may have suffered the side effects of air pollution. The body of an Eskimo woman who apparently died in an earthquake or landslide some 1600 years ago was discovered on Saint Lawrence Island in the Bering Sea in 1972. Because the body must have been frozen shortly after death, medical specialists were able to perform a detailed autopsy; they found that the woman had black lung disease, which resulted form breathing some form of highly polluted air. Experts speculate that years of inhaling fumes from lamps that burned seal oil or whale blubber could cause black lung, a disease frequently found in coal miners. Human beings have been capable of modifying their environments, including the air they breathe, for centuries, and air pollution (caused by people changing the environment around them) may have a long history.

*From Associated Press story in *Rocky Mountain News*, February 12, 1977.

---

being produced by pollution. We know that we are walking around in air that is filled with toxicants, that exhaust gases from automobiles, aerosol spray emissions, factory discharges, gaseous and solid airborne particles from industrial wastes, and even the smoke from forest fires and cozy fireplaces in the home can have seriously adverse effects on health. Among the common pollutants are carbon monoxide, sulfur dioxide, nitrogen dioxide, particulate matter, hydrocarbons, and photochemical pollutants formed from the reaction of other pollutants with light and heat. Fortunately, with increased social consciousness and passage of such legislation as the Clean Air Act, we are well on our way to reducing many types of air pollution. Nevertheless, the air is still being contaminated and will continue to be for many years to come (see preceding box). In this section we will examine some of the available research on air pollution and behavior. We will start with how we perceive air pollution and then examine the health effects, performance effects, and social effects of air pollution (for a more thorough review of air pollution and its behavioral effects, the reader is referred to Evans & Jacobs, 1982).

Perception of Air Pollution

Perception of air pollution depends on a number of physical and psychological factors. What do you think of when you hear the term "air pollution"? Probably, you think of two bad things—bad odors and smog-like conditions. Unfortunately, we depend primarily on our sense of smell and on atmospheric visibility to perceive air pollution. We say *un*fortunately because many of the most harmful types of air pollution are not detectable in these ways. Carbon monoxide, for example, is both odorless and colorless. Moreover, airtight homes designed to restrict heat loss may be two or three times more polluted than outside air (Guenther, 1982; see also Sterling, 1979).

Perception of air pollution is also likely to be affected by factors such as annoyance. Attitudes toward the source of pollution or the attractiveness of this source may, for example, affect our perception of pollution or how we report it when asked. Winneke and Kastka (1987) found that pollution from a chocolate factory produced less annoyance among nearby residents than did emissions from a brewery, a tar oil refinery, or an insulation plant. It is possible that this was because odor exposure was perceived as less intense near the chocolate factory. Other studies suggest that perception of pollution or annoyance caused by it do not always correspond to physical levels of pollution, and that asking people to rate pollution may provide only rough estimates of actual exposure (e.g., Perrin, 1987). Partly because of this, a number of researchers have begun to develop measures of pollution exposure or consequences that are "indirect, behavioral impacts of air pollution" (Evans & Jacobs, 1982, p. 117). The problem of separating one's awareness of a pollutant and one's affective and cognitive reactions to it will be discussed again later in this chapter.

To detect particulate pollution, we may, of course, observe dust on our belongings; for some pollutants, eye and respiratory irritation are cues (cf. Barker, 1976). For our purposes, however, we will first examine perception of air pollution through smell and vision, and then look at an alternative means of perception.

Perception of Air Pollution Through Smell
When pollution is detectable through smell, how do we perceive the smell? The answer appears to be chemically, through the **olfactory membrane**. The olfactory membrane lies at the top of the nasal passage, just behind the nose. This membrane, which is similar to the basilar membrane in the cochlea, is lined with hair cells. By a mechanism we still do not understand, gaseous chemicals stimulate these cells as they pass by, sending signals to the brain, which interprets the signals as various odors. Several factors determine whether the olfactory membrane detects a specific odor. For one thing, the chemical stimulating the membrane usually has to be heavier than air. Also, sufficient quantities of the chemical have to be present. This is one reason "sniffing" the air helps you detect odors. To the extent that pollutants are capable of stimulating the olfactory membrane, humans can detect air pollution through smell (for reviews of odor detection, see Berglund, Berglund, & Lindvall, 1976; Turk, Johnston, & Moulton, 1974).

Perception of Air Pollution Through Vision
In addition to noticing smells, most of us infer air pollution from smog-like conditions. That is, we use visual perception to determine the presence or absence of pollution. If a scene looks hazy, especially if the haze is brown, we perceive that there is considerable pollution present. At least two research studies have suggested that visibility is the primary cue that average citizens use to detect air pollution (Crowe, 1968; Hummel, Levitt, & Loomis, 1973). These researchers asked the open-ended question, "What do you think of when you hear the term 'air pollution'?" There was a strong tendency for respondents to specify effects of pollution, such as smoke or smog, rather than to specify causes, such as factories or automobiles (see Table 7–2).

Other Means of Detection   As stated at the beginning of this section, really harmful pollution is often not detectable by its smell or visibility. What, then, can be used to perceive the presence of pollution? Although sophisticated chemical detection equipment is one possibility, much simpler means are available to everyone. We might turn to pollution experts to find out what to use. According to Hummel, Loomis, and Hebert (1975), experts use automobile concentration as the primary cue in detecting pollution. Since automobiles account for about 50 percent of urban pollution, this certainly makes sense. Hummel and colleagues (1975) found that experts base their judgments of pollution far more on the concentration of automobiles than do nonexperts, and nonexperts tend to use visibility as a cue more than experts do. Other cues useful in detecting air

Table 7–2 *Classification of Typical Definitions of Air Pollution**

Component of Definition	Percentage of Respondents Using Each Component	
	Urban Sample	Student Sample
Specific manifestation (smoke, haze)	43	14
Causative source (cars, industry)	22	43
Effects (health or property damage)	18	9
Combination (two or more of the above)	17	34

*Note that causes are specified less than half the time. (from Hummel, Levitt, & Loomis, 1973).

pollution include the absence of rain (rain cleanses the air), the presence of tall buildings (which block winds), and the presence of stop-and-go traffic as opposed to freeway traffic (idling and accelerating automobiles produce more pollution than automobiles moving at a constant speed). Why not instruct the public in the use of such cues as a means of detecting pollution that otherwise would go unnoticed? Hummel (1977) presents evidence that such instruction is indeed possible.

Other Factors Affecting Perception of Pollution   In concluding our discussion of perception of air pollution, we should note that our perceptual awareness of pollution may change with our exposure to it, and may also depend on other factors (see also Evans & Jacobs, 1981). For example, lower socioeconomic status individuals tend to be less aware of air pollution than other groups (Swan, 1970). Moreover, time of day and the particular season also make a difference (Barker, 1976). Interestingly, we tend to think ''the other guy'' has more pollution than we do. That is, we think our own immediate geographic area is less polluted than adjacent areas (DeGroot, 1967; Rankin, 1969).

Does prior exposure to air pollution decrease or increase our awareness of it? Unfortunately, the evidence is mixed on this question. For example, Wohlwill (1974) compared two groups of people in one location: those who had

moved there from a highly polluted region, and those who had moved there from a relatively unpolluted area. The current location was considered more polluted by those from the unpolluted area than by those from the highly polluted area; this suggests that the two groups were using different adaptation levels in making their assessments. In essence, these findings suggest that the more people were familiar with pollution, the less they were bothered by it (see also Evans, Jacobs, & Frager, 1979). Data from Lipsey (1977) and Medalia (1964) support the opposite position: The more people encounter pollution, the more concerned they become about it. For example, Medalia (1964) found that the longer people had lived near a malodorous paper mill, the more aware they were of its pollution. Whether we actually adapt perceptually to the presence of air pollution or become more sensitive to it with exposure, then, is unclear. As we will discuss in the next two sections, however, there is some evidence that we adapt physiologically and behaviorally to air pollution.

Air Pollution and Health

The hazardous effects of air pollution on health are becoming well known (see Table 7–3). From time to time, very high concentrations of pollutants have been known to increase the death rate for urban areas, as in the December,

1952, disaster in London, in which 3,500 deaths were attributed to excessive levels of sulfur dioxide (Goldsmith, 1968). Such disasters, however, are rare. More worrisome are adverse health effects of high concentrations of pollutants that occur more frequently (Coffin & Stokinger, 1977; Evans & Jacobs, 1982; Garland & Pearce, 1967; Goldsmith & Friberg, 1977; National Academy of Sciences, 1977; Rose & Rose, 1971; Schulte, 1963). In the U.S., for example, 140,000 deaths are attributable to pollution each year (Mendelsohn & Orcutt, 1979), and the annual cost of air pollution in the U.S. has been estimated at 16.1 billion dollars (and dollars for the year 1973, at that) (Lave & Seskin, 1973).

Carbon monoxide (CO), the most common pollutant, prevents body tissues (including those of the brain and heart) from receiving adequate oxygen, a condition known as hypoxia. Its primary sources include motor vehicles, coal and oil furnaces, and steel plants. Prolonged exposure to heavy concentrations of CO can lead to very serious health problems, including visual and hearing impairment, epilepsy, headache, symptoms of heart disease, fatigue, memory disturbance and even retardation and psychotic symptoms. **Particulates**, such as those containing mercury, lead, or asbestos from industrial sources, leaded gasoline, and so on, can cause respiratory problems, cancer, anemia, and neural problems, among other things. **Photochemical smog** can cause eye irritation, respiratory problems, cardiovascular distress, and possibly cancer. **Oxides of nitrogen and sulfur**, also produced by cars, trucks, and furnaces, impair respiratory function and may lower resistance to disease. Finally, furnaces, smelters, wood stoves, dry cleaning plants, and petroleum refineries produce arsenic, benzene, cadmium, and hydrocarbons, all of which can cause irritation or illness. For most pollutants, the elderly and the ill are the most likely victims. Physicians have identified an **air pollution syndrome (APS)** caused by combinations of pollutants and characterized by headache, fatigue, insomnia, irritability, depression, burning of the eyes, back pain, impaired judgment, and gastrointestinal problems (cf. Hart, 1970; LaVerne, 1970). Indeed,

---

Table 7–3 *What You Can't See in the Air Can Hurt You: The Major Components of Air Pollution Have a Variety of Health Effects**

Respiratory symptoms: *Ozone*, formed in sunlight when nitrogen oxides and hydrocarbons combine, aggravates respiratory problems by damaging epithelial cells in the trachea.

Skin problems: *Arsenic*, produced by furnaces, can cause skin cancer. Depletion of the ozone layer of the atmosphere may also contribute to skin cancer.

Nervous system diseases: *Arsenic* and *lead* can disrupt development in children or cause central nervous system problems.

Liver: *Lead* can cause liver disease.

Reproductive difficulties: *Cadmium* can retard development of the fetus.

Eyes: *Hydrogen chloride* causes irritation; *carbon monoxide* and *ozone* affect eye–hand coordination.

Heart: *Carbon monoxide* can reduce blood's ability to carry oxygen and cause symptoms of heart disease.

Lungs: Almost all *particulates* and metals accumulate in lungs and can contribute to cancer.

*Based on *Newsweek*, 29 August 1988, p. 47.

Figure 7–9   Exposure to air pollutants, such as carbon monoxide, oxides of nitrogen, oxides of sulfur, particulates, and photochemical smog, can lead to many adverse health effects, including cardiovascular problems, visual and hearing impairment, epilepsy, memory disturbances, and even retardation and psychotic symptoms. Pollution also affects performance and social behavior.

the list of ailments aggravated, if not caused, by air pollution seems endless. Some experts believe that 50 to 90 percent of human cancer is related to some form of pollution, including air and water pollution and food contamination (*Time,* June 13, 1977).

Some research has considered behavioral and mental health consequences of air pollution. Data suggest, for example, that people are less likely to engage in outdoor recreational activities when air quality is poor, but these effects are not as clear as one would expect, partly because subgroups of people were not considered. Evans, Jacobs, and Frager (1982) reported that people who exhibited more internal locus of control and who were newly arrived from low-pollution areas more clearly reduced outdoor activities during periods when air quality was poor. Data suggest that air pollution can increase hostility and aggression and reduce the likelihood that people will help each other

(Cunningham, 1979; Jones & Bogat, 1978). Finally, there is some evidence that psychological disturbance can follow exposure to air pollution. Symptoms of depression, irritation, and anxiety have been observed after indoor air pollution exposure (e.g., Weiss, 1983), and epidemiological studies have revealed correlations between air pollution levels and psychiatric hospital admissions (Briere, Downes, & Spensley, 1983; Strahilevitz, Strahilevitz, & Miller, 1979) (see Figure 7–9). Rotton and Frey (1982) found evidence of increased emergency calls for psychiatric problems when air pollution levels were high, and Evans et al., (1987) found that poor air quality increased the likelihood of distress following major life stressors.

Interestingly, there is some evidence that we can adapt physiologically to some pollutants, including photochemical smog (Hackney et al., 1977) and sulfer dioxide (Dubos, 1965). However, the extent of such reduced physiological reactivity is unknown (see also Evans & Jacobs, 1982), and there are certainly limits to the extent to which any organism can adapt to changes in the chemical environment.

Air Pollution and Performance

Most available research on pollution and performance involves studies of carbon monoxide (CO), which results from the incomplete burning of substances containing carbon (see Evans & Jacobs, 1981; National Academy of Sciences, 1977, for reviews). It has been found that concentrations of CO at 25 to 125 parts per million (ppm) are typical on freeways at rush hour. In one study, Beard and Wertheim (1967) exposed volunteers to concentrations of CO ranging from 50 ppm to 250 ppm for various periods of time and asked them to make discrimination judgments about time intervals. It was found that 90 minutes of exposure to CO at 50 ppm significantly impaired performance on the time judgment task. As CO concentration increased, shorter periods of exposure were required for similar levels of impairment. Using rats, these researchers also found that 11 minutes of exposure to 100 ppm adversely affected learning in an operant conditioning situation.

Breisacher (1971) has reviewed research indicating that air pollutants, including CO, also adversely affect human reaction time, manual dexterity, and attention (see also Beard & Grandstaff, 1970; Gliner et al., 1975; O'Donnel et al., 1971; Putz, 1979; Ramsey, 1970; Rummo & Sarlanis, 1974). Such research suggests that air pollution on major traffic arteries may impair driving ability enough to increase the frequency of automobile accidents. This possibility is supported by results of a study by Lewis et al. (1970), in which subjects were exposed to "clean" air or to air drawn 15 inches (38 cm) above ground at a traffic site handling 830 vehicles per hour. Performance decrements occurred in three out of four information-processing tasks for subjects breathing

the polluted air (see also Horvath, Dahms, & O'Hanlon, 1971). In sum, carbon monoxide appears to be quite deleterious to performance.

Interestingly, there is at least some evidence that we adapt to air pollution behaviorally. That is, after prolonged exposure, our behavior differs from that of those who have experienced only brief exposure. Evans, Jacobs, and Frager (1979), for example, found that long-term residents of the Los Angeles area tended to deny the threat of pollution, felt they were less vulnerable to its effects, and felt they knew more than they actually did about pollution hazards. Those who were newcomers to the area, however, felt more positively about the value of mass transit to reduce pollution and more readily looked for information about pollution. Moreover, those newcomers who were internal in locus of control (i.e., felt they controlled their own destiny) were more likely to avoid outdoor activity on high smog days. Feeling that one is in control of the situation has also been shown to reduce the effects of malodorous pollution on frustration (Rotton, 1983). In sum, pollution affects performance negatively, but we may develop ways of coping with some of these negative effects.

Air Pollution and Social Behavior

Research has shown that malodorous air pollution influences at least three types of social behavior. First, recreation behavior in particular, and outdoor activity in general, are restricted by pollution (Chapko & Solomon, 1976; Peterson, 1975). Second, Rotton et al. (1978) examined the effects of ammonium sulfide and butyric acid on interpersonal attraction. In one experiment, it was found that ammonium sulfide increased attraction for similar others with whom subjects thought they were interacting. That is, if subjects thought they were sharing the experience of exposure to the unpleasant odor, attraction toward similar others increased. In a second experiment, however, the same researchers found that subjects who did not expect to interact with others

Does Cigarette Smoke
Pollute the Air?

For a number of years we have known that tars and nicotine can have major effects on the health of smokers. There is now some evidence that nonsmokers breathing the air in a room where others are smoking may also suffer ill effects. For example, cigarette smoke has been shown to contain significant quantities of carbon monoxide and probably some degree of DDT and formaldehyde as well. A nonsmoker inhaling the air around a person who is smoking may experience an increase in heart rate, blood pressure, and breathing rate (Luquette, Landiss, & Merki, 1970; Russell, Cole, & Brown, 1973). Further, the 1986 Surgeon General's report on involuntary smoking concludes that **passive smoking** can cause disease, that children of smokers have more respiratory infections than do children of nonsmokers, and that we must act as a society to minimize exposure of children and nonsmoking adults to others' tobacco smoke (Koop, 1986).

Opposition to smoking in public places is growing. Many states have adopted laws prohibiting or restricting smoking in elevators, stores, and some restaurants. A number of antismoking groups, including ASH (Action on Smoking and Health), GASP (Group Against Smokers' Pollution), and SHAME! (Society to Humiliate, Aggravate, Mortify, and Embarrass Smokers) have adopted tactics ranging from mildly to overtly hostile in efforts to discourage smokers from "lighting up" in front of them. THANK YOU FOR NOT SMOKING signs are becoming more common, as are such signs as YES, I MIND IF YOU SMOKE, SMOKERS STINK, and KISSING A SMOKER IS LIKE LICKING A DIRTY ASHTRAY. Hostile tactics include plucking cigarettes from smokers' mouths and dunking one's hand in a smoker's water glass with the explanation, "You don't pollute my air, I won't pollute your water!" We need not comment on the behavior that is likely to follow such action except to say that it is likely to be consistent with theories of aggression.

Increasing evidence suggests that so-called passive smoking is bad for our health. Research has certainly confirmed that nonsmokers are disturbed by cigarette smoke. In one study (Bleda & Sandman, 1977), smokers were evaluated negatively by nonsmokers if they smoked in the presence of the nonsmokers. Other research indicates that nonsmokers have increased feelings of irritation, fatigue, and anxiety when exposed to cigarette smoke (Jones, 1978). In another study (Bleda & Bleda, 1978), it was found that persons sitting on a bench in a shopping mall fled faster if a stranger next to them smoked than if he or she refrained from smoking. Interestingly, smoke-induced irritation in nonsmokers may occur primarily when individuals are less involved in tasks at hand, rather than when they are intensely motivated by their activities (Stone, Breidenbach, & Heimstra, 1979). Finally, cigarette smoke may not just lead to feelings of irritation and dislike, but to overt hostility as well. Both feelings of aggression (Jones & Bogat, 1978) and hostile behavior (Zillmann, Baron, & Tamborini, 1981) increase in the presence of others' cigarette smoke.

evaluated those others less favorably if exposed to ammonium sulfide or butyric acid than if not exposed. It seems that the unpleasant affective states associated with pollution lead to decreased attraction if not shared with others, but to increased attraction if shared. Malodorous air pollution affects more than just attraction to people. Interestingly, foul odors also reduce liking for paintings and photography (Rotton et al., 1978).

In another experiment, Rotton et al. (1979) investigated the effects of exposure to ethyl mercaptan and ammonium sulfide on aggression. Using the shock methodology common in aggression research (see p. 145), the researchers ostensibly allowed subjects to shock a confederate. In accordance with the research on heat and aggression, it was anticipated that exposure to a moderately unpleasant odor (ethyl mercaptan) would increase aggression, but that exposure to a more unpleasant odor (ammonium sulfide) would decrease aggression. Consistent with these predictions, it was found that relative to a no-odor control group, the moderate odor increased aggression. In addition, there was suggestive evidence (though not statistically reliable) that the stronger odor decreased aggression.

Two other studies show that air pollution affects our social behavior and the way we feel about other people. Rotton and Frey (1985) found that complaints about household disturbances, including child abuse, were elevated when ozone levels were high compared to when they were low. Pollution may contribute to such behavior by making us more hostile or depressed, a possibility suggested by a study showing that a combination of high life stress and high air pollution predicts how hostile or depressed people feel (Evans et al., 1987).

Summary of Air Pollution Effects on Behavior

Air pollution consists mainly of carbon monoxide, photochemical smog, particulates, and oxides of nitrogen and sulfur. We primarily detect pollution through reduced horizon visibility, smell, and eye and respiratory irritation. Unfortunately, some deadly forms of pollution cannot be detected readily using these means. Respiratory and cardiovascular problems are the most notable effects of various pollutants, although a number of other adverse health effects are associated with pollution. Performance deteriorates upon exposure to pollutants in sufficient quantities, especially carbon monoxide. In addition, maladorous pollutants may either decrease or increase attraction and aggression. Physiological and psychological stress, arousal, perceived control, and adaptation level all seem to have some mediational influence in pollution effects.

SUMMARY

Stressors may be categorized as cataclysmic events, personal major stressors, or daily hassles and background stress. This categorization is based on both the power of the event and the number of people affected. At one extreme, cataclysmic events are potent events that demand a great deal of effort from people trying to cope with them. However, they often pass quickly. Disasters are a primary example of such events. At the other extreme are hassles, minor, transient stressors that by themselves demand little effort in order to cope with them. However, they are repetitive or constant, and over time may exact a substantial cost. Air pollution is one of these background stressors.

Natural disasters are powerful, destructive events that require a great deal of adaptation. They involve threat to life or loss of property, but are usually brief in duration. Most disaster events last for less than a day, some for only a few minutes. Once the disaster has passed, various means of coping may be directed at recovery and a number of effects may occur. Beneficial effects due to the formation of cohesive groups in the face of adversity have been found when these groups stay together long after the disaster. Though there is some concern for negative long-range effects of these events, research evidence of this is equivocal and most research suggests only short-lived stress reactions.

Technological catastrophes are similar to natural disasters, but are also different in several ways. They are caused by human actions rather than by natural forces, are not necessarily as destructive, are less predictable, and lack a clear low point, after which recovery may begin. These accidents and disasters seem to have few, if any, positive effects and longer-lasting negative consequences, including stress, negative mood, and uncertainty. One reason for this is that the events are human-caused, providing a better focus for blame than in natural disasters. Another is that technological accidents occur when control is lost over something previously under control (natural disasters are never controllable). A final possibility is that technological catastrophes often also involve toxic substances, and we have seen that the possibility of exposure to toxic substances can cause many long-term problems.

We have also discussed a very prevalent but often ignored source of toxic exposure, air pollution. Air pollutants cause or aggravate a variety of ailments, most notably respiratory and cardiovascular problems. Carbon monoxide in sufficient quantities impairs performance. Malodorous pollutants can increase or decrease aggression and attraction, depending on other factors. However, for the most part, we seem readily able to adapt to the threats and irritations that air pollution poses. In part, this may be due to the fact that air pollution effects occur in combination with other variables, such as weather, temperature, and behavioral goals.

SUGGESTED PROJECTS

1. Interview some people who have lived through severe storms, tornadoes, floods, or earthquakes. Ask them how they felt during and just after the event, how they coped, and what they worried about. Now interview some people who experienced some kind of technological accident. Are there differences in their reports?

2. Talk with homeowners in your area. Have they ever heard of radon? How much do they know about it? How concerned are they about it, and how likely are they to test for it? Is knowledge about radon related to fear of it and likelihood of remedial action?

3. Keep a log for two weeks in which you enter your local air pollution and pollen indexes each day. Also, write down your observations about your and others' apparent mood, behavior, and level of activity. Is pollution related to any of these measures of mood and behavior? If so, are people aware of it?

8 PERSONAL SPACE AND TERRITORIALITY

KEY TERMS

arousal
behavior constraint
compensatory behaviors
equilibrium
ethological models
expectancy-discrepancy models
field methods
individual difference variables
individual personality traits
internality-externality
interpersonal distance
laboratory methods
overload

personal space
privacy
privacy regulation model
reciprocal response
simulation methods
situational conditions
sociofugal
sociopetal
stress
symbolic barriers
territoriality
territory

INTRODUCTION

Imagine you are in a part of the world that is in some ways quite different from where you live. Although the people look just like you do, their behavior is unfamiliar. It is common for them to walk up to others, even strangers, and to stand right against them. People seem to have no concept of the need to maintain a personal space "buffer" around one's body. They do not mind if total strangers touch their most private parts. When waiting for a bus, instead of distributing themselves evenly and maintaining space between each person, individuals simply form a mass of bodies, each touching the other. And on the beach, people who are together lie on top of each other, rather than spacing themselves evenly on a blanket.

In addition to these differences, you find there is no such thing as territorial behavior. People move randomly from one dwelling to another and have no place to call "home." They do not knock before entering a new place but simply walk in and

Figure 8–1 In addition to constant spacing between various groups, members of individual groups maintain relatively constant personal space from each other.

use what is there. The next day they move somewhere else, taking some of the things that were in the place they had been with them. They seem not to mind that they have nowhere to call their own, or that at any moment a complete stranger might walk in on whatever they are doing.

What would life be like in such a place? How would you feel, and what would you be able to accomplish in life, if you had to live there? While this "fantasy" may seem extreme, it should make you aware of your need to maintain a portable personal space "bubble" between yourself and others, and of the importance of territorial functioning. In this chapter we will discuss personal space and territoriality, two ways in which people create different types of boundaries to regulate their interactions with others in their environment (cf. Altman, 1975). The importance of such boundaries is evident from our chapter opening example (Figure 8–1).

Personal space is defined as a portable, invisible boundary surrounding us, into which others may not trespass. It regulates how closely we interact with others, moves with us, and expands and contracts according to the situation in which we find ourselves. In contrast, **territories** are relatively stationary areas with often visible boundaries that regulate who will interact. The person is always at the center of personal space—it is always with you. On the other hand, territories, which often center around the home, can be left behind. While territoriality is more of a group-based process, personal space is more of an individual-level process. We will provide a more comprehensive discussion of personal space and territorial behavior in this chapter, and will elaborate on the role each plays in our lives. For now, it is important only to note some of the similarities and differences between personal space and territoriality which we have described above.

Thus far in the book we have examined how we perceive the environment and how various elements of it impact us. As we move toward an examination of the built environment, this chapter and the next mark a transition in which we describe spatial relationships between humans and their environment. As we will see, these spatial relationships have design implications, as well as commonalities with other environment-behavior relationships.

PERSONAL SPACE

The term "personal space" was coined by Katz (1937). The concept is not unique to psychology, since it also has roots in biology (Hediger, 1950), anthropology (Hall, 1968), and architecture (Sommer, 1959). Both popular and scientific interest in personal space have intensified greatly during the last two decades. In fact, over 700 published experiments have been done in this area since 1959 (Aiello, 1987).

Functions of Personal Space

What is the function of the personal space bubble we maintain around ourselves? A number of conceptual explanations have been suggested, some of which correspond to the theoretical formulations we reviewed in Chapter 4. An **overload** interpretation of why we maintain an interpersonal distance between ourselves and others is that such a boundary is necessary to avoid overstimulation. According to this notion, too close a proximity to others causes us to be bombarded with excessive social or physical stimuli (e.g., facial details, olfactory cues). An alternative formulation, the **stress** interpretation, assumes that we maintain personal space to avoid a variety of stressors associated with too close a proximity. Further, the **arousal** conceptualization posits that when personal space is inadequate, people experience arousal. This may elicit attributions in individuals who are attempting to understand why they are aroused, and the quality of these attributions can determine how people respond to inadequate personal space. A fourth conceptual perspective is the **behavior constraint** approach, which suggests that personal space is maintained to prevent our behavioral freedom from being impinged upon.

In addition to the above formulations, which we have discussed in detail earlier in this book, many other explanations have been suggested for why we maintain personal space. We will elaborate on a number of these here. One, proposed by anthropologist E. T. Hall (1963, 1966), conceptualizes personal space as a form of *nonverbal communication*. In this context, the distance between individuals determines the quality and quantity of stimulation that is exchanged (e.g., tactile communication occurs only at close proximity). Distance also communicates information about the type of relationship between individuals (e.g., whether it is intimate or nonintimate), and about the type of activities that can be engaged in (e.g., lovemaking cannot occur between individuals who are far apart).

Another formulation, proposed by Altman (1975), views personal space (and territoriality as well) as a boundary regulation mechanism to achieve desired levels of personal and group **privacy**. Privacy is an interpersonal boundary process by which people regulate interactions with others. Through variations in the extent of

their personal space, individuals ensure that their desired and achieved levels of privacy are consistent. When it is impossible to regulate these boundaries so they are within desired levels, negative effects and coping will ensue.

Related in some ways are the intimacy–equilibrium model proposed by Argyle and Dean (1965) and the comfort model formulated by Aiello (1987). According to these approaches, in any interaction (or relationship) people have an optimal level of intimacy they want to maintain. Lovers aspire to more intimate relations than friends, and so on. Intimacy is a joint function of personal space and other factors such as eye contact, facial gestures, and the intimacy of the topic under discussion. If the level of intimacy in an interaction becomes too great (e.g., the people are interacting about too intimate a topic and too much eye contact is being maintained), **equilibrium** will be restored through **compensatory behaviors** in some other modality (e.g., moving physically farther away). If the level of intimacy is too small, equilibrium will be restored as well (e.g., by moving closer or maintaining more eye contact). While nonoptimal levels of intimacy will typically prompt compensatory behaviors, Aiello (1987) suggests that these may not result from small deviations from an optimal level of intimacy, and that really large deviations may cause people to completely lose interest in the interaction.

Other investigators (Cappella & Greene, 1982; Patterson, 1982) have taken a somewhat different approach. They have articulated **expectancy–discrepancy models**, which propose that expectancies for appropriate interpersonal spacing between people who are interacting are formed based on norms, situational factors, the interactants' personalities, and their past experiences and relationships. Thus, a complex set of variables is involved in determining the distances at which people *expect* to interact with others. When such expectancies are violated, behaviors such as compensation, reciprocation, and withdrawal occur with the goal of alleviating the discomfort created by disconfirmed expectations.

A final perspective is afforded by **ethological models** (cf. Evans & Howard, 1973). These assume that personal space functions at a cognitive level and has been selected out by an evolutionary process to control intraspecies aggression, to protect against threats to autonomy, and thereby to reduce stress. We should note, however, that in contrast to the contention of ethological models that personal space evolved naturally, most researchers (e.g., Altman, 1975; Cappella & Greene, 1982; Duke & Nowicki, 1972) would probably argue that it is more a product of learning. However, once learned, our spatial behavior seems to be governed unconsciously (i.e., we do not have to "think" about how to position ourselves in different situations).

If all of the conceptual perspectives we have discussed are integrated, personal space may be seen as an interpersonal boundary regulation mechanism which has two primary sets of purposes. First, it has a *protective* function and serves as a buffer against potential emotional and physical threats (e.g., too much stimulation, overarousal leading to stress, insufficient privacy, too much or too little intimacy, physical attacks by others). The second function we have discussed involves *communication* (cf. Hall, 1963, 1968). The distance we maintain from others determines which sensory communication channels (e.g., smell, touch, visual input, verbal input) will be most salient in our interaction. To the extent that we choose distances that transmit intimate or nonintimate sensory cues and that suggest high or low concern with self-protection, we are communicating information about the quality of our relationship with another person (i.e., the level of intimacy we desire to have with them).

Size of Personal Space   What determines the size of the personal space we prefer to maintain between ourselves and others? The distance we maintain must be appropriate to fulfill the two functions of personal space—protection and communication. One determinant of the amount of space necessary to accomplish these functions is the situation (i.e., whom we are with and what we are doing). Certain relationships and activities demand more distance than others for appropriate communication and adequate protection. Situational conditions are not the only determinants of the size of our personal space, however. Some individuals habitually preserve minimal personal space zones, while others maintain relatively large personal space zones. Individual differences in spatial behavior probably reflect different learning experiences concerning the amount of space necessary to fulfill the protective and communicative functions (cf. Montagu, 1971). Individual differences that affect spatial behavior include gender, race, culture, and personality.

One of the first observational studies of the effect of **situational conditions** and **individual difference variables** on spatial behavior was conducted by E. T. Hall. Concerning the effect of situational conditions, Hall (1963, 1966) suggested that Americans use one of four personal space zones in their interactions with others. The particular zone that we use depends upon our relationship with the others and the activity we are engaged in. The four zones (which are labeled *intimate distance, personal distance, social distance,* and *public distance*) vary in terms of the quality and quantity of stimulation that is exchanged (see Table 8–1). Hall's assertions were corroborated in an extensive review of the personal space literature by Altman and Vinsel (1977).

With respect to the effect of individual differences on spatial behavior, Hall observed in cross-cultural investigations that cultures vary widely in terms of spatial behavior, an observation which has been corroborated in another review of a large number of studies (Aiello & Thompson, 1980b). Cultural differences were attributed by Hall to different norms regarding the sensory modalities seen as appropriate for communication between people who are interacting. A quotation from Hall (1968) nicely summarizes this finding and suggests how cultural differences in spatial behavior may be the source of considerable miscommunication:

> Americans overseas were confronted with a variety of difficulties because of cultural differences in the handling of space. People stood "too close" during conversations, and when the Americans backed away to a comfortable

conversational distance, this was taken to mean that Americans were cold, aloof, withdrawn, and disinterested in the people of the country. It was quite obvious that these apparently inconsequential differences in spatial behavior resulted in significant misunderstanding and intensified culture shock, often to the point of illness, for some members of the American overseas colonies (p. 84).

Table 8–1 *Types of Interpersonal Relationships, Activities, and Sensory Qualities Characteristic of Hall's Spatial Zones**

	Appropriate Relationships and Activities	*Sensory Qualities*
Intimate distance (0 to 1½ feet)	Intimate contacts (e.g., making love, comforting) and physical sports (e.g., wrestling)	Intense awareness of sensory inputs (e.g., smell, radiant heat) from other person; touch overtakes vocalization as primary mode of communication.
Personal Distance (1½ to 4 feet)	Contacts between close friends, as well as everyday interactions with acquaintances	Less awareness of sensory inputs than intimate distance; vision is normal and provides detailed feedback; verbal channels account for more communication than touch.
Social distance (4 to 12 feet)	Impersonal and businesslike contacts	Sensory inputs minimal; information provided by visual channels less detailed than in personal distance; normal voice level (audible at 20 feet) maintained; touch not possible.
Public distance (more than 12 feet)	Formal contacts between an individual (e.g., actor, politician) and the public	No sensory inputs; no detailed visual input; exaggerated nonverbal behaviors employed to supplement verbal communication, since subtle shades of meaning are lost at this distance.

*Based on Hall, 1963.

- -

Is Personal Space Really a Bubble?

Researchers, including the authors of this text, have a tendency to liken personal space to a bubble of sorts that surrounds us and fulfills a number of functions. While the bubble analogy is attractive because it gives us a concrete image to visualize and may thereby aid our understanding, it has some drawbacks that may lead to misunderstanding if taken too literally. First, it has been suggested that the notion of a personal space "bubble" emphasizes the protective function of personal space more than the communicative function (Aiello, 1987). Second, one might begin to think that if personal space is analogous to a bubble, it is the same size for all individuals and in all situations. Clearly, this is not the case. As we will see in this chapter, people have varying spatial zones, and the amount of space we desire between ourselves and others expands and contracts depending on the situation. Personal space is really an interpersonal distance continuum.

In addition to the bubble analogy, there are problems with the term "personal space." One could easily get the idea that since it is "personal," personal space is somehow attached to an individual in all situations. This is also not true; the concept has meaning only with respect to another individual and does not apply to distance between people and desks, for instance. Also, the label "personal space" may emphasize the idea of space and thus suggest that researchers are concerned only with distance. As we will see in this chapter, those studying personal space must also focus on other behaviors, such as body orientation and eye contact, in order to get a complete understanding of spatial behavior (Aiello, 1987; Knowles, 1978; Patterson, 1975). The latter behaviors are interpersonal rather than personal and imply that the *personal,* as well as the *space,* components of the term "personal space" may be misleading.

Due to these possibly misleading aspects of the term "personal space," should we consider replacing it with something else? Some researchers, such as Aiello (1987), have suggested that a term such as **interpersonal distance** might be better to use than personal space. Such a term implies that distance is a continuous dimension in which a variety of behaviors can occur. However, even Aiello admits that the concept is probably too well engraved in our minds—and in the literature—to be readily abandoned!

- -

Methods of Studying Personal Space

While Hall's studies were primarily observational and qualitative in nature, many *experimentally-based* investigations have considered the effect of situational and individual difference variables on personal space. In this re-search, several different methodologies have been employed. Many of the experimental studies exploring factors that affect personal space have used **laboratory methods**. Some of this work involves real interaction between people. Here, the personal space between subjects is measured as a function of experimental conditions (e.g., degree of mutual attraction).

Other laboratory methods include **simulation methods**—techniques in which subjects manipulate the personal space between dolls or symbolic figures, or approach an inanimate object under various experimental conditions. Another set of studies has used **field methods**. These involve observing and experimenting with interpersonal positioning in naturally occurring situations, as a function of individual difference or situational variables.

Fortunately, many of the important relationships between situational and individual difference variables and the size of personal space have been corroborated using different experimental approaches. While this has occurred with some regularity (Duke & Nowicki, 1972; Knowles, 1980; Little, 1965), in other cases there have been dissimilar findings for studies that used different methods to assess the same spatial relationship. Knowles and Johnson (1974) suggested that although there is sometimes a general association between the various methods used to measure personal space (i.e., they can be considered to be indicators of the same dimension), the level of convergence is only moderate. Others (e.g., Aiello, 1987; Hayduk, 1983, 1985) have suggested that the different measures of personal space are *not* measuring the same thing. In general, since it appears that laboratory and field methods that involve actual interaction between subjects are better measures of our spatial behavior than simulation techniques (Aiello, 1987; Hayduk, 1983; Jones & Aiello, 1979; Love & Aiello, 1980), they should receive preference from investigators both when planning research and in interpreting discrepant results.

Having discussed the methodologies used to study interpersonal distancing behavior, we now shift our focus to some of the more representative findings that have accumulated. Our review will deal first with the relationships observed between situational conditions and personal space. Next, we will discuss findings on the effects of individual difference variables on spatial behavior.

Situational Determinants of Personal Space: Research Evidence

Experimentally-based studies have explored the effects on spatial behavior of attraction between individuals, of interpersonal similarity on various dimensions (e.g., age, race), and of the context of the interaction (e.g., positive versus negative). Such studies have identified a number of rather consistent relationships.

Attraction and Interpersonal Distance   How does attraction between people who are interacting affect the size of the interpersonal distance between them? Love songs often lament one lover's longing for physical closeness with a distant other and suggest that the greater the attraction between individuals, the more physically close they wish to be. There is some truth to this popular notion, but the relationship between affection and personal space is somewhat more complex and depends on the gender of the interactants.

Studies (Allgeier & Byrne, 1973; Byrne, Ervin, & Lamberth, 1970; Edwards, 1972) indicate that when males and females interact, increased attraction is associated with closer physical distance. In one study, Byrne and his colleagues (1970) manipulated attraction by sending male–female pairs, who were similar or dissimilar on a variety of personality traits, on a brief date. From research in social psychology, we know that similar individuals tend to be more attracted to each other than dissimilar individuals (Byrne, 1971). When the "matched" or "mismatched" couples returned from the date, the experimenter measured their degree of mutual liking, as well as the distance between them as they stood in front of his desk. The "matched" couples liked each other more and stood closer together than the "mismatched" couples. Additional studies have examined whether the attraction-proximity relationship for opposite sex dyads occurs because the male moves closer to the female, because the female moves closer to the male, or because both the male and the female move closer to each other. These studies (e.g., Edwards, 1972) suggested that the smaller distances between close friends of the opposite sex were primarily attributable to females moving closer to males they were attracted to (i.e., females respond more to attraction by their spatial positioning than do males).

If the spatial behavior of females is primarily responsible for the attraction-proximity relationship, then the distance between female–female pairs should be determined by their degree of mutual attraction, while the distance between male–male pairs should not. In line with this assumption, it has been shown that while female–female pairs position themselves closer together with increased liking, positioning does not vary with liking for male–male pairs. In one experiment (Heshka & Nelson, 1972), pairs of adults were unobtrusively photographed by researchers as they walked down the street. The use of a standard in each of the pictures permitted a fairly accurate estimate of the distance between interactants. After taking the photograph, the experimenter approached the unknowing "subjects" and asked them what type of relationship they had. It was observed that female–female pairs interacted at closer distances as their relationship became more intimate, while distance between male–male pairs did not change as a function of friendship.

Why is it that the attraction–proximity relationship holds for females but not males? One explanation derives from socialization differences between the sexes, which could be reflected in spatial behavior with liked others. For males, who may be socialized to be fearful of homosexual involvement and to be independent and self-reliant overall (Maccoby, 1966), and who have less experience with intimate forms of nonverbal communication (Jourard & Rubin, 1968), spatially immediate situations with liked males or females are ambivalent. Close distances with liked males may trigger concerns about homosexuality, close distances with liked females may evoke concerns about

dependency, and for males physical closeness and its attendant high degree of sensory stimulation is generally somewhat foreign. On the other hand, females may be socialized to be more dependent, to be less afraid of intimacy with others of the same sex, and generally to be more comfortable in affiliative situations (Maccoby, 1966). They also have more experience as senders and receivers of intimate nonverbal messages (Jourard & Rubin, 1968). Thus, it is not surprising that they have less difficulty responding spatially to liked others. (See also Bell, Kline & Barnard, 1988.)

The research demonstrating that in some cases people in dyads interact at closer distances with increasing friendship suggests that closer personal space is an outcome of increased attraction. Do individuals viewing people interacting at close range infer higher degrees of attraction? The available research evidence suggests that closer distances do serve as indicators of attraction to observers. Mehrabian (1968) found that photographs of people interacting at four feet were judged to show a more positive interpersonal relationship than photographs of individuals seated 12 feet apart. Other studies (Haase & Pepper, 1972; Wellens & Goldberg, 1978) have reported similar findings.

Effect of Other Types of Similarity on Interpersonal Distance   We mentioned earlier that one type of similarity (personality similarity) leads to attraction, which elicits closer interpersonal positioning (Byrne et al., 1970). Since other types of similarity have been shown to affect attraction in the same manner as personality similarity (Byrne, 1971), similarity on these other dimensions should also lead to closer interpersonal positioning. This has been found to be true in a number of studies. For example, closer distances are maintained between individuals of similar rather than dissimilar age (Latta, 1978; Willis, 1966), race (Campbell, Kruskal, & Wallace, 1966; Willis, 1966), sexual preference (e.g., heterosexual vs.

bisexual) (Barrios et al., 1976), and status (Lott & Sommer, 1967). One setting where status is highly salient is in the military. When initiating an interaction with a superior, the greater the similarity between the initiator and the other in terms of rank, the smaller the interpersonal distance maintained (Dean, Willis, & Hewitt, 1975). Finally, it is at once interesting and unfortunate that ''normals'' prefer to interact at closer interpersonal distances with other ''normals'' (i.e., similar others) than with people who are stigmatized or have handicaps (dissimilar others) (Dabbs & Stokes, 1975; Rumsey, Bull, & Jahagan, 1982).

Why should similarity and attraction lead to closer interpersonal distances than dissimilarity and dislike? People generally anticipate more favorable interactions with similar (liked) than with dissimilar (disliked) others (Byrne, 1971). Since one of the functions of personal space is protection against perceived threats, we *should* be willing to interact at closer distances with similar than dissimilar others because we anticipate fewer threats from them. Maintaining close interpersonal distances with liked others is also a means of fulfilling the communicative function of personal space. By choosing closer distances, we convey information to liked others that we are attracted to them and that we expect to communicate intimate sensory cues to them.

Type of Interaction and Interpersonal Distance   If qualities such as degree of friendship and similarity create expectations of pleasant interactions which in turn affect interpersonal positioning, then situational qualities (e.g., type of interaction, discussion topics) which can be placed on a pleasant–unpleasant dimension should also affect the size of our personal space. This line of reasoning is supported by studies that have varied the affective quality of the interaction situation and observed that negatively toned situations precipitate larger spatial zones (Karabenick & Meisels, 1972; Mandal & Maitra, 1985; Rosenfeld,

1965). In one study, Karabenick and Meisels found that subjects who were given negative feedback about their performance stayed farther away from a confederate than subjects who were given positive feedback. In another, subjects in a stressful interaction maintained more distance than those in a low stress condition (Ugwuegbu & Anusiem, 1982). An analysis of the literature further suggests that women, as opposed to men, are especially apt to react to threatening situations by expanding their personal space (Aiello, 1987) (Figure 8–2 A–D).

While it appears that affectively negative situations generally lead to more distant interactions, there is a special case in which contrasting results are sometimes found. When subjects are angered as a result of personal insults, they may show closer interaction distances than nonangered subjects (Meisels & Dosey, 1971). This may be seen as a retaliatory stance that facilitates communication of anger. However, some studies (O'Neal et al., 1979; O'Neal et al., 1980), suggest that anger, like the other negative affects, may also produce farther distances. Additional situational conditions probably determine when anger leads to closer distances (for retaliation), or to farther distances (for protection).

Individual Difference Determinants of Personal Space: Research Evidence

In addition to situational conditions, differences between individuals or groups that reflect diverse learning experiences also determine the size of personal space (Aiello, 1987). For example, cultural or subcultural norms may affect whether individuals believe it is appropriate to communicate by means of touch, and thus govern the distance chosen to fulfill the communicative function. In terms of the protective function, learned values relevant to the amount of space needed for protection against perceived threats, and experiences which deter-

Figure 8–2 A–D Interpersonal distance and such nonverbal behaviors as eye contact, body angle, and facial expression vary with the affective tone of the interaction context. Can you suggest the affective tone of the interaction situation and relate it to personal space and nonverbal behavior in each of these pictures?

mine the amount of sensory stimulation one is accustomed to, will affect spatial behavior. Although we will find that there *are* consistent relations between individual difference variables and personal space preferences, some findings are inconsistent. In part, this may be due to the use of different methods in different studies (e.g., simulation vs. other techniques). Generally, we have tried to "weight" results from studies using simulation techniques less in arriving at our conclusions.

Cultural and Racial Determinants of Personal Space Assuming that individuals raised in different cultures and subcultures have diverse learning experiences (Edwards, 1972, 1973), we might expect cross-cultural differences in interpersonal distancing as well as dissimilarities among subcultural groups within a single culture.

There is evidence relating to *cross-cultural* variations in spatial behavior, although the patterns revealed in the research are sometimes inconsistent (Aiello, 1987; Altman & Vinsel, 1977; Hayduk, 1983). Hall (1966) proposed that in highly sensory "contact" cultures (e.g., the Mediterranean, Arabic, and Hispanic cultures), where individuals use smell and touch as well as other sensory modalities more, people should interact at closer distances. In contrast, more reserved "noncontact" cultures (e.g., northern European and Caucasian American cultures) should exhibit larger interaction distances. This assertion has received support (cf. Aiello, 1987). Hall (1966), Watson and Graves (1966), and Little (1968) have found that Hispanics, French, Greeks, and Arabs maintain smaller interaction distances than Americans. Further, Sommer (1969) and Little (1968) reported that the English, Swedish, and Swiss are similar to Americans in the size of their spatial zones. Thus, although the research is not entirely consistent and many cultures have yet to be studied (Aiello & Thompson, 1980b), various cultural groups may need different distances to fulfill the protective and communicative functions of personal space.

The research on *subcultural differences* in spatial behavior within our culture is more confusing (Hayduk, 1983). As was indicated earlier, there is evidence that subcultural groups tend to interact at closer distances with members of their own subculture than with nonmembers (Aiello, 1987; Willis, 1966). Also, it seems as if Hispanic-Americans interact more closely than Anglo-Americans (e.g., Aiello, 1987; Ford & Graves, 1977). Unfortunately, findings for other subcultural differences (e.g., black–white differences) have often been inconsistent. It has been suggested (Hayduk, 1978; Patterson, 1974) that socioeconomic status may be a better predictor than subculture of learning experiences related to spatial behavior (cf. Scherer, 1974). Although members of a particular subculture may vary greatly in their living conditions, those in a particular socioeconomic group tend to live under relatively similar conditions. However, support for the view that socioeconomic status should have consistent effects on spatial behavior has been mixed (Aiello, 1987).

Gender Differences in Personal Space We mentioned earlier that males and females display different spatial behavior with *liked* than *disliked* others. Females interact at closer distances with liked others, while males do not differentiate spatially as a function of attraction. Another interesting question centers around the relative distances at which females and males interact with others, regardless of degree of attraction. Do males generally maintain closer interpersonal distances than females when interacting with people, or is the reverse true?

In terms of interpersonal distance from others of the same sex, it is typically found that in same-sex dyads, female–female pairs maintain closer distances than male–male pairs (Aiello, 1987). This has been shown in a wide variety of situations, ranging from playground interactions among children (Aiello & Jones,

1971), to structured interviews (Pellegrini & Empey, 1970), to simulation techniques (Barnard & Bell, 1982). Again, these findings may be seen as reflecting a stronger female socialization to be affiliative, more experience by females with intimate nonverbal modalities (Jourard & Rubin, 1968), and a greater male concern about not being intimate with others of the same sex (Maccoby, 1966). The tendency for women to interact more closely than men does not hold for all situations. While it occurs in affiliative situations, in contexts that imply threat women interact at greater distances than men (Aiello, 1987).

How do mixed sex dyads compare spatially with male–male or female–female pairs? When dyads are of mixed sex, distancing depends on the relationship of the interactants. Acquaintances maintain an intermediate distance (between that used by male–male and female–female pairs), while mixed sex dyads who are in a close relationship maintain less personal space than either male–male or female–female pairs (Aiello, 1987). Interestingly, some research suggests that a woman's point in the menstrual cycle affects the personal space she chooses to maintain with opposite sex others. Females' personal space zones tend to be larger during the menstrual flow than during the middle of the cycle (Sanders, 1978). This has been interpreted as reflecting the midcycle peak in sexual desire (e.g., Benedak, 1952). In effect, hormonally-determined sexual receptivity may affect personal space in opposite sex interactions.

Age Differences in Personal Space Research focusing on personal space from a developmental perspective has been directed at answering two questions: the age at which personal space is first established and the extent to which children's spatial behavior changes as they become older. There are many estimates concerning when children begin to exhibit personal space preferences. Duke and Wilson (1973) and Eberts and Lepper (1975) found behavioral evidence of personal space in children between 45 and 63 months of age, but other studies (e.g., Meisels & Guardo, 1969) have found that exhibition of personal space begins at a later age. Unfortunately, none of this research sheds much light on how the learning from which spacing mechanisms evolve takes place.

The second question concerns whether personal space changes with age. It has been found that: (a) children less than five years old show inconsistent spatial patterns, and (b) after age six (grade 1 in Figure 8–3), the older the child (until adulthood), the greater the preferred interpersonal distancing (Aiello, 1987; Hayduk, 1983; Willis, Carlson, & Reeves, 1979). This pattern has held up across cultures (e.g., Lerner, Iwawaki, & Chihara, 1976; Lomranz et al., 1975). Adult-like spatial norms are first exhibited around the time of puberty (Aiello, 1987; Aiello & Cooper, 1979; Altman, 1975).

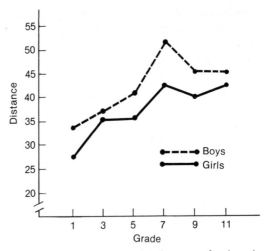

Figure 8–3 Mean interaction distances of male and female dyads at six grade levels. (From Aiello, J.R., and Aiello, T., 1974. The development of personal space: Proxemic behavior of children 6 through 16. *Human Ecology, 2,* 177–189. Reprinted by permission.)

Personality Determinants of Spatial Behavior A major attempt has been made by researchers to identify **individual personality traits** associated with differential concern about maintaining personal space. Since personality represents one's way of looking at the world and reflects learning and experience, it seems reasonable that personality orientations should be reflected in spatial behavior.

One personality variable that has been explored in terms of its implications for interpersonal distancing is **internality–externality**. A study by Duke and Nowicki (1972) demonstrated differences in personal space between internals and externals and provided an excellent example of how spatial behavior may reflect learning experiences. The theory of internality–externality views an individual's orientation (internal or external) as a reflection of past learning about internal or external causation of events. *Internals* view reinforcements as under the control of the self; *externals* view reinforcements as controlled by external sources. Consistent with this theoretical framework (and with the assumption that learning is reflected in spatial behavior), Duke and Nowicki found that externals desired more distance from strangers than internals. It appears that if past learning leads to the belief that one is in control of a situation, one feels more secure at close distances with strangers than if past learning leads to the belief that events are controlled externally.

Several other studies have found that spatial behavior differs as a function of personality. In this context, Horowitz, Duff, and Stratton (1964) and Sommer (1959) compared the spatial needs of schizophrenics and "normals" and found that schizophrenics require more space. Using simulation techniques, Weinstein (1965) found that emotionally disturbed children placed toy figures farther apart than normal children. It has been observed in several studies that anxious individuals maintain more personal space than nonanxious people (Karabenick & Meisels, 1972; Patterson, 1977), and that extraverts maintain less space than introverts (Cook, 1970; Patterson & Holmes, 1966). Also, those with high self-esteem have smaller personal space than those with low self-esteem (Frankel & Barrett, 1971), people high in need for affiliation prefer closer distances than those low in need for affiliation (Mehrabian & Diamond, 1971$_a$), and field dependent persons maintain closer distances than field independent ones (Kline, Bell, & Babcock, 1984).

How do violent and nonviolent prisoners compare in their use of space? Kinzel (1970) compared the body buffer zones of violent and nonviolent prisoners. He found that violent prisoners required nearly three times as much space around themselves as nonviolent prisoners to feel comfortable. Similar patterns of results are reported by Roger and Schalekamp (1976). Interestingly, when prisoners increase in psychological stability, they allow closer approach distances (Wormith, 1984). Again, it is reasonable to assume that such patterns of spatial differences reflect learning and experience. All of the above differences have potential implications for the design of physical environments.

The above research notwithstanding, many of the studies that have attempted to relate individual personality traits to spatial behavior have not been terribly enlightening and have resulted in conflicting findings (cf. Aiello, 1987; Hayduk, 1983). Patterson (1974, 1978) has proposed a procedure that may be more fruitful than the individual personality trait approach. Rather than studying single personality traits and their relationship to spatial behavior, Patterson conceptualized personality dimensions in more general terms. He looked at *clusters* of personality variables related to a general approach tendency for social situations (e.g., need for affiliation, extraversion), and related these to personal space preferences. His research demonstrated that such a strategy may yield better, more stable predictors of interpersonal distancing than focusing on individual traits. Another way to maximize the possibility of observing relationships between personality variables and personal space was suggested by Karabenick and Meisels (1972). Specifically, it may be necessary to study such relationships in

situations in which the personality trait in question is salient (e.g., studying the relationship between aggressiveness and personal space in an anger-provoking situation), as opposed to the neutral contexts generally employed.

Physical Determinants of Personal Space

Although we have focused primarily on situational and individual difference determinants of personal space (as has past research), studies also suggest some interesting *physical* determinants of interpersonal spacing. First, a number of architectural features affect personal space. For example, Savinar (1975) found that males had more need for space when ceiling height was low than when it was high. White (1975) reported that personal space increased with reductions in room size and decreased with increases in room size, and Daves and Swaffer (1971) found that individuals desire more space in a narrow than a square room. Also, Baum, Reiss, and O'Hara (1974) suggested that installing partitions in a room can reduce feelings of spatial invasion. Do we maintain closer distances with others when "in the dark," than when there is light? Gergen, Gergen, and Barton (1973) report that we are more likely to touch others (the ultimate in closeness) when it is dark than under more typical lighting conditions.

In addition to architectural features, people's position in a room, whether they are sitting or standing, and whether they are indoors or outdoors, also affects personal space. Concerning position in a room, several studies (cf. Dabbs, Fuller & Carr, 1973; Tennis & Dabbs, 1975) found that over a variety of subject populations, people exhibit greater personal space when in the corner of a room than when in the center. Also, it seems that we maintain closer distances when standing than while seated (Altman & Vinsel, 1977). With respect to spatial differences as a function of being indoors or outdoors, Little (1965) and Pempus, Sawaya, and Cooper (1975) found that subjects kept more distance between themselves and others when indoors than when outdoors. The "corner–center," "sitting–standing," and "indoor–outdoor" relationships may all reflect differential physical availability of escape; when we know we can get away, we are content with less space.

Interpersonal Positioning Effects

Do the same variables that determine the *size* of our personal space affect other aspects of spatial positioning? Studies have shown that besides determining the distance between interactants, individual difference and situational variables affect the body orientation that we maintain between ourselves and others.

One individual difference variable that has been found to affect spatial positioning is gender. While males prefer to interact with liked others in an across (i.e., face-to-face) orientation, females prefer to have liked others adjacent to them. In two related studies, Byrne, Baskett, and Hodges (1971) manipulated the attraction between a subject and two confederates so that the subject liked one of the confederates but disliked the other. The subject was then asked to join the confederates in another room where his or her choice of seats with respect to the liked and disliked confederates was recorded. In the first experiment, which involved side-by-side seating, females sat closer to the liked confederate than to the disliked one, while males showed no preference. In the second experiment, which involved face-to-face seating, males sat closer to the liked confederate, while females showed no preference.

The cooperativeness or competitiveness of the interaction situation also affects spatial positioning. In an initial study, Sommer (1965) observed the spatial arrangement of individuals who were cooperating or competing and found that cooperating pairs sat side-by-side, while competing pairs sat across from each other. A second study found corroborative results. Sub-

jects anticipated either a cooperative or a competitive interaction and sat opposite a decoy in competitive conditions and adjacent to him or her in cooperative conditions.

Spatial Zones that Facilitate Goal Fulfillment

What distances lead to the best results in a dyadic learning situation? What seating position in a classroom will promote the most teacher–student interaction? And where should a therapist position him- or herself to elicit the most self-disclosure on the part of a client, or a doctor sit when giving a patient important health recommendations? These are obviously important questions, and show the applied significance as well as the design implications of research on personal space. Unfortunately, at present there are no completely satisfactory answers, though there is research that makes an attempt to provide some preliminary ones.

Optimal Spacing in Learning Environments
We know that the distance between a teacher and a student may affect learning, at least when the two are in a dyadic interaction. Although the results are slightly contradictory, they suggest, in general, that interactions at Hall's personal distance zone (Skeen, 1976), and even at his intimate zone (Miller, 1978), may lead to better performance by the student than the other spatial zones. For example, in the study by Skeen (1976), a subject performed a serial learning task either six inches (intimate distance) or three-and-one-half feet (personal distance) from the experimenter. For tasks of varying levels of difficulty, the learner's performance was better at the personal distance than at the intimate one. In the study by Miller (1978), subjects received instruction at a distance from the instructor corresponding to one of Hall's four zones. Here, the students did better when taught at the intimate distance than at the other three. While the results of these studies are somewhat inconsistent, taken to-

gether they suggest that Hall's closer zones, rather than his farther ones, may lead to the best learning by students in teacher–student dyads.

What about typical classroom situations, where there are many students present? Although there is currently no research which definitively identifies how far from the instructor you should sit in order to get the best grade, a study by Kinarthy (1975) may at least provide a hint. In this experiment, trained observers recorded the amount of communication between the students and the instructor. It was reported that seating position does affect communication in the college classroom, even after statistical procedures were used to control for the fact that in many cases students chose their own seats. (Without such controls, it could be the type of person who chose a particular position, rather than the position itself, which caused the effects.) Where is the best place to sit? It seems as if the middle, front section of the classroom is a relatively high communication zone. Sitting there promotes verbalization (except for those who are very low verbalizers) and facilitates attention (Koneya, 1976; Schwebel & Cherlin, 1972; Sommer, 1969) (see Figure 8–4). It has been found that people who choose middle-front seats also get the best grades in the class (Becker et al., 1973; Sommer, 1972). While the relationship between seating position and grades is just correlational, there is also some *experimental* evidence that partially supports it (Stires, 1980) (Figure 8–5).

Optimal Spacing in Professional Interactions
An interesting question concerns the distance at which people feel most comfortable disclosing

Figure 8–4   Where you sit in a large lecture hall can make a big difference.

personal information about themselves to clinical psychologists. Again, this topic has not been thoroughly researched, although there are preliminary data. Generally, an intermediate distance is preferred for a counseling situation (Brokemann & Moller, 1973), and psychiatric patients talk most about their fears and anxieties at that distance (Lassen, 1973). This pattern of effects also holds for college students. When Stone and Morden (1976) had students discuss personal topics with a therapist at a distance of two feet, five feet, and nine feet, they found that students volunteered the most personal information at the five-foot distance. Since this distance is culturally appropriate for such communications and is expected for them (Brokemann & Moller, 1973), these data support Hall's (1968) prediction that deviation from the appropriate distance elicits negative effects. It should be noted, however, that these data do not generalize to self-disclosures between two strangers in nonclinical interactions (cf. Skotko & Langmeyer, 1977).

How far should a physician position him- or herself from a patient so that the patient's compliance with medical regimen will be highest? According to available evidence, the answer depends on whether the doctor is delivering basically "accepting" or "neutral" evaluative feedback for the patient's self-disclosures. In a study by Greene (1977), close physical proximity strengthened adherence to dieting recommendations when "accepting" feedback was offered, but lowered compliance when "neutral" feedback was given. It may be that the feedback suggested to the patient the type of relationship she had with the practitioner. When feedback was accepting, the closer distance was appropriate and led to more positive effects than the less appropriate, farther distance. On the other hand, when feedback was neutral a farther distance was viewed as appropriate and led to more positive effects than a close distance. Another way of saying this is that when the intimacy of both the verbal and environmental "channels" was consistent,

more positive effects occurred than when there were inconsistencies.

Optimal Spacing to Facilitate Group Processes Can the spacing between people be manipulated to affect group processes in order to accomplish some desired end? A number of studies suggest that the answer is "yes." Suppose that an environmental psychologist wants to promote interaction within a group. This calls for **sociopetal** spacing (spacing that brings people together, such as the conversational groupings found in most homes), rather than **sociofugal** space (space that separates people, like the straight-line arrangement of chairs found in airports or bus terminals) (Osmond, 1957). In an early study, Sommer and Ross (1958) were called in to examine conditions at a Saskatchewan hospital, where a newly opened ward with a lovely, cheerful decor seemed to be having a depressing and isolating effect on patients. They observed that chairs were lined up against the walls, side-by-side. All the chairs were facing the same way, and rather than seeing each other, people

Figure 8–5 Students' participation in class activities as a function of seating positions. (From Sommer, R., 1967. Classroom ecology. *Journal of Applied Behavioral Science, 3,* 500. Copyright 1967 by NTL Institute Publications.)

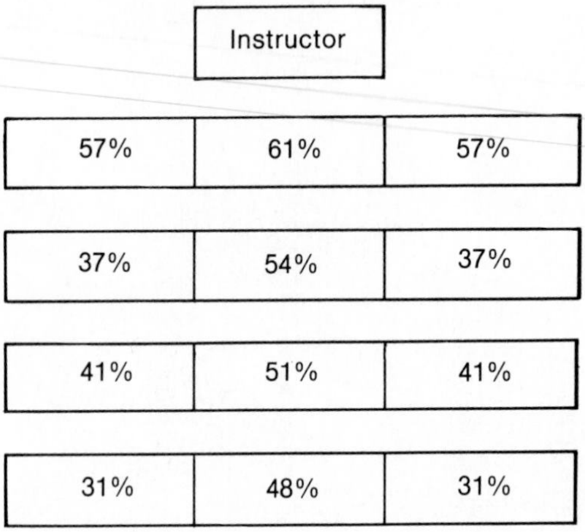

Instructor		
57%	61%	57%
37%	54%	37%
41%	51%	41%
31%	48%	31%

just gazed off into the distance. When Sommer and Ross rearranged the chairs into small, circular groups, the frequency of interactions among patients almost doubled. Other studies have similarly found that arranging space so that people face each other more directly results in greater interaction between group members (Mehrabian & Diamond, 1971b). A nonfacing orientation may elicit longer pauses, more self-manipulative behaviors and postural adjustments, and perhaps even more negative ratings of group interaction (Patterson et al., 1979).

How could one manipulate his or her spatial positioning in a group in order to become its leader? It seems that in small group settings, people direct most of their conversation to the person sitting across from them (i.e., the one who is the most highly visible) (Michelini, Passalacqua, & Cusimano, 1976; Steinzor, 1950). Also, people who occupy a central position in a group initiate the most communications (Michelini and colleagues, 1976). This suggests that one could become highly influential merely by choosing a central spatial orientation where others eye them directly. This assumption has received some support. Those who choose the end of a rectangular table are more likely to be elected foreman in simulated jury studies (Strodtbeck & Hook, 1961) or to otherwise dominate group interaction. Of course, this could be due to the fact that dominant individuals *choose* to sit at the "head" of the table, or it could be a reciprocal relationship. Experimental work still needs to be done to identify the cause of this effect.

Consequences of Too Much or Too Little Personal Space

We have seen that situational, individual difference, and physical-environmental variables determine our preferred personal space zone. And we have also seen that some spaces facilitate goal fulfillment more than others. At this point, it is interesting to consider what happens when we are forced to interact with another person under conditions of "inappropriate" (i.e., too much or too little) personal space. For example, imagine an interaction with a vacuum cleaner salesperson who insists on extolling the virtues of his or her product at an inappropriately close distance (e.g., three inches) or an inappropriately far distance (e.g., 10 feet). Would you be likely to buy anything from this person? Since personal space serves some important functions, we can assume that inappropriate distancing often has negative consequences for the interactants.

Predicting the Effects of Inappropriate Distances The effects of inappropriate positioning can be described in the context of the general environmental stressor model introduced in Chapter 4 and presented in Figure 8–6. Before we discuss the model, however, recall that we have observed throughout our coverage of research on personal space that situational conditions and individual differences determine optimal interpersonal distances. It is evident in Phase I of the model that whether we perceive our personal space as optimal or nonoptimal at a particular objective distance from another person depends on situational conditions (e.g., attraction) and individual differences (e.g., personality). If we perceive our personal space as within an optimal range, homeostasis is maintained. If we perceive it as outside this range, a variety of responses may occur.

What is the nature of our response to nonoptimal personal space? The same conceptual formulations used earlier to explain *why* we maintain personal space (e.g., overload, arousal, and behavior constraint) predict the effects of inappropriate interpersonal distancing. For example, *overload* notions predict that stimulus overload occasioned by an inappropriate personal space should cause performance decrements and elicit coping responses directed at lowering stimulation to a more reasonable level. Coping responses may include giving different priorities to inputs so that only impor-

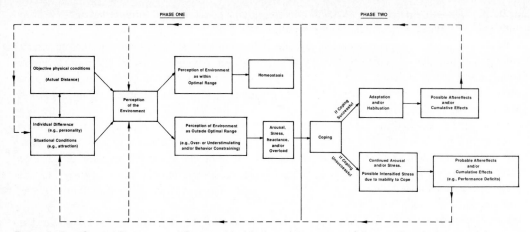

Figure 8–6 General Environmental Stressor Model adapted to conceptualizing reactions to inappropriate personal space.

tant stimuli are attended to (e.g., ignoring some of the incoming information) and erecting interpersonal barriers (e.g., acting coldly toward others). In terms of the *stress* approach, inappropriate positioning leads to a stress reaction, which may have emotional, behavioral, and physiological components. Coping responses are directed at reducing stress to a more acceptable level.

The *arousal* conceptualization assumes that being too close leads to overarousal and to attributions, and suggests coping mechanisms designed to lower arousal. According to *equilibrium, "comfort,"* and *expectancy–discrepancy* models, distances which are too close or too far will lead to compensatory reactions in other modalities (e.g., changes in body orientation or eye gaze) and, when these are impossible, to a loss of interest in continuing the interaction. Altman's (1975) **privacy regulation model** implies that inadequate personal space will elicit attempts to "shore up" boundary control mechanisms and thus ensure privacy. Finally, the *behavior constraint* approach suggests that inadequate personal space should

lead to an aversive feeling state and to coping responses that attempt to reassert freedom.

We noted earlier that Hall (1966) proposed a model based on *communication properties* to explain personal space and that ethological models have also been applied (cf. Evans & Howard, 1973). In terms of Hall's formulation, it might be predicted that inappropriate distance constitutes a negative communication and leads to negative attributions and inferences. The *ethological approach* makes still another set of predictions. It assumes that when personal space is inadequate, fear and discomfort are experienced due to feelings of aggression or threat (cf. Evans, 1978).

How can we integrate all these formulations? Although each of the approaches proposes a somewhat different reaction to inappropriate positioning, we should not view them as competing with each other. Rather, it is probable that inappropriate personal space may at times lead to each of the responses we have described. Further, the predictions of all of the conceptual schemes may be integrated into the sequence of events shown in Phase II of Figure

8–6. When personal space is inadequate, various types of coping responses are employed, which may or may not be successful. When coping is successful, it leads to adaptation or habituation, and aftereffects are less likely. If coping is unsuccessful, inappropriate positioning can lead to aftereffects such as dislike for the other, poor performance, and so on.

The Consequences of Inappropriate Spacing

What type of research evidence exists to support the assertions of our model concerning the consequences of inadequate personal space? Which of the above conceptual approaches have received support? Several studies have shown that when an environmental setting forces two people to interact in an inappropriate spatial zone, unfavorable feelings and inferences are elicited. In an experiment on the effects of distance between a subject and a communicator on persuasion, Albert and Dabbs (1970) hypothesized that negative feelings and attributions would be elicited if a communicator and a subject were positioned more or less than five feet apart, an appropriate distance for such interpersonal contacts. Accordingly, the communicator (actually an experimenter) and the subject were constrained to interact at the "appropriate" distance of five feet (1.5 m), or at one of two inappropriate distances (i.e., 2 feet or 15 feet, 0.6 m or 4.6 m). Several effects were measured, and the findings basically supported the prediction. It was observed that subjects paid more attention to the communicator and rated him or her as more of an "expert" at the five-foot distance than at either of the other distances.

Boucher (1972) found parallel results using schizophrenics as subjects. First, interviewers sat down with patients at a distance that was inappropriately close, appropriate, or inappropriately distant. The distance manipulation was accomplished by fastening both chairs to the floor at one of the three ranges so that people in "inappropriate" positions could not adjust their

proximity to a more comfortable zone. Following a 10-minute interview under these conditions, the subject's attraction to the interviewer was assessed. It was found that more attraction was expressed for the interviewer at the appropriate distance than at distances that were inappropriately close or far.

Several studies suggest that maintaining inappropriate interpersonal distance is associated with considerable stress. For example, Dabbs (1971) found that a persuasive communicator who was positioned too close caused subjects to feel more pressured, unfriendly, and irritated than they did when a more appropriate distance was maintained. And when Aiello and Thompson (1980a) had subjects converse at either a comfortable distance or an uncomfortably far one, subjects who sat too far apart not only felt ill at ease, but blamed the other for their discomfort, even though the other was clearly not responsible!

Patterson and Sechrest (1970) reported that subjects evidenced more positive feelings when interacting with a confederate at a moderate distance (4 feet, 1.2 m) than at either a closer distance (2 feet, 0.6 m) or a far distance (8 feet, 2.4 m). Similarly, Bergman (1971) found that subjects in discussion groups with chairs separated by two inches (5 cm) on each side showed more palmar sweat (a measure of arousal) than subjects in discussion groups with chairs separated by three feet (.76 m). All of the above studies on the effects of having to interact under conditions of inappropriate spacing have design implications.

In another study, Hayduk (1981) found a linear relationship between the *degree* to which a spatial arrangement was inappropriate and the amount of people's discomfort. Also, he observed that subjects with smaller personal space zones responded more positively to an inappropriately close distance than subjects with larger zones. Interestingly, a study by Fisher (1974) suggests that inappropriate distances with a similar (liked) other lead to less negative

Compensation Versus Reciprocation: Too Close Is Not Always Too Bad

Up until now, we have suggested that inappropriate interpersonal distancing leads primarily to negative consequences (e.g., dislike) and to compensatory reactions (e.g., indirect body orientation). However, we have also noted that there is some conflicting evidence. One conceptual formulation (Patterson, 1976, 1978) suggests a way of integrating both sets of data. Patterson hypothesizes that when two individuals are interacting, a sufficient change in the intimacy of one of them (e.g., moving too close) produces a changed state of arousal in the other. Depending on cognitions about the situation (e.g., attributions), this arousal may be labeled as either a positive or a negative emotional state by the other person. If the arousal is negatively labeled, a compensatory response (such as moving farther away) will occur. On the other hand, if the arousal is positively labeled, a **reciprocal response** (moving still closer to the other) will occur. This model makes an important point; the situation should determine whether the effects of interacting at a very close range will be negative (i.e., eliciting compensatory reactions and dislike) or positive (i.e., eliciting reciprocal reactions and liking). For example, reciprocity may occur when two people like each other, while compensation may occur when they are unsure about the relationship or dislike

one another (Firestone, 1977; Ickes et al., 1982).

A study by Storms and Thomas (1977) supports the notion that the situation determines whether interacting at close range is positive or negative. In this study subjects interacted with another who was either friendly or similar, or unfriendly or dissimilar at a very close or normal distance. The other was liked more when he sat close than at a "normal" distance in the friendly or similar conditions. In effect, when the situation is positive, closeness may facilitate a desire for reciprocal intimacy. On the other hand, the subject was liked less when he sat close than farther away in the unfriendly or dissimilar conditions. Closeness in this situation promoted disliking and a desire for a compensatory response.

While Patterson's model received some support from research, it has been criticized on theoretical grounds (Ellsworth, 1977; Hayduk, 1983). Hayduk has suggested that it is often difficult to make predictions with the model since it does not specify what causes a positive or negative evaluation of a change in intimacy. Ellsworth believes that the degree of cognitive self-focusing it implies is overstated. Attempts to modify the model (Anderson & Anderson, 1984) have met with some success.

reactions than the same distances with a dissimilar other.

In addition to lowering attraction and persuasibility and causing negative affect, what other effects can inappropriate spatial positioning have? According to Argyle and Dean (1965), nonverbal compensatory coping reactions should occur to restore a comfortable "equilibrium'' when the physical distance between two individuals is too close or too far. Although all the implications of this proposition have yet to be tested, a number of studies have provided support for Argyle and Dean's formulation. In one study (Patterson, 1974), subjects interacted with an interviewer at both an appropriate and an inappropriate distance, and changes in eye contact and body orientation were recorded. In this study and others (e.g., Rosenfeld et al., 1984), the results of the distance manipulations on eye contact and body orientation were in line with the equilibrium hypothesis. It was found that with too much proximity, body orientation became less direct and percentage of eye contact decreased.

Other studies consistent with the equilibrium hypothesis have shown that decreased directness of body orientation leads to greater proximity among individuals in the situation (Aiello & Jones, 1971; Felipe & Sommer, 1966). In addition, the longer subjects interact under inappropriate conditions the greater the degree of compensation which is observed (Sundstrom & Sundstrom, 1977). However, research has not always supported the predictions of the equilibrium notion (cf. Altman, 1973), and some studies find opposite results (i.e., closeness begets closeness). One way of resolving this apparent conflict is indicated in the box. Others have suggested modified equilibrium theories (i.e., the "comfort" model reviewed earlier), which better correspond to certain experimental findings (e.g., Aiello, 1977; Aiello & Thompson, 1980b).

Consequences of Personal Space Invasions

Research on the consequences of too much or too little personal space suggests that when *ongoing interactions* take place at inappropriate distances, they may lead to lower attraction, negative inferences, and compensatory behaviors. However, what happens when a person is sitting alone minding his or her own business,

with no intention of interacting with anyone, and a stranger sits down at an uncomfortably close proximity?

The Effects of Being Invaded on Flight Behavior An early study of the effects of personal space invasions was conducted by Felipe and Sommer (1966). At a 1500-bed mental institution where patients spent a great deal of time outdoors, a stranger (actually an experimental confederate) approached lone patients at a distance of six inches (15 cm). If the subject attempted to move away, the confederate moved so as to maintain a close positioning. The flight behaviors of the "invaded" group were compared with those of patients who were not invaded but who were watched from a distance. As can be seen in Figure 8–7, after one minute 20 percent of the experimental subjects and none of the control subjects had fled. After 20 minutes, 65 percent of the experimental subjects had left their places, and

Figure 8–7 Cumulative percentage of patients departing at various intervals. (Based on data from Felipe & Sommer, 1966.)

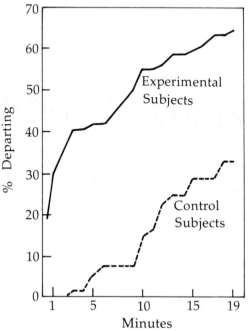

only 35 percent of the control subjects displayed such a reaction.

Similar results for flight behavior after personal space invasion were reported by Konecni et al. (1975). In this study (see Table 8–2), it was observed that both male and female pedestrians crossed the street more quickly as personal space invasions became more severe. Smith and Knowles (1979) reported the same thing, and also observed that invaded pedestrians formed more negative impressions of the invader, and experienced more negative moods, than those in control conditions. In addition, Patterson, Mullens, and Romano (1971) reported that ''invaded'' subjects turned away, avoided eye contact, erected barriers, fidgeted, mumbled, and displayed other compensatory and coping reactions more than ''noninvaded'' control subjects. Such reactions are especially common in individuals who choose not to escape altogether, or who do not have the option of escape. In a study by Terry and Lower (1979), it was found that in the latter group the more severe the invasion, the more intense the attempts at perceptual withdrawal. Finally, in research with children, it was found that personal space invasions caused behavior to become more primitive, and to be characterized by increasing movements (e.g., fidgeting) (Bonio, Fonzi, & Saglione, 1978).

Effects of Being Invaded on Arousal   If ''invasions'' are uncomfortable experiences for the target, invasion victims might be expected to evidence higher levels of physiological arousal than noninvaded controls. Only a few studies (e.g., Evans & Howard, 1972; McBride, King, & James, 1965) have systematically considered the effects of invasion on physiological arousal. A very ingenious study by Middlemist, Knowles, and Matter (1976) bears directly on this question. The setting for the study was, of all places, a three-urinal men's lavatory! The unknowing subjects were lavatory users who were ''invaded'' by a confederate at either a close or a moderate distance. In the control condition, the confederate was not present. How was arousal measured under these three levels of personal space invasion? Since research indicates that stress delays the onset of urination and shortens its duration, it was reasoned that if closer invasions cause stress, greater delay of onset and shorter duration of urination should result. Accordingly, an experimenter stationed in a nearby toilet stall with a periscope and two stopwatches recorded the delay of onset and persistence of urination. As can be seen in Figures 8–8A & B, and 8–9, results confirmed the assumption that personal space invasions are stressful. Close interpersonal distances increased the delay and decreased the persistence of urination. Perhaps installing partitions could add to people's comfort in lavatories.

One implication of the arousal elicited by personal space invasions is its effect on task performance. In line with the Yerkes–Dodson Law (page 96), available evidence suggests that

Table 8–2 *Time in Seconds Taken to Cross the Street by Experimental Condition**

| | Experimenters' Lateral Distance from Subjects (in feet) | | | |
Sex of Subjects	1	2	5	10
Male	7.65	8.45	9.09	9.08
Female	8.94	8.95	9.41	9.79

*Based on data from Konecni et al., 1975.

Figure 8–8 A&B   Observation apparatus which was used to study the effects of arousal from personal space invasions in a men's room. As you can see, the periscope is quite unobtrusive when hidden by the stall. (Eric Knowles)

the consequences of invasion-induced arousal for performance depend on the complexity of the task. With simple tasks, performance does not seem to be negatively affected by having another too close. With more complex tasks, invasions take a toll. For example, Evans and Howard (1972) and Barefoot and Kleck (1970) found decrements in performance on information-processing tasks as a function of personal space invasion. Thus, it may be that if somebody invades your space when you are in the library studying, the quality of your work will suffer.

Other Effects of Being Invaded   If personal space invasions are aversive for the target, they should elicit a host of additional behavioral reactions. For example, it would seem reasonable to assume that if your personal space were invaded by someone, you would be less likely to help him or her if given the opportunity. Two

Figure 8–9* Mean persistence and delay of onset for urination at three levels of personal space invasion.

*(From Middlemist, R. D., Knowles, E. S. and Matter, C. F., 1976.) Copyright © 1976 by The American Psychological Association. Reprinted by permission of the author and publisher.

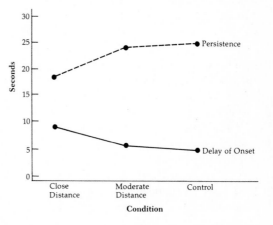

Too Close for Comfort: Gender Differences in Response to Invasions of Personal Space

A study by Fisher and Byrne (1975) found gender differences in victims' responses to personal space invasions and demonstrated that invasions affect victims on a broad array of dimensions.

As you recall from earlier in the chapter, it has been found that males prefer to position themselves *across from* liked others, while females prefer to position themselves *adjacent to* liked others (Byrne, Baskett, & Hodges, 1971). On the basis of these findings, Fisher and Byrne reasoned that for each sex the spatial position most favored for "liked" others should be the one least favored for an invading stranger. Specifically, it was hypothesized that females should respond more negatively than males to side-by-side invasions of personal space, while males should respond more negatively than females to face-to-face invasions.

The subjects were males and females who were sitting alone at tables in a library. As they attended to their business, they were "invaded" by a male or female "invader" from either a face-to-face or an adjacent position. After five minutes, the invader appeared to have concluded his or her work and left the area. Three minutes later, an experimenter arrived, claiming to be a student who was conducting a study of people's impressions of various stimuli for an introductory psychology class. The experimenter also claimed to have noticed that someone had been sitting at the subject's table and wondered if the subject could indicate his or her impressions of that person as well as impressions of the library environment on questionnaires. The questionnaires specifically tapped the subject's affective state, attraction toward the invader, perception of the aesthetic quality and crowdedness of the environment, and the positiveness of motivation attributed to the invader.

How did invasion victims respond to the questionnaires? Regardless of the invader's sex, males responded negatively on all measures when the invader sat across from them but were not affected by an adjacent invasion. Females responded negatively when the invader sat adjacent to them but were not affected by one who sat across from them. It is as if special significance is associated with opposite positioning for males and adjacent positioning for females, and invading these "special" zones leads to particularly negative reactions.

The results of the study led Fisher and Byrne to make a simple prediction that, if confirmed, would lend additional support to their findings. It was assumed that if males dislike invasions from across, they should place their books and personal effects between themselves and facing seats in a library, and if females dislike adjacent invasions, they should place their possessions between themselves and adjacent seats. To test these hypotheses, an observer was sent into the library to record where males and females placed their possessions. The hypotheses were confirmed: Males erect barriers primarily between themselves and facing positions, while females erect barriers between themselves and adjacent positions.

Why is it that the sexes seem to attribute special significance to different spatial positioning arrangements? One possible explanation lies in the socialization process, with males taught to be relatively competitive and hence more sensitive to competitive cues, and females taught to be relatively affiliative and more sensitive to affiliative cues (Maccoby, 1966). Adjacent seating (which occurs in affiliative situations) may signal affiliative demands to females. Females like to have someone they "feel safe with" in this relatively intimate affiliative position and react negatively when it is occupied by a stranger. On the other hand, facing

seats (which occur in competitive situations) may signal competitive demands to males. Males like to have a trusted (and nonthreatening) friend in this competitive position.

It is rather humorous, but the gender differences observed in the Fisher and Byrne research may be the source of considerable miscommunication between the sexes. A female who wants to befriend an unknown male may be surprised to find that a nonthreatening (to her) eyeball-to-eyeball approach causes consternation and alarm. In the same way, a male who attempts to ingratiate himself with an unknown female by sitting down next to her in a nonthreatening (to him) position may be surprised to find he elicits a "Miss Muffet" reaction.

- -

sets of studies have looked at the effect of personal space invasions on helping and have reached conflicting conclusions. In one group of studies (Konecni et al., 1975; Smith & Knowles, 1979), a confederate first violated the subject's personal space and then dropped one of several objects. It was found that when the personal space violation was severe, victims failed to retrieve even objects that seemed to be important. In addition to failing to help the *invader,* Smith and Knowles (1979) reported that the reluctance to help on the part of those who had experienced "severe" invasions also generalized to an unwillingness to assist others in need of aid. A second set of studies (e.g., Baron & Bell, 1976) found the opposite: Personal space invasions facilitated helping. However, in these studies confederates asked the subject for help when at either an "invaded" or an appropriate distance. These conflicting findings can be readily resolved. In the first set of studies, the victim may have

attributed the invasion to negative intent, dismissed the invader as a "nasty" person, and refused to help him or her. In the second, the invader's violation may have been attributed to the importance of the request rather than to negative personal qualities and therefore resulted in greater helping.

Thus far, we have seen that personal space invasions can cause physiological arousal and cognitive and behavioral responses. Although there are many possible ways to view the relation between these, Smith and Knowles (1979) suggest an interesting possibility, which supports Patterson's theory of compensation versus reciprocation (see the box on page 246). Based on some studies they did, Smith and Knowles imply that our initial response to a personal space invasion involves *arousal.* As we know, arousal can have many behavioral consequences, in and of itself. However, they argue that arousal is also followed by a secondary, cognitive response (e.g., attributions). In effect, our arousal response draws our attention to the invader and causes us to try to understand why we are aroused, and why the invader behaved as he or she did. Characteristics of the invader and the situation affect the explanations at which we arrive. These, in turn, determine our attributions to the invader, our liking for him or her, whether we will help the invader if in need, etc. While Smith and Knowles' proposed interrelation between the various responses to personal space invasions has received some support, further research is needed.

After exploring the effects of personal space invasion on a wide array of behaviors, an interesting question remains: Do all personal space invaders elicit the same reactions in their victims, or is it more aversive to be "victimized" by some people than others? The model proposed by Smith and Knowles (1979) would suggest the latter. The more negative our attribution for why someone invaded our space, the more uncomfortable the invasion will make us. While relatively few studies have looked at this question, there are some suggestive findings. First, it appears that people flee more slowly after having their personal space violated by an attractive rather than an unattractive confederate (Kmiecik, Mausar, & Benziger, 1979). Second, some evidence indicates that it may be more upsetting to be invaded by a male than a female. Specifically, Murphy-Berman and Berman (1978) and Bleda and Bleda (1978) observed that male intruders were evaluated more negatively and elicited more movement in their victims than female intruders. Perhaps this is because we attribute more negative motives to male than female invaders. Other research suggests that more negative reactions to male invaders may be limited to *ambiguous* settings (Aiello, 1987). In less ambiguous settings, such as on the beach or in a bar, a male's invasion of a female's personal space may elicit a favorable response (Skolnick, Frasier, & Hadar, 1977). Additional studies suggest that the degree of

choice invaders have in their action affects how negatively they are evaluated (Murphy-Berman & Berman, 1978) and it seems that invaders who smoke elicit more flight reactions in their victims than those who do not (Bleda & Bleda, 1978).

What about the effect of invaders of different ages? Fry and Willis (1971) had children who were 5, 8, and 10 years old stand six inches (15 cm) behind adults in theater lines. It was found that 5-year-olds were given a positive response, 8-year-olds were ignored, and 10-year-olds were given a cold reaction. Thus, as children get older, they are treated more as adult invaders. Finally, in a study that examined whether the status of the invader affects reactions to him or her, Barash (1973) varied the clothing confederate invaders wore and found that those who wore "faculty-like" attire evoked faster flight than those who wore casual clothing.

How could one ameliorate some of the negative effects in the victim, when forced to invade someone's personal space? Research by Quick and Crano (1973) found that just saying "Hello" lowered the number of victims who fled, while Sundstrom and Sundstrom (1977) suggest that asking permission can make a difference. And Schavio (1975) reported that invaders who were reading newspapers elicited more favorable responses in victims than a "no newspaper" control. But perhaps the best way to avoid torturing those you invade comes from research by Smith and Knowles (1979), who suggest that "negative reactions occur only when there is no immediately apparent and appropriate reason for the invader to be standing close." So, as long as you behave so that your victim believes you have a good reason for your invasion, you may be able to avoid inflicting pain on others.

Are there gender differences in reaction to personal space invasions? It is interesting to note that males generally react more negatively to invaders than females (Garfinkel, 1964;

Patterson, Mullens, & Romano, 1971), although there are exceptions (Bell, Kline, & Barnard, 1988). On airplanes men use the common armrest three times as much as women, and are more apt to get annoyed if their neighbor uses it. In part, the larger spaces taken up by men and their more negative reactions to invasions may be responsible for the fact that women are typically approached more closely than are men (Long, Selby, & Calhoun, 1980). Overall, women have more tolerance for distances that are inappropriately close than men (Aiello, 1987).

The Effects of Invading Another's Personal Space We have spoken about how it feels to be the victim of a personal space invasion, but have said nothing about how it feels to be the invader. Investigators have been looking at what happens when people are placed in dilemmas that require them to become personal space "invaders." Several studies have found that people do not even like to *approach* the personal space of others. In one study (Barefoot, Hoople, & McClay, 1972), a lone confederate was stationed 1, 5, or 10 feet (0.3, 1.5, or 3.0 m) from a water fountain. Fewer passersby approached the fountain when doing so would violate the confederate's personal space (i.e., at the 1-foot distance) than when it would not (i.e., at the 5- or 10-foot distances). While people will avoid a water fountain when the setting is uncrowded, it becomes easier to invade someone's personal space (and take a drink) under crowded conditions (Thalhofer, 1980). This may be because we become "overloaded" when it is crowded, and are less attentive to social cues (e.g., that we may cause another person discomfort). Another study demonstrated that it may be aversive to approach the personal space of a group, as well as a lone individual. Knowles and Bassett (1976) positioned groups of varying sizes on a hallway bench and observed "deflection" in the walking patterns of passersby as they walked past the

seated confederates. As the number of confederates on the bench increased, passersby were "deflected" farther away. Thus, it appears that approaching the personal space of either lone individuals or groups is a threatening experience, to be avoided if possible. Design features that allow us to avoid invading others' personal space would probably be appreciated.

Several other experiments have looked at the invader's reactions to physically penetrating, rather than merely approaching, the personal space of interacting dyads. One study suggests that for females it is easier to invade the personal space of someone who is smiling than of someone displaying a neutral face, while for males the reverse is true (e.g., Hughes & Goldman, 1978; Lockhard, McVittie, & Isaac, 1977). And, at least for males, it may be still easier to violate the space of one who has his or her back toward the invader (Hughes & Goldman, 1978). Efran and Cheyne (1973) found that passersby are less likely to "invade" if the individuals in the dyad are conversing, if they are occupying Hall's personal space zone rather than social distance, and if they are of the opposite sex. Similar results were reported by other studies (e.g., Bouska & Beatty, 1978), which also found that an "invasion" was less likely if the interactants appeared to be of high status (e.g., a businessman, a priest). When it is necessary to invade, the status of the victims also determines how the invader treats them. High-status individuals receive "positive deferential" behaviors (e.g., signals of appreciation), while those with low status receive signs of negative deference (e.g., derogation) from the invaders (Fortenberry et al., 1978). Finally, dyads comprised of individuals who are black are more likely to be invaded than white or mixed race dyads (Brown, 1981).

Even though it is easier to invade some people's personal space than others, it is generally aversive to violate the personal space of others under any conditions. In a finding that shows how taxing it is to invade interacting

How do Groups Respond to
Personal Space Invasions?

In general, we have restricted our attention to the effects of personal space invasions on lone individuals. In a very interesting study, Knowles (1972) extended this line of research to an exploration of how *groups* of people respond to personal space invasions. His findings suggest that groups, like individuals, engage in compensatory responses when their space is invaded, constituting evidence for a group analog to personal space.

What did Knowles do to establish that groups, like individuals, engage in compensatory responses when invaded? On a city street he had a confederate approach a pair of pedestrians (subjects) walking in the opposite direction. The invader walked so it appeared that he or she intended to walk right between the two pedestrians. It was found that over half the pairs moved together to avoid an intrusion and that some reprimanded the invader; this suggests that groups try to maintain their personal space—even in the face of invasion. Further, avoidance of intrusion was more frequent when the pedestrians consisted of a male and a female rather than individuals of the same sex. In a later study, Knowles and Brickner (1981) found that the more cohesive the dyad, the more it resisted the intrusion, i.e., protected its "group space." (Additional evidence of personal space at the group level is also provided in this chapter where we discuss research by Knowles on the other side of this question: how we respond when we have to invade the space of interacting groups.)

dyads, it was observed that subjects forced to invade tended to look at the floor rather than ahead and to close their eyes (Cheyne & Efran, 1972; Efran & Cheyne, 1973). Further, Efran and Cheyne (1974) reported that the act of invading interacting dyads has affective consequences: Subjects in "invasion" conditions displayed more negative moods and more hostile facial responses than noninvading control subjects.

How does the invader react to penetrating a group larger than a dyad? Knowles (1973) created "targets," groups of two or four persons who were interacting in a hallway so that passersby had two choices: to violate the group space or to go around the interactants. Fewer people penetrated the four- than the two-person group, and low-status individuals were invaded more often than high-status individuals. Thus, not only individuals and dyads but larger groups appear to be aversive to invade. For the invaders, the permeability of interacting targets depends on such factors as status, group size, and sexual composition. Further, it is apparent that groups, like individuals, are recognized as having a sort of personal space. (Note that the study reviewed in the box, in which groups responded as a unit to a confederate invader, also supports the idea of personal space at the group level.)

Summary of Personal Space

Personal space is an invisible, portable boundary which regulates how closely we interact with others. There are many conceptual perspectives which may be applied to suggest different functions of personal space. A combination of these approaches implies that personal space serves two major functions: protection and communication.

Personal space expands and contracts depending on situational conditions, and as a function of individual differences. People interact more closely with similar than with dissimilar others, and in pleasant than in unpleasant interaction situations. Individual differences that affect personal space preferences include gender, certain cross- and subcultural differences, age, and several personality factors (e.g., internality–externality, anxiety, introversion–extraversion, self-esteem, need for affiliation). Physical factors (e.g., ceiling height, position in room) also affect personal space preferences.

Some of the same factors, such as gender and interpersonal attraction, which impact on personal space also affect interpersonal positioning. In addition, the appropriateness of spacing (e.g., too close vs. too far) affects goal fulfillment and group processes. Inappropriate spacing also leads to negative affect and to compensatory responses.

Similarly, personal space invasions elicit negative affect, arousal, negative inferences, and compensatory reactions. The intensity of negative reactions varies as a function of situational conditions and individual differences. Finally, being placed in the role of personal space invader is aversive, and is avoided if possible. With this in mind, we move on to a discussion of territorial behavior.

TERRITORIAL BEHAVIOR

We mentioned at the beginning of this chapter that both personal space and territoriality are interpersonal boundary regulation mechanisms with certain differentiating characteristics. Personal space tends to be invisible, movable, person-centered, and regulates how closely individuals will interact. Territory is visible, relatively stationary, visibly bounded, and tends to be home-centered, regulating who will interact (Sommer, 1969). Also, territories are generally much larger than personal space; and whether or not we are on our own territory, we still maintain a personal space zone.

One way of viewing *territories* is as places that are owned or controlled by one or more individuals. Anyone who has ever been on the sending or receiving end of a statement like, ''Don't you ever set foot on my property again,'' has confronted the concept of *territoriality* head on. In addition to the notion of demarcation and defense of space, territories

also play a role in organizing interactions between individuals and groups, can serve as vehicles for displaying one's identity, and can be associated with feelings, valuation, or attachment regarding space (Figure 8–10).

Figure 8–10 Fences and signs are among the many ways people demarcate and defend their territories.

Although most of us have an instinctive feeling of what territoriality is, it is difficult to define, and there is considerable controversy among researchers about what constitutes the best definition. Our definition of territoriality in humans is representative of "mainstream" views in the field (for commentaries on the definitions used by diverse groups of researchers, see Altman & Chemers, 1980; Brown, 1987; Taylor & Brooks, 1980). For us, *human* **territoriality** *can be viewed as a set of behaviors and cognitions an organism or group exhibits, based on perceived ownership of physical space.* Perceived ownership as used here may refer either to actual ownership (e.g., as with your home) or to control over space (e.g., you may control but not own your office, if it is part of a building owned by another). Territorial behaviors serve important motives and needs for the organism and include occupying an area, establishing control over it, personalizing it, thoughts, beliefs, or feelings about it, and in some cases defending it (Brown, 1987). Note that the concepts of "territory" and "territoriality" illustrate the interdependent nature of human–environment transactions. Without a territory there would be no territoriality, and vice versa (Carpenter, 1958).

According to Altman and his colleagues (Altman, 1975; Altman & Chemers, 1980), there are three types of territories used by humans, and this distinction has been supported in research by others (Taylor & Stough, 1978). These differ in their importance to the individual's or group's life—*primary* territories are most important, followed by *secondary* and *public* territories. They also differ in the duration of occupancy, the cognitions they foster in the occupant and others (e.g., the extent of perceived ownership), the amount of personalization, and the likelihood of defense if violated. (These differences are highlighted in Table 8–3.) As we will discuss later, different

Table 8–3. *Territorial Behaviors Associated with Primary, Secondary, and Public Territory**

	Extent to Which Territory Is Occupied/Extent of Perceived Ownership by Self and Others	Amount of Personalization/Likelihood of Defense if Violated
Primary Territory (e.g., home, office)	*High.* Perceived to be owned in a relatively permanent manner by occupant and others.	*Extensively personalized;* owner has complete control and intrusion is a serious matter.
Secondary Territory (e.g., classroom)	*Moderate.* Not owned; occupant perceived by others as one of a number of qualified users.	*May be personalized to some extent during period of legitimate occupancy;* some regulatory power when individual is legitimate occupant.
Public Territory (e.g., area of beach)	*Low.* Not owned; control is very difficult to assert, and occupant is perceived by others as one of a large number of possible users.	*Sometimes personalized in a temporary way;* little likelihood of defense.

*Based on Altman (1975).

types of territories provide different benefits for individuals (e.g., primary territories such as a bedroom promote privacy and control and allow for the expression of one's identity, functions *not* promoted in a public territory). Therefore, based on the type of activity we want to engage in and the needs it poses, we choose a particular type of territory (Taylor & Ferguson, 1978).

The Origins of Territorial Functioning

Territorial behavior is practiced by humans and animals. Some researchers consider human territoriality to be *instinctive,* some consider it to be *learned,* and some consider it an *interaction* of the two (cf. Alland, 1972; Ardrey, 1966; Klopfer, 1968). According to the instinct view, territorial behavior in humans and animals is instinctively determined: There is a drive to claim and defend territory (e.g., humans and animals mark off their turf to keep others out, and respond with vocal warnings and bodily threats to invaders) (Ardrey, 1966; Lorenz, 1966). Since the earth has a limited amount of space, and we are all driven to make and defend territorial claims, conflict is inevitable. Needless to say, this set of beliefs makes some fairly pessimistic predictions regarding the future of humankind. However, few investigators hold that territorial behavior is entirely instinctive.

The position that territoriality is learned suggests that in humans it results from past experience and from culture. For example, people learn through socialization that certain places are associated with particular roles. And the patterns of learning that occur depend on culture (e.g., some cultures are nomadic and relatively aterritorial, while others are highly territorial). Some proponents of learned territorial behavior assume that such learning is limited to humans; in animals territoriality is instinctively driven. For them, even when humans and animals exhibit similar behaviors,

such as aggression against an intruder, the same mechanisms may not be responsible.

Finally, there is the perspective that human and perhaps even animal territorial behavior results from an interaction of instinct and learning. This view holds that both processes contribute to territorial actions. The exact way in which this may occur is yet to be specified (Altman & Chemers, 1980). However, it is quite possible that we are predisposed toward territorial behaviors through instinct, but that learning determines the intensity and form of our territorial actions. Alternatively, it has been proposed that instinct guides some types of elementary territorial behaviors, while learning is responsible for more complex ones (Esser, 1976).

It should be noted that while instinct theories have historically been invoked more to explain animal territorial behavior and learning and interactive perspectives have been used more to explain human territoriality, recent research suggests replacing the instinct perspective on animal territoriality with a more complex conceptualization. Based on this work, the notion of a territorial instinct in animals which is "unresponsive to learning and driven to expression" is becoming less accepted (Brown, 1987; p. 508). Instead, animal territoriality is viewed more as an adaptive mechanism which is responsive to ecological considerations (e.g., resource availability) and which is flexible across time and different types of settings (Brown, 1987). Given that the conceptualization of animal territoriality has become less biological, the argument that human territoriality is strictly biologically based has come to hold even less weight than before.

Functions of Territoriality

Just as there may be differences between humans and animals in the mechanisms responsible for territorial behavior, there are differences in the functions territorial behavior plays for each. While it should not be forgotten that there are variations between species (e.g., Carpenter, 1958), animals maintain territory for such important functions as mating, dispersing the population more evenly, food gathering and protecting food supplies, shelter, rearing of young, and minimizing intraspecies aggression. Thus, territories are often quite essential to their survival. Also, animals tend to defend territories vigorously when violations occur (Edney, 1976), though this depends on resource distribution and competition.

Humans are more flexible with respect to the use of territories for functions such as those mentioned above. For us, many of the purposes territories serve are not as closely related to survival, and they may be seen primarily as "organizers" on a variety of dimensions (e.g., they promote predictability, order, and stability in life) (e.g., Edney, 1975). For example, territories allow us to "map" the types of behavior we can anticipate in particular places, whom we will encounter there, what someone's status is, etc. In this way they help us plan and order our daily lives. Territories also contribute to order due to their relationship to social roles (e.g., the boss controls his or her office, the company lounge, the lunchroom, etc.). Precisely how territories function to "organize things" depends on the particular space in question (for some examples, see Table 8–4). In addition to their organizing function, territories may lead to feelings of distinctiveness, privacy, and a sense of personal identity. People may experience higher self-concept due to the territories they possess, and the ways they have personalized them. They may even proudly refer to themselves as "the man who lives in the red house on Oak Street." In sum, social, cultural, and cognitive elements are more characteristic of human than animal territoriality. While animal territoriality is rooted in survival needs, human territoriality is also associated with "higher order" needs (e.g., self-image, recognition) (Gold, 1982).

How do humans and animals differ with regard to territorial defense? In general, humans very rarely resort to aggressively defending

Table 8–4. *The Organizing Functions of Human Territories in Some Everyday Settings**

For People in . . .	Organizing Function of Territory
Public places (e.g., a library, the beach)	Organizes space; provides an interpersonal distancing mechanism.
Primary territories (e.g., a bedroom)	Organizes space by providing a place that promotes solitude; allows intimacy; expresses personal identity.
Small face-to-face groups (e.g., the family)	Clarifies the social ecology of the group and facilitates group functioning; may provide home court advantage.
Neighborhoods and communities	Promotes an "in-group" who "belongs" and can be trusted; differentiates it from an "out-group" who doesn't belong and can't be trusted. In some urban areas, territorial control makes a space safe to use.

*After Taylor, 1978.

their turf. When they must deal with territorial invasions, their defense is typically based on laws that defend territorial rights, rather than brute force (Brown, 1987). This is not to suggest that relatively dramatic forms of territorial defense never occur in humans. Indeed, many international problems (e.g., the continuing Arab–Israeli conflicts), as well as interpersonal difficulties (e.g., fights with a roommate over use of the VCR) involve territorial issues and associated aggression. However, one reason for the typically lower degree of territorial defense in humans than animals is that people generally recognize and avoid each other's territory. This varies, of course, with the type of territory (as depicted in Table 8–3 on page 256). In addition, humans routinely entertain others on their turf without aggression. When human territorial aggression does occur, it often takes a different form from that of animals. While human territory-related fighting tends to occur more often at the group level (e.g., one nation versus another), animal fighting is more frequently at the individual level, though it occurs at the group level as well. Unfortunately, humans now have the capacity to destroy one another's territory without physically invading, through the use of long-range weapons (Edney, 1976).

A broad concept of the functions of territory for humans may be achieved through an analysis in terms of the environment–behavior theoretical formulations (e.g., arousal, overload) discussed in detail in Chapter 4, and earlier in this chapter in the context of personal space. For example, in terms of the *overload* approach, clearly defined territories reduce environmental load by lending a sense of order that lowers the amount and complexity of incoming stimulation and makes life easier to cope with. In effect, they afford role organization (e.g., the host has one role and the visitor another); allow us to assume continuity in the future (e.g., we'll always be able to sleep in our house); and afford us control over inputs from the outside world (e.g., "No Trespassing" signs keep out extraneous inputs). *Stress* formulations view territories as functioning to reduce stress by controlling the amount of stressful stimuli we must contend with. According to Altman's (1975) *privacy regulation model,* territories are used to maintain a consistency between desired and achieved levels of privacy. From the *arousal* perspective, territories hold down arousal (e.g., by moderating the amount of stimulation we are exposed to). In the context of the *ethological* conceptualization, territories may be seen as preventing aggression and affording identity. Finally, in line with the predictions of *control* models, the fact that territories facilitate unhindered performance of chosen behaviors should be quite beneficial. Territories should also have favorable effects because the "owner" of a territory controls access to it and what goes on there.

Methods of Studying Territoriality in Humans

Past research on territorial behavior has focused mostly on animal populations; a relatively smaller amount of work has dealt with territoriality in humans. Those studies which have been done with humans have looked at territorial behavior in both groups and individuals, employing methodologies that range from controlled laboratory and field experimentation to naturalistic observation. In some cases these methodological approaches have inherent problems when applied to human territorial behavior, which may account for the overall lack of research.

Laboratory experiments are difficult to perform with humans because territoriality implies a strong attachment between an individual and a place, which is not easy to approximate under artificial laboratory conditions. Introducing experimental manipulations (e.g., territorial invasions) into real world settings (e.g., dormitories) where people do perceive a degree of territorial "ownership" avoids this problem, and has provided some rich data. In addition, many researchers have relied on nonmanipulative (and nonexperimental) field observation of behavior in naturally occurring territories.

Unfortunately, nonmanipulative observation is often fraught with interpretive problems. For example, Vinsel et al. (1980) reported an interesting relationship between the way in which students personalized their dorm room (or primary territory) with decorations, and whether or not they dropped out of college during the following year. Students whose decorations showed diversity and commitment to the university setting were more likely to survive the rigors of college than those whose decorations did not. However, what these data mean is very unclear. It could be that the way non-dropouts personalized their territory led to feelings of security, which promoted success in school. On the other hand, personalizing one's dorm room may reflect commitment to it, and lack of personalization may indicate a sense of alienation from that setting. Other studies employing nonmanipulative observation of territorial behaviors are similarly difficult to interpret.

Research Evidence of Territorial Behavior

Territorial behavior occurs between groups, within groups, and when alone. It is manifested in many ways, and it will become clear that it has some important consequences.

Territorial Behavior Between Groups   Suttles (1968) observed the territorial actions between various ethnic groups on Chicago's South Side (public territory). Each group claimed and defended a separate territory, and there were some "shared territories" in which certain community resources were used separately by each ethnic group in a prescribed fashion. Different groups could use them but never at the same time. Another interesting example of group territoriality stems from an analysis of street gang behavior in Philadelphia (Ley & Cybriwsky, 1974a). It was found that street gangs are highly territorial, taking their names from a street intersection at the center of their territory. Each gang demarcates its territory, and territorial domains are recognized by gang and nongang youth. Outsiders usually avoided the in-group's turf, but were greeted with hostility when they entered.

What functions does territoriality between groups serve? Such actions tend to facilitate trust *within* the group. Just sharing a territory can lead to feelings of group identity and security, perhaps because people in the same territory share common experiences (Taylor, 1978). And the security afforded by a territory is important: In some areas of a city having territorial control of a space makes it safe to use (Taylor, 1978). However, the in-group cohesion resulting from territories can have negative effects (e.g., the formation of gangs). It may also cause "outsiders" to be viewed with suspicion. Both of these consequences could elicit aggression.

Territorial Behavior Within Groups   Group members often adopt certain areas as "theirs." In primary territories, families have territorial rules that facilitate the functioning of the household (McMillan, 1974; Sebba & Churchman, 1983). These support the social organization of the family by allowing certain behaviors by some members, in particular areas (e.g., the parents can engage in intimacy in the bedroom undisturbed) (Taylor & Stough, 1978). In one study of territoriality in family life, it was found that people who share bedrooms display territorial behavior, as do individuals at the dining table (e.g., through seating patterns). Family members generally respect each other's territorial markers, such as closed doors (Altman, Nelson, & Lett, 1972), and a violation of territorial rules often leads to punishment of the one at fault (Sheflen, 1976).

Territorial behavior within groups is not limited to primary territories. Lipman (1967) found that residents of a retirement home made almost exclusive claims to certain chairs in the day rooms. They defended their "territory" despite considerable psychological costs and physical inconvenience. Even students stumbling into their 8:00 A.M. class display territorial behavior. Haber (1980) found that in formal-style (e.g., traditional lecture) classes, about 75 percent of the students claimed a particular seat, and occupied it more than half the time. In informally run classes this occurred for only 30 percent of the students. Also, of those students who claimed a seat to be their territory, 83 percent chose the one that they occupied during the first, second, or third class period. In addition to choosing a seat as their territory, many students used markers to delineate their turf. "Marking" (e.g., placing books and possessions to defend one's turf) is also frequent in libraries and cafeterias, among other places (e.g., Fisher & Byrne, 1975; Taylor & Brooks, 1980).

A number of researchers have investigated whether some members of intact groups are more territorial than others. One line of research has searched for gender differences, and it is reliably found that males are more territorial—have larger territories—than females (Mercer & Benjamin, 1980). In addition, some studies with animals show a strong relationship between dominance within a group and territoriality, generally finding that more dominant animals are more territorial. This finding, however, depends on resource scarcity and competition. Although research with humans has sometimes demonstrated mild support for the dominance–territoriality relationship found in animals, in some studies opposite results have been observed. Whether this inconsistency is the result of methodological difficulties (e.g., problems in defining dominance and territoriality operationally; use of unusual subject populations) or the absence of reliable relationships between dominance and territoriality in hu-

mans, is at present somewhat uncertain (cf. Edney, 1975). In any event, it seems that the relationship between dominance and territoriality is quite complex (Brown, 1987).

One attempt to interpret these conflicting findings is an analysis made by Sundstrom (1976). Sundstrom suggested that whether more dominant individuals will display higher or lower territorial behavior depends heavily on the situational context. He posited that in environments where there are only a few desirable places (e.g., private rooms in a boys' home), dominant individuals should end up with them and hence appear to be highly territorial. In contrast, when a setting has no areas that are more desirable than others, dominant individuals should roam over large amounts of space and appear to be very low in territoriality. This hypothesis has been supported, at least in a suggestive sense, by a series of studies. In the stark and rather uniform confines of a mental hospital, Esser et al. (1965) obtained suggestive evidence of an inverse relationship between dominance and territoriality (i.e., more dominant individuals displayed less territoriality). In a home for juvenile delinquents, which presumably had more environmental variation, a direct relationship was found between dominance and territoriality. In addition to its dependence on the level of environmental variation in a setting, the dominance–territoriality relationship also depends on group composition and social organization. It has been shown that adding and removing group members or changing the social organization of the group can significantly affect the nature of dominance–territoriality relationships (DeLong, 1973; Sundstrom & Altman, 1976).

Researchers (e.g., Esser, 1973; Taylor, 1978) suggest that where a dominance–territoriality relationship does exist, it should facilitate group functioning. This has yet to be tested experimentally—but why do *you* feel this represents a viable hypothesis? Investigators propose that if those with high dominance are recognized as having access to the best space, this helps clarify the ecology of the group and thus reduces conflicts within it (e.g., Taylor, 1978).

Territorial Behavior When Alone   Territoriality also exists for individuals who are alone. In fact, research suggests that people may feel a stronger ownership of a setting when alone than when part of a group (Edney & Uhlig, 1977). Thus, members of a family or roommates may feel lower responsibility to maintain their turf, and may individually exert less surveillance over it, than single occupants. This also implies that there may be more vandalism, theft, etc. in group than in individual residences.

Signals of Territoriality: Communicating Territorial Claims   What do a backyard fence, a chair with a coat on its back, a nameplate on an office door, and a blanket at the beach have in common? All are ways of communicating territorial ownership to others as well as, perhaps, reassuring oneself regarding ownership or propriety over something (Truscott, Parmelle, & Werner, 1977). We engage in these types of behaviors in primary, secondary, and in public territories. How effective are our various defense strategies in warding off territorial invaders? While it might be speculated that they would be increasingly effective as one moves from public to primary territories, this has yet to be demonstrated. It has been suggested, however, that in certain public territories (e.g., an airport, bus station), rather than provide protection from invasion, valuable markers (e.g., a suitcase, fur coat) are apt to be stolen (Brown, 1987)! In general, research has focused on assessing the relative effectiveness of different types of territorial signals in a particular setting (Figures 8–10 and 8–11).

Sommer (1969) conducted studies that looked at the relative effectiveness of various strategies for warding off territorial invaders in libraries. At low levels of overall density, people were less likely to sit down at tables with any kind of marker (e.g., a sandwich, a sweater, books) than at tables without such personal effects. However, under conditions of high density, it appears that potential invaders take an attributional approach to interpreting whether or not particular markers really represent someone who intends to return. To the extent that markers are personal and valuable (a sports coat, a notebook with a name on it), territorial ''ownership'' tends to be respected. However, when attributions of intent are not clear, as when the marker is a library book or a newspaper, the resulting uncertainty coupled with the fact that there are few available seats tend to lead to invasions. Are markers belonging to men and women equally effective at defending territories? Research indicates that ''male'' markers are much more effective at territorial defense than ''female'' markers, and that territories belonging to males (e.g., a man's vs. a woman's desk) are less apt to be invaded (Haber, 1980; Shaffer & Sadowski, 1975). It should be noted that although we and others (e.g., Taylor, 1978) consider such markers as books and coats to be territorial indicators, there is debate as to whether they function mainly as territorial markers or as interpersonal distance maintainers (cf. Becker & Mayo 1971). Resolution of this subtle point is left to future researchers.

Ley and Cybriwsky (1974a) suggested another interesting means of indicating turf ownership. They found that in Philadelphia, wall graffiti offer an accurate indication of gang territorial ownership. As a general rule, gang graffiti (i.e., graffiti that includes a gang's name) become denser with increasing proximity to the core of the gang's territory. These graffiti are readily accepted by neighborhood youth as an accurate portrayal of each gang's area of control. It was also found that often, when street gangs invaded each other's territory, they spray-painted their name in the rival gang's turf. The ''invaded'' gang generally responded by adding an obscene word after the rival gang's name! Gangs that were not respected (or feared) generally had turf covered with a large amount of graffiti put there by neighboring gangs.

Finally, in addition to traditional (e.g., books, coats) and nontraditional markers, such as graffiti, it has been suggested that *nonverbal* markers may be used to communicate territorial claims. Studies have found that restaurant patrons touch their plates when they have reason to assert a territorial claim (Truscott, Parmelle, & Werner, 1977), and in a video arcade Werner, Brown, and Damron (1981)

found that standing close to or touching a machine protected it from violation by others. In addition, people were more apt to touch their video machine to assert ownership when others were approaching.

Personalizing Territories In addition to staking territorial claims, people tend to *personalize* their territory. Some means of personalizing territory (e.g., working on one's lawn or garden, making improvements to one's property) may provide opportunities for neighbors to get to know each other better, to become more

Figure 8–11 Note the various forms of territorial defense which people employ.

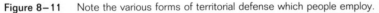

cohesive (Brown & Werner, 1985), and thus enable residents to better distinguish between residents and strangers. This may lead to more surveillance and less problems with outsiders (Taylor, Gottfredson, & Brower, 1981). Personalization may also elicit greater feelings of attachment to a place and instill the feeling that it is "comfortable" and "home-like" (Becker & Coniglio, 1975). In addition, personalizations often reflect the self-identity of the owner. For example, artifacts in people's living rooms reflect their social status (Laumann & House, 1972), and decorative complexity of housing interiors correlates with materialistic values (Weisner & Weibel, 1981). Further, observers form impressions of others' idealized self-images (Sadalla, Burroughs, & Quaid, 1980) or ethnic identities (Arreola, 1981) from their personalizations. Are there gender differences in the extent to which people personalize and feel attached to territories? The literature suggests that women engage more in personalization and have greater feelings of attachment to their homes than men (Sebba & Churchman, 1983; Tognoli, 1980).

Territory and Aggression

One of the most interesting aspects of territoriality is the relationship between territory and aggression. Although it is not always realized, territory may serve either as an instigator to aggression *or* as a stabilizer to prevent aggression. The function it serves depends upon a number of situational conditions. One factor that affects the relationship between territoriality and aggression is the status of a particular territory (i.e., whether it is unestablished, disputed, or well established). When territory is unestablished or disputed, aggression is more common. Observational evidence to this effect is provided by Ley and Cybriwsky (1974a), who found that street gangs engaged in more intergang violence when territorial boundaries were ambiguous or unsettled than when they were well established. Parallel evidence is

available for animals: It has been found that animals fight more when territories are being established or are under dispute than after territorial boundaries have been well drawn (Eibl-Eibesfeldt, 1970; Lorenz, 1966). This seems to be because under the former conditions, resource competition is more intense.

While unestablished or disputed territory promotes aggression, established territorial boundaries often lend stability and lead to reduced hostility in humans as well as in animals (O'Neal & McDonald, 1976). For example, Altman, Nelson, and Lett (1972) observed that confined groups that established territories early in their confinement evidenced smoother interpersonal relationships and were more stable socially than groups that failed to establish territories early. O'Neill and Paluck (1973) reported a drop in the level of aggression in groups of retarded boys after the introduction of identifiable territories. What are the dynamics of the process by which territorial boundaries decrease aggression? We mentioned earlier that territorial behavior serves an organizing function, indicating what is "ours" and what is "theirs." Thus, well-established territories should be less subject to intrusion, which tends to elicit aggression. In line with this analysis, several investigators (e.g., Mack, 1954; Marine, 1966) have found that the separation of neighborhood ethnic groups by clearly defined boundaries led to decreased territorial intrusion, and less intergroup conflict.

When territorial invasions do occur, what are the consequences? Predicting reactions to territorial invasions is complex because our responses appear to depend on situational conditions. For example, Altman (1975) proposed that the attributions we make for a violation will mediate our response, and that we will only consider aggression when we feel the other's behavior was malicious. And generally, we try other verbal adjustive responses (e.g., warning the individual to leave, threatening them), as well as physical ones (e.g., putting up a fence, or a "No Trespassing" sign) first, resorting to aggression only when these are unavailable or unheeded. In addition, Edney (1974) suggested that for humans many forms of "appropriate" territorial invasion exist (e.g., when guests are present) that do not elicit aggression.

One additional factor that may determine whether invasion leads to aggression in humans is the location of the territory "under siege" along a primary territory–public territory dimension (Brown, 1987). Invaders of primary territories are likely to elicit the most intense aggression (see Table 8–3). By definition, primary territories are more central to the owner's life, symbolize his or her identity, and are associated with more legitimate feelings of control than public territories. Invasions of primary territories (e.g., homes) are also more apt to be intentional and to involve a deliberate crossing of boundaries or markers than invasions of secondary or public territories. Thus, invaders are seen as more threatening and hence are dealt with more harshly. The intensity of the territorial invasion–aggression relationship for primary territories is reflected in the ambiguity of many local laws dealing with the prosecution of a homeowner accused of killing an intruder (Geen & O'Neal, 1976). One possibility for preventing invasion of primary territories is for homeowners to erect markers of territorial defense (e.g., "No Trespassing" signs). Edney (1972) compared homeowners who displayed such markers with those who did not. He found that individuals who erected forms of territorial defense had lived in their houses longer and intended to stay longer than people without territorial markers. Further, residents who displayed markers answered their door bells faster, which may be interpreted as a sign of defensive vigilance.

In contrast to the defensive posture assumed by holders of primary territory, a study by O'Neal, Caldwell, and Gallup (1975) found weaker evidence for territorial defense in public territory. This study was conducted with children who were exposed to a manipulation designed to induce possessiveness toward a carpeted play area. Children were led to another room, where they could press a button to electrically shock a clown who was advancing toward their turf. Invasions under these conditions did not lead to a convincing demonstration of aggression. However, other research suggests that even in public territories, people may exhibit defensive behaviors toward intruders. Haber (1976) found that when a participant-observer intruded onto a seat in a class that a person had sat in consistently, about one-quarter of the victims demanded a return of their seat while three-quarters retreated. If the class was characterized by low density, or if the "owner" had "marked" the seat, the probability of demanding its return was much higher.

Attempts to regain public territory are generally preceded by expressions of surprise or intimidation (Taylor & Brooks, 1980). Also, research by Taylor and Brooks (1980) indicates that as the *value* of the invaded public territory increases (e.g., a library carrel vs. a seat at a table), the likelihood of its defense rises. On the other hand, even under some of the conditions identified above as maximizing the likelihood of defense (e.g., marking), several studies (e.g., Becker, 1973; Becker & Mayo, 1971) suggest a strong reluctance on the part of subjects to defend public territories. It seems that flight is the most frequent reaction to invasions of public turf (Brown, 1987).

Also relevant to the "primary"–"public" territory distinction, it has been found that whether a territory is perceived as temporary or permanent affects our level of aggression in defending it. Schmidt (1976) reported that occupants of permanent territories challenged invaders more quickly and gave them more hostile treatment than occupants of temporary territories. For example, they were more punitive to invaders, and also more aggressive to strangers following an invasion, than those in temporary territories. So, invasions of permanent territories may promote more aggression toward the instigator, as well as more generalized aggression, than violations of temporary territories.

An Analysis of the "Home Court Advantage"

Just how pervasive is the "home court advantage" in professional and college sports? A study by Schwartz and Barsky (1977) looked at the outcomes of 1,880 major league baseball games, 182 professional football games, 542 professional hockey games, and 1,485 college basketball games which took place in a one season year. They assumed that in the absence of a home court advantage, about half of a team's total wins for the season should occur at home and half "on the road." What did they find? The results are shown in Table 8–5. For all sports, there is a decisive home court advantage. This varies somewhat according to the sport in question, ranging from professional baseball, where 53 percent of the total wins occur at home, to professional hockey, where 64 percent of the wins during the season occurred at home. The analysis of basketball records, which employs slightly different techniques and which is therefore not incorporated into the table, suggests that still a higher proportion of college basketball contests are won on the home court. This implies that the advantage of the home team becomes more pronounced for indoor than for outdoor sports.

Other studies suggest that the "home field advantage" may be greater for better teams. While even mediocre teams benefit, the better the team, the greater the benefit (James, 1984). However, when pressure to succeed is very high, being at home may be a disadvantage. While being on home turf is beneficial to teams in the first few games of the world series, when the series goes to a "sudden death" seventh game, home teams win less than 40 percent of the time (Baumeister, 1985)!

When being at home is advantageous, what types of differences in team play occur? Schwartz and Barsky found that the underlying factor in the home court advantage is that superior offensive play occurs at home compared to "on the road;" there are no differences for

Table 8–5 *Percentage of Games Won By Home Team in Baseball, Football, and Hockey in a Given Year.**

| | | Sport | | |
| | | Football | | |
Home Team Outcome	Professional Baseball	Professional	College	Professional Hockey
Win	53	58	60	64
Lose	47	42	40	36
Total	100	100	100	100

*Ties are excluded. After Schwartz & Barsky, 1977.

defensive play. How strongly should the home court advantage be "weighed," as compared with factors like team quality? Strikingly, analyses of the data suggested that the advantage from just being on one's own turf can actually be as significant in determining the outcome of a game as the quality of the team!

Are the same factors (e.g., control) responsible here as were responsible for the dominance of the individual who was on "home turf" in the dormitory studies described earlier? While these factors undoubtedly play a role, there is one additional element—home audience support. And Schwartz and Barsky (1977) feel that this factor—the applause for the home team and jeers for the visitors—is an important determinant in the home court advantage in sports. This may also be why the home court advantage is greater for indoor sports, where sounds do not get lost in the air. Also, distance between noisy fans and players is also greater outdoors than indoors.

Territory as a Security Blanket: Home Sweet Home

If individuals are willing to defend territories from invasion by resorting to aggression, it would seem that such areas must be associated with a number of important benefits. The assertion that territories have beneficial aspects is supported by the conceptual analysis we put forward earlier, which suggested that many properties of territories are associated with positive effects. The truth of the saying "Home Sweet Home" has been assessed in a number of experiments. In a study which also supported the assumptions of Altman's (1975) conceptual distinction between primary, secondary, and public territory, Taylor and Stough (1978) found that subjects reported the greatest feelings of control in primary territories (e.g., dormitory rooms), followed by secondary territories (e.g., a fraternity house) and public territories (e.g., a bar). In a great deal of research, feelings of control are related to a sense of well-being, as well as other positive effects (e.g., beneficial implications for health). And a study by Edney (1975) using Yale undergraduates highlights additional benefits of being on one's turf. The experiment took place in the dormitory room (primary territory) of one member of the pair, where the other member was a "visitor." Subjects who were in their own territory were rated by visitors as more relaxed than residents rated visitors, and residents rated the rooms as more pleasant and private than visitors did. Residents also expressed greater feelings of passive control. In a related study, Edney and Uhlig (1977) reported that subjects induced to think of a room as their territory felt less aroused, and found the setting to be more pleasant than others in the control group.

While being on one's own turf is typically associated with enhanced perceived and actual control, in offices at least, this may depend in part on status. Katovich (1986) had subjects role play a conversation between an employer and an employee which took place either in the boss's or the employee's office. It was found that the office holder always initiated the handshake at the start of the interaction, but that the power to invite the "visitor" to enter depended on status. While the boss invited the employee to enter when the meeting occurred in his office, he sat down *without* waiting for an invitation when it was in the employee's office! Thus, in certain places, one's territorial "rights" depend on one's status.

An additional advantage of being "at home" is that under conditions that do not promote liking (e.g., competition, disagreement, or unequal roles), the resident has a "home court" advantage that allows him or her to dominate the visitor. Martindale (1971) reported that dormitory residents were more successful at a competitive negotiation task on "their own turf" than were visitors. Similarly, Conroy and Sundstrom (1977) found that when resident–visitor dyads held dissimilar opinions (conditions that cause disliking), residents talked more and exerted more dominance over the conversation than visitors. When the two had similar opinions (conditions that promote liking), visitors talked more and dominated the conversation. The authors interpreted residents' allowing this as a sort of "hospitality effect." In addition, Taylor and Lanni (1981) have shown that residents have an advantage under conditions that do not facilitate liking in triads as well as dyads, and for both low and high dominance individuals. The effect is even true of larger groups and in settings other than primary territory. In a comparison of the "home" and "away" records of the University of Utah football team over a three-year period, Altman (1975) found that the team won two-thirds of its home games and only one-fourth of its away games (see the box).

Some Design Implications

Given that territories may be quite beneficial, it is unfortunate that the design of many settings, especially institutions, does not foster these benefits. Most mental hospitals, old age homes, residential rehabilitation settings, prisons, etc. do not contain architectural features or permit behavior (e.g., bringing personal possessions, personalizing an area) that promote feelings of personal territory. The contention that these would benefit patients has been demonstrated in research (Barton, 1966). When areas were redesigned to increase territoriality, or residents were allowed to personalize the environment, the social atmosphere of the ward improved and there were more positive feelings toward the environment (Holahan, 1976; Holahan & Saegert, 1973).

Designing space so that it appears to be someone's turf has other advantages as well. When spaces have clear boundaries that signal they "belong" to somebody, there is evidence that less crime and vandalism occur. In a study of low-cost urban housing developments, Newman (1972) found that public areas having no clear symbols of ownership were more likely to be vandalized than those with well-marked boundaries. (Expanded coverage of this relationship and the factors that may account for it is provided in Chapter 10). Although Newman's findings have been subjected to methodological criticism (cf. Adams, 1973), supportive evidence is provided in a study that observed the locations where cars were vandalized in inner-city Philadelphia (Ley & Cybriwsky, 1974b). It was suggested that more vandalism took place near "public" places such as factories, schools, and vacant lots than in areas that signaled territorial ownership, such as private dwellings and small businesses. While the nature of the research precludes a definitive statement, it seems that people tend to respect properties that can be identified as someone's territory more than properties that cannot be easily identified.

An interesting study by Brown (1979) identified a number of specific characteristics of residential areas in general, and homes in particular, that are associated with burglary. Before we tell you what she found, take a look at the houses in Figure 8–12. Which do *you* think you would rob if you were a burglar? Brown found that signs of defensibility, occupancy, and territorial concern were different in a sample of homes that were not burglarized, than in a corresponding sample which were. Specifically, burglarized homes differed in that the **symbolic barriers** they possessed were public, as opposed to private. For example, burglarized homes had fewer assertions of the owner's private identity (e.g., name and address signs), more signs of public use (e.g., public street signs in front of them), and fewer

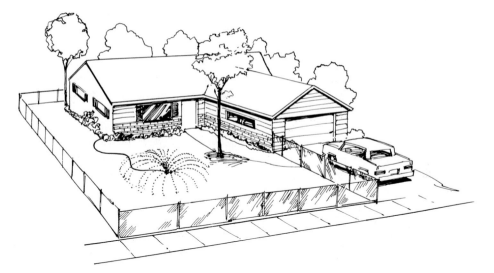

Figure 8–12A   A nonburglarized house on a nonburglarized block. (From Brown, 1979; reprinted by permission.)

Figure 8–12B   A burglarized house. (From Brown, 1979; reprinted by permission.)

attempts at property demarcation from the street (e.g., hedges, rock borders). They also had fewer *actual barriers* (e.g., fewer locks or fences to communicate a desire for privacy, and deter public access). Also, on streets where burglaries occurred, there were fewer *traces* (e.g., signs of occupancy) that showed the presence of local residents. Burglarized houses had fewer parked cars and sprinklers operating, and residents were less apt to be seen in their yards by the researchers. In this regard a garage was significant, since it often makes it ambiguous whether or not people are home (e.g., a garage without windows can disguise the absence of the car). More burglaries occurred in homes without garages, perhaps because for them the absence of cars makes it likely that the house is empty. Finally, in houses where burglaries occurred, *detectability* (the potential for exercising surveillance) was lower, and neigh-

Territorial Behavior And Fear
of Crime In the Elderly

We have seen that when symbols of ownership are present, less crime and vandalism may occur. Are people who display more territorial markers (e.g., "No Trespassing" signs, fences, external surveillance devices) less fearful of being victims of crime than people who do not display such markers? In an interesting study, Patterson (1978) explored this problem with an elderly population in central Pennsylvania. Since fear of crime is a major source of anxiety for older citizens (some studies have shown it to be greater than fear of illness), determining the effectiveness of territorial markers in ameliorating such fears is important from both an applied and a conceptual perspective.

Patterson had interviewers approach the homes of elderly citizens to record unobtrusively any territorial markers.

After gathering these data, the interviewer approached the homeowner and conducted an interview. The interview consisted of several sets of questions, including fear of property loss (e.g., "When I am away, I worry about my property") and fear of personal assault (e.g., "There are times during the night when I am afraid to go outside"). What were the results of the study? It was found that displaying territorial markers was associated with less fear of both property loss and assault, especially for males. (See Figure 8–13.)

What do these data mean? It is clear that there is an important relationship between reduced fear of crime in the elderly and territorial behavior. However, since this study is correlational, the mechanism by which territoriality is associated with reduced fear is not clear. One possibility is that erecting territorial markers gives one perceived and perhaps actual control and thus leads to feelings of safety. A study by Pollack and Patterson (1980) as well as research by Normoyle and Lavrakas (1984) tentatively supports this interpretation. If this is the case, there is a clear design implication: Encourage people to display territorial markers to enhance their feelings of security. But there is another explanation that cannot entirely be ruled out: Those elderly homeowners who feel sufficient mastery of the environment to erect territorial boundaries are also those who would feel secure from victimization in any event. If this is the case, the implications of the research would seem less clear.

Figure 8–13   Fear of property loss by males and females high and low in territoriality. (From Patterson, A. H., 1978, Territorial behavior and fear of crime in the elderly. *Environmental Psychology and Nonverbal Behavior, 3,* 131–144.)

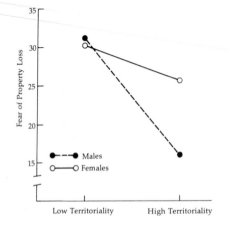

boring houses were less visually accessible.

Designers should consider the above findings. Too often areas do not communicate the types of territorial messages they should, or are ambiguous with regard to their territorial status, due to designed-in characteristics. In addition, some territories do not promote the sorts of activities people need to use them for (e.g., the value of primary territory may be hampered due to a lack of adequate soundproofing, or too much visual access). This often leads to lack of use, to use by the wrong parties, or to various types of misuse. Care during the design process could prevent this.

SUMMARY

Personal space is invisible, mobile, and body-centered, regulating how closely individuals interact. It has two purposes—protection and communication. The size of the spatial zone necessary to fulfill the protective and communicative functions changes according to situational variables (e.g., attraction, activity being engaged in) and individual difference variables (i.e., race, personality). Individuals find it aversive (1) when they are constrained to interact with another person under conditions of inappropriate (too much or too little) personal space; and (2) when their personal space is "invaded" by others. Interacting at inappropriate distances leads to negative affect and negative inferences; personal space invasions precipitate withdrawal and compensatory reactions.

Territory is visible, stationary, and home-centered, regulating who will interact. It serves somewhat different functions in humans and animals; in humans it serves a variety of organizational functions. Human groups and individuals exhibit territorial behavior and have adopted a variety of territorial defense strategies that vary in effectiveness. Territorial invasion by others may or may not lead to aggressive responses by the target, depending on the situation. Further, being on one's own turf has been shown to have a number of advantages and elicits feelings of security and improved performance. Finally, areas that appear to be someone's territory are less likely to be vandalized.

SUGGESTED PROJECTS

1. A scale called the C.I.D.S. or Comfortable Interpersonal Distance Scale (Duke & Nowicki, 1972) permits us to diagram the shape of our personal space without even getting out of our seat! It works like this.

   Imagine that Figure 8–14 represents an imaginary round room, for which each radius is associated with an entrance. You are positioned at dead center, facing position number 8. For each of the 8 radii, respond to an imaginary person approaching you by putting a mark on the radius indicating where you would prefer the stimulus person to halt (i.e., the point at which you think you would begin to feel uncomfortable by the individual's closeness). After you've marked all 8 radii, connect the points you've marked and you'll know the shape of your personal space.

   The C.I.D.S. may also permit you to verify some of the relationships that we have described between situational and individual difference conditions and personal space without leaving your chair. For example, imagine that the approaching

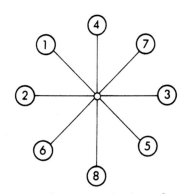

Figure 8–14 Diagramming the shape of personal space. (From Duke, M. P., & Nowicki, S. "Diagramming the shape of personal space: A new measure and social learning model for interpersonal distance." *Journal of Experimental Research in Personality,* 1972, *6,* 119–132.)

individual is a friend and mark the radius; then do the same imagining that he or she is a stranger. Does your experiment confirm the results of Byrne and his coworkers (1970), who found that people maintain smaller personal space zones for friends than for strangers? Do the same for an approaching individual who is racially similar or dissimilar to yourself or for any of the other relationships we have discussed. You'll see how the C.I.D.S. is a useful means of assessing the effects of many factors on spatial behavior. But before you begin, we have one note of caution. Be sure to remember that because the various measures of personal space are not perfectly related (see discussion on page 233), failure to replicate studies with the C.I.D.S., which originally used different methods, does not necessarily mean that the original measures are invalid. Thus, while a replication on the C.I.D.S. of earlier findings that employed other methods is valuable supportive evidence, failure to replicate should not be seen as terribly damaging.

2. Your nearby library offers an opportunity for you to study the fine art of territorial defense. Before you go, make some hypotheses about the relative effectiveness of various types of territorial markers for repelling potential invaders. Consider the possible effects of a wide range of markers, including some you expect to be highly effective and some you expect to be less effective. Collect the necessary materials and report to the library for your experiment.

   When you arrive at the library, make a mental note of the overall level of population density, and place each of the artifacts you brought at a separate empty table, trying not to use too many of the study tables in any one room for your experiment. After you have distributed them all, "make the rounds," of all your experimental tables at 15-minute intervals, noting which markers are more effective and which are less so in preventing territorial invasion. Repeat the procedure using different levels of population density.

3. Position yourself and a same-sex other on either side of a busy doorway through which many people must pass. Face each other and engage in a lively conversation for 15 minutes. Watch the reactions of the passersby, whom you have placed in the role of personal space "invaders." What do they do? Do they force their way through, wait for you to invite them to pass, or look for an alternative exit? Next, remain in your positions but stop conversing for 15 minutes and note whether the reactions of passersby change. Is your personal space more or less difficult to invade when you are talking? Finally, follow the same procedures with an opposite-sex other positioned across the arch from you. Do you find that passersby find it more difficult to violate the personal space of same- or opposite-sex dyads?

9 HIGH DENSITY AND CROWDING

KEY TERMS

anticipated crowding
behavioral interference
behavioral sink
control
correlational research
crowding
density-intensity
field experiments

high density
inside density
learned helplessness
outside density
privacy regulation model
quasi-experimentation
social density
spatial density

INTRODUCTION

Suppose you are put in charge of a large experimental device called a "mouse universe." You begin with eight "colonizer" mice (four males and four females) in the apparatus and are told female mice can bear a litter of four to eight pups once a month. You are instructed that your job as keeper of the mice is to create a veritable paradise for them, in which they can live and bear young in complete harmony and protection from their natural enemies. As an incentive for you to do your job well, your employer offers you a bonus if the population of the "universe" increases dramatically under your guidance. To ensure that you obtain the bonus, you study what can be done to provide a utopian setting for the residents. You decide to supply unlimited food, water, and nest-building materials and to provide an ideal air temperature. Furthermore, although you don't enjoy it, you vow to clean the feces that accumulate on the floor of the "universe" frequently so as to minimize disease and further assure collecting your reward.

After creating your "ideal" environment, you sit back and watch, thinking of how you'll spend your new riches. At first, things run smoothly; the males are establishing territories and mating with the females in their areas. The females are constructing nests, bearing young (very quickly, to your satisfaction), and successfully raising them to weaning. However, when the population begins to get very large, you observe that the inhabitants start behaving quite differently from before. Their odd behavior increases with expanding population size. Although some animals are still able to maintain their normal lifestyle, most males no longer function effectively as territorial defenders and procreators, and most females no longer function well as bearers and rearers of young. The birthrate declines rapidly. In addition, the mortality rate of the young becomes extremely high, and some animals become hyperactive, homosexual, and cannibalistic. You envision your bonus disappearing and wonder why these ungrateful creatures are doing this to you. You gave them everything they could possibly need—or did you?

Although the strange behavior of the mice as the population increased may have been unexpected and seemingly bizarre, it really is not. Experiments have shown that if animal populations are allowed to multiply unchecked, the resulting **high density** conditions lead to considerable disease and behavioral disorders, even when other aspects of the environment (food, water) are seemingly ideal (Calhoun, 1962; Christian, 1963; Marsden, 1972; Ng, Marsden, et al. 1973). In fact, this description of high density behavior is based on the results of actual experiments. Such research with animals provided a major impetus for studying the effects of high density on humans, which is the major focus of this chapter.

Another impetus to research on how high density affects humans was the environmental movement (e.g., the writings of Barry Commoner, 1963; Paul Ehrlich,

Figure 9–1   Crowding refers to the way we feel when there are too many people and/or not enough space.

1968) and the awareness of impending overpopulation problems that these writers generated. It seems as if we are going to live in a world characterized by higher and higher population densities, which makes the importance of studying the effects of high density on humans paramount. For example, the present population of the world is about 5 billion, and it is increasing by approximately 1.7 percent annually (U.S. Bureau of Census World Population Profile, 1985). If current growth patterns continue for the next 40 years, world population will approximately double, which will intensify the crowding caused by an expanding population (Figure 9–1).

Will the expected high density on "Spaceship Earth" lead to negative behavior in humans as it did with the mice in our imaginary universe? A final impetus for studies on human crowding was correlational work done by sociologists, which examined the association between human population density and behavior and health abnormalities. As you may remember from Chapter 1, correlational research does not allow us to draw strong conclusions concerning causes and effects. However, some of the early studies of this type did suggest that increases in human population density may be associated with pathology.

In this chapter, we will discuss research and theory on the effects of high density. Our discussion will begin with a brief overview of experimental and conceptual work on the reactions of animals to this condition. We will then proceed to the primary focus of the chapter—the effects of high density on humans. After a review of this area, some conceptualizations that attempt to explain human response to high density will be discussed. The last section of the chapter will focus on several means of alleviating the causes and effects of high density.

EFFECTS OF POPULATION DENSITY ON ANIMALS

Two basic types of research methods have been used to explore the effects of density on animals. These include laboratory methods (which tend to be experimental) and naturalistic observation (which tends to be descriptive). In laboratory research with animals (and humans as well), density is manipulated in one of two ways. **Social density** manipulations vary group size while keeping area constant, while **spatial density** manipulations vary area while keeping group size constant. For a discussion of social and spatial density manipulations, see the box on page 279.

In contrast to laboratory methods, studies employing naturalistic observation assess behavior in "real world" settings, as it is affected by naturally occurring density variations. An example of naturalistic observation is provided by Dubos (1965). Dubos found that when Norwegian lemmings become overpopulated, they migrate to the sea where many drown. He attributed this to density-induced malfunctions of the brain. Similarly, Christian (1963) observed the rising and falling population patterns of a herd of deer isolated on an island in the Chesapeake Bay. In both of these instances, density occurred independently of the attempt to study it.

Given these brief examples of how research with animals is done, let us turn to what has been found in past studies. Our discussion will first highlight some of the more consistent physiological and behavioral responses to being "densely packed," and will then attempt to place these findings in a conceptual perspective.

Physiological Consequences of High Density for Animals

Past research has shown that when animals interact under high population densities, negative physiological effects occur. Interestingly, many of these effects parallel the characteristic reactions of Selye's General Adaptation Syndrome, discussed in Chapter 4. For example, high density is associated with changes in a number of body organs, such as the kidneys,

liver, and brain (Myers et al., 1971). Such changes are hardly indicative of good health. Another consistent finding is that high social and spatial density lead to abnormalities in endocrine functioning, which may be seen as an indicator of stress (Christian, 1955).

One important effect of high density on endocrine functioning is that it leads to decreased fertility in both males and females (Christian, 1955; Snyder, 1966). For example, it has been found that male rats living under high density conditions produce fewer sperm than those living under low density (Snyder, 1966). With females, estrus cycles of "low density" animals have been found to begin at an

Figure 9–2* The "universe" used by Calhoun (1962) to study the effects of high density on rodent behavior. There are no ramps between pens 1 and 4, which means that they are essentially "end" pens. This eventually precipitates a behavioral sink in pens 2 and 3.

*From "Population Density of Social Pathology" by John B. Calhoun. Copyright © 1962 by Scientific American, Inc. All rights reserved.

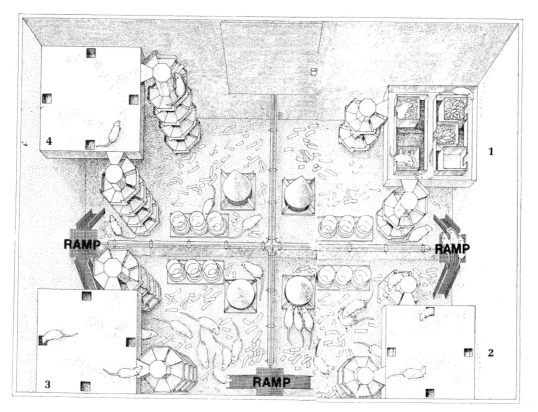

earlier age, occur more frequently, and last longer than those of "high density" animals (Snyder, 1966). Given such differences, it is not surprising to find both smaller litter sizes and less frequent births in crowded populations (Crew & Mirskowa, 1931; Snyder, 1966).

Behavioral Consequences of High Density for Animals

Some extremely interesting and provocative studies have found that various high density manipulations can cause significant disturbance to normal social organization in animals (Calhoun, 1962; Christian, 1963; Snyder, 1966; Southwick, 1955). The pioneering work of John B. Calhoun in this area serves as an excellent example of how high density affects populations of animals. Calhoun has studied both rats and mice, but his most startling study was based on rat colonies. He placed a small number of male and female rats in the apparatus pictured in Figure 9–2 and allowed them to bear young and eventually overpopulate. (Note the similarity to the situation described in our introduction.) The "universe," which can comfortably handle 48 animals, consists of a 10 ft. × 14 ft. (300 × 420 cm) platform divided into four cells, each with a capacity of 12 animals. One important feature of the universe is that ramps connect all the pens except two "end" pens, which eventually causes many animals to crowd into the central pens. Pens labeled "1" and "4" take on the role of end pens, while the other two become more central. (See Figure 9–3.)

Before they become extremely crowded, "average" male rats busy themselves accumulating a harem, mating with members of the harem, and defending territory. They roam freely around the environment, do not fight much, and do not mate with females in other harems. Females occupy themselves with building nests and raising the young. They do not fight, and resist advances from males outside their harem. How do rats behave under condi-

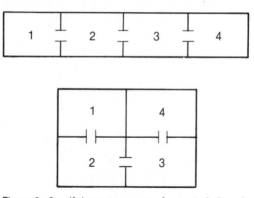

Figure 9–3   If the arrangement of pens 1, 2, 3, and 4 is changed from the one in the top diagram to the one depicted below it, pens 1 and 4 remain "end" pens with only one entrance/exit.

tions of high density? As we shall see, Calhoun observed that under high density the normal social order disintegrated, and a new one emerged.

Allowing the animals to overpopulate had adverse effects on the social behavior of all the occupants of the universe, and these effects were particularly negative in pens 2 and 3, where high density was acute. (Calhoun calls this extremely crowded area, which is described in the box on page 280, a **behavioral sink**.) In the two end pens, males and females still attempted to enact their normal social roles, as females engaged in nurturant behaviors and dominant males guarded the sole entrance and maintained a semblance of territorial behavior. But in the behavioral sink, neither males nor females carried out their roles effectively. For example, although females in the less crowded pens tried to nurse their young, to build nests for them, and to transfer them in the event of harm, none of these behaviors was effectively engaged in by mothers in the behavioral sink. This accounts, at least in part, for the fact that the infant mortality rate in the behavioral sink was extremely high, with 80 to 96 percent of all pups dying before being weaned. In contrast (but nothing to be pleased about) only about 50 percent of the pups in the less crowded "end"

The Components Of Population Density In Laboratory And Naturalistic Research

At first thought, it probably seems to you that density is simply an animal-to-space ratio. However, population density can be measured (and manipulated by experimenters) in a number of ways. For example, if you were planning to study the effects of population density on sexual behavior in animals, how would you create high and low density conditions? Two predominant approaches have been used in past research with animals and humans. These approaches focus on one or another component of the density ratio (number of people to amount of space available). One is to vary group size while keeping area constant, which is a manipulation of *social density*. This might entail putting 15 rats in an apparatus in the low density condition and 75 in the same device for high density. Or, it might entail starting out with 15 rats and observing behavior change as they reproduce, and density increases. The second approach is to vary area while keeping group size constant, a manipulation of *spatial density*. To manipulate spatial density you might place 15 rats in a 4 ft. × 5 ft. (120 × 150 cm) apparatus in the low density condition, and 15 rats in a 3 ft. × 4 ft. (90 × 120 cm) device in the high density condition.

As we will see later in this chapter, there is quite a bit more to the distinction between social and spatial density. They are not simply ways of manipulating density and are *not* interchangeable. Rather, they reflect different conditions with different problems and consequences.

Is it better to manipulate social density than spatial density, or vice versa? The answer to both is, "no," and, "it depends on what you are studying." Both manipulations are somewhat imperfect. Social density variations include the confounding of group size and space supply (i.e., group size and space per individual are changed at the same time). In contrast, spatial density manipulations confound room size and space per individual (i.e., room size and space per occupant are changed at the same time). One thing we will find in our literature review is that the way in which density is manipulated sometimes affects the results obtained (i.e., social and spatial density manipulations do not *always* yield the same results).

---

pens suffered this fate. While dominant males protected estrous females in the less crowded pens, packs of socially deviant males in the crowded inner pens relentlessly pursued estrous females, who were unable to resist their advances. This led to a high rate of mortality from diseases in pregnancy (almost half of the females in these pens died by the 16th month of the study), which was not experienced by female residents in the less crowded pens.

Within the bizarre setting of Calhoun's "universe," several social classes emerged, varying in the extent and type of their pathological behavior. There were four groups of males. First, there was a group of dominant males that generally lived in the less crowded

What Is A Behavioral Sink?

At this point, you probably have the general (and correct) impression that a "behavioral sink," such as existed in pens 2 and 3, is an area in which the negative effects of high density are intensified. However, up to now we have not discussed the dynamics by which behavioral sinks are formed. According to Calhoun (1967), a behavioral sink develops when a population that is uniformly distributed becomes nonuniformly distributed in groups far exceeding optimal size. Two processes are involved in "behavioral sink" formation. First, some aspect of the environment or the behavior of the animals makes population density greater in some places than in others (the absence of ramps connecting pens 1 and 4 did this in Calhoun's study). Second, animals come to associate the presence of others with some originally unrelated activity. For example, in Calhoun's studies, animals came to associate food (a reinforcer) with the presence of others, which caused them to be attracted to areas where there were many animals. As we have seen,

the intense crowding and the attendant need to make accommodations to so many others was clearly detrimental to the social order. Can you think of any areas in the human environment that would qualify as "behavioral sinks"?

Given an understanding of the dynamics of the behavioral sink, how can this condition and its associated pathology be remedied? One approach taken by Calhoun was to substitute granular food (which can be eaten very quickly) for the hard food pellets (which were very time-consuming to eat) used in his earlier studies. Consequently, it took much less time for animals to eat, decreasing the probability that two or more animals would be eating simultaneously and that the conditioning process previously described would occur. In these studies, behavioral sinks failed to develop, and the pathological behavior associated with high density was less intense, although by no means low. Can you think of a similar means of eliminating the human behavioral sinks you thought of earlier?

---

pens. As noted earlier, these were the most normal animals in Calhoun's "universe." They were also the most secure, since the majority of the other animals were victims of almost continuous aggressive attacks. The second group, which Calhoun called the "beautiful ones," consisted of pansexual males. These animals could not discriminate between appropriate and inappropriate sex partners and made advances to females who were not in estrus as well as to males. The third class of males was completely passive and ignored other rats of both sexes. The fourth and most unusual group

of males Calhoun termed "probers." These animals lived in the behavioral sink and were hyperactive, hypersexual, homosexual, and cannibalistic. Classifying the female rats was relatively simple. One group (which lived in the behavioral sink) was completely abnormal, could fulfill no sexual and maternal functions, and "huddled" with the male rats. The second group (which lived in the less crowded pens) behaved much more like "normal" rats.

While Calhoun's work is clearly important, it is not without criticism. Because of the design of his apparatus, some have claimed that

Calhoun, in addition to studying high density, was also manipulating territoriality. Some rats became territorial due to design features, while others were constrained from having territories. The fact that rats in the high density pens were also less territorial suggests that both high density and lack of territoriality may be responsible for the negative effects. Others have criticized the work for having low ecological validity. In the wild, rats are not penned in as in Calhoun's "universe," and tend to emigrate when density becomes too high (Archer, 1970). The latter critics suggest that the way the apparatus was designed, "behavioral sinks" were inevitable. They imply that while the research provides a look at how things could be in the worst of all possible worlds, it may not portray a completely accurate picture of rats' behavior under high density.

Nevertheless, Calhoun's work has been central to the study of the behavioral consequences of high density in animal populations, and some of his results find parallels in that literature. For example, Southwick (1967) reported increases in aggression with increasing density in a group of monkeys. Other studies (e.g., Anderson et al., 1977) have found density-related increases in withdrawal rather than aggression among monkeys. Still other researchers have found, like Calhoun, that crowding affects the sexual behavior of rats born in high density settings (e.g., Chapman, Masterpasqua, & Lore, 1976; Dahlof, Hard, & Larsson, 1977).

Having discussed the effects of high density on social behavior and physiological responses, we might ask what other consequences high density has for animals. While a complete discussion is beyond our scope, a final effect worthy of mention is that high density is associated with decrements in learning and task performance. Goeckner, Greenough, and Maier (1974) raised rats in groups of 1, 4, and 32. It was found that animals raised in the most crowded conditions showed poorer performance on complex tasks, though no performance deficits were found for simple tasks.

Further, Bell et al. (1971) reported decreased maze exploration and activity levels in settings with high social density.

Conceptual Perspectives: Attempts to Understand High Density Effects in Animals

Given that animals respond negatively to high density, what is responsible for these reactions? A number of attempts have been made to explain the negative effects of high density on animals. In a sense, these perspectives view the negative responses of animals to high density as *adaptive* mechanisms that act to prevent extinction due to overpopulation. Although none of the conceptual schemes has received the unqualified support of the scientific community, they are useful in adding to our understanding of the effects of density on animals. At this point, we should consider the various viewpoints as "possibilities" and expect the eventual explanation to be an integration of several approaches.

One conceptualization of the effects of high density on animals has been proposed by Calhoun (1971). This formulation can be used to explain both the extremely negative consequences that occurred in the behavioral sink and the relatively less negative effects that occurred elsewhere. First, Calhoun assumes that species of mammals are predisposed by evolution to interact with a particular number of others. This is termed their "optimal group size." It leads to a tolerable number of contacts with others each day, some of which are gratifying and some of which are frustrating. Calhoun suggests that as the group increases beyond the optimal size, the ratio of frustrating to gratifying interactions becomes more unfavorable. Further, interruptions in necessary periods of solitude increase, and these are experienced as aversive. This state of affairs becomes extremely debilitating when the number in the group approaches twice the optimal number, and a sustained period under such conditions produces the sort of effects observed in Calhoun's "rat universe" (Figure 9–4).

Another conceptualization of the negative effects of high density on animals is social stress theory (Christian, 1955). From this perspective, it is assumed that the social consequences of high density (e.g., increased social competition, effects on social hierarchies) are stressful, and that stress produces an increase in the activity of the adrenal glands as part of a stress-like syndrome. (Recall the evidence described earlier that high density is associated with changes in endocrine functioning.) It is believed that increased adrenal activity is responsible for many of the negative physiological and behavioral effects associated with high density. Interestingly, social stress theory predicts that glandular activity may also moderate a population *increase* when populations are very small. Since its social consequences are not stressful, low density does not elicit negative physiological and behavioral effects, and thus facilitates higher birthrate, longer life span, and so on. Social stress theory involves a type of endocrine feedback system that keeps density at an acceptable level.

An explanatory framework based on territorial behavior has been proposed in the work of Ardrey (1966) and Lorenz (1966). It assumes that the negative effects of density on animals are caused primarily by aggression induced by territorial invasions. These writers suggest that as population density increases beyond an optimal level, violations of territorial "rights" increase, precipitating high levels of aggression. (The relationship between territorial invasion and aggression in animals was discussed in Chapter 8.) Such aggression results in the negative physiological and behavioral effects described earlier as associated with high density. Under conditions of low density, territories are not violated, aggression is low, and the population can increase toward the optimal level. This formulation, however, cannot ex-

Figure 9–4 Calhoun suggests that animals are evolutionarily predisposed to interact with a particular number of others. When more than the "optimal group size" are present, interactions become aversive, and at twice the optimal size conditions may become debilitating.

plain the effects of density on species of animals that are relatively nonterritorial.

Another way to integrate these formulations as well as others (cf. Frank, 1957; Krebs, 1972; Pearson, 1966, 1971; Pitelka, 1957) has been proposed by Wilson (1975). He assumes that there is a tendency for populations to return to an optimal level of density. How does this occur? It is accomplished by "density-dependent controls" (e.g., by varying levels of aggression, stress, fertility, emigration, predation, and disease). According to Wilson, such controls operate through natural selection. For example, at high density, selection may favor an aggressive organism, which will bring the population into decline. At low density, aggressive organisms would be at a disadvantage, and the gene frequencies would change to favor more gentle behavior, permitting the population to expand. In effect, such a process protects the species from extinction caused by under- or overpopulation.

Summary Animals experience various severe, negative physiological and behavioral reactions to high density conditions. These include changes in body organs, glandular malfunctions, and extreme disruption of social and maternal behavior. Calhoun's research with rodents powerfully demonstrates many of these effects and shows that they are intensified when behavioral sinks develop. Before we conclude, however, we should add one caveat. Although the findings we discussed in this section are quite consistent, it is important to note that there are some variations among species in the reactions that occur. Finally, several different conceptual schemes have been proposed to explain animal reactions to high density.

EFFECTS OF HIGH DENSITY ON HUMANS

After reviewing a series of studies on the physiological and behavioral effects of high density on animals, as well as some conceptual frameworks in which to view them, it is tempting to speculate about whether this same pattern of effects can generalize to humans. (Figures 9–5, 9–6). Scientists and philosophers have puzzled over the differences between humans and animals for centuries, and endless arguments have emerged. (See the box on page 285 for a discussion of what we can assume about humans from our study of the literature on animal behavior.)

Differences between humans and animals notwithstanding, most early research on human crowding assumed that for us, like animals, high density would lead to uniformly negative effects. To the surprise of everyone, this was not the case. While for animals high density is generally aversive, for humans it depends more on the situation. For the most part, the effects of high densities on people are neither severe nor uniform (Baum & Paulus, 1987). Our discussion of human response to high density will first highlight research findings and then integrate them in terms of the general environment-behavior model presented in Chapter 4. Before proceeding, however, we will pause to consider the methodologies used to study human reactions to high density.

Methodologies Used to Study High Density in Humans

The method most often used to study high density in humans is laboratory experimenta-

Figure 9–5 While it is generally the case that animals respond negatively to high density, for some it constitutes "standard operating conditions" and does not lead to negative consequences. Optimal population densities for some species may appear quite crowded to us. (James O. Whittaker)

tion. Laboratory studies have a number of advantages over other techniques, as discussed in Chapter 1. However, for exploring high density in humans, they have two disadvantages worthy of mention. First, creating high density conditions in the laboratory is somewhat artificial, which may affect generalizability to the "real world." Second, laboratory studies can explore only very short-term high density effects, which is a serious problem. In attempts to remedy these deficiencies, researchers have increasingly turned to field research techniques (i.e., **field experiments** and field studies). These offer greater realism than laboratory experiments and permit us to study longer-term density effects. However, while field experiments permit us to make causal inferences, field studies do not. **Quasi-experimentation**, a field study technique that permits one to more closely approximate a causal inference through the use of certain experimental designs, allows both the realism of field settings (e.g., prisons, dormitories) and some ability to infer causality.

A final research technique for studying high density in humans is **correlational research**. This is used primarily by sociologists and involves correlating different indices of population density with the frequency of various abnormal behaviors. These studies have generally looked at correlations between pathology and two types of density: **inside density** (e.g., number of persons per residence or per room) and **outside density** (e.g., number of persons, dwellings, or structures per acre). Unfortunately, early sociological-correlational research failed to control for a number of variables that may vary along with density (e.g., income, education), and the results are of questionable value. A "second generation" of studies has statistically controlled for these confounding variables.

Although these later studies represent an improvement over earlier sociological-correlational research, several important weaknesses remain. First, so many different indices of inside and outside density are used that meaningful comparison among studies is difficult.

Figure 9–6 In general, humans evidence more variable reactions to high density than animals do. Sometimes we like it; sometimes we don't. (James O. Whittaker)

What Does Animal Research Tell Us About Humans?

As a rule, it is difficult to assume that generalization from animals to humans will occur (although in reading this chapter you will find that both sometimes respond similarly). Why shouldn't we expect findings that hold for animals to necessarily be true for humans?

First, animal behavior appears to be determined largely by biological factors, whereas humans depend much more on learning and cultural inputs (Swanson, 1973). Unlike other animals, thought processes and learning play an important role in determining the extent of human stress reactions (Baum & Paulus, 1987). Also, humans have more means at their disposal to adapt to high density. For example, when the number of interactions between people gets too great, humans have many ways of moderating them (Baum & Paulus, 1987). In addition, while naturalistic high density for animals is almost always accompanied by lack of food, humans are able to live under such conditions and feed themselves adequately. Finally, the fact that most animal data are based on organisms that exist only in high density settings limits their generalizability to humans, who often have at least brief opportunities to escape (Evans, 1978). Are there situations in which animal responses to high density may be especially likely to generalize to humans? Interestingly, the similarities between human and animal responses to high density may be greatest for human populations whose ability to cope with stressors has broken down and become ineffective (Baum & Paulus, 1987).

If there are often difficulties in generalizing from animal research to humans, what value does animal research have? We should view animal studies as important in their own right for what they say about the impact of density on animals and as a rich source of hypotheses concerning how humans *may* respond to high density. For example, the notion of unwanted interaction and social regulation that forms the basis of Baum and Valins' (1977) studies of college dormitories (page 291) was directly derived from Calhoun's notion of balancing frustrating and gratifying interactions. As with animal populations, Baum and Valins and others have found that in humans, exposure to large numbers of others has negative effects, as does a lack of social structure. The value of animal work as a source of hypotheses—and sometimes generalizable data—about human reactions to high density is enhanced by several methodological strengths of animal research over human research:

1. There are ethical problems in studying *long-term* high density in humans: These make it difficult to do the type of well-controlled studies commonly done with animals.

2. Since animals bear young more quickly than humans, it is possible to observe the cycle in which they reproduce and overpopulate in a much shorter period of time.

3. It is easier to study physiological and behavioral responses of animals without disturbing the process being monitored than it is with humans.

Second, it appears that the more fruitful of the studies have focused on relating smaller scale indices (e.g., persons per room) rather than larger scale indices (e.g., persons per acre) to pathology (Gove & Hughes, 1983). Third, while they can tell us whether various disorders are associated with density, sociological-correlational studies can give us very little information about the specific cause of pathology. We will review some of the research employing this approach in the present chapter, but since much of it focuses on the relationship between levels of urban density and urban pathology, this work will also be considered more fully in Chapter 10.

Having reviewed the methodologies used in human research on high density, we now turn to the research itself. Our review will be organized into conceptually related areas: how density makes us feel (e.g., its consequences for affect, arousal, and illness), how density affects our social behavior (i.e., its effects on interpersonal attraction, aggression, and prosocial behavior), and how density affects task performance. While we will discuss the effects of density on each of these areas separately, it is important to keep in mind that density may have simultaneous effects in several domains, and that these effects may be interrelated.

Feeling the Effects of Density: Its Consequences for Affect, Arousal, and Illness

Affect   One of the most common assumptions that people make about crowding is that it makes people "feel bad." In line with this observation, several studies report that high social density may cause negative affective states (Evans, 1975; Sundstrom, 1975). One field study (Saegert, MacIntosh, & West, 1975) had subjects perform a series of tasks in either crowded or uncrowded settings. It was observed that subjects reported more anxiety in the dense than in the nondense conditions, although this probably does not surprise anyone

who has ever had to perform a task with hordes of others "breathing down your neck." Also, a study by Baum and Greenberg (1975) found that the mere anticipation of being in a crowd elicits a negative mood.

Before concluding that crowding invariably leads to negative mood, however, we should consider some evidence that suggests the negative feelings caused by high spatial density may be stronger in males than in females. Several studies (Freedman et al., 1972; Ross et al., 1973) found that while males experience more negative moods in high than in low spatial density conditions, the reverse is true for females (Figure 9–7). One way to explain these effects is the finding in the personal space literature (see Chapter 8) that males have greater personal space needs than do females.

Alternatively, in our culture these findings may reflect the female socialization to be more affiliative (and therefore to have more of an affinity for others at close range) and the male socialization to be more competitive (and thus to view others at close proximity as sources of threat) (Maccoby, 1966). Research indicates that women may approach high density settings in more cooperative ways than do men (Karlin,

Figure 9–7   Ratings of affective states for males and females in high and low spatial density conditions. Higher scores = more negative affect. (After Ross et al., 1973.)

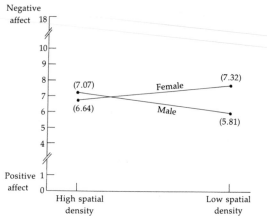

Epstein, & Aiello, 1978; Taylor, 1978). Or, it is possible that density does not cause any kind of mood in and of itself but rather serves to intensify the prevailing mood in the situation—a **density-intensity** effect (Freedman, 1975). We discuss this notion in the box on page 305.

It is important to note that the studies discussed above that found uniformly negative moods were primarily studies of high *social* density. In contrast, those that reported gender differences in affective response were studies of high *spatial* density. Recall that we said earlier that social and spatial density refer to more than just methodological differences—they reflect very different kinds of problems. It is possible that high social density is equally aversive to men and women, but that high spatial density is bothersome only for males.

Physiological Arousal   If high density affects our feelings, can it also lead to physiological effects, such as increased heart rate? As we have seen, stress has an arousal component, and several studies have examined such arousal as it applies to high density. In one experiment, Evans (1979a) had mixed-sex groups of five males and five females participate in a three and one-half hour study in either a large or a small room. Participants' heart rate and blood pressure were recorded both before the experiment began and after three hours. Results indicated that in high density conditions, subjects showed higher pulse rate and blood pressure readings than in more spacious conditions. Similarly, research by D'Atri et al. (1981) found that increasing levels of population density in prisons were associated with higher levels of blood pressure. When prisoners were transferred back to lower density accommodations, these effects were reversed.

Several other physiological indices of arousal are affected by high density (cf. Baum & Paulus, 1987). For example, skin conductance (a measure of arousal) has been found to increase significantly over time for subjects in high but not low spatial density conditions

(Aiello, Epstein, & Karlin, 1975a). And Saegert (1974) found that exposure to a large number of others leads to arousal as measured by palmar sweat. Finally, Heshka and Pylypuk (1975) compared cortisol levels (indicative of stress) of students who spent the day in a crowded shopping area and students who stayed on a relatively uncrowded college campus. When compared with the control group, males who had been in high density conditions had elevated cortisol levels indicative of higher stress, but females did not.

Field studies in Sweden have also investigated stress-related arousal in high density settings (e.g., Lundberg, 1976; Singer, Lundberg, & Frankenhaeuser, 1978). Lundberg (1976) studied male passengers on a commuter train, comparing their response to trips made under high and low density conditions. Despite the fact that even under the most crowded conditions there were seats available for everyone, negative reactions increased as more people rode the train. Further, Lundberg collected urine samples from the subjects and found higher levels of epinephrine after high density trips than after low density ones. (Epinephrine is an endocrinological marker of stress-related arousal.)

Other results, however, qualified the nature of these findings. Regardless of how densely packed the train was, riders who boarded at the first stop experienced less negative reactions and had lower levels of epinephrine in their urine than passengers boarding halfway to the city. Despite the fact that their ride was considerably longer (72 minutes vs. 38 minutes), those boarding at the first stop entered an empty train and were able to choose where to sit and with whom they traveled. For example, groups of commuters who were friends could be assured of finding seats together. In this way, they could buffer themselves from the high density that would occur by structuring the setting before it became crowded. Apparently, the **control** afforded initial passengers reduced the effects of high density, while the lack of control associated with boarding an already crowded train resulted in increased arousal (Lundberg, 1976; Singer and colleagues, 1978).

Illness   It would seem reasonable that if high density leads to negative feeling states and to physiological overarousal, residing under such conditions would have negative health consequences. High density can contribute to illness due to stress, but can also be associated with poor health because disease can "spread" more quickly in high than low density settings (Paulus, 1988). There is evidence to support the assertion that high density is associated with decrements in health. Corroborative evidence is provided by McCain, Cox, and Paulus (1976), who report that in a prison setting inmates who lived in conditions of low spatial and social density were sick less than those who lived in high densities. Recent work similarly reported that requests for medical attention in inmates were related to absolute levels of density (Wener & Keys, 1988). Other studies indicated that high density was related to blood pressure increases in inmates and even to increased death rates (Cox, Paulus, & McCain, 1984; Epstein, 1982; Paulus, McCain, & Cox, 1978). (See Figure 9–8.)

Researchers also report high density-related increases in skin conductance and sweating (Cox et al., 1982), and further evidence of the health effects of high density is provided in studies done with college dormitory residents. For example, Stokols and Ohlig (1975) observed an association between reports of high density and visits to the student health center, and Baron et al. (1976) found evidence of more visits to the infirmary by residents in high than low social density dormitories. Finally, Dean, Pugh, and Gunderson (1975, 1978) have reported associations between high density and illness complaints aboard naval vessels.

The relationship between high density and illness has also been assessed by sociological-correlational studies. Although there are indi-

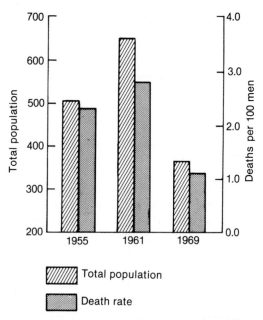

Figure 9–8   As population size increased in prison settings, the death rate in the prison also increased. Decreased population size was associated with lower mortality. These findings controlled for a number of factors, including violent deaths. The correlation between death rates and population size was .81. (Based on data in Paulus, McCain, & Cox, 1978.)

vidual studies in this literature that support a link between density and pathology, as a whole it is characterized by methodological inadequacies and inconsistent findings. When all of the research is taken as a whole, it does *not* suggest that high density is an important factor in medical pathology (Choldin, 1978; Kirmeyer, 1978). The reason for the inconsistency between sociological-correlational work and the research we reviewed above is unclear.

Summary   Having considered the effects of high density on affect, arousal, and illness, we can draw several tentative conclusions. First, it appears that high density leads to more negative affective states (especially in males) and to higher levels of physiological arousal, as measured on a wide variety of indices. Further, there is evidence (although somewhat inconsistent) that high density is associated with illness. With this capsule summary in mind, we now turn our focus to the effects of high density on such social behaviors as interpersonal attraction, withdrawal, prosocial behavior, and aggression.

Effects of Density on Social Behavior

Attraction Will we tend to like a stranger more if we meet him or her in a crowded subway car or in a more spacious setting? Generally, it seems as though high density leads to decrements in attraction, whether we are merely anticipating confinement, are confined for a relatively short period, or are confined for a long time. For example, Baum and Greenberg (1975) found that merely expecting high social density elicited dislike; students who were told ten people would eventually occupy a room liked those they waited with less than subjects who were told only four others would be present. In a study of short-term high density confinement, groups of eight males who were together for an hour attributed more friendliness to other group members under low than high spatial density (Worchel & Teddlie, 1976). Looking at long-term density effects, Baron and his colleagues (1976) reported that dormitory residents living in "triples" (three students in a room built for two) were less satisfied with their

roommates and perceived them to be less cooperative than students living in "doubles" (Table 9–1). We discuss other studies on "tripling," and elaborate on the above findings, later in this chapter.

Although it appears that high density leads to lower attraction, there is evidence (as noted earlier for affective state) that for high *spatial* density, this response is more characteristic of males than females (cf. Epstein & Karlin, 1975; Freedman, Klevansky, & Ehrlich, 1971; Ross et al., 1973; Stokols et al., 1973). For example, in an experiment by Epstein and Karlin (1975), male and female subjects participated in same-sex groups of six. Consistent findings on a variety of measures indicated that while males responded more negatively to group members in high than low spatial density conditions, females liked group members more under high density conditions (Table 9–2). We speculated earlier that gender differences in response to high spatial density may be due to different size personal space zones or to differential cooperative and competitive socializations.

Epstein and Karlin (1975) suggest another possibility. They state that while both males and females experience arousal from high spatial density, social norms permit females to share their distress at being "packed like sardines" with others in their group, which leads to greater liking and cohesion. The same norms prohibit males from sharing distress, which causes a more negative response. In a follow-up experiment (Karlin et al., 1976), it

---

Table 9–1. *Satisfaction With Roommate Under Crowded And Uncrowded Conditions**

	Uncrowded	Crowded
Satisfaction with roommate	4.9	3.7
Perceived cooperativeness of roommate	4.7	3.9

*Higher numbers indicate more positive responses. (Based on data from Baron et al., 1976.)

Table 9–2. *Ratings Of Perceived Similarity Under Crowded And Uncrowded Conditions**

Sex	Crowded	Uncrowded
Male	5.7	4.4
Female	4.2	5.7

*Lower numbers indicate greater perceived similarity. (Based on data from Epstein & Karlin, 1975)

was found that when females were not permitted to interact with each other, their positive reactions to high spatial density were attenuated. Support for this interpretation has been limited, however (cf. Keating & Snowball, 1977).

Withdrawal   In support of Baum and Valins' observation that withdrawal may be associated with high levels of social contact (see the box on page 291), studies have reported that withdrawal may function as an anticipatory response to high density, as a means of coping with ongoing high density, and as an aftereffect. For example, the mere expectation of high social density elicits withdrawal responses, including lower levels of eye contact, head movements away from others (Baum & Greenberg, 1975; Baum & Koman, 1976), and maintenance of greater interpersonal distances (Baum & Greenberg, 1975). Withdrawal also occurs during ongoing high density interactions: Subjects are more willing to discuss intimate topics under low density conditions (Sundstrom, 1975), and both children (Hutt & Vaizey, 1966; Loo, 1972) and psychiatric patients (Ittelson, Proshansky, & Rivlin, 1972) interact less frequently as room density increases. Finally, it appears that withdrawal can constitute an aftereffect of exposure to density. Males were less likely to volunteer for another experimental

session after high social density (Dooley, 1974), and groups of males preferred larger personal space and recalled fewer names after exposure to high density (Joy & Lehmann, 1975). Further evidence for withdrawal in high density environments is reviewed in Chapter 10, which considers the effects of city life.

Prosocial Behavior   If high density leads to lower attraction and to withdrawal responses, how might it affect helping? For example, suppose you lost something of value. Where would you be most confident of finding someone who would help you look for it: in a building characterized by high or by low density? In a cafeteria which is full, or one that is empty? Interestingly, most research on how density affects prosocial behavior has been done in field settings like these.

In studies that explored helping as a function of building density, it was found consistently that greater density leads to less helping. For example, Bickman et al. (1973) compared prosocial acts in high, medium, and low density dormitories. Envelopes, which were stamped and addressed, were dropped in the dormitories, and helpfulness was measured by the number that were picked up and placed in the mail. The results showed that 58 percent were mailed in the high density condition, 79 percent in the medium density condition, and 88 percent in the low density condition. In an interesting corroborative study, Jorgenson and Dukes (1976) observed the effect of social density on compliance with a prosocial request (printed on signs) for cafeteria users to return their trays to designated areas. It was found that fewer users complied during high density periods. A final set of studies which address the effects of high density on helping has compared prosocial behavior in urban and rural areas. These studies are reviewed in Chapter 10.

Aggression   If density can make us less likely to help others, does it also make us more apt to

High Density In The Dorm: Where Would You Like To Live Next Year?

One of the most often studied residential environments is the college dormitory. Some important effects of high residential density in this setting were reported by Baum and Valins (1977). These investigators performed a number of studies comparing the responses to high density of students assigned to suite-style dormitories and students assigned to corridor-style dormitories. Corridor residents shared a bathroom and a lounge with 34 residents on the floor; suite residents shared a bathroom and a lounge with only four to six others (see Figure 9–9A and B). All students shared a bedroom with one other student. While the suite and corridor designs were identical in terms of space per person and number of residents per floor, as you might guess, they led to dramatic differences in the number of others that residents encountered constantly.

What were the behavioral effects of the greater number of interpersonal contacts in corridor-style dormitories? Corridor residents responded differently from suite residents in a number of ways. They perceived their floors to be more crowded, felt they were more often forced into inconvenient and unwanted interactions with others, and indicated a greater desire to avoid others. Corridor residents were also far less sociable, perceived less attitude similarity between themselves and their neighbors, and were less sure of what their neighbors thought of them as people. Not surprisingly, a significantly lower number of corridor residents reported that the

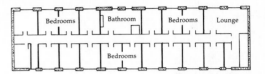

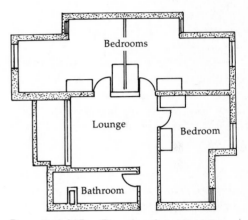

Figure 9–9 A&B   Floor plan of corridor-style dormitory (above) and suite-style dormitory (below). (From Baum & Valins, 1977. Published with permission of Lawrence Erlbaum Associates.)

majority of their friends lived on the same floor.

It was also found that living in a suite- or a corridor-style dormitory led to different behaviors in other places and with other people. For example, Baum and Valins reported that corridor residents looked less at confederates and sat farther away from them while waiting for an experiment. Corridor residents also performed significantly worse than suite residents on tasks under cooperative conditions, although they performed better under conditions that inhibited personal involvement with an opponent. In another study, Reichner (1979) found that when ignored in a discussion, residents of corridor-style dorms felt less badly than those living in suite-style dorms.

What do these data mean? It may be that corridor residents find themselves "overloaded" by their high level of interaction with others, or that they experience frequent *unwanted interactions,* and their withdrawal responses may be interpreted as coping strategies that prevent such involvement. Baum and Valins suggest that high density living in suites and corridors may be considered as a type of social conditioning process. Obviously, this process results in a more positive orientation to others in suite-style than in corridor-style dormitories. Subsequent studies have linked this difference to prosocial behavior, interpersonal bargaining, and response to violations of social norms (e.g., Davis, 1977; Reichner, 1979; Sell, 1976).

Is there any way to make life in corridor-style dormitories more tolerable? Baum and Valins found that membership in small local groups, when it occurred, tended to reduce many of the negative effects of corridor living. Baum and Davis (1980) found that an architectural intervention—that of dividing the long corridor into two shorter ones by adding a door in the middle—reduced overload and eliminated many negative outcomes. How does your own experience as a dormitory resident correspond to these observations and conclusions?

. . . .

hurt them? One research approach to this question has explored the effects of density on aggressiveness of children's play. This strategy has led to inconsistent results. Some studies (e.g., Aiello et al., 1979; Ginsburg et al., 1977; Hutt & Vaizey, 1966) have found that increased density leads to more aggression; others have found the reverse (e.g., Loo, 1972) and still others (e.g., Price, 1971) have reported no effect. Loo suggested the possibility that density affects children's aggression in a curvilinear fashion. This assertion was supported by a study that observed that moderately high density led to increased aggression in males, while very low and very high density led to decreased aggressiveness (Loo, 1978). Subsequent research, however, has shown increases in aggression under conditions of very high social density among boys (Loo & Kennelly, 1979).

In another attempt to relate density to agression, Rohe and Patterson (1974) suggested that competition over scarce resources is a major determinant of children's aggression in high density situations. If there are more kids than toys and each child wants a toy, aggression is more likely than if there are enough toys to go around. Rohe and Patterson hypothesized and found that increases in spatial density led to more aggression only if resources were limited. This relationship was also reported by Smith and Connolly (1977), who observed that increased aggression occurred during play if playground equipment was made more scarce.

Other research has suggested that children's responses to high density change with continuing development (Aiello et al., 1979; Loo & Smetana, 1978). Since children are presumably less restrained and more outwardly aggressive than adults, it may be that high density has more subtle effects on adult aggressiveness. Several studies have addressed the aggression-enhancing effects of high density among adults. Often, it appears that increased density leads to aggression in adult males but not in females, a familiar pattern in high density research. For example, Stokols and his associates (1973) studied same-sex groups under high and low spatial density and found that males rated themselves as more aggressive in the small room, while the reverse was true for females. Freedman et al. (1972) also found that increasing spatial density was associated with increasingly aggressive behavior among men but not women. When Schettino and Borden (1976) used the ratio of people in a classroom to the total number of seats as an index of density, they found that density was significantly correlated with self-reported aggressiveness for males but not females.

Baum and Koman (1976) found gender differences in aggressive response to **anticipated crowding** as well, but *only* when spatial density increased. Men in small rooms expecting to be crowded behaved more aggressively than did women in the same situation. Further, men were more aggressive in a smaller room than when a larger room was used. However, increases in *social* density did not produce increased aggression. In fact, under conditions where subjects expected large numbers of people rather than limited space, they tended to withdraw rather than act aggressively.

From the studies reviewed thus far, it appears that the aggression-enhancing effects of density may be related more to spatial and resource-related problems than to issues created by the presence of too many people. It also seems that the magnitude of the effect of density on aggressiveness is less than overwhelming (Baum & Paulus, 1987). The studies that have found increases in aggressiveness during high density have reported them primarily among men, and the effects have been mild at worst. However, the indices of aggression employed in this research (e.g., subjects sentencing a hypothetical criminal to a longer prison term) have been artificial. They are not the sort of aggression one finds in "real world" crowded environments. One reason for this artificiality is the settings in which the research has been done. Most investigations of adult aggression during high density have been conducted in the laboratory, where subjects are confined only briefly, and where the measures one can use to assess aggression are limited. Overall, these research methods pose serious limitations to our understanding of the density-aggression relationship.

These problems are only partly resolved by the sociological-correlational work that has been attempted. Such research contains methodological flaws, and shows a tenuous relationship between high density and various indicators of crime (e.g., Galle, Grove, & McPherson, 1972). However, the more "fine grained" the measure of density used in the study (e.g., room density as opposed to people per acre), the higher the correlation with aggression. In addition, there is evidence that high density is even more strongly associated with fear of crime than with actual victimization (Gifford & Peacock, 1979).

An exception to some of the above criticisms of extant research on the density-aggression link is research that has been done in prisons. Here, people are confined for long periods of time under high density, "real life" aggression does take place, and there are accurate records of both population density and aggressive behaviors. In this context, Paulus, McCain, and Cox (1981) observed that increases in disciplinary infractions were associated with increased population density, and studies by Cox, Paulus, and McCain, (1984) found extremely high correlations between prison density and inmate aggression. In one prison, a 30 percent decrease in the census resulted in a 60 percent decrease in assaults. When a 20 percent increase in the census occurred, it was followed by a 36 percent increase in assaults! Similar results are reported by Ruback and Carr (1984). It should be noted, however, that some prison studies have been less conclusive (Bonta, 1986). In addition, the extent to which this body of research could be expected to generalize to other populations living under high density is unclear. Obviously, prison inmates are different from the "person in the street," and prisons are not a typical high density setting. While this research points to the possibility of stronger relations between density and aggression in the general population than occurred in artificial laboratory studies, the extent of its generalizability is uncertain.

Summary   Our discussion of the effects of density on social behavior (i.e., attraction, withdrawal, helping, and aggression) allows us to draw several tentative conclusions. First, it appears that high density leads to less liking of both people and places, and that this relationship is stronger for males than for females. High density also causes withdrawal and less helping behavior in a variety of situations. Concerning aggressive behavior, the findings are somewhat inconsistent, but there seems to be at least a weak relationship between high density and aggression, for certain populations. The differences between social and spatial density also appear to be important. With these ideas in mind, we turn our focus to the effects of high density on a final and extremely important dimension—task performance.

Effects of High Density on Task Performance

One of the most critical questions that can be asked about high density is whether it affects task performance. The answer has important implications for the design of all types of living and working spaces (e.g., schools, factories). Most early studies used simple tasks and were consistent in finding no performance decrements under high social or spatial density (Bergman, 1971; Rawls et al., 1972). For example, Freedman and his associates (1971) reported that density variations did not affect performance of any of a series of tasks.

Later work, generally using more complex tasks, supports a somewhat different conclusion (Dooley, 1974; McClelland, 1974; Saegert, 1974; Saegert, MacIntosh, & West, 1975). As shown in Table 9–3, Paulus et al. (1976) found that both high social and spatial density led to decrements in complex maze task performance, but these decrements were more pronounced

Table 9–3. *Errors In Maze Performance As A Function Of Spatial Density And Social Density**	
Low spatial density	34.20
High spatial density	37.44
Low social density	32.13
High social density	39.50

*Based on data from Paulus et al., 1976.

under conditions of high social density. In a field setting, Aiello, Epstein, and Karlin (1975b) observed decrements in complex task performance over time in overcrowded dormitory rooms (three persons in a room built for two), as compared with less crowded rooms (two persons in a room built for two). Evans (1979b) also found poorer complex task performance under high density conditions but no impairment in simple task performance, and Klein and Harris (1979) reported poorer complex task performance in individuals who were anticipating crowding. Finally, Knowles (1983) reported decrements in maze learning under conditions of high social density when all the individuals in the room were watching the subject perform, but *increased* retention of the task, once learned.

How can we reconcile our findings of high density decrements on some tasks but not on others? One explanation centers around the fact that high density leads to arousal (cf. Evans, 1975; Worchel & Brown, 1984). The Yerkes–Dodson Law (see Chapter 4), a formulation that relates arousal to task performance, states that arousal *should* interfere only with complex task performance. In terms of this law, our observation that high density causes decrements only in complex task performance would be expected, rather than discrepant. Since the

Yerkes–Dodson Law has been supported in numerous research contexts in the psychological literature, it seems quite tenable as an explanation here. In addition, Paulus (1977) offers other suggestions for why density has not consistently affected task performance. He concludes that such factors as the psychological salience of the others present, the feelings of being evaluated, and the number of tasks subjects must perform may be important as well.

An alternative explanation for the past inconsistent findings has been offered by Heller, Groff, and Solomon (1977). They propose that many studies of high density have focused only on the physical aspects of a setting at the expense of the kinds of interactions that are typical of high density situations. For example, some studies occupy subjects with tasks so that interaction is minimized. Heller et al. suggest that this kind of procedure reduces the likelihood of finding effects of high density on task performance. In support of this, they showed that decrements in task performance occurred only under conditions characterized by high density *and* interaction among subjects. High density settings in which subjects did not interact very much did not produce task performance decrements (see Figure 9–10).

Another potential explanation is provided by a study reported by Schkade (1977). She manipulated spatial density and expectancy (how well subjects thought they would do on the task.) Results showed that the poorest task performance occurred when density was high and expectations were low—that is, subjects did not expect to do well on the task. Problems with task performance under high density conditions may be evident primarily when negative outcomes are anticipated.

A final and very important question is whether high density can cause *aftereffects,* as well as immediate effects, on performance. As you will recall, noise is a stressor that has been linked to consequences occurring *after* exposure, and some studies suggest that crowding

has lingering effects as well. For example, it was found that subjects exposed to high density later showed less persistence at working on unsolvable puzzles than those exposed to low density (Dooley, 1974; Evans, 1979a; Sherrod, 1974). In an attempt to determine whether perceived control would lessen aftereffects, Sherrod (1974) gave some subjects the option of leaving a crowded room to complete the study in a spacious setting (i.e., perceived control). Although no one took advantage of the option, this group showed fewer aftereffects than a group that was not offered an opportunity to leave. The similarity of these findings to those observed by Glass and Singer with noise (reviewed in Chapter 5) further suggests that noise and high density may affect people in similar ways.

Putting the Pieces Together: Conceptualizations of Density Effects on Humans

Up to this point, we have explored a number of density-behavior relationships, finding that high

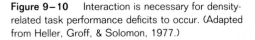

Figure 9–10   Interaction is necessary for density-related task performance deficits to occur. (Adapted from Heller, Groff, & Solomon, 1977.)

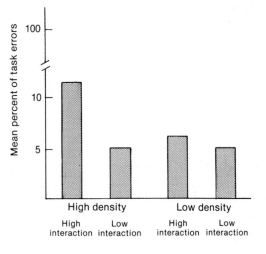

density may lead to various negative effects. As suggested in the general environment-behavior model from Chapter 4, we have seen that high density, like other potential stressors, may lead to (1) immediate effects such as physiological arousal and negative affect; (2) coping responses (e.g., withdrawal); and (3) aftereffects and cumulative effects (e.g., illness). However, high density does not always have negative consequences. For example, it impinges on task performance in some situations but not in others. Hence, the most appropriate conclusion might be that density negatively affects some of the people some of the time in some ways.

Basic Models   What is it about high density that causes those negative effects which do occur? Stokols (1976) identified three conceptual perspectives (overload, behavior constraint, and ecological approaches) used by different researchers to answer this question. All the approaches have been covered in detail in Chapter 4. Briefly, the *overload concept* posits that high density can be aversive because it may cause us to become overwhelmed by sensory inputs. When the amount and rate of stimulation occasioned by high density exceeds our ability to deal with it, negative consequences occur. In contrast to the overload approach, the *behavior constraint approach* views high density as aversive because it may lead to reduced behavioral freedom (e.g., fewer behavioral choices, more interference). Thus, whether or not we will experience negative effects depends on what we want to do and whether high density constrains us. Finally, the *ecological model* assumes that high density can have negative consequences since it may result in insufficient resources for people in the setting. Resources are broadly defined and include anything from materials to roles. When density causes them to become insufficient, negative effects occur.

Not surprisingly, additional explanations have been offered to account for how density affects us. *Arousal theory* (Evans, 1978; Paulus

& Matthews, 1980) suggests that high density may increase arousal. As we noted in Chapter 4, arousal has effects on performance in and of itself. Also, arousal may be attributed to various factors depending on situational and cognitive cues. For example, Worchel and Teddlie (1976) argue that personal space violations associated with high density settings cause arousal, which results in a negative experiential state attributed to others being too close. If arousal is misattributed, the likelihood of a negative emotional state being linked to high density is lessened (Aiello, 1983a).

Baum and Valins (1977) build upon an overload framework and propose that the negative consequences of high density are caused by *unwanted interaction*. While too many contacts (overload) may be distressing, this is not always the case—sometimes a large number of social interactions may be bearable or even fun. However, when these interactions are unwanted, or when one cannot predict whether they will be wanted or not, problems are more likely. Thus, difficulties in regulating when, where, and with whom one may interact can lead to a surfeit of unwanted interactions, and eventually, to stress. In support of this notion, Baum and Valins (1977) consistently found that "tripled" dormitory residents complained about unwanted or unregulable contacts with neighbors.

Another explanation, the **behavioral interference** formulation (e.g., Schopler & Stockdale, 1977), asserts that when inadequate space or large numbers of people interfere with goal-directed behavior, negative effects are experienced. This explanation is loosely derived from the behavior constraint model discussed earlier, and is supported by studies showing that interference increases the negative effects of high density (Heller, Groff, & Solomon, 1977; Sundstrom, 1975). Unwanted interaction can be subsumed by this model, since it, too, can disrupt or prevent goal achievement. Also consistent with the model are findings that the presence of social structure, or rules governing conduct (which lessen interference) reduce the negative consequences of high density (Baum & Koman, 1976; Schopler & Walton, 1974). Finally, studies have directly linked the type of interference which occurs and the importance of blocked goals to the intensity of stress (McCallum et al., 1979; Morasch, Groner, & Keating, 1979; Schopler, McCallum, & Rusbult, 1978).

Related in some ways is Altman's (1975) **privacy regulation model**. According to Altman, high density has negative effects when there is a breakdown in the achievement of desired levels of privacy. As we stated in the previous chapter, privacy is an interpersonal boundary process by which a person or group regulates interactions with others (Altman,

1975; p. 67). When achieved privacy is less than desired, control of social interaction is inadequate, and the person cannot regulate his or her level of interaction with others. Under these conditions, there may be negative consequences of high density. According to Altman, people cope with the inadequate privacy characteristic of high density by using stronger, or additional, privacy control mechanisms.

So, we now have a number of different, potentially critical determinants of when high density will lead to negative effects (see Table 9–4). There is no doubt that all of them are relevant, and that there are probably other ways of conceptualizing the negative effects of high density as well. How can we resolve these

Table 9–4. *Summary Of Theoretical Perspectives On Crowding*

Conceptual Approach	Critical Cause(s) of Crowding	Primary Coping Mechanisms	Reference
Social overload	Excessive social contact; too much social stimulation	Escape stimulation; prioritize input and disregard low priorities; withdrawal	Milgram, 1970; Saegert, 1978
Behavior constraint	Reduced behavioral freedom	Aggressive behavior; leave situation; coordinate actions with others	Stokols, 1972; Sundstrom, 1978
Ecological	Scarcity of resources	Defense of group boundaries; exclusion of outsiders	Barker, 1968; Wicker, 1980
Arousal	Personal space violations plus appropriate attributions	Lower arousal to more optimal level	Evans, 1978; Paulus & Matthews, 1980
Unwanted interaction	Excessive unregulable or unwanted contact with others	Withdrawal; organization of small primary groups	Baum & Valins, 1977; Calhoun, 1970
Interference	Disruption or blocking of goal-directed behavior	Create structure; aggression; escape	Schopler & Stockdale, 1977; Sundstrom, 1978
Privacy regulation	Inability to maintain desired privacy	Privacy control mechanisms	Altman, 1975

*Adapted from Stokols (1976).

Figure 9–11   Although some members of this crowd are displaying signs of discomfort due to loss of individual control, many members of this crowd are enjoying this rock 'n roll festival near Paris, France—but imagine being confined under such conditions for a week.

competing explanations? Or, must we resolve them so much as combine them into a more unified perspective? Bear in mind that some of these orientations are more theoretically sophisticated, such as the overload or ecological models, but that these are far more speculative and untested than the constraint, interference, or unwanted interaction models. However, despite the fact that the different formulations were presented as competing with one another, it is probably true that too much stimulation, overarousal, too many constraints on behavior, inadequate privacy, excessive unwanted social contact, interference, and resource inappropriateness *each* accounts for some negative effects of high density (Baum & Fisher, 1977).

More recent conceptual efforts have focused on more parsimonious explanations for why high density has the effects that it does. One of these, the *control perspective*, has been used in this regard because it crosses the lines of the models in Table 9–4 and unifies diverse theoretical currents. We will discuss the control formulation in some detail here.

The Control Perspective As you recall from Chapter 4, *perceived control* is a potent mediator of stress. When we believe that we can control a stressor or other aspects of a situation, the aversiveness of stress appears to be reduced. On the other hand, even if no other problems are apparent, losing or not having control can be stressful. Several researchers have proposed that high density can cause a loss of control (or prevent someone from ever having control), and that this loss of control is the primary mechanism by which density causes stress (Baron & Rodin, 1978; Baum & Valins, 1979; Schmidt & Keating, 1979; Sherrod & Cohen, 1979).

Can we really explain many of the negative effects of high density as a loss of control? All of the theories outlined above—with the exception of arousal theory—can be readily subsumed by the concept of control. *Overload models* assume that under conditions of high density we are bombarded by more stimuli than we can process—a situation where a loss of control is likely. And Baum and Valins' notion of *unwanted interaction* is a control-based perspective. Negative effects are the result of contact that is too frequent, which makes control over when, where, and with whom people interact difficult to maintain. As a result, interactions become unpredictable and frequently unwanted. The *behavior constraint* notion is also control-based, viewing high density as eliminating behavioral options and reducing freedom to behave as one might like. For example, having inadequate space can constrain our behavior by making it impossible to control the nature of interaction with others (Figure 9–11).

In addition, *privacy regulation models* are related to the concept of control. We can typically control the degree of intimacy in one-on-one interactions by adjusting the distance we stand from people, but in a very high density room, we may find ourselves with no choice—we must stand close to people whether we know them well or not. In this manner, we can lose control over intimacy regulation. *Interference* can also be viewed as a threat to control, because our attempts to achieve one goal or another are repeatedly blocked or disrupted. And resource problems, the focus of *ecological* models, can limit our choices and restrict our ability to exercise control. Thus, to some extent, many of the "consequences" of high density that have been related to negative effects do cause a reduction in control. But, is there any direct research evidence for the relation between density and control? (See Figure 9–12.)

Research examining the links between high density and loss of control has taken two different tacks. The first has been to manipulate personal control (i.e., provide some subjects, but not others, with perceived control), and to see if this has any effect on experience in high density settings. Rodin, Solomon, and Metcalf (1978) attempted to manipulate whether or not

Figure 9–12   At least part of the anguish evidenced by the expressions on the faces of these young baseball fans is due to the difficulty of achieving their goal—obtaining an autograph.

people riding in a crowded elevator had control. First, they observed people's response to riding in crowded elevators, and found a tendency for them to gravitate toward the floor selection panel (a control panel, if you will). In effect, people attempted to "take control" in a high density elevator by standing near the panel which regulates entry, exit, and floor selection. Next, Rodin and colleagues manipulated whether subjects were able to stand near the control panel (high control condition) or not (low control condition). The results indicated that subjects allowed to stand near the panel (i.e., those who were given control) felt better, and thought the elevator was larger, than subjects not near the panel. Rodin and coworkers (1978) also examined the effects of control on the experience of high density in a laboratory context. Again, subjects were provided with varying degrees of control over the setting, and those with control felt better than those without.

A somewhat different approach to demonstrating the importance of control was taken by Sherrod (1974). Recall that in research on noise (see Chapter 5), Glass and Singer (1972) found that the negative aftereffects associated with exposure to noise were reduced if subjects had control over it. Sherrod conducted a similar study with density instead of noise as the environmental stressor. As in research on noise, negative aftereffects were associated with exposure to high density only when control was not available. Subjects who had perceived control did not exhibit negative aftereffects following exposure to high density.

Taken together, the above studies all demonstrate that high density associated with loss of control is more aversive than high density with control, and that introducing control can reduce the potential negative effects of high density. They do not, however, demonstrate that high density itself has consequences similar to those associated with loss of or lack of control.

Fortunately, that bit of evidence has been reported by other researchers. Rodin (1976) conducted two studies in field settings charac-

Crowding In The Home
And In The Schools

Imagine yourself growing up in a small apartment with five other people who are continuously interacting with each other and with you. With so many people in so little space, you may grow up to feel the world is a complex place in which you have little power to influence events (cf. Altman, 1975; Baron & Rodin, 1978). What consequences does this have? Seligman (1975) has demonstrated that when we come to believe we cannot control our outcomes by responding appropriately (as may result from living in high density conditions), we no longer perform effectively in a number of situations. This syndrome is called "learned helplessness."

Two interesting and provocative studies by Rodin (1976) demonstrated the relationship between residential density and susceptibility to "learned helplessness." In her first experiment, Rodin hypothesized and found that children who lived in high density conditions were less likely than those in low density to try to control the administration of rewards they were to receive. In a second experiment, she exposed subjects from both groups to an initial frustrating task on which responses and outcomes were noncontingent. Rodin found that children from high density homes did significantly worse on a subsequent task for which outcomes were contingent. Thus, it appears that density in one's home is an important determinant of both the use of control and of performance after frustrating noncontingent reward situations.

A third study, by Saegert (1982), also focused on the consequences of residential density for low income children, but this time on its effects for school performance. Children from high density homes were more apt to be rated behavior problems by teachers, and exhibited more evidence of distractibility and hyperactivity than children from low density homes. In addition, reading scores were lower and vocabularies less developed for children from high density homes. Though these effects could be due to various factors, evidence suggested that density played a role.

Besides the home environment, what other settings may be sources of "learned helplessness" training? As surprising as it may seem, one important culprit may be the schools. Baron and Rodin (1978) suggest that as class size increases, learned helplessness training begins to occur. They argue that larger classes lead to lower student expectations for control of reinforcement, because teacher feedback concerning student work becomes less discriminative. For example, as class size goes up, individualized student-teacher interactions decrease, and generalized (rather than individualized) praise and criticism increase. Clearly, such conditions could lead to a state of learned helplessness and its negative consequences for performance. If Baron and Rodin's hypothesis proves to be correct, it could have a profound impact on our educational system. What have *your* experiences been in small and large classes?

terized by chronically high residential density. She attempted to ascertain whether living under high density was associated with helplessness-like behavior. **Learned helplessness** is a syndrome in which people who are exposed to uncontrollable settings learn that they cannot control the setting, and hence stop trying to do so (Seligman, 1975). This manifests itself in reduced motivation and cognitive activity. Does chronic exposure to high density result in learned helplessness? It was found that Rodin's subjects, who were children and adolescents, showed symptoms of helplessness that were associated with the high density in their homes (see the box on page 301).

Baum and Valins (1977) also found symptoms of helplessness among people exposed to high density in a residential environment over a prolonged period of time. While neither Rodin (1976) nor Baum and Valins (1977) linked helplessness *directly* to loss of control in residential settings, this has been accomplished by Baum, Aiello, and Calesnick (1978) and Baum and Gatchel (1981). It was established in these studies that as people in high density situations relinquished their beliefs that they could control their environment, their behavior became increasingly like that associated with helplessness.

Overall, there is compelling evidence that control is involved in the negative effects of high density. When control is available, high density has less impact on people than when it is not available. Further, chronic exposure to high density appears to be associated with learned helplessness. Additional evidence of the links posited by the control model is needed, but it is fairly clear that the effect of high density is at least partly determined by people's perceptions of control.

A Summary Perspective on High Density Effects Given that high density involves an array of potentially disturbing elements (e.g., loss of control, overarousal, overstimulation), how can we explain the fact that it only *sometimes* influences our behavior? Many researchers (Desor 1972; Loo, 1973; Rapaport, 1975; Stokols, 1972) have addressed themselves to this issue. A conceptualization of the effects of density on humans is presented in Figure 9–13. As you will notice, the conceptual scheme is a special case of the general environment–behavior model presented in Chapter 4.

In Phase I of our conceptualization, an important distinction is made that explains why high density is sometimes stressful (leading to

Figure 9–13 A conceptualization of the effects of high density on behavior.

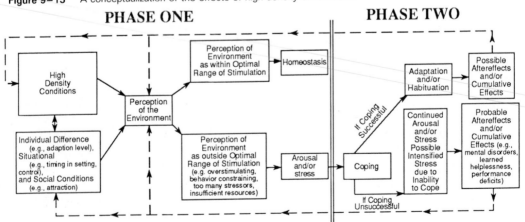

More Than 57 Varieties
of Crowding

The research we have reviewed thus far suggests that crowding has situational antecedents, an emotional component, and, of course, behavioral consequences. The theoretical notions introduced have pinpointed some of the situational factors associated with crowding, and the research we have reviewed has highlighted some of its affective and behavioral consequences. While we have "pieced the crowding story together" from a variety of sources, a study by Montano and Adamopoulous (1984) had subjects rate how they would feel and act in a variety of crowded situations, applied sophisticated statistical techniques, and yielded a picture of crowding quite consistent with the themes of this chapter—all in a single study.

The researchers found that there were four major situations in which people felt crowded, three major affective consequences, and five typical behavioral responses. The situations in which people became crowded were: feeling that one's behavior was constrained, being physically interfered with, being uncomfortable due to the mere presence of many others, or when high density caused expectations to be disappointed. What types of affective response did crowding elicit? It was associated with negative reactions to others and the situation, and under certain conditions, positive feelings. When is positive affect associated with crowding? According to Montano and Adampoulous, this occurs only when people feel that they have coped successfully with it. Regarding the types of behaviors caused by crowding, the researchers identified five: assertiveness, rushing to complete activities so that one can flee to less dense environs, physical withdrawal, psychological withdrawal, and adaptation—making the best of a bad situation! While this research did not involve people engaged in "real world" experiences with high density, it is useful as corroborative evidence for earlier findings, and it suggests some new approaches. By crossing the four situations crowding was found to occur in and the three affective and five behavioral responses, it implies that crowding comes in at least 60 different varieties!

---

negative effects) and other times is not. In terms of this distinction (first proposed by Stokols, 1972), *high density* is viewed as a physical state involving potential inconveniences (e.g., loss of control, stimulus overload, lack of behavioral freedom, resources, or privacy), which may or may not be salient to a person in the situation. Whether or not these conditions are salient depends on: (1) individual differences between people (gender, personality, age); (2) situational conditions (what the person is doing; time in the setting; presence of other stressors); and (3) social conditions (relationships between people, intensity of interaction). If the negative aspects of high density are not salient, the environment is perceived as being within an optimal range, homeostasis is maintained, and no negative effects occur. If the constraints of high density are salient, crowding occurs. **Crowding** is conceptualized as a psychological state characterized by stress and having motivational properties (e.g., it elicits attempts to reduce discomfort).

Having incorporated the density–crowding distinction into our model, we turn now to Phase II, which specifies the consequence of the psychological state of crowding. As in other stressful situations (see Chapter 4), it is assumed that the stress associated with crowding involves coping responses that are directed toward reducing stress (e.g, withdrawal). Interestingly, the overload, behavior constraint, and ecological approaches, as well as the others, each predict qualitatively different types of coping responses (see Table 9–4 for a description of these varying responses). However, the sequential links specified in our model between stress, coping, adaptation, and aftereffects conform to the general environment–behavior model found in Chapter 4. It is assumed that when coping is successful in handling stress, adaptation or adjustment occurs, and the individual is less likely to experience aftereffects or cumulative effects. If coping is unsuccessful, the stress continues, and the individual is extremely likely to experience aftereffects and cumulative effects (e.g., illness).

Coping is an important part of any model of crowding for two reasons. First, it is usually directed at reducing the causes or effects of crowding, and second, it is a continuous process. From the moment that crowding is first experienced or anticipated, people attempt to deal with it. These attempts are dynamic, continuously unfolding until adaptation is achieved, the crowding dissipates, or fatigue makes further coping impossible (e.g., Altman, 1975). This notion of dynamic coping underlying crowding suggests that responses to crowding change with the situation. Such a coping process has been addressed by research examining adjustments to high spatial and social density (Greenberg & Baum, 1979; Greenberg & Firestone, 1977). For example, Greenberg and Firestone observed adjustments of verbal and visual behavior in contexts where other

forms of coping were blocked. Greenberg and Baum reported continuing adjustment and readjustment of social behaviors among subjects who anticipated changing degrees of crowding in their experimental session.

How well is our application of the general environment–behavior model to high density situations supported by relevant data? Unfortunately, most of the studies of high density to date have had a practical rather than a conceptual focus, and few *explicit* attempts have been made to test the various relationships proposed in the model. While many of the studies we discussed in our literature review are implicitly supportive, they apply only to small parts of the ''whole'' encompassed by the model. However, a few experiments that have been done allow us to draw suggestive evidence about the sequential links we have posited. Such studies (e.g., Worchel & Teddlie, 1976) support many of the assertions, but we will have to await future research for a more precise test. At this point, we should view the model as a tentative but viable means of understanding the effects of high density on behavior. It can also serve as a source of hypotheses concerning the moderation and control of high density effects. (For an alternative model of high density effects, see the box on page 305.)

Eliminating the Causes and Effects of Crowding

At this point in our dicsussion, you might be wondering how we can eliminate the causes and the effects of crowding. We will explore the predictions derived from our general environment–behavior model, and apply them to address this issue.

Predictions from Our General Environment–Behavior Model Applied to High Density
One extremely valuable feature of our model is that it provides a framework for speculation and research about how to moderate the causes and effects of crowding. This can be of great

. . . .

An Alternative Approach:
the Density–Intensity Model

We have summarized a model that distinguishes between density and crowding and that specifies a number of factors that may cause crowding and its attendant effects. Freedman (1975) takes another position, which has been a source of great debate among environmental psychologists. In general, he does not support the density–crowding distinction accepted by most researchers.

He also argues that density intensifies reactions that would occur in any case in a particular situation. High density heightens the importance of other people and magnifies our reactions to them. Thus, for Freedman, high density will intensify the pleasantness of positive situations and intensify the negativeness of aversive ones. From this viewpoint, any number of factors can cause a negative reaction in a high density situation.

In his intensification notion, Freedman has provided a link between density and *contagion*, which is said to occur when the behaviors or emotions expressed by one person spread rapidly throughout a group of people. In a study using different room sizes and group sizes to vary density, Freedman, Birsky, and Cavoukian (1980) observed people's reactions to humorous films. After viewing the films, a confederate began to applaud, and the spread of this reaction throughout the group was noted. As one would expect from the intensification notion, contagion was more extensive in high density groups. Freedman and Perlick (1979) similarly found intensification of contagion with high density; and Freedman (1975), Schiffenbauer and Schiavo (1975), and Aiello, Thompson, and Brodzinsky (1983) reported additional evidence consistent with the general model. On the other hand, several studies have found reduced appreciation of humor under high density conditions (Prerost, 1982; Prerost & Brewer, 1980).

There is no doubt that among the effects of density is the magnification of response to various situational variables. At baseball or football games, excitement is often intensified by larger crowds, while negativity may be amplified if the home team loses and the drive home is in bumper-to-bumper traffic. Yet, this is only one of the many effects of density. Freedman and coworkers (1980) are careful to point this out, and it remains clear that high density can exert independent effects as well as intensifying the affect that would otherwise be present. Identification of those cases in which intensification is the primary mechanism underlying response to high density and when it is not is an area for future research.

. . . .

conceptual and applied significance. As you recall, the model specifies that individual differences among people, situational conditions, and social conditions determine whether or not high density is perceived as "crowding."

Research has supported the assertion that these factors can produce the experience of crowding either alone, or by interacting with each other. We will briefly discuss representative individual differences, situational, and social conditions found to affect our reactions to high density.

Identifying *individual difference* variables that determine whether high density is experienced as crowding is of practical value, since it allows us to select those individuals who will be most and least sensitive to the constraints of limited space. For example, we have found that in a variety of situations, males are more apt to experience crowding than females, and have suggested several explanations for this. There is some evidence, however, that this pattern of gender differences may be limited to laboratory settings, where there is no possiblity of escape (Aiello, Thompson, & Brodzinsky, 1983). Under such conditions, women seem to handle stress better, perhaps because they are more apt than men to share their distress with others. In long-term high density contexts, however, women may cope more poorly than men. For example, in dormitory crowding studies (e.g., Aiello, Baum, & Gormley, 1981) women sometimes report more crowding and negative effects. This may be because men cope with high density by leaving their rooms, whereas women are more involved with their roommates and spend more time in their room, which results in increased stress (Aiello, Thompson, & Baum, 1981).

In addition to gender, the amount of personal space people desire to maintain between themselves and others constitutes an individual difference variable which may affect the degree to which crowding is experienced. For example, Aiello et al. (1977) found that subjects with preferences for large interpersonal distances were more adversely affected in a high density setting than those with smaller preferred distances. Individuals who liked to sit far away from others showed greater physiological arousal, discomfort, and poorer task performance than those who preferred to sit closer. Dooley (1974) has found evidence of similar effects.

Research has focused on whether personality characteristics moderate our reactions to high density. Some of this work has focused on locus of control (i.e., whether people believe they, or outside forces, control their outcomes). It has typically but not always been found (cf. Walden, Nelson, & Smith, 1981) that internals (individuals who feel they control their fate) display a *higher* threshold of crowding than externals (individuals who feel events are controlled by outside forces) (Schopler & Walton, 1974; Schopler, McCallum, & Rusbult, 1978). One setting in which internals experienced crowding as *more* aversive than externals was in a dormitory setting where students were "tripled up" (Aiello, Vautier, & Bernstein, 1983). This may be because while externals "gave up" and stopped trying to control this difficult situation, internals persisted without success, experiencing stress along the way. Not surprisingly, people who are highly affiliative are more tolerant of high density than those who are less affiliative (Miller & Nardini, 1977). In fact, high affiliative subjects experienced more stress in a low- than a high-density dormitory living situation (Miller, Rossbach, & Munson, 1981).

When considering individual differences it is important to note that the characteristics of a particular high density setting may affect how an individual difference variable will impact on coping. For example, Baum et al. (1982) found that people who screen themselves from interaction and organize their surroundings were better able to cope with high *social* density than individuals who did not screen themselves. One would expect that this "screening" variable would be less important under conditions of high *spatial* density.

One should also keep in mind that the individual differences we have discussed were found for North American subjects, and may not hold cross–culturally. Indeed, the personal space literature (see Chapter 8), sociological–correlational studies (Sundstrom, 1978), and work on privacy (Altman, 1975) suggest that there should be cultural differences in reactions to high density. Research corroborates this assertion. For example, studies find that high density is related to social pathology in some places but not in others (Draper, 1973; Galle & Gove, 1979; Levy & Herzog, 1974). Similarly, Nasar and Min (1984) predicted and found that Mediterraneans would respond more negatively than Asians when placed in a small, single dormitory room.

What differentiates the cultures where high density may be more, and less, associated with pathology? One factor could be the *age* of the culture. Young, as opposed to older cultures may have had less time to develop means of coping with high density. According to this logic, as cultures evolve, ways are developed to cope with density, and negative effects may decrease (Gifford, 1987). Some suggestive data support the above line of reasoning, although more research is clearly needed. One society which is very old, in which people may cope especially well with high density, is the Chinese culture. It has been suggested that the Chinese may have become so familiar and comfortable with high density that, when given the choice, people often opt for high as opposed to low density conditions (Aiello & Thompson, 1980a). Further, it has been suggested that the Chinese have developed an elaborate set of norms, rules, and coping strategies to support them in a "densely packed" existence. There are rules about access to space, a low level of emotional involvement is expected with others, and interaction between different groups (e.g, men and women; high vs. low status individuals) is regulated. Further, sounds that others might view as noise are regarded as acceptable (Aiello & Thompson, 1980a; Anderson, 1972). Similar practices are found in other cultures that have adapted successfully to high density (Munrowe & Munrowe, 1972).

However, other research casts doubt on the assumption that the Chinese have an affinity for high density. In a study of people living in Chinatown in San Francisco, Loo and Ong (1984) found that residents view crowding as undesirable and even harmful. The experience of crowding was also a major reason why they might want to move. Overall, this research suggests that the Chinese like crowding no more than anyone else, and presents a forceful challenge to work implying that they bear up especially well under high density.

A final, related, individual difference variable that has been linked to reactions to high density is one's adaptation level from past experience under high density conditions. Some investigators hypothesize that people with a history of high density living are less likely to experience crowding in a novel situation than those with a history of isolation. In support of this hypothesis, it has been found that the Japanese, residents of Hong Kong, and the Logoli (all of whom live under extremely high density) have developed social mechanisms that may be viewed as adaptive for high density living. Further, Booth (1976) reported that men who grew up in high density situations were less apt to contract stress-related diseases if they lived in high density when they were adults. While several additional studies (Eoyang, 1974; Gove & Hughes, 1983; Sunstrom, 1978; Wohlwill & Kohn, 1973) support this "high density experience-adaptation" hypothesis, Paulus and his colleagues (1975) found that the longer an inmate was imprisoned, the *lower* his or her tolerance for crowding. Inconsistent evidence is also reported by Rohe (1982) and by Loo and Ong (1984). Thus, the relationship between adaptation level and the experience of crowding may be seen as only suggestive.

In addition to being moderated by individual difference variables, reactions to high density are affected by *situational conditions*. An important situational condition is the degree of control we have. Complementing the studies we discussed earlier, additional research has found that allowing people increased control over a situation leads to less perceived crowding (Langer & Saegert, 1977) and to fewer negative effects (Baum & Fisher, 1977; Langer & Saegert, 1977; Sherrod, 1974). The applied potential for introducing control into high density situations is great. For example, providing individuals who live under high density with training that enhances control (e.g., giving pointers about how to share space and ensure privacy) may help alleviate crowding and its negative effects. Schmidt and Keating (1979) have identified three types of control which might be introduced: cognitive control (accurate information), behavioral control (ability to work toward a goal), and decisional control (having choices available). They suggest that providing one or more of these to people in high density could ameliorate crowding stress.

Other situational conditions may affect reactions to high density as well. For example, at a constant level of density, men experience more negative effects when others are touching them, than when this is not the case (Nicosia et al., 1979). This supports Knowles' (1983) assertion that in addition to the more traditional measures of social and spatial density, the physical proximity of others is important to consider. All current measures of density assume that people are evenly distributed across space. However, it may not be only how many square feet per person there are in a room, but how close the others are to you that counts.

Does the amount of time we are confined to high density conditions moderate our reaction? The relationship between time under high density and crowding is somewhat unclear, but it is probably fair to suggest that the longer the period of confinement, the more aversive the response (Aiello, Epstein, & Karlin, 1975b; Loo & Ong, 1984; Ross et al., 1973). Of course, as we noted earlier, very prolonged confinement under high density may affect one's adaptation level, and for such individuals, density *may* become less problematic. Whether we are in a primary environment (like a home) or a secondary environment (like a restaurant), and the extent to which other stressors (e.g., noise) are involved may also affect crowding. When we are in a primary environment (Stokols, 1976, 1978; Stokols, Ohlig, & Resnick, 1979) and when other stressors are operating, we may be more likely to experience crowding.

This will be especially true when we view others as responsible for our distress (Sundstrom, 1978). Finally, there is suggestive evidence that we are more likely to experience crowding when engaged in work than when engaged in recreation (Cohen, Sladen, & Bennett, 1975).

In addition to individual differences and situational conditions, *social conditions* can be manipulated to affect whether or not we are crowded. These variables make up the social "climate" of a high density situation (e.g., the degree of friendship, and the level of social interaction and interference.) For example, our relationship with the people we are with may determine how crowded we feel: Less crowding is experienced with liked rather than disliked others (Fisher, 1974; Schaeffer & Patterson, 1980), with others who engage in activities we approve rather than disapprove of (Gramann & Burdge, 1984; Womble & Studebaker, 1981), and with acquaintances rather than strangers (Cohen et al., 1975; Rotton, 1987). To the extent that we experience social interference (interruptions) by others (especially if these are perceived as intentional—Stokols, 1978), or experience excessive proximity or immediacy (too direct eye contact or body orientation) (Sundstrom, 1975), crowding is more likely. Finally, crowding is more often experienced in unstructured than in structured task situations (Baum & Koman, 1976).

High density within primary social groups (e.g., families) has repeatedly shown fewer negative effects than in other groups. For example, when density *within* apartment units is examined, it appears to be negligible as a factor associated with illness or behavior difficulties (e.g., Giel & Ormel, 1977). Degree of acquaintance with others and one's relative position in a group's dominance hierarchy also affect crowding: The presence of friends or the possession of high status tends to reduce the aversiveness of large numbers of people or cramped spaces (Arkkelin, 1978).

The dynamic way in which social conditions can affect crowding may be illustrated by considering, once again, studies on the effects of overassignment of student residents to dormitory rooms. You recall that this research assessed the consequences of having three students live in a room designed for only two. Initial study of this phenomenon (e.g., Aiello et al., 1975b, 1983; Baron et al., 1976; Karlin, Epstein, & Aiello, 1978; Walden et al., 1981) revealed that the "tripling" of dormitory rooms was associated with negative mood, increased health complaints, and suppressed task performance. These findings made sense, given the increased difficulties of sharing resources, coordinating activities, and achieving privacy created by the addition of a third roommate. Yet the question remained—was this a problem of too many people or too little space? Baum et al. (1979) reasoned that it was neither. Going back to the social psychological literature on groups, they found confirmation of a notion that many of you already know: Three-person groups are very unstable and susceptible to coalition formation such that two people get together and exclude the third (e.g., Kelley & Arrowood, 1960). Given this, it seemed possible that the primary problem in "tripling" was not that there were too many roommates or insufficient space. Instead, it was that there were three roommates, one of whom was likely to feel left out and, as a result, to have less control over the shared bedroom. This "isolate," when compared with the other two roommates, would have less input into how the room was arranged and used, feel generally more "left out," have greater difficulty achieving privacy, and feel more crowded.

Research examining the formation of coalitions in "tripled" dorm rooms provided support for this interpretation (e.g., Aiello et al., 1981a, 1983b; Baum et al., 1979; Gormley & Aiello, 1982; Reddy et al., 1981). These studies indicated that students living in tripled rooms were especially likely to feel "left out" by roommates. Those who felt like isolates reported more problems related to using the room and more perceived crowding. Tripled residents who did not feel "left out" reported experiences and moods more like students living in doubled rooms (Baum, et al., 1979).

An extension of this research examined the effects of tripled and quadrupled rooms (Reddy et al., 1981). If the instability of three-person groups was responsible for the effects of "tripling," one would expect residents of four-person rooms to feel less crowded than residents of three-person rooms. If, on the other hand, the primary problem was the absolute number of roommates, then quadrupled rooms would be associated with greater crowding. Results indicated that isolates were more likely in the tripled than in quadrupled rooms and that nonisolate residents of tripled rooms reported experiences similar to quadrupled residents. Isolates, on the other hand, reported more problems with crowding than either of the latter two groups. From this research, we can see the importance of considering social processes in attempting to understand crowding.

Architectural Mediators of Crowding Now that we have tried to provide you with a feeling for some of the conditions that moderate the experience of crowding, it should be interesting to consider how we can modify existing environments or plan new ones so that crowding is less of a problem. (For a complete discussion of the design process, see Chapters 11 and 12.) What would you do if you were a planner charged with evaluating (and possibly modifying) some of the plans for a building which might affect the level of crowding residents are likely to experience? First, you would probably assess objective physical conditions (i.e., space allotted to each resident) in terms of its adequacy for the type of functions to be performed in that space. Next, you would estimate how spatial needs would be affected by anticipated situational conditions (e.g., how well the individuals occupying the space could be expected to get along) and individual differences (e.g., adaptation level). From your evaluation of objective physical space plus situational, social, and individual difference conditions, you would have an idea of how much of a crowding problem there would be. If you anticipated insufficient space, you could institute some of the architectural modifications we will describe below.

How can environments be designed or modified to alleviate crowding and its consequences? A number of studies suggest alternatives that can be incorporated into existing structures or planned into new ones. For example, for males, greater ceiling height is associated with less crowding (Savinar, 1975), and it has been found that rooms with well-defined corners elicit less crowding than rooms with curved walls (Rotton, 1987). In addition, rectangular rooms seem to elicit less crowding than square rooms of the same area (Desor, 1972), and rooms that contain visual escapes (e.g., windows and doors) are rated as less crowded than similar areas without such escapes. The latter findings suggest that in some cases, the *design* of a building affects how crowded people feel in a constant amount of objective space. Rapoport (1975) makes the important point that the level of density that people perceive, rather than the actual level of density, is apt to determine their behavior. Therefore, designs which lessen perceived density could be expected to be associated with less crowding and negative effects.

One type of design that seems to lessen perceived crowding is low- as opposed to high-rise buildings. High-rise buildings are associated with greater feelings of crowdedness, and less perceived control, safety, privacy, and satisfaction with relations with other residents, than low-rise buildings (McCarthy & Saegert, 1979). Some research suggests that residents of higher floors in high-rise buildings are less crowded than those on lower floors (Nasar & Min, 1984; Schiffenbauer, 1979), but other studies are equivocal on this point (e.g., Mandel, Baron, & Fisher, 1980).

Clearly, the above types of features would be fairly difficult to change in a structure that has already been built. In terms of more feasible modifications, placement of activities in the center of rooms rather than in a corner or along a wall elicits less crowding (Dabbs, Fuller, & Carr, 1973), and a number of studies (Baum, Reiss, & O'Hara, 1974; Desor, 1972; Evans, 1979b) provide evidence that adding flexible partitions to rooms lessens feelings of crowding. In one study, "privacy cubicles" (areas surrounded by high partitions and containing a desk and storage space) were placed in dormitory-style prison rooms. Inmates having the cubicles in their dormitories had more positive reactions to their environment and lower rates of noncontagious illnesses (McGuire & Gaes, 1982). Similarly, segmenting large dormitory rooms in prisons into smaller rooms by building a lounge area in the middle lowered illness complaints (Baum & Paulus, 1987). These studies suggest, incidentally, that at least in prisons, the number of people one must have contact with is a more important determinant of outcome than the amount of space one has. For a discussion of whether it is generally worse to experience high social or spatial density, see the box on page 311.

It has also been found that brightness (provided by wall and accent colors or appropriate light sources) leads to less perceived crowding (Mandel et al., 1980; Nasar & Min, 1984; Schiffenbauer, 1979), and that the presence of visual distractors (e.g., pictures on walls, advertisements on transportation vehicles) leads to more perceived space (Baum & Davis, 1976; Worchel & Teddlie, 1976). In addition, sociofugal seating arrangements (when people face away from each other) are associated with less crowding than sociopetal ones (when people face each other) (Wener, 1977). However, this may not be the case when relations between interactants are good.

Interventions in High Density Settings

While many intervention strategies can be derived from the various models of crowding, only a few have actually been implemented. Some have attempted to prevent crowding from occurring in the first place (e.g., by providing

Social vs. Spatial Density:
Which is More Aversive?

Should a designer faced with the unenviable choice worry more about creating a design with high social density or high spatial density? Each type of density offers different problems to individuals experiencing it (Baum & Paulus, 1987). Increasing numbers of people bring with them more interaction, more need for social structure, more social interference, and greater threats to control. Too little space, on the other hand, may be associated with physical disruption, loss of intimacy regulation, spatial invasion, and physical constraint (Baum & Paulus, 1987).

Not surprisingly, then, research on high density suggests differences in the effects of high social and spatial density. And, based on a careful analysis, researchers have tentatively concluded that manipulations of social density are more aversive than manipulations of spatial density (cf. Baum & Valins, 1979; Paulus, 1977). Specifically, they have found that high social density will produce negative effects more consistently than high spatial density, and that while social density manipulations are *generally* aversive, spatial density manipulations are often problematic only to males in same-sex groups (Paulus, 1977). In natural settings social density is clearly a more serious concern for people (Paulus, 1980). For example, Cox et al. (1984) report that

while high social density led to very negative effects in prisoners, high spatial density had few negative effects. They conclude that the best way to house prisoners would be in small, single rooms. Others report consistent findings. For example, Ruback and Carr (1984) reported that prisoners who lived in single rooms liked their accommodations more, had higher perceived control, and experienced less stress than those in accommodations characterized by higher social density.

Why might an overabundance of others be more distressing than too little space? The answer is unclear, but there are some hypotheses. One explanation put forth by Baum and Valins suggests that people are more immediately aware of problems created by large numbers of others than by spatial limitations. Also, the loss of control that results when too many people are in a room is frequently more serious than that caused by being in too small a room. In addition, people may be threatened by the presence of many others. What are the theoretical consequences of the assertion that social and spatial density may affect us differently? While we should not draw the conclusion that the effects of spatial limitations are inconsequential, we should develop predictive frameworks that account for the differences in the two manipulations.

people with information on how to exert "control" over the situation, or by modifying high density environments in ways that would help people to cope, thereby reducing or preventing

crowding). Others have focused on treating the consequences of crowding (e.g., dealing directly with the negative mood created by high density).

Preventing Crowding From Occurring
One form of intervention has involved providing what is often referred to as heightened *cognitive control* to people in high density situations. Cognitive control is the increased sense of predictability or controllability that people gain when given prior warning or information about a situation. Much of the initial work in this area was done in medical settings; only later was it applied to high density contexts. For example, providing patients with information about how they will feel, what will happen, or what they can do about their feelings *before* surgery can reduce distress and complications later on (e.g., Johnson & Leventhal, 1974). When behavioral control is limited, providing such information increases a person's sense of control, and, as we noted in Chapters 4 and 5, perceived control can reduce the aversiveness of stress.

Some important work has found that increasing cognitive control is beneficial in high density situations as well as in medical contexts. Langer and Saegert (1977) reported an experiment in which information about crowding was given to some subjects, but not others, before they entered grocery stores varying in actual levels of density. The information subjects were given focused on how they would feel if the store became crowded. All participants were given a task to perform that required them to move around the store to find a number of items. Not surprisingly, the results suggested that when density was higher, task performance was poorer. In addition, subjects who had been given prior information about crowding performed better and reported a more positive emotional experience than those who did not receive information. Having information about how they might feel allowed subjects to better select appropriate coping strategies and to behave more confidently (Langer & Saegert, 1977). This pattern of effects has been replicated both in laboratory and field settings (Baum, Fisher, & Solomon, 1981; Fisher & Baum, 1980; Paulus & Matthews, 1980). In

one related study, Wener and Kaminoff (1983) introduced informational signs into the crowded lobby of a federal correctional center. Visitors reported less perceived crowding, discomfort, anger, and confusion.

Additional strategies for preventing crowding have involved architectural, as opposed to cognitive, interventions. Baum and Davis (1980), for example, reported a successful architectural intervention in high density dormitories (see box on page 291). By altering the arrangement of interior dormitory space, they were able to prevent residents from experiencing crowding stress. Other strategies are sure to arise. What is important is to understand that architectural interventions into high density settings can be effective only if they consider the specific dynamics of the situation they are addressing.

Another thing to keep in mind in planning *any* intervention is that high density is not invariably negative, and one must consider the complexities of the situation before deciding whether it is even desirable to intervene. For example, a study by Szilagyi and Holland (1980) revealed that when an organization moved into a new building characterized by higher social density, employees reported less role stress and job autonomy, but greater feedback about their job performance from others, increased friendship opportunities, and work satisfaction. While it is not clear that higher social density is uniquely responsible for the reported effects, there may be situations in which, rather than decreasing social density, one might actually want to increase it!

Treating the Consequences of Crowding In addition to interventions which determine whether or not crowding occurs, a second set of interventions focuses on moderating the effects of crowding when it does occur. Karlin, Rosen, and Epstein (1979) reported a study which sought to lower the anxiety and arousal associated with crowded transportation settings. Three therapeutic interventions were used to treat subjects in a laboratory analogue of a transportation context. Participants were given training in *muscle relaxation, cognitive reappraisal* (in which they were told they could improve their mood by focusing on the positive aspects of the situation), or *imagery* (in which they were instructed to concentrate on a pleasant, distracting pastoral image). A fourth group received initial instructions to relax, but was given no other training. Responses to crowding among subjects in these four groups provided mixed support for the value of therapeutic intervention. Subjects given cognitive reappraisal instructions showed more positive responses to the setting than subjects in the other groups. The effectiveness of muscle relaxation and imagery treatments in reducing the impact of high density was less marked.

SUMMARY

Considerations of global overpopulation make the study of high density effects particularly important. This area of investigation has become increasingly popular and has included research with both human and animal populations. Two types of density manipulations are commonly used: varying *spatial density* (in which space is manipulated and group size held constant), and varying *social density* (in which group size is manipulated and space is held constant). With animals, it appears that the physiological and behavioral effects of high density are almost uniformly negative. It has been found that animals experience changes in body organs and glandular malfunctions that affect birthrate and also experience severe disruptions of social and maternal behaviors. A number of conceptual schemes have been developed to account for animal reactions to density.

Human reactions to high density depend more on the particular situation. While density does not have a totally consistent negative effect on humans, it leads to aversive consequences on a variety of dimensions. Concerning its effect on feeling states, high density leads to negative affect (especially in males) and to higher physiological arousal. There is also some evidence that it is associated with illness.

In terms of effects on social behavior, high density has been found to result in less liking for others (especially in males), and it is associated with withdrawal from interaction. Also, there is suggestive evidence that high density leads to aggression and to lower incidence of prosocial behavior. Finally, for task performance, it leads to decrements for complex but not for simple tasks, and it may also be associated with aftereffects.

Overall, high density causes (1) immediate effects on behavior; (2) coping responses; and (3) aftereffects. A number of explanatory schemes (e.g., overload, behavior constraint, and ecological models) attempt to explain why high density is aversive, and each stresses a different element of density as critical. Why does high density not always lead to negative consequences? A model that differentiates between high density and crowding accounts for this finding. It is suggested that while high density contains negative aspects, it is individual difference and situational and social conditions that determine whether these are salient and whether "crowding" occurs. The model specifies a progression of effects that follow when crowding is experienced and also offers ways to eliminate the causes and effects of crowding.

SUGGESTED PROJECTS

1. In our discussion about eliminating the causes and effects of high density, we stated that individual differences, situational, and social conditions moderate perceived crowding. A simple procedure used by Desor (1972) allows us to verify this relationship and many more that have been highlighted throughout the chapter. The procedure is the "model room technique." First, get a shoe box, or a somewhat larger size carton. Modify it a bit so that it looks something like a room. (You may be creative and include elaborate windows, draperies, and so on if you like, but be sure to leave the top off.) Next, take a large number of clothespins, small blocks, pieces of styrofoam, or the like, which can be modified to stand up and to look something like people. Now you are ready to start doing "model room" experiments.

   How do you begin? First, decide what relationship you want to test. Let's assume you want to test the assertion that people will feel more crowded in primary environments than secondary ones. Have a willing subject imagine that the box is his or her living room (a primary environment). Tell the subject to place figures in the box up to the point at which he or she feels the room is crowded. Count the number of figures in the box, and then remove the figures. Next, tell the subject the box is a restaurant (a secondary environment) and ask him or her to place figures in the box until the space seems crowded. Determine how the number of figures placed in the box varies, depending on whether it is described as a primary or a secondary setting. You now have data concerning the "threshold" of crowding in primary and secondary environments. If you find a lower threshold of crowding in primary than in secondary environments, you may have supportive evidence for Stokols' (1976) assertion that we experience crowding more readily in a primary than in a secondary setting. Some other hypotheses to test using this procedure are listed below:

   a. Test Baum and Valins' (1977) assertion that people who live in corridor dormitories avoid social contact situations more than people who live in suite-style dormitories. (To do this, you will need two groups of subjects, one living in corridor dormitories, the other living in suite dormitories.)

   b. Test whether different personality types have different thresholds of crowding by first administering personality tests and then relating the test results to the number of figures the subjects place in the box.

2. By comparing other people's reactions in high and low density natural settings, you can get a feeling for how high density affects you. Select a "real world" setting that varies over time in the number of people who are present. For example, a bus or train that becomes more crowded as it approaches the end of the line would be ideal. Your school cafeteria or library, which varies in terms of density over time, would also work. Then, pick a number of dimensions (e.g., friendliness of people toward one another, eye contact, defensive postures, object play) to observe for behavioral changes as population density increases. Compare how people respond on these dimensions in high and low density situations. By employing this procedure in a variety of settings, you can gain firsthand experience about how people react to high density.

3. We cited some evidence showing that people who like each other respond more favorably to high density than people who dislike each other. One reaction to high

density confinement with a disliked other should be a variety of coping strategies. Check whether high density with a disliked other leads to coping by making an informal study of residents on your dormitory floor. First, list five residents who like their roommates, and five who do not. Look into the rooms of both groups, and note the arrangement of furniture. If confinement with a disliked other leads to coping, furniture should be arranged so as to block interaction and ensure privacy.

4. Make several comparisons concerning environmentally destructive behavior between high-rise and low-rise (i.e., high and low density) dormitories on your campus. Compare graffiti, damage to furniture and public telephones, and so on to assess whether aggressive behavior accompanies higher levels of density.

10

THE CITY

KEY TERMS

affiliative behavior
behavior constraint
block organizations
defensible space
deindividuation
diffusion of responsibility
environmental stress
familiar stranger
gentrification

homelessness
overload
overstaffing
propinquity
prosocial behavior
Pruitt-Igoe
urban homesteading
urban renewal
Weber-Fechner function

Imagine yourself watching television coverage of a monumental press conference taking place in New York City. It seems that after more than 350 years New Yorkers have decided that Peter Minuit's agreement to buy New York from a tribe of Native Americans may not have been fair and equitable. In an attempt to remedy the situation, they have located the present chief of the tribe, who is working as a riveter on a new skyscraper in midtown Manhattan. The cameras zoom in on the following conversation between the chief and three officials of New York City, who have climbed up the girders and are speaking to the chief while he eats his lunch.

"Chief, we're here on behalf of the City of New York, and we understand that your ancestors sold the island of Manhattan for 24 dollars."

The chief said, "That's true. The Dutch drove a hard bargain in those days. We were robbed."

"Well," said the second official, "we New Yorkers have always felt very bad about it, and we want to make it up to you. How would you people like to buy the place back?"

"For how much?" the chief asked suspiciously.

"Twenty-four dollars."

"That's a lot of money," the chief said.

"We're willing to throw the Bronx, Brooklyn, Queens, and Staten Island in the package."

The chief stared down at the traffic jam below him. "I don't think my people would be interested," he said.

"If it's a question of financing," the third official said, "you could give us four dollars down and four dollars a month."

Smoke and smog kept drifting up, and the chief wiped his eyes with a red bandanna. "It isn't a question of the money. We just don't want it."

The first official said, "Chief, this is a golden opportunity for your people. Not only would you get all the land, but you'd have Lincoln Center, the Metropolitan Museum of Art, the Verrazano Bridge, and Shea Stadium."

The chief said, "White man speaks with forked tongue. Who gets the subway?"

"Why you do, of course."

"The deal's off," the chief said.

While they were talking, police sirens sounded and three men down below came running out of a bank, guns blazing.

The first official said, "It's obvious you don't know a good thing when you see it. We're sorry we even brought it up."

The three officials started their long climb down. Waiting nervously at the bottom was the mayor.

"What did he say?" the mayor wanted to know.

"No dice."

"I was afraid of that," he said. "Well, I'll have to think of something else."[1]

[1]From Buchwald, *Son of the Great Society.* Copyright 1965, 1966 by Art Buchwald. Reprinted by permission of the G. P. Putnam's Sons.

Obviously, this story by humorist Art Buchwald doesn't portray cities (especially New York City) very favorably, and we should note that urban areas have many positive aspects. As we will see in this chapter, urban life can offer very satisfying interpersonal and social relationships with others. And nowhere is there such diversity, novelty, intensity, and choice as in the city. Cities provide an immense variety of cultural and recreational facilities, such as concert halls, museums, sports stadiums, educational facilities, and all types of restaurants. Further, there is a much wider variety of services available to the average city dweller than to the resident of a small town. A quotation from the *Wall Street Journal,* which describes a unique *official service* offered by the city of New York makes this point in style. The paper asked, "How do you get rid of a dead elephant?" It answered its question as follows: "Bring it to New York: City's offal truck will take expired rhinoceroses, yaks, and mules off your hands" (October 3, 1972).

One way to think of the city is as a place characterized by *multiple and contrasting realities.* Within the city both ends of almost any continuum (e.g., excitement and boredom; safety and danger) can and do exist simultaneously. Cities can potentially pull people apart and bring them together, yield opportunities for us and in other ways constrain our behavior. There are good and bad, rich and poor, isolation and integration within the city's limits. Urban life is good for some people and bad for others, optimal for some activities but not for others (Krupat, 1985).

However *you* choose to view cities, they are an environmental feature that you will probably have to contend with throughout your life. In fact, cities and their suburban outgrowths are where most of us live. Today, more than 76 percent of the population of the United States lives in small or large metropolitan areas (*Statistical Abstract of the United States,* 1988), compared with 6 percent in 1800 (Gottman, 1966). In 1850, only 2 percent of the world's population lived in metropolitan areas with over 100,000 population, but by the end of the century, 40 percent will live in such areas (Davis, 1972). Further, there were only seven metropolitan areas in the world in 1800 with a population of over 500,000, 42 in 1900, and there are almost 500 today (World Development Report, 1987). A key feature of the next twenty-five years will be "mega cities" such as Mexico City, with populations in the dozens of millions. All of this has caused Davis (1973, p. 5) to conclude, "In all industrial nations it is the rural population which is abnormal, not the cities." (Figure 10–1)

In this chapter, we will discuss cities in some detail. Our working definition of cities is a slightly modified version of that proposed by Proshansky (1976$_a$). Specifically, cities are considered to be a large number of people and activities concentrated in a given geographical area for the purpose of providing the dimensions of human life we call organized society. It will become evident that cities are complex, large-scale environments that combine many of the environmental features already discussed in this book. As you read this chapter, keep in mind that there are important differences *between* cities in their desirability and livability (see the box on page 322) which probably affect the consequences of residing in them. Too many studies on the effect of urban life have been done in New York City, which many would argue is hardly a representative city, and other cities may have received less attention than they deserve.

Our chapter will begin with a consideration of some conceptual perspectives that have been proposed for understanding and predicting the effects of urban life. We will then move on to a discussion of studies on how city life affects us. Finally, we will highlight various solutions that have been proposed to ameliorate some of the problems associated with urban life.

EFFECTS OF URBAN LIFE ON THE CITY DWELLER: CONCEPTUAL EFFORTS

What types of conceptual efforts are concerned with understanding and predicting some of the effects of urban life? As you read the descrip- tions of the various theoretical perspectives below, try to make predictions from them concerning how and when urban life can be

Figure 10–1 A&B   The city is a mixture of multiple and contrasting realities.

All Cities Aren't
The Same: Finding
The Best City in America

We have mentioned some of the positive and negative aspects of cities (e.g., cultural diversity and crime, respectively), and suggested that all cities are not the same. Some have more of the good and less of the bad, and vice versa. One attempt to classify urban areas according to their desirability as places to live was made by Boyer and Savageau (1985). Based on data obtained from agencies of the federal government, professional organizations and nonprofit organizations, scoring systems were devised and points awarded for features of cities which people view as desirable or beneficial. In addition, points were subtracted from the total accumulated by a city for certain negative features. Ratings were made for nine categories of "quality of life" (i.e., health care, climate, education, recreation, transportation, arts, crime, economics, and housing), for a total of 329 metropolitan areas. When the ranks on all of the dimensions were summed for each city, what were the top 50 cities in America? They are listed in Table 10–1.

While the work of Boyer and Savageau that resulted in these ratings is both useful and interesting, it is not without its detractors. Loftus (1985) argued that the method of simply summing the rankings of each city on each dimension to arrive at the best places to live was inadequate. He argues that from a psychological perspective, "simply summing is simply wrong." Loftus' reasoning goes like this. Suppose City A and City B rank 1 and 25, respectively, on arts, but 276 and 246, respectively, on climate. By Boyer and Savageau's method, City B is a better place to live than City A, since its overall rank is *better* (i.e., closer to number 1). According to Loftus, this is inconsistent with our intuition. From a *psychological perspective*, Loftus argued that the difference between a rank of 1 and 25 is much more important than the difference between 246 and 276. City A is first rate in the arts, City B is second rate, and *both* have relatively miserable climates. Overall, Loftus feels that a psychological interpretation would view differences in ranks near the top of the distribution as more important than similar differences in the middle or bottom. Such an approach would conclude that City A is best, and is consistent with the **Weber–Fechner function** in psychology (see p. 36). In contrast, the method used by Boyer and Savageau came to a different conclusion.

To "correct" the original ratings in line with the Weber–Fechner function, Loftus recalculated the rankings by giving equal importance to equal rank *ratios*, rather than equal rank *differences* (which happens when rankings are added). Calculating the overall ratings in this way led to some dramatic changes, as evidenced in Table 10–2. Perhaps *your* preference for a ranking scheme depends on whether you come from Pittsburgh or San Francisco!

Whatever rating scheme you prefer, you should keep in mind that objective social and environmental conditions, such as described in Boyer and Savageau's (1985) *Places Rated Almanac*, do not necessarily imply

Table 10–1 *America's Top 50 Metro Areas*

Rank	Metro Area	Rank	Metro Area
1.	Pittsburgh, PA	28.	San Diego, CA
2.	Boston, MA	29.	Middlesex–Somerset–Hunterdon, NJ
3.	Raleigh–Durham, NC		
4.	San Francisco, CA	30.	Denver, CO
5.	Philadelphia, PA–NJ		
		31.	Cleveland, OH
6.	Nassau–Suffolk, NY	32.	Rochester, NY
7.	St. Louis, MO–IL	33.	Charlottesville, VA
8.	Louisville, KY–IN	34.	Wilmington, DE–NJ–MD
9.	Norwalk, CT	35.	Tampa–St. Petersburg–Clearwater, FL
10.	Seattle, WA		
11.	Atlanta, GA	36.	Asheville, NC
12.	Dallas, TX	37.	Omaha, NE–IA
13.	Buffalo, NY	38.	Los Angeles–Long Beach, CA
14.	Knoxville, TN	39.	Bridgeport–Milford, CT
15.	Baltimore, MD	40.	Norfolk–Virginia Beach–Newport News, VA
16.	Washington, DC–MD–VA		
17.	Cincinnati, OH–KY–IN		
18.	Burlington, VT	41.	Greensboro–Winston-Salem–High Point, NC
19.	Albany–Schenectady–Troy, NY		
20.	Syracuse, NY	42.	New Haven–Meriden, CT
		43.	Bergen–Passaic, NJ
		44.	Nashville, TN
21.	Albuquerque, NM	45.	Johnson City–Kingsport–Bristol, TN–VA
22.	Harrisburg–Lebanon–Carlisle, PA		
23.	Richmond–Petersburg, VA		
24.	Providence, RI		
25.	New York, NY	46.	Oklahoma City, OK
		47.	Monmouth–Ocean, NJ
		48.	Anaheim–Santa Ana, CA
26.	Chicago, IL	48.	Jacksonville, FL
27.	San Jose, CA	50.	Stamford, CT

subjective well-being (i.e., the top rated cities do not necessarily have the least psychosocial pathology) (Levine, Miyake, & Lee, 1988). Levine et al. defined pathology in terms of levels of alcoholism, crime, suicide, and divorce. When they looked at the relationship between objective conditions such as used in *Places Rated* and pathology, they found that better climates, higher

Table 10–2 *The New Top 20 Cities in America (Original Ranks are in Parentheses)*

1. San Francisco (4)	11. Atlanta (11)
2. New York (25)	12. Pittsburgh (1)
3. Washington, DC. (16)	13. San Diego (28)
4. Boston (2)	14. St. Louis (7)
5. Chicago (26)	15. Dallas (12)
6. Philadelphia (5)	16. Raleigh–Durham (3)
7. Los Angeles (38)	17. Cleveland (31)
8. Seattle (10)	18. Denver (30)
9. Nassau–Suffolk, N.Y. (6)	19. Burlington (18)
10. Baltimore (15)	20. Oakland (68)

Due to errors in calculation, some of the numbers in parentheses may differ from those in the *Places Rated Almanac*. Discrepancies will be changed in the next printing of the *Almanac*.

average incomes, and better economic conditions in cities (all of which would make a city rank high in *Places Rated*) were all associated with *more* pathology. In addition, higher crime rates were associated with better climate and economic conditions. These data contradict the assumption that negative social/environmental conditions are related to pathology and suggest that *Places Rated* measures provide valuable information about the quality of social and environmental conditions, yet ratings may be unrelated to the *psychological* quality of life. What explains the finding that more attractive places may have greater pathology? It is difficult to tell, but Levine et al. suggest that migration patterns may play an important role. Individuals who have high levels of pathology may tend to migrate to "attractive" places.

expected to affect those who live in cities. Also think about the suggestions offered by each theory for preventing the negative aspects of city life and preserving the positive ones. Keep in mind that while these formulations are useful for understanding some of the effects of city life and some ways for ameliorating urban problems, they do not tell the whole story. Other factors are also operating, and we will attempt to highlight them, where applicable, throughout this chapter.

Overload Notions

How do **overload** notions (cf. Milgram, 1970) apply to understanding and predicting urban behavior? Overload theorists hypothesize that an urban existence involves being exposed to a profusion of stimulation, including too much exposure to the actions and demands of others, confrontation with endless choices, and exposure to excessive visual and auditory stimulation. This plethora of stimuli is frequently more than we can deal with and requires us to employ coping strategies in order to lower stimulation to a more reasonable level. Coping strategies for dealing with urban life are many and varied and include setting priorities on inputs so that only important stimuli are attended to (which may result in ignoring those in need of certain types of help), erecting interpersonal barriers (e.g., behaving in an unfriendly fashion), establishing specialized institutions (e.g., welfare agencies) to absorb inputs, and shifting burdens to others (e.g., requiring exact change on buses). Even successful coping may be costly, leading to such aftereffects as exhaustion, fatigue, or disease. When successful coping does not occur, the individual will be subject to continued overload and is extremely likely to suffer serious physical or emotional damage (Figure 10–2).

Environmental Stress

A number of researchers (cf. Glass & Singer, 1972) have applied the **environmental stress** approach to understanding and predicting reactions to urban life. In general, this approach views the presence of *particular* negative stimuli (e.g., noise, crowding) as critical for the negative effects of city life, as opposed to the overload assumption that too much stimulation

per se is the critical element. The negative elements of city life may be experienced as threatening and may elicit stress reactions, which have emotional, behavioral, and physiological components. Stress reactions lead to a variety of coping strategies, which may be either constructive (e.g., using reasonable means to control the stressor) or destructive (e.g., aggression). If coping is successful in eliminating threat, adaptation occurs, and long-term consequences of the stressor are often prevented. If coping is unsuccessful, long-term costs are likely to result.

Behavior Constraint

Besides overload and environmental stress notions, the **behavior constraint** formulation can be applied to the analysis of urban behavior. This formulation assumes that city dwellers experience constraints on their behavior (such

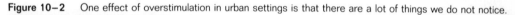

Figure 10–2   One effect of overstimulation in urban settings is that there are a lot of things we do not notice.

as those caused by fear of crime, or getting "stuck" in traffic jams) that are not generally shared by people who live in rural areas. Such constraints often determine whether or not they can achieve their goals in a setting (Stokols, 1978).

What kinds of consequences result from the feeling that one's behavior is constrained? Initially, behavior constraint notions predict that individuals experiencing this situation will evidence a negative feeling state and will make strong attempts to reassert their freedom. However, predictions of the consequences of long-term adaptation may be more pessimistic. If our efforts at reasserting control are repeatedly unsuccessful, or if we are overwhelmed by too many uncontrollable events, we may be less likely to attempt control of urban settings even when it is actually possible to control them. In effect, we may experience learned helplessness. While city life does impose many constraints on behavior, it should be noted that in some ways it is *less* constraining than small town life. For example, urbanites probably have more control over the information others obtain about their activities than those living in small towns.

The City as an Overstaffed Environment

A final approach to understanding urban behavior makes use of staffing theory (Wicker, McGrath, & Armstrong, 1972). As you recall from Chapter 4, **overstaffing** occurs when the number of participants exceeds the capacity of the system. How does this concept apply to understanding behavior in urban settings? A brief look at any city is sufficient to convince us that we are looking at an overstaffed environment. In terms of overstaffing theory, city dwellers should respond to such conditions by experiencing feelings of competition and marginality, by establishing priorities for interaction, and by attempting to exclude others from their lives. If overstaffing is habitual, these behaviors may come to characterize everyday

existence. However, it should be kept in mind that cities offer more diverse behavior settings and more behavior settings overall to choose from, and this could have positive effects.

Integrating the Various Formulations

Each of the views we have presented posits a different element of urban life as the critical factor in potential negative effects. Moreover, each suggests somewhat different reactions to urban life. How can we resolve the discrepancies in the various conceptual perspectives? We should bear in mind that these formulations are relatively speculative and untested and therefore should be viewed in a tentative light. Although the approaches are presented as competing with one another, it is probably the case that too much stimulation, too much stress, too many behavioral constraints, and overstaffing probably *each* accounts for some of the negative effects that may result from an urban existence. Eventually, a "compromise" model may emerge, which subsumes the valid predictions of each approach by using a more parsimonious construct.

Overall, it should be noted that on a general level all the views can be integrated into the sequence of events presented in Figure 10–3. As indicated in the figure (which you will recognize as a special case of the general environment–behavior model presented in Chapter 4), objective urban conditions interact with differences among individuals, situational conditions, and social conditions to determine one's experience of the environment. If the environment is outside the individual's optimal range (i.e., if it is overstimulating, contains too many stressors, constrains behavior, or is overstaffed) stress is experienced, which elicits coping. The ways in which people are assumed to cope differ for the various models we have discussed. Nevertheless, when coping is successful in handling stress, adaptation or adjustment occurs, and the individual is less likely to

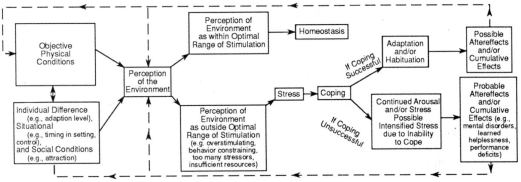

Figure 10–3   A conceptualization of the effects of urban life on behavior.

experience aftereffects or cumulative effects. If coping is unsuccessful, the stress continues, and the individual is likely to experience aftereffects and cumulative effects (e.g., illness).

How well is our model supported by existing data? In the next section, in which we summarize results of research on the effects of urban environments, we will see that none of the studies can be considered an *explicit* attempt to test the relationships proposed in the model. However, many of the experiments we will discuss are implicitly supportive, even though they apply to only a small part of the whole encompassed by the model. One problem with the model is that it does not sufficiently take into account the potential *positive* effects of city life (see the box on page 328).

EFFECTS OF URBAN LIFE ON THE CITY DWELLER: RESEARCH EVIDENCE

Having reviewed conceptual efforts that deal with the effects of the city, we now turn to past research focusing on how urban life affects city dwellers. This research has relied on two methodological approaches. One (the "single variable" approach) attempts to synthesize a picture of urban life from studies of how various *individual* stressors present in the city (e.g., noise, pollution) affect urbanites' behavior. These studies have often been done in "real world" settings, where the stressor under study varies naturally, rather than at the will of an experimenter. To explore the effect of urban noise on psychiatric disorders, one might compare the mental health of the residents on two streets that differ only in their closeness to a noisy factory. This strategy may allow us to approximate a cause-and-effect relationship between a potential urban stressor and behavior, although the nonrandom assignment of subjects to conditions may lead to problems in causal inference.

While the "single variable" approach allows us to synthesize a picture of urban life (after considering the separate effects of various stressors), it forces us to piece the picture together from a multitude of individual elements. The city represents the simultaneous

Predicting the Positive
Effects of City Life

The conceptual frameworks that have been developed by researchers to understand and predict the effects of urban life (e.g., overload theory), focus primarily on the negative aspects of urban existence (cf. Proshansky, 1976[a]). Are there any perspectives that enable us to specify the conditions under which positive effects of city life will occur? A few notions that predict such effects have emerged.

Contrasting with overload theory, which suggests that the high level of stimulation characteristic of the city will have negative effects, an adaptation level approach (cf. Geller, 1980) implies that this is not necessarily the case. Drawing on the concepts of optimal level of stimulation and adaptation level, which we have discussed in Chapter 4, Geller argues that stimuli (such as the urban setting) which are intense, complex, and/or novel may lead to positive *or* negative effects. The effects will vary across persons (e.g., depending on their past experiences). For certain people the city may offer an optimal level of stimulation: Many people cannot live anywhere else but a city. For others, urban settings are horribly aversive. However, it could also be argued that the city offers so much diversity (e.g., quiet parks, busy streets) that somewhere within its environs it could harbor an optimal level of stimulation for everyone. The effects of urban life will also vary over time. Those not used to the city often find it to be too noisy, too crowded, etc., but after they adapt, more complex stimuli are tolerated and may even be preferred. Also, we may find the city to be a perfect setting for some activities, but awful for others.

Proshansky (1976[a]) assumes that the complex physical properties of cities impose behavioral and experiential requirements on the individual, which in turn affect the way he or she deals with the environment in the future. To Proshansky, the elements of city life may render the urban dweller a relatively versatile person, who can approach new situations in a particularly adaptive fashion. Further, Freedman's (1975) density–intensity theory, reviewed in the box on page 305 in Chapter 9, suggests that urban density may sometimes intensify positive experiences. This would predict that urbanites respond to certain positive events (e.g., a festive Thanksgiving Day parade) more heartily than their rural counterparts because of high density.

A final viewpoint that implies positive consequences of city life has been proposed by Fischer (1976), who suggests that cities may sometimes serve to strengthen interrelationships within a subcultural group (such as Chinese-Americans). Strengthened relationships can lead to positive effects that could not otherwise happen (e.g., bringing people with common values together).

While the above assertions are interesting and may prove to be important, it should be noted that they have not yet entered the mainstream of environmental psychology. Since the most popular theories tend to dictate research questions, it is not surprising that past research on the effects of cities has tended to place a greater emphasis on the negative rather than on the positive views.

presence of a great many stressors, and the effects of cities on human behavior are multiply determined in a very complex manner. A realistic view of the consequences of urban stressors may come from considering how they affect us collectively. Research using this approach generally compares cities (which obviously contain a full range of urban stressors) with nonurban areas on various dependent variable dimensions. One might attempt to assess how urban and rural life affect willingness to help others by comparing prosocial behavior in urban and rural settings. Such studies give us a feeling for how urban and rural conditions affect aspects of human behavior, but sacrifice the ability to identify a specific cause. Since cities and nonurban areas vary in many ways besides the presence or absence of environmental stressors, we must be aware that differences between urban and rural behaviors could be caused by different populations, social conditions, physical conditions, or a combination of these (cf. Korte, 1980). It should be noted, however, that urban versus rural comparisons are still one of our best opportunities to determine how city life affects behavior.

In the sections that follow, we will discuss the effects of urban life on a variety of dimensions (e.g., stress, coping strategies, affiliative behavior). Whenever possible, our coverage will include the findings of relevant studies that use both the "single variable" and the "urban versus rural" methodological approaches. This should yield a balanced coverage in which the two methods complement each other.

Stress

Clearly, urban areas differ from each other. As noted in the box on page 322, some are obviously much better places to live than others. Nevertheless, comparisons of urban and rural areas generally suggest that cities contain more stressful environmental features. A number of stimuli identified as potential stressors are more prevalent in cities than in small towns. For example, noise levels have been found to increase with the size of a community (Dillman & Tremblay, 1977). One study showed that the quietest times in inner city apartments were noisier than the noisiest moments in small town living areas (EPA, 1972). Pollution is also greater with increasing city size (Hoch, 1972), and serious pollution is almost unique to cities. In fact, one breath of New York City air contains 70,000 dust and dirt particles, and just living in that city is equivalent to smoking 38 cigarettes a day (Rotton, 1978). In addition, both crowding and crime are much more frequent in urban than in rural areas (Fischer, 1976).

Cities also tend to be warmer than surrounding areas, since large numbers of people,

Table 10-3 *Walking Speed in Cities of Various Sizes**

Country	Town/city	Population	Observed velocity (m/sec)
Ireland	Galway	29,375	1.25
	Limerick	57,161	1.27
	Dublin	679,748	1.56
Scotland	Inverness	53,179	1.43
	Edinburgh	470,085	1.51
United States	Seattle	503,000	1.46

*After M. H. Bornstein. The pace of life: revisited. *International Journal of Psychology*, 1979, 14, 84.

automobiles, and industries produce heat, and large buildings and pollution trap it (Fischer, 1976). The pace of life is faster in the city. For example, it has been found that residents' walking speed varies as a linear function of the size of the local population (Bornstein, 1979) (see Table 10–3). In addition, urban areas have less sunshine, more rain, and more wind due to air pollution, the high density of city buildings, and the greater heat in urban areas (e.g., Elgin, Thomas, & Logothetti, 1974). Also, there is greater exposure to a class of events we will call "extra demand and inconvenience" (Figure 10–4). What is "extra demand and inconvenience"? An example is spending time commuting on crowded highways (see box on page 331). Finally, urbanites are exposed to more bureaucratic hassles, which we all know can induce stress (Glass & Singer, 1972).

It is sad to note that in some ways, the urbanites most intensely exposed to urban stressors are those with other problems as well. It seems that people who are poor, poorly educated, and generally discriminated against by society live in those areas of the city with the greatest pollution (McCaull, 1977). The poor are probably exposed to more urban crowding, noise, and crime as well. Given the fact that these people are already vulnerable to stress, adding the environmental stressors characteristic of urban life can be especially problematic.

With all the evidence indicating that living in the city should be experienced as more stressful, do urban and rural dwellers really *perceive* different levels of stress? Although there are few data from studies comparing urbanites and ruralites that bear on this point, a study of individuals who had recently migrated to the city or to a rural area suggested that this may be the case (Franck, Unseld, & Wentworth, 1974). Investigators interviewed a sample of students who were newcomers to either a small town or a large city. It was observed that the urban newcomers reported experiencing significantly more tension when living in the city than in their previous residence; the reverse was observed for rural newcomers. When sources of stress were broken down into those associated with the physical environment and those associated with the social environment, some additional differences emerged. For physical stressors (e.g., pollution, noise, crowding),

Figure 10–4 A&B When trying to "get around" in urban areas, crowds can be a source of extra demand and inconvenience. (Peter Oliver)

Commuting Stress:
Dangerous to Your Health?

In most cities, workers wake up to face a huge traffic jam. This occurs because so many of us refuse to use public transit or carpools, and insist on driving personal automobiles to work. In Chapter 14, we will discuss strategies which have attempted to change this practice, but for now, let us focus on the emotional, behavioral, and health consequences of sitting for interminable periods of time in snarled traffic.

A number of investigators have addressed this issue. For example, early field studies found significant relationships between exposure to rush hour traffic and negative physiological responses, like chest pains and cardiac arrhythmia (cf. Aronow et al., 1972; Taggart, Gibbons, & Sommerville, 1969). Other studies found positive correlations between traffic volume and heart rate, blood pressure, and electrocardiogram irregularities, as well as heightened catecholamine and adrenocortical secretion (cf. Aronow et al., 1972; Bellet, Roman & Kastis, 1969; Hunt & May, 1968). These problems are especially severe among drivers with coronary artery disease, but prolonged exposure to city traffic is associated with physiological disturbances even for healthy drivers. Another study, by Singer, Lundberg, and Frankenhaeuser, (1978), suggested that the conditions of

the commute (e.g., whether one has a seat on a commuter train or not) may be a more important determinant of stress reactions than the amount of time spent en route.

Perhaps the most complete study of commuting stress was done by faculty and students in the Social Ecology Program at the University of California— Irvine (Novaco et al., 1979; Stokols & Novaco, 1981). The research was a longitudinal field experiment, using urban commuters traveling varying distances to work. Subjects were tested twice in their work settings— 18 months apart— to determine the effects of commuting stress. The data mostly corroborate earlier studies, but give a more complete picture of things. It was found that conditions that interfere with a commuter's movement (e.g., congestion) elicit stress reactions such as physiological arousal, negative mood, and performance deficits, and that the intensity of these responses depends on personality characteristics of the commuter. Also, when people view commuting in a negative light they attempt to change the situation (e.g., move closer to work, try other routes). Importantly, such coping often makes them feel better at the psychological level.

urbanites reported being affected far more adversely than rural dwellers. For social stressors, results depended on the particular stressor. *Public* social stressors (e.g., slums, aversive individuals one must deal with) were experienced more strongly by urban newcomers.

However, some rural newcomers complained about the lack of cultural diversity in their environment. *Personal* social stressors (stressful personal relationships) did not differ significantly for the two groups. These findings are suggestive and should be interpreted with caution, as should all studies involving urban and rural comparisons.

A study by Wohlwill and Kohn (1973) suggested that perception of stressors in urban and rural areas depends on one's adaptation level (measured by the size of the town one resided in previously). In their study, people from small, middle-size, and large communities who had migrated to Harrisburg, Pennsylvania, were asked to make judgments concerning extent of crowding, frequency of crime, and feelings of safety. Although the results were not totally consistent, it was found that individuals coming from relatively large communities assessed Harrisburg as safer, less crime-ridden, and less crowded than those coming from smaller communities. (These findings support Geller's conceptualization of the effects of city life, portrayed in the box on page 328). It is important to note that in addition to adaptation level, many other types of individual differences may affect the perception of stressors in cities. For example, variables such as one's length of residence, one's need for stimulation, and one's socioeconomic status might influence the way urban stressors are experienced. Unfortunately, little research has been done in this area, and what exists has been inconclusive. Further, although future research is clearly needed before we can draw such a conclusion, in addition to affecting people's experience of environmental stressors, individual difference variables will probably also be found to affect other responses to urban settings (such as coping).

Coping

If urban life is more stressful than rural life, our general stressor model would assume that active coping strategies would be more characteristic of urban populations. Again, there is evidence that this is the case. In their study, Franck and her coworkers (1974) found that urban newcomers seemed to adopt a cognitive mode involving more planning and deliberation than

rural newcomers did. For example, 67 percent of all urban newcomers reported becoming more purposeful and deliberate since their move, while 73 percent of all rural newcomers reported becoming less deliberate. Over the period of a year, significantly more urban than rural newcomers reported some "strategy" for dealing with life in their new setting. For urbanites, this included increased vigilance, safety precautions, and repression of fear. In addition to these coping strategies, the theoretical perspectives of overload and overstaffing would predict other coping responses. For example, based on overload and overstaffing theories, it might be predicted that urbanities would attempt to exclude others from their experience. This should affect city dwellers' willingness to affiliate with strangers, and might also affect their willingness to help others who are in need.

Affiliative Behavior

On a number of dimensions, city life seems to be associated with a decreased desire for **affiliative behavior**. This ties in well with several of the conceptual notions we have discussed as well as with conceptual formulations discussed elsewhere (e.g., Wirth, 1938), but can also be explained in terms of reinforcements derived from past experience with city life (e.g., more experiences with crime). In one study suggesting a lower degree of affiliation, Newman and McCauley (1977) found that subjects' eye contact with strangers who looked them in the eye was relatively rare in center city Philadelphia, more common in a Philadelphia suburb, and very common in a rural Pennsylvania town (Table 10–4). In a study extending these findings, McCauley, Coleman, and DeFusco (1977) showed that commuters were less willing to meet a stranger's eye when they arrived at a downtown terminal than when they were in a suburban train station. How did urbanites and ruralites respond facially to attempts by strangers to take candid photos of

Table 10–4 *Percentage of Passersby Making Eye Contact with Male and Female Experimenters at Post Office and Store in Parkesburg, Bryn Mawr, and Philadelphia**

Sex of Experimenter	Parkesburg		Bryn Mawr		Philadelphia	
	Post Office	Store	Post Office	Store	Post Office	Store
Female	80	82	45	50	15	18
Male	75	73	40	45	12	10

*Reprinted from Joseph Newman and Clark McCauley, Eye contract with strangers in city, suburb, and small town, *Environment and Behavior*, 9, No. 4 (December 1977), 547–558.

them? When the pictures were given to college students to rate, it was found that urbanities in the photos appeared to be less friendly, less easygoing, and more tense than ruralites (Krupat, 1982). Finally, Milgram (1977) reported that when undergraduate students approached strangers on the street and extended their hands in a friendly manner (as if to initiate a handshake), only 38.5 percent of city dwellers reciprocated, compared with 66 percent of small town dwellers.

While this pattern of effects suggests that city dwellers are apt to avoid contact with strangers, it is important to assess whether this behavior extends to friends and acquaintances. In an experiment designed to test this hypothesis, McCauley and Taylor (1976) did a survey in which they asked small town and large city residents about yesterday's telephone conversations with friends and acquaintances. Phone conversations in the city were as often with close friends and as intimate in subject matter as conversations in small towns. This pattern is corroborated by additional research (see Korte, 1980). Many other studies (e.g., Glenn & Hill, 1977; Key, 1968) show no urban–rural differences in contact with relatives. This urban behavior of coldness to strangers and cursory acquaintances but not to friends and relatives was also observed in a study in which newcomers to a city and a small town were interviewed (Franck et al., 1974). Initially, individuals

moving to the city rated themselves as having fewer friends, as finding it harder to make friends, and as experiencing the city as a more difficult place to form close relationships, than people moving to a small town. However, after a few months (when they were no longer strangers), all of these self-reported differences disappeared.

Prosocial Behavior

Does the urbanite's lack of desire to affiliate with strangers extend to a disregard for strangers who are in need? One group of studies assessing urban–rural differences in willingness to help (i.e., **prosocial behavior**) consistently suggests this (cf. Korte, 1980). When a child claiming to be lost asked for aid in New York City and in several small towns, he or she was more likely to receive a helping hand in the smaller towns (Milgram, 1977). In a similar vein, Milgram found that willingness to allow a needy individual into one's house to use the telephone was higher in a small town than in a large city. Also, in Milgram's study 75 percent of all city respondents answered the person in need by shouting through a closed door, while 75 percent of all rural respondents opened the door, reinforcing our earlier conclusion about urbanite avoidance of affiliation with strangers. Additional studies (Gelfand et al., 1973; Korte & Kerr, 1975; Milgram, 1970) have also found

The Familiar Stranger

One thing our discussion has suggested is that urbanites are less likely to acknowledge strangers (e.g., by shaking hands and making eye contact) than rural dwellers. Some extremely interesting research by Milgram (1977) indicates that while city dwellers fail to display such amenities in everyday situations, they may show their feelings in other ways.

Milgram and his students found that many city residents have a number of people in their lives who may be called **familiar strangers**. What is a familiar stranger? It is someone they observe repeatedly for a long period of time but never interact with, probably because of overload. Milgram found that commuters to New York City had an average of four individuals whom they recognized but never spoke to at their train station, and that 89.5 percent of the commuters had at least one "familiar stranger." How did the researchers find this out? They took pictures of groups waiting for a train at the station and had subjects tell them how many of those present met the definition of a "familiar stranger."

What is the difference in urbanites' behavior toward "familiar strangers" and other strangers? First, many passengers told the researchers they often think about their "familiar strangers" and try to figure out what kinds of lives they lead. There is evidence that urbanites are more likely to help a familiar stranger in need than an ordinary stranger. Finally, Milgram found that under some circumstances, familiar strangers do interact with each other, although it is rarely in the place where they usually meet. He suggests that the farther they are away from the scene of their routine encounter (a foreign country, for instance), the more likely they are to interact.

that urbanites are less helpful than rural dwellers, and a meta analysis (i.e., a statistical summary of all past research on the subject) by Steblay (1987) strongly supports the nonurban–urban difference in helping, though decreases in helping were found to begin at a higher threshold (i.e., communities with a population of 300,000 or more) than previously thought (cf. Amato, 1983).

There are a number of possible explanations for the lower helpfulness of urbanites, one of which is overload theory. As that model would predict, the high levels of stimulation characteristic of the city make passersby less attentive to novel stimuli, such as someone needing help (Korte, 1980). In addition, Fischer (1976) suggested that the diversity of appearance and behavior characteristic of others in urban areas may make people feel insecure and thus less likely to help, and Wirth (1938) has proposed that being brought up in an urban as opposed to a rural area elicits an "urban personality," which is simply not characterized by prosocial behavior. Overstaffing theory (detailed earlier) could offer a fourth explanation, and diffusion of responsibility notions (cf. Latané & Darley, 1970), a fifth. Work on **diffusion of responsibility** suggests that when there are many people around who *could* help (as would occur more in cities than in small towns), perceived responsibility to help lessens, which affects the likelihood of giving aid. Interestingly, meta analytic work by Steblay (1987) suggests that it is the urban context rather than personality factors which is responsible for lower levels of urban helping. This discounts Wirth's "urban personality" theory, while lending a measure of support to several of the others.

Although much research suggests that there may often be less prosocial behavior in cities, other studies imply some important moderators of this pattern (Forbes & Gromoll, 1971; Korte, Ypma, & Toppen, 1975; Weiner, 1976). Korte and his colleagues suggested that urban and rural settings may lead to differences in helping only insofar as environmental input level (i.e., amount of incoming stimuli) is higher in cities. Their findings led them to conclude that input level may be the critical determinant of helping, rather than the urban–rural distinction per se. Similarly, others (e.g., Kammann, Thompson, & Irwin, 1979) suggest that pedestrian density in the area where help is to be given, rather than city size, is the major factor in whether or not aid will occur. And House and Wolf (1978) report intriguing evidence of lower urban helping only where crime rates make involvement inadvisable, suggesting that this may account for lack of prosocial action. Finally, Steblay (1987) reported that urban–nonurban differences were great only when the individual requesting help was male, and when the request for help was either very trivial or very serious.

Some studies have even found *more* helping in urban than in nonurban contexts. Weiner (1976) and Forbes and Gromoll (1971) found greater helping by individuals raised in cities than by those raised in small towns. Interpreting her findings, Weiner posited that different patterns of social-perceptual learning in the city and the country may cause urbanites to be more socially effective in certain circumstances. In effect, she suggests that the experience of growing up in the city allows one to learn skills that may be particularly adaptive in certain dependency situations. Also, it seems that deviants are *more* apt to receive aid in cities than in small towns (Hannson & Slade, 1977) and that the pattern of less helping in cities

extends only to strangers and not friends (Korte, 1980). Given the above qualifications, it is safe to conclude that additional variables may be operating.

Performance

While there are very few, if any, "urban versus rural" studies that compare performance, a large number of "single variable" studies suggest that the types of stressors prevalent in urban areas take a toll. For example, in an experiment by Cohen, Glass, and Singer (1973) reviewed in Chapter 5, we noted that noise in a city apartment building from a nearby highway adversely affected reading scores in children. In the same vein, city children whose classrooms are parallel to train tracks read more poorly than children on a quieter side of the building (Bronzaft & McCarthy, 1975). And Cohen et al. (1980) reported that children from schools with high noise levels near the Los Angeles airport were more likely to fail on a cognitive task, and more apt to "give up" before time had elapsed, than children from quieter control schools. Adverse effects also result from pollution. The air pollution index in Los Angeles is correlated with the number of automobile accidents, an effect that is attributed by investigators to decreased mental effectiveness and vigilance (Ury, Perkins, & Goldsmith, 1972). The oxidant level in Los Angeles smog has also been related to poor athletic performance (Wayne, Wehrle, & Carroll, 1967), and high pollution levels are associated with complete avoidance of outdoor and certain indoor activities (Chapko & Solomon, 1976; Peterson, 1975).

Levels of crowding, heat, and "extra demand and inconvenience" present in cities also affect performance adversely. Some studies have related urban crowding to performance decrements. Saegert, MacIntosh, and West (1975) did an experiment with shoppers in a midtown Manhattan department store during periods of high and low social density. The participants' task was to remember several aspects of the setting accurately. While no differences were found in recall of the merchandise (the main task), memory of incidental details was impaired in high density conditions. Langer and Saegert (1977) found that city shoppers' efficiency was impaired by high density, and that this could be ameliorated by affording shoppers a means of control (i.e., informing subjects in advance that high density may be arousing). And studies reviewed in Chapter 9 revealed that living in high density apartment settings led to poorer performance in school, and to symptoms of learned helplessness. Although no studies have specifically related heat in cities to performance, research reviewed in Chapter 6 indicates that heat negatively affects performance in certain situations (cf. Bell, Provins, & Hiorns, 1964; Provins & Bell, 1970). Finally, Shaban and Welling (cited in Glass & Singer, 1972) found evidence that hassles with bureaucrats can have negative consequences for performance on subsequent tasks and can even lead to learned helplessness.

Crime

Studies of victimization suggest that even what could be thought of as trivial crimes may have long-lasting consequences for victims' well-being (Greenberg & Ruback, 1984), and there is ample evidence that crime is more prevalent in urban than rural areas (Fischer, 1984). The rate of violent crimes per person is almost eight times greater in the largest cities than in extremely rural areas, and the rate of murders is three times as high (Fischer, 1984). When asked to list the top 10 problems facing their neighborhoods, residents of cities listed crime as the number one problem (Gallup Opinion Poll, April 4, 1981). An amusing anecdote related by Zimbardo (1969) suggests the intensity of crime in and around many cities. While repairing a flat tire alongside a highway in Queens, New York, a motorist was startled

when he observed that his car hood was being raised, and a stranger was removing his battery. "Take it easy, buddy," said the thief to his assumed car-stripping colleague, "you can have the tires—all I want is the battery!"

Why, as depicted in Table 10–5, is there more crime in cities than in small towns? Although these findings can be interpreted in terms of overload, stress, behavior constraint, or overstaffing notions, several other explanations have been offered. One is the theory of **deindividuation**. It was used by Zimbardo (1969) to explain why an "abandoned" car he left in New York City was stripped of all movable parts within 24 hours, while a similar car left in Palo Alto, California, was untouched. According to this theory, when we feel we are an anonymous member of a crowd (i.e., deindividuated), our inhibitions against antisocial behavior are released. This is partly because we feel it is very unlikely that we will be identified and punished. Under such conditions, criminal behavior is clearly less costly and is more likely to be engaged in. Other explanations for the higher levels of crime in urban areas include a lack of employment opportunities, the greater number of antisocial role models available, and the fact that there may be fewer prosocial models available than in nonurban areas. Another explanation, which is at least in part a cause of urban crime, is that there are simply more possible victims, more goods to steal, and more outlets for stolen goods in cities than elsewhere. Individuals who want to pursue crime may even migrate to the city for the above reasons.

Not surprisingly, feelings of being unsafe and concern about being a potential crime victim are greater for city residents (Fischer, 1984). This is due to the fact that crime rates are higher in cities, but also because "urban incivilities" (e.g., physical deterioration) may make people feel more vulnerable. Feelings of vulnerability to crime can have several types of consequences. First, individuals residing in cities with populations over 50,000 trust others

Table 10–5 *Crime Rates by Population Groups.* (Violent Crime Includes Murder, Forcible Rape, Robbery, and Aggravated Assault. Property Crime is Burglary, Larceny–Theft, and Motor Vehicle Theft)*

Size of Area	Number of Violent Crimes/100,000 Inhabitants	Number of Property Crimes/100,000 Inhabitants
>1,000,000	1,433.7	6,498.2
500,000–999,000	1,104.0	7,585.1
250,000–499,999	1,082.5	7,923.0
100,000–249,999	701.5	7,125.2
50,000–99,999	525.5	6,135.4
25,000–49,999	420.1	5,543.2
10,000–24,999	315.3	4,674.4
<10,000	278.6	4,225.3
Suburban Areas	355.5	4,477.4
Rural Areas	194.0	2,076.1

*From *Uniform Crime Reports*, 1979.

less than those living in areas with lower populations (NORC, 1987). Second, urbanites have greater fear of crime, which may lead to stress (see the box, page 338).

What are the effects of crime stress? Overall, there is little empirical evidence about its effects and the data are contradictory. Roberts (1977) found that crime stress was associated with emotional reactions of worry, fear of injury, fear of material loss, and feelings of loss of control. It would seem reasonable to assume that continued stress associated with crime (which is likely since the objective threat of crime does not dissipate) could have extremely negative effects (e.g., it may be associated with nervous disorders and learned helplessness). Also, fear about victimization through crime and associated stress could lead to a reduction in people's activities. In fact, compared to suburbanites, city dwellers report that they restrict their activities much more of the time due to fear of crime (Lavrakas, 1982). Far worse, fear of crime and crime stress has led a few, especially the elderly, to refrain entirely from leaving home (Ginsberg, 1975). Nevertheless,

a number of studies have found few effects of fear of neighborhood crime on mental health and well-being (Kasl, 1976; Kasl & Harburg, 1972; Lawton, Nahemow, & Yeh, 1980). For example, one recent study showed only scattered effects of crime on the well-being of adults and no effects on children (White et al., 1987).

Long-Term Behavioral Effects

While there have been too few studies to permit a definitive statement, moving to an urban area involves some consequences that may be interpreted as long-term behavioral effects. Importantly, these effects have both positive and negative aspects. On the negative side, Franck and her associates (1974) reported that urban newcomers were far more likely than rural newcomers to report becoming more cynical, fatalistic, helpless, distrustful, and callous after a year in their new home. On the positive side, they were more likely than rural newcomers to report that they had become more adaptive in a variety of situations, broadened their perspec-

Environmental and Individual Difference Factors and Fear of Crime

Imagine being afraid to go outside of your apartment to buy food or cash a check, or opening the door in terror when someone knocks, hoping he or she is not a criminal. Fear of crime and associated stress are major problems in urban areas. Interestingly, it has been found that fear of crime is increasing faster than actual crime rates (Taylor & Hale, 1986). In fact, in some cases, fear of crime in a subpopulation is not related to its true likelihood of being victimized (Maxfield, 1984).

Several rather complete conceptualizations have been offered of the various factors which affect fear of crime (for a review, see Taylor & Hale, 1986). However, our interest here is primarily to explore how fear is influenced by *environmental factors*. In the chapter on personal space and territoriality we discussed how territorial markers can moderate fear of victimization; here we will mention some other environmental determinants of crime stress.

Various aspects of the urban environment may impact on fear of crime, which varies from neighborhood to neighborhood (Maxfield, 1984). Teenage loitering, which can be facilitated or inhibited by environmental features, can elicit crime stress (Lavrakas, 1982; Lewis & Maxfield, 1980). It has also been suggested that physical decay of the environment and signs of urban "incivilities" (e.g., reports of crime; vandalism, graffiti, litter) can imply to people that the social order has broken down, and elicit fear of victimization (Lewis & Maxfield, 1980; White et al., 1987). This is especially likely when residents attribute the cause of the incivilities to factors residing "within the neighborhood" (Taylor & Hale, 1986). Importantly, studies have shown that *perceptions* of incivilities are more strongly related to fear than the objective number of incivilities (Taylor & Hale, 1986). Finally, perceived loss of territorial control appears to be associated with fear of crime (Taylor & Hale, 1986).

While there is no evidence that street lighting affects actual levels of crime, it does decrease fear of crime (Tien et al., 1979). And while it had been hypothesized that in urban areas with more pedestrian activity there would be less fear of crime, there is some evidence (albeit weak), that the *reverse* may be true (Baumer & Hunter, 1978). In addition, **propinquity** (discussed in detail in Chapter 12) affects how afraid people are of being victimized. The closer we live to a known crime victim, the more we fear that we could suffer the same fate (cf. Lavrakas, 1982). Finally, social interaction between neighbors may increase fear of crime to the extent that it increases knowledge of crime victims (Newman & Franck, 1981).

In urban areas certain types of people seem to fear crime more than others. Those who are most concerned are those with lower incomes, females, blacks, the aged, and residents of the inner city (Clemente & Kleiman, 1977; Gordon et al., 1980). There are many possible reasons for this, ranging from greater victimization of some groups to less ability of others (e.g., the aged, women) to defend themselves. Interestingly, in areas with the highest crime, age is *not* related to fear of crime. Where crime is a regular feature of daily life, the physical vulnerability associated with age may be a less important determinant of fear than other factors (Maxfield, 1984).

People with high fear of crime feel they must restrict their activities greatly to avoid being victimized (Lavrakas, 1982). Environmental designs which help promote social cohesion among residents (e.g., **defensible space**; see p. 343) may moderate fear and make people feel more comfortable "moving about." Also, having supportive neighbors who are accessible may act to quell fear of being victimized (Gubrium, 1974; Sundeen & Mathieu, 1976). For the aged, this seems to occur more often in socially homogeneous living

situations (e.g., retirement communities) than in other settings.

In a study which is only suggestive because residents assigned themselves to living situations that differed in *many* respects, elderly living in a heterogeneous central city core reported fewer support systems and perceived themselves to be less safe than those in a socially homogeneous retirement community. Residents in a typical suburban community were in between "core" and "retirement" residents on both measures (Sundeen & Mathieu, 1976). This suggests that environmental design may facilitate social cohesion and lower fear of crime. Of course, we must ask ourselves whether *all* the implications of homogeneous housing for the elderly are as good as those we have noted above. It may be that there are other, more negative effects in some areas that could counteract the good ones mentioned here.

. . . .

tive, and experienced personal growth. This is not surprising: Cultural innovations (e.g., new ideas) are "born" in urban areas and may take years to "trickle down" to smaller towns. The speed with which they spread to a particular area is a function of its size. The same holds for material innovations (Fischer, 1978) (Figure 10–5).

Other positive effects of urban life have been described quite eloquently by Proshansky (1976). In line with his conceptualization, it appears that the experiences characterizing the urban existence (cultural opportunities, noise, crowds, crime) can sometimes lead to important benefits (see the box on page 344). They may make the urbanite a more versatile and adaptable individual than his or her rural counterpart. For example, Jain (1978) reports that urbanites have more tolerance for competition than ru-

ralites. This can be viewed as an adaptive response to urban conditions. Overall, urban life may allow the individual to learn many roles, to engage in many activities, and to shift roles and activities when settings demand. Further, the urbanite may learn to make choices among diverse environmental alternatives and to cope with the constant presence of many others. Future research should be directed toward testing Proshansky's assertions and to looking more at the positive side of urban life.

Health

Caution should be used in interpreting data relating health to urban and rural settings. First, specialized medical care is generally more available in cities. Specialists, such as cardiologists and surgeons, are in especially short

Figure 10–5   Nowhere but in the city are such diverse opportunities available to people.

supply in rural areas (Dillman & Tremblay, 1977), and urban hospital facilities are superior. Second, individuals who are ill often migrate from the country (where they became sick) to the city (Srole, 1972). Because these factors make it difficult to interpret the findings of studies on urban–rural differences in health, the actual data are rather equivocal and depend on the particular disease.

Hay and Wantman (1969) studied the rate of hypertension and heart disease (both associated with stress) and found that hypertension rates were only slightly higher in New York City than in the nation overall. A recent study by Levine et al. (1988) found that in those cities where the "pace of life" was faster (which the authors termed "type A cities"), death rates from coronary heart disease were greater. Interestingly, arthritis and rheumatism rates were found to be lower in New York City than in the country as a whole (Srole, 1972). On the other hand, tuberculosis, emphysema, bronchitis, and other respiratory diseases (often associated with pollution) occur more frequently in urban areas (Ford, 1976), and the incidence of lung cancer in cities is double that in rural areas (National Academy of Sciences Study, reported in the *Los Angeles Times,* September 11, 1972). Some experts predict that 25 percent of the annual deaths in the U.S. due to respiratory diseases could be avoided if urban air pollution were reduced by 50 percent (Weinstein, 1980). Overall, it may be said that the effects of city life on health are not inherently pathological, and that the relationship between urban and rural environments and disease is complex.

Turning from physical to mental health, we begin by looking at urban–rural differences in self-reported life satisfaction. Again, any urban–rural differences must be interpreted cautiously, due to patterns of migration from rural to urban areas (e.g., people who are unhappy or mentally ill may migrate from the country to the city, contributing to any urban–rural differences.) Nevertheless, there are survey data which indicate urban–rural differences in overall happiness and in optimism about the future (urbanites are less happy and less optimistic), and which suggest that such differences are becoming more intense (Gallup Opinion Index, 102, 1973; Hynson, 1975). Urbanites also show much lower levels of interpersonal trust than ruralites (NORC, 1987).

How are these differences reflected in rates of mental illness? While it is clear that mental hospital admissions are higher in cities than in rural areas (Clinard, 1964; Mann, 1964), it is not certain that urbanites are actually less mentally healthy (Srole, 1972). For example, of 17 studies comparing paper-and-pencil measures of adjustment in areas of different size, three found more personality problems in larger cities, five found that such difficulties were more common in small communities, and nine found no differences (Fischer, 1976). Srole (1976) reports that inhabitants of large cities are less likely to show symptoms of imminent nervous breakdown than residents of small towns. On the other hand, Dohrenwend and Dohrenwend (1972) contend that some forms of mental illness (e.g., psychoses) are more prevalent in rural areas, while other forms (e.g., neuroses, personality disorders) predominate in urban areas.

While mental illness may not differ reliably in urban and rural areas, two afflictions that are symptomatic of such disorders may show urban–rural differences. First, in the United States, it is sometimes found that alcoholism is more common in large cities than in small towns (Trice, 1966), though other data (Fischer, 1976; Ross, Bluestone, & Hines, 1979) suggest that this is not always the case. Second, drug addiction is much more common in urban than in rural areas (Fischer, 1976). Obviously, these differences can be accounted for in terms

of the overload and stress notions we reviewed earlier. Some other explanations include: greater availability of drugs and liquor, better treatment of alcoholics and drug addicts and hence more reporting of these afflictions, and better record-keeping in cities. Finally, and rather surprisingly, there is no consistent difference in the suicide rate between urban and rural areas (Gibbs, 1971).

Homelessness

While **homelessness** occurs in rural areas, it is disproportionately an urban malady. Not surprisingly, most of the studies of homelessness have been done in cities, though it has been noted that the problems of the rural homeless differ somewhat from those of the urban homeless (Committee for Health Care for Homeless People, 1988). Although there have always been homeless people, their number has increased dramatically in the last few years, and their plight has become the focus of more and more public attention (Figure 10–6).

How is homelessness defined? The U.S. Government defines it as occurring when a person is without a fixed, regular, and adequate nighttime residence, or when someone has a primary nighttime residence that is: (a) a shelter designed for temporary accommodations, (b) an institution that provides temporary residence for people intended to be institutionalized, or (c) a public or private place not designed for, or ordinarily used as, a regular sleeping accommodation for human beings. While it is difficult to count the number of people who qualify as homeless under those criteria, estimates suggest that on any given night in the U.S., there are 735,000 homeless people, of whom many are children; that during 1988, 1.3–2.0 million people were homeless for one night or more; and that there are about 6 million Americans at risk of becoming homeless, primarily because of the high cost of housing relative to their income (Alliance Housing Council, 1988).

The characteristics of the homeless differ dramatically from place to place, but there are some consistent patterns. Men make up 56 percent of the homeless population and women 25 percent; the remainder are adolescents and families with children. The composition of the homeless is changing over time: middle-aged men now make up a *shrinking* percentage of the homeless, and families with small children are the fastest growing segment of this population (U.S. Conference of Mayors, 1987). Homeless adults are most likely never to have been married. In fact, a lack of support systems is one of the reasons for homelessness. In a study of single parent homeless families, many women actually named their major source of support as their children (McChesney, 1986). In the larger cities, minorities are overrepresented among the homeless. Interestingly, most homeless are long-term residents of particular cities, which negates some public officials' arguments that if they do more to help them, increased numbers of homeless will come to their city (Committee for Health Care for Homeless People, 1988).

Why are so many people homeless? Many individuals are homeless because their incomes have failed to keep up with sharply increased housing costs. Especially for those with few close family ties who have marginal incomes, the loss of even a few days' pay due to an injury, losing a job, etc., can quickly result in homelessness. Another factor in the homelessness problem is society's failure to provide adequate community-based housing and care for people. Urban renewal and gentrification can also cause homelessness. Gentrification occurs when middle- and upper-income people move back to the city and occupy and improve areas formerly lived in by poor people (see p. 355). There are other reasons for homelessness as well. Many homeless families are "multiproblem families" (Bassuk, Rubin, & Lauriat, 1986) with fragmented social networks, and difficulty utilizing available public welfare services. In addition, certain health problems tend to cause homelessness (e.g., major mental

Figure 10−6 Homelessness is becoming a significant urban problem.

illnesses like schizophrenia). In fact, some studies suggest that a very large percentage of the homeless have psychological or addictive disorders (Bassuk et al., 1986), or diseases like AIDS, which may render one unable to pay rent and/or undesirable to landlords and even family due to stigma.

In addition to being a *cause* of homelessness, health and psychological problems can *result* from homelessness. Homelessness may increase the risk of developing many diseases, the likelihood of incurring trauma, and of being victimized (rape for women; violent assault for both sexes) (Kelly, 1985). For those with medical problems, homelessness makes treatment extremely difficult. How can someone be on "bed rest" when they do not have a bed? How can they be on a restricted diet if they do not have food preparation facilities? Homelessness is also associated with other risks (e.g., the fires used by street people to keep warm often cause burns). Finally, while mental illness was mentioned as a factor associated with becoming homeless, it can also be a result of homelessness. The trauma of being homeless has negative psychological consequences and is associated with anxiety and depression. Homelessness can also contribute to alcoholism or drug addiction as an attempt to ''medicate'' the psychological pain of not having a place to live.

Summary

Environmental stressors are more intensely present in urban than in rural settings. Stressors include noise, pollution, heat, crowding, ''ex-tra demand,'' crime, and homelessness. Studies suggest that individually and collectively these stressors have at least mildly negative effects on various dimensions of urban existence. Urban stressors are associated with increased coping behavior, less desire for affiliation with strangers, performance decrements, long-term behavioral effects, and differences in some health-related indices. These effects can be interpreted in terms of the urban stress model we have proposed. While there are many urban problems, future research needs to focus more on the positive effects of city life. This type of research is described in the box on page 344.

ENVIRONMENTAL SOLUTIONS TO URBAN PROBLEMS

As is painfully obvious, the modern city has a wide variety of problems. Not surprisingly, many people and businesses have attempted to find true happiness by escaping from urban areas. Those who remain behind are often individuals whose social or economic position makes them incapable of departing. What effect has this had on the cities? It has left them with a deteriorating physical condition, a dwindling tax base, and a population composed heavily of minority groups with high levels of unemployment and attendant social problems, such as crime. How can this situation be ameliorated? Many very significant social, economic, and physical changes are needed. Since such disciplines as political science and economics are beyond the scope of this text, we will restrict ourselves to discussing physical-environmental attempts to solve urban problems. However, a unified attack on many fronts will be needed to change the situation, and when compared with the possible effects of potential social and economic programs, the impact of the physical interventions we are proposing may be relatively slight.

Several possibilities exist for physical/environmental approaches to certain urban problems (e.g., the high crime rate and the destruction of property in cities). It has been proposed that with proper environmental modifications and appropriate designs for new settings, such urban problems could be attenuated. Simultaneously, the design process could precipitate improvements in urban social and psychological life, yielding among other things more cohesive neighborhoods, more ''neighborly'' behavior, less fear of crime, and greater perceived control for urbanites.

Defensible Space

Newman and his colleagues (Newman, 1972, 1975; Newman & Franck, 1979, 1982) have focused on how physical aspects of a setting may affect resident-based control of the environment and ultimately lead to lower crime. Their ideas are captured in the concept of **defensible space**. What are ''defensible spaces''? They are clearly bounded or semi-private spaces that appear to belong to some-

Looking for the Good
as Well as the Bad:
Benefits of A
Positive Focus

For reasons mentioned earlier, most studies comparing life in urban and rural areas have focused primarily on the intensity of aversive environmental conditions (such as stress) across the two settings. Such studies are interesting and important, but we should design future research that allows us to make comparisons on positive as well as negative dimensions. Haney and Knowles (1978) employed such an evenhanded approach in assessing the characteristics of neighborhoods described by inner city residents, outer city residents, and suburbanites. The results, depicted in Table 10–6, are consistent with earlier studies in suggesting that the inner city has more negative characteristics than the outer city or the suburbs. However, observe that it was also found that the number of positive characteristics mentioned by

each group was approximately equal, although the particular characteristics varied with the setting. The "positive characteristics" dimension, which is not tapped by most studies, can provide valuable supplemental information for research on cities.

A similar evenhanded approach was taken by Krupat, Guild, and Miller (1977), who created a composite list of positive and negative adjectives and had a group of students rate the extent to which each was characteristic of large cities and small towns. While the results are complex, the procedures yielded both positive and negative information not usually obtained in urban–rural comparison studies. For example, cities were characterized by such *positive* traits as "offers much entertainment," "allows choice of lifestyle," and "is liberal," along with the common negative

Table 10–6 *Percentage of Residents Citing Positive and Negative Characteristics of Their Neighborhoods**

Neighborhood Characteristic	*Inner City*	*Outer City*	*Suburb*
Positive Respones			
Nice neighborhood	62	58	74
Friendly people	38	58	64
Closeness to services, stores	62	32	31
Quiet	25	26	22
Negative Responses			
Traffic and noise	44	26	8
Undesirable residents	19	5	0
Malodorousness	12	11	0

*From W. G. Harey and E. S. Knowies. Perception of neighborhoods by city and suburban residents. *Human Ecology* 1978. 6, 201–214.

traits "crowded," "competitive," "makes one feel anonymous and isolated," and "impersonal and untrusting." Small towns were characterized by such *negative* traits as "people gossip a lot," "people don't like outsiders," and "people are prejudiced," in addition to such common positive traits as "peaceful," "safe," "healthful," "intimate," and "relaxed."

. . . .

one. Defensible spaces allow surveillance because they are visually accessible. Newman argued that if we create such spaces through design, they will lead residents to feel propriety over them, foster informal surveillance, and promote social cohesion between neighbors. These behaviors should reduce certain types of crime and antisocial acts and elicit improved social relations among urbanites.

Defensible spaces could actually lead to lower crime for several reasons (Taylor, Gottfredson, & Brower, 1984). First, they could have a direct effect. It may be that spaces which look "defensible" lead potential offenders to assume that residents will actively respond to intruders, a notion which has been supported in work by Brower, Dockett, and Taylor, (1983). Second, as suggested by Newman, defensible space may cause the formation of local ties among residents. This may occur because it makes people feel safer, which causes them to use the space more, to come into increased contact with neighbors, and ultimately, to develop more common ties. Individuals with more ties are more apt to intervene to "defend" their neighborhood, are better able to discriminate neighbors from strangers, and, because shared norms develop, to know what types of activities should go on and what types should not (Taylor & Brower, 1985). The latter analysis was supported in research by Taylor et al. (1984). Finally, defensible space could lessen crime, since it may strengthen people's territorial functioning (i.e., because areas characterized by defensible space are well bounded and more defensible, they may elicit more proprietary attitudes).

Does the concept of defensible space have the predicted effects? There is definite support for at least parts of the model. Newman (1972) compared two public housing projects in New York, one of which was high in defensible space, the other of which was low. The latter project had more crime and higher maintenance costs, and this could not be explained by tenant characteristics. However, while increased defensible space was associated with less crime, whether this was due to greater cohesion among neighbors and stronger territorial attitudes and behaviors, as suggested by defensible space theory, is unclear since this mediating link was not measured. Another study, a demonstration project in Hartford, Connecticut, implemented both physical and social changes designed to increase defensible space (Fowler, McCall, & Mangione, 1979). While the mediating variables posited by defensible space theory were again unmeasured, the changes which were implemented led to fewer burglaries, and residents perceived themselves to be less at risk. They reported walking in the neighborhood more, and believed it was easier to recognize strangers. In making changes that will enhance defensible space, it is important for residents to participate in the decision process, and they must view modifications as positive, not punitive (Taylor, Gottfredson, & Brower, 1980).

In addition to physical changes to enhance defensible space, other interventions that will increase neighborhood cohesion or feelings of "ownership" should also lower crime. These could include increasing the extent of home ownership in an area, assisting neighborhoods in the development of local social ties, etc. For example, block organizations can be sponsored and supported, and neighborhood clean-up and beautification contests can be run. (Taylor et al., 1984). All of these may impact on some of the same types of social processes which the physical changes advocated by defensible space theorists are assumed to affect.

There has been criticism of the way the defensible space theory was originally formulated (e.g., Taylor et al., 1980) and of how some of the research on it has been carried out (e.g., Patterson, 1977). One of the problems, as noted above, is that the social processes defensible space is assumed to affect were not measured in most studies. While the research suggests that factors associated with more defensible space may affect crime and other outcomes in a favorable way, there is little evidence that this occurs, as Newman believes, because defensible space creates feelings of ownership and affects the social fabric of a setting. Recent research (e.g., by Taylor and his associates and Newman and his) has tried to clarify and extend the model, and to measure the links between cognitions and behavior.

Other research suggests that the link between the physical design features advocated by the theory and lower crime, while sometimes significant, are not terribly large and may be influenced by other factors (Taylor et al., 1984). In addition, not all research has found that defensible space works to lower crime, increase neighborhood cohesion, and so on (e.g., Mawby, 1977; Merry, 1981). Social and cultural factors (e.g., groups of residents from different ethnic groups who do not form cohesive bonds even when living in "defensible space") may sometimes cause defensible space to remain "undefended."

In addition to architectural features affecting defensible space, as suggested by Newman, Taylor and his associates (e.g., Taylor et al., 1980) believe defensible space research and application should draw more heavily on the concept of territoriality (see Chapter 8). They suggest that some critical environmental fea-

Figure 10—7 Social networks, such as those involved in Neighborhood Crime Watch organizations, can be effective in ameliorating crime.

tures for controlling crime are signs of defense, signs of appropriation, and signs of incivility (Hunter, 1978). Signs of defense are symbolic and real barriers directed toward strangers that keep unwanted outsiders away. Signs of appropriation are territorial markers suggesting that a space is used and cared for. Signs of incivility are physical and social cues (e.g., environmental deterioration) that indicate a decay in the social order. These territorial signs give information to other residents and to strangers which affects whether or not crime occurs. Taylor et al. believe that territorial signs which deter crime are more common in homogeneous neighborhoods, and where there are strong local social ties. As opposed to Newman's model, then, these authors suggest that sociocultural variables and social conditions, in addition to design, determine territorial cognitions and behaviors and ultimately the level of crime in a neighborhood. This model has been tested and has received support (e.g., Gottfredson, Brower, & Taylor, 1979; Newman & Franck, 1982; Taylor & Ferguson, 1978; Taylor et al., 1980, 1984).

Land Use

Another approach implies that land use in an area will affect the crime rate. Jacobs (1961) has suggested that diverse land use is an important factor in deterring urban decay. Neighborhoods should contain commercial, residential, institutional, and leisure-oriented areas. These areas would attract a continuous flow of people and ensure informal surveillance. In effect, planning and zoning for heterogeneous rather than "specialized" urban districts would lead to positive effects. Research implies that there may be problems with this approach. Greenberg, Williams, and Rohe (1982) found that low crime neighborhoods had fewer people on the streets than those with high crime. The flow of people into low crime neighborhoods was limited by *homogeneous* land use, fewer major arteries, and by the nature

of residential boundary streets. And Dietrick (1977) reported that residential burglary occurred more near commercial areas. This suggests that maintaining the residential character of neighborhoods and limiting access to outsiders may inhibit crime. Overall, it does seem that land use affects crime, but whether or not heterogeneous land use yields the best overall results is an open question.

Additional research helps clarify how land use may affect crime. O'Donnell and Lydgate (1980) catalogued the types of "physical" resources (e.g., restaurants, financial services) in different police beats in metropolitan Honolulu. The criminal acts occurring in the area were then related to the physical resources. Increased burglary was related to the presence of permanent and transient residences and facilities offering alcohol consumption and entertainment. Forgery occurred in police beats where there were physical resources allowing one to obtain goods, services, or cash through this means (e.g., stores, bars, or restaurants). Fraud, larceny, and robbery were related to a cluster of tourist facilities, such as retail stores, restaurants, bars, transient residences, and entertainment. Violent offenses were most highly correlated with the presence of sex-related activities. The authors view these findings as suggesting that certain physical resources in the environment provide "opportunities" for crime. By cataloguing these resources we can better plan for police protection, and through zoning perhaps we could attempt to control crime rates.

Social Factors

It has been suggested that in coping with urban problems, neighborhood social networks could play a significant role. Neighborhood social networks are people living nearby who care about and depend on each other. People with strong social networks enjoy better physical health and psychological well-being, are less fearful of victimization, and respond better to crisis events (e.g., Antonovsky, 1979; Holahan & Moos, 1981). Also, the presence of social networks helps regulate access to an area by strangers, leads to less reliance on police for dealing with disturbances, and can exert significant pressure to conform on social deviants living inside a neighborhood (e.g., Suttles, 1968; Wheeldon, 1969). When social cohesion is absent, urban decay can get a strong foothold. Under these conditions, diffusion of responsibility effects (Darley & Latané, 1968), in which people assume it is "someone else's" responsibility to deal with social problems, may occur. In addition, deindividuation (Zimbardo, 1969), in which people feel "lost in the crowd," unrecognizable, and therefore not responsible for their antisocial behavior, may occur.

Viable social networks are most likely to occur in certain situations. "Neighboring" in urban environments is greater when there is racial similarity, shared socioeconomic status,

psychological "investment" in a neighborhood, satisfaction with conditions there, and a positive sense of well-being (Unger & Wandersman, 1983). Social networks can also be fostered or inhibited through environmental means. We will see later that they are very often strong in so-called "slums," and very weak in many urban renewal housing projects. Research by Newman (1972, 1975) and Newman and Franck (1982) has also shown that defensible space works to facilitate local social network formation (Figure 10–7).

One way in which social networks can function effectively for the good of an urban area is to form local organizations (often called "**block organizations**"). These work for improvements such as better lighting, police protection, street repairs, or other common goals. Residents' participation in block organizations may be predicted by several factors: how important the block environment is to the

Figure 10–8 Unfortunately, what urban designers consider to be "slums" are often not viewed as such by area residents. (Peter Oliver)

individual, whether a person believes he or she could perform the behaviors necessary to participate, the perceived existence of common needs among residents, and how much a person generally participates in activities with other residents (Wandersman & Florin, 1981).

Urban Renewal

A major physical–environmental means of improving urban life is through urban renewal programs, which in the United States have caused the relocation of many people each year. The assumption behind urban renewal was that it would provide better housing and solve other problems of the poor as well. A better physical environment was expected to lead to enhanced health, a more stable family, less crime and delinquency, greater motivation, an improved self-concept, and greater satisfaction with life (e.g., Schussheim, 1974). In effect, urban renewal was to be a panacea for many urban problems: There was assumed to be a causal relationship between poor housing and a "grab bag" of social ills. In fact, aside from studies relating poor housing to problems with physical and mental health (e.g., Duvall & Booth, 1978), there is little evidence to support this assumption.

Urban renewal can be defined as an integrated series of steps taken to maintain and upgrade the environmental, economic, and social health of an urban area (Porteus, 1977). To accomplish this, massive physical changes are often made in the environmental setting, which may involve demolishing housing and relocating residents. There is frequently a conflict of interest of sorts between planners and those living in the slums that are torn down to make way for renewal. Planners hope to attract wealthy individuals and businesses back into the city, to destroy eyesores, and to keep the city sufficiently attractive so that people will make use of its cultural resources (Porteus, 1977). They tend to replace slums with luxury apartments and office buildings, forcing residents to move elsewhere. Unfortunately, the people who are relocated often do not perceive their area as a slum at all but as a pleasant neighborhood (Fried & Gleicher, 1961). The "slum" residents are usually the losers in a conflict with planners. They are forced to leave and are often adversely affected by it (see Figure 10–8).

What are the psychological consequences of demolishing neighborhoods and forcing people to relocate? Clearly, this depends on a large number of situational conditions, including attraction to the former neighborhood. Overall, however, while forced relocation may occasionally have a mildly positive effect on family relationships (cf. Wilner et al., 1962), it often has negative consequences. It must be kept in mind that destroying a neighborhood not only eliminates buildings, but destroys a functioning social system and a sense of identity for people. According to Gans (1962), slum areas provide not only cheap housing, but offer the types of social support people need to keep going in a crisis-ridden existence.

An intensive study was made of the effects of an urban renewal project built in Boston's West End, in an Italian working-class area that residents identified with greatly and liked very much. What were the consequences of relocation? Loss of home, neighborhood, and daily interactions with well-known neighbors caused an extreme upheaval in people's lives and disrupted their routines, personal relationships, and expectations. This led to a grief reaction in many of those who were displaced, especially in people who had been most satisfied with the status quo. It can be explained, in part, in terms of the relationship between the strength of social networks and physical and psychological well-being, discussed earlier. Among women who reported liking their neighborhood very much, 73 percent displayed short-term reactions of extreme grief, including vomiting, intestinal disorders, crying spells, nausea, and depression. About 20 percent of the residents were depressed for as long as two years after moving. These types of reactions, and more severe health effects, may be most common in people who are already ''vulnerable'' (e.g., those with previous problems) (e.g., Freeman, 1978). Interestingly, people's reactions were mediated by knowledge of their former neighborhoods. The greater the familiarity, the stronger the grief (Fried, 1963).

In addition to the kinds of losses caused by the demolition of neighborhoods, there is the problem of where people go when forced to relocate. Forced relocation frequently results in one of two housing options. Although affected individuals are generally promised alternative housing, the promise is often unfulfilled, and they tend to drift into other slums and may even become homeless. There is a tremendous lack of affordable, alternative housing in the United States today. Because of this, the net result of urban renewal is often to lower the population of one slum neighborhood while increasing the population of another. Alternatively, people are relocated in public housing, which is low-rent housing built for those with a relatively low income. Public housing often provides physical settings that are objectively much better than the residents' original homes, but such projects are often unsuccessful. In fact, even the physical improvements reflected in new public housing projects are often temporary, since in many cases they are destroyed by residents. And fear of crime and anxiety about being physically harmed are very important concerns of housing project residents (Argrist, 1974).

A classic example is the **Pruitt–Igoe** project in St. Louis, which was built in the inner city in 1954. In this project, 12,000 persons were relocated into 43 buildings 11 stories high, containing 2,762 apartments, and covering 57 acres. The buildings contained narrow hallways with no semiprivate areas for people to congregate—a design that was praised in *Architectural Forum* (April 1951) for having no ''wasted space.'' The project was expensive to build but very institutional in nature, containing such ''features'' as institutional wall tile (from

which graffiti was easily removed), unattractive (but indestructible) light fixtures, and vandal-resistant radiators and elevators.

In spite of the way Pruitt–Igoe was built, within a few years it was a shambles. Take a walk with us through the project several years after it opened. First, there is a display of broken glass, tin cans, and abandoned cars covering the playgrounds and parking lots. Some of the building windows are broken; others have been boarded up with plywood. Inside, you smell the stench of urine, trash, and garbage. The elevator is in disrepair, and the presence of feces indicates it has been used as a toilet. Next, you notice that plumbing and electrical fixtures have been pulled out of apartment and hallway walls. When you come upon a resident and ask her about Pruitt–Igoe, she says she has no friends there; there is ''nobody to help you.'' She also tells you that gangs have formed and that rape, vandalism, and robbery are common. Since crime frequently took place in elevators and stairwells, the upper floors have been abandoned. (See Figure 10–9.)

These conditions destroyed Pruitt–Igoe, and by 1970, 27 of the 43 buildings were vacant; they have now been totally demolished. Why did Pruitt–Igoe fail so miserably? There are multiple reasons. One explanation was proposed by Yancey (1972), who centered his argument around the fact that space in the buildings was primarily sociofugal. Since there were few semiprivate, sociopetal spaces or other facilities that could promote the formation of a social order, the informal social networks which can play an important role in lower-class neighborhoods did not develop. Lower-class families like to congregate in informal spaces, typically along the street outside their home. This is facilitated in ''slums'' by low-rise tenements, narrow streets, and lots of doorways to businesses in which to stop and talk. The design of many urban renewal projects does not facilitate such interaction. This architectural failure results in a lack of cohesion among residents, as well as in conflict and crime.

The Personal Toll
of Relocation:
A Descriptive Account

While most of the research we have presented has been quantitative, often a descriptive account may add greatly to our understanding of environmental phenomena. The following commentary (Jacobs, 1961) describes the local culture in a high density urban neighborhood, characteristic of many targeted for urban renewal. It will give you an idea of the type of loss experienced when such neighborhoods are torn down. Jacobs observes that in such high density urban areas, sidewalks teem with excitement. Children play with each other on front stoops, and individuals stroll down the street conversing with merchants and looking into shop windows. In fact, such interactions constitute an important part of neighborhood life. Typically, residents know the merchants as well as many of the passersby from years of interaction. Relations with neighbors are very important to them. Over time, an atmosphere of trust develops. As Jacobs puts it:

> The trust of a city street is formed over time from many, many little public sidewalk contacts. It grows out of people stopping by at the bar for a beer, getting advice from the grocer and giving advice to the newsstand man, comparing opinions with other customers at the bakery and nodding hello to the two boys drinking pop on the stoop, eyeing the girls while waiting to be called for dinner, admonishing the children, hearing about a job from the hardware man and borrowing a dollar from the

druggist, admiring the new babies, and sympathizing over the way a coat faded.

The atmosphere described by Jacobs has many important consequences for people's lives. First, it leads to a social structure characterized by a large number of individuals with whom one may have social contact and feel secure and accepted. Further, parents feel safe allowing their children to play outside in such settings, since they know others care. For example, when the neighborhood tailor spots a child who is lost and then calls the child's parents, the parents and the child benefit directly, and the child also learns that even people who are not formally related should display social responsibility to each other. In addition to experiencing social benefits and a degree of security about their children's welfare, Jacobs suggests that adults gain other benefits from the neighborhood culture. Thus, it is common in such neighborhoods for residents to leave apartment keys with a friendly shopkeeper when they are expecting company before they arrive home. The merchant may also receive packages for residents who are at work or let children playing in the street use the shop's bathroom.

In effect, the longstanding history of contacts between individuals forms a cement for mutual aid between neighborhood residents and for dealing with problematical situations. This is jeopardized when neighborhoods are demolished and long-term residents are forced to relocate. In many other ways, too, slum living provides sources of satisfaction for residents that are not visible to people from outside their culture and value system. For example, kinship and extended family ties play an important role in the life of people living in "slums." Unfortunately, urban designers, planners, and others fail to recognize these sources of support. Because they have different values and backgrounds, these groups have often concluded that the inner city is not characterized by a meaningful social life because it does *not* correspond to that common in middle-class communities.

. . . .

Yancey also contended that the high-rise architectural design of the project was greatly to blame. It put children beyond their parents' sight and control whenever they were outside their house and gave them many hidden areas, such as stairwells and elevators, in which to cause mischief. Such areas also provided sanctuaries for teenagers and adults to engage in illicit activities almost anonymously. As one resident said, "All you have to do is knock out the lights on the landings above and below you. Then when someone comes . . . they stumble around and you can hear them in time to get out" (Yancey, 1972, p. 133).

Other explanations have also been put forward for the demise of Pruitt–Igoe. One suggested by Rainwater (1966) is that such "features" as vandal-proof radiators and walls may convey a self-threatening message of inferiority to residents and may actually challenge them to destroy these objects. In another context, Sommer (1974) and Stainbrook (1966) proposed that the environment can convey negative information that may adversely affect behavior. In a sense, the stigma of poverty was highlighted by the design of Pruitt–Igoe. It, like many public housing developments, had a look that set it off from other types of housing,

Figure 10–9   The demolition of part of Pruitt-Igoe in 1972. (United Press International).

How to Design
Public Housing

Our discussion of Pruitt–Igoe has read like a "how-not-to" guide for designing public housing. We now turn to some general guidelines for designing public housing so as to avoid these errors. Although few of our assertions have been extensively tested, they appear to be reasonable means for improving the functioning of public housing projects.

Our plan involves several elements. First, semiprivate spaces should be "designed in" to facilitate social interaction between residents and thus encourage the development of a social order. These areas should exist both inside and outside the building and should be planned so as to make pleasant social interactions almost inevitable. Can you think of any design schemes used in your dormitory or in other places that have successfully attained such a result? This strategy does have the desired effect. It has been shown experimentally that greater liking for housing and more interaction occur when such designs are incorporated into public housing (Holahan, 1976; Mullins & Robb, 1977). Semiprivate spaces also encourage neighborliness and mutual helping (Wilner et al., 1962).

The second element in our plan is derived from Newman's concept of defensible space. Buildings should be designed so that all space appears to "belong" to some individual or group. It is also important that residents both use and control the spaces outside their apartments (Newman & Franck, 1982). Such areas are defended and promote surveillance, which tends to reduce crime. How can this be accomplished in

a housing project? Newman suggested that projects be divided into "subprojects" to promote territoriality. The areas around the buildings (e.g., playgrounds, parking spaces) should appear to "belong" to the building, as an external extension of internal living space. Public areas, such as hallways and elevators, should be eliminated to the extent possible (e.g., through horizontal rather than high-rise construction). When this is not possible, "open air" hallways outside the building, combined with porches, or hallways and elevators that are accessible only to small groups of residents, can serve as territorial markers. Alternatively, fitting traditional corridors with windows can promote surveillance.

While Newman (1972, 1975) suggests that architectural features which create "defensible space" can lower crime, and offers empirical evidence to that effect, research by Merry (1981) suggests some important moderators of this finding. Merry reports that spaces may be defensible, yet remain undefended if the social fabric necessary for effective defense is lacking. This may occur when there are ethnic groups in conflict or in isolation from each other within the project, when people do not believe the police would respond if they were called or if calling them would result in retribution, or if respondents are unable to distinguish a criminal from a neighbor's dinner guest. Overall, Merry suggests that enthusiasm for the notion of controlling crime through design should be moderated somewhat, and that the social context of the setting must be taken more into account.

Several other guidelines should also be followed. The design of public housing should allow for surveillance by the police. Often, public housing has tried to create a "park-like" atmosphere. There is a large interior open space surrounded by housing units. Vehicles, passersby (and also police) are denied visual access to the interior. Patrol cars cannot reach the area (Reppetto, 1976). To deal with this problem, more direct access to the interior should be available to police (by building roads that go

there), and the interior space should be visible to those in the street. Projects should also be kept small (between 150 and 350 units), only a limited number of large families should be allowed to live in each project, and a good management firm should be chosen (*Chicago Tribune*, 1974).

The above suggestions should be taken into account when designing or renovating public housing. Degree of compliance with them could also be used to predict the probability of problems and to plan for police protection.

. . . .

and it was easily identified as "housing for the poor." The lack of "defensible space" (see the box) has also been suggested as an important explanation (Newman, 1972). Finally, it should be mentioned that Pruitt–Igoe was plagued by a poorly administered housing authority and by its isolation from the surrounding community.

Pruitt–Igoe is unfortunately not unique in its effects on residents, which has prompted other housing projects to be studied by social scientists. One study was conducted in Puerto Rico by Hollingshead and Rogler (1963). Their findings will give you a feeling for the obstacles a public housing project is up against, even if it incorporates the types of improvements we have suggested. The project in question was less crowded and had better facilities, lower rents, and a healthier atmosphere than the slums from which the residents had moved. However, while only 35 percent had disliked the slums, 86 percent of the men and 71 percent of the women disliked the project. When their reasons were examined, they reflected many complaints that could not easily be remedied by design changes. One problem was loneliness, since the designers had not made provisions for housing the extended family that people had lived with in the slums. Residents also resented their

unknown neighbors and felt bored because they had lost the companions and pastimes they were used to. Finally, some were unhappy because they could no longer engage in certain illegal activities they had practiced in the slums (e.g., selling stolen goods, prostitution) due to greater surveillance.

What factors are associated with satisfaction by residents of low-income housing? A study by Rent and Rent (1978) surveyed residents from many housing projects in South Carolina. Those who lived in single family or "duplex" dwellings liked their residences much more than others. This satisfaction probably occurred, in part, because these residences were more often owned, which is another predictor of satisfaction in low-income housing. For other reasons, too (e.g., greater privacy), such dwellings produce more satisfaction. Not surprisingly, then, 75 percent of those surveyed said they would prefer to live in a single family dwelling, and 83 percent wanted to own one. Another important predictor of housing satisfaction was having friends in the neighborhood (often these turn out to be neighbors). Generally, the more satisfied one was with his or her neighbors, the greater the attraction to the living situation. An interesting finding was that overall life satisfaction was associated with liking one's residence. The happier one was with his or her life, the more satisfied one was with living arrangements. Overall, then, social as well as physical factors may be important determinants of housing satisfaction among low-income individuals.

Fortunately, some of the recent trends in government housing assistance have more elements associated with residential satisfaction than earlier project housing. When government assistance is provided, the U.S. government has more or less stopped building "high-rise" projects for low-income families. No "public housing" has been built for over a decade. Instead, people are placed more often in townhouses or small apartment buildings. There have also been increased government assistance with home ownership, direct housing subsidies for the poor (e.g., rent vouchers), and attempts to renovate or preserve current housing instead of demolition. This serves the admirable function of "fixing the building and leaving the people." Another recent innovation is "**urban homesteading**," where abandoned urban property is given to individuals who agree to rehabilitate it to meet existing housing codes and occupy it for a prescribed period of time. It has sometimes been quite successful, but in other instances the practical problems of having low-income families with limited resources play the role of "general contractor" have been overwhelming. There has, unfortunately, been one "backlash" from earlier fiascoes with public housing such as Pruitt–Igoe: Some municipalities refuse altogether to have any form of it within their boundaries.

When people *must* be moved due to urban renewal, are there some means of accomplishing this in a more humane way? One possibility would be to move people to a new setting in established social groups. This would maintain the social cohesion of the former neighborhood (Young & Willmott, 1957). It could also be maintained, to some extent, by moving people to redeveloped areas near their old neighbor-

hood. Another important factor is citizen participation in planning the move and the new setting in which they will live (e.g., Arnstein, 1969). Designers and planners should encourage this, and be especially sensitive to cultural or subcultural differences in housing preferences.

Gentrification

While urban renewal has had an effect on cities for many years, a more recent trend has been gentrification. **Gentrification** can be defined as the emergence of middle- and upper-class areas in parts of the inner city that were formerly deteriorated (London, Lee, & Lipton, 1986). Frequently, this takes the form of renovating buildings which were once attractive and desirable, but which have fallen into disrepair. After the renovation, wealthier tenants often move in. Those who have lived there before the renovation (if anyone), must find alternative housing. While gentrification is good for cities in many ways (e.g., it encourages "resettlement" by people with greater means, raises the tax base, and improves the environment), like urban renewal, it can be "bad news" for poor residents of the city. In addition, while gentrification and urban renewal continue to occur, it should be kept in mind that a major threat to cities is *still* the disintegration and abandonment of urban housing (Henig, 1982).

Why is gentrification becoming more pervasive these days? Several conceptual perspectives have been proposed to explain the emerging trend of gentrification, though they must be viewed as tentative since most renovation has occurred only in the past 10 years or so (Figure 10–10).

Demographic explanations suggest that gentrification is due to several factors: the increasing numbers of "baby boomers" reaching adulthood and putting demands on the housing supply, the declining fertility rate, and the increasing number of women in the work force. Affluent, childless, working couples are not

Figure 10–10   Gentrification has both positive and negative effects.

concerned with the quality of inner-city schools, and may want to live in the city, close to their jobs and recreational opportunities (London et al., 1986). In contrast, *ecological approaches* suggest that the ecology of the setting determines whether or not there will be gentrification (London et al., 1986). From this perspective, cities high in white-collar businesses, low in manufacturing, low in noxious land use, and which have long commuting distances should be most apt to experience gentrification (e.g., Lipton, 1977).

A third approach, *sociocultural explanations,* assume that changing values, attitudes, and lifestyles are responsible for gentrification. They suggest that while the values of most Americans may have formerly been antiurban (Allen, 1980), this may be changing. In fact, it

may even be becoming "in vogue" to live in the city among some population subgroups (e.g., yuppies).

Finally, *political–economic explanations* may take several forms. One implies that the decreasing availability of suburban land, rising transportation costs, inflation, the low cost of urban, inner city dwellings, and antidiscrimination and school desegregation laws are all conspiring to encourage gentrification. Another perspective suggests that economic interests and political factors are responsible for gentrification, and that, in some sense, it has been willfully planned. Powerful interest groups first allow the city to deteriorate, mindful that gentrification could yield major profits. They pursue gentrification for their own benefit, with little regard for individuals who would be displaced by it (London et al., 1986).

How have the above hypotheses fared when subjected to research? While little work has been done, a study by London et al. (1986) suggests that *each* explanation has received some support. All of the processes proposed above appear to contribute, to a greater or lesser extent, to gentrification.

Do only the wealthy benefit from gentrification? While at first it may appear so, a closer analysis suggests that this may not be entirely correct. It has been found that while the *owners* of gentrified housing are "urban gentry" (e.g., young, highly educated professionals), the "renters" of such housing typically have much lower incomes, and pay a large proportion of them for rent. Thus, two types of people are moving into gentrified areas (DeGiovanni & Paulson, 1984).

There are various "costs" of gentrification. It has been found that gentrification often results in an increase in violent crimes (Taylor & Covington, 1988), as well as an increase in larceny and robbery (Covington & Taylor, 1988). This may occur, in part, from the close juxtaposition of the "haves" to the "have nots" in gentrifying areas. One of the major urban trends of the past decade, in fact, is an increasing gap between the very poor households and the other households in urban areas. This is the source of many current urban problems (e.g., violence and crime) and will probably play an even greater role in the future.

Another negative aspect of gentrification is that the poor who originally lived in the "slums" are often pressured to move out. Because they have few political advocates and little power, they are in a difficult situation. Henig (1982) argues that collective mobilization or other forms of protection for the victims of gentrification (e.g., those whose rents or property taxes are raised, or who are pressured or forced to relocate) is even more important than for victims of urban renewal. The federal government has not found effective means of monitoring gentrification for possible harm, and leaves much of the responsibility for dealing with those displaced to state and local officials. When these officials weigh their concerns over displacement of existing residents with their desire for an increased tax base, they often find

it difficult to support the former (Henig, 1982). In addition, the private sector is resistant to policies to limit displacement due to gentrification. Not surprisingly, as with urban renewal, it has been found that being forced to relocate due to gentrification is associated with threats to health and well-being (Henig, 1981; Myers, 1978).

Summary

Urban renewal is an environmental means that has been used in an attempt to solve the problems of cities. Unfortunately, while renewal and gentrification may have beneficial effects on the city as a whole, they have often been quite costly to those whom they displace. These "costs" could be reduced if planners and city officials attended to the needs of resident populations more closely, but some costs of forced relocation are probably unavoidable. With this in mind, we briefly turn to an alternative to city life, which usually is open only to the more affluent.

ESCAPING FROM THE CITY

The great American dream appears to be to leave the city. Evidence of the dislike most city dwellers have for their environs is suggested by the finding that almost four in ten would like to move out of the city, though seven in ten say they could be induced to stay if conditions would improve (Gallup Poll, March 1978, vol. 2). Only 15 percent of those living in communities with less than 50,000 residents express a desire to leave (Gallup Poll, April 19, 1981). In addition to crime, urbanites cite overcrowding, pollution, housing, traffic congestion, and noise as major reasons for leaving. Where would people rather live? A 1985 survey asked a representative American sample, "If you could

live wherever you wanted, would you prefer a large city, a suburban area, a small town, or a rural area?" The results were: city, 9 percent; suburbs, 29 percent; small town, 37 percent; rural area, 25 percent (ABC News/Washington Post Survey, February 22, 1985). However, it does not appear that the city is being totally rejected: Many of those expressing a preference for suburban or rural areas still wanted to be near a medium-size or large city (Figure 10–11).

This explains the massive move to suburbia, but what exactly are suburbs? They are areas within a metropolis that are relatively distant from the center of the population (Fischer,

Figure 10–11   Many people prefer to leave the city entirely.

1976). Suburban living has increased dramatically, especially since World War II, and at present more Americans live in the suburbs than in the center city or nonmetropolitan areas (Fischer, 1976). Why is this happening? Quite simply, because suburban living offers an answer to a number of urban problems. As one moves farther from the city, he or she is subjected to fewer crowds and to less dirt, noise, and pollution. In addition, although suburban crime rates are increasing, they are still much lower than in the city.

What are the consequences of the move to suburbia for those who make it? There is some evidence that the move has a positive effect. Suburbanites are generally happier with their housing, their communities, and their lives than city dwellers, even when socioeconomic status and other differences between urban and rural populations are statistically controlled (Fischer, 1973; Marans & Rodgers, 1975). Also, people

who move to the suburbs are much less afraid of crime victimization, and restrict their behavior less due to fear of crime (Lavrakas, 1982; Skogan & Maxfield, 1981). However, not all is well in suburbia. The price of typical suburban houses is rising tremendously, and it appears that fewer and fewer people will be able to afford or to maintain a suburban life style in the future. Further, as more and more people escape the city for the suburbs, crowding, pollution, and other urban problems are becoming suburban problems. As noted earlier, crime in the suburbs is increasing, and the use of drugs in suburban schools is cause for great concern. All this leaves one wondering if the suburban areas of today will be characterized by a full complement of ''urban'' problems in the future. But perhaps the worst problem created by the move to suburbia has its roots back in the cities. Cities are experiencing decreased populations, populations that are poorer, and that are more minority dominated than ever before. There is a declining tax base and an increasing demand for city services (e.g., police protection). This has occurred at a time when federal support has decreased. Unfortunately, the trend toward abandoning urban areas and moving to suburbia has jeopardized all that the city has to offer. We will have more to say about urban-suburban living in Chapter 12.

SUMMARY

The city is a salient environmental element in almost everyone's life. How does the urban setting affect individuals who live in it? A number of conceptual formulations have been derived to understand and predict the effects of the city on individuals; these include overload, environmental stress, behavior constraint, and overstaffing notions. Although they are often presented as competing concepts, it is probably true that overload, stress, constrained behavior, and insufficient resources each explains some of the consequences of an urban existence. Further, the predictions of each of the models can be integrated into the general environment–behavior formulation presented in Chapter 4. While this model has not been tested explicitly in research on cities, many of its assertions have been supported.

What are the results of experiments on the effects of city life? Two methodological perspectives (the "single variable" approach and the "urban versus rural" approach) have been used in past research. Each has its strengths and weaknesses. Overall, such urban stressors as noise, pollution, heat, crowding, and "extra demand," have at least moderately detrimental effects on city dwellers; the effects of homelessness and crime are much more severe. Further, when cities and nonurban areas are compared, there are urban–rural differences in terms of affiliative behavior, prosocial behavior, crime, stress, coping behavior, long-term aftereffects, and health. On most of these dimensions, urbanites come out on the short end. However, on dimensions not often studied by researchers (e.g., ability to adapt to diverse situations), urbanities may come out ahead.

Finally, a number of solutions have been tried to alleviate urban problems. One major attempt has been urban renewal. Unfortunately, this has often involved a conflict of interest between slum dwellers and city planners, with the former being forced to relocate. Forced relocation into public housing sometimes has disastrous consequences, which might be ameliorated by proper design of public housing. Gentrification is a more recent trend. Individuals return to the city and renovate housing that was formerly in bad condition. While this improves the urban area, it again causes relocation of original residents. The dream of most urbanities, however, is suburbia. This is attainable only for those whose socioeconomic level permits it. Research on suburban living shows that it offers a solution to some of the negative aspects of the city for those who can make the move.

SUGGESTED PROJECTS

1. One assumption we have made is that cities differ from small towns on a number of dimensions. To test this hypothesis, first buy copies of a few newspapers from large cities and small towns. Compare the following sections: entertainment, sports, and reports of local crime. Next, locate some telephone directories from large cities and

small towns. Compare listings for the following: medical specialists, tradespeople, specialized restaurants of diverse nationalities, museums, religious institutions, educational facilities, and theaters. What pattern of urban–rural differences emerges on these various dimensions?

2. Think of three cities you have visited, and attempt to rate them in terms of "atmosphere." Can you identify specific physical or social aspects that led you to make these judgments?

3. Now that you have been exposed to an empirically-based discussion of the city, what are *your* views of urban life? Has our assessment led you to become more positive or more negative toward cities than before? Write down your views and compare them with those of classmates.

4. Do a mini-experiment similar to that done by Bronzaft and McCarthy (1975) on the effects of noise on performance. First, find a classroom building or dormitory in which some areas are noisier than others. Next, choose some representative performance dimensions (e.g., grades, test scores, attendance, illness), and see if noise leads to performance decrements. If this type of measure is not available, construct one that is (e.g., favorability of nonverbal cues given). Try to use a context where people in the noisy and quiet areas are randomly assigned to their particular setting. If this is not possible, be sure to allow for the limitations that nonrandom assignment places on your findings.

5. Obtain from the library several urban newspapers that include the daily pollution index for their metropolitan areas. Plot the index for a week, along with the number of reported crimes in various categories, and reports of serious traffic accidents and deaths in the same geographic area. See if you find evidence for a relationship between pollution levels and accidents or crime.

6. Try to replicate the studies Newman and McCauley did on reciprocation of eye contact (which signals accessibility for interactions). In a small town and then in a city, position yourself near a doorway. When people passing by are a few feet away, initiate eye contact. Record the number of reciprocal gestures you receive in both settings. Do your results replicate those of Newman and McCauley?

7. Write a paragraph or two stating your agreement or disagreement with the following: "The 'bright side' of urban life has been missed by researchers." Give as much evidence as possible to support your position.

11 ARCHITECTURE, DESIGN, AND BEHAVIOR

Illumination

Windows

Furnishings

Privacy

CHAPTER SUMMARY

SUGGESTED PROJECTS

KEY TERMS

aesthetics	master plan
applicability gap	modern design
brightness	normative theory
chromatic aberration	organic growth
commodity	participation
congruence	pattern language
delight	possibilism
design alternatives	positive theory
design cycle	post-occupancy evaluation
determinism	preindustrial vernacular design
firmness	primitive design
folk design tradition	probabilism
gaps	procedural theory
Gestalt perception	saturation
grand design tradition	sociofugal
habitability	sociopetal
Hawthorne effect	substantive theory
hue	transient adaptation

INTRODUCTION

You are finally moving out of the dormitory and into the "real world." A local newspaper ad reads, "Immaculate two-bedroom apartment close to campus, recently redecorated." You become excited, and rush over to take a look. From

mental influence on behavior, probabilism is a compromise. It assumes that while an organism may choose a variety of responses in any environmental situation, there are *probabilities* associated with specific instances of design and behavior. These probabilities reflect the influence of both nonarchitectural factors and design variables on behavior. Thus, one can say that, given all we know about people and the particular environment they are in, some behaviors are more likely to occur than others.

A simple example will serve to illustrate environmental probabilism. Let us assume that you have a class with a small number of others in a very large room. Under these conditions, discussion is minimal. After studying everything you can find about classrooms, you decide to change the arrangement of the desks. You have learned that, in most cases, if you arrange seating in a circle, people will talk more. Thus the chances are good that if you rearrange your classroom in this way, you will help to create more discussion. However, if the class was scheduled late in the day, or if the instructor has "turned students off," you may not succeed. There are no "sure bets," according to probabilism.

THE DESIGNER'S PERSPECTIVE

According to Lang (1987, 1988) there is general agreement among architects that buildings and other designed environments must fulfill three basic purposes: **commodity**, **firmness**, and **delight**. Commodity refers to the functional goal of a design (what is the building to be used for?), firmness to the structural integrity or permanence (will it last?), and delight encompasses aesthetic concerns. Different architects may place different emphasis on these interrelated dimensions, but in each case the designer must draw on his or her professional expertise in order to face the challenges of a specific design. Of course, this need not be a lonely task. As we shall see, there are a number of reasons why it is often wise for designers to collaborate, both with other professionals and with the eventual occupants of a design. To be responsive to each of these concerns, designers must draw upon an accumulation of data and ideas organized as theories and models.

In this instance, we use the term "theory" loosely to refer to a system of organized ideas that describe or explain the world. This use of the term is informal, but it is consistent with our definition of theory in Chapter 4. Theory provides a source of information to which a designer can refer. Lang (1987, 1988) distinguishes between positive and normative theory. **Positive theory** attempts to discover predictable relationships between variables, in this instance, the effect of modifications of the physical environment on commodity, firmness, and delight. **Normative theory**, on the other hand, is based upon value-laden descriptions and explanations of what *ought* to be done. Normative theory may express itself in design manifestos, identification with a particular design movement, or other differences in style (see Figure 11–1). As psychologists we prefer to limit ourselves to empirical or positive theory, but we would be foolish not to recognize that even this choice represents the normative stance of our field.

We have also noted that Lang (1987, 1988) differentiates between procedural and substantive issues (again refer to Figure 11–1). "Pro-

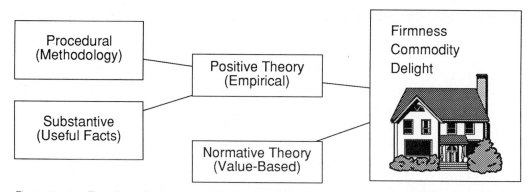

Figure 11-1 The relationship between normative and substantive theories and design. (After Lang, J., 1987. *Creating architectural theory: The role of the behavioral sciences in environmental design.* New York: Van Nostrand Rinehold.)

cedure'' refers to the method of gathering data or making decisions, and ''substance'' to a series of useful facts about the relationship between environmental variables such as color,

privacy, or furnishings and the ability of a design to provide commodity, firmness, and delight.

THE PROCESS OF DESIGN: PROCEDURAL CONTRIBUTIONS

The architect is faced with quite a challenge in attempting to design original structures that address the needs of his or her clients. With hindsight it is probably an easy task for you to think of instances in your own home or campus environment in which building design is not congruent with the needs of you, the user. Ironically, the premium our society places on originality and the explosion of building technology make errors almost inevitable (e.g., Alexander et al., 1975; Rapoport, 1969).

History, Culture, and Design Procedures

If someone were to ask you right now to name five things you associate with ancient Egypt it is likely that among them you would name the

Pyramids or the Sphinx. For Ancient Greece a similar list might bring the Parthenon to mind, and symbols of modern Paris are likely to include the Eiffel Tower (see Figure 11-2).

Surely these are impressive (and relatively permanent) examples of their respective culture's design achievements, but are they really representative of the environments that most affect the average member of their societies? Rapoport (1969) notes that monuments and other ''important'' buildings represent a self-conscious attempt of the designer (or his or her patron), to impress—what Rapoport refers to as the **grand design tradition**. By intent, these constructions are unusual, specialized, and not representative of the variety of environments experienced by the common person. On the other hand, the **folk design tradition** (as

Figure 11–2   The Eiffel tower is an excellent example of high-style architecture.

expressed, for example, in the home of the common person) is a more direct expression of the day-to-day world of people as they live, shop, and work. Environmental psychology should concern itself with both the monumental architecture of public buildings and the more personal design of individual dwellings, but Rapoport's summary of folk design across cultures will serve to highlight some of the broad issues confronting both designers and environmental psychologists in a variety of contexts.

Within the folk tradition Rapoport distinguishes between **primitive** and **preindustrial vernacular** architecture. In so-called "primitive" societies there is little specialization, and nearly everyone is capable of building his or her own shelter according to time-honored techniques that result in a standard design across all dwellings within the culture. The term "primitive" does not imply unsophisticated. Indeed,

these shelters have evolved over time under the unforgiving challenges of survival, and they represent successful integrations of unique cultural and environmental demands. Given the resource and cultural constraints, a modern designer would be hard-pressed to create a more durable and portable dwelling for a family than the Cheyenne tepee, or a more successful adaptation to Northern winters than the snow igloo (see Figure 11–3). Furthermore, these and other examples of primitive architecture are sensitive adaptations to climatic conditions such as temperature, wind direction, and moisture rather than attempts at overcoming them with the huge energy expenditures needed to make the standard North American frame home habitable from Florida to Alaska.

As construction methods become somewhat more complex, families may begin to rely on the knowledge and assistance of specialists. Rapoport refers to this as *preindustrial vernac-*

Figure 11–3 Shelter in so-called "primitive" societies is often a very sophisticated solution to the challenges of a particular environment.

ular architecture, characterized by slightly more individual variation in the design of individual buildings and by needing the assistance of tradespersons. Again however, design in these societies is based upon an evolved construction tradition. Each building is simply a variation on an established and time-tested theme.

As Figure 11–4 illustrates, **modern building design** in industrial nations differs from design in these traditional societies on a number of dimensions. For example, the designer is likely to be an architect or some other professional rather than a member of the family, the design is less constrained by climatic conditions, and the changes in building styles and construction techniques are likely to occur at a dramatically faster pace. Furthermore, shelter and survival are expectations rather than concerns for the middle- or upper-class citizens who commission designs or purchase homes. Therefore, in addition to obvious structural

concerns such as durability and safety, modern criteria for building design are likely to include aesthetic evaluation, comfort, efficiency, and the performance of the people living and working within a design. Particularly in the industrialized nations, survival in comfort has led to a high dependence on technology, and typically, heavy use of nonrenewable sources of energy to fuel our furnaces, power our air conditioners, and light our homes and factories. Unfortunately, it is easy to cite instances of technological mishaps as the price of our dependence. (See Chapter 7 for a discussion of human reactions to technological catastrophes such as nuclear power plant accidents.)

The Design Process

What can psychology contribute to the *process* of design? One of the most important is an emphasis on objectivity and logic in research and theory-building. Psychology can offer in-

Figure 11–4   Modern buildings often emphasize aesthetics, individuality, and changing technology.

sights into the complex process of information-gathering and decision-making that occurs in the design process (Lang, 1987; Zeisel, 1981). In discussing how designs are planned and implemented, we need to consider several basic concepts. Here we will discuss two: congruence and design alternatives.

Congruence Congruence is a major goal of the design process (Michelson, 1977). This construct refers to the degree of "fit" between user needs and preferences and the design features of a given setting. The emphasis here is on the match between form and function. If they match well, the design supports or facilitates the behaviors necessary for the function of the space, and positive outcomes typically occur (Studer, 1970). Designs that support or facilitate the desires and needs of the people using them are said to be congruent. However, arrangements of space inevitably restrict behavioral options (we cannot walk through a wall unless a door is there), and to the extent that these restrictions inhibit preferred ways of behaving, users will be dissatisfied and negative reactions will be manifested. One way to achieve greater congruence is to "design in" flexibility, thereby ensuring that the space can support a variety of behaviors (Zeisel, 1975). Congruence is often referred to as **habitability**, particularly in residential settings. Habitability also refers to how well a particular environment fits the needs of its inhabitants (Nelson, 1976), which can range from basic survival (such as seeking shelter from the weather), to improvement of a setting that is already safe and secure.

Design Alternatives Another important concept is that of **design alternatives**. Our adaptation or adjustment to the physical environment is determined in part by the number of potential design alternatives (or different ways we can think of to design or redesign a setting). If there are few design alternatives available, we will probably have to adapt to current conditions, which may be quite costly in some cases. When there are many design alternatives, we are apt to adjust environmental conditions through one means or another. Each different possible adjustment of our environment, then, can be called a design alternative. In effect, the various combinations or isolated uses of design elements, such as color, lighting, furnishings, or the arrangements of space, all reflect design alternatives. In a given setting there may be an extremely large number of these, but as different criteria are brought to bear, more and more alternatives will be ruled out. For example, some alternatives may be too expensive, and others may be inappropriate due to their behavioral effects. The process of determining the proper design alternatives and weighing the importance of various criteria forms the heart of the design process. It is a complex undertaking, since there are many interrelationships among design alternatives as well as many different social, economic, artistic, and cultural pressures that affect it (see Figure 11–5).

In practice, there are usually an enormous number of acceptable, or even equally good design solutions, so there may be no such thing as the *best* solution. Because there is such a variety of apparently acceptable solutions, and because even poor designs may appear successful until after a great deal of effort has gone into developing them, one of the designer's most difficult problems may be in deciding when to *stop* design and begin construction. Instead of proceeding in a smooth, directed path, Zeisel (1981) suggests that a spiral metaphor is a better representation of the design process (see Figure 11–6). In separate cycles, architects propose, test, and refine possible solutions to sets of related problems. The result of each cycle will be a possible response to a particular design problem, but this decision may limit the alternative solutions to another set of problems. By testing ideas, finding conflicts, then retesting, the spiral will gradually narrow until it lies within the domain of acceptable solutions, at which point construction will begin.

Figure 11–5A and B   The solution to a design problem may require weighing a number of possible design alternatives. Aesthetic and space needs prompted renovation of the building above, but plans were modified by other utilitarian requirements. Thus, the need to eliminate wooden floors dictated a new internal structure, and handicapped access required the addition of an external atrium to house an elevator. In this instance, both requirements are expensive, but not inconsistent with functional and aesthetic desires.

Stages in the Design Process

Each time we employ a design alternative to adjust our environment to make it more congruent (or habitable), we use the design process. (See Figure 11–6 for one outline of the various stages involved in the design process.) It begins with an *awareness* both of needs that have been met, and of potential design alternatives (environmental adjustments). Once a need and a possible design alternative have been specified, it is necessary to develop *criteria* for determining how effectively the proposed alternatives resolve the need. Although criteria may be physical in nature, as in the quality specifications of building materials, our discussion of the design process will focus on behavioral criteria, such as ease of movement.

Frequently, some kind of research or *evaluation* must be performed in order to know

Figure 11–6 Zeisel's design spiral. (Adapted from Zeisel, J., 1975. *Sociology and architectural design: Social science frontiers*, No. 6. New York: Russell Sage Foundation.

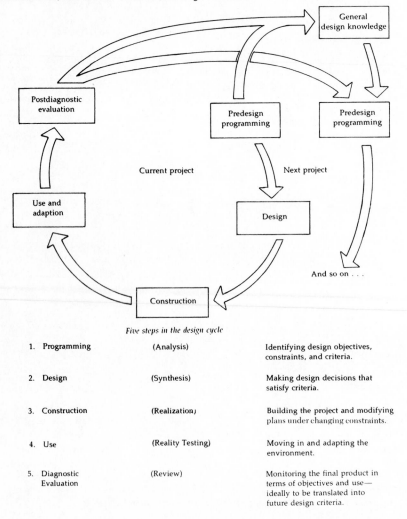

Five steps in the design cycle

1. Programming	(Analysis)	Identifying design objectives, constraints, and criteria.
2. Design	(Synthesis)	Making design decisions that satisfy criteria.
3. Construction	(Realization)	Building the project and modifying plans under changing constraints.
4. Use	(Reality Testing)	Moving in and adapting the environment.
5. Diagnostic Evaluation	(Review)	Monitoring the final product in terms of objectives and use— ideally to be translated into future design criteria.

whether specific design alternatives measure up to the criteria established for them. When such evaluation indicates the desirability of a particular alternative, additional steps must be taken to *implement* the design. Models of the design process that stress cooperation among different professions, consideration of environmental quality, and post-occupancy evaluation (POE) can be effective tools in going beyond this step and arriving at the goal of a habitable environment.

Implementing the Design Process: Models for the Future

We have seen how design awareness and careful selection of behavioral criteria lead to research on the behavioral effects of design alternatives. Given this body of research, how can we implement the environmental design process to ensure an end product such that future-built environments are more habitable? Design professionals, such as architects, must keep many factors in mind—building site problems, projected costs, availability of materials, and performance standards for construction materials, to name a few. What can we do to make sure that habitability is included in these considerations? In this section, we will examine a model that has been proposed with this end in mind. We should note that other equally useful models, which we do not have the space to describe, also exist. (Interested readers might wish to consult Broadbent, 1973; Kaplan & Kaplan, 1982; and Weisman, 1983.)

A Model of the Design Cycle   How can we be even more certain that improved design will follow awareness of environmental quality and environmental design alternatives? Ideally, a continuous cycle of design planning and evaluation should occur for every building project (Zeisel, 1975, 1981). Such a **design cycle** would permit information gained from an existing project to be applied immediately to the next project, which in turn should be evaluated for

the planning phase of still another project. Zeisel's model of this process includes five distinct steps that would be repeated for every new design project (Figure 11–6).

This model begins with a programming step intended to identify design criteria, then moves into a stage at which the criteria are synthesized into design features. In the third stage of the model, design modifications are made as construction conditions demand. In the fourth stage, the newly constructed environment is tested in actual use for habitability and other performance standards. The final, or diagnostic, step is to make follow-up evaluations of how well the finished project measures up to the behavioral design criteria developed during the planning stage. Note that Zeisel's model emphasizes the importance of **post-occupancy evaluation**. This step might be most simply stated as learning from past mistakes and successes and integrating the findings into future research and design. Although recognition of the importance of POE as a formal step in the design process may be relatively recent, a number of articles have sought to formalize or describe the POE process (e.g., Moore, 1982; Zimring & Reizenstein, 1980) and to offer examples of successful evaluation (Marans & Spreckelmeyer, 1981). Such diagnostic data can then be used in the planning stage of the next project.

Altman (1973, 1975) suggests that the model might be extended. His suggestions include adding a second dimension to allow for different design emphases for environments whose scale or size differs. The design of a bedroom, for example, would probably emphasize different factors than the design of a community. A third dimension in Altman's model allows for different behavioral emphases (or for more than one behavioral criterion) in any given project. Privacy needs and personal space requirements might be evaluated differently for a hospital than for a neighborhood, and the planning and evaluation stages in the design cycle might approach these behaviors somewhat differently.

Altman emphasizes that the design process must reflect the different approaches of the various people involved in environmental design. In particular, he feels that practitioners, such as architects, are inclined to attend primarily to design criteria and to particular places or settings. Researchers, on the other hand, are more likely to stress ongoing behavioral processes, such as privacy, territoriality, or personal space. Consequently, the practitioner may think of privacy more in terms of a setting, such as the home, or in terms of a design decision, such as locating bedrooms away from living areas to ensure privacy. The social science researcher tends to think of privacy more as a continual coping behavior to control the level of social interaction in one's environment. Moreover, practitioners are apt to want information that can be used immediately to solve a given problem, whereas researchers are often more interested in long-range projects that will reveal new discoveries. By including three dimensions in his model, each of which contains considerable breadth, Altman hopes to include the point of view of numerous practitioners and researchers.

In concluding our discussion of broad design principles, we would like to repeat Altman's emphasis on the necessity of interdisciplinary teamwork in the environmental design process. Interdisciplinary cooperation offers an important means of implementing behaviorally-oriented environmental design. One hopeful sign that this goal is closer to being attained is the occurrence of interdisciplinary design conferences. For example, each year the Environmental Design Research Association (EDRA) holds a conference that attracts behavioral scientists and designers who share an interest in behaviorally-based design (Werner & Szigeti, 1987).

Decisions, Communication, and Research: The Gaps

Despite the advantages of interdisciplinary collaboration, several authors (e.g. Alexander, 1979; Alexander et al., 1975; Kaplan & Kaplan, 1982) suggest that design is still likely to fail unless **participation** is expanded even further. These theorists believe that modern design practices have isolated the eventual occupants of buildings from the designers and builders who are responsible for creating them (Kaplan & Kaplan, 1982; Zeisel, 1981). The problem may become one of encouraging substantive communication between the professional design team and those who pay for or inhabit their creations.

In most introductory treatments of behavioral design it has become common practice to speak of the **gap**. In fact, there are several gaps, but the one to which these authors refer (Figure 11–7) represents our earlier observation that unlike primitive or preindustrial vernacular cultures, the eventual users of a building or other environmental design (*using clients*) are often never directly consulted in the design process. As several authors (e.g., Mitchell, 1974; Zeisel, 1975, 1981) have noted, the architect often has direct contact with only the *paying client*, often some corporation or governmental agency. The problem is easy to illustrate. Were you (or some other student before you) consulted by the architect responsible for the classrooms in which you learn or the residence halls in which you or your classmates dwell? Because most individuals buy either an older home or from a developer, it is almost as unusual for a family to have an opportunity to participate directly in the design of their home.

Social or behavioral research may be a useful tool for the architect who wishes to understand the complex behavioral needs of the strangers for whom he or she builds. The implication for our present discussion is that behavioral science offers a likely avenue for bridging the gap between designers and the using client. Increased communication between designers and their clients is something to which no one really objects, but successful communication is not accidental. It has been suggested that design

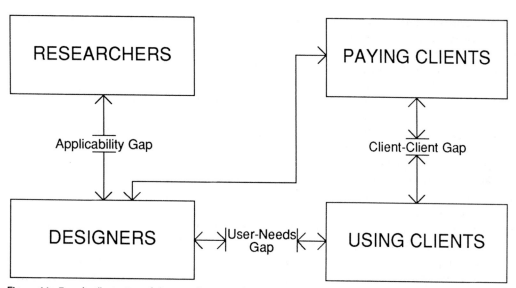

Figure 11—7 An illustration of the gaps between the paying and the using client, between designers and the clients, and between behavioral scientists and designers. (Adapted from Zeisel, J., 1981. *Inquiry by design.* Monterey, CA: Brooks/Cole.)

education and training shapes and changes the expert's perceptions of the environment (Kaplan & Kaplan, 1982; S. Kaplan, 1987). Designers may have developed ways of visualizing design alternatives and communicating with other professionals that may not be comfortable for laypersons.

Fostering Participation There are several ways to improve the chances that the needs and wants of the using client are incorporated in new design. One way to close the gap would be to train experts to be more sensitive to people's concerns (Kaplan & Kaplan, 1982). Perhaps the most straightforward approach to involving users is to include them in the actual design process. Unfortunately, Kaplan and Kaplan (1982) lament that the single most striking aspect of participation as it is now practiced is how badly it works. Although design experts are likely to recognize the complexity and ambiguity of many design questions, they are asked to make quick, confident, and cost-effective decisions—a requirement that in the

short term at least, is likely to conflict with the laborious process of gathering and assimilating data from the public.

Several themes that seem to characterize instances of successful participation were suggested by Kaplan and Kaplan (1982):

1. *Involving the public at an early stage in design so that their suggestions can be fairly integrated into design alternatives.* The public will rightfully feel offended if their participation is invited only when most of the decisions have already been made.
2. *Availability of several concrete alternatives to react to.* The designer's expertise can demonstrate the scope of design alternatives and present options that allow straightforward responses.
3. *Presentation of possibilities in a format that is comprehensible.* In particular, the use of visual or spatial material can make it possible for lay persons to visualize design alternatives.

To summarize, a concerted effort needs to be made to accurately communicate design alternatives to laypersons so that they may make substantive and informed decisions. Simulations such as models or drawings are frequently employed by designers in communicating with clients and other designers. In many instances these models are themselves almost works of art. In communicating with the public, at least, the Kaplans emphasize that too much attention to detail and exactness in simulation may actually be counterproductive. A model that pretends to be a perfect replica of an actual design is likely to be expensive, and may simply activate the human tendency to try to find all of the little discrepancies between the model and reality. Instead, the Kaplans propose very rough models, sometimes as simple as building blocks. These are inexpensive, adaptable, and enlist the viewer as a collaborator.

We might add that if a psychologist wishes to serve as a liaison between professionals and their clients, the psychologist would profit from a basic understanding of the graphics and technical references used by designers. In a sense, a successful liaison must be able to translate between the dialects spoken by both the professional and lay participants.

A Pattern Language for Participation The best known, most ambitious, and perhaps most controversial proposal for user participation is probably that developed by Christopher Alexander and his colleagues (Alexander, 1979; Alexander, Ishikawa, & Silverstein, 1977; Alexander et al., 1975). Although this approach is quite normative, it does directly address the three themes outlined by the Kaplans. Like Rapoport, Alexander believes that modern design has lost many of the advantages of participation and slow evolution that were characteristic of primitive and preindustrial cultures. In particular, Alexander attacks the modern approach in which roads are built by engineers, buildings by architects, and tract housing by developers. In Alexander's view,

the average citizen has lost the ability to affect design, and designers have lost touch with the needs of those they serve. *The Oregon Experiment* (Alexander et al., 1975) illustrates the participative process as Alexander would implement it on a college campus (in this case the University of Oregon).

Most colleges and universities have a **master plan**, a map or series of maps with supporting documents which seek to coordinate future building projects. The goal of these planning documents is to prevent haphazard growth and isolated constructions that lack coordination with other campus facilities or design styles. Yet Alexander finds these plans to be too rigid, too likely to constrain growth to patterns devised decades earlier, and too likely to overlook the need for small, evolutionary renovations. Instead of a master plan, Alexander favors piecemeal, **organic growth** in which buildings are initiated and designed by their users and built by architects and contractors. Change and adaptation are constant, but piece-by-piece growth achieves a long-term order as each new space is carefully fit into the existing environment.

In order to allow lay persons such unusual prominence in design, Alexander created what he calls a **pattern language** (Alexander et al., 1977) which contains prescriptions for hundreds of different design problems or situations. We can get a flavor for the content of these prescriptions by examining two for the University of Oregon:

4. UNIVERSITY SHAPE AND DIAMETER

When a university is too spread out, people cannot make use of all it offers; on the other hand, a diameter for the university based strictly on the 10-minute class break is needlessly restrictive.

Therefore: Plan all classes evenly distributed within a circular zone not more than 3000 feet in diameter. Place non-class activities such as athletic fields, research offices, administration within a wider circle, not more than 5000 feet in diameter (p. 110).

16. STUDENT COMMUNITY

If dormitories are too small and too communal, they become constraining. If they are too big or too private, then the idea of group living is lost.

Therefore: Encourage the formation of autonomously managed cooperative housing clusters that bring 30 to 40 units together, around communal eating, sports, etc. Unlike dorms, however, make the individual units rather

autonomous, with sink, toilet and hot plates, and with private entrances (p. 119).

Regardless of your orientation, we hope you will agree that social and psychological phenomena are to some extent influenced by architecture and design. We will now turn to a consideration of some specific, individual interior design elements which have been found to affect our behavior across a wide variety of settings. In contrast to our focus here on individual design elements—the pieces which make up the whole—Chapters 12 and 13 will consider the behavioral effects of design in entire behavior settings.

ENVIRONMENTAL PSYCHOLOGY'S SUBSTANTIVE CONTRIBUTIONS

In addition to facilitating design decisions and promoting communication between designers and their clients, environmental psychology ought also to serve as a source of substantive theory, that is, empirical data of use to designers. Indeed, this role as an archive of research findings is a more familiar one to many academic psychologists. Again, if the results of research are to be useful they must be:

1. *Reliable and valid;*
2. *Responsive to the pragmatic needs of designers;*
3. *Communicated in a manner that is comprehensible to nonscientists.*

Certainly the behavioral sciences are just one of several sources of substantive knowledge. An architect must employ a variety of information very foreign to both this text and the skills and knowledge of psychologists. For example, firmness will depend largely upon the design-

er's knowledge of construction materials, commodity requires an understanding of much more than just behavior, and the aesthetic concerns subsumed under delight may also be understood from the perspective of art rather than science. But how are designers integrating relevant behavioral information in their designs? "Cautiously" would be the simplest answer. In fact, some (e.g., Sime, 1986) suggest that architecture in the late 1970s began to react against the idea of collaboration with social scientists.

Many environmental psychologists are most comfortable with the academic research models of experimental and social psychology. Academicians often value their independence, that is, their ability to choose to investigate almost any question that interests them. They are also typically (rightfully) committed to cautious interpretation of their data. Unfortunately, at least for those who wish to see the early application of behavioral design, these goals of experimental science sometimes result in a situation that encourages psychologists to ask simple research questions of statistical elegance but that hold little promise for application. Furthermore, the design implications of the research literature can be difficult for design professionals to extract from the jargon and statistical descriptions of research journals. If behavioral science is to offer designers useful data, it should be more responsive to practical questions of design. This is likely to pose one of the thorniest problems for environmental psychology in the years to come. If, as Kaplan and Kaplan (1982) assert, research that is trivial and not worth doing is not worth doing well, psychology will also suffer painfully from sloppy or misinterpreted findings. The long-term answer to this problem will appear only as the field and its database of well-documented research matures. For now, the task has just begun.

The **applicability gap** (Russell & Ward, 1982; Seidel, 1985) is a name given to miscommunication between psychologists trying to understand the needs of architects, and designers who try to come to grips with the data and the implications of social and behavioral sciences. There has long been a conflict between the scientist's desire for rigor and control and the designer's need for data addressing relevant questions. Recognition of the applicability gap prompts questions regarding research methodology and philosophy of science, and represents an unresolved tension in the youthful field of environmental psychology.

Earlier we said that three fundamental purposes of design are to provide firmness, commodity, and delight (Lang, 1987). Psychology may serve as a resource for designers wishing empirical data regarding aesthetics and the ability of an environment to support certain behaviors (commodity). Of course much of this text is a summary of theory with potential design applications, and Chapters 12 and 13 will consider entire behavioral settings such as

schools, museums, and the workplace. The balance of this chapter will first provide a brief review of architectural aesthetics and, subsequently, five specific substantive design elements that can affect our behavior across a wide variety of settings.

Aesthetics

One of the primary goals of a design is to evoke a pleasurable response from people viewing the finished setting. The study of **aesthetics** in architecture is an attempt to identify, understand and, eventually, to create those features of an environment that lead to pleasurable responses. The problem is that aesthetic considerations in design may operate contrary to behavioral ones. Some of the most beautiful structures are also among the most impractical. However, one cannot simply dismiss aesthetic quality as less relevant than the behavioral effects of design. Indeed, there is evidence that aesthetics may be important in determining behavior (e.g., Steinitz, 1968). (For another discussion of general aesthetic principles, see Chapter 2.)

According to Lang (1987), formal aesthetics has traditionally been heavily dependent on the **Gestalt theory of perception** (see the box on page 380), which views the organization of elements of visual form as units which can be perceived as either simple or complex. Although these principles have been widely demonstrated, Gestalt theory is now considered to apply only to a rather limited number of situations, and this approach is just one of many in the psychology of perception (e.g., Goldstein, 1989). Nevertheless, the Gestalt approach appeals to the designer's need for an understanding of visual forms at a broad, holistic level. For many designers, the implication is that environments ordered according to these principles of "good form" will also be good environments, whereas other designers (e.g., Venturi, 1966) deliberately violate Gestalt principles as a means for obtaining visually richer environments. Unfortunately, most of these applications remain rooted in the Gestalt principles of the 1930s. Applications of empirical aesthetics may profit from consideration of more current perceptual theories. For example, in Chapter 2 we reviewed Berlyne's psychobiological approach (1974), which proposes that pleasure is related to the achievement of a moderate, but not too high level of stimulation. There is also evidence to suggest that aesthetic qualities can reduce the monotony of the city and maintain gratifying levels of stimulation (e.g., Berlyne, 1960). Other research emphasizes the aesthetic importance of functional environments (Gibson, 1966; Kaplan & Kaplan, 1982) or legible environments like those discussed by Lynch (1960). Studies of images of urban areas also suggest that aesthetic qualities influence people's ability to find their way through a cityscape (Lynch, 1960; Smith, 1984).

Research has indicated that the aesthetic quality of a room—the extent to which it is pleasant or attractive—may affect the sorts of evaluations we make while in that setting. In one classic study, Maslow and Mintz (1956) compared subjects' ratings of a series of photographs of individuals in a "beautiful" room (well-decorated, well-lit, etc.), an average room (a professor's office), and an "ugly" room (resembling a janitor's closet). Their results showed that subjects rated the persons in the photos most positively if they had been in the beautiful room, and most negatively if they had been in the ugly room.

Attractive environments also make people feel better. Research has shown that decorated spaces make people feel more comfortable than ones which have not been decorated (Campbell, 1979). Also, the good moods that are associated with pleasant environments seem to increase people's willingness to help each other (Sherrod et al., 1977). How does aesthetic quality affect one's work output? We can guess that for some kinds of work and in certain settings the positive feelings associated with pleasant spaces may improve work efficiency and accuracy, while in

other contexts an aesthetically pleasant environment may be disruptive. People feel more like talking to one another in pleasant settings (Russell & Mehrabian, 1978), and to the extent that socializing in the office detracts from efficient performance, aesthetic quality can be a problem. Research has also suggested that decoration may be distracting (e.g., Baum & Davis, 1976), but whether this is necessarily a problem appears to depend on other factors (Worchel & Teddlie, 1976).

Color

At least in popular literature, color is recognized as an important consideration in the design of residential and business environments. Certainly, as Heimstra and McFarling (1978) noted some time ago, color is one of the most easily manipulated dimensions of the physical environment. In a business setting, for example, a coat of paint is far less costly than structural remodeling. Surprisingly, there is very little recent research directed specifically at the effectiveness of various manipulations of environmental color. Granted, several authors have provided prescriptions for color combinations which are said to alter spatial perception, temperature, and mood, and these notions have been enthusiastically adopted by some designers. Unfortunately, these prescriptions are typically not based upon strong empirical foundations (Holahan, 1982; Sanders & McCormick, 1987). Like Sanders and McCormick, we are forced to conclude that the literature addressing the application of color is dominated by opinion rather than research.

Dimensions of Color Colors are described along three dimensions. **Hue** is the dominant wavelength of light, and is probably the primary dimension we think of when we describe a color. Luminance is based upon the amount of light and results in the sensation of **brightness**. Finally, **saturation** refers to the degree to which a color is pure (uncontaminated by other

. . . .

Principles of Perceptual Construction

When perception theorists say that we construct our perceptions, they do not mean that we "make them up," but rather that we add to the simple sensations we experience so that these sensations are interpreted as part of a larger whole. To illustrate, let us examine some perceptual principles, often called Gestalt principles. This term refers to the German word "Gestalt" (pronounced guess-TALT), which means "form" or "figure," or more literally "good form." The term is also associated with the Gestalt psychologists who proposed these perceptual principles (see also, Lang et al., 1974).

Examine the lines in Figure 11–8(A). What do you see? There are six lines in the drawing, but you tend to see them not as six separate lines, but as three pairs of lines. This phenomenon illustrates the principle of *proximity*, or the tendency to group together those things that are spatially close. Now look at Figure 11–8(B). Do you see a circle and a square? Technically you do not, and you would receive a poor grade in geometry if you drew them this way. Note that the figures are not complete (i.e., they contain gaps), yet you interpret them as complete. This phenomenon illustrates the principle of *closure*, or the tendency to join lines together to make a more perfect or complete figure.

Next, examine Figure 11–8(C). Although the spacing is essentially the same between the Xs and Os, you tend not to see the figure as one of five rows and five columns but rather

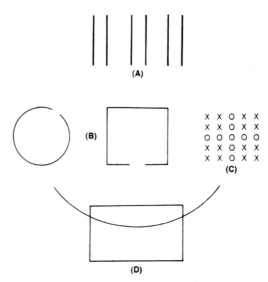

Figure 11–8   Principles of Gestalt construction.

as a central cross and four groups of four Xs each, illustrating the principle of *similarity*, or the tendency to make a pattern out of similar stimuli. Finally, examine Figure 11–8(D). You probably see it as a rectangle with a curved line across it (i.e., a geometric parabola). Or you could interpret the figure as the back of an envelope with two lines drawn off to the sides. However, because the curved line is continuous, you initially interpret the drawing as a curved line superimposed over a rectangle. This illustrates the principle of *continuity*.

Governing all of these principles of organization is the *law of pragnanz*, or good form, which emphasizes that the composition of one's field of vision will be perceived in the simplest way possible. In our examples of closure, for instance, it is cognitively simpler to perceive one circle rather than a series of arcs.

The Gestalt psychologists believed that these were innate functions of human biology rather than learned. In practice, examples of Gestalt laws are typically most applicable to simple line drawings of the type illustrated in Figure 11–9 which convey little depth. Principles developed with these simple figures probably underestimate the importance of three-dimensional depth cues, familiarity, and learning. Furthermore, the Gestalt perspective has been criticized as offering descriptions applicable to one situation but not explanations that might be more broadly applied (Goldstein, 1989).

. . . .

wavelengths) and not "washed out" (see Figure 11–9). Certain color effects result from the direct physiological action of colored light on the human visual system. Other effects seem more likely to be subject to the vagaries of human perception, including the influence of culture, fashion, and idiosyncratic life events.

Physiological Color Effects At one level, the existence of differential response to various colors is hardly controversial. Clearly, since humans without visual defects do perceive differences in hue, brightness, and color saturation, there is a color-specific physiological response at the sensory level. Consequently, the human sensory system possesses several characteristics with straightforward implications for design. We will provide just one of many possible examples. One aspect of color of traditional interest to psychologists has been the apparent tendency of red surfaces to "advance" and blue surfaces to "recede." Most people judge equidistant objects differing in highly saturated colors to be at different distances, with red objects appearing to be in front of blue ones. This phenomenon seems to be due to **chromatic aberration**, which occurs because the lens of the eye (unlike that of a well-designed camera) is not completely color corrected. Refraction caused by the eye's cornea and lens causes short wavelengths (blues) to converge in front of the retina and long wavelengths (reds) to converge behind it in a mid-range accommodated eye.

Therefore, in order to focus light of these different wavelengths, the eye must accommodate differentially. This is interpreted by the perceptual system as a depth cue (see Sundet, 1978, for a more thorough review of several theoretical explanations for this effect). Stolper (1977) presents experimental evidence that accommodation to alternating red and blue

Figure 11–9 The color dimensions of hue, brightness, and saturation.

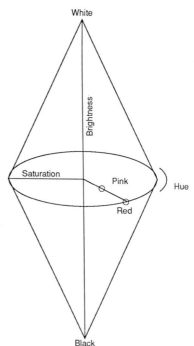

backgrounds may cause adverse stress for someone reading or performing other visual tasks. In some other instances the same sensory effect may presumably be useful, adding perceptual contour to a flat wall or emphasis to some design element.

In addition to its obvious effects on visual sensation, color may also affect other parts of the nervous system. For instance, Wilson (1966) has reported that galvanic skin response (GSR), an indicator of physiological arousal, was significantly higher when subjects were shown slides of highly red hues than when the slides were green. Other transient effects such as changes in blood pressure, heart rate, and respiration rate are occasionally reported (Birren, 1969; Stolper, 1977), but perhaps the only physiological responses that have been systematically investigated and documented regard a decreased ability on tasks requiring muscular inhibition (hand steadiness, for example). Laboratory data suggest that red light may slightly increase hand and finger tremors (Cockerill & Miller, 1983; Nakshian, 1964).

Color and Temperature A number of investigators have examined the possibility of a relationship between color and temperature. Early investigations (e.g., Newhall, 1941; Ross, 1938; Wright & Rainwater, 1962) reported that warm temperatures were most often associated with reds and oranges, whereas coolness was associated with blues and greens. But were these early investigations successful in delineating the psychological effects of color in a way that can be applied to design? That is, does the color of the walls in the room in which you are now reading affect your perception of the room's temperature? Many aspects of color are tangled in a web of symbolism. Simply asking subjects to report color–temperature associations may only tap an individual's ability to repeat these learned, perhaps wholly symbolic associations. The answer came from studies in which experimenters actually manipulated room color and temperature, while elim-

inating the demand upon subjects to repeat learned color–temperature associations.

As a rule, investigators who have adequately controlled the tendency for subjects to try to respond ''correctly'' with the usual color–temperature symbolisms have failed to find useful effects (Bennett & Rey, 1972; Berry, 1961; Greene & Bell, 1980; Fanger, Breum, & Jerking, 1977). The study by Berry (1961) neatly makes our point. Berry chose to investigate the effects of color on the comfort of subjects seated in a heated room. Participants were ostensibly performing a task designed to determine the effects of colored light on performance in an automobile driving simulator. They were told that the lights generated a great deal of heat and that they should notify the experimenter when they became uncomfortably warm. Berry concluded that the color of the illumination (green, blue, yellow, amber) did not affect the level of tolerable heat. Subsequently, however, Berry asked the same subjects to rank samples of the experimental colors in terms of the amount of heat they transmitted. Thus cued, most ranked the colors in the conventional hue–heat order (again, warmth with amber, coolness with blue and green).

Spatial Effects Perception of spaciousness, or conversely, crowding, is also influenced by color. Acking and Kuller (1972) had subjects rate a series of slides depicting rooms which varied in color. Results indicated that lighter rooms were seen as more open and spacious. Similarly, Baum and Davis (1976) found that different intensities of the same color affected subjects' response to model rooms. Light-green rooms appeared larger and less crowded than identical rooms painted a darker green. The latter study suggests that color can affect the ways in which we perceive settings.

Illumination

How does interior lighting affect our behavior? Investigations of performance effects of different lighting conditions date back to the beginning of this century (see the box on page 384). Lighting can affect how well we perform in many contexts, ranging from an examination, to an experimental task in a laboratory, to a job on an automobile assembly line. At a very basic level, lighting affects performance by making it harder or easier to see what we are doing. At one extreme, the absence of light makes it impossible to take an exam because we cannot read the questions. On the other hand, we may not be able to see the questions on the exam if there is too much light.

As it turns out, illumination engineering is a rather complex task. Not only does one need to consider the amount, color, and location of a light source, but also reflectance from walls and ceilings, the contrast in luminance between a given area (the work table, for example) and the surroundings, and glare. Fortunately the Illuminating Engineering Society has adopted recommendations for determining the appropriate levels of illumination for a variety of tasks and environments (Kaufman & Christensen, 1984). Generally, the data indicate that increasing illumination results in smaller and smaller improvements until performance levels off or drops because of glare or a reduction of the clarity of patterned visual stimuli (Logan & Berger, 1961; Sanders & McCormick, 1987). The disabling effects of glare can include light scattered by irregularities within the structure of the eye, and **transient adaptation**, which occurs as the eyes are drawn to a bright light source and become adapted to it, thus reducing their sensitivity to less bright objects (Trotter, 1982). In general, greater performance improvements are achieved by improving the visual features of the task itself, such as the size and contrast of objects or messages, than by increasing illumination (Boyce, 1981). Nevertheless, Sanders and McCormick (1987) note that over the years the recommended levels of illumination have increased and are about five times greater than the levels recommended for the same tasks 30 years ago.

Different lighting conditions may also have subtle effects on social behavior and mood. There is relatively little information regarding these effects of lighting on social relationships, and some of it seems contradictory. Two commonly held beliefs are that low levels of light lead to both greater intimacy and to quieter or reduced conversation (e.g., Feller, 1968; Saunders, Gustanski, & Lawton, 1974). Several studies support these common beliefs. For example, Gergen, Gergen, and Barton (1973) reported that when college students who were strangers to each other were placed in a dark room for several hours, considerable verbal and physical intimacy occurred between them. Darkness and anonymity had apparently removed some customary barriers to intimacy. More recently, Butler and Biner (1987) used a questionnaire format to determine the lighting preferences of a large sample of college students. Participants in the studies reported their preferred lighting levels, the importance of these lighting levels, and the degree to which they desired control over the lighting levels. Having the proper lighting level was rated as most important in instances in which individuals reported preferences for either a rather dark (e.g., during a romantic interlude) or very bright (cutting vegetables with a knife) lighting level. Predictably, control over the level of lighting was more important in some environments than others, and particularly important for those expressing strong lighting preferences.

In spite of these findings, the effects probably depend on the environmental context we are in. For example, dark spaces in the inner city may be depressing or frightening, while in other settings they can be quite romantic, facilitating intimacy. The importance of further investigation is highlighted by two recent studies which conflict with the two common beliefs about the social effects of illumination we cited above. With respect to the amount of intimate communication, Gifford (1988) reports a laboratory study of the effects of illumination levels on the

A Hawthorne in the Side of
Environmental Psychology?

In the early 1900s Frederick Taylor proposed a management system based upon the assumption that workers are primarily motivated by economic incentives. It was assumed that production would be greatest when pay was adequate and production techniques and the work environment were optimal. This approach was labeled *scientific management* and led to several investigations of environmental qualities such as heating and lighting. It also led to routine and standardized jobs and what some consider a rather unflattering picture of workers and their motivations.

One of the first real breaks with scientific management was promoted by a series of studies that took place beginning in the 1920s in the Hawthorne plant of the Western Electric Company near Chicago (Roethlisberger & Dickson, 1939). One of the early questions addressed by this project, which became known as the Hawthorne studies, was the effect of illumination on productivity. According to many reports, lighting levels were systematically varied for an experimental group, whereas a control group worked under constant illumination. Amazingly, *both* the experimental and control groups increased production. In follow-up observations, an experimental group was reported to have maintained their initial level of performance in spite of the fact that illumination had been reduced by 70 percent! Eventually the researchers only *pretended* to change

the illumination level and still workers continued to increase their production and to express pleasure with what they perceived to be better illumination. These bizarre results were interpreted at the time as suggesting that workers' performance increased as a result of novelty and the fact that workers knew they were being observed, rather than because of experimental changes. This interpretation came to be known as the **Hawthorne effect**.

In hindsight, the true meaning of the Hawthorne studies is open to discussion. A number of reviewers have pointed out methodological flaws that cast doubt on many of the conclusions drawn by the researchers (e.g., Franke & Kaul, 1978; Landesberger, 1958; Parsons, 1978). Indeed, the illumination studies which are so often recounted were never formally published and seem to have served mainly as an impetus for subsequent investigations of work schedules, supervision, and work group functions (Parsons, 1978).

Nevertheless, the illumination studies and the others that followed have had powerful effects, and in fact, probably led to a revolution in industrial/organizational psychology. In particular, the Hawthorne studies are often cited as the beginning of the human relations movement in American management (Landy, 1989; Saal & Knight, 1988). On the other hand, in focusing on the importance of the placebo-like "Hawthorne effect," these studies may have shifted research attention away from environmental variables such as illumination and delayed the development of what we now know as environmental psychology.

. . . .

amount and intimacy of written communication between female college students. As expected, a brightly lit room stimulated general communication, but brighter light actually encouraged more rather than less intimate communication. Furthermore, another recent study (Veitch & Kaye, 1988) found that sound levels were actually *lower* in the brighter of two experimental rooms for female students engaged in a discussion. Among several explanations for these results is the possibility that early studies may have tapped responses in situations in which people have learned to speak quietly (e.g., restaurants) because they have learned that it is appropriate, rather than because of some direct effect of low light levels on conversations.

Windows

Windows figure prominently in the general ambience, as well as the illumination, of a setting. Studies have considered the behavioral effects of windows in several environments. In factories, Pritchard (1964) has argued that the lack of windows does not reduce worker efficiency. On the other hand, research on underground factories in Sweden has suggested that workers in windowless environments tend to suffer more fatigue and somatic distress (e.g., headaches) and to express more negative feelings about the setting (Hollister, 1968). To some extent, lack of windows can be compensated for by providing high levels of lighting and air conditioning, but the general conclusion to be drawn is that workers do not like windowless settings (Collins, 1975).

In office environments, the presence of windows also appears to be important. Research has indicated that regardless of whether occupants are satisfied with most aspects of their offices, not having windows leads to dissatisfaction (Ruys, 1970). The desire for windows in an office environment appears so strong that Ruys (1970) concluded that the problems created by windowless offices could not be corrected without installing windows. According to Collins (1975), windowlessness is particularly troublesome for those in sedentary jobs or restricted environments. Presumably, windows may provide these workers with stimulation and variety in an otherwise routine workday. Of course windows are important sources of information about the weather or time of day (Ruys, 1970; Sommer, 1983), but visual contact with the natural environment may be even more important (e.g., Heerwagen & Orians, 1986; Ulrich, 1984). For example, workers may attempt to compensate for a lack of windows by hanging landscape pictures, travel posters, and other decorations. In a study conducted in a university setting, Heerwagen and Orians (1986) found that decorations in windowless offices were dominated by nature scenes, such as landscape paintings.

Other evidence of the importance of windows comes from studies of windowless schools. Originally designed to reduce distraction in the classroom, as well as to lower heating costs and vandalism, these school buildings typically contain few if any windows. Research has suggested that the absence of windows in classrooms has no consistent effect on learning (some students improve; others show poorer performance), but that it does have a *negative* impact on mood (Karmel, 1965; see also Chapter 12).

Perhaps the most persuasive support for the generous use of windows comes from a growing literature documenting therapeutic effects of hospital windows overlooking pleasant landscape views (e.g., Ulrich, 1984; Verderber, 1986). For example, Ulrich (1984) reports that patients with pleasant landscape views outside their hospital rooms had shorter postoperative hospital stays, required lower doses of painkillers, and had fewer negative evaluative comments from nurses.

Although we might conclude that windows are generally appreciated, preferences for the amount of window space vary across different types of spaces. For example, one survey found that large windows were preferred for family rooms, dorm rooms, and libraries. In these environments, factors such as a view, sunlight, and mood influenced window preferences. On the other hand, an absence of windows was desirable in public bathrooms where privacy seemed to be somewhat more important (Butler & Biner, 1989).

Furnishings

Furniture, its arrangement, and other aspects of the interior environment are also important determinants of behavior. In classroom settings, for example, it appears that the use of nontraditional seating patterns can influence student performance; horseshoe arrangements, circular patterns, or other less formal departures from the standard "rows of desks facing the teacher" seem to generate more student interest and participation (Sommer, 1969). There is also some evidence that within traditional classroom arrangements there are differences in performance according to where people sit. These findings are discussed in Chapter 8.

The arrangement of furnishings in a room can also affect the way in which the room is perceived. Some studies have served simply to confirm what most of us have always known or suspected. For example, Imamoglu (1973) found that empty rooms were perceived to be larger than furnished rooms, which were seen as larger than "overfurnished" rooms. This verifies the common experience reported by college students looking for off-campus housing: Furnished apartments look smaller than unfurnished ones, and unfurnished apartments seem smaller once students have moved in.

Many studies of furniture arrangements have been conducted in institutional settings. Reusch and Kees (1956) have noted that the way in which patients arrange their furniture expresses their feelings regarding interaction in their space. Some arrangements (called **sociopetal**) are open and welcome interaction, while others (called **sociofugal**) are closed and discourage social contact. Sommer and Ross (1958) described the relation between furniture arrangement and behavior in a geriatric hospital. When chairs were arranged in rows along the walls, patients did not interact very much. This arrangement was simply not conducive to talking; it did not suggest that interaction was appropriate. When Sommer and Ross changed the arrangement, clustering the chairs in small groups, people began to talk to each other. The new juxtaposition facilitated conversation while the old one seemed to inhibit it. Holahan (1972) found the same kind of effect in a psychiatric hospital—patients seated around a table talked to each other more than patients seated in rows against the walls. (For a thorough discussion of design in selected institutional environments, see Chapter 12.)

Furniture arrangements can also communicate status or a desire for distance from others. For example, some studies considering the effects of furniture placement in offices have found that the use of a desk as a "barrier" between the office occupant and a visitor can communicate a desire for physical and psychological distance, as well as status differences. For example, Joiner (1971) observed that high-status office occupants were more likely to use a closed desk arrangement (the desk sits between the visitor and the office occupant) rather than an open placement (in which the desk is placed against the wall). Furthermore, desk arrangement can also have implications for the pleasantness of the interaction and the visitor's level of comfort (Morrow & McElroy, 1981). Consider the arrangements of office space in a college psychology department. Some professors arrange their offices so that visitors sit across a desk from them. Others arrange their offices to suggest less distance, placing no barriers between them and their students. Each arrangement can evoke different reactions (for an additional discussion of office design, see Chapter 13).

Furniture arrangements can be used to help structure the preexisting architectural layout of a setting. In most environmental contexts, the walls, the location of the doors, and so on are fixed—they are rather difficult to move. To some extent, these elements do structure the space inside a building. However, the placement of furniture often provides additional organization. For example, if you have a large living room, you may arrange the furniture to suggest two rooms. Or, you may arrange it to unify the room.

Arrangement is not the only aspect of furnishings that can affect mood and behavior. The quality of the furnishings is also important. Earlier, we discussed studies on the effects of "pretty" and "ugly" rooms and found that being in a pretty room could sometimes have beneficial psychological effects. Unfortunately, studies varying the quality of single pieces or sets of furniture have not been done systematically. However, there is research on the effects of large-scale improvements in furnishings. Holahan and Saegert (1973) reported on a large-scale refurbishing of a psychiatric hospital admissions ward, comparing it to another ward that was not redone. The refurbishing included bringing in new furniture, repainting, and creating different types of space. These improvements in the quality of the environment led to increases in social activity on the ward and demonstrated that the quality of an environment can influence mood and behavior. However, because the improvements were so extensive, it is difficult to know what was primarily responsible for the observed results.

Ultimately, any decision about furnishings will be based on several criteria, including cost, aesthetics, and the function of the setting. This latter criterion is often the most difficult to

evaluate. Sometimes a given space is expected to facilitate communication between employees working near each other, to serve as a meeting room on occasion, and to impress clients who come for consultations. Some of these functions are at odds with each other, and the choice of arrangement of furnishings must be accomplished with these complex issues in mind.

Privacy

One of the most important aspects of the design of interior space is the amount of privacy it provides. (For a definition of the concept of "privacy," see the box on page 388.) All of us sometimes need to be able to "get away from it all." Architectural design can increase or decrease the ease with which people can do so. In some settings we may find it very difficult to "be alone" while in others, getting away may be easier. For example, dormitories that house students one instead of two to a bedroom promote greater privacy. Likewise, the use of barriers around one's work area may increase the sense of privacy there. Often, then, privacy adjustment is centered around the structures that partition interior space. Some designs make privacy easy to achieve, while others make it more difficult.

One way in which an environment can directly affect feelings of privacy is by increasing or decreasing the possibility of seeing and being seen by other people. This refers to *visual intrusion*—that sense of privacy that is more difficult to achieve when people can still be seen. If you lived in a glass house and could see people outside and vice versa, your sense of privacy would be less than if you could block them out. Consistent with this, research has indicated that barriers that block views of other people decrease the impact of these people, while barriers that do not obscure the view (e.g., clear panels) do not reduce their impact (e.g., Baum, Reiss, & O'Hara, 1974; Desor, 1972).

When an environment does not provide enough privacy for those using it, problems

Defining and Conceptualizing Privacy

Altman (1975) has defined privacy as the "selective control of access to the self or one's group." This definition has two important parts. The first is the notion of privacy as an *ability to withdraw or separate ourselves from other people.* In effect, this refers to the need or desire for seclusion. At the same time, Altman recognizes a second important aspect of privacy—*the ability to control information about ourselves.* Similarly, Ittelson et al. (1974) define privacy in terms of freedom to regulate the type or amount of self-information made available to others. Thus, privacy also refers to regulating what other people find out about us. We all keep some aspects of our personalities or some of our thoughts to ourselves, and this need is part of our requirement for privacy.

Privacy means different things to different people. Marshall (1972) has studied students' notions of privacy and compared them to their parents' definitions. Marshall reported evidence of six basic definitions, three of which loosely conform to Altman's description of "need for seclusion," and three of which parallel information regulation. The first three were the *desire to be able to be alone; having space that is away from where other people congregate;* and *having the ability to govern intimacy and maintain interpersonal distance.* More related to the availability of personal information were the *abilities to keep secrets; limit self-disclosure;* and *regulate when and with whom one might interact.* Designs that optimize privacy have to consider both elements of Altman's definition, as well as the fact that privacy means different things to different people.

develop. Vinsel et al. (1980) found that students who dropped out of college for "nonacademic" reasons were less likely to have been able to achieve adequate privacy in their dormitories than those who stayed in school. Among the problems the "dropouts" mentioned were an inability to find a quiet place to be alone and a reluctance to invite people to their rooms. Studies have also shown that apartment building designs that do not promote privacy between apartment units are associated with resident dissatisfaction (Zeisel & Griffin, 1975).

Finally, the lack of privacy in prisons may cause prisoners to learn antisocial behaviors. Glaser (1964) had suggested that young prison-

ers may learn criminal behavior from older ones as a function of being housed in more open, less private dormitory units. Private quarters are often used as a reward, and a younger prisoner may have to wait some time to earn the privilege of a private cell. During this period, the youthful prisoner must cope with the demands of older inmates. These demands may be in the form of physical attacks and homosexual advances. Glaser recommended greater privacy for young prisoners to help them resist the demands of older ones. Instead of waiting for private cells, younger prisoners should be housed in them at the start until they have developed coping skills for dealing with a prison environment.

SUMMARY

We began this chapter with a comparison between the design traditions of the industrialized nations and other less technological societies. We concluded that there is frequently a gap between modern designers and those who will eventually use or live in their constructions. We suggested that user participation may be one avenue to bridging this gap, and that a more responsive relationship between designers and researchers provided another.

We also examined formal models of the design process. For any given building there are several important criteria: cost, durability, aesthetic quality, and the like. Among these are behavioral considerations such as the congruence of fit between design and user needs. These criteria are used to decide between different design alternatives in a rather complex process.

Finally, we considered the behavioral effects of several different individual features of built settings, such as lighting, color, ambience, furnishings, and so on. Each is capable of influencing mood and behavior by itself, but most work together. Thus, while the color of a room may influence your mood, the combination of lighting and color is more likely to affect you than is either one alone.

We have also considered the notion of arrangement of space. Architectural designs have many functions, but the most basic is to structure space. Designs shape the space within buildings as well as outside, and arrangements of furnishings can further structure space. This, too, can have a strong effect on mood and behavior.

SUGGESTED PROJECTS

1. Ask several friends to list their most and least favorite buildings on your campus and to indicate the reasons for their choices. Is there any agreement between their likes and dislikes? Are these based upon firmness? Commodity? Aesthetics? Does what you have learned about environmental psychology offer any insights into the reasons for their opinions or ways to improve the least-liked buildings to facilitate human behavior?

2. According to NASA, humans may soon establish a permanent settlement on the moon. What would be your goals in designing living and working quarters for these pioneers? Outline a proposal for acquiring the behavioral requirements for a successful design.

3. The design process is complicated and sometimes resistant to behavioral input. Assume that your college is building a new student union. How would you approach the possibility of providing information for the process? What design alternatives would you suggest?

DESIGN IN SELECTED ENVIRONMENTS

INTRODUCTION

THE RESIDENTIAL SETTING
>   Preferences
>   Use of space in the Home
>   Satisfaction with the Home Environment
>   Propinquity: The Effect of Occupying Nearby Territories

LEARNING ENVIRONMENTS
>   Classroom Environments
>>   Windowless Classrooms
>>   The Open Classroom Concept
>>   Environmental Complexity and Enrichment
>   Libraries
>   Museum Environments
>>   Fatigue in Museum Exploration

PEDESTRIAN ENVIRONMENTS: SHOPPING MALLS, PLAZAS, AND CROSSWALKS

HOSPITAL SETTINGS
>   Designing for Hospital Visitors

DESIGNING FOR THE ELDERLY
>   Residential Care Facilities for the Elderly
>   Specialized Facilities for the Cognitively Impaired: Alzheimer Units
>   Noninstitutional Residences for the Elderly

SUMMARY

SUGGESTED PROJECTS

KEY TERMS

age-segregated
Alzheimer's Disease
attraction gradient
custodial care
day–night reversal
dementia
discontinuity
double corridor design
environmental spoiling hypothesis
exit gradient
friction–conformity model
functional distance
intermediate care
museum fatigue
objective physical distance

open classrooms
orientation
perceived control
person–environment congruence
privacy gradient
propinquity
radial ward design
residential care
residential preference
residential satisfaction
single corridor design
windowless classrooms
wind tunnel effect
you-are-here maps

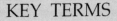

INTRODUCTION

Your first breaths are taken in a sterile room with very institutional surroundings. Your parents take you "home," and place you in a strange container that looks like a cell with bars on two sides (which they call a crib), and when you look around, you see stuffed toys, a changing table, and a rocking chair. When you get a bit older you begin to explore your house, and continue to be affected greatly by its environment. Soon it's time for you to attend school. On your first day you are amazed by the large number of desks, their arrangement, and the whole educational environment. In some ways the classroom setting is stimulating, but in other ways it constricts your behavior—you must get permission to move from your personal work station to another part of the setting. More time passes and you go to work. The work environment bears some similarity to the school setting, but in many ways it is different. You work in a large "open" office and, while you like the fact that you have easy access to your coworkers, you also feel you have insufficient privacy. You value your annual vacation, and enjoy spending time in recreational environments, away from the work setting. As you move up the organizational ladder, you experience other work environments, and note their positive and negative effects on yourself and your coworkers. After you retire, you live in a large retirement community. Although you appreciate having other retired people as well as medical facilities nearby, you miss aspects of the more heterogeneous environment you lived in before. But, in general, you have positive feelings about your living situation.

In previous chapters we have examined how specific aspects of the environment interact with our behavior. In Chapter 11 we saw how we can use knowledge of these environment–behavior relationships to design environments that will facilitate the behavior we want to occur. In this and the next chapter we will see how these principles can be brought together in specific environments. That is, we will select some settings that have been studied extensively by environmental psychologists and show how those particular environments influence behavior, and how the design of those environments can be modified to achieve desired effects.

This chapter will examine environmental psychological research on residential settings, learning environments, pedestrian environments, hospitals, and facilities for the elderly. The next chapter will continue the same theme by examining work environments and leisure settings. We should caution that numerous books and articles have been written on behavior in each of these environments, and that we have room to discuss only an outline of the relevant material on each of these topics. What we will emphasize is how some of the principles of environmental psychology can be applied to these settings.

Two concepts in particular, covered in detail in Chapter 4, will be common threads from one setting to the next. First, **person–environment congruence** is paramount: The setting facilitates the behaviors and goals appropriate to the setting—a major proposition in Barker's ecological psychology. Second, the setting has much to do with our perception of personal control (or lack thereof) in it: Our behavior in the setting is in part a function of the degree of **perceived control** the environment offers. Moreover, we can add design features to enhance personal control.

THE RESIDENTIAL SETTING

We have talked about residential environments in earlier chapters and will consider them in more detail in this one. It is no surprise that they have been mentioned so often—residential settings are so familiar and important to most of us that there has been a great deal of research interest in residential design and improvement. (For recent reviews and bibliographies, see

Altman & Werner, 1985; Cooper Marcus & Sarkissian, 1985; Rullo, 1987; Tognoli, 1987.)

Homes are important for reasons other than shelter. They also provide meaning and identity in our lives. For example, they signify status (e.g., Duncan, 1985), they structure our social relationships, they afford a location for major activities of daily living (e.g., eating, bathing), they are centers of regular and predictable events, and they trigger many of the memories central to our formative past, all of which contribute to a form of psychological bonding with this environment (Werner, Altman, & Oxley, 1985).

As you know, there are a number of different kinds of residential settings. The most common type, at least away from the core of the city, is the single-family detached house that many of us grew up in. In urban settings, row houses or two- or three-story apartment buildings may be the rule, while in many areas townhouses are becoming a predominant form. Also, of course, there are high-rise apartment buildings. Each of these kinds of environments is associated with a different style of living, and research has begun to address the similarities and differences among them.

Preferences

With all of these different forms of housing, it has become important to examine **residential preferences**. Research seems to suggest that people in North America and the British Commonwealth tend to describe the detached, single-family house as the "ideal" home (Cooper, 1972; Thorne, Hall, & Munro-Clark, 1982). This tendency does not appear to be a matter of socioeconomic class—people seem to reject apartment settings and prefer suburban homes regardless of ethnic or social background or the kind of housing environment they occupy (Dennis, 1966; Hancock, 1980; Hinshaw & Allcott, 1972; Ladd, 1972; Michelson, 1968).

Although you may have suspected that most people want a "nice little house in the suburbs," the reasons for this preference are not clear. The growth in popularity of the suburban detached house is attributable to many factors, including among others, pride in home ownership, government incentives (such as for tax-deductible mortgage interest), and the growth of transportation systems leading into and out of large cities (e.g., Gans, 1967; Jackson, 1985;

Warner, 1978). To environmental psychologists, however, the most compelling explanation is the way these settings structure space. Michelson (1970), for example, has argued that the ways in which space is distributed in areas dominated by single-family homes allows residents to avoid intense interaction with neighbors. Urban areas are sometimes characterized by close neighborhood ties, extended families, and extensive social interaction. The single-family house appears to permit residents to avoid or control these social factors to a greater degree. Michelson also reports some evidence that single-family housing is generally regarded as family-oriented. Thus, people seem to want the family privacy afforded by these settings. Not all areas, of course, have close neighborhood ties and extensive social interaction (e.g., Altman & Wandersman, 1987; Wellman & Leighton, 1979). In these situations, as well, the single-family house seems to offer a sense of security along with perceived control over relationships.

Choice of type of housing may be restricted by economic factors. Economic factors may make it difficult for young families to purchase single-family houses, in which case they may opt for townhouse or condominium settings, or apartment living (cf. van Vliet, 1983). There are also factors that appear to determine the location that one lives in —where the house, townhouse, or the like is situated. Again, economic factors are important, since some areas of a city or its suburbs may be more expensive than others. Choices are often made between locations and types of housing. A family may be able to afford a single-family house in suburb A, but only a townhouse in suburb B. A number of things are ordinarily considered before making choices between locations and housing type (e.g., Shlay, 1985). The status communicated by housing types is very distinguishable, even for homes of 100 years ago (Cherulnik & Wilderman, 1986).

Given the basic preference for the detached house, why might a family opt for a townhouse

Life in the Suburbs:
Is It Really
What You Think?

We have noted that living preferences fairly consistently show the majority of people want a single-family house, and that most envision the suburbs as the best location for such an arrangement. Schools, transportation, and recreational opportunities have some role in this vision. But just how ideal are suburbs? Jackson (1985) offers the history of the suburban movement in America, with a book appropriately titled *Crabgrass Frontier*. Although development on the outskirts of cities has been around since cities began, most of us think of "contemporary" suburbs as they have developed after World War II. The "prototype" planned development by William Levitt is alleged to have started the suburbanization boom. Said Levitt, reflecting the atmosphere of the times in 1948, "No man who owns his own house and lot can be a Communist. He has too much to do." Jackson observes that in seeking our private, suburban ownership, we also evolve along a sameness dimension—everyone has the same dreams, the same fence, the same yard, same cars, same commuting route, same "little boxes," and it still seems preferable to the city!

But is all well in paradise? Lublin (1985), among others, has summarized some of the ills befalling suburbia. Homeowners must worry about flight paths for new airports. Office buildings, commerce, and industry are retreating to suburbs to cut costs and eliminate commuting. Growth, traffic snarls, pollution, noise, strains on public services, and lack of workers to fill low-end jobs accompany these developments. Housing becomes more expensive. Developers buy up houses to put in commercial projects. Restricting the heights of these buildings to preserve views means development spreads out and traffic congestion becomes worse. The 1980 census showed that 27 million Americans actually commute from one suburb to another (Lublin, 1985)! Ah, life in the suburbs!

in a different suburb? Status may be an issue, if one of the two suburbs is very high or very low in prestige. Security and crime rates may be another—the detached home in suburb A may also be closer to high crime areas. Commuting time, closeness to and quality of schools, and availability of shopping and services may also be important. Clearly, preferences for and actual choice of housing is complex, with factors about the residential environment and its surrounding area being considered in each instance (see also Cook, 1988).

Use of Space in the Home

Despite differences in the ways in which people arrange their homes, consistent space-use patterns emerge. Black (1968), for example, found that leisure reading was most common in the living room and least common in the kitchen and dining room. The kitchen is often the center of family activity (Mehrabian, 1976). Bedrooms are the most frequently occupied areas of the home (Parsons, 1972), and may become personalized or private areas for individual family members. Home interior designs clearly mediate social interactions (Bonnes et al., 1987; Werner, 1987).

The intended function of a room has important implications for its design and how it is used. Bedrooms are, for one thing, intended to be private space, and thus are likely to be set off from less private areas. They may be located down a hallway from the living and kitchen areas, or on a different floor altogether. Bedrooms are also supposed to be for sleeping and therefore must be quiet. However, as Parsons (1972) notes, some sleepers prefer noisier settings. Individual preferences are a problem for designers who wish to generalize designs across large numbers of residences (see box, page 397).

The bathroom is an especially interesting design problem. Consider the many functions or purposes of a bathroom. Kira (1976) identifies over 30 functions, including among others: brushing teeth, rinsing mouth, gargling, expectorating, cleaning and soaking dentures, vomiting, treating skin blemishes, cleaning ears, applying cosmetics, shaving, defecating, urinating, bathing, washing wounds, applying bandages, taking medicine, and inserting contact lenses. Each one of these functions can serve as the basis for bathroom design criteria. To the physical hygienic functions that we are all familiar with, we can also add some social functions. Many people use the bathroom as a "sanctum" for privacy. Social conventions frown on people interrupting one another while in the bathroom and, as a result, one can often escape there for a moment of peace and quiet. Thus, even though the bathroom can take on attributes of shared space, it can also serve as a place where privacy can be achieved on a transient basis. Of course, this is not the case with large bathrooms, such as those in a college dormitory. There, the small stalls within the bathroom may serve the same privacy function as the entire bathroom. The role of the bathroom in affording pivacy should not be under-

estimated. Inman (cited in Meer, 1986) surveyed 200 households in Indiana. Regardless of how much space the rest of the house had, about half of all families with only one bathroom felt stressed because of a perceived lack of living space, compared to about 20 percent of those with more than one bathroom. She cautioned, however, that having more than three bathrooms increased stress because of problems related to cleaning and stocking!

Kira (1976) has examined the relationship between the design of bathrooms and their functions. Many of his suggestions are intended to increase convenience, including changes in sink and vanity design and placement of shower control knobs, electrical outlets, and so on. Other suggestions are more adventurous, and one goes completely against the notion of privacy in the bathroom. Kira (1976) proposes the creation of a living room bath which could be used for entertaining guests. He views such an unusual situation as a logical response to economic pressures. As residential settings become smaller because of energy and land costs, designers often include multipurpose space in homes. Because bathrooms are not used all of the time, they are prime candidates for new functions, and Kira argues that they can be used as living rooms as well as bath areas (Figure 12–1).

So far, our discussion of space use has been for a typical middle-class setting. Scheflen (1971) provides an alternative view of space use in the urban ghetto. Because many children share the same room, each can claim perhaps only one drawer and a quarter of a closet in the bedroom—if there is a separate bedroom at all. The kitchen is 9 feet by 12 feet (2.7m by 3.7m), but a bed, cabinets, and closets take up much of this space. The refrigerator is across the room because the original space for it was designed in 1920 and is too small for any refrigerator available today. How does one adapt to such a kitchen where two adults cannot maneuver in it at the same time? Scheflen noted two options:

Preferences for Messy
And Neat Rooms:
The Odd Couple

Residential satisfaction applies not only to entire neighborhoods but also to single rooms. Recall the Neil Simon play, movie, and television series about the "odd couple" who had to cope with each other's preference for a neat or messy apartment. A definite preference for a neat or messy room may be more than just a scriptwriter's whim. Personality and cultural background may influence whether a person will find satisfaction or annoyance with a room that is kept tidy or disorderly. Samuelson and Lindauer (1976) asked college students to describe rooms that were experimentally changed to look either messy or neat. The messy room had papers and pencils scattered about, an overflowing wastebasket, and a general look of disorder. In the neat room, objects were arranged in an orderly manner.

Students described the rooms differently and also showed different levels of preference for each room. Students who indicated they preferred more exciting or varied experiences were more satisfied with the messy room. Students less inclined toward experience-seeking (as measured by test scores) were more satisfied with the neat room. Just as each member of the odd couple found the apartment most satisfying when arranged his way, students differ in their preference for order or disorder in a setting. Those with adaptation levels closer to the "orderly" end of a "disorderly—orderly" dimension seem to find it easier to adapt to (and are more satisfied with) a neat room, whereas those whose adaptation levels lie closer to the "disorderly" end tend to be more comfortable in a messy room.

(1) all dining occurs in the living room, or (2) an end table or child's play table is the kitchen table, so adults do not eat in the kitchen. There is one sofa and one chair in the living room, and a dominance hierarchy develops around their use, which varies from household to household. Territorial defense within the apartment is not achieved with physical partitions, but rather with behavior: Extending an elbow or leg keeps others a little farther away, and contours of posture help block visual access. Noise and lack of privacy are such problems that studying is difficult at best and frequently nonexistent. Although many factors contribute to the social ills of the inner city, these adaptations to spatial restriction should be considered by anyone

exploring solutions (cf. Merry, 1981, 1987; Oxman & Carmon, 1986).

Satisfaction with the Home Environment

As we become accustomed to a specific residential setting, we develop more and more satisfaction with our ability to perform basic tasks in it. The more easily and conveniently these functions can be performed, the more satisfied we usually become. Steidl (1972) found that the size and floor plan of rooms were often mentioned as problems that affect the performance of tasks. Not having enough room to work, having too many rooms to clean, and

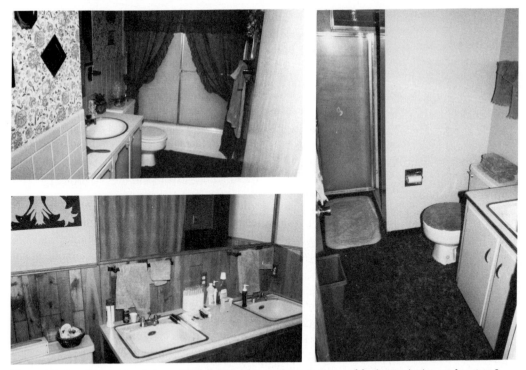

Figure 12–1   How do the designs of these bathrooms compare in terms of facilitating bathroom functions?

being too close to noisy areas of the house are among these problems. Another study, however, suggests that some people are less likely to be satisfied with their residences regardless of their characteristics (Galster & Hesser, 1981). Younger people, female heads of households, blacks, married couples, and couples with many children appear to be somewhat dissatisfied with their housing on the average. Galster and Hesser also found that certain physical or environmental factors were associated with dissatisfaction. Poor plumbing, heating, or kitchen facilities were strongly related to dissatisfaction, as were neighborhood characteristics such as racial makeup, high density, or condition of the structures in the area (see also Michelson, 1977). Physical and social factors are clearly interdependent in determining satisfaction (Weidemann & Anderson, 1982), but there are cross-cultural differences (e.g., Hourihan, 1984; Tognoli, 1987; Zube et al., 1985).

Several concepts we have seen before appear very applicable in understanding these preference relationships. First, recall from Chapters 2 and 3 that environmental preference models, such as that of Kaplan and Kaplan, posit psychological dimensions such as complexity and legibility to be predictive of evaluations of environments. Similar dimensions apply to dwellings, such as contrast, complexity, and naturalness (Gobster, 1983), and cleanliness, silence, privacy, and energy efficiency (Volkman, 1981). Second, we have noted that success with adaptation has much to do with environmental satisfaction. The same applies to residences: The better we are able to adapt to the features of our residence, the greater the satisfaction (Tognoli, 1987). Also recall that in the previous chapter we mentioned design alternatives as components of the design process. If an alternative dwelling is available for comparison that makes our own seem superior,

Homes and the
Privacy Gradient

Understanding people's social values and practices is extremely important for developing a home design that will provide desirable levels of privacy. In the U.S., a number of modern designs are based on open architecture that includes the kitchen as part of the area for entertaining guests. In Peru, however, a **privacy gradient** exists that restricts certain areas in terms of entertaining (Zeisel, 1975). Formal friends and acquaintances are permitted only in the room intended for social activities. As guests become better known, they may be invited into other areas, but only those closest to the homeowner are ever permitted into the kitchen. Alexander (1969) suggested that a Peruvian house should be designed along a privacy gradient that places the sala (room for entertaining) at the front and the kitchen at the rear.

In French upper-middle-class homes, privacy is marked by distinct barriers. Carlisle (1982) observed that residents of these homes isolate intimate areas of the house with hallways, doors, grills, or curtains.

Why do we place so much emphasis on home ownership? Although there are many obvious economic and status reasons, Tognoli (1987) suggests that ownership implies less permeable boundaries (i.e., more control over privacy) than renting.

we are more likely to be satisfied than if our own seems inferior (Tognoli, 1987).

Social ties also appear to be important in determining **residential satisfaction**. Fried and Gleicher (1961) found this to be more the case for residents of urban slums than for suburbanites. In urban areas, social ties appear to contribute to a sense of neighborhood and the sharing of outdoor space by residents. Greenbaum and Greenbaum (1981) found that group identity in a neighborhood is related to territorial personalization and social interaction. When people were able to establish social bonds with those around them, they took more care in decorating the exteriors of their residences and the neighborhood took on the aura of group-owned territory. Neighborhood ties are stronger on cul-de-sacs than on through streets. This effect is often reflected in more decorations at Christmas and Halloween on cul-de-sacs (Brown & Werner, 1985; Oxley et al., 1986).

Even teenagers show differences in neighborhood evaluations. Van Vliet (1981), for example, found that teenage Canadian residents of suburbs, relative to counterparts in a city, were more satisfied with neighborhood safety, "nice looks," friendliness, and quietness. City dwellers, however, rated their environment as having more things to do.

Other social factors can be significant sources of satisfaction or dissatisfaction for many people. We have already mentioned privacy regulation as an important consideration in the design of environments. How a residence is designed can affect the ease with which we achieve privacy. Individuals differ, however, in the amount of privacy they want. Privacy in the single-family home, as reported by the male members of the household, could take two forms (Altman, Nelson, & Lett, 1972). One type of family controls privacy without using physical features of the environment as a means of control. In these families,

Designing for
Energy Conservation

With the advent of the energy crisis in the 1970s and price increases in the cost of home heating, some designers have turned to an energy-wise alternative for home building. Reversing our high-rise trend, more and more underground homes are appearing. Properly called earth-sheltered homes, they are built several feet into the ground.

The temperature of the ground just three or four feet below the surface is remarkably constant at about 50°F (10°C). By building a home into the earth at or below this level, it can cost as much as 75 percent less to heat it in the winter and to cool it during the summer. On a 0°F (−17.5°C) morning, a good deal more energy is required to warm your home to 65°F (18.5°C) if it is above ground than if nestled in the 50°F (10°C) earth.

Earth-covered houses have very little surface area exposed. This also helps to keep energy use low, but is associated with perhaps the largest problem the houses offer—the psychological effects of living underground. Although storms may pass harmlessly overhead, the common image of dark humid caves can be a problem. Earth-covered homes must be built to avoid this dungeon-like quality. There can be no windows, of course, and as a result designing for psychological well-being can be a challenge (e.g., Volkman, 1981; Weber, 1981).

Several solutions have evolved. The most common is to build the home into the side of a hill so that one side is open to the world. This results in some loss of energy efficiency, but the design still yields great savings. Another alternative

is to build atria into the home—large vertical shafts or rooms that reach to the surface and are either roofed with glass or contain skylights. This brings light into the deepest of homes and helps to minimize the negative aspects of living underground.

Figure 12-2   Examples of earth-covered houses.
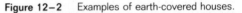

Courtesy Ken Tremblay

Courtesy Ken Tremblay

Color use can also change the appearance of underground buildings. Bright colors that suggest an open, well-lighted room will do more to change the feeling of being underground than will the use of darker colors. Furnishings might also help. For example, landscape paintings in strategic wall spaces can be used to suggest windows.

Arrangement of space in underground structures can help reduce the negative aspects of such a design. If a central atrium is included, walls between this naturally lighted area and adjacent rooms should be minimal. In this way, more of the spaces in the building receive some natural light. Frequently used rooms should also be those nearest the atrium.

Recently, radon gas (which is carcinogenic—see Chapter 7) has been identified as a major problem in many American homes (e.g., Kerr, 1988c; Nero, et al., 1986; Sun, 1988). Underground homes are especially vulnerable, since the radon comes from decaying uranium in the soil and surrounding rock. Proper ventilating techniques can usually solve the problem.

Life underground is not the same as life above ground. Despite the attractiveness and efficiency of building underground homes and offices, savings may not be sufficient to overcome the problems associated with this kind of environment. If these environments are to remain feasible, intelligent use of design variables to counter potential problems will be necessary (Figure 12–2).

. . . .

bedroom doors are rarely closed and few areas of the home are considered the domain of one family member. A second family type is more likely to use environmental controls over privacy. These families help to ensure privacy by designating rooms as specific territories for individual use (cf. Edney et al., 1985; Keeley & Edney, 1982). Clearly, one cannot use a single residential design and expect both types of families to be satisfied. Variety of interior design of homes helps to ensure that individual family styles can be accommodated (cf. Morris, 1987; Shlay, 1987; see box, page 399).

Before concluding, we should note that it is impossible to cover all aspects of residential design in this discussion. Included in the concept of the home are survival-oriented needs for shelter, culturally-bound preferences, expressions, and guidelines, and a highly personal conception of hearth and home. We know that people use the space in their homes in many different ways and that this use often reflects an individual's cultural background or preferred lifestyle (Weisner & Weibel, 1981). Despite some common uses (e.g., most of us prepare food in the kitchen), the wide variety of other uses of different forms of residential space makes designing it difficult. The more flexible spaces are, the better they should suit a range of activities, as long as the basic function of a room can be carried out.

Propinquity: The Effect of Occupying Nearby Territories

Thus far we have considered several variables associated with residences. Another factor important in residential design is **propinquity**, or "nearness" between places people occupy. How close you are to other residents in a housing development, an apartment building, or even a dormitory or an office building will affect your social outcomes with them (cf. Webber, 1963).

Two types of propinquity have been found to lead to favorable social outcomes. First, it has been observed that the closer the **objective physical distance** between two individuals, the more likely the individuals are to be friends.

The classic study was conducted by Festinger, Schachter, and Back (1950), who investigated friendship patterns of apartment dwellers in Westgate West. When residents (who were randomly assigned to apartments) were asked, "Which three people do you see most often socially?" it was found that people were friendliest with those who lived near them. In fact, residents were more likely to be friendly with a neighbor one door away than with a neighbor two doors away, and so on. Furthermore, this finding was replicated in a study by Ebbsen, Kjos, and Konecni (1976). Another study (Segal, 1974) provided corroborative evidence for the data on objective distance–friendship choice. In this experiment, Segal noted the friendship choices among trainees at the Maryland Police Academy, where trainees were assigned to rooms and to seats in classrooms on the basis of the alphabetical order of their last names. In effect, alphabetical order served as a manipulation of propinquity, and it was found that individuals were most likely to become friendly with others whose last initials were close to theirs in the alphabet.

Objective physical distance is not the only predictor of attraction, however. It has been found that **functional distance**, defined as the likelihood of two individuals coming into contact, also predicts whether people will become friends or like each other (Ebbesen et al., 1976; Festinger et al., 1950). Functional distance becomes a more accurate predictor of friendship than objective physical distance when architectural features of a building constrain individuals whose apartments or offices are physically distant from frequent interaction. For example, the concept of functional distance would best predict attraction between two individuals who live five floors apart in an apartment building (distant in an objective sense), but who have adjacent mailboxes in the lobby (Figure 12–3).

Why does propinquity lead to friendship? Sears et al. (1988) offer some fairly convincing explanations. First, it is impossible to find grounds for friendship with someone we have never met, and those who are close to us in terms of physical or functional distance are clearly more readily accessible to us and to each other than individuals who are more distant. Second, since we have to continue to interact in the future with others who live in close proximity to us, perhaps we try a bit harder to "see the good side" of them and exert ourselves a bit

Figure 12–3 The distinction between functional distance and objective physical distance. The A and B units which share the same number are back-to-back and very close in objective physical distance. The functional distance for walking from Unit A-3 to B-3, however, is much greater. As a result, occupants of Unit B-3 are likely to be closer friends with occupants of any of the B units than with the occupants of any of the A units.

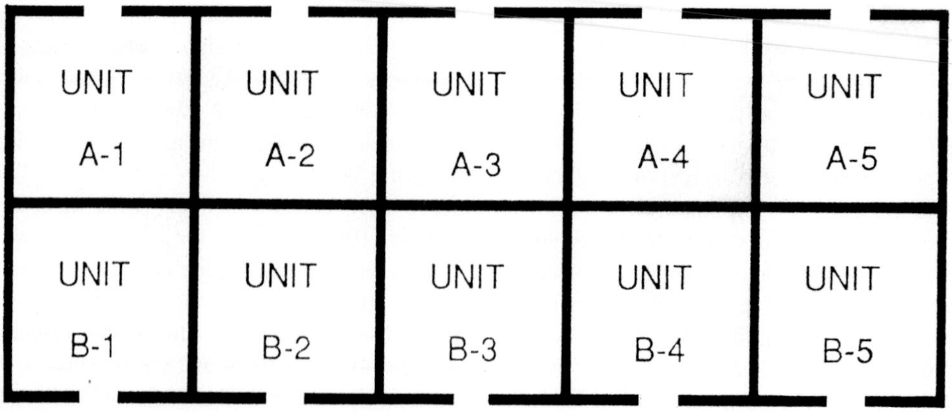

UNIT A-1	UNIT A-2	UNIT A-3	UNIT A-4	UNIT A-5
UNIT B-1	UNIT B-2	UNIT B-3	UNIT B-4	UNIT B-5

harder to "make it work." Third, continued interaction with individuals obviously leads to feelings of predictability and to a sense of security, which may make friendship more likely. Fourth, familiarity in and of itself may lead to attraction (Moreland & Zajonc, 1982; Saegert, Swap, & Zajonc, 1973; Zajonc, 1968).

However, it should be noted that propinquity is more likely to lead to attraction under cooperative conditions where there is equity between individuals than under competitive conditions where there is inequity. Familiar persons whom we see as rewarding are liked most (Swap, 1977). In addition, conditions of equality and cooperation promote enhanced attraction more effectively if prior attitudes toward another individual are neutral or mildly positive than if they are highly negative. Studies of functional and objective distance and friendship formation often examine homogeneous population groups—often newcomers needing help adjusting. Under these conditions, friendships are likely to form out of propinquity. On the other hand, propinquity can also create enemies. Ebbesen et al. (1976) found that more disliked than liked others lived close to subjects. They interpreted their results in terms of an **environmental spoiling hypothesis**: Positive social relationships follow from frequent contacts (which may or may not stem from propinquity), but the activities of *some* can spoil the perceived quality of the living environment.

Much of the work in environmental psychology concerning housing and neighborhoods has to do with the ethnic mix of a neighborhood (cf. Tognoli, 1987). One important attempt to promote propinquity, which many had hoped would lead to liking, has involved the integration of blacks and whites in American residential neighborhoods, schools, and workplaces. Unfortunately, in many cases where propinquity occurs between racially dissimilar others, the optimal conditions for positive relations are not met. In fact, conditions often more closely parallel those which elicit negative responses.

For example, when school desegregation occurs, there is generally not equality between whites and blacks, who have had inferior educational opportunities. The climate is often somewhat competitive, and the attitudes expressed by parents and others may be far from neutral. Thus, it is not surprising that reviews of the school integration literature suggest some negative outcomes. While the studies that the results are based on are nonexperminental and there are many uncontrolled variables, the findings have been rather consistent (Stephan, 1978). Racial attitudes are more likely to improve under conditions of equal status, equal power, and common goals (e.g., Taylor, 1974).

Research has also focused on the effects of interracial propinquity in residential areas. This has involved studies on the sudden integration of public housing, and the effects of desegregating the "suburbs." Public housing projects built by the government feature low rent and are "reserved" for those with low incomes (see also Chapter 10). Until the early 1950s, many public housing projects were segregated. When many were suddenly desegregated, research was done to compare racial attitudes of whites toward blacks for those living in integrated and segregated units. Results generally showed that propinquity led to less anti-black prejudice (e.g., Deutsch & Collins, 1951; Ford, 1973). There still may be a bit of prejudice remaining, however. It has been found that while most friendships between dissimilar others (e.g., blacks and whites) occur for those who live in very close proximity to one another, a greater proportion of friendships between similar others occurs for those who live farther away (see also Merry, 1987; Scheflen, 1971). In effect, propinquity may be the major factor in friendships between dissimilar others, while friendships between similar others can occur without it (Nahemow & Lawton, 1975).

Integration of suburban neighborhoods came much later, and many of our suburbs are still segregated. Also, there are several differences between public housing and suburban life which could suggest a different response to propinquity (e.g., people have a large financial investment in their homes; the socioeconomic status of residents differs). What happens when a black family buys a house down the street in a white neighborhood? Residents of the area report feeling that there is a significant change in the nature of the neighborhood, discuss the event with a disapproving tone, and try to gather as much information as possible about the newcomers. They are also very concerned about property values. Over time, however, some positive changes often occur. From three months to a year after the newcomers move in, discussions about them become less negative and eventually quite positive. The apprehension about property values subsides, and it has even been found that there is eventually a decrease in racism scores (i.e., people in integrated neighborhoods hold less racist attitudes than those in segregated ones) (Hamilton & Bishop, 1976). As an example, content of discussions about new residents in one study changed from 27 percent negative before they moved in to only 8 percent negative a year later; positive content, on the other hand, went from 0 percent to 42 percent (Hamilton & Bishop, 1976). Thus, residential propinquity can have favorable effects, at least in the long run (see also Fairchild & Tucker, 1982; Shumaker & Stokols, 1982).

LEARNING ENVIRONMENTS

Education is a central component of the socialization of youngsters and provides them with the tools for life. Accordingly, the effects of the design of learning environments on the activities within them has been of great interest to researchers. These environments may range from small dormitory study areas, such as the one depicted in Figure 12–4, to large formal library settings. If design features are causing problems, they must be remedied in order to allow educational goals to be attained. If a design change can increase the effectiveness of education, so much the better. Let us now look at several design factors in a variety of educational settings.

Classroom Environments

Changes in classroom environments have been made more or less continuously since we abandoned the one-room schoolhouse. However, as we shall see, we are no longer bound to traditional designs for physical reasons, and

research has indicated that changes in classroom design can result in more positive student attitudes and greater participation in class (Gump, 1984, 1987; Rivlin & Wolfe, 1985; Sommer & Olsen, 1980). Let us consider some of these innovations.

Windowless Classrooms One innovation, the building of **windowless classrooms,** has not proven overwhelmingly successful. Originally designed to reduce distraction in the classroom, as well as to reduce heating costs, these new school buildings typically contain few if any windows. Research has suggested that the absence of windows in classrooms has no consistent effect on learning (some students improve, others show worse performance), but that it does reduce the pleasantness of students' moods (Ahrentzen et al., 1982; Karmel, 1965).

The Open Classroom Concept The traditional design of classrooms, rectangularly shaped with straight rows of desks, dates back

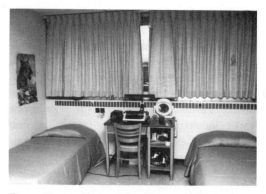

Figure 12–4 How good a place would this be for studying?

to medieval times, when the only source of light was natural light that came in through windows. Modern buildings, of course, do not rely solely on sunlight, so that new design alternatives are possible. **Open classrooms**, like open offices, are designed to free students from traditional barriers, such as restrictive seating. In such settings, students should have more opportunity to explore the learning environment.

Research evaluating these designs is confounded by the fact that the environment is typically not the only difference between open and traditional schools. That is, an "open education" philosophy implies freedom for students to move around and less structure in class activities. However, these could occur in a traditionally designed classroom and do not necessarily occur in open classrooms. Interestingly, Rivlin and Rothenberg (1976) found that behavior and performance in open-plan settings were not always consistent with the general philosophy of open education. In many open classrooms, students behave much as they do in traditional classrooms, and teachers often do not use all of the space provided. As is the case in traditional settings, students spend a great deal of time engaged in solitary tasks such as reading and writing. For example, Rothenberg and Rivlin (1975) found these percentages of total activities observed in one open classroom: writing 26 percent; arts and crafts 11.8 percent;

talking 11.3 percent; reading 6.3 percent; working at projects 5.7 percent; and teaching 4.3 percent. However, Gump (1974) observed that students in open classrooms spend less time in directed activity than students in traditional settings, and that groups in open classrooms show greater variability in size. Such heightened flexibility in open-plan rooms is often accompanied by greater activity than in the traditional classroom.

Two serious problems with open-plan designs are that they provide inadequate privacy and foster too much noise (e.g., Ahrentzen et al., 1982; Brunetti, 1972; Rivlin & Rothenberg, 1976). The flexibility provided by the open space can cause coordination problems, and frequently teachers do not know how to arrange furnishings so as to get the most use out of the space provided. Variable height partitions can reduce noise but still give the open feeling (Evans & Lovell, 1979). It is conceivable that by combining aspects of traditional and open-design classrooms, better environments may be created. At present, however, reviews of this kind of physical design are mixed. Interestingly, Traub and Weiss (1974) found that suburban students' learning was not impaired in open classrooms, but city-dwelling students performed better in traditional than open classrooms. Moreover, the style of the teacher (e.g., lecture-oriented vs. interactive), the age of the pupils, and whether they are learning disabled or have attention deficit disorders may be critical factors in the suitability of the open design. Overall, data-based studies indicate that open classroom designs are noisy, provide undesirable distractions, and do not foster adequate educational benefits to outweigh these problems (Bennett et al., 1980). As we will see in the next chapter, open plans in offices are also mixed blessings.

Environmental Complexity and Enrichment
What is the proper amount of environmental complexity in an educational setting? As we have seen elsewhere in this book, studies have

indicated that the complexity of an environment can affect arousal and performance in that setting (e.g., Evans, 1978). Too many stimuli may distract students, create overload, or increase fatigue. However, extremely simple settings may be boring and equally detrimental to performance (cf. Sommer & Olsen, 1980).

Some researchers believe that classrooms should tend more toward the complex rather than the simple (Rosenweig, 1966; Thompson & Heron, 1954). Having more stimuli and opportunities for environmental exploration present provides an enriched environment that facilitates learning. Others disagree, arguing that complex learning environments are distracting and make it difficult for the student to concentrate on school work (Vernon & McGill, 1957; Wohlwill, 1966). Comparative research is scant, but one study has examined the effects of variations in complexity of learning environments (Porteous, 1972). This study showed greater learning in less complex settings, supporting the position that overload and distraction are important problems in complex classrooms. Of course, classrooms serve more purposes than just learning content relevant to a specific topic. They also involve learning *how* to learn, learning social responsibility, and acquisition of cultural values. Different classroom environments may facilitate one of these purposes but not the others. How happy the pupil is in the setting may be the most important factor of all (Santrock, 1976), and working for the right fit between pupil and learning environment is probably worth the effort.

Libraries

Library designers have a number of unique problems with which they must deal. One familiar problem at university libraries is that patterns of use for study and reading areas move through periods of over- and underuse (e.g., Cziffra et al., 1975). Because underuse wastes space that could be used for books, a proposed design alternative for a university library would reserve the library for the storage and dispensation of materials. Reading and study areas would be eliminated from this setting and dispersed to other areas on the campus (Figure 12–5). For many students, such a separation of library and study functions would mean a major change in work style and would sometimes prove inconvenient. After all, the campus library often is the one place where students know they can get school work done!

In another library use study, Lipetz (1970) observed how a sample of over 2,000 patrons used a library card catalog. Since a large proportion of users go to the catalog upon entering the building, the catalog is usually located near the entrance. It may come as little surprise that Lipetz found that students used the catalog system far more than the faculty did. Furthermore, the rate of library use varied across periods of the academic year, with some of the heaviest use occurring after vacations and semester breaks. Now that most libraries are using a computerized catalog system, it will be much easier to track catalog user patterns. After using the card catalog, people often have a difficult time locating the right stacks in a library, so Lipetz recommends better orientation aids than are typically available (see box,

Figure 12–5 Books or people? Libraries have traditionally provided space both for books and reading or study. However, many libraries are caught in a conflict between space needs for a never-ending stream of new books and study space that is used only part of the time.

Locating a Book
at The Library:
A Problem in Orientation

Finding a book in a library is partly a problem of **orientation** to a large setting. Where do we start? Where do we go for help? Do we ask for information or try to find our way by reading signs? Pollet is one librarian who is interested in helping libraries improve their orientation aids (e.g., Pollet, 1976; Pollet & Haskell, 1979). One of the most important observations she makes is that library patrons must cope with information overload. Adding signs to help people find their way around contributes even more information to the environment. In particular, Pollet notes that clustering many signs together makes orientation information ineffective. People who are already receiving too much information are not apt to stop and look at a cluster of signs.

Libraries are learning to reduce the number of signs used and to experiment with critical locations of signs throughout the building. People need information at the point of making a decision about

where to go next. One helpful technique is to use a specific color for orientation information. No matter where people are, they can look for that color and become oriented. However, Pollet concludes that using too many colors for different areas simply adds more information to be processed, and can cause disorientation. (See also Chapter 3 on wayfinding.)

As found in similar museum studies, many patrons will not ask for help in libraries. Pollet advocates a good sign system that will give patrons a sense of control over the environment instead of relying on attendants to answer questions. She also comments that it is hard to find attendants who can put up with answering the same questions all day. While library patrons may be experiencing stimulus overload, information attendants may experience understimulation, which can leave them bored and irritable.

---

this page). Campbell and Shlechter (1979) suggest that library designs have so much impact on student behavior and satisfaction that planning for new or remodeled facilities should involve behavioral scientists as well as designers and librarians.

Museum Environments

Museums are, in a sense, learning environments, but they are quite different from classrooms. Since we use museums less regularly than classrooms, the museum environment is

somewhat more novel to us. Museums are also larger and do not provide a home base, such as a desk does in a classroom. In addition, the primary mode of activity in museums is exploration, as we make our way through halls and rooms, past endless cases of exhibits.

The ability to find things in a museum is related to wayfinding in any setting. Museums that are confusing or hard to explore may result in less satisfaction with the visit (Winkel et al., 1976). If you miss the exhibits you came to see because you could not find them, or if you find yourself constantly backtracking and going in circles, you probably have less fun than if everything were simpler. However, the complexity of museum environments is an almost inherent feature of their purpose—to display as many exhibits as possible.

One way of overcoming this inherent complexity is to provide aids for finding one's way through the museum. Winkel et al. (1976) suggest that people prefer to consult signs and maps and are uncomfortable if they have to ask museum employees for help. Maps that clearly depict a setting and identify the viewer's location on the map in relation to the setting seem to be particularly helpful. Such **you-are-here maps** show the position of the viewer and how to get from "here" to other parts of the setting (Levine, 1982; Levine, Marchon, & Hanley, 1984; see also Chapter 3). Not surprisingly, orientation aids such as maps and suggestions for what to see appear to increase satisfaction with the environment (Borun, 1977).

Overload notions may help explain why orientation aids are so valuable in museums. It has been found that the most popular museum exhibits are those that are of moderate complexity (Lakota, 1975; Melton, 1972; O;Hare, 1974; Robinson, 1928). Fatigue in a museum is not only a simple matter of walking around, but is also affected by the stimulation provided by the exhibits (Robinson, 1928). It may be, then, that museums can create overload if they are too complex or if it is difficult to get around inside (see Figure 12–6 A and B).

Research has also addressed the ways in which people explore museums. For example, people appear to have a right-handed bias; upon entering a gallery in a museum, they typically turn right and move around the room in that direction (Melton, 1933, 1936; Robinson, 1928). Once inside a museum, people usually stop at the first few exhibits and then become more selective, stopping at fewer the longer they explore (Melton, 1933). The higher the **attraction gradient** of an exhibit, the more likely visitors are to explore it. Exits to other exhibit rooms are also important because people tend to use the first exit they see. Museum researchers refer to this "pull" of exits as the **exit gradient**. Due in part to attraction gradients and exit gradients, most people see only a part of each exhibit room rather than seeing everything before moving on (Parsons & Loomis, 1973). These patterns are depicted in Figure 12–7.

Fatigue in Museum Exploration Predictable though it is, the pattern of physical movement within a museum shows some signs of being maladaptive. Walking in a museum should facilitate exploration of the environment. Yet, as we have seen, visitors frequently move past much of the exhibit without stopping or looking, thereby missing many of the rewards to be gained from a museum visit. Why is exploratory movement not more complete? One explanation is that fatigue interferes with completing more thorough patterns of visual exploratory behavior.

Robinson (1928) first studied fatigue in museums many years ago. In spite of his work being old, many of his observations on exploratory fatigue are still important. He concluded that fatigue was not due just to physical exertion but also to the visitor growing tired of maintaining a high level of attention. Robinson coined the term **museum fatigue** to describe the phenomenon.

In a clever laboratory study, Robinson was able to demonstrate that museum fatigue was more than just physical exertion. He had persons seated at a table look at a series of copies of paintings from a gallery, presented in the same order as they hung in the gallery. Attention time for each painting was recorded and compared with the attention time observed in the gallery itself. It turned out that subjects seated at the table and looking through the stack of pictures began to show a drop in attention at about the same point in the sequence as visitors walking through the museum. Robinson concluded that museum fatigue was due to psychological satiation or boredom as well as to fatigue

Figure 12–6 Modern museums have recognized the problem of environmental complexity and fatigue by creating exhibits that pace the amount of complexity so as to reduce fatigue and orient the visitor. (From A. Neal., 1969. *Help! For the small museum.* Boulder, CO: Pruett Publishing.)

from physical activity. He did not mean that visitors were bored by the exhibits. Rather, he noted that after visitors concentrated on several stimulating exhibits for a long period, they became so satiated with the museum's environ- ment that additional exhibits were relatively unstimulating. Recall from our discussion of information overload in Chapter 4 that when we receive the massively complex stimulation typ- ical of many museum environments, we tend to

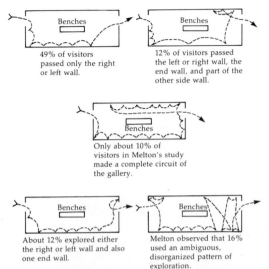

49% of visitors passed only the right or left wall.

12% of visitors passed the left or right wall, the end wall, and part of the other side wall.

Only about 10% of visitors in Melton's study made a complete circuit of the gallery.

About 12% explored either the right or left wall and also one end wall.

Melton observed that 16% used an ambiguous, disorganized pattern of exploration.

Figure 12–7 Typical movement patterns found in one study of visitors to an art museum. (Adapted from A. W. Melton, 1933. Studies of installations at the Pennsylvania Museum of Art. *Museum News, 10.* Used with permission.)

ignore less important cues in order to attend to more important ones. This is the sort of phenomenon that occurs with museum fatigue: We become so satiated with complex informa-tion that we spend less and less time looking at the details of various exhibits.

Museum fatigue can be alleviated somewhat by building what Robinson called **discontinuity** into the design of an exhibit. Discontinuity refers to a change of pace in the stimuli presented. For example, a series of paintings might be broken up with a piece of sculpture or an arrangement of furniture. The number of paintings or objects displayed can also be reduced, since a single gallery may contain a collection large enough to tax the attention span of the most ardent art lover. Alleviating mu-seum fatigue helps visitors gain more satisfac-tion from their exploration of the museum environment. For further discussion of these museum exploration and exhibit design princi-ples, see Bitgood, Roper, and Benefield (1988); Loomis (1987); Robillard (1984); Thomson (1986).

Finally, we should add that the principles of exhibit design and visitor behavior that hold for museums are also valid for visitor-oriented settings such as interpretive exhibits at national parks and zoos (e.g., Bitgood, Patterson, & Benefield, 1988). The entire July 1988 issue of *Environment and Behavior* is devoted to this topic as it relates to zoological parks.

PEDESTRIAN ENVIRONMENTS: SHOPPING MALLS, PLAZAS, AND CROSSWALKS

Nearly every environment has characteristic patterns of pedestrian movement through it. People select paths and avoid obstacles in regular fashion (Figure 12–8). By understand-ing the development of these patterns, we can obtain important information about the design of several kinds of settings (e.g., Whyte, 1980).

Research has revealed a number of principles of pedestrian movement patterns. One basic rule of thumb is that people choose simple, direct routes, whether formalized as landscaped paths or freely chosen, as in walking across lawns (Preiser, 1972). The well-worn paths across lawns on most college campuses, despite the presence of nearby sidewalks, illustrate this principle. Another observation about movement patterns regards the speed with which people walk. Generally, people conform their speed to that of people around them (Preiser, 1973).

Figure 12–8   People walking in an open plaza, as in the campus scene shown here, appear to be moving in a totally random manner. However, systematic observation of pedestrian movement has revealed that there is a predictable pattern to most movement. Some pathways, such as the most direct diagonal route across a plaza, will draw a heavy flow of foot traffic.

Larger crowds appear to move more slowly, and people walk slower on carpeting than on bare floors. Moreover, pedestrians match their speed somewhat to the pace of background music. These and other basic movement patterns apply in several different settings (e.g., Bovy, 1975).

We mentioned that movement patterns must also consider the effects of obstacles, such as automobile traffic. Frequently, people must negotiate traffic while walking somewhere. They may have to cross a street in order to get to a classroom building, or pass through a crowded parking lot en route to a shopping mall. People walk slower in such situations and often experience uncertainty in deciding whether to cross the traffic or wait (Henderson & Jenkins, 1974). In addition to traffic, large crowds can inhibit our movement and change patterns. The presence of people in one's way

leads to frequent changes in speed and deviations from the most direct route one can take. For example, people will walk around a small group of persons who are standing and talking rather than following a direct route between or through the group (Cheyne & Efran, 1972; Knowles et al., 1976). Preiser (1973) has incorporated all of these influences on pedestrian movement into a **friction–conformity model**. That is, "frictions" such as those mentioned above impede pedestrian flow, and conformity pressures (e.g., the speed of others) exert additional influence on movement.

Knowles and Bassett (1976) have considered social cues that people use in deciding whether to stop or move in crowded settings. Their perception of whether a group is an interacting entity or a casual gathering of strangers appears to be important in determining behavior. When pedestrians encountered a group of people

Pedestrian Malls:
Progress or Eyesore?

A relatively new development in cities is the use of pedestrian malls to enhance city life. A street in a commercial downtown area is blocked off and turned into a plaza for pedestrians—no automobiles are allowed. The idea is to reduce traffic congestion, beautify the area, and encourage commerce in previously deteriorating areas. Whyte (e.g., 1974) has observed that pedestrian plaza areas can indeed liven up the environment. Food vendors, sunny areas, places to sit, and fountains promote the habitability of such spaces. Amato (1981) even observed that people were more likely to help another in need along an area converted to a pedestrian mall compared to when it was a "normal" street.

On the other hand, pedestrian malls can be a disappointment. Grossman (1987) summarizes some of the problems that can occur. A mall in Eugene, Oregon

. . . became a wasteland. Pedestrians stayed away, partly out of fear that the mall's many trees and fountains were hiding muggers. Motorists skirted the area, confused by the reconfigured street routes.

With sales much slower than expected, merchants departed and storefronts were vacant.

Downtown Eugene began to rebound two years ago when one block of the mall was reopened to traffic. Now the city is considering reopening two more of the mall's original eight blocks to vehicles. If it does, Eugene will have spent more than twice the mall's original $1 million development cost on revamping the mall (p. 27).

Grossman observes that Galveston, Burbank, Minneapolis, Grand Rapids, Chicago, and Little Rock faced similar decisions with pedestrian malls. What went wrong? For one thing, shoppers accustomed to suburban mall shopping did not have the convenience of free parking, a variety of stores, and short drives to shop in the evening. Derelicts, delinquents, drug dealers, and "boom boxes" could find their way to the malls and scare away customers. What can be done to change the situation? Solutions include allowing some motorized transportation along the malls, building hotels there to provide a ready shopping population, removing obstructions where muggers could hide, and sponsoring festivals along the mall to attract crowds.

talking to one another, they moved on. When they encountered a casual group of people who were simply standing and looking up in the air, they were more likely to stop and join in the gazing.

Sometimes we like to watch others pass by us. "People watching" occurs when people seek out benches or seats where they can watch others (Preiser, 1972). Snyder and Ostrander (1972) observed this phenomenon among residents of retirement homes, who often locate themselves in areas where they can watch staff and other residents. Similarly, Zeisel and Griffin (1975) reported that elderly residents of an apartment complex preferred to sit along sidewalk areas so that they could watch other people

Design Research For
Pedestrian Wind Discomfort

No matter how efficient public transportation becomes, some pedestrian movement will be needed to get people to their final destination. Modern cities usually have high concentrations of pedestrian movement around business areas that consist of numerous high-rise buildings or skyscrapers. These buildings make it possible to locate many activities, such as work, shopping, entertainment, and living quarters, in a relatively small geographical area. However, there is increasing evidence that concentrated areas of high-rise buildings can alter ground level climate and pollution conditions because of the effects of building design on wind patterns (Hunt, 1975).

Engineers are now able to test the wind effects of proposed building designs in elaborate simulations that make use of wind tunnels (Peterka & Cermak, 1975). Such tests involve fitting models of proposed and existing buildings with pressure-sensitive recording devices. When the models are subjected to simulated wind levels typical of that city, researchers can examine structural stress effects as well as possible wind problems for pedestrians. Two common problems occur if a smokestack on a tall building is too short, or if a tall building is located too close upwind from a short one. Resulting wind patterns can force pollutants toward the ground and trap them there, causing a variety of discomforts for pedestrians. Another problem arises when high-speed winds 30 or more feet (9m) off the ground strike a tall building. Typically, these winds are forced straight down. If the building has an open passageway at ground level, the winds rush through it, causing a **wind tunnel effect**. Pedestrians, especially those carrying opened umbrellas, may be literally sucked through the passageway. Design alternatives that include wind deflectors are one means of solving this problem.

Such wind tunnel simulations enable researchers to test potential wind effects on entire city blocks (Peterka & Cermak, 1977). Design solutions to anticipated problems can also be tested. In one case, tests revealed that high winds in a plaza could be avoided by erecting partial walls at the entrance (Peterka & Cermak, 1973). The beauty of this type of research is that design alternatives can be tested before construction commitments are made.

go by. People watching is certainly not restricted to the elderly. For example, teenagers who use an area shopping mall as a "hangout" may sit for hours watching people pass, looking for friends and visiting with those they find.

Understanding pedestrian patterns is useful in several ways. Knowing how people move through shopping areas, for instance, may help in designing malls and arranging shops so that they are optimally patronized. In other settings, obstacles can be minimized and short, direct routes between places can be provided. By doing these things we can facilitate comfortable movement through a number of settings.

HOSPITAL SETTINGS

Much of what we know about design in hospital settings is derived from research on acute care and psychiatric hospital environments (Reizenstein, 1982). Most data-based investigations have considered psychiatric patients, perhaps because of greater ease and accessibility in using these subjects. Whatever the reason, this fact necessarily limits what we can conclude about design in hospital settings, since there is no guarantee that hospital patients respond comparably regardless of their reasons for being patients.

In addition, the literature on hospital environments is limited by methodology—much of it is based on descriptive or other nonexperimental approaches. In other words, a lot of what we know about these settings is based on observation and opinion rather than on careful study of behavior in them, although there are some notable exceptions (e.g., Canter, 1972; Noble & Dixon, 1977; Wolfe, 1975).

One aspect of hospital settings that has received attention is the low control or "low choice" forced upon patients and visitors (Olsen, 1978; Taylor, 1979). Hospitals typically have a great number of rules and allow patients only minimal control over the small spaces that they use. Olsen has pointed out that hospital designs can communicate this message—that people are "sick and dependent and should behave in an accordingly passive manner . . ." (Olsen, 1978, p. 7). Provision of greater spatial complexity or providing more options or variations in design can improve the situation and lead to more positive emotional responses (Olsen, 1978). Originally, hospitals for the mentally ill resembled prisons more than hospitals (Figure 12–9 A and B). Today, the design of psychiatric facilities tends to resemble that of a dormitory or hotel built around a central nurses' station and lounge (Figure 12–10 A and B).

Ronco (1972) observed that hospital settings are usually designed for staff rather than patient needs. For example, it is conceivable that a ward design that facilitates staff functioning might also cause a patient to sense an overwhelming loss of personal control and privacy. Such feelings in turn may contribute to the patient's becoming overdependent on the hospital and withdrawing from normal activities. These and other considerations have led researchers to look for design alternatives that alleviate the negative effects of hospitalization and stimulate the healing process, as well as facilitate staff needs.

Do some designs and locations of nurses' stations promote more efficient patient care (i.e., behavioral facilitation), as some suggest (cf. Lippert, 1971)? In order to answer this question, Trites et al. (1970) investigated nurse efficiency and staff satisfaction with three different hospital ward designs (Figure 12–11). In general, a **radial ward design** was found to be the most desirable (relative to **single** and **double corridor designs**), both in terms of saving unnecessary ward travel and of increasing time with patients. Moreover, members of the nursing staff indicated a preference for assignment to the radial ward. The fact that nursing staff in the radial unit had more free time was interpreted as an indication that more patients could be housed on the ward. In another ward study, however, Lippert (1971) found no one ward design particularly superior to another, using efficiency in patient care stops as the behavioral criterion. Nevertheless, it is clear that hospital design can have significant impact on the well-being of both patients and staff.

Another issue that has received attention is the degree to which different designs affect social interaction among patients. Beckman (1974) suggests that an appropriate design is

Figure 12–9 A and B   Exterior and interior of the first hospital in the United States built specifically for the mentally ill. This facility was built in 1773 in Williamsburg, Virginia.

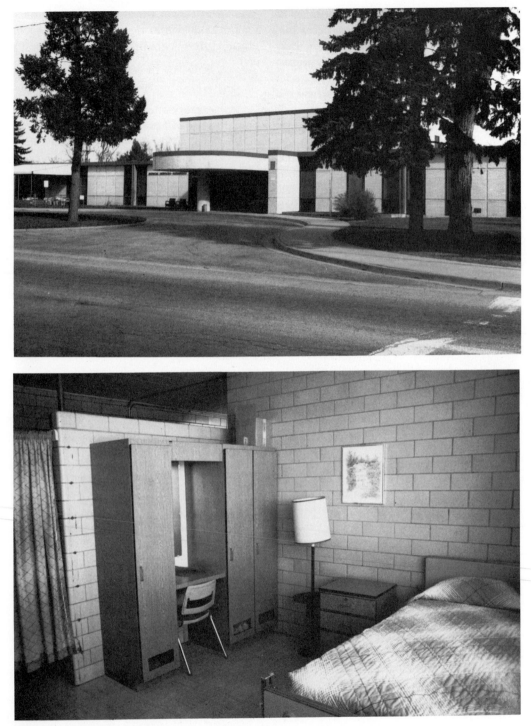

Figure 12–10 A and B   Exterior and interior of a contemporary facility for the mentally ill.

one which encourages patients to leave their rooms and seek out others, and which supports social interaction. Of course, for some types of patients (e.g., those in an intensive care unit), one might want to discourage some of this movement. This design goal reflects an understanding and concern for the same kinds of issues raised in studies of residential environments—the recognition that the arrangement of space can affect the frequency and quality of social contact (Baum & Valins, 1979).

We noted in the previous chapters that some types of furniture arrangements (i.e., sociopetal vs. sociofugal) facilitate patient interaction more than others. In addition, keeping down the number of beds on a ward promotes social interaction and reduces withdrawal (Ittelson, Proshansky, & Rivlin, 1970). Social interaction concerns extend to other relationships as well. Pill (1967), for example, discusses how designs that place nursing staff in close proximity to patients do not allow nurses to satisfy their privacy needs. Another important form of interaction, disclosure between patient and physician, is facilitated by pleasantly designed institutional settings (Reizenstein, 1976).

Still other environmental features have been shown to have direct impact on well-being. One study has shown that windowless intensive care units have a higher incidence of postoperative problems, ranging from negative psychological outcomes to physiological complications (Wilson, 1972). Still another (reviewed in Chapter 11) compared surgery patients assigned to rooms looking out over a natural setting with patients in rooms whose windows faced a brick building. Patients in the rooms with a nice view had shorter postoperative stays in the hospital and used fewer pain-killing medications (Ulrich, 1984). Moreover, a study of uncontrollable noise in the hospital showed that it increases experienced pain and is associated with greater use of painkillers by surgery patients (Minckley, 1968).

A series of studies by Wolfe and Rivlin (Rivlin & Wolfe, 1972; Wolfe, 1975) has

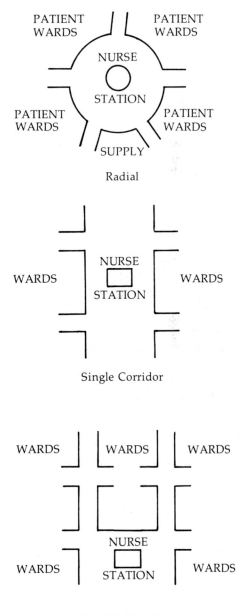

Radial

Single Corridor

Double Corridor

Figure 12−11 These designs represent three types of hospital wards. The radial unit appeared to be the most desirable in terms of staff satisfaction and amount of time spent with patients. (Adapted from Trites, D., Galbraith, F. D., Sturdavant, M., & Leckwart, J. F., 1970. Influence of nursing unit design on the activities and subjective feelings of nursing personnel. *Environment and Behavior, 2,* 303–334.

Prison Design
and Behavior

Even during economically difficult periods, one thing society seems to be able to fund is the building of more prisons. Given that prisoners are confined for long periods of time, it would seem that prison design could have important consequences. Recall from Chapter 9 that research by Paulus and his colleagues has led to some important conclusions regarding the behavioral effects of prison design. Among other things, they found that different architectural layouts of residence space in prisons affected behavior and health. Grouping prisoners together in large numbers was less healthy than grouping them together in small numbers (Cox et al., 1982, 1984; Schaeffer et al., 1988). Single or double occupancy cells were better (i.e., judged as less crowded) than were cells grouping small numbers of prisoners. Further, if large groups were "broken up" by partitions or segmentation of space (so that the large group became several smaller ones), psychological and physical health was improved.

These findings provide strong evidence that the design of prisons influences mood and behavior of prisoners. At one level, this is not surprising. Prisons are usually designed along functional criteria and are not built for aesthetic reasons. Space is designed to facilitate order and regimentation. Bars and walls are deliberate attempts to constrain behavior, and economy is usually an important factor in determining the use of space. However, it is also clear

Figure 12–12 A and B The top picture displays a traditional prison gun tower and security wall. The bottom picture is a more contemporary facility with windows so narrow they do not require bars.

that prison designs can have unintended, demoralizing effects, and new prisons have been increasingly designed to avoid some of these consequences (Luxenberg, 1977). This has occurred in spite of objections based on differing penal philosophies and increased costs.

The ethic that guided traditional prison design evolved from nineteenth-century concepts of correctional activity. Treatment was seen as being best accomplished by isolation from society, both physically and symbolically. To some extent, prisons' clear separation from society may be traced to this ethic. At another level, so are the economic considerations that we have already mentioned. Most people see prisoners as nonproductive elements of society, so we place a special emphasis on economy. As a result of these pressures, prisons are usually large, located in remote areas, and surrounded by high exterior walls that

Figure 12–12C Floorplans of three generations of jails showing changes in surveillance and privacy. In third-generation jails, passive surveillance is replaced by active supervision; the officer becomes a service-providing professional rather than a turnkey, and must have skills in counseling, crisis intervention, and interpersonal communication. These changes can result in an increased sense of professionalism and the feeling that the job is challenging and desirable. (From Wener, Frazier, & Farbstein, 1987. Reprinted with permission from *Psychology Today Magazine*. Copyright 1987, PT Partners, L.P.)

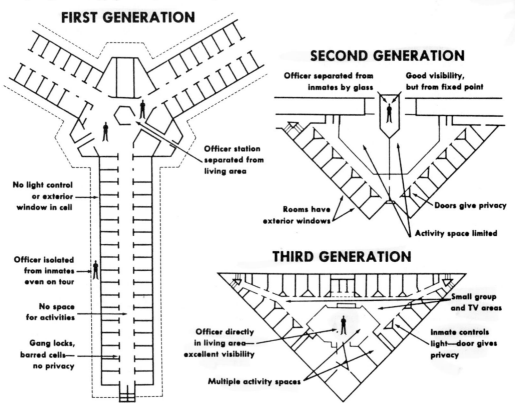

FIRST GENERATION

No light control or exterior window in cell

Officer station separated from living area

Officer isolated from inmates even on tour

No space for activities

Gang locks, barred cells— no privacy

SECOND GENERATION

Officer separated from inmates by glass

Good visibility, but from fixed point

Rooms have exterior windows

Doors give privacy

Activity space limited

THIRD GENERATION

Officer directly in living area— excellent visibility

Multiple activity spaces

Small group and TV areas

Inmate controls light—door gives privacy

deny inmates visual access to the outside world.

"New" prison designs usually seek to do several things. First, they attempt to provide more "humane" environments, replacing gun towers with natural barriers, adding color and lighting to otherwise drab settings, and increasing opportunities for privacy by providing more single occupancy cells and by designing windows so narrow they do not need bars (Figure 12–12A and B). There has also been an attempt to build more cells into exterior walls so that inmates can have a view of the outside world. Control over the environment has also been heightened in some prisons, with inmates gaining control over heating, lighting, and even privacy in their own cells. Rather than separate observational booths or rooms for guards, the guards are placed directly in the living quarters of the inmates to increase interaction. These improvements have been made in conjunction with changing philosophies in dealing with people who break the law. Wener, Frazier, and Farbstein (1985, 1987) have indicated that such designs help remove the fear of violence at the hands of other inmates, resulting in 30 to 90 percent reductions in violence, similar drops in vandalism (e.g., to mattresses and light fixtures) and graffiti, and the virtual disappearance of homosexual rape (Figure 12–12C).

. . . .

examined a number of design variables and their effects on behavior in a children's psychiatric hospital. One important variable turned out to be bedroom size and occupancy. Ittelson et al. (1970), for example, found that the more patients in a room, the fewer types of behavior were observed. Wolfe (1975) similarly reported that design elements which increased the number of children assigned to a hospital room decreased its use and had inhibiting effects on patients' behavior.

Design of play space in psychiatric facilities for children has also received attention (Rivlin, Wolfe, & Beyda, 1973). In general, little consideration is given to age level differences in planning play space in these facilities. Younger children, especially, seem to have difficulty in adapting to highly controlled hospital ward space. Rivlin and her colleagues suggested that the behaviors younger children display in handling their disorientation to ward space may be interpreted by staff members as part of their disorder. In reality, the younger child may be reacting as any child might to restrictions on play caused by inadequate space. Consequently, special care facilities should be designed not only for treating illnesses, but also for encouraging the normal activities of a particular age group.

Designing for Hospital Visitors

Thus far we have discussed some considerations for hospital residents and staff. Zimring, Carpman, and Michelson (1987) point out that hospitals should attend to design needs of visitors, as well. They note that in this day of cost-saving efforts, visitors can often perform basic caregiving tasks instead of the staff, such as adjusting pillows, feeding the patient, or providing psychosocial support. Yet, many visitors are themselves worried about the condition of the patient, and they are in an unfamiliar environment. Numerous design flaws—many of which are readily rectified—add more stress for the visitor.

For example, how easy is it to find your way through all the corridors? Most visitors have a difficult time with wayfinding (e.g., Carpman, Grant, & Simmons, 1983–84). Good signs in everyday language instead of medical terminology would help, as would frequent "you-are-here" maps, or paper maps visitors could carry. As another example, visitors find hospital noise disturbing (Reizenstein et al., as cited in Zimring et al., 1987). Sound-absorbing materials (carpeting, furnishings) would help. Television sets are often positioned in patient rooms so that patients can see them from the bed, but visitors have to sit in uncomfortable positions for a good view (Carpman & Grant, 1984, as cited in Zimring et al., 1987). Privacy is also an issue: Visitors have no place to go for a private conversation. Conference rooms accessible to visitors, or screened portions of waiting areas could alleviate this design problem (Reizenstein et al., as cited in Zimring et al., 1987). The list of design concerns for visitors includes many other dimensions we have discussed previously in other contexts, such as lighting, segregation of smokers and nonsmokers, odors, and furniture arrangements in waiting areas and patient rooms. Indeed, all of these components communicate whether or not the visitor has been considered when the design was developed.

DESIGNING FOR THE ELDERLY

Those over age 65 are the fastest growing segment of the population in the industrialized world, and those over age 85 are the fastest growing subgroup of the elderly. In the U.S., 12 percent of the population was over 65 in 1987, and that figure will rise to 20 percent by 2020. Japan is the most rapidly aging country in the world, where the elderly population will grow from 10 percent in 1987 to 23 percent by 2020 (Dickson, 1987). As a greater proportion of our population becomes aged, providing specialized short- and long-term residential care facilities for them becomes very important. Certain characteristics of the elderly should be kept in mind when designing such environments. Especially important to consider is that the elderly are a heterogeneous lot. Too often, designers have assumed that the elderly are a homogeneous group, when actually they have only age and certain health problems in common. In fact, there is probably no other segment of the population with such a broad diversity of individual problems and needs. Some elderly citizens have trouble hearing, others have difficulty with vision, and still others have difficulty with locomotion. Many have no physical disabilities at all. Some elderly people suffer from psychological difficulties (e.g., withdrawal, distorted thought processes) while others do not. Another source of diversity in the elderly is the fact that indivduals have established long-term behavior patterns, and these differ greatly among people. All of these considerations argue for "designing in" flexibility in any facility for the elderly. In general, these facilities can be discussed as either institutional or noninstitutional. Institutional facilities are nursing homes and similar settings providing a relatively high level of care for residents, such as nursing care (e.g., administration of medications) and what is termed **custodial care**, or care for everyday needs such as meals and laundry. When the emphasis is on custodial care rather than medical care, the setting is often called **intermediate care** or **residential care**. Noninstitutional settings include retirement villages or similar housing where residents provide most of their own daily care. In Chapter 4 (box page 105), we described Lawton's model of environmental press and competence in the elderly, which holds that if the press of a specific environment is within the competence of the elderly to handle it, positive adaptation will occur. Let us see how some design principles might be applied to institutional and noninstitutional facilities for the elderly to help them maintain competence (see also Altman, Lawton, & Wohlwill, 1984; Carp, 1987). Moos (1980) observed that two million elderly live in specialized settings, whereas 10 times that number live in other (more conventional) settings. Nevertheless, we will put most of our emphasis on institutional settings because that is where most of the design-related research has occurred.

Residential Care Facilities for the Elderly

How should designers approach the task of planning residential care facilities for this population? They should attempt to compensate as much as possible for the physical and psychological difficulties which some aged individuals have, without unduly constraining the lives of people who have no particular problems (e.g., Baltes et al., 1987). That is, designs should foster adaptation. A variety of environmental options should be provided, so that people can continue to engage in the same activities as they did prior to institutionalization. Also, it is important for designers to attempt to view things from the perspective of aged residents, which may differ from the ideas and needs of the staff of the facility or those of the designer. Too often facilities for the elderly are designed in accord with an architect's vision (which may not be sufficiently informed about the elderly), or are planned so that they make life easy for the nursing, cleaning, or maintenance staff of the institution (e.g., Fontaine, 1982). A study by Duffy et al. (1986), for example, found that designers and nursing home administrators were biased in favor of nursing home designs

that emphasized social interaction, whereas residents who were not cognitively impaired actually preferred designs that fostered privacy.

A number of design features would seem to be useful to incorporate in a short- or long-term residential care facility for the elderly. First, it is important for the environment to provide for safety and convenience. To promote safety, a facility should permit sufficient staff surveillance to prevent accidents or to detect them when they do occur, while not eliciting the feeling that there is no privacy. In addition, specific design features should be included to prevent accidents (e.g., handrails in halls, "nonslip" surfaces), and aspects of the design certainly should not cause accidents. For example, entrances should be protected from the elements: Many elderly are not steady on their feet, and snow, ice, rain, or wind around entrances can be extremely hazardous. Also, elements should be included that permit clients to notify staff if they have a problem in a private area (e.g., call buttons in bathrooms). The design should promote convenience by providing orientation aids (e.g., color-coded floors, cues to differentiate halls), as well as by affording comfort (e.g., chairs should be easy to get in and out of). Convenience is also fostered to the extent that the setting is "barrier free," and allows a large proportion of the population to move about independently. Finally, important facilities (e.g., bathrooms, communal areas) should be within easy access of rooms. In many ways, facilities conforming to the above criteria will promote feelings of personal control, prevent helplessness, and elicit positive effects in residents. (For a review of the concepts of control and helplessness, see Chapter 4 and Rodin, 1986).

The design of a residential care facility for the elderly should also foster choice (and in doing so, feelings of control). The location of the facility should be sufficiently close to a community to allow residents to choose among a variety of available services (e.g., grocery stores, movie theaters). Choice is also facilitated when the design contains various types of spaces which can be used for special purposes (e.g., recreation, privacy, dyadic as opposed to large group communication). Recreation areas should be designed to elicit communication (i.e., should be sociopetal), but some areas should afford privacy (i.e., should be sociofugal). It is very important that there be a range of social and recreational choices available to each resident (Lawton, 1979). Also, each resident should have access to both a bathtub and a shower, and it is preferable for each room to have individual heating controls. Without adequate degrees of choice being promoted by physical design, the environment can promote loss of perceived control and helplessness.

In addition to providing choices, objective physical conditions of the facility should be adequate and appropriate. Rooms should be of sufficient size, there should be enough recreational space for the resident population, and the construction should be of reasonable quality. Objective physical conditions affect patient behavior in many ways. When large sitting areas are occupied by relatively few residents, there seems to be a low level of physical interaction. Designs including long corridors appear to discourage resident mobility. When physical arrangements cause residents to be grouped in areas closely accessible to staff, some positive outcomes occur (e.g., the staff has more surveillance over accidents and danger, and interacts more with residents). However, some negative outcomes also occur under these circumstances (e.g., the staff may behave in ways that encourage patient dependency) (Harris, Lipman, & Slater, 1977). It is also important for patients to have their own kitchen facility, or else residents tend to depend on staff members even to get a cup of coffee (Lipman & Slater, 1979). This situation encourages helplessness.

In addition to the physical environment, the social environment is extremely important to the well-being of the institutionalized elderly. A great deal of recent research has found that when the social environment fosters perceived choice and personal control, the well-being of the elderly is enhanced (cf. Rodin, 1986; Rowe & Kahn, 1987; Woodward & Wallston, 1987). Unfortunately, both the social conditions under which many people arrive at institutions and institutional life itself typically promote a loss of control. The new resident is often stripped of his or her accustomed relationships and satisfactions, and must give up personal property which has served as a means of self-identification. Also, people frequently come to a residential care facility after having problems with illness, financial setbacks, and family difficulties, all of which foster a loss of control. Often, the family decides that the person cannot remain at home any longer and to which institution the person will go (Fontaine, 1982). The very character of institutional life (e.g., one must submit to rules and regulations, to authority, to ''standardized'' schedules and procedures) adds to one's loss of control (Wack & Rodin, 1978).

One's response to being relocated and entering a long-term residential care facility is more positive if he or she is afforded a degree of control over the process. Reactions are more favorable when the person has chosen to be institutionalized, has picked the particular facility that he or she will live in, and when the difference in control between the pre- and post-relocation environments is not great (Ferrari, 1960; Schulz & Brenner, 1977). In addition to providing control, one way to increase predictability (and hence resident well-being) is to give people preparatory information about their forthcoming move, which actually decreases mortality rates after relocation (Pastalan, 1976; Zweig & Csank, 1975). Another helpful procedure is to familiarize the resident with the building prior to the move by means of a three-dimensional model and slides of the various rooms and corridors (see Chapter 3). Among other things, this procedure aids wayfinding (and cognitive mapping) once the resident moves into the building (Hunt, 1984).

One problem for residents is that with subsequent declines (or improvements) in health, further relocation may be necessary. In order to minimize the negative effects of this movement, multilevel facilities—those that offer many levels of care and supervision in one place—are becoming popular. These are beneficial because they minimize the effects of relocation by making the move from one part of the facility to another, rather than from one facility to another. People can still have access to their friends and can be moved easily if their condition again improves or deteriorates. While there are benefits to this type of design, there are criticisms as well. Some say that the presence of people in deteriorated states of health can undermine the morale and create dependency (and even illness) in relatively more healthy residents (Gutman, 1978). The verdict still is not in on multilevel designs, and further research is necessary (Figure 12–13A and B).

Once one has relocated and is living in an institution for the elderly, aspects of the institutional environment (both physical and social) can foster a sense of loss of control. For example, a great deal more is done for residents of nursing homes than was the case in their former environments. What can we do to reverse this loss of control, which can eventually result in helplessness? One important element in solving the problem is for residents to be encouraged to do more things for themselves. In Chapter 4 we noted a study by Langer and Rodin (1976) in which one group of institutionalized elderly was treated in a way designed to increase feelings of control. In the group where control was fostered, residents were happier, their conditions had improved somewhat after several months, and they showed more activity (e.g., were more apt to attend a movie, and to participate in a contest) than in the condition where control was not encouraged.

Similar results were reported by Mercer and Kane (1979) and, in general, it seems that increasing control consistently leads to important psychosocial effects. Not only does it improve individual functioning, but it improves the overall atmosphere of the institution (Fontaine, 1982). Do the effects of control-increasing interventions persist? Here, the evidence is mixed: Some studies (e.g., Rodin & Langer, 1977) show long-term effects, while others (e.g., Schulz & Hanusa, 1978) do not. (We should note that Rodin and Langer instilled control by encouraging residents to make more decisions for themselves, whereas Schulz and Hanusa in part encouraged visitation and then discontinued it.)

Specialized Facilities for the Cognitively Impaired: Alzheimer Units

Although most elderly are not cognitively impaired, about 5 to 10 percent or so of those over 65 have **Alzheimer's Disease**, which is characterized by loss of memory, confusion, impaired judgment, and progressive decline to more and more dependent states of existence. It is the fourth leading cause of death in the U.S., afflicts about three million Americans, and accounts for half of all nursing home admissions (e.g., Cook-Deegan, 1987). We have emphasized above the need to permit choice among nursing home residents. What happens when residents are so cognitively impaired that free choice can be dangerous? One answer is the creation of specialized Alzheimer units or dementia units within nursing homes. (**Dementia** is a medical term meaning loss of cognitive capabilities. Although Alzheimer's disease accounts for over half of all dementias, there are many causes of dementia and the behavioral consequences of these diseases are such that the environmental interventions for them are essentially the same.)

Alzheimer units are designed with the idea that dementia patients display diminished judgment capabilities and progressive confusion. These residents are very prone to wandering off

Figure 12–13 A and B   Providing several levels of care in a facility for the aged can minimize difficulties associated with relocation, but can also reduce the morale of healthier patients.

and can easily become lost. Traditionally, dementia victims have had to be physically or chemically restrained to prevent wandering and other potentially dangerous behavior. An Alzheimer unit attempts to minimize the need for these restraints: The setting is designed to make life safe and less restrictive by adjusting the environment to the behavior. For example, the units have locked access so that a key (or combination) is needed to leave the unit. Such an arrangement may sound cruel, but if it is carefully designed, it permits minimal use of restraints: The residents can wander within the unit all they want without wandering off or otherwise endangering themselves. Most of the time the unit includes a secured outdoor area with open access for the residents, so they may wander in and out of the building but never away from the unit. A very important feature of these units is extra staffing and thorough training of the staff in behavioral management techniques, such as the use of reminiscence and diversion. Also, activities to keep the residents occupied are specially planned. Environmental considerations include non-glare floors (glare can increase confusion about orientation), extra orientation aids (such as pictures indicating locations of toilets; names of residents in large letters on the room door), pictures firmly affixed to walls (to prevent their inadvertent falling when touched out of curiosity), absence of "busy" interior decorations (which can add to confusion), and a lounge area with a Dutch door (i.e., a door with a bottom half that can be closed separately from the top half). The reason for this door is that at night, some residents will not be able to sleep, a phenomenon in Alzheimer's known as **day–night reversal**. If sleepless residents are forced to stay in their rooms, they will likely wake others. If permitted to roam in the lounge (with only the bottom half of the door closed to permit staff supervision), they typically do not disturb others. Although there are numerous variations of these dementia unit designs, a representative one is shown in Figure 12–14. How well do Alzheimer units

work? Although they have not been around long enough to determine for sure, initial evidence suggests they have some merit. For example, Bell and Smith (1989) found that walking on these units was twice as likely to occur as sleeping—they are much more active than conventional nursing home units. Moreover, the unnerving behaviors of hitting and shouting, which are common in some stages of Alzheimer's, were extremely rare on the units studied. From a preliminary perspective, at least, the design of dementia units may have some desirable consequences. (For additional reading on these units, see Calkins, 1987; Lawton, Fulcomer, & Kleban, 1984; Ohta & Ohta, 1988; Rhodes & Houser, 1986).

Noninstitutional Residences for the Elderly

While it becomes necessary for many elderly to enter an institution, this is not uniformly the case. In many ways, it is probably better if one can stay at home or in a relatively "homelike" setting without having to endure certain almost inevitable problems associated with institutional environments. Accordingly, special residential housing facilities for the elderly have been planned and built. Also, many services (e.g., "Meals on Wheels," home-based health care) are now made available to elderly citizens who are living "at home."

What type of residential housing for the aged seems to be best? Various elements (e.g., high and rising rents for people on fixed incomes, long-term residences being turned into condominiums) can make it difficult for the elderly to find a decent place to live at a reasonable price. Overall, studies suggest that providing planned housing specifically for the elderly is superior to leaving them to find a residence on the "open market" (e.g., Carp, 1976; Lawton & Cohen, 1974). Is it best for the elderly to live in **age-segregated** or in heterogeneous environments? While arguments could be made citing costs and benefits of each environmental arrangement, the confluence of evidence suggests that the elderly prefer age-segregated housing. Living with others one's own age is associated with housing satisfaction, neighborhood mobility, and positive morale (Grant, 1970; cf. Normoyle & Foley, 1988). Why is this the case? Perhaps it is because more similar others are in close proximity when the neighborhood is age-segregated, and both similarity and propinquity elicit attraction (Byrne, 1971). In addition, age segregation probably results in more activities that are appropriate to an elderly population. There are other possibilities as well, such as the provision of more medical and other services needed by the elderly in age-segregated settings, and avoidance of some annoyances such as certain forms of noise (see box, page 428).

What other factors should be taken into consideration when planning noninstitutional residences for the elderly? One important element in residential living for the aged population is adequate transportation. Too often, transportation is not sufficiently accessible for the elderly in the community. Planners should be certain there are bus routes running through

Figure 12–14   An example of a floor plan for a dementia unit. Note that the locked access still permits wandering through the facility, indoors and out.

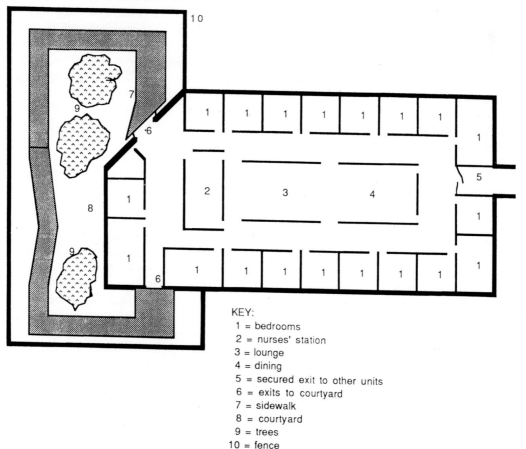

KEY:
1 = bedrooms
2 = nurses' station
3 = lounge
4 = dining
5 = secured exit to other units
6 = exits to courtyard
7 = sidewalk
8 = courtyard
9 = trees
10 = fence

areas with many senior citizens, and these should include stops at places where these individuals must go (i.e., medical complexes, shopping areas). Buses should also be accessible to elderly citizens (and others) with handicaps. In addition to making transportation systems physically available to the elderly,

designers must explore means of making other aspects of the community accessible as well (e.g., Evans et al., 1984). Many elements in the environment (e.g., exterior stairways, nonautomatic doors) may be discouraging and dangerous to an elderly population.

An Ideal Residential Care Facility for the Elderly: Increasing Environmental and Social Control

We have suggested that aspects of the physical and social environments that afford control will have favorable effects on elderly residents of institutional care facilities. While some attempt has been made to increase control in such institutions, there are many more steps that can be taken. One impediment is that in the short run, giving control to residents may be perceived by staff as causing more work for them, or taking away their authority. But as we have seen, in the long run it could lead to better functioning residents who are much more able to care for themselves, rather than depending on staff members.

What would an ideal residential care facility for the elderly be like? In an interesting speculative essay based on past research on the effects of control in institutional settings for the elderly, Fontaine (1982) suggests several important elements. The ideal facility would be relatively small, which would afford residents more control in dealing with staff, the environment, and other residents. People would be given a choice of large single or double rooms. All rooms would contain movable, rearrangeable furniture so people could control their immediate environment, and each room would have a private bathroom. Residents would be

encouraged to bring their own furniture, pictures, and certain other possessions with them. This is important for maintaining one's self-image and a sense of continuity in life. Double rooms would have partitions which residents could arrange to suit their needs. It would be the job of residents, where possible, to maintain and to clean their rooms, again affording control over the immediate environment. There would be a shop on the premises where residents could buy their own personal effects and disposable items, thus promoting control and reducing dependency on staff and family members.

Complementing the institutional kitchen would be a kitchen for people who do not want to eat what everyone else is eating on a particular day, or who want to prepare food for guests or friends. (Each patient would have a food storage closet and refrigerator space.) An ideal facility would also permit residents a great deal of choice in the planning of institutional meals, and there could be choices of what dishes they would be served at a particular meal.

Choice would also be heavily incorporated into recreational offerings. Television sets would be available for use in rooms by request, as well as in one of the day rooms. All sorts of recreational areas would be available, some fostering large-group, and others promoting individual and small-group, activity. Outside there would be a large courtyard where residents could plant flowers (which they could give as gifts or use to decorate their rooms) and vegetables (which they could eat).

Choice would also be incorporated into the everyday routine. Within reason, residents would be allowed to get out of bed and get washed whenever they wished. They would help choose daily activities, which would ensure that they had interesting things to do. Any complaints would be handled in a democratic way, giving residents some control over the way the facility is run.

While the above means of establishing environmental control for residents sound good, there are some caveats. Fontaine notes that the amount of control one can handle depends on one's physical and psychological condition. Having more control than one can exercise could be bad, rather than good, for people. However, almost anyone can exercise some degree of control (e.g., which side to lie on in bed, what they would like to eat). And even those who cannot exercise much control can benefit from information about what will be occurring in the facility, which affords a feeling that events are predictable, if not entirely controllable.

We should add that an "ideal" care facility would follow the design process described in Chapter 11, with continual evaluation and feedback from residents and staff. Objective measures of environmental quality for nursing homes have been developed (e.g., Lemke & Moos, 1986, 1987), and can be used in part to evaluate design components.

SUMMARY

In American culture, strong preferences exist for single-family detached homes, apparently because such housing provides high control over social interaction. Economic and other factors, however, often lead to choices of other types of housing.

The more easily we can perform given tasks in a setting, the more satisfied we are with it. Other factors affecting residential satisfaction include noise, ease of cleaning, and adequate plumbing, heating, and kitchen facilities. For inner-city residents, satisfaction with a neighborhood is closely tied to social bonds.

Privacy is a significant mediator of activities in residences but is not a simple process. Whereas some families have a very open structure, others use design within the home to structure privacy for all family members. Another important issue is functional criteria in residential design. One current consideration is to combine several functions in one room, such as using a sunken bathtub as a conversation pit in a living room.

Propinquity involves both objective physical distance and functional distance, or the likelihood that two individuals will come into contact. Both types of propinquity facilitate the formation of friendships. Designing for optimal conditions has attempted to use propinquity to promote racial harmony and other favorable social relationships.

Research on classroom design has shown

that windowless classrooms have no consistent effects on academic performance, but that presence of windows promotes pleasant moods. Open-plan classrooms also show mixed results, with some research showing an increase in activity associated with open classrooms, as well as increases in noise and decreases in privacy. Apparently, an optimal level of complexity in the classroom environment promotes learning.

Libraries have a problem of periodic overuse of facilities. One proposal would separate the "normal" library functions from the study function it often serves. In addition, evidence indicates additional orientation aids would help many libraries. Orientation is also a problem in museums, with some evidence suggesting improved orientation enhances satisfaction. Exploration of a museum tends to be systematic and is heavily influenced by the attraction gradient of exhibits. Museum fatigue may be caused by overstimulation, and can be alleviated by designing discontinuity into exhibits.

Pedestrian movement also tends to be systematic, with people preferring the shortest route. Crowds slow down pedestrian movement, as does carpeting. People tend to match their walking speed to the flow of the crowd and to background music. A friction–conformity model has been proposed to explain these relationships.

Hospitals are often oriented toward a high-control, low-choice atmosphere to facilitate staff functioning. This tendency, however, reduces perceived control on the part of the patient, as well as privacy. Designs that restore control and foster social interaction can help in this regard, and can also facilitate patient recovery. A radial design of wards around a nursing station can improve staff efficiency and increase the amount of time staff spends with patients. Design features which could help hospital visitors include orientation maps, private areas, low-noise designs, and considerations for comfort.

Care facilities for the elderly need to consider the fact that characteristics and needs of the elderly vary widely, so designs should allow for flexibility. Safety and convenience, choice and control, and physical conditions are important considerations. Large sitting areas may discourage social interaction. Long corridors may discourage mobility. Whereas proximity of residents to staff facilitates surveillance, it may also encourage dependence. Although providing several levels of care in one facility minimizes negative effects of relocation, morale of healthier residents can suffer from too much interaction with those in deteriorated states of health. Clearly, providing perceived control is one of the most effective interaction strategies for the institutionalized elderly. With dementia units, the idea is to adapt the environment to the special behavioral characteristics of the cognitively impaired. For those outside of institutions, planned housing in age-segregated areas seems to enhance satisfaction and morale, and adequate transportation and shopping are also important.

SUGGESTED PROJECTS

1. Tour some model homes in the community. Compare the privacy available in the bedrooms, kitchen, and baths. What behavioral adaptations do you anticipate once someone occupies the homes?

2. Observe the activities of an entire floor of a dormitory. In what ways do the behavioral adaptations resemble those of a private home? In what ways do they resemble those of a ghetto described by Scheflen?

3. Try to visit open classrooms and conventional classrooms in your area. Which seem to have the most activity? Which seem to have more noise?

4. Visit your local museum or zoo and note exploration patterns of visitors. Can you

identify attraction gradients and disconti-
nuities? Do visitors tend to use the same
route through displays?

5. Visit a nursing home or retirement home
    and note the location of lounge areas.
    Look for lounge areas that have a lot of
    interaction, and those with little interac-
    tion. What factors account for the differ-
    ences? Can you identify design features
    intended to promote competence?

13
WORK AND LEISURE ENVIRONMENTS

KEY TERMS

adventure playgrounds
assigned workspace
behavior constraint
behavior settings
carrying capacity
contemporary playgrounds
controls
displays
electronic cottage
encapsulation
experience
extrinsic motivation
freedom of choice
human factors
human-machine system
individual difference variables

intrinsic motivation
landscaped office
legibility
link analysis
loose parts
open office
overload
population stereotypes
scientific management
solitude
stress
traditional playgrounds
video display terminal (VDT)
workflow
workspace
workstation

INTRODUCTION

Harry and Sue were looking forward to the weekend. Harry's job at the factory was getting more and more unpleasant. The machines were so loud the company doctor had informed him last week he was losing his hearing in the sound frequencies most necessary for conversation. What was worse, relationships among his coworkers were deteriorating. Management was pressing for increased productivity, and the only way for him to produce more was to make faster trips between the supply room and his workstation. Other workers were doing the same thing, though, and they were all getting in each other's way. If his workstation could be closer to the supply room, at least one problem would be solved.

Sue was equally hassled. Her firm had just moved into a new office without interior walls. It was supposed to reduce maintenance costs and increase ease of communication to have everyone in one large room. She couldn't stand it, though. She had to reprimand a secretary yesterday and there was no place to do it except at her desk where everyone else could hear the conversation. Her new workstation was attractive enough, and bristled with the latest in computer technology. Everything was efficient. The computer word processing program eliminated much of the time spent in rewriting. Company records were carefully filed in a database, and her computer could easily "talk" to those in various branch offices. Still, Sue seemed to be more tired lately. Her eyes hurt from staring at the computer screen, and she wondered if the pain in her back wasn't simply from spending too much time hunched over the keyboard. To make matters worse, her doctor had called today with unfavorable news on some lab tests, and it seemed as if everyone in the office heard at least her end of the conversation. Noise was a problem for her, too. She worked hard on a marketing report due today, but it took much longer than necessary because of all the distraction from phones ringing and everybody else talking. The chatter of the computer printer 10 feet from her desk didn't help much either.

To get away from these headaches, Harry and Sue decided to go camping in the state park in the next county. After all, the convenience of the park was one reason they had chosen Rockport as a home. Arriving at the park entrance, the ranger informed them they were just in time to get one of the last two campsites available. They felt fortunate, though when they pulled into the campground it was discouraging to see that one of the remaining campsites was too muddy to

pitch a tent on and the other was next to a motorcycle gang having a loud party. This was getting away from it all?

Have you had experiences similar to those described above? Unfortunately, they occur more often than we would like. Environmental psychologists and others concerned about these kinds of situations have asked whether or not environmental design and management can make a difference in our lives of work and play. Are there ways of designing the factory, the office, and the leisure setting so that undesired effects are minimized and desired results are maximized? Admittedly, work and leisure seem worlds apart—unlikely companions in a chapter you might think. As we will soon see, however, the difference between work and leisure is often neither the activity we engage in nor the setting in which it takes place, but rather our psychological motivation for performing those behaviors and the experiences we obtain. As with the previous chapter, our discussion will be organized around the setting itself—first workplaces, then recreation areas and playgrounds.

WORK ENVIRONMENTS

In previous chapters we have discussed the effects of noise, temperature, and territorial identification on behavior, and in Chapter 11 we saw how such factors as lighting, color, and furnishings need to be considered in environmental design. In the present section we will examine how these and other components of the environment can be incorporated into the pro-

cess of designing the work environment, which is sometimes called the **workspace**. For those who wish to study the design of the work environment more thoroughly, detailed reviews of previous research exist elsewhere (Becker, 1981; Sundstrom, 1986, 1987; Wineman, 1982). For our purposes, we will highlight some of the important findings of this research.

A Brief History of Workplace Design

Before the Industrial Revolution, nonfarm work was typically done in small spaces, often in the craftsperson's or businessperson's home. Of course, even in early times, some specialized products required the labor of several persons, and the specialized work places sometimes took a shape dictated by their product. Ropewalks, for example, were buildings in which rope was woven. Before the introduction of modern coiling machines, the maximum length of a rope was dictated by the length of the building in which it was manufactured (Kostof, 1987). Hence, ropewalks were simple, but extremely long (one built in Charlestown, Massachusetts, in 1838 was a quarter of a mile long). Early factories were limited by their reliance on water for power and the sun for lighting. Because they required swiftly flowing streams, often they had to be constructed on remote sites far from the populated (but flat) coastal strip. Mill towns became self-contained communities, often wholly owned by one partnership (Kostof, 1987). The reliance on water to power these early mills and factories also dictated their shape. A water wheel outside the factory turned a long shaft that extended inside the building. Off this shaft ran a series of belts that powered the factory's machinery. Thus, the technology of the power source dictated a long buiding, and the need for sunlight limited building width to about 60 feet, or 18 meters (Sundstrom, 1986).

Working conditions in early American factories were miserable, a situation which persisted through the early 1900s. At that time several factors combined to cause rapid improvements (Sundstrom, 1986). First, a tragic disregard for human safety led the popular press to pressure for reforms that eventually led to a variety of laws to protect worker health and safety. Second, there was a growing belief that comfortable working conditions would lead to increased productivity. Finally, managers began to discover Frederick Taylor's (1911)

scientific management. As we mentioned briefly in Chapter 11, this was a management philosophy that emphasized the importance of optimal pay, the analysis of work activities to improve efficiency, and the development of work environments to support efficient movement.

Like the factory, the office building was restricted by construction technology. Stone construction and the absence of elevators meant that buildings could not be more than six to ten stories high, and the need for adequate lighting through windows dictated a fairly narrow building. Two developments in technology changed both the factory and the office. First, iron and later structural steel, combined with concrete, made it possible to span larger spaces as well as to build higher and higher. (With stone construction, walls had to be so thick at the base for support of upper floors that tall buildings were impractical.) Second, commercially available electricity allowed for more extensive indoor lighting and elevators in tall buildings, as well as the ability to separate manufacturing machines from a central power shaft. It then became technologically possible to set up a factory or office in an almost infinite number of ways (Sundstrom, 1986).

Human Factors and the Work Environment

Can careful design of the tools, machines, and workspaces in an office or factory increase productivity? If so, managers and others would want to take advantage of design principles for this purpose. Indeed, interst in work-related design considerations has a long history, and easily predates the establishment of the field of environmental psychology. Historically, the work environment has been the domain of **human factors** psychologists (human factors psychology is also sometimes referred to as engineering psychology, or, especially in Europe, as ergonomics). Many of the early efforts of these investigators and practitioners focused not on the ambient work environment, but on specific tools or procedures such as link analysis that might increase worker efficiency. For example, Taylor (1911) demonstrated dramatic improvements in efficiency when steel workers were issued the optimal-sized shovel for each shoveling task—smaller ones for heavy iron ore and larger ones for ashes (Figure 13–1 shows an example of particularly poor human factors design). More recent human factors research emphasizes either the interactions between humans and machines (computers, aircraft, nuclear power plants), the workstation, or ambient environmental conditions such as noise, light, and temperature which we have discussed throughout much of this text.

We have already discussed one of the most dramatic incidents of poor human factors design in Chapter 7. On March 29, 1979, an accident at Three Mile Island Unit 2 resulted in a crisis that lasted for several days, costing the plant owner over $1 billion and subjecting people living nearby to persistent stress. During the incident operators searched frantically to discover what was wrong with the reactor. Of the 1600 windows and gauges in the control room (some 200 of which were flashing), several critical displays were in out-of-the-way locations, hidden by maintenance tags, or absent altogether. You may recognize this as a situation of information overload, discussed in Chapter 4. Resulting investigations revealed that many of the human errors that contributed to the accident resulted from grossly inadequate control room design (Smither, 1988).

Communicating with Machines Perhaps you agree that features of a person's immediate work environment such as the displays and controls in an airplane's cockpit can greatly affect safety and health. In general, human factors psychologists focus on the **human–machine system**, perhaps most easily understood as a communications cycle. The human being (pilot, driver, operator) makes decisions and communicates them to a machine through **controls** such as knobs, levers, steering wheels, or pedals (see Figure 13–2). As it functions, the machine communicates to the human operator through **displays** such as dials, gauges, or warning lights. No doubt all of this seems simple enough, and it is unlikely that any engineer would knowingly design a machine that was impossible to control. The problem is making the human–machine system as efficient and error free as possible.

Note the display-control pair in Figure 13–3A. You might think of the display as a pressure gauge and the knob as the control that increases the pressure in some fictional machine. Which direction would you turn the knob in 13–3A to increase the machine pressure? Which direction would you turn the knob in 13–3C? Although most people would turn the knob clockwise in the first two instances, many would switch to counterclockwise for Figure 13–3C. We are actually discussing **population stereotypes**, learned expectations about the relationships between controls, displays, and their movements. In 13–3C, one population stereotype conflicts with another. According to the clockwise-for-increase principle, people will turn a knob clockwise to increase the value on the display. On the other hand, Warrick's principle states that a pointer on a display will be

Figure 13–1 A student design for an air-cooled coffee cup.

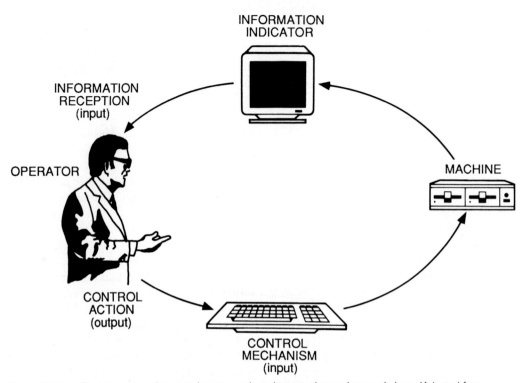

Figure 13-2 The interactions between humans and machines in the modern workplace. (Adapted from Chapanis, A. (1976). Engineering Psychology. In M. D. Dunnette (Ed.), *Handbook of industrial and organizational psychology*. Reprinted by permission of John Wiley & Sons, New York.)

expected to move in the same direction as that part of the control nearest it. You may not have considered these before, but perhaps we can suggest a more familiar example of conflicting stereotypes. What direciton do you turn the knob on your stereo to turn up the volume? What direction do you turn a water faucet in order to turn on or increase the water flow? These problems may be trivial enough, but consider the implications of a mistaken control movement by a pilot traveling in a military jet at several times the speed of sound!

The Electronic Office Another impetus to increasing interest in human factors and workplace design is less dramatic, but perhaps more important. Modern advances in computer technology have already made dramatic changes in the workplace (e.g., Grandjean, Hunting, & Piderman, 1983; Kleeman, 1982). At many colleges both faculty and students make extensive use of computer word processing programs for writing and revising memos, papers, and book chapters. Mail can be electronically shipped to destinations across campus or across the world, and your academic records may reside in a university database that allows your advisor to instantly review your transcript. Soon trips to the business office, registrar, or filing cabinet will be unnecessary, and we will have the ''convenience'' (and misfortune) of never having to leave our desks. Certainly as the time we spend using computer terminals increases, so does the importance of carefully designed seating (Shute, & Starr, 1984), keyboards, and computer screens (see box, page 440).

Workflow The principle of **workflow** (originally called straight-line flow of work) is based

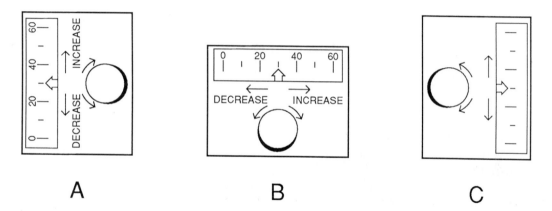

A　　　　　　　　**B**　　　　　　　　**C**

Figure 13–3　Warrick's principle. If your turn the knob in 13–3A to the right to increase "pressure," and the knob in 13–3B to the right for an increase, which direction do you turn the knob in 13–3C? (Adapted from Saunders, M. S., & McCormick, E. J., 1987. *Human factors in engineering and design.* New York: McGraw-Hill Book Company.)

on the idea that the layout of a factory or office should provide for the shortest possible distance between workstations along which the work moves (e.g., Hicks, 1977). For example, an assembly line should be arranged so that workers do not have to spend long amounts of time walking from the point where they finish their assignment on a product back to the point where they start the assignment on the next item. Also, space for supplies should be provided as close to the assembly line as possible so that workers do not have to spend excessive time moving from the supply area to the assembly area. Similarly, an office should be arranged so that related departments are close to each other. If paperwork moves from office A to office B to office C to office D, in that order, the offices should not be arranged with A on the tenth floor, C next to it, B on the fifth floor, and D on the sixth floor. Rather, the offices should be located in the order that the paperwork actually flows.

On a smaller scale, similar considerations apply to the placement of the components of a **workstation** (the area of a factory or office assigned to an individual), such as tables, computer equipment, or even the knobs and dials on a control console. **Link analysis** is a term applied to the systematic investigation of the number of times a movement is made to adjust a control or read a display. Proper positioning of workspace elements will minimize the distances required for common or sensitive activities to reduce errors and fatigue (Sanders & McCormick, 1987).

Ambient Work Environments

As a student of environmental psychology you will not be surprised to learn that physical comfort and safety also affect productivity in work environments. Prior to the twentieth century, choking fumes and deafening noise, for example, were considered part of the normal manufacturing process. Concern for the safety and health of workers, along with studies showing that productivity and accident rates could be influenced by physical working conditions, has led to standards for lighting, ventilation, noise, and so on which not only provide for greater safety, but also avoid conditions that reduce productivity. In general, this means providing the appropriate amount of lighting, noise reduction, ventilation, organization of space, and other physical considerations as necessary. The effects of these various physical

The Electronic Office:
Panacea or Curse?

Perhaps the most important changes in the "office of the future" will result from the continued development of inexpensive microcomputers. Whether this technology is a blessing or a curse may depend in part upon our ability to exploit the computer's strengths and adjust to its demands. With the proliferation of **video display terminals (VDTs)** workers began complaining of eyestrain, headaches, back pain, and fatigue. Others suggest that terminals may emit certain types of electromagnetic radiation with as yet undocumented effects on human health (Kirkpatrick, 1988).

These concerns have sparked a number of investigations. Unfortunately, not all researchers have been able to control for task characteristics, office and workstation design, gender, pay, and benefits (Starr, Thompson, & Shute, 1982). In fact, several studies that have held these confounding variables constant have concluded that VDTs are not themselves responsible for most of the health complaints attributed to them. For example, in a comparison between directory assistance operators who used good quality VDTs and a similar group working from paper documents, Starr et al. (1982) found no evidence that the terminals were more likely to lead to eyestrain or decreases in comfort or morale. Although several studies have concluded that people read text from VDT screens more slowly (e.g., Gould & Grischowsky, 1984), Gould et al. (1987) found reading rates similar to those for good quality paper printing when displays were designed to combine dark letters on a light background, a high quality display terminal, and specially adjusted lettering.

This is not to say that VDTs are necessarily benign. Glare from lights and windows is likely to cause discomfort if not systematically avoided, and careful location of the display along with occasional breaks to rest the eyes are recommended (Garcia & Wierwille, 1985; Rose, 1987). Furthermore, job-related stress may occur in part because of the indirect effects of VDTs on jobs. Computers reduce the need for workers to move around the office to accomplish their jobs and this, combined with the possibility of computer monitoring of a worker's progress, may usher in an era of greater workloads, fewer breaks, and less autonomy (Sundstrom, 1986).

On the other hand, the same technology is capable of allowing exciting new freedoms to workers. For some, a trip to the "office" involves walking into a different room in the house. Communications networks now allow workers to perform many of their chores from home-based work stations, an **electronic cottage** (Toffler, 1980). As Sundstrom (1986, 1987) notes, such an arrangement might eliminate much of the cost and inconvenience of commuting, but such a decentralized work force will put new demands on supervisors and weaken some of the organization's control. Indeed, the role of the employee may change to that of a contractor, and the office building may become essentially a conference center for those meetings that require face-to-face encounters rather than telephone or video conferences.

conditions on job performance may be conceptualized within the framework of the environment–behavior theories discussed in Chapter 4. For example, noise or poor ventilation can increase arousal, narrow attention, or elevate stress to such an extent that performance is impaired. Considerations of these psychological mediators, then, is important in designing the work environment (For a discussion of an office environment that is no doubt familiar to you, see the box on page 442).

Personalization   There are a number of reasons for people's desires to personalize and decorate spaces in which they work. It is one's way of making the space his or her "own." By placing objects or decorating walls in certain ways we can identify spaces as being ours and project some of our feelings, goals, and values. In addition, decoration of spaces makes them more pleasant. Research has indicated that pleasant or attractive rooms make people feel better than do stark or ugly rooms (Campbell, 1979; Maslow & Mintz, 1956). Another factor that may affect people's moods at work is the provision of music (see box, page 444).

What are the effects of a pleasant workspace? Is it reasonable to assume that if attractive work areas make people feel better, such environments will help to increase your efficiency or the efficiency of your instructors? Research has shown that decorated spaces make people feel more comfortable than do undecorated spaces (Campbell, 1979), and that good moods associated with pleasant environments seem to increase people's willingness to help each other (Sherrod et al., 1977). Yet we can also guess that for some kinds of work, the positive feeling associated with decorated space may also be disruptive. People feel more like talking to one another in pleasant settings (Russell & Mehrabian, 1978), and to the extent that socializing in the office detracts from effective or efficient working, pleasantness can be a problem. Research has also suggested that room decorations may be distracting (e.g.,

Baum & Davis, 1976), but whether this is a problem depends on how a setting is perceived (Worchel & Teddlie, 1976).

Territoriality and Status in the Work Environment   We discussed territoriality in Chapter 8 as it relates to many of our relationships with the environment. Some researchers also believe that territories are important in work environments. Often the concept relates to assignment of a specific area or machine to a worker, and is termed **assigned workspace** (Sundstrom, 1986). It is often believed, for example, that if a large machine in a factory is assigned to one worker, that worker will take better care of it than if all workers roam from machine to machine. The same concept is often called the *fixed workspace*. Sundstrom (1986) suggests that the right to treat a workspace as a territory might lead to more personal attachment to it, more perceived control over it, and thus more of a sense of responsibility for it and more signs of personalization of the workspace. Whether workers in fact prefer clearly defined territories and whether territories improve job satisfaction or productivity is open to question. Most likely, territories become more important to workers the higher the rank they have in the organization. At higher ranks, territories may become symbols of status (Sundstrom, 1986).

Status symbols in the office or factory may be important in several ways. For example, they communicate status and power to others, they compensate employees as a nonmonetary benefit, and they serve as props or tools (such as larger desks, filing cabinets, computer terminals), which the worker is privileged to use on the job (Sundstrom, 1986). In addition to furnishings, such as desks and size and comfort of chairs, typical status symbols include amount of floorspace, the capacity to regulate privacy and accessibility (e.g., through an enclosed office), and the right to personalize the workspace. One large firm, for example, provides carpeting, a bottled water dispenser, and plants

The Faculty Office

One environment ripe for investigation, and one with which you are no doubt familiar, is the university faculty office. Have you strolled down a hallway of professors' offices and speculated on the character of their occupants? Is a neat office the sign of a neat mind, or is it sterile and cold? Do decorations or living things make workplaces more hospitable? Does a particular office convey a sense of distance or welcome? Research on faculty offices has centered on three issues: the placement of the desk, aesthetics, and overall neatness.

Placement

Much of the interest in desk placement probably began with a survey of 10 London firms conducted by Joiner (1971). He found that higher status individuals tended to place their desk between themselves and the door rather than against a side or back wall. This finding led Zweigenhaft (1976) to hypothesize that faculty who placed their desks between themselves and visiting students would be using the desk as a physical barrier (perhaps inadvertently) and would be perceived as more behaviorally distant than those who used a more barrier-free arrangement. Consistent with Joiner's observations regarding status, Zweigenhaft's survey found that senior faculty (full professors and associate professors) were more likely to use the closed desk (desk-between) arrangement. Furthermore, those faculty members who used an open desk arrangement, in which the desk did not separate the faculty person and his or her visitors, were more likely to be rated positively by students. Other researchers have also observed open desk placement to be associated with more positive student feelings (Morrow & McElroy, 1981) and also with positive evaluations by other faculty members (McElroy & Morrow, 1983). On the other hand, at least one attempt at replication failed to confirm the effect of desk placement (Campbell & Herren, 1978), and another found only a weak effect (Campbell, 1979). Perhaps a study by Hensley (1982) clarifies the situation. Hensley hypothesized that although there is a relationship between faculty desk placement and student evaluations, instead of the office arrangement causing more positive evaluations, *both* the evaluations of the teacher and the desk placement result from the influence of a third variable, the professor's formality or attitude toward education. Thus, a formal teacher is also likely to choose a more formal office, and an informal teacher is likely to have an open, informal desk arrangement. Hensley's results support his contention in that more traditional educational philosophies were more often associated with a closed desk arrangement. In addition, the desk arrangement was also affected by the number of advisees a professor had. Perhaps because a more open desk arrangement facilitates activities such as reviewing records or completing schedules, even traditional professors with a large number of advisees tended to adopt an open desk placement.

Aesthetics and Neatness

Campbell (1979) used slide photographs to investigate the effects of the

Figure 13–4 What would be the effect of this messy faculty office on students' perceptions of its occupant?

presence or absence of living things (four potted plants and two aquariums with fish) or art objects (four wall posters and a macramé hanging). Students associated these decorations with feelings of welcome and comfort, and expected the professor to be friendly and unhurried. Overall neatness may be even more important than decorations (see Figure 13–4). Very messy offices make the occupant appear to be busy and rushed, and to make visitors report that they would be less comfortable and welcome (Campbell, 1979; McElroy & Morrow, 1983; Morrow & McElroy, 1981). Morrow and McElroy also introduced an intermediate level of tidiness they refer to as "organized stacks." Interestingly, the organized stacks level of tidiness was evaluated as significantly more friendly, welcoming, and comfortable than either the messy or extremely neat office conditions (McElroy & Morrow, 1983; Morrow & McElroy, 1981).

as one moves up the corporate ladder. Apparently, the more one can attach status to the office space, the more satisfied one is with the job (Konar et al., 1982).

Designing the Office Landscape

We have mentioned that the use of structural steel in buildings has allowed architects to design larger and larger open spaces. With previous construction methods, the need for support walls required a building to be separated into smaller rooms. Accordingly, a relatively small number of workers shared an office. Typically, a manager or executive would have a totally private office, and several clerical workers would share an adjoining space. Such office designs are still common today, but there is also an alternative permitted by a large open

space. To facilitate workflow, for example, work stations for 100 or more clerks could be put in the same large room, with supervisors' offices along the sides of the large room. With the growth of the human relations movement in the 1950s, more open communication between workers and managers was encouraged, employees were allowed and even encouraged to participate in decision-making, and barriers of status and authority became less prominent. These developments encouraged what is now known as the **landscaped** or **open office** (Figure 13–5A and B). This concept probably originated in Germany with work by the Schnelle brothers and their Quickborner Team consulting firm (Sundstrom, 1986). Basically, the idea involves arranging desks, filing cabinets, and other office furniture in such a manner as to make maximum use of the large open

. . . .

Music To Work By

Although the noise from office machines and conversations is usually found to be intrusive in the work environment, there is some belief that music may actually improve the work setting, though the evidence is mixed. Sundstrom (1986) reviews the evidence on music in the workplace and report that although much of the research is the private, inaccessible property of firms that sell music systems to businesses, published research may or may not support the idea that music enhances the work environment. At one time it was actually thought that singing and/or listening to music with a steady, somewhat upbeat rhythm improved productivity. Later it was felt that pleasant music made employees cheerful and the environment enjoyable. Research indicates that in factories, music may or may not slightly improve productivity, but employees like it anyway. In offices, music may facilitate vigilance tasks (e.g., where an employee must monitor a screen), though it can be distracting for some. Employees often report that music helps provide a pleasant atmosphere, and the mere belief that it does so probably ensures that it will always be found in some work settings.

. . . .

space but still provide for efficient workflow. The office landscape design typically places a supervisor very near workers and arranges work areas close together or far apart so that workflow and communication between related areas is unimpeded by myriad enclosed offices. In some schemes, portable screens are used to set areas off from others, or shelving and filing cabinets may accomplish the same purpose. As you might expect, such an office design has a number of advantages, but also carries with it a number of disadvantages (e.g., Becker et al., 1983; Brooks & Kaplan, 1972; Oldham, 1988; Oldham & Brass, 1979; Sundstrom, 1986). Let us examine some of these separately.

Advantages of the Open Plan Office   We have already mentioned one advantage of the open office: It provides for a more efficient flow of work and communication. In addition, it often costs less because there are no internal walls to construct, and lighting and ductwork can be shared by several workspaces. Maintenance costs may also be reduced due to less painting and faster cleaning of work areas, and more people can be accommodated in the same interior space without walls. Moreover, it is easier to make changes in the design of the office when new jobs are added or eliminated or the number of people working on a project changes, because there are no fixed walls to move or add to change spatial arrangements. Finally, the open office permits easier supervision of workers. That is, a supervisor can see all workers from his or her desk without having to walk through several offices. Furthermore, there is evidence for social facilitation in non-private offices (Block & Stokes, 1989). A number of researchers have demonstrated that the mere presence of others improves performance, at least for simple tasks.

Disadvantages of the Open Plan Office   Typically, changes in any environment cannot be made without trade-offs, and open offices are no exception. For all the potential advantages of the open office, it carries disadvantages that fall into two major categories: increased noise and distraction and lack of adequate privacy. When offices are separated by walls,

Figure 13–5   Traditional (on the left) versus open office design. (Courtesy of John Rundell)

the noise from typewriters, phones, and duplicating machines in one area seldom penetrates into the next office. With the open office plan, however, the noises may be very distracting to those in neighboring workstations. Similarly, conversation travels, and as we saw in Chapter 5, noise that is interpretable as conversation is quite distracting. Indeed, although open offices may facilitate social conversations, there is little evidence that organizationally relevant communication improves (Wineman, 1982). Movement of people as they walk about doing assigned tasks is also more noticeable in the open office plan, and adds still another source of distraction. Solutions to the problem of noise and distraction include office machinery designed to be quieter, and the use of portable barriers (partitions, shelving, cabinets) to help screen out the distraction.

Loss of privacy is also very noticeable in open offices. Personal conversations are easily overheard and communication between supervisors and workers becomes more difficult to keep confidential. Just as open offices facilitate supervision, so they also reduce privacy. Every move a worker makes is open for public view.

Phone calls with family members are overheard. Errors and embarrassing behavior are there for all to see, and personalizing the workspace with artwork or mementos may be discouraged. As with noise and distraction, use of portable barriers may help solve the privacy problem in the open office, but these barriers cannot provide the privacy of an enclosed, individual office (e.g., Hundert & Greenfield, 1969; Pile, 1978; Sundstrom, 1986). Employees who move from a conventional office to an open arrangement may complain of loss of privacy and suffer from reduced job satisfaction (Oldham & Brass, 1979). More recently, Oldham (1988) demonstrated the therapeutic effects of moving employees from an open office to either a partitioned office or a lower-density open plan office that allowed more space per employee.

In sum, open office plans provide both advantages and disadvantages. The increased opportunity for communication may facilitate some flow of work, but also increases distraction and reduces privacy. Depending on the functions to be accomplished in a given office, the disadvantages may outweigh the advantages (see also Becker et al., 1983; Block & Stokes, 1989; Goodrich, 1982; Marans & Speckelmeyer, 1982; Sundstrom, Herbert, & Brown, 1982; Wineman, 1982).

Job Satisfaction and the Work Environment

In addition to productivity, managers and others have become concerned that design of the work environment can influence job satisfaction. Although most research suggests that job satisfaction does *not* directly increase productivity (e.g., Landy, 1989), it is sometimes believed that the more satisfied the worker, the better an employee he or she makes in terms of such factors as loyalty, absenteeism, and turnover. In general, employees do list physical conditions as important for job satisfaction, although the physical environment is not as important in this regard as such factors as job security, pay, and friendly coworkers (e.g., Herzberg, Mausner, & Syderman, 1959). One influential theory suggests that an adequate work environment does not substantially enhance job satisfaction, but a substandard environment definitely leads to *dissatisfaction* (Herzberg, 1966; Herzberg, Mausner, & Snyderman, 1959). Whatever the case, it is clear that appropriate working condi-

tions are important considerations in the design process (Sundstrom, 1986).

Summary of Design in the Work Environment

Technological developments permit great flexibility in designing work environments. Central to workspace design are the issues of: (1) productivity, especially as it relates to workflow, safety, and health; and (2) job satisfaction. In general, work environments can be designed to maximize productivity through facilitating workflow and providing safe and healthy working conditions. Job satisfaction is related to quality of the work environment, although other factors are usually more important. Open offices may save on construction and maintenance costs, facilitate communication and workflow, increase flexibility of floorspace, and enhance supervision. On the other hand, open offices increase noise and other distractions and reduce privacy. Finally, the ability to treat a workspace as a territory and to personalize it serves as a form of status and may increase job satisfaction, although the issue is likely more relevant at higher ranks in the organization.

LEISURE AND RECREATION ENVIRONMENTS

Before beginning our discussion of leisure environments, perhaps it would be useful for you to reflect on your personal understanding of the term. Of course all of us have an intuitive idea of what leisure is, but there seems to be general agreement among researchers that leisure will be experienced when an individual is intrinsically motivated and perceives **freedom of choice** (Neulinger, 1981; Tinsley & Tinsley, 1986). **Intrinsic motivation** is a popular term

that has resisted precise definition by psychologists but is basically the degree to which a behavior leads to personal satisfaction and enjoyment (Smither, 1988). Perhaps the term is best understood by contrasting it with **extrinsic motivation** that is given to us by some external agent, such as pay, gifts, or praise. Several researchers have examined the importance of these dimensions. For example, Iso-Ahola (1986) found that students were more likely to perceive an activity as leisure if their participation had been voluntary, the rewards were intrinsic, and if the activity was not work-related. Similarly, Shaw (1985) found that freedom of choice, intrinsic motivation, enjoyment, and relaxation were associated with day-to-day periods of leisure.

Of course a simple way of summarizing all of this discussion might be to say that leisure means "being able to do what you want to do," but notice also that our definition emphasizes leisure as an **experience** rather than as an activity (e.g., Gunter, 1987; Tinsley & Tinsley, 1986). According to this view, different activities may lead to similar psychological experiences, or conversely, the same activity might yield different experiences depending upon the personality of the participant, the setting, or other factors. For example, the psychological experience of risk-taking might be met by mountain climbing or by downhill skiing. On the other hand, the experience of skiing for one person might focus on speed, for another the accomplishment of good form, and for a third individual, an opportunity to enjoy the company of a loved one. Furthermore, several very different environments might support quite similar kinds of leisure experiences. For example, with a few small changes in decor (and somewhat larger changes in attitude), an office can support a lively holiday party. Thus, the leisure experience is jointly determined by environmental, social, and **individual difference variables** (see Figure 13–6). This observation is quite consistent with the concept of **behavior settings** (Barker, 1987) discussed in Chapter 4.

What sorts of rewards or benefits do we receive from different activities? One recent classification of the psychological benefits of leisure participation (Tinsley & Johnson, 1984) names nine categories:

Figure 13–6 Natural environments provide a wealth of leisure experiences and opportunities.

Intellectual stimulation (e.g., working crossword puzzles or watching television).

Catharsis (e.g., playing volleyball, jogging, or swimming).

Expressive compensation (e.g., canoeing, camping, and hiking).

Hedonistic companionship (e.g., drinking and socializing).

Supportive companionship (e.g., picnicking or visiting friends and relatives.

Secure solitude (e.g., collecting stamps or collecting autographs).

Routine, temporary indulgence (e.g., shooting pool or playing cards).

Moderate security (e.g., bowling or playing guitar).

Expressive aestheticism (e.g., playing chess, woodworking, or painting).

The magnitude of the leisure experience probably varies from time to time and between individuals. For some, the feeling of freedom, increased sensitivity, and decreased awareness of the passage of time are profound. Indeed, several researchers suggest that the leisure state can be similar to mystic or peak experiences (Mannell, 1980; Tinsley & Tinsley, 1986).

Clearly, our needs for recreational involvement differ at different points in our lives, so that the types of recreation environments we require change over time as well. We probably engage to some extent in each type of recreational involvement at each point in the life cycle, although for certain periods some needs become more "primary." Children need recreation areas in or close to home in which they can play and socialize with other children. Playgrounds have a role in this regard, as do back yards and play areas in an apartment or home. For young adults it is essential to have a place to meet others, to form social groups, and

to engage in courtship behaviors. Since North Americans are waiting longer to marry and since divorce is more common than was the case in earlier years, such recreation environments are, of course, important. But many of us do marry and have families—in fact, the statistical norm is still to be married and to raise a family. Families center most of their recreational activities around their community, and children join Little League, Cub Scouts, Brownies, etc. Mothers and fathers join local clubs and fitness programs, and use neighboring pools and tennis courts, along with children. In the "middle years" (for parents), children become relatively independent, and parents often need more recreational activities during this period, since they have more leisure time. Finally, during retirement, needs for specialized recreational facilities (e.g., senior centers, golden age clubs) become evident.

Given the various types of recreational involvement at different points in the life cycle, and the fact that personality (e.g., Driver & Knopf, 1977) and socioeconomic status also affect one's type of recreational involvement (Marans, 1972), a very wide variety of environmental settings must be designed and made available to allow satisfaction of our needs. In addition to aspects of individuals (e.g., age, personality) affecting their use of recreation environments, the availability of recreational facilities in an area determines to some extent how we recreate (Marans, 1972). The presence of community swimming, tennis, and boating facilities increases the frequency of these recreational activities (Marans, 1972), and more people will probably spend their time skiing if there are ski slopes nearby. For some activities (e.g., water for swimming), an environmental setting is a necessary and sufficient condition to afford a particular recreational goal. For other recreational activities, the environmental setting may vary (e.g., we can listen to music at home, in a car, in a concert hall, or at an outdoor amphitheater). In an overall sense, variation in recreational behavior may be viewed as an interaction between individual

People–Plant Interaction:
The Garden as a Recreational Environment

Even for city residents, the impact of the natural environment can be striking. In this instance, "nature" can be as close as the nearest tree, windowbox, or garden plot. As we noted in Chapters 2, 11, and 12, simply having an opportunity to observe a natural scene through a window can have beneficial effects on hospital patients (e.g., Ulrich, 1984; Verderber, 1986). In a survey of public housing residents, Rachel Kaplan (1985) determined the availability of views of natural features such as trees, large open spaces, and garden plots. Despite the popularity of expansive lawns in many apartment complex designs, Kaplan's data suggest that open "greenbelt" space is not the most important component of nature. Instead, the best predictors of residential satisfaction were small-scale pieces of nature—a view of some trees or a place to take a walk.

Gardening is a common form of recreation, and one which may have important environmental and psychological benefits for both rural and urban residents (Kaplan, 1983, 1985; Kaplan & Kaplan, 1987; Lewis, 1973). For example, Lewis (1973) researched the effects of providing recreational gardening environments for residents of run-down urban areas in New York City. The New York City Housing Authority sponsored recreational gardening opportunities, in which any group of tenants wanting to garden could apply to the Authority, which gave them a garden site close to their project, turned over the ground for them, and also provided money for seeds and plants and a gardening manual.

Providing garden plots for residents had many beneficial effects. Lewis (1973) reports that recreational gardening by inner-city residents led to pride in acomplishment, to increased self-esteem, and to reduced vandalism outside as well as inside the buildings. Social factors are important as well. In Kaplan's (1985) study cited above, residents who had adequate access to gardens found their neighbors to be more friendly and felt a stronger sense of community. Gardens add social cohesion in the community by providing a meeting place and a chance for people to work together toward a common end (Lewis, 1973). Gardening may also increase the proprietary sense of territoriality, and thus make nearby space more apt to be defended and defensible (see Chapter 8).

Why is recreational gardening beneficial? In addition to their natural beauty and potential as a food source, gardens may provide a restorative experience that allows people to recover from the stresses of day-to-day life (Kaplan & Kaplan, 1987). The chance to be outside, to labor, to see things grow, and to experience a diversion from the routine involves many of the same benefits observed in wilderness recreation (R. Kaplan, 1984; Talbot & Kaplan, 1986).

differences in people (e.g., their recreational wants and needs) and available recreation environments. Recreational behavior is also affected to some extent by the times (e.g., snow boarding, windsurfing, or water "adventure" parks in the 1980s); it reflects to some extent the current perception of the "good life." Unfortunately, however, at present there is no encompassing theory or model of recreation behavior or a model that can accurately explain or predict the types of recreational facilities people want.

The range of leisure environments is almost endless. Some of us recreate in bars, some on golf courses, some in senior centers, some in gardens (see box, page 449), and others in wilderness areas of parks. Many of us spend our leisure time walking in shopping malls, people watching, window shopping, and stopping for an occasional slice of pizza, a chocolate chip cookie, or a drink. Some have even moved to "planned recreational communities," which offer tennis courts, swimming pools, golf courses, and even boating and skiing in certain cases. Recognizing the variety of settings, we will restrict ourselves to two types of environments in which recreation activities are particularly important—natural areas and playgrounds.

Wilderness and Other Natural Areas

One recreational setting that has received a relatively large amount of research attention is publicly-owned natural land, such as forests, deserts, and other natural and wilderness areas. (See box, page 451, for an account of changes in North American attitudes toward the wilderness.) One factor underlying this research interest is the fact that many of our national parks and other similar facilities are overcrowded, and environmental planners need to know how to deal with the demand. Clearly, more and more of us are trying to "get away from it all"—to spend some of our time in the wilderness, preferably not in a crowd.

Environmental managers have historically been trained in professions such as forestry, wildlife and fisheries biology, or range management. Especially since World War II there has been a dramatic increase in the number of citizens who desire to maintain options for uses such as recreation, aesthetic appreciation, or wildlife observation not associated with hunting

or fishing. Managers trained in the natural sciences to support the sustained yield of commodities such as timber now find themselves managing for the enjoyment of recreationists (Pitt & Zube, 1987).

How can we add additional capacity to national parks and wilderness areas to accommodate more visitors without changing the characteristics of the natural setting that attracts people to them? Also, how do current and projected levels of crowding affect user satisfaction? Recreational use often competes with other economically important resource capabilities (timber cutting or mining, for example), and may cause long-term damage to fragile natural environments (Pitt & Zube, 1987). Many of these questions have traditionally been the domain of economists; however, recreation is a resource use characterized by the behavior and experiences of people, and psychologists are increasingly involved in forest recreation research. The ability of an area to absorb use is termed its **carrying capacity**. In the case of recreation, carrying capacity may include the resistance of an area to ecological damage, the availably of facilities such as campsites, and social carrying capacity, which refers to the desired level of social interaction (Pitt & Zube, 1987). As illustrated in Figure 13–9, the recreation production process can be seen as one of attempting to meet human recreational demands by managing the basic resources of a given site (Driver & Brown, 1983).

Perhaps an example will highlight some of these issues. Let's begin with a question: How much wilderness does our society require? Many nations have created wilderness areas by legislative action and are considering establishing more. The acreage encompassed by national parks and monuments, national forests, and other generally natural areas far exceeds that which has been officially designated "wilderness." Should more land be reserved as "true" wilderness and be lost forever for lumbering, resort development, or even campground construction? Will as *many* different people enjoy a

Historic North American Attitudes Toward The Wilderness

It seems that the commonly held attitudes of Americans toward wilderness landscapes have changed since the colonial period (Burdick, 1980; Jackson, 1975; Nash, 1982; Turner, 1920). Most of the eastern United States was, of course, forest land before European settlers began clearing it for farming. Roderick Nash (1982) compares the environmental attitudes of the Puritan settlers of New England and those held by the Colonialists of the mid-Atlantic and southern states. The Puritans found themselves in a threatening environment of harsh winters and poor soil. The combination of this environment and their conservative religious tradition led the Puritans to view the wilderness around them as a hostile, threatening landscape inhabited by servants of the devil (referring to Native Americans). Thus, the Puritans saw themselves as envoys from God whose mission was to pacify the wilderness and break the power of evil. As their already poor farm land was exhausted by ill-advised farming practices, the descendants (both genetic and intellectual) of the Puritans moved westward, clearing forests and fencing prairies in an effort to conquer the vast American wilderness.

Although their principal attitude toward nature was also utilitarian, the settlers of the Middle Atlantic colonies benefited from a more hospitable environment and expressed a quite different attitude toward nature (Nash, 1982). Many were of the Anglican faith, and most were better educated, wealthier, and more likely to study and appreciate natural phenomena than were the Puritans. Virginian Thomas Jefferson may epitomize the attitudes of the late eighteenth-century gentleman/naturalist (Figure 13–7). He believed that nature could be better managed through understanding rather than conquest (Burdick, 1980), and as president, Jefferson charged the Lewis and Clark expedition of 1803 with providing detailed reports of natural phenomena. Jefferson and his contemporaries shared a somewhat more benign attitude toward nature than the Puritans of New England, but the vistas they most appreciated were still the pastoral, rural landscapes of farms and country lanes, not the true wilderness. Yet in Jefferson, and those like him, we can see the beginnings of an attitude of conservation and curiosity rather than exploitation and loathing for nature and wild things.

Ironically, it may have taken the development of Romanticism in Europe in the eighteenth and early nineteenth centuries to persuade Americans to look at the true wilderness with pleasure rather than disdain. This tradition grew largely from an urban literary elite who found themselves attracted to an idealized primitive landscape described as "picturesque" or "sublime." America did not have the cultural traditions, material wealth, or power of the Europeans, but size and diversity of

Figure 13—7   Thomas Jefferson's estate at Monticello.

Figure 13—8   *Looking up the Yosemite Valley.* Albert Bierstadt's painting from the Hudson River School of American landscape painters.

wilderness lands was one domain in which the New World could compare favorably with the older cultures (Burdick, 1980; Nash, 1982). In the decades following the American Revolution, the wilderness became a source of national pride with at least a growing minority of Americans. Soon American writers like James Fenimore Cooper and painters like Thomas Cole and Albert Bierstadt (see Figure 13–8) began to celebrate and romanticize the vistas of the great untamed lands of North America. Those who celebrated wild lands were still a small minority compared with those who viewed them with hostility, but we can see, at least for some, the establishment of the wilderness (in addition to pastoral landscapes and designed gardens) as a place of beauty.

For Americans near the end of the twentieth century, reactions to the wilderness are still often ambivalent. On the one hand there is a literary, artistic, and philosophical tradition that associates the wilderness with beauty, and even religious experiences. This appreciation of wild lands has been passed to us from Jefferson, Cooper, and Cole through nineteenth-century environmentalists like Henry David Thoreau and John Muir. On the other hand, the wilderness is, by definition, unaltered for the convenience or enjoyment of humankind. It can be an uncomfortable, confusing, even dangerous place. Perhaps wild lands will always inspire both fear and sublime appreciation.

. . . .

given parcel of land if it is declared wilderness as would use it if it were developed with an access road, sanitary facilities, and picnic tables? The answer to the latter question is probably "no." If one measures the value of an area based only on the number of users, the wilderness seems to be an expensive luxury. On the other hand, it might be demonstrated that the wilderness provides unique experience opportunities that can be received nowhere else, and that, in the long run, the effects of recreation are beneficial not only to the individual, but to society in general. Furthermore, what are the moral rights of wildlife to their particular habitat requirements if providing them forces the withdrawal from use by hu-

Figure 13–9   The recreation production process. (After Driver, B., & Brown, P., 1983. Contributions of behavioral scientists to recreation resource management. In I. Altman & J. F. Wohlwill (Eds.), *Behavior in the natural environment.* New York: Plenum Press.)

Resource	Activities	Experiences	Long–Term Benefits
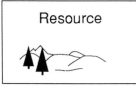	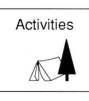	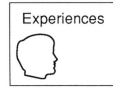	

Recreation Management Production Process

mans? An understanding of the experiences and long-term benefits people receive from recreating is an important management tool.

Why *do* people spend time in the "wilderness"? One answer may be derived from the environment–behavior models reviewed in Chapter 4. We may visit national parks to escape the **overload** or **stress** associated with daily life. This may partially explain why urbanites visit them more than ruralites. The **behavior constraint** approach would suggest that visits to the wilderness allow us to engage in many behaviors we are constrained from in everyday life, although due to their primitive nature, wilderness settings probably also constrain our behavior in some ways. Overall, one way of viewing the wilderness experience is as a way of coping with stressful aspects of everyday life. Unfortunately, however, crime, overcrowding, littering, and other problems currently associated with the wilderness experience are probably making it less of an optimal experience than it once was.

Other motivations for spending time in the wilderness may include the need to: develop, maintain, or project a particular type of self-image; retain or develop a new social identity; affiliate with certain other people; enhance our self-esteem; develop or display certain skills; exercise power; engage in self-fulfillment; or achieve mastery (Driver, 1972). In addition, one could add the aesthetic delight associated with many wilderness areas (e.g., breath-taking views) and the emotional experience such visits can generate (see Figure 13–10).

Who uses national parks and wilderness areas? Interestingly, some evidence suggests that while all types of people use them, users tend to be disproportionately higher income individuals, people with professional and technical occupations, those who live in urban areas, and people who have done college and postgraduate work (U.S. Department of the Interior, 1979).

What characteristics do we prefer in wilderness areas, and what do we find distasteful? The

Figure 13–10 Natural scenery: One benefit of wilderness recreation.

answers to these questions have important implications for resource planners. Several authors have remarked on the importance of **solitude**, for example (e.g., Hammitt, 1982). This probably refers to solitude from unknown others, since very few of those studied were traveling alone. Overall, people in wilderness areas prefer to interact and to develop relationships with those in their own party, but not to meet others along the trail. Thus, although the absolute number of encounters with other people in wilderness areas is very low, federal recreation resource managers are regularly concerned with user complaints of overcrowding (Anderson & Brown, 1984; Manning, 1985). Of course this is consistent with our discussion of crowding in Chapter 9, which emphasized that increasing density is perceived as crowding when it becomes inconvenient or restricts our freedom to engage in some desired behavior. Manning (1985) reviews some of the factors associated with perceived crowding in back-country settings:

Characteristics of visitors. Several user characteristics are related to the likelihood of perceived crowding. For example, those who seek solitude are more likely to perceive crowding than those seeking excitement (e.g., Ditton, Fedler, & Graefe, 1982). In addition, more experienced users and those with "purist" attitudes toward the wilderness are likely to perceive more crowding (e.g., Schreyer & Roggenbuck, 1978).

Characteristics of those encountered. The type of the other group encountered affects perceived crowding. Most groups object to loud, inconsiderate behavior (e.g., Owens, 1985; West 1982), but if others are perceived to be similar to one's group in behaviors and apparent values, the conflict and perceived crowding are minimized. In general, recreationists employing higher levels of technology are more likely to disrupt the experiences of their lower technology counterparts than the reverse. Canoeists tend to dislike meeting motorboats (Lucas, 1964); backpackers dislike encountering horses (Stankey, 1973). Thus, the low-technology recreationists are likely to be the first to be displaced.

Characteristics of the situation. Manning concludes his review by noting that characteristics of the situation can also affect tolerance for others. For example, people are usually more sensitive to others in nearby campsites than those met briefly on the trail, particularly if there is competition for facilities.

It should be noted that there are strong individual differences in people's preferences in natural settings (e.g., how much solitude they desire, and which aesthetic features they prefer) (Lucas, 1964). For example, while wilderness campers prefer solitude, others who could be called "general campers" (e.g., families who go camping) actually desire to meet and interact with people outside their immediate group. Part of what makes camping attractive to them is the expectation of meeting new people (Pitt & Zube, 1987). Also, more educated people, urbanites, males, and older people insist on an extremely pristine environment for their wilderness experience more than those with less education, ruralites, females, and younger people (Cicchetti, 1972). One's expectations for a setting also importantly affect his or her reactions to it (Westover, 1989). If we do not expect to meet other people and we do, this will be more disturbing than if we do expect to meet others and encounter them. Moreover, campers who expect good facilities and a particular level of comfort will be more disturbed if these conveniences are not present than will campers with lower expectations. In the same vein, whether or not we meet our objective in visiting a recreation area can affect our reactions to it (Driver & Knopf, 1976). Different recreational facilities carry with them different objectives. If we go fishing and fail to catch fish, we will be more dissatisfied than if we just came for the view.

What are the effects one actually experiences from spending time in wilderness settings? Presumably some of these benefits might be improvements in the health or well-being of individuals, regional or national economic development, or even useful changes in society as a whole (Driver & Rosenthal, 1982; Talbot & Kaplan, 1986). Many positive outcomes have been suggested (e.g., improved physical and mental health, realization of human potential, social benefits), but few have been documented through actual research. It is probably true that the outcomes one experiences from recreating in wilderness environments (and in other outdoor settings as well) depend jointly on physical elements (e.g., the scenery), facilities or equipment (e.g., having a good or a bad tent), characteristics of the user (e.g., the state of one's health), and on managerial decisions (e.g., whether or not what we want to do is "allowed") (Driver, 1975). What sorts of outcomes has research shown to be associated with spending time in wilderness settings? A number of studies suggest the potential for positive changes in self-concept or personality following a wilderness experience (e.g., Risk, 1976). For a group of psychiatric day-care patients, a five-day backpacking trip in the Sierras led to improvement in many areas (e.g., less obsessive thought patterns, fewer dependency needs, lower feelings of helplessness) (Slotsky, 1973). Talbot and Kaplan (1986) reported the results from a long-term research program to determine the effects of the Outdoor Challenge program on teenage boys. Individuals began to notice more subtle details in their wilderness environment and developed an attitude of living with, rather than controlling, nature.

Recreation Environments for Children

Having focused on recreational environments for the "older set," we now turn our attention to settings used by children. Children spend their recreational hours in all types of environmental contexts, including playgrounds, recreation rooms, museums, vacant lots, alleyways, street corners, and driveways. Very little research has been done on these diverse recreational environments, or their effects on children (Brown & Burger, 1984). Nevertheless, play activity has great significance for children, and serves as an important vehicle for learning about the world. The various types of recreational environments available or unavailable to a child (e.g., because they do not exist, or are considered dangerous or unsafe) could have a

significant impact on the child's development. Also, the way in which available play spaces are designed can impact greatly on what children realize from their interaction with them.

How are children's play spaces designed? A number of researchers believe that environmental designers do not sufficiently weigh the preferences or concerns of children and parents (e.g., Bishop & Peterson, 1971; Moore, 1973). The reasoning that goes into play space design often involves untested assumptions about the nature of children and play (Brown & Burger, 1984; Hayward, Rothenberg, & Beasley, 1976). Consequently, we should ask how well the resultant play spaces actually meet the needs of the user population. Due to design-related problems and an overall inadequate number of good play spaces in many areas, children may spend too many of their recreational hours in inappropriate (and sometimes dangerous) environments.

Most of the research which has been done on children's play environments has focused on playgrounds. Although this may overemphasize the importance of environments *designed* for play (neglecting back yards, streets, and vacant lots), it provides some of the standardization necessary for our discussion. The beginning of the playground movement in America occurred in 1885 when a pile of sand was provided for a "sand garden," a play area for the children living near a mission in Boston (Dickason, 1983). This structured play experience was well supervised, and was apparently intended to "Americanize" the children of immigrants by enticing them to a site where they would be subject to instruction or propaganda. Although this goal may seem rather heavy-handed, it represents an early recognition of the usefulness of formal play facilities in creating effective educational environments. Even today, unfortunately, some teachers view time spent on the playground as "recess from the children time" (Brown & Burger, 1984), so some educational opportunities are overlooked.

Figure 13–11 A, B, and C   A traditional playground in Wyoming (top), a contemporary playground in New York state (right), and an adventure playground in Toronto (bottom left).

Although there are relatively few empirical studies of playground design, those available (e.g. Hayward et al., 1976) often distinguish between three broad playground styles: **traditional**, **contemporary**, and **adventure playgrounds** (see Figures 13–11A, B, and C). Perhaps you are most familiar with the traditional and contemporary playground types. Traditional playgrounds contain the standard apparatus (e.g., swings, monkey bars, jungle gyms). This is still the most widely spread playground type in the United States, and seems primarily geared toward exercise. Unfortunately, these playgrounds are often dangerous places with a variety of metal parts, chains, and (with a curious insensitivity to life and limb)

concrete or asphalt paving. Aesthetics are not necessarily ignored. Sometimes pipes are fashioned into rocket ships or stagecoaches, and sometimes concrete is molded into animal shapes (Shaw, 1987).

Contemporary playgrounds include many of the same elements found in traditional designs, but with a flair for aesthetics and abstract shapes (e.g., the slide may extend from a multileveled wooden structure with a variety of ladders, balancing beams, ramps, bridges, and other delights). Note that in a contemporary playground a single apparatus often serves multiple rather than single play functions.

What is an adventure playground? (To get a preliminary idea, it might help to know that they are also referred to as "junk" playgrounds.) Adventure playgrounds began in Denmark during World War II and encouraged youngsters to use scrap wood and other castoff materials to build their own world of fantasy— and dirt. Instead of traditional play equipment, scraps of materials such as wood and tools like hammers, nails, and saws are supplied. Children are encouraged to build structures and to modify old ones as time goes on and interests evolve. Clearly these playgrounds require careful supervision, and the presence of adult supervisors makes possible activities such as cooking and gardening in addition to less structured digging and hammering. Some believe the adventure playground can expand the range of play opportunities available to children (Cooper, 1970; Nicholson, 1970), while others (often members of the community) complain about their unplanned nature and unattractive appearance.

When studying the three types of playgrounds, Hayward et al. (1976) found that each attracted a somewhat different clientele. Practically no preschool children attended the adventure playgrounds, while about one-third of the users in the other two settings fell into this age group. In contrast, older children were more likely to patronize the adventure playgrounds (Hayward et al., 1976). Finally, fewer adults were present in adventure playgrounds than in the contemporary or traditional playgrounds. This latter finding is in all likelihood due to fewer young children being present, but it nevertheless has implications for the level of supervision in the three settings. The presence of adults may be one reason why fewer school-age children attended the traditional or contemporary playgrounds than the adventure playgrounds, since school-age children desire a degree of independence.

The activities engaged in at the three playgrounds differed as well, and the data clearly imply that environmental features had a strong effect on behavior. In the traditional playground, swinging was the most common activity; but at the contemporary playground, children engaged in a continuous mode of activity which included playing on varied equipment. This result was probably due in part to the equipment at the contemporary playground (e.g., there was much more "multipurpose" equipment). At the adventure playground the most popular activity was playing in the "clubhouse," an option that did not exist in the other two settings.

The degree of novelty of an apparatus also seemed to affect its use: There were traditional slides at the traditional playground, but at the contemporary playground a slide was built on a cobblestone "mountain" with tunnels running through it. Whereas the novel slide was extremely popular, the traditional one was used relatively infrequently. Overall, for the three playgrounds, it may be seen that the opportunities and constraints provided by the environment predict the predominant activities engaged in by children. Such opportunities and constraints also affect *how* the children play (e.g., alone or in groups) and the focus of their interaction (e.g., on the "here and now" versus fantasy). For example, fantasy play was least common in the traditional playground.

There seems to be general agreement among architects and educators that traditional playgrounds fall short of providing the desirable variety of educational, physical, and experiential challenges (Frost & Klein, 1979). On the other hand, not all empirical research demonstrates that contemporary playgrounds as a class are necessarily superior to more traditional designs. Brown and Burger (1984) for example, observed children at three contemporary and three traditional playgrounds. Although one of the three contemporary playgrounds was the most successful at promoting educationally desirable social, language, or motor behaviors, the overall levels of the measured behaviors were actually *lowest* at one of the other contemporary sites. The researchers concluded that although the poorly functioning playground appeared contemporary in design and was

pleasing to the adult eye, these visual characteristics were not successful in promoting the
desired play behaviors. In sum, children's play
is affected by the success of each individual
playground apparatus, the choice of sites for the
playground, and the integration of the play
spaces more than the particular design style
(traditional or contemporary).

We will paraphrase the playground design
guidelines suggested by Shaw (1987) as a
summary of desirable playground amenities.
They should possess:

A sense of place. Just as adults seem
to prefer **legible** environments (those
that can be easily understood or
cognitively mapped), children will be
most comfortable when spaces form a
context that reflects an overall order.

Unity. The environment's overall image
should be unified. Individual parts should
be connected physically and spatially;
otherwise, most activity will center on
the most complex pieces. Unity may also
improve children's ability to develop and
sustain workable cognitive maps.

A variety of spaces. Playgrounds should
include large spaces, small spaces,
enclosed spaces, and open spaces. In
particular, children may especially enjoy
enclosed defensible spaces, a
phenomenon Brown and Burger refer to
as **encapsulation.**

Key places. Key places are complex
play structures that support a variety of
activities.

A system of pathways. Key places need
to be linked by a carefully chosen
system of paths that provide children
with choices and lead them to discover
the variety of play options.

Three-dimensional layering. The
playground should not be thought of as a
series of structures seated on a single
plane, but as a three-dimensional
arrangement of ramps, slides, tunnels,
and ladders that allow children access to
different elevations.

Loose parts. **Loose parts** are things to
manipulate that are not part of the
playground apparatus itself. Examples
include balls, games, or building
materials.

Summary of Leisure and Recreation Environments

There are a variety of different types of
recreation and leisure. We have emphasized
that it is a psychological experience, rather than
a particular activity that motivates recreational
behavior. Our interest in specific modes of
recreation varies with age, personality, socioeconomic status, and availability of facilities.
Wilderness hiking or camping may be viewed
as ways of coping with stressful aspects of
everyday life, although crowding, littering, and
other problems associated with camping may
work against the coping function, and desire for
personal growth may be equally important in
our wilderness experiences. Solitude is a major
expectation of wilderness campers, and if the
experience provides it, the outing can have
positive psychological and health benefits for
us. Play activities also have significant consequences for children, and the design of a
playground affects the behavior in it. In one
study, for example, play behavior in a contemporary playground was more continuous than
play in a traditional one. In an adventure
playground, however, children were more creative. Clearly, recreation and leisure opportunities are important for people of all ages, and
design considerations are paramount in determining what opportunities are available in
given recreation and leisure environments.

SUMMARY

Work environments have developed flexibility because of technological innovations allowing removal of equipment from rigid power sources and construction of expansive and high-rise spaces. Modern technology has also created difficulties in the interactions between humans and machines. Human factors specialists continue to search for principles that will minimize conflicts. One, the principle of workflow, states that workstations should be arranged in the order that provides immediate flow of work from one point in the work cycle to the next necessary point. Attention to the principle of workflow enhances productivity; attention to design factors that promote safe and healthy working conditions also facilitates productivity. The quality of the work environment also affects job satisfaction, although job security, working relationships, and other factors are usually found to have more impact on job satisfaction than does quality of the environment.

A major innovation in office design is the open office plan, or office landscape. The advantages of the open office include reduced maintenance costs, easier communication, better workflow, and easier supervision. Disadvantages of open offices, which may in some circumstances outweigh advantages, include increased noise and other distractions, as well as reduced privacy. Portable partitions may help overcome some of these disadvantages, however.

The ability to treat one's workspace as a territory, as well as the right to personalize it, may serve as a form of status in the organization. Especially at high ranks in a firm, such territorial treatment and personalization may correlate with job satisfaction.

Recreation and leisure opportunities are important for people of all ages, and design alternatives help determine which opportunities exist in a given recreation or leisure environment. The type of recreation and leisure opportunity we most prefer varies with age, personality, and socioeconomic status. Wilderness and camping experiences permit opportunities for personal growth and can help with everyday stresses. However, crowded camping areas and other problems can defeat the stress-reducing aspects of camping. Among the most important expectations of wilderness campers are solitude and aesthetic appreciation. Benefits of solitude, aesthetic experiences, and other encounters during camping can improve our psychological outlook and benefit our health. Similarly, recreational exercise benefits our health and psychological outlook and can improve family and other social relationships. Poorly designed exercise facilities, however, often result in accidents that are clearly not beneficial to our health. For children, opportunities for play have a significant socializing impact. Adventure playgrounds, for example, result in more creative interactions among children.

SUGGESTED PROJECTS

1. Take a tour of various offices around your campus and note various types of personalization. Does personalization seem to vary with status, gender of the occupant, type of job, or academic specialization?

2. In this chapter we discussed several population stereotypes regarding the human-machine system. Can you think of others? Make up a short survey to give to your friends to determine the relative strength of your proposed stereotypes. There will probably be some disagreements. What are the implications of ambiguous situations?

3. Explore several types of recreation environments and note the concentration of ages in them, as well as the experiences or benefits people seem to be getting from them. Are there systematic differences? What design changes would be necessary to provide other recreational opportunities?

4. If your school has a large computer terminal room, conduct an informal observation of human factors in the student workplace. Are the terminals and furniture designed with an eye to human factors? Are there signs of fatigue among users? How do users adapt the workplace to their needs (keyboards in laps, books shading glare, etc.)? Can you offer suggestions for design improvements?

14 CHANGING BEHAVIOR TO SAVE THE ENVIRONMENT

SUMMARY

SUGGESTED PROJECTS

KEY TERMS

antecedent behavioral change
   techniques
approach prompts
avoidance prompts
commons dilemma
dominant Western world view
environmental education
feedback
foot in the door
free-rider
greenhouse effect
individual good—collective bad trap
missing hero situation
negative reinforcement

new ecological paradigm
nuts game
one-person trap
ozone hole
perceived inequity
positive reinforcement
prompts
public goods problem
punishment
self-trap
social dilemma
social traps
vandalism

INTRODUCTION

Imagine that you are a shepherd and that you share a pasture known as "the commons" with the other shepherds of your village. Further assume that the commons cannot be enlarged—it constitutes all the land you and the others have on which to graze your animals. Although you share the pasture land, the economic benefits you gain from your herd are yours, and from time to time you are confronted with the decision of whether to purchase another sheep for your flock. The commons is becoming depleted, but you feel that you would enjoy the economic advantage of owning another animal. After all, the commons could support one more sheep without too much further damage. You reason that the cost (to you) of one additional sheep grazing on the commons is quite low, and you conclude that you are acting rationally by deciding to make the purchase. However, force yourself to consider what would happen if all the shepherds added one extra animal. The eventual result would be complete depletion of the commons, and all would suffer. After you have ruminated on this for a while, you become disturbed and uncertain about what to do.

This story is taken from Hardin's "The Tragedy of the Commons" (1968). As you have probably realized, it offers an excellent analogy with many aspects of contemporary life. Many resources are being consumed at too high a rate, which is endangering the future availability of the resource. At a personal level we often find ourselves faced with resource-related decisions that are modern-day equivalents of whether or not to add another sheep to our herd. Should we avoid buying paper plates in order to save trees? If we use paper plates can we avoid wasting water to wash dishes? In a sense, our needs are pitted against those of the larger community. We are faced with a choice between satisfying our immediate needs with the prospect of negative future consequences to society, and restricting our present consumption for the future good of the community. The way we resolve such dilemmas obviously has important implications. Hardin argues that if we want the commons to survive, each of us must give up some of our freedom. While the individual shepherd will benefit by adding to his or her flock, one must refrain for the greater good. But as logical as this seems, your experience may suggest to you that it will require more than reasoning to make people refrain from behaviors that are environmentally destructive, although personally satisfying. Unfortunately, people frequently fail to respond to reason alone.

John Platt (1973) considers situations like the **commons dilemma**, in which short-term personal gains conflict with long-term societal needs, to be types of **social traps**.

In general, Platt feels that social traps are hard to break out of, but claims it is essential for researchers to design strategies enabling us to do just that. Various methods have been suggested to help us break out of the commons dilemma (cf. Edney, 1980; Platt, 1973). For example, researchers have tried to increase short-term costs of environmentally destructive behaviors so that they become less attractive behavioral alternatives, and have attempted to decrease the costs of environmentally constructive acts. Environmental psychologists have also tried to educate people (e.g., by conducting environmental seminars) to make them realize their interdependence and to make the long-term societal costs of squandering resources more salient, and have advocated adding reinforcers to encourage behaviors incompatible with those that waste precious resources. Some have also supplied people with feedback about the extent to which they are depleting the commons and have assessed the effects on resource overconsumption of dividing up available resources (e.g., through rationing).

In this concluding chapter we will discuss a broad range of techniques that have been used by environmental psychologists in an attempt to study and change an array of human behaviors that are not in our best interests environmentally. Some environmentally destructive behaviors are easily amenable to conceptualization in terms of the "commons dilemma" and "social trap" analyses we have described, while others require a different type of conceptualization. Therefore, the approaches we will discuss for dealing with environmentally destructive behavior include the sorts of techniques mentioned as useful for attacking the "commons dilemma" type of problem, as well as other methods.

ENVIRONMENTAL PSYCHOLOGY AND SAVING THE ENVIRONMENT

Clearly, changing human behavior to save the environment is an extremely important topic. However, past research in environmental psychology has focused more on the effects of environmental variables (e.g., crowding, deteriorated environments) than on how to modify our behavior to save the environment. Environmental psychologists have documented that certain environments affect us adversely, but have done less research on how to change our behaviors so they do not have adverse effects on the environment. There is a big difference between knowing that people react negatively to filthy urban areas or to energy or other resource shortages, and getting them to do something about solving these problems. We need to devote more research attention to studying how we can have a positive effect on the environment, as opposed to focusing on how it affects us.

What unique contribution can environmental psychology make to help deal with the many environmental problems we face (e.g., insufficient and expensive fuels, air and water pollution, a generally deteriorating environment)? The approaches other disciplines have taken have emphasized physical technology. For example, a great deal of attention has been focused on developing nuclear and solar energy, and pollution abatement techniques. Many seem to think that solving our environmental problems only requires the right technologies. In contrast, relatively less attention has focused on strategies for preserving the environment which involve changes in people's behavior. Where these techniques have been used they are often regarded as "stopgap" measures—until technology bails us out of our current problems. We will argue that although physical technology certainly has a role, behavior change—sometimes involving substantial modifications in how we act on an "everyday" basis—will have to make a significant contribution if things are to improve. In fact, sometimes behavior change will be more important than physical technology in effecting solutions.

Why do we (and many other environmental psychologists) feel this way? First, in some cases physical technologies have gotten us into this mess. Modern transportation has solved problems in locomoting, but has caused pollution, an energy shortage, unsightly commercial "strips," etc. Modern packaging allows us to preserve all types of food, but has created a tremendous litter problem. Most technologies have unfortunate "side effects," and in this chapter we will see that psychological techniques for behavior change could help eliminate them. Second, in some cases (e.g., dealing with littering) there is no efficient physical technology, so changing behavior is our best means of coping. Even when there is an efficient technology for dealing with environmental problems (e.g., building smaller, more efficient homes; retrofitting existing ones), particular behaviors are often necessary to ensure that people use available technology. For example, motorists have disconnected catalytic converters in automobiles in order to increase gas mileage and eliminate attendant smells. By doing so, they subvert pollution control technology. More generally, we could say that the impact of any technology depends on people's behavior—how they *use* the technology. Finally, behavior does have strong effects on the environment: We would not be exaggerating if we asserted that almost everything anyone of us does has either a positive or a negative impact on our environment.

Two questions remain: (1) Will changing our behavior to save the environment require a lower quality of life, and (2) can it be done?

Generally, the answer to the first is "No." If we changed our behavior so fewer of us drove cars and more used public transportation, there would be less pollution, we would have significantly more money to spend, we could walk or ride bicycles anywhere, inflation would not be particularly linked to the price of foreign oil, and so on. In many ways, the quality of life would actually improve. We rephrase the second question: Do the behavior change techniques that we will be describing in this chapter work? We will leave that for you to decide after reading our presentation of the evidence in the coming pages. We will, however, suggest that there is lots of room for environmental psychologists to improve our environment-relevant behaviors. For example, energy consumption often varies by a factor of two or three for similar people living in identical homes (Socolow, 1978; Winnett et al., 1979). Their apparently different behavior seems to show up in energy use!

If we could influence environmentally relevant behaviors to improve the environment, what would we focus on? We would probably want to promote environmentally protective behaviors (e.g., picking up litter, recycling things), and discourage environmentally destructive ones (e.g., throwing litter on the ground, driving cars that are "gas hogs") (Cone & Hayes, 1980). It should be noted that both types of behaviors impact on the same problems. Encouraging environmentally protective acts (e.g., rewarding people for picking up litter) and discouraging environmentally destructive behavior (e.g., high fines for littering) will improve the litter situation. Unfortunately, programs that encourage protective behaviors do not necessarily inhibit destructive behaviors, and vice-versa (Cone & Hayes, 1980). Also, not all environmentally protective and destructive behaviors have the same impact on the environment. A program that stops people from littering is sure to have direct environmental impact; one that encourages people to vote for conservation-oriented legislators will probably have a more diffuse impact.

Finally, we should stress that the effects of any environmentally protective or destructive behavior are complex. Suppose we could get people to recycle all newspapers. This would save trees, but might cause water pollution from the ink removal process. It would save energy since we would not need to process virgin wood, but the recycling process itself uses a great deal of energy. Sometimes it is hard to figure out when we are really "ahead" (Figure 14–1).

What is the range of environmental problems that we would like to improve if we could? These may be categorized as (1) problems of environmental aesthetics (e.g., prevention and control of litter, protection of natural resources, preventing urban deterioration); (2) health-related problems (e.g., pollution, radiation,

Figure 14–1 A and B Actions to "save" the environment often involve trade-offs. Using paper plates saves water that would be used in washing dishes, but costs trees. Using porcelain plates saves trees but costs water. Recycling newspapers saves trees, but removing the ink can pollute water.

high levels of noise); and (3) resource problems (e.g., overconsumption of nonrenewable resources, such as oil) (Cone & Hayes, 1980). These categories are neither exhaustive nor mutually exclusive. Often, specific environmental problems, such as overdependence on the automobile, impact on all three categories. While we will not be able to deal with all of the environmental problems needing solutions, later in this chapter we will discuss specific approaches for coping with several of them in detail.

At this point, let us examine the commons

dilemma in more detail to see how we can modify the situation to improve the outlook for the environment. We will then consider a range of general techniques used by environmental psychologists that can be applied to almost any sort of environmental problem. These methods are (1) environmental education; (2) appropriate environmental prompts and cues; (3) various reinforcement strategies; and (4) techniques that combine several of the approaches. Some of these methods may hold great promise for solving the critical problems that now confront us.

THE COMMONS DILEMMA AS AN ENVIRONMENT–BEHAVIOR PROBLEM

Hardin's (1968) depiction of the tragedy of the commons has spawned numerous attempts to examine factors which might help us work out favorable solutions to the commons dilemma. To see how generalizable Hardin's propositions have become, it might be useful to enumerate examples of commons-like behavior beyond that of Hardin's shepherds. Hardin himself was interested in the problem of overpopulation: Seemingly self-serving motives for reproduction (e.g., having more labor to run the family farm) have a long-term negative consequence if the total population outstrips the food supply. Other examples of the commons dilemma are apparent when we consider some scenes typical on many college campuses. Parking lots are often jammed, with long lines of cars waiting for a space. The parking lot can be thought of as a commons: It is shared by all and owned by none of those who use it. Because parking spaces may be scarce, individuals acting in self-interest may arrive early to get a share of the valued resource. But as demand for spaces increases, you must arrive earlier and earlier to

be assured of one. The result is that people who really need access early may be deprived of access because others have rushed in before them. Or consider space in campus dining areas around the noon hour. Space is limited, and many students use dining tables to socialize or to study for the next class. If they studied elsewhere, there would be room for all to eat. Libraries are not immune from commons-type behavior. Toward the end of each semester or quarter, demand for certain valued reference materials soars and access becomes constricted. In self-interest, someone may hold the material for an inordinate amount of time. If students (and faculty!) would use these materials throughout the term, the "crunch" disaster would not strike so badly at the end of the term. Scheduling of classes is also a type of commons. It appears that 10 A.M. is the most popular time for faculty to teach and for students to want to be in class. Accordingly, classroom space is scarcest at that hour, but is underutilized at other times of the day. Budgets also have the characteristics of a commons. If

Simulating the Commons Dilemma: How It's Done and What is Found

To test different techniques for helping us break out of the "commons dilemma," a number of simulations have been developed which incorporate the central elements that people face in such contexts. In these simulations, various interventions are attempted to determine those which would cause us to behave in a more constructive way. Thus far, the simulations have included computer analogs (e.g., Brechner, 1977; Cass & Edney, 1978), as well as noncomputerized methods involving portable (e.g., Edney, 1979) and nonportable apparatus (e.g., Edney & Harper, 1978b). In addition to being useful for exploring strategies for helping us to break out of the commons dilemma, simulations can be used as teaching devices to aid us in understanding the dynamics of our environmentally destructive behaviors.

To give you a feel for these simulation techniques, we will discuss Edney's (1979) **nuts game** simulation in some detail. Recall that commons dilemmas include: (1) a limited resource that may regenerate itself somewhat, but which can be endangered through overconsumption; and (2) people who have the choice between restricting current individual consumption for the good of society (and the future of the resource pool), and exploiting the resource for their own immediate good. A successful simulation would have to include these elements.

How can this be done? Edney's "nuts game" accomplishes it quite nicely. A small number of subjects enter the lab and sit around an open bowl that originally contains 10 hexagonal nuts, obtained from a hardware store. The bowl symbolizes the pool of resources (e.g., trees, whales, or oil), and the nuts symbolize the individual resources themselves. Participants are told that their goal is to obtain as many nuts as possible. (This simulates the fact that typically we try to maximize our outcomes in life.) Players can take as many nuts as they want at any time after a trial begins. The experimenter also states that the number of nuts remaining in the bowl after every 10-second interval will be doubled by him or her. This replenishment cycle simulates natural resource regeneration rates. The above events continue until the time limit for the game is exceeded, or until the players empty the bowl.

How do subjects behave during the "nuts game"? We would hope that they would take at most a few nuts out of the pool per 10-second period, which would allow the game to continue and maximize the long-term outcomes. However, in his research, Edney (1979) found that 65 percent of the groups depleted the pool completely before the first replenishment stage. They took out all 10 nuts (i.e., depleted the resource pool completely) during the first few seconds of the game. As in the "real world," people exploit the commons, with unfortunate results.

Figure 14–2 A and B   The commons dilemma applies to many shared resources.

the members of a group allocate a fixed amount from which they all draw, such as for phone calls or photocopying, the tendency is for everyone to spend more than their share from that part of the budget. If each participant decides, then, that it is in his or her best interest to spend a fair share before someone else uses it, the resource becomes depleted very quickly—to the detriment of all. Can you think of other examples of this type of dilemma? (See Figure 14–2.)

We mentioned that Platt (1973) conceptualized the commons dilemma as a type of social trap. Platt described three such categories of social traps, each of which is relevant to environmentally destructive behavior. The *commons* type of trap, or **individual good–collective bad trap**, involves a group competing for a valued resource, such that destructive behavior by one participant has minor impact on the whole, but if all engage in the same individual behavior, the impact on the commons is disastrous. The **one-person** trap, or **self-trap**, involves a disastrous consequence to one person. Typical of these traps is addiction to drugs or food. The momentary pleasures of the present have disastrous consequences in the long run. The third type of trap is the **missing hero situation**. Whereas the commons trap and self-trap involve unfortunate actions which we take, the missing hero trap involves an action which we fail to take, such as refusing to help someone in need or failing to warn others of the toxicity of a substance they work with.

Interestingly, Platt (1973) notes that all three of these traps can be analyzed in terms of the rewards and punishments (i.e., reinforcements) associated with them. There is a positive side to the situation which we seek, and a negative side which we want to avoid. The problem is that the positive and negative have become separated in time, or the negative has been diluted across the members of a group, so that the behavior leading to the short-term positive consequence is more likely to occur. For example, in the commons problem of overharvesting whales, the immediate reward of taking one whale seems more prominent than the long-term consequence of everyone else taking more whales. In a self-trap of overconsuming food, the short-term pleasure of an extra dessert seems overwhelming relative to the long-term consequence of damage to the body and to our appearance. In a missing-hero trap, there is an unpleasant component to the behavior we should be performing: The punishment is short-term but the reward is long-term, so we avoid the behavior. For example, we may fail to pick up litter because the inconvenience seems to outweigh the long-term benefit of an aesthetically pleasing environment.

How, then, do we resolve social traps? Platt argues that we simply rearrange the positive and negative consequences of our behavior. If we engage in a destructive behavior because it has immediate rewards, such as using an automobile rather than mass transit, we can impose a system of penalties for automobile use (such as heavy freeway tolls) and rewards for mass transit use (such as free rides on high-pollution days). Or, we could increase the unit cost of a resource, such as electricity, for those who use a large quantity, and reduce the unit cost for those who use little. We will examine these ideas in more detail when we discuss specific use of rewards and punishments to prevent environmentally destructive behavior.

Edney (1980) points out that although this reinforcement interpretation of the commons dilemma is appealing in its simplicity, it ignores a number of human elements. For one, it ignores the long-established evidence that individuals are different from one another: They do not all respond in the same way to the same rearrangement of the circumstances for rewards and punishments. Reinforcement approaches also sidestep questions of conscience, altruism, ethics, and humanistic tendencies, and suggest that reason is dominated by questions of reward.

We should mention that there are other formulations of commons-type problems. To social psychologists, the problem is one of a class of **social dilemmas**, where individual interests are pitted against group interests (e.g., Messick et al., 1983). Economists refer to a variation of the issue as the **public goods problem** (e.g., Marwell & Ames, 1979). In this situation, individuals must all contribute to a common cause, such as paying taxes for mutual self-defense or contributing to a public television station. Any one person can fail to contribute, and the public cause will survive. However, if too many people get the idea of not contributing, the common good suffers. Those who do not contribute are termed **free-riders**, since they not only do not contribute, but also benefit from the public cause. For example, a person who sneaks onto a subway without paying or who poaches wildlife without a hunting license could be termed a free-rider.

In our discussion above we showed how Platt would rearrange rewards and punishments to solve the commons dilemma. Hardin (1968) suggests that some form of government is necessary to manage the commons in a nondestructive manner. In his terms, we must have "mutual coercion mutually agreed upon" in order to regulate our tendencies toward overconsumption. Laboratory investigations using commons dilemma simulations (see box, page 469) have explored a number of factors, including forms of "government," which might help us conserve the commons. It is instructive to review some of these laboratory findings.

Consistent with Platt's notions, laboratory studies do show that adding rewards for cooperative behavior and punishments for selfish behavior can help preserve the commons (e.g., Bell, Petersen, & Hautaluoma, 1989; Kline et al., 1984; Komorita, 1987; Yamagishi, 1986). It has been found that cooperation among players is essential for proecological (preservation) outcomes; consequently, there must be trust between participants (Edney, 1979; Moore

et al., 1987). Also, if groups are allowed time to study the game and to communicate, they derive their own strategies, which frequently are proecological. Other research shows that giving groups immediate and detailed resource feedback about the effects of their behavior (Kline et al., 1984; Seligman & Darley, 1977; Stern, 1976), or the ability to communicate about the commons (Brechner, 1977; Dawes, McTavish, & Shaklee, 1977; Edney & Harper, 1978a, 1978b), leads to maintaining the commons for a longer period of time. Groups who are afforded both feedback and communication are especially successful at maintaining the commons (Jorgenson & Papciak, 1981).

When one's individual behavior in commons dilemma situations is subject to the scrutiny of others, he or she is less apt to overexploit the commons (Jerdee & Rosen, 1974). Other studies have explored the effects of knowing one is interdependent with others for a resource, rather than having his or her own supply (e.g., Edney & Bell, 1984). Generally, individually owned resources are handled more efficiently than common or "pooled" resources. In fact, obtaining knowledge of resource interdependence seems to increase the intensity of behaviors aimed at "getting as much as possible for oneself," which ends up depleting the commons (Brechner, 1977; Cass & Edney, 1978). This suggests that rationing resources could be a useful strategy.

Structural changes to the commons are usually more effective management strategies than trying to influence individuals (e.g., Messick et al., 1983; Samuelson et al., 1984). For example, experiments have studied whether educating people about the optimal strategy for using resources in commons dilemma situations leads to proecological actions. As we will see later when we discuss environmental education, often it is quite ineffective (Edney & Harper, 1978b). Moral exhortation to be altruistic helps, but not much (Edney & Bell, 1983). On the other hand, when the structure of the situation is changed to promote communication, subjects arrive at an optimizing strategy themselves (Edney & Harper, 1978a, 1978b). Another structural change, that of breaking down the commons into individually owned territories, also improves conservation (e.g., Edney & Bell, 1983). This territorial solution actually eliminates the commons, and is not very practical for some resources, such as national parks. It is, however, a type of solution that manipulates the ''government'' structure of the commons. Another ''government'' structural solution, that of requiring that all members harvest in equal amounts, also has proecological results (Edney & Bell, 1983). Freedom of choice and equality of harvesting outcomes seem to improve harvesting efficiency (Edney & Bell, 1987). If those sharing the commons like each other, they seem to manage it more efficiently (Smith, Bell, & Fusco, 1988). If those sharing the commons identify with each other as a group, preservation is more likely

. . . .

The World as a Commons: New and Old Ecology

Although there are a number of examples of individual commons dilemmas, we might also consider the entire world as a commons. Environmental sociologist Riley Dunlap, drawing on the views of others, has suggested that a shift is occurring in how we view world resources (e.g., Dunlap, 1980; Dunlap & Van Liere, 1978, 1984). This shift takes the form of a contrast between a long-held **dominant Western world view** and a **new ecological paradigm** approach to the world's resources. We summarize these contrasting attitudes below.

The dominant Western world view holds that

1. Humans are unique and have dominion over all other organisms.
2. We are masters of our own destiny—we have the intellectual and technological resources to solve any problem.
3. We have access to an infinite amount of resources.
4. Human history involves infinite progress for the better.

The new ecological paradigm holds that

1. Humans are interdependent with other organisms, such that their preservation is to our advantage.
2. Many things we do have unintended negative consequences for the environment.
3. Some things, such as fossil fuels, are finite.
4. Ecological constraints, such as the carrying capacity of an environment, are placed upon us.

You may agree or disagree with some of the above contentions. The ones you endorse probably have much to do with how palatable you find the various strategies for managing the commons.

. . . .

(Brewer & Kramer, 1986; Kramer & Brewer, 1984). Also, different leadership and decision-making rules have been related to commons dilemma outcomes. A study by Shippee (1978) found that personal participation in choosing a group's leadership and in implementing decisions to limit resource use led to quite successful conservation results. This, coupled with the earlier findings on being involved in choosing an optimizing strategy, highlights the importance of individual participation.

What does all of the above mean? Clearly, commons dilemma analogs can give us useful hypotheses regarding how to deal with "real-life" situations. They might eventually provide important partial solutions to pressing contemporary problems. However, we must keep in mind that the external validity of these laboratory simulations has not been demonstrated, and thus it is still an open question as to whether or not the sorts of interventions which are successful in simulations would work in the real world. There is certainly some evidence that these laboratory studies have implications for the real world, although the linkage is not complete. Clearly, social—as opposed to technological—solutions must be considered. For example, we mentioned that Edney and Bell (1983) demonstrated the efficacy of dividing the commons into territories. Acheson (1975) observed that Maine lobstermen who are highly territorial in defending their ocean claims are more successful in maintaining productivity than those who are less territorial. Such outcomes raise the question of whether some environmental policies might be better than others in achieving desired outcomes. We must keep in mind that outcomes involve trade-offs. For example, if we were to divide a national park into privately-owned territories as a strategy for preserving it, we would defeat the purpose of holding the park as a "common" good. Moreover, Edney and Bell (1983) found that a strategy of everyone sharing equally preserved the commons as well as did dividing

it into territories. However, Edney (1981) observed that the sacrifices that must be made to preserve the commons are often unequally shared among the population (i.e., some harvest less than others; see Samuelson & Messick, 1986), and concluded that honesty and interpersonal trust are extremely important psychological qualities in any solution to the commons dilemma.

As individual action has more and more impact globally, the relevance of the commons dilemma becomes more and more apparent. For example, (1) in the **greenhouse effect**, individual use of fossil fuels seems harmless but collectively it dangerously warms the entire planet (e.g., Kerr, 1988a); (2) the individual use of chlorofluorocarbons (e.g., for air-conditioning) seems harmless but collectively it creates an **ozone hole** over the South Pole (e.g., Kerr, 1988b); (3) the locally harmless use of fossil fuels creates acid rain when the collective output of the fuels precipitates over neighboring areas (e.g., Schindler, 1988); and (4) the singular launch of a space vehicle seems strictly an advancement of science, but the total output of waste products left in orbit from multiple launches endangers future launches (e.g., Marshall, 1985) and, along with night lighting from urbanization, interferes with astronomical studies of outer space (e.g., Waldrop, 1988). While it is easy to adopt a fatalistic attitude that we are hopelessly locked into one collective ecological disaster after another, there remains hope. Research has indeed shown that a variety of strategies can modify environmentally destructive behavior. We turn now to some strategies that have known outcomes in their applications, with the knowledge that the commons dilemma is a useful foundation for the implications of these strategies. Moreover, some of the same factors that influence outcomes in the commons are important for these strategies, such as rewards and punishments, communication, feedback, and social cohesion or attraction toward those who participate in the strategy.

ENVIRONMENTAL EDUCATION: TEACHING US WHAT IS WRONG AND HOW TO RESPOND TO IT

Essentially, **environmental education** involves making people aware of the scope and nature of environmental problems and of behavioral alternatives that might alleviate them. This approach has been used to promote energy conservation, to lower the levels of pollution and littering, and to encourage other pro-ecological attitudes and behavior. The guiding assumption of most such programs is that education will lead to environmental awareness and attitude change, which in turn will affect behavior advantageously (Bruvold, 1973; O'Riordan, 1976; Winston, 1974).

Environmental educators employ all manner of techniques to attain these goals. One strategy makes use of the mass media to reach large segments of the population. Such techniques are employed by agencies of the federal and state governments, by public utilities, and by private industry. Another method involves formal coursework at the elementary, secondary, or college level. In this context, special texts, workbooks, comic books, and simulations have been developed to help "get the point across." Diagnostic tests have been designed to pinpoint deficiencies in student knowledge and to provide an index of learning. Less formally, environmental workshops and displays are set up locally at shopping malls and regionally at state fairs and museums. Finally, although this does not complete the list of sources of environmental education, organizations such as the Sierra Club regularly disseminate educational information (Figure 14–3).

Figure 14–3   Sample of environmental education. (From "Fun with the Environment," U.S. Environmental Protection Agency, Washington, D.C.)

How effective are environmental education programs? Research suggests that people sometimes lack environmental knowledge (Ditton & Goodale, 1974; Towler & Swan, 1972), and that educational programs may be helpful in enhancing awareness as well as in changing attitudes for the better (Allen, 1972; Cohen, 1973). However, the link between environmental education and behavior appears to be weak (Cone & Hayes, 1980; Heberlein, 1976). For example, it was reported that of all the persons who attended one of the first environmental "teach-ins" in 1970, only a few decided to make substantial alterations in their behavior. Specifically, 60 percent of the participants did not plan any changes on the basis of what they had learned; the 40 percent who planned to take action mostly chose very moderate measures (e.g., writing Congresspersons). Of the latter group, only 13 percent indicated a desire to modify their lifestyle significantly (Lingwood, 1971). These findings are striking for two reasons. First, individuals had voluntarily attended the workshop for the express purpose of finding out what behavioral alternatives were available. Second, the dependent measures were of *behavioral intentions* rather than of actual behavior. If actual behavior had been measured, possibly even less commitment to change would have been seen.

Are the rather weak results reported by Lingwood typical of other environmental education programs? Unfortunately, there is evidence that many other programs also have been ineffective in changing environmentally destructive behavior. In one study, Howell and Warmbrod (1974) reported no difference in attitudes between students whose classes used a manual oriented to environmental problems and solutions and those whose classes did not. If environmental education is not even effective in changing attitudes, it is unlikely to bring about behavioral change. Similarly, Winston (1974) found no relationship between a measure of environmental awareness and an index of positiveness of environmentally oriented behavior,

a finding that casts serious doubt on the worth of environmental education efforts.

In spite of these discouraging data, you should not prematurely conclude that all environmental education will fail to yield positive effects. A two-year study by Asch and Shore (1975) found that compared to a control group, school classes that had been taken on field trips to a nature area (a form of environmental education) displayed greater respect for wildlife, plant life, soil, and water. Thus, it could be that environmenal education is most successful with young children who do not have well-established habits. Some researchers believe that the effectiveness of environmental education would be improved if it focused more on presenting solutions to problems than on increasing awareness of them (Rankin, 1969). More and more people seem to recognize the existence of an "environmental crisis," but many have little or no knowledge of specific ways to deal with it. Finally, it seems likely that the effectiveness of environmental education would be especially high under certain circumstances. This may be the case when we are unaware that a problem exists, when we have little or no information about how to deal with it, and when the information provided suggests a specific, relatively low-cost solution.

Although they are sometimes successful, why do environmental education programs so often fail to have a positive effect on behavior? What do *you* think interferes with the effectiveness of environmental education? Many reasons have been proposed, most centering around the lack of correspondence that social psychologists often find between attitudes and behavior (Wicker, 1969a).

As we mentioned earlier, proponents of environmental education programs (cf. Leff, 1974) assume that information will lead to awareness, to attitude change, and finally to behavior change. Unfortunately, in view of social psychological work (e.g., Petty & Cacioppo, 1981) and work in environmental psychology indicating that attitudes frequently fail to predict behavior, these assumptions are not very sound (Wicker, 1969). An example should bring home our point about attitude–behavior discrepancies. Bickman (1972) planted trash on a path and watched students' *behavior*—they walked right past it. Although 98.6 percent did not pick up the litter, 94 percent endorsed the *attitude* statement, "It should be everyone's responsibility to pick up litter when they see it" (p. 324).

O'Riordan (1976) has listed several attitude–behavior assumptions on which environmental education may mistakenly rest:

1. The assumption that human beings are rational and consistent creatures who will modify their motivations on the basis of new information from self-interest to altruism.
2. The assumption that by concentrating upon one set of cognitions, we can change other relevant cognitions.
3. The assumption that attitude shifts will be sufficiently strong and long-lasting to influence behavior.

It is also the case that attitudes are only one possible determinant of behavior (Petty & Cacioppo, 1981). The behavior of lowering one's thermostat may depend less on one's attitudes toward conservation than on one's feelings of comfort, the reaction of one's family, etc. (Pallack, Cook, & Sullivan, 1980). And we should keep in mind that sometimes attitudes may follow from behavior (Bem, 1972) rather than precede it, as environmental educators typically assume.

These criticisms undermine the bedrock on which environmental education stands. Indeed, some argue that we have generally turned to environmental education after realizing that physical technology has been unable to provide a solution to environmental problems, only to find that education, too, is ineffective (Cone & Hayes, 1980). But there are those who disagree with such a dismal appraisal: They feel it is far too soon to display such pessimism about environmental education.

Some have suggested that environmental education has failed because it has often been attempted without sufficient understanding for why people engage in environmentally destructive behavior (Stern & Oskamp, 1987). For example, researchers have found that many believe that conserving energy by lowering the heat in their house could adversely affect their health and comfort. This belief is associated with nonconservation (Olsen, 1981). Environmental education could be aimed at attacking such beliefs (which would result in greater conservation), rather than simply making people aware that they may be using too much energy, and that lowering the thermostat would help to conserve. Studying what types of educational approaches are most effective at encouraging conservation (e.g., approaches that focus on the societal versus individual harm associated with nonconservation) and incorporating them into educational strategies would also be useful. It appears that communications that foster the belief that energy crises will have direct, negative effects on individuals are associated with increased conservation behavior (Olsen, 1981; Seligman et al., 1979).

Advocates of environmental education also point out that the methodological problems inherent in assessing the relationship between attitudes and behavior cast doubt on the conclusion that educational strategies to change attitudes will not lead to behavior change (Schuman & Johnson, 1976; Weigel & Newman, 1976). Overall, we might tentatively conclude that while research has not strongly supported the effectiveness of environmental education, future studies may reveal programs that have value, and methodological refinements may allow us to assess the effects of these better. Even if environmental education programs do not *change* behavior, they may serve a useful function in *reinforcing* proecological behavior and attitudes in people already committed to proecological action.

PROMPTS: REMINDERS OF WHAT TO DO AND OF WHAT NOT TO DO

In addition to environmental education, appropriate **prompts** (cues that convey a message) are commonly used to encourage environmentally constructive behavior and to discourage environmentally destructive acts. Signs such as those represented in Figure 14–4 are examples of typical prompts. However, this should not give you the idea that prompts are restricted to such mundane causes—they have been used for all types of proecological purposes. Prompts are **antecedent behavioral change techniques**. They occur before the target behavior and are designed to increase the likelihood of favorable acts (approach prompts) and to decrease the probability of unfavorable ones (avoidance prompts).

Some prompts are general in nature (e.g., "Help keep our community clean") while others are specific (e.g., "Drive 55 mph to save energy"). Some prompts signify incentives or disincentives for certain behaviors (e.g., "$100 fine for littering;" "5 cents for each bottle returned"), and others (e.g., the presence of police cars) may remind us of disincentives (e.g., speeding tickets if we exceed speed limits). Typically, **approach prompts** specify an incentive for engaging in some behavior, **avoidance prompts** a disincentive for enacting it (Geller, Winnett, & Everett, 1982). While prompts are generally administered in written or spoken form, the actions of social models (i.e., other people) and the condition of the environment may also function as prompts. How do the various types of prompts affect the way we act? It is assumed that they moderate environmentally destructive behavior by making certain social norms (e.g., the norm that we should not litter) either more or less salient in a given situation.

Clearly, the most common type of prompt consists of simple written and verbal messages. These have the advantage of being relatively inexpensive, and are effective in a number of contexts. For example, in an attempt to decelerate environmentally destructive lawn-walking behavior in a new "mini-park," Hayes and Cone (1977a) erected signs that read, "University Mini-Park—Please Don't Trample the Grass." This accounted for a significant reduction in the rate of lawn-walking behavior. As we will see later in this chapter, simple written prompts can also encourage energy conservation and decrease littering. In Beaver Stadium (capacity 60,000) at Pennsylvania State University a written prompt accounted for a 45 percent reduction in littering at a football game (Baltes & Hayward, 1976).

While written and verbal prompts *may* be effective, under certain conditions they are not. Pirages and Ehrlich (1974) reported that despite an appeal from the San Francisco Bay Area Pollution Control District for people to avoid using their cars during a serious smog episode, there was no demonstrable reduction in traffic flow. Generally, when the cost of obeying a prompt is too high, or when the prompt deals with a very essential behavior, it may go unheeded. Prompts accompanied by *contingencies* (e.g., offering a reward for the correct behavior or a penalty for the incorrect one) make it more likely that inconvenient proecological behaviors will be adopted (Geller et al., 1982). Prompts *without* such contingencies are most effective when they suggest responses that are easy to emit or avoid, are specific (say exactly which behavior should or should not be enacted), and are given in close proximity to an opportunity to perform the act (Stern & Oskamp, 1987).

Another determinant of the effectiveness of prompts is the specific wording of the message. Under some conditions, psychological reac-

Figure 14–4 A&B Signs such as these exemplify typical prompts.

tance (described in Chapter 4) may be aroused. While anti-litter prompts of the "Please don't litter" variety can be effective, overly forceful prompts ("Don't you *dare* litter," or "You *must* not litter") are quite ineffective (Reich & Robertson, 1979) because they may elicit reactance. Such prompts can actually cause people to do exactly the opposite of what is desired (Reich & Robertson, 1979). The size and the salience of prompts would also be expected to impact on effectiveness, though the relationship is somewhat complex. Obviously, a prompt must be sufficiently large and salient to be seen in order to have an effect, but when it is too large or salient, it may be perceived as overly forceful and elicit reactance (e.g., Luyben, 1980).

In addition to prompts that employ verbal or written messages, the state of the environment and the behavior of models can also function as prompts that affect behavior. A clean or dirty environment may convey information about how one is expected to behave there, and thus make the anti-littering norm more or less salient. In this way, it may serve as an anti- or pro-litter prompt (e.g., Krauss, Freedmen, & Whitcup, 1978; Reiter & Samuel, 1980). Similarly, a human model who litters or does not litter may undermine or bolster the anti-littering norms with which we are socialized, and thus serve as a prompt (Stern & Oskamp, 1987). Models can consist of other live individuals or people portrayed in the media. As well as demonstrating a specific behavior, models often provide information for us about the positive or negative consequences of an act.

A final type of prompt is the physical presence of an environmentally constructive alternative. This is usually an object which, if used, could prevent an environmentally destructive act. For example, a nearby sidewalk might serve as a prompt not to walk on newly planted grass, or a nearby garbage can might function as a cue not to litter. Of course, such objects do not serve as prompts in a strict sense, since they provide a behavioral alternative to environmentally destructive behavior. Be that as it may, many researchers (especially those doing work on littering) consider such objects to be a type of prompt and have measured how they affect environmentally destructive acts. (Figure 14–5).

REINFORCEMENT TECHNIQUES: WHAT YOU DO DETERMINES WHAT YOU GET

In addition to environmental education and the use of prompts, reinforcement techniques have been employed to modify environmentally destructive behavior. In contrast to prompts which are *antecedent* strategies (i.e., occur before an event), reinforcers are *consequence* strategies (come after it). Some of the most successful efforts to date have involved reinforcement methods.

One such strategy is termed **positive reinforcement**. In this technique, individuals are given positively valued stimuli for performing environmentally constructive acts (e.g., they may be offered money for turning in paper at a recycling center). The purpose of positive reinforcement is to increase the probability that a desirable response will occur in the future. As opposed to positive reinforcement, **negative reinforcement** increases desirable behavior because we are motivated to escape some ongoing noxious stimulus (e.g., high electric bills) or avoid an aversive stimulus (e.g., a fine). A third

Figure 14–5 Sometimes the physical presence of an object, which if used could prevent environmentally destructive behavior, can be considered a prompt. In the case of this trash can, the prompt appears to have been quite effective!

the same reinforcer can often be perceived as a positive or a negative reinforcer or as punishment, depending on the context and the observer's perspective. For a program to be successful, it is essential that the target population perceive things in the same way as the program director or designer (Geller et al., 1982).

We turn now to a general discussion of the efficacy of using positive reinforcement, negative reinforcement, punishment, and feedback. While reinforcement strategies are often effective, like prompts they can backfire (e.g., when they elicit reactance). Consequence techniques may affect one's perception of control, and when we believe we have lost our freedom and are being ''manipulated,'' we may work against the goals of the program and refuse to emit the target behavior. Skinner (1971) suggests that positive reinforcement is less apt to cause reactance than negative reinforcement or punishment.

Positive Reinforcement: Encouraging Good Behavior

Positive reinforcers have been used in the vast majority of studies employing reinforcement techniques. These have ranged from financial rewards (either small or large) to nonmonetary benefits (e.g., decals stating, ''I protect the environment''). Positive reinforcers are the most socially acceptable of all the reinforcement strategies, are the easiest to administer, and are probably the most cost-effective in the long run (Geller et al., 1982). Because they require an elaborate enforcement apparatus, negative reinforcers and punishment are sometimes more expensive to administer than positive reinforcers.

In some cases, positive reinforcers are administered continuously, while in others they are given less frequently. Sometimes positive reinforcement is made to be contingent on performing a particular *response;* in other instances it is given when a particular *outcome* is achieved. Examples of response-contingent

technique is called **punishment**. It usually entails administering a noxious or painful stimulus to those who engage in environmentally destructive behavior (e.g., a reprimand or fine to someone who litters). Behaviors are decreased in frequency when followed by punishment, at least in the short run.

The final reinforcement-related technique may be termed **feedback**. This method provides information about whether one is attaining or failing to attain an environmental goal (e.g., reducing fuel consumption). As such, feedback may constitute positive reinforcement or punishment, depending on whether the recipient is succeeding or failing. It is important to note that positive reinforcement are raffle tickets for bringing paper to a recycling center (e.g., Ingram & Geller, 1975) and a token redeemable for merchandise for using public transportation (Deslauriers & Everett, 1977). Examples of outcome contingent reinforcement are giving someone money for cleaning up a yard to criterion (Chapman & Risley, 1974) and payment for maintaining a 10 percent reduction in home heating energy (Winett & Nietzel, 1975). Since response contingent reinforcers provide us with information about what specific behaviors are appropriate while outcome contingent reinforcers often do not, the latter may ultimately be less effective in encouraging proecological behavior (Geller et al., 1982).

Studies using positive reinforcement strategies can be divided into two groups. One has used these techniques to improve environments that are already disturbed (e.g., littered, noisy); the second has used them to prevent negative consequences from occurring in the first place. In studies employing positive reinforcements to restore disturbed environments, strong changes in behavior have occurred, at least for the period in which the reinforcement contingency remains in effect.

An especially interesting set of such studies has dealt with eliminating excessive noise in elementary and secondary schools. In one project, Schmidt and Ulrich (1969) monitored noise levels in a second- and a fourth-grade classroom and found an average of 52 dB. When students were told they could earn extra minutes of gym for each 12-minute period in which sound levels did not exceed 42 dB, dramatic and stable reductions resulted. Similarly, Wilson and Hopkins (1973) used automated equipment to record the percentage of time that sound in seventh- and eighth-grade home economics classes exceeded 70 dB. When the sound level dropped below the 70 dB threshold, the students' favorite radio station was played. Although the noise before treatment exceeded 70 dB for 30 percent of the time, during the treatment it exceeded the threshold

for only 5 percent of the time. Clearly, the appropriate use of positive reinforcers may be an important technique in improving disturbed environmental conditions.

Up until now we have discussed positive reinforcement techniques in terms of their capacity to restore disturbed environments. However, as we noted earlier, a second group of studies has used these methods to prevent negative environment-related effects from occurring in the first place. Studies in this area involve anticipatory attempts to forestall negative effects by reinforcing people when they engage in appropriate behaviors. In this research, both monetary and nonmonetary reinforcers have been used. Some projects have offered nonmonetary benefits, such as faster commuting times, to promote energy conservation. For example, in many cities, faster passage (a nonmonetary reinforcer) is offered to cars with three or more passengers by allowing them to travel in special lanes with less traffic. Similar nonmonetary benefits are provided by special buses operated by many cities that take commuters from suburban parking areas to the city center. These buses make it unnecessary to search for a parking space (a considerable benefit) and reduce the tension associated with driving in city traffic. Unfortunately, the effectiveness of such programs is not well researched.

In contrast to programs using nonmonetary positive reinforcers to prevent negative effects on the environment, research has measured the effects of monetary reinforcers. These studies show that offering money can increase behaviors that forestall environmental damage. Encouraging results were found in a study that employed monetary reinforcers to increase student ridership of a campus bus system (Everett, Hayward, & Meyers, 1974). Increased ridership means less pollution, less gasoline consumption, and so on. As we will see later in this chapter, studies also suggest that monetary reinforcers can be employed to increase energy conservation in the home (Hayes & Cone,

1977b; Kohlenberg, Phillips, & Proctor, 1976; Winett & Nietzel, 1975).

In general, the use of various types of positive reinforcers is an effective technique both for restoring disturbed environmental conditions and for preventing environmentally destructive behaviors. However, while we have painted a rather glowing picture thus far, we should mention some negative aspects that are associated with such techniques. First, they are often quite expensive. In some studies on energy conservation, the costs of the program exceeded the value of the energy saved (Stern & Oskamp, 1987). Second, in some instances it has been found that target behaviors that improved during the reinforcement period returned to baseline levels soon after reinforcement contingencies were removed (Stern & Oskamp, 1987). This is sometimes a problem in other reinforcement-related methods as well. Since people are responding to externally-imposed contingencies, they may have little motivation to retain desirable behaviors once reinforcements are removed. While such studies show the *potential* of environmental psychology for suggesting public policy alternatives to alleviate environmental problems, at this time they do not offer clearcut possibilities for environmental policymakers (Stern & Oskamp, 1987). This is because of their sometimes unfavorable cost–benefit ratio, and because proecological behaviors may be difficult to maintain after the reinforcers are terminated.

Negative Reinforcement and Punishment: Alternatives to Positive Reinforcement

We have devoted considerable attention to positive reinforcement as a moderator of environmentally destructive behavior, but what of the effects of negative reinforcement and punishment? In general, negative reinforcement as conceptualized here involves avoiding unpleasant aspects of a situation, and punishment consists of adding aversive elements to it. Not

surprisingly, researchers have used these methods much less than positive reinforcement to control environmentally destructive behavior. We will discuss some suggestions for employing negative reinforcement and punishment, but it should be noted that few such programs currently exist.

Many possible applications of negative reinforcers to combat unfavorable environmental conditions have been suggested. For example, Cone and Hayes (1980) suggest that we might prohibit aircraft that exceed certain noise standards from landing at convenient airports, so that airline companies and aircraft manufacturers might reduce noise levels in order to avoid the prohibitions. Another use of negative reinforcement would be to threaten to cut off important corporate tax benefits for companies polluting our water and air. While all of these options may be promising, most have not yet been implemented, and those that are in operation have not yet been subjected to scientific study.

How might punishment be used to discourage behaviors that are not in our environmental best interests? Some uses of punishment are rather common, e.g., fines for companies that pollute and for people who drop trash along the roadside. Another suggestion, which would lower traffic in urban centers and on nearby freeways, is to change parking and toll rates to make it much more expensive for those who travel by private automobile during peak hours. Unfortunately, since programs employing them have not yet been implemented or studied in many cases, we will have to reserve judgment on the use of negative reinforcement and punishment to regulate environmentally destructive behavior. They may hold great hope, but only the future can tell.

Feedback: Letting Us Know How We Are Doing

The final reinforcement-related strategy is termed ''feedback.'' Feedback may be viewed as a form of response-contingent reinforcement. As we noted earlier, it may be either positive or negative, depending on whether the performance it refers to is successful or unsuccessful. In this way, it may constitute either positive reinforcement or punishment, although it may actually be intended only to inform, not to reward or punish. How has feedback been used to improve environment-related behavior? Examples of its use include feedback on energy use given monthy or weekly (e.g., Kohlenberg et al., 1976) and placing estimates of commu-nity litter on the front page of the local newspaper (Schnelle et al., 1980). In general, feedback has been employed alone or in combination with other strategies (e.g., environmental education, prompts), as well as with certain reinforcers, such as money. While it is often difficult to separate the effects of the feedback component of the treatment from the other elements, studies we will review later in this chapter suggest that feedback can be a very effective technique.

INTEGRATING AND EVALUATING THE VARIOUS APPROACHES TO ELIMINATING ENVIRONMENTALLY DESTRUCTIVE BEHAVIOR

We have considered environmental education, use of prompts, and reinforcement-related techniques as separate strategies for improving the quality of the environment. While it is true that these methods have often been employed separately by researchers, and that such a presentation makes the material easier for the reader to digest, it is also true that many studies have used several methods simultaneously. Often, a combined strategy enables the researcher to tailor his or her attack to the specific qualities of the problem and yields the strongest possible program. While we could never hope to survey the many combined strategies that have been used to combat environmentally destructive behavior, we would like to offer an example that will be relevant to many of our readers.

As you undoubtedly know if you have ever resided in a college dormitory, noise can become a tremendous problem. Further, you have probably observed that the coping strategies of dormitory residents are many and varied. In an attempt to combat the "noise nemesis," Meyers, Artz, and Craighead (1976) structured a program that included elements of both reinforcement-related techniques and environmental education. The treatment package consisted of: (1) an *educational* component, in which residents were given information about noise and how to deal with it; (2) a *feedback* component, which included a doorbell set to ring when a serious noise transgression occurred; and (3) a *reinforcement* component, which took several forms, including monetary reward. What were the effects of this combined approach? It accounted for a striking decrease in noise transgressions from 345 per day during the baseline period to 148 per day during treatment. Thus, the combination of a reinforcement approach with environmental education and feedback may have yielded unique benefits otherwise unavailable. It should be noted that combined programs have also been successful in other contexts.

While it is apparent that combined strategies may often be quite effective, you may be wondering at this point how various individual methods (environmental education, prompts, and reinforcements) measure up relative to each other. In general, reinforcement strategies are strongest, prompts are moderately effective, and environmental education is weakest (Cone & Hayes, 1980). One study that allows us to draw these conclusions involved an ingenious attempt to measure the effectiveness of several anti-littering strategies in theaters (Clark, Hendee, & Burgess, 1972). It evaluated the following approaches: (1) showing a Walt Disney anti-littering cartoon (environmental education); (2) adding extra trash cans, distributing litter bags, or distributing both litter bags and instructions (all of which are prompts); and (3) providing money and movie tickets as incentives for full litter bags (reinforcements). To evaluate the effectiveness of the various strategies in each condition, the proportion of the total litter that was deposited appropriately was measured. As can be seen in Figure 14–6, environmental education had little effect. The use of prompts proved quite variable, with some strategies having a mildly positive effect and others not. However, when reinforcements in the form of money or free tickets were added, the positive effects were truly formidable.

How representative is this pattern of results? It can be stated that it generally reflects other studies designed to allow a comparison of all three approaches, as well as studies designed to compare the relative effectiveness of only two of the strategies (Geller, Chaffee, & Ingram, 1975; Kohlenberg et al., 1976; Luyben & Bailey, 1975). But relative effectiveness is not all that should be taken into account in designing a program to counter environmentally destructive behavior. As noted throughout this chapter, each of the techniques we have mentioned has *unique* costs and benefits, which should be assessed completely before deciding on a strategy (Stern & Oskamp, 1987). For example, reinforcements appear to have strong effects but are often relatively expensive to administer. In contrast, prompts are somewhat less effective but are relatively inexpensive. Thus, the dictates of the situation should determine which combination of costs and benefits is most appropriate.

Something to include in any program are elements that increase proecological behaviors along with elements that decrease undesirable ones (e.g., tax benefits for proper waste dis-

Figure 14–6 Percentage of total litter returned by the audience under environmental education, prompt, and reinforcement-related conditions. (From Clark, R. N., Hendee, J. C., & Burgess, R. L., 1972. The experimental control of littering. *Journal of Environmental Education, 4,* 22–28.)

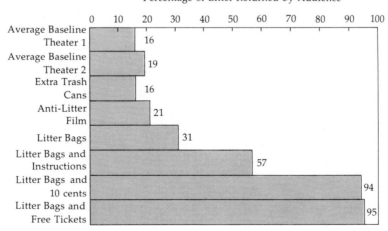

Percentage of Litter Returned by Audience

posal, along with fines for dumping toxic wastes). To ensure this, a mixture of strategies is frequently necessary. Further, it should always be ascertained that the selected treatments do not have unintended negative side effects. In the end, the choice is quite complex, and can best be made by individuals who are familar with the situation and who weigh all the relevant factors carefully before reaching a conclusion (Stern & Oskamp, 1987). It should be ascertained what type of action, taken by whom, would have the largest effect on the environment. Such an analysis may sometimes suggest that interventions other than the types we have discussed above would be most effective. For example, the use of strategies such as reinforcement or feedback to encourage energy conservation would probably pale when compared to the relatively more dramatic effects of the government imposing mandatory average fuel economy standards on automakers (Stern & Oskamp, 1987).

APPROACHES TO SPECIFIC ENVIRONMENTAL PROBLEMS

Armed with an understanding of some useful general techniques for curbing environmentally destructive behavior, we will consider some specific approaches which have been applied to cope with several major environmental problems—littering, energy overconsumption both at home and in transportation settings, and finally, vandalism.

Littering

In the United States, hundreds of millions of tons of trash are "created" each year, and too much of this ends up as litter. A great deal of such litter collects annually alongside our highways (Ward, 1975). It costs a tremendous amount of money to clean up this mess in public areas (e.g., highways, parks) and in private ones (e.g., business and industrial property). In addition to being profoundly ugly, litter represents a hazard to our health and safety and may cause damage to plant and animal life. Who helps to create these unseemly conditions? Young people litter more than older ones; some studies suggest that males litter more than females; and people who are alone litter more than those in groups (Osborne & Powers, 1980).

The whole range of strategies we have discussed (e.g., prompts, reinforcers) has been used in attempts to prevent people from littering, and to motivate them to clean up litter left by careless individuals. We will discuss the various techniques, and find that some methods have been more effective than others. (For detailed reviews, see Brasted, Mann, & Geller, 1979; Cone & Hayes, 1978; Geller, 1987; Osborne & Powers, 1980). In addition, bottle bill legislation (requiring a deposit on all bottles and cans) has been effective in reducing this type of litter at the roadside by 75 percent and in saving energy through recycling (Levitt & Leventhal, 1984; Osborne & Powers, 1980).

Many studies have employed prompts and cues as antecedent strategies to prevent littering. For example, handbills with an anti-litter prompt are less apt to be littered than those without a prompt (Geller et al., 1982) (Figure 14–7). Generally, prompts that state the specific anti-litter response desired (e.g., "Place this paper in a trashcan") are more effective than general ones. Anti-litter prompts are also more effective when given in close temporal proximity to an opportunity to dispose of litter, when proper litter disposal is relatively convenient, and when the prompt is phrased in polite, nondemanding language (Geller et al., 1982; Stern & Oskamp, 1987). Even under optimal circumstances, the absolute magnitude of change effected by these sorts of prompts is often relatively small (though statistically significant), and to have a meaningful effect they may have to be experienced by many people over a long time frame.

Other antecedent factors which may serve as prompts include the amount of litter already in a setting, the behavior of models, and the presence of trash receptacles. Generally, "litter begets litter"—the more littered an environment the more littered it becomes. In fact, studies have shown up to a five-fold increase in littering in "littered" as opposed to "clean" settings (e.g., Finnie, 1973; Geller, Witmer, & Tuso, 1977; Krauss, Freedman, & Whitcup, 1978). Extrapolating from these findings, we could expect vandalism to beget more vandalism and graffitti to prompt more of the same (Sharpe, 1976). In addition to the pattern noted in the box on page 488, an exception to the "litter begets litter" finding has been reported

Figure 14–7   Type of prompt utilized in a number of littering studies. (Adapted from the work of E. Scott Geller.)

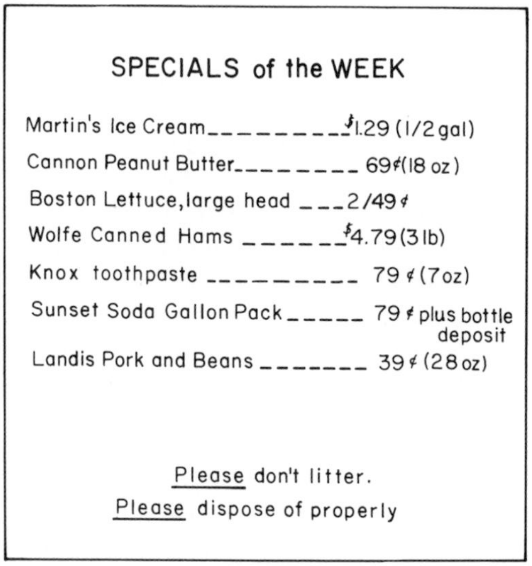

```
┌────────────────────────────────────────┐
│                                          │
│        SPECIALS of the WEEK              │
│                                          │
│   Martin's Ice Cream_____$1.29 (1/2 gal)│
│                                          │
│   Cannon Peanut Butter_____ 69¢(18 oz)│
│                                          │
│   Boston Lettuce,large head ___2/49¢     │
│                                          │
│   Wolfe Canned Hams _____$4.79(3 lb)     │
│                                          │
│   Knox toothpaste _____ 79 ¢(7oz)    │
│                                          │
│   Sunset Soda Gallon Pack_____ 79 ¢ plus bottle│
│                                         deposit│
│   Landis Pork and Beans _____ 39¢ (28 oz)│
│                                          │
│                                          │
│         Please don't litter.             │
│       Please dispose of properly         │
│                                          │
└────────────────────────────────────────┘
```

in some natural settings, where people are less apt to litter and more apt to pick up other people's trash when their picnic areas are littered than when clean. This may be because in such settings environmental cleanliness plays an especially important role for people, since they are there to appreciate natural beauty (cf. Geller et al., 1982).

Like the state of the environment, directly observing the behavior of models can serve as a prompt that reduces or produces environmentally destructive behavior. Cialdini (1977) exposed subjects to a model who littered or did not litter in a clean or dirty environment. After seeing the model fail to litter in the clean setting, subjects littered the least; after seeing him litter in the dirty setting they littered the most. And Jason, Zolik, and Matese (1979) found that observing a proecological model who showed people how to pick up dog droppings with a "pooper scooper" led to a target area more free of feces. Unfortunately, other studies are less optimistic about the potential of models to prevent environmentally destructive behavior (cf. Geller et al., 1982). From social psychological research we can predict that modeling will be most effective when the model is liked and respected by the target person, and is reinforced for his or her proecological actions (Bandura, 1969; Bandura & Walters, 1967).

A final antecedent strategy to prevent littering is the presence of waste receptacles. Finnie (1973) reported that compared to a condition in which no trash cans were in sight, their presence reduced littering by about 15 percent along city streets and by nearly 30 percent on highways. When a greater number of trash cans were present, littering decreased still more. (Imagine a world with trash cans placed every two feet in an attempt to efficiently control littering!) The value of trash cans or similar objects as anti-litter prompts may depend on their attractiveness or distinctiveness. Finnie (1973) observed that colorful garbage cans reduced littering by 14.9 percent over baseline

. . . .

Is A Little Litter a
More Effective Prompt
Than None At All?

We suggested that more environmentally destructive behavior typically occurs when there is evidence of previous misdeeds (litter on the ground) than when there is not. While this is usually true, work by Cialdini, Reno, and Kallgren (1989) brought out an interesting caveat. While they found (like previous investigators) that a perfectly clean environment produces less littering than a dirty environment, they also observed that the *least* littering occurs in a setting that is clean except for one piece of litter. The studies were run as follows: Subjects were handed a public service-related circular as they walked down a path. Beforehand, the experimenter had positioned 0, 1, 2, 4, 8, or 16 pieces of litter in front of them. As indicated in Figure 14–8, 18 percent of the subjects littered in the "no litter" condition, but only 10 percent littered in the "one piece of litter" condition. Beyond that, littering by subjects increased proportionate to the amount of litter positioned by the experimenter.

Why did Cialdini et al. observe such a "check mark" pattern for the relationship between the amount of litter in the environment and subsequent littering? They reasoned that while a perfectly clean environment makes the "no littering" norm salient, an environment clean except for one violation makes it

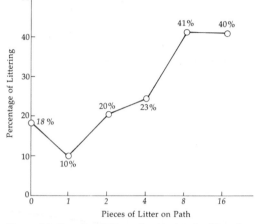

Figure 14–8 Percentage of subjects who littered as a function of pieces of litter on the path. (Used by permission of Dr. Robert Cialdini, Arizona State University.)

even more salient. With increasing violations, however, the norm becomes undermined, and littering is facilitated. These findings are provocative, and if replicated in other contexts they could have practical implications for environmental education as well as for environmental design. For example, do you think you would be more likely to return your shopping cart at the supermarket if all but one of the remaining carts were neatly stacked or if there were no violations of the "return your cart" norm?

. . . .

levels, while ordinary cans led to a reduction of only 3.15 percent. Similarly, Miller et al. (1976) reported that brightly colored cans resembling birds were much more effective than plain cans in eliciting appropriate disposal.

Finally, an ingenious garbage can in the shape of a hat worn by students to Clemson University football games greatly reduced trash in the area of the college football stadium (Miller et al., 1976; O'Neill, Blanck, & Joyner, 1980). Such cans serve both as prompts to prevent litter from being disposed of inappropriately and to motivate people to pick it up, since it can be reinforcing to deposit litter in them. (The Clemson hat dispenses a mechanical "Thank you" to anyone who deposits litter in it.)

We turn now to consequence strategies for litter control (i.e., methods to encourage people to pick up existing litter), which have generally been more effective than antecedent techniques (Cone & Hayes, 1980). Prompts have been used as a consequence technique, in addition to being employed as an antecedent strategy. Unfortunately, picking up someone else's litter and putting it in a receptacle is often a more costly behavior than depositing one's own litter, and it seems to be relatively unresponsive to prompts. For example, 10 experiments by Geller and associates (Geller, 1976; Geller, Mann, & Brasted, 1977) found that prompts have minimal effects on people's likelihood of picking up others' litter and disposing of it. The only exception may be in natural areas, such as campgrounds, where prompts may elicit such behavior (cf. Crump, Nunes, & Crossman, 1977). The ineffectiveness of prompts is especially unfortunate, since much money is spent on them by state litter control authorities and organizations such as Keep America Beautiful. (See the box, page 490.)

Reinforcement-based techniques are more successful than prompts in motivating people to clean up littered environments. In fact, when prompts are coupled with reinforcements for obeying them, they can be rather effective. Kohlenberg and Phillips (1973) positioned a prompt which said, "Depositing Litter May Be Rewarded," and then proceeded to reward litter depositors on different reinforcement schedules. This technique precipitated a dramatic cleanup. Another study involved a combination of prompts, environmental education, and reinforcers (in this case feedback). Investigators organized local newspaper coverage about the littering problem (which served as a prompt and a form of education), along with daily feedback

on littering in certain target areas. These methods accounted for a decrease in litter compared to baseline conditions (Schnelle et al., 1980). Other experiments have similarly coupled reinforcers with educational techniques and prompts. In these studies, the rewards generally account for much more of the resultant improvement in the litter situation than the other methods (Cone & Hayes, 1980). However, while reinforcement methods are useful, they sometimes require costly supervision to monitor behavior and dispense reinforcers. What alternatives are there for reinforcing litter depositors without supervision?

One group of studies has used novelty trash cans, which reinforce litter depositors by talking to them, displaying a "Thank you" sign, or emitting some other response. There is short- but little long-term research suggesting that these may be effective in motivating people to pick up litter (Geller et al., 1982). Reinforcements can also be administered on the "honor system." A sign in a U.S. forest area offered people either 25 cents (sent to them by mail) or a chance to win a larger reward if they filled a plastic trash bag with garbage and completed an "information card" stating their name and address. Compared to a prompt-only condition (which asked people to fill up a bag but offered no reward), the "honor system" reinforcement condition was much more successful (Powers et al., 1973).

A clever and effective use of positive reinforcement that motivates people to pick up litter is the "litter lottery." A litter lottery offers people an opportunity to win valuable prizes just for depositing litter appropriately. In one version of the technique (Bacon-Prue et al., 1980; Hayes, Johnson, & Cone, 1975), experimenters distribute specially marked items on the ground amidst the litter that is habitually present. People are told some litter is marked in an undetectable fashion, and if an experimenter verifies that they have collected a marked item, they will be awarded a substantial prize. In another version (Kohlenberg & Phillips, 1973),

Keep America Beautiful:
The Clean Community System

A national organization called Keep America Beautiful has developed the Clean Community System (CCS), a hybrid set of strategies which has had widespread impact on litter control. The CCS has been implemented in hundreds of U.S. communities and in other countries, and is an excellent model for community action aimed at solving environmental problems.

How does CCS work? A community must apply for CCS certification by showing its commitment to an anti-litter program. To join, the city's mayor must endorse CCS, the public works director must submit an evaluation of the litter and solid waste situation in the community, and a committee must be formed representing the commercial, government, and consumer sectors. There are other requirements as well. When a community is accepted for membership, CCS gives a workshop for the local "project team," provides program modules, and many other types of useful supports.

What is the philosophy of CCS? It includes elements of both environmental education and the behavioral techniques we have discussed. CCS assumes that unacceptable norms and attitudes cause littering, and that these can be changed by using behavioral principles. It is believed that when negative attitudes change, littering will decrease. What types of tactics does the CCS program include? Among other things, educational programs are developed and presented, media are used to focus attention on people who engage in commendable anti-litter activities, incentive programs

are developed to reward appropriate waste disposal, punishment contingencies are clarified so they can be enforced effectively, and new anti-littering laws may be added (e.g., those who litter may be required to pick up litter along the highway). Also, prompts and cues may be placed appropriately, as well as increased trash receptacles. Finally, a major part of CCS is an evaluation component, to check up on how well the procedures are working and to suggest modifications to enhance effectiveness.

How do environmental psychologists evaluate the CCS system? Geller et al. (1982) commend it as a model for community participation in dealing with environmental problems, but pinpoint a number of interesting conceptual and methodological issues. First, they disagree with the assumption that changing attitudes about litter is a necessary prerequisite for dealing with the litter problem. In fact, some environmental psychologists argue that CCS works not due to its attitude change component, but because of its other elements. (We noted earlier in this chapter that anti-littering attitudes will not guarantee non-littering *behavior*, due to the persistent discrepancy between attitudes and behavior). Second, Geller et al. (1982) suggest that the procedures could be even more effective if they held more closely to behavioral principles. Third, they point out a number of methodological problems in the way the effectiveness of CCS is evaluated.

the experimenter merely observes litter deposits and rewards ecologically-minded people intermittently. Both techniques have achieved dramatic results toward cleaning up the environment, but both require costly human intervention. The "marked item" strategy can, however, be "automated" and introduced widely. Imagine the following scenario for improving litter control throughout the United States. Litter marked with radioactive isotopes (or in some other way) would be distributed at random, as would special trash cans (indistinguishable from ordinary ones) that would deliver valuable reinforcers automatically if a "marked item" were deposited. Whenever you had some spare time, you might find yourself absentmindedly picking up garbage, throwing it in a trash can, and fantasizing about future wealth! Of course, the "novelty" of such a program might wear off after a while, and it would be expensive to administer, which could detract from its overall usefulness (Figure 14–9).

In conceiving of any technique for improving environmental conditions, one should be careful to think about ways in which it could be "subverted." One problem with the litter lottery is that it may not prevent people from throwing litter on the ground—the piece they throw away cannot possibly be "marked." Children participating in a litter lottery still disposed of litter inappropriately (La Hart & Bailey, 1975). On the other hand, the more garbage litter-lottery participants deposit inap-

Figure 14–9 Paying for the collection of litter from highways, parks, and other public places costs Americans over $1 billion in taxes per year. It is important to find ways to motivate people to pick it up. (Andrew Fisher)

propriately, the more difficult it should be to find "marked" items. Adults may be aware of this contingency, and it may keep them from littering. When reinforcements are given per bag of litter collected (as in Powers et al.), this too may be problematic because it encourages people to pick up large but not small pieces of litter, and perhaps even to throw it on the ground in the first place. They may not pick up litter from the target area at all, but may bring it from home. And when rewards are based on some criterion (e.g., a clean campsite), this may encourage some people to clean the area by throwing trash somewhere else.

To summarize, several strategies have been used to prevent littering, and to encourage people to pick up extant litter. Prompts and cues (e.g., signs, verbal appeals, a clean environment, availability of trash cans) may be somewhat effective antecedent techniques. They are especially effective when depositing litter is convenient, the request is specific, and certain other conditions are met. However, antecedent prompt techniques rarely improve the litter situation by more than about 20 percent. Prompts without accompanying reinforcements

---

When the heat is on . . .

- Lower your thermostat to 65 degrees during the day and 55 degrees at night. You can save about 3 percent on your fuel costs for every degree you reduce the *average temperature* in your home. In addition, you can save about 1 percent on your heating bills for every degree you dial down *only at night.*

- Keep windows near your thermostat tightly closed, otherwise it will keep your furnace working after the rest of the room has reached a comfortable temperature.

- Have your oil furnace serviced at least once a year, preferably each summer to take advantage of off-season rates. This simple precaution could save you 10 percent in fuel consumption.

- Clean or replace the filter in your forced-air heating system each month.

- Check the duct work for air leaks about once a year if you have a forced-air heating system. To do this, feel around the duct joints for escaping air when the fan is on.

- Relatively small leaks can be repaired simply by covering holes or cracks with duct tape. More stubborn problems may require caulking as well as taping. You could save almost 9 percent in heating fuel costs this way.

- If you have oil heat, check to see if the firing rate is correct. Chances are it isn't. A recent survey found that 97 percent of the furnaces checked were overfired.

- If your oil furnace doesn't run almost constantly on a very cold day, call a service man.

- Don't let cold air seep into your home through the attic access door. Check the door to make sure it is well insulated and weatherstripped, otherwise you'll be wasting fuel to heat that cool air.

- Dust or vacuum radiator surfaces frequently. Dust and grime impede the flow of heat. And if the radiators need painting, use flat paint, preferably black. It radiates heat better than glossy.

- Keep draperies and shades open in sunny windows; close them at night.

- For comfort in cooler indoor temperatures, use the best insulation of all—warm clothing.

- The human body gives off heat, about 390 BTU per hour for a man, 330 for a woman. Dressing wisely can help you retain natural heat.

- Wear closely woven fabrics. They add at least a half a degree in warmth.

- *For women.* Slacks are at least a degree warmer than skirts.

- *For men and women.* A light longsleeved sweater equals almost 2 degrees in added warmth; a heavy long-sleeved sweater adds about 3.7 degrees; and two lightweight sweaters add about 5 degrees in warmth because the air between them serves to keep in more body heat.

are *not* effective in motivating people to pick up extant litter. Reinforcements coupled with prompts, or reinforcements used along with other techniques, are often quite effective in facilitating cleanup of a littered environment. In fact, their use can often effect a speedy cleanup of an environmental setting, and cleanups that account for a large percentage of the extant litter are not uncommon. However, some such programs may be costly due to supervision and the cost of reinforcers. Also, without careful planning, reinforcement programs may be subverted.

Saving Energy at Home: Residential Energy Conservation

Another environmental issue which has received research attention is energy conservation. While at present there is sufficient energy to meet our needs, this was not the case during the 1970s when various forms of rationing had to be enacted. Since the Western countries are *still* dependent on OPEC, we may again find ourselves facing insufficient fuel supplies if OPEC ministers decide to reduce production, or if other events (e.g., war, political instability)

If every household in the United States lowered its average heating temperatures 6 degrees over a 24-hour period, we would save more than 570,000 barrels of oil per day or more than 3.5 percent of our current oil imports.

Cooling Energy Savers

Overcooling is expensive and wastes energy. Don't use or buy more cooling equipment capacity than you actually need.

Regarding air-conditioning equipment . . .

- If you need central air-conditioning, select the smallest and least powerful system that will cool your home adequately. A larger unit than you need not only costs more to run but probably won't remove enough moisture from the air.

- Ask your dealer to help you determine how much cooling power you need for the space you have to cool and for the climate in which you live. (For further information, see page 19. Energy Efficiency-Ratios.)

- Make sure the ducts in your air-conditioning system are properly insulated, especially those that pass through the attic or other uncooled spaces. This could save you almost 9 percent in cooling costs.

- If you don't need central air-conditioning, consider using individual window or through-the-wall units in rooms that need cooling from time to time. Select the smallest and least powerful units for the rooms you need to cool. As a rule, these will cost less to buy and less to operate.

- Install a whole-house ventilating fan in your attic or in an upstairs window to cool the house when it's cool outside, even if you have central air-conditioning.

- It will pay to use the fan rather than air-conditioning when the outside temperature is below 82 degrees. When windows in the house are open, the fan pulls cool air through the house and exhausts warm air through the attic.

When you use air-conditioning . . .

- Set your thermostat at 78 degrees, a reasonably comfortable and energy-efficient indoor temperature.

- The higher the setting and the less difference between indoor and outdoor temperature, the less outdoor hot air will flow into the building.

- If the 78°F setting raises your home temperature 6 degrees (from 72°F to 78°F, for example), you should save between 12 and 47 percent in cooling costs, depending on where you live.

Figure 14–10   A typical page from an informational brochure. "Tips for Energy Savers," Federal Energy Administration. (Reprinted from Geller, E. S., Winnett, R. A., & Everett, P., 1982. *Preserving the environment: New strategies for behavior change.* New York: Pergamon.)

occur in the world. We can reduce the impact of such occurrences if we conserve energy both "at home" and "on the road." We will discuss saving energy at home first, followed by a discussion of energy conservation in transportation settings.

About 20 percent of all the energy used in the United States is consumed in private residences, and much of this is wasted (Cone & Hayes, 1980). In fact, the energy used in the "typical" American home could be reduced by 50 percent by making some simple physical and behavioral changes (Socolow, 1978). A way to accomplish this is suggted in the box on page 493.

One approach to residential energy conservation has been through environmental education. Various brochures and pamphlets have been prepared by local utilities and by the federal government (Figure 14–10). Even though people are frequently misinformed about energy use and its consequences (e.g., they believe that turning down thermostats in evenings during the winter will lead to increased energy use when turned up in the morning), studies have suggested that educating them is not effective at changing energy-relevant behaviors (e.g., Heberlein, 1975; Palmer, Lloyd, & Lloyd, 1978; Winnett et al., 1978). For example, Heberlein (1975) gave people either a typical booklet of energy-saving tips prepared by the electric company, an informational letter educating them in the personal and social costs of not conserving energy, or an informational pamphlet urging people to use *more* energy! What were the effects of the educational strategies? None of them had any appreciable effect on behavior. In a similar vein, Geller (1981) gave educational workshops on energy use, and found they were very effective in changing attitudes and intentions regarding energy use, but follow-up audits of participants' homes revealed that the changes suggested in the workshops had not been implemented. Correct information should thus

be conceptualized as a necessary element in any intervention, and as something which may affect attitudes, but it is not sufficient to promote behavior change.

Under what conditions do educational programs on home energy conservation have the greatest potential for success? An educational program for high school students which included an energy audit and teaching students how to monitor home consumption positively affected student behaviors and those of parents (Stevens et al., 1979). This program may have been productive because it taught *specific* conservation behaviors, not general ones. An energy audit (especially a "type A" audit in which an auditor comes to the home, makes specific suggestions, and discusses them with the owner or occupant) also shows special promise, though more evaluation is needed (Geller et al., 1982). In effect, *specificity* of conservation targets and behaviors seems to be an important element in programs targeted at improving home energy conservation.

Involving homeowners actively in an energy audit (e.g., having them go up to the attic with the auditor to examine it) also makes a difference (Stern & Aronson, 1984). In addition, a study (Gonzales, Aronson, & Costanzo, 1988) compared homeowners' reactions to auditors trained to utilize certain social psychological principles (e.g., to personalize their recommendations, to induce commitment, and to frame recommendations in terms of loss rather than gain). Auditors were also trained to use "vivid" language (e.g., telling people that the cracks under their doors were equivalent to having a hole the size of a basketball in their living room, or that their attic, which had little insulation, was "naked"). While the trained auditors elicited greater compliance with their recommendations and led to more applications for finance programs to pay for home retrofitting, no differences were found in actual energy use.

In addition to environmental education, the use of models has been applied to the problem of residential energy overconsumption. Winnett et al. (1981) produced a series of videotaped programs on how to adapt to cooler temperatures at home (e.g., change thermostats gradually, wear warmer clothing, use extra blankets). Models who enacted these behaviors were rewarded (i.e., the vignette ended with them being happy with each other); those who approached the situation inappropriately were punished (i.e., the vignette ended with them being angry with each other). To enhance modeling effects (cf. Bandura, 1977), models in the tapes were similar to the target population of viewers in age, dress, and so on. Did the modeling intervention work? The answer is yes: Overall electricity use was down 14 percent and energy used for heating decreased 26 percent.

More typical sorts of prompts have also been utilized. Television announcers may prompt us to use energy wisely, or signs in university dormitories may remind us that "Empty rooms love darkness." These procedures are certainly cheaper than some other strategies we will discuss, but do they work? As we noted earlier in this chapter, they are more apt to if they are specific, well timed, well placed, and the behavior they request is easily enacted (Geller et al., 1982; Stern & Oskamp, 1987). The "Empty rooms love darkness" prompt would work best if placed on the back of the door you open to leave, and if it also said, "Turn off the lights when going out!" An effective use of prompts to curtail unnecessary use of air conditioners was devised by Becker and Seligman (1978). They strategically placed a light in the kitchens of homes that would turn on when air conditioning was on and outside temperatures were below 68°F (20°C). The prompt indicated that air conditioning was unnecessary, and the light went off only when the air conditioner was turned off. This achieved an energy savings of 15 percent.

The energy conservation technique that has perhaps been used most successfully is an array of reinforcement-based strategies (e.g., financial payments). One set of studies using reinforcers has been done in master-metered apartments where people do not get information about their energy use and frequently do not pay for it; the other has been done in individually metered residences. An energy conservation method used in master-metered apartments is rebating all or some part of the money saved by energy conscious residents to them. If $10,000 is saved through energy conservation in an apartment building, half might be divided among residents, the other half kept by management. This procedure becomes more effective for conservation as the proportion of savings given to residents increases, and when there is greater cohesion among residents (Slaven, Wodarski, & Blackburn, 1981). Walker (1979) tried another reinforcement strategy with people living in master-metered apartments. It was publicized that people with thermostats set above 74°F (23°C) in summer who had their windows closed when air conditioning was on would receive a $5.00 payment. Apartments were selected randomly for inspection, and those meeting the criteria were reinforced. This technique led to a 4–8 percent savings in energy use throughout the apartment complex.

More research has been done in individually metered residences (e.g., private homes or apartments with separate meters). Here, too, researchers have used financial incentives to motivate people to save energy. Some studies have used such reinforcers to change the *pattern* of our energy use. Utilities save money when they can rely on their least expensive sources of power, which is typically the case during hours of "non-peak" demand. When demand "peaks," they must augment their supply with more expensive sources of power. Therefore, it is advantageous to utilities to shift the pattern of energy use from peak to nonpeak periods. To decrease peak demand in some places financial incentives are provided (i.e., rates are lowered for consumers during non-peak hours and raised

Thermal Adaptation and Adjustment at Home

Could you get used to a mean winter temperature of 62°F (16.5°C) in your home and feel as comfortable as you did at the previous setting? If you could it would certainly save money since studies show up to a 3.7 percent savings in electricity for each degree a thermostat is lowered (Socolow, 1978). A group of researchers at Virginia Tech attempted to answer that question

(Winnett, Neale, & Grier, 1979; Winnett et al., 1979). Subjects were people living in all-electric homes, who were provided with a schedule for *gradually* turning down their thermostats. The schedule employed day and night setbacks, and was designed to produce the greatest conservation with the least discomfort (Beckey & Nelson, 1981). In addition to the temperature reduction

Table 14–1 *Samples of Clothing and Associated clo Values**

Samples of Women's Clothing

Description	Fabric Construction	Typical Fiber Content	clo
Underwear			
Bra		Cotton	0.02
Panties		Acetate	0.02
Long Underwear			
Tops	Knit		0.25
Bottoms	Knit		0.25
Socks and Hosiery			
Panty Hose		Nylon	0.01
Tights	Knit		0.25
Shoes			
Low Shoes			0.03
Knee High Boots, Leather Lined			0.30
Blouses			
Short Sleeve Blouse	Plain Weave	Rayon	0.17
Heavy Long Sleeve Shirt	Plain Weave	Wool	0.37
Pants			
Light Pants	Knit	Polyester	0.26
Jeans	Twill Weave	Cotton	0.26
Dresses and Skirts			
Heavy Skirt	Twill Weave	Wool	0.22
Sweaters			
Long Sleeve Sweater	Knit	Wool	0.37
Blazers and Vests			
Light Vest	Weave		0.20
Heavy Blazer	Weave	Wool	0.43

schedules, participants were shown videotapes of models enacting conservation behaviors, given feedback on their electric usage, and a listing of the insulation value (clo value) of different articles of clothing (see Table 14–1). Warmer clothing was suggested as one way of dealing with the cooler indoor temperature, and models were shown wearing it.

The results showed that you *could* get used to a mean winter temperature of 62°F! Subjects who got daily feedback on conservation and/or were exposed to models successfully reduced their thermostats to an average of 62°F (18°C) by the end of the study, and saved 26 percent of the energy used for heating and 15 percent of overall electric consumption. They also expressed no change in perceived comfort from before the study, perhaps because they increased the clo value of their clothing by 10 percent (see Table 14–1). In contrast, subjects in a control group experienced no changes in energy use. The researchers at Virginia Tech have also shown that similar procedures could reduce electric usage in summer by up to 20 percent.

Samples of Men's Clothing

Description	Fabric Construction	Typical Fiber Content	clo
Underwear			
Briefs	Knit	Cotton	0.05
Sleeveless Undershirt	Knit	Cotton	0.08
Long Underwear			
Tops	Knit		0.25
Bottoms	Knit		0.25
Socks			
Light Socks	Knit		0.03
Heavy Knee High Socks	Knit		0.08
Shoes			
High Shoes			0.15
Shirts			
Short Sleeve Light Knit	Knit	Cotton	0.22
Long Sleeve Woven	Plain Weave	Polyester and Cotton Blend	0.29
Pants			
Heavy Trousers	Twill Weave	Wool	0.32
Sweaters			
Sleeveless Sweater	Knit	Orlon	0.17
Sports Coats and Vests			
Heavy Vest	Weave		0.30
Heavy Sport Coat	Twill Weave	Wool	0.49

*From Geller, E. S., Winett, R. A. & Everett, P. B (1982). *Preserving the environment: New strategies for behavior change.* New York: Pergamon Press. Reprinted by permission.

during peak demand). These price incentives and disincentives may be effective in switching some discretionary energy-consuming activities (e.g., washing and drying clothes) from peak to non-peak periods, with benefits to both the utility and the consumer.

Other studies have employed reinforcers to decrease the overall amount of energy we use rather than to affect our pattern of use. Rate structures have been suggested which favor low utilization by increasing the cost per kilowatt hour as consumption increases, and are employed in some states. (At present, rates *decrease* with increasing use in most areas.) Another approach to conservation has simply been to let costs float with prevailing conditions, as is exemplified in deregulating oil and natural gas pricing in the United States. This approach does not seem to be very effective in reducing consumption. Doubling the price of energy leads to only a 10 percent decrease in use (Stern & Gardner, 1981). Other data suggest that it is not energy cost per se, but the percentage of the budget devoted to energy cost, that predicts conservation (Stern & Oskamp, 1987). Unfortunately, little study has been done on the effects of most energy rate structures. In addition to adjusting utility rates, some studies have simply paid residents of individually metered residences to lower their energy utilization. These techniques have proven quite effective alone, and when combined with feedback (Cone & Hayes, 1980). Paying people for lowering residential energy use seems to have quite a bit of potential, yet it may be difficult to implement in a way that is cost-effective. Finally, in one study financial incentives in the form of tax credits were offered for home retrofitting, but were not sufficient to encourage a high level of this behavior (Stobaugh & Yergin, 1979).

In individually metered residences, the most extensively studied method of improving energy conservation has been feedback. Relatively immediate feedback may be effective in reducing energy use for several reasons. It can familiarize users with the units electricity is measured in, and strengthen the relation between patterns of use and energy-related outcomes. Feedback can tell people when they are wasting energy, and it can also reinforce (and thereby bolster) energy-conserving behaviors (Table 14–1).

Often, energy use feedback compares our consumption this year with the same period last year. Good feedback should correct for differences between current weather and weather during the corresponding period last year, so that doing better or worse is not an artifact of warmer or cooler temperatures. It should also focus on an individual's *own* outcomes, rather than a group's conservation outcomes. However, combining both types of feedback—our own outcomes and those of others—can be very effective (Winnett et al., 1979). Studies have typically given energy consumption feedback in written form—a paper with appropriate data is supplied to consumers at agreed upon intervals—though in other experiments more sophisticated feedback devices (e.g., energy meters) have been used. At present, we do not know which mode is most effective, or whether feedback on energy use is more effective if represented as a percentage change in use (compared to the previous year), the amount of money saved, absolute differences in kilowatt hours consumed, and so on (Cone & Hayes, 1980).

The more frequent the energy consumption feedback, the more conservation occurs (Seligman & Darley, 1977), though relatively infrequent feedback can sometimes be surprisingly effective (Hayes & Cone, 1981). Feedback is more effective at decreasing energy use when the cost of energy relative to peoples' income is high (Winkler & Winnett, 1982), when people believe that the feedback accurately reflects their energy-consuming behavior, and when the household has made a commitment to save energy (Stern & Oskamp, 1987). Some studies

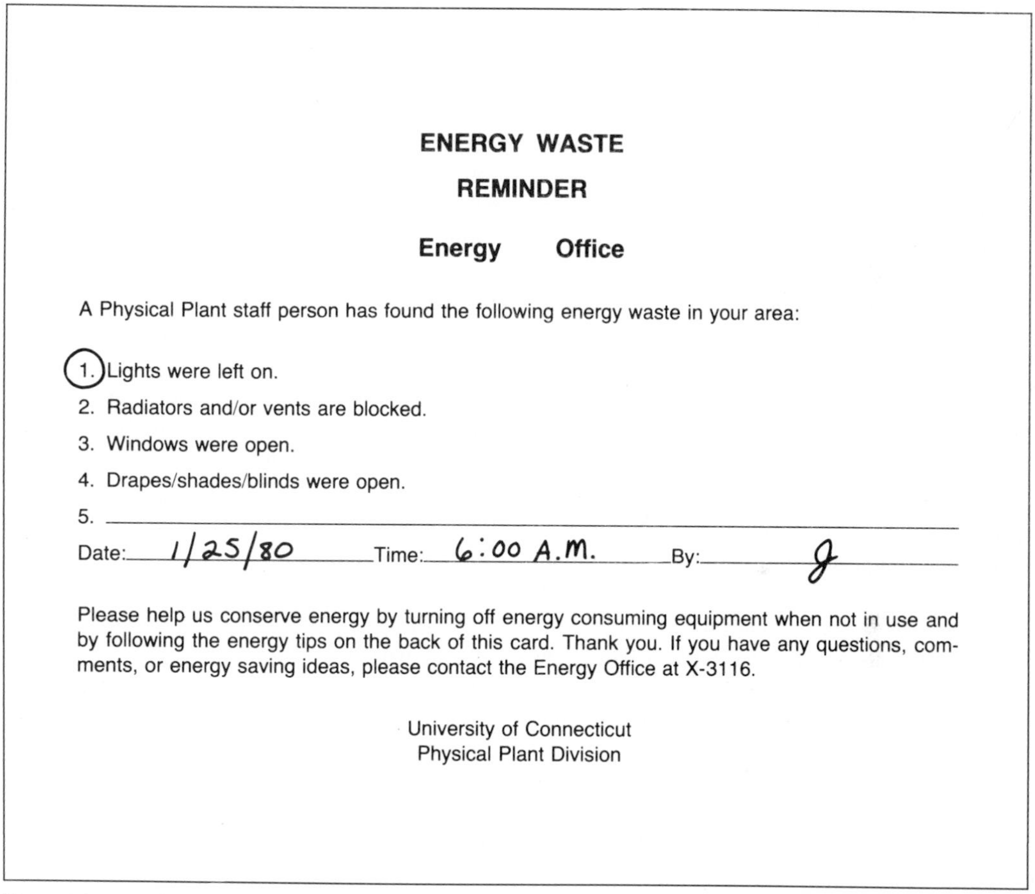

ENERGY WASTE

REMINDER

Energy   Office

A Physical Plant staff person has found the following energy waste in your area:

(1.) Lights were left on.

2. Radiators and/or vents are blocked.

3. Windows were open.

4. Drapes/shades/blinds were open.

5. _____

Date: _1/25/80_   Time: _6:00 A.M._   By: _J_

Please help us conserve energy by turning off energy consuming equipment when not in use and by following the energy tips on the back of this card. Thank you. If you have any questions, comments, or energy saving ideas, please contact the Energy Office at X-3116.

University of Connecticut
Physical Plant Division

Figure 14–11   In institutional settings, "energy waste reminders" may function as a form of feedback.

suggest that feedback is especially effective during periods of high energy use (e.g., hot humid days of summer; the coldest days of winter) (Cone & Hayes, 1980), and giving customers energy reduction goals along with feedback enhances its effect (Becker, 1978). Conservation efforts due to feedback may be retained for as long as 12 weeks after the feedback program ends (Winnett et al., 1981).

While feedback is often effective in reducing energy use, giving it in some forms is not cost-effective. Having someone read the meter and supply written feedback, at least on a frequent basis, can be quite expensive (Geller et al., 1982). Sometimes recording and/or signaling devices (cf. Becker & Seligman, 1978) may be more cost-effective, at least in the long run. But the least expensive form of feedback is self-monitoring—teaching people how to read their own power meters and encouraging them to do it regularly. Although much prompting may be necessary to get people to do this consistently, studies show it is possible and that such procedures result in conservation (Winnett, Neale, & Grier, 1979).

Overall, research suggests that feedback may be the single most effective technique for promoting residential energy conservation. Ellis and Gashell (1978) posit that to conserve energy in the home, people must be *motivated* to conserve and must *learn* how the home energy system works (i.e., what behaviors have what consequences for energy use). Thus, information and prompts do not motivate people, incentives motivate them but do not teach them the necessary relationships, and only feedback can (under ideal circumstances) provide both the motivational and informational elements which are necessary.

What other methods have been used to promote home energy conservation? Some residential energy conservation can be legislated. For example, Davis, California, is an extremely energy-efficient town, in part due to housing codes. Building specifications require heavily insulated homes, and actually give priority in construction permits to builders with the most energy-efficient plans. They also limit the number and size of windows, specify that most must face north and south, and indicate that some windows must be shaded. If a homeowner wants more windows, he or she must "compensate" by putting in more insulation, adding water-filled columns to retain heat or cold, or use concrete slab construction (*The Hartford Courant*, November 25, 1979). Another method that has been suggested to improve energy conservation is for the government to develop simple, understandable indices of energy efficiency, similar to miles per gallon, for furnaces, buildings, appliances, and so on (Stern & Oskamp, 1987). These indices should be publicized and their use encouraged. For an interesting additional means of conserving energy, see the box on page 501.

A final and theoretically different approach to energy savings in the home relies on the finding in social psychology that the greater one's degree of commmitment to an issue (e.g., energy conservation), the more likely it is that his or her future behavior will follow. In a series of studies, Pallak, Cook, and Sullivan (1980) manipulated the degree of commitment homeowners had to energy conservation and mea-

sured subsequent energy use. Homeowners all agreed to participate in a study to see if home energy could be saved. One group (high commitment) was told that the list of people in the energy conservation study would be publicized along with the experiment's results; another group (low commitment) was assured of anonymity. Subjects in the high commitment condition used less energy than those in the low commitment or control conditions, and these effects persisted for as much as six months after the study had terminated. Thus, the more committed we can make people to conserving energy, the more likely they will be to enact energy-saving behaviors.

Energy Conservation and Transporation

About 30 to 40 percent of all of the fuel we use is for transportation (Everett, 1977). Unfortunately, our choices among the available forms of transport are often inefficient and lead to overuse of fuel, to problems with air and noise pollution (see Chapters 5 and 7), and to other difficulties (e.g., ugly "strip" areas in urban and suburban neighborhoods). What means have been employed to improve energy efficiency in our use of transportation? One group of studies has focused on the inefficiency in our use of private "family" automobiles. Strategies have been directed toward reducing the overall number of miles we drive and toward increasing the number of miles we get per gallon. Another set of studies has tried to encourage us to use more efficient forms of transportation (e.g., vanpools, instead of cars), which also reduce traffic congestion.

Let us turn first to our over-reliance on the private family car, which wastes a great deal of energy and causes much congestion on the roads, compared to mass transit and ridesharing arrangements. Our general use of private automobiles corresponds in many ways to the social trap analysis we described earlier. The short-term benefits of the passenger car (e.g., pri-

. . . .

The Marketplace
As a Source of
Energy Efficiency

Another way of achieving home energy savings, quite different from those we have discussed so far, involves psychological strategies to encourage people to purchase the most energy-efficient equipment that exists whenever they buy any energy-consuming device (e.g., air conditioner, water heater, automobile). If we can understand the dynamics of the purchase situation sufficiently well and structure it so people make energy-efficient purchasing choices, we will go a long way toward solving the energy problem. Stern and Gardner (1981) have suggested that this strategy, rather than the types of techniques we have discussed, represents the best way to save energy. For example, purchasing the most energy-efficient automobile on the market today would achieve a 20 percent savings over the average car on the road, buying the most efficient heating equipment an 8 percent savings, the most efficient refrigerator about a 2 percent savings, and so on.

In comparison to the savings from buying the most efficient equipment, Stern and Gardner suggest that the types of behavioral techniques focused on most by researchers often save less energy. For example, replacing six major equipment items with the most efficient alternative yields an energy savings of 33.2 percent, compared to 12.5 percent from using existing devices in the most energy-efficient way. This argument is clearly interesting, and there are valuable insights to be gained from it. However, Geller et al. (1982) suggest that the Stern and Gardner estimates of savings from efficient use may be underestimates, and that they have not considered all the energy waste involved in replacing old equipment with new (e.g., costs of disposal, energy used in the manufacturing process). Regardless of these points of contention, there is much to be said for developing psychological and other techniques for encouraging our purchase of the most energy-efficient equipment available.

. . . .

vacy, prestige, speed, and convenience) accrue to the driver, while some of its negative consequences (e.g., pollution, furthering our energy problems) are longer range, and are shared by the driver and others. (Note that the traffic jams created by overuse of the automobile are immediate, and are shared by the individual and others.) Later we will discuss how we can wean ourselves away from this energy hog and use more efficient forms of transportation. But first let us consider environmental psychologists' attempts to reduce the number of miles we travel in our cars, and to increase the number of miles we get per gallon.

If each car in the United States were driven 10 miles less per week, 5 percent of the annual demand for gasoline would be saved (Federal Energy Administration, 1977), and bumper-to-bumper traffic could be reduced as well. Foxx and Hake (1977) offered subjects various rewards (e.g., cash, tours) to lower the number of miles they drove. The rewards led to a 20 percent reduction in miles driven, compared to a control group where mileage increased by about 5 percent. In an extension of the initial study, Hake and Foxx (1978) replicated their original findings and documented that when a leader of one type or another (e.g., a teacher, a supervisor) was in a particular experimental group, the energy savings in that group were greatly enhanced. This may prove to be a potent added force in favor of conservation for programs based in educational or business settings, for example. Other studies have found that competitions between teams enhance mileage reductions, and that giving lottery tickets (instead of cash payments) can be an effective motivator to drive less (Reichel & Geller, 1980).

We could also compel people to drive fewer miles through some sort of fuel rationing. Studies of the commons dilemma suggest that rationing may lead to conservation of resources (e.g., Cass & Edney, 1978). When we divide the "commons" up, people may use their portion more carefully. There are some experiments, however, that find no effect of rationing on conservation (Stern, 1976), and whether rationing would work when applied on a broad scale is an open question. Also, from a political standpoint, rationing could be very difficult to implement.

Another approach to saving transportation energy involves increasing mileage per gallon. Laws have accomplished this by forcing automakers to market more fuel-efficient fleets, but proper driving habits (e.g., driving more slowly, not accelerating rapidly from a stop) can make vehicles yield even better gasoline mileage. While few studies have been done in this area, people can be motivated to improve their mpg. Lauridsen (1977) did a small pilot study involving feedback and a lottery. Drivers received either continuous miles per gallon feedback or the same feedback after each hour they drove. For each tenth of a gallon improvement in mpg they received a ticket to a lottery, so the more they conserved the better the chance of winning. Results were encouraging, but do not allow us to determine whether they were due to the feedback or the lottery, or to some combination of the two.

A larger scale study was run by Runnion, Watson, and McWhorter (1978), and involved 195 long distance drivers for a textile company. Drivers were given instructions on how to save fuel, as well as certificates commending them when they reduced consumption. Public feedback was provided by charting fleet and individual mpg each day, and peer competition was fostered by a weekly lottery in which chances to win were based on improvements in mpg. The program had impressive results: Mileage improved up to 9 percent, and the company saved enough money over two years to run its entire truck fleet for a month!

Although it is obviously useful for us to drive less and more efficiently, we also need to abandon our love affair with the car for more efficient ways of "getting around." These include car- and vanpools, mass transit, walking, and riding bikes. Most of the research has focused on encouraging people to join some type of "pool," or to use mass transit. Ridesharing (i.e., either car- or vanpooling) is very efficient compared to driving to work by private auto. An average eight-passenger vanpool can save 5,000 gallons of gasoline in just one year! (Pratsch, 1977). How can we encourage people to ride together in carpools and vanpools? One way is to offer them some sort of benefit. As we mentioned earlier, this has sometimes involved providing special lanes of highways for cars with more than a particular number of passengers. These are sometimes called "HOV" (high occupancy vehicle) lanes. Using these lanes makes for a faster, less congested commute. Most of the situations where this has been implemented have not been evaluated, but in one case, a priority lane seems to have increased carpooling (Rose & Hinds, 1976). Unfortunately, priority lanes for carpoolers are difficult to enforce: People pick up unknown others at bus stops to "qualify," and some have even bought inflatable dummies to place in the car! In addition to priority lanes, other incentives to promote carpooling have involved giving people preferred parking spaces (e.g., closer to the place they work), or offering them free or reduced rates for tolls or parking. These incentives can have the desired effects (Hirst, 1976). Note that some of these techniques not only reward carpoolers, but make solo driving more difficult.

A major problem in starting carpools is finding others in similar locations with compatible work schedules. Many programs have tried to match people via computer matching procedures. Employees are given lists of potential carpools, and must then organize a working carpool. It is consistently found that the mere distribution of lists of names without other employer-initiated incentives does little to increase carpooling. Although employees typically express positive attitudes toward ridesharing, they rarely do it when provided with lists of convenient partners. When employers provide incentives along with listing partners, programs can be effective (Jacobs et al., 1982). However, it seems that the incentives are the major factor in this success (Geller et al., 1982).

Why would you avoid joining a carpool or other ridesharing plan? The chances are that in addition to inconvenience factors (e.g., it takes longer to get to work, less privacy, more potential for stress), social factors may play a role. Carpooling is actually a social arrangement, so social aspects of the situation may be important. Barkow (1974) reported that a major impediment to carpooling is our hesitancy to deal with strangers. He found that we would prefer to carpool with an acquaintance rather than a stranger, and if one has to carpool with a stranger, both sexes would prefer that their "poolmate" be female. Other major social impediments to ridesharing center on constraints to freedom (e.g., the necessity of being "on time," and being civil to others on a repeated basis). To be successful, carpooling seems to require mature individuals who are flexible and willing to accommodate to each other. What did carpoolers view as the major benefits? They appreciated the monetary savings and avoiding the tension and responsibility

of driving. Based on this study, one could suggest that appeals to promote carpooling should focus on lowering our fear of interacting with strangers (e.g., by allowing members to meet each other beforehand), and highlighting financial savings and the relaxation of "not being in the driver's seat."

Vanpools accomplish the same conservation goals as carpools, but they are even more fuel-efficient. Like carpools, they necessitate fewer parking spaces at the work site and relieve traffic congestion, but unlike carpools the van often belongs to one's employer or sponsoring agency. With vanpools, income from the operation (e.g., charging customers 7 cents per mile) often pays for the program. Usually there is a van coordinator who drives the van, maintains it, bills participants, and who may make a small profit from the operation. Reactions to vanpooling have often been quite positive (Owens & Sever, 1977), and more vanpools are being "born" each year. However, before vanpools will become truly pervasive they will have to overcome many of the social and other objections associated with carpools.

If we cannot interest you in a car- or vanpool, how about riding the bus or another form of mass transit? Some studies have tried to increase mass transit ridership by adding positive elements (e.g., cost savings, offering merchandise coupons as rewards). Others have removed unpleasant aspects typically associated with mass transit (e.g., it is perceived as slow, uncomfortable, dangerous due to crime, noisy, and unreliable).

Attempts to provide rewards for use of mass transit have been successful. Giving passengers hamburger coupons for buying a monthly bus pass increased sales by 86 percent in Syracuse, New York (American Public Transit Association, 1975). Others have increased bus ridership by giving money to people as they entered the vehicle (Everett, 1973). Deslauriers and Everett (1977) increased ridership on a campus bus system by giving riders tokens that could be redeemed at local stores. The tokens were passed out either to all of the bus riders, or to a preset proportion of them. Both reinforcement schedules increased ridership compared to controls, and the lower, "proportionate" payoff schedule did not occasion lower ridership than continuous reinforcement. This suggests that less costly reinforcement schedules may often be just as effective. The trick is to find the optimal "payoff ratio."

In addition to adding reinforcers, bus ridership would increase if the punishments many of us associate with it (e.g., paying fares, crowding, a slower ride) were removed. It has been found that removing bus fares (i.e., giving people a free ride) leads to increased ridership (Everett et al., 1978). Making commuting time shorter by adding bus lanes also improves ridership (Rose & Hinds, 1976). Hopefully, in the future it will be possible to remove other negative aspects from the public transit setting so that more of us will participate in it.

Vandalism

A final environmental problem which we will discuss, along with some means of ameliorating it, is vandalism. While vandalism shares some characteristics with the environmental problems we have covered thus far, there are often differences in the motivations behind it and in the means of solving the problem. **Vandalism** can be defined as the "willful or malicious destruction, injury, disfigurement, or disfacement of any public or private property" (*Uniform Crime Reporting Handbook*, 1978, p. 90). There are several types of vandalism: *acquisitive vandalism* (looting, petty theft), *tactical/ideological vandalism* (to draw attention to oneself or to an issue of concern), *vindictive vandalism* (aimed at revenge), *play vandalism* (to combat boredom), and *malicious vandalism* (due to diffuse frustration and rage, often occurring in public settings).

How big of a problem is vandalism? Its cost in American schools, parks, recreation areas, public housing, and transit systems is estimated at billions of dollars per year, and these costs are increasing rapidly. In one recent year the costs of U. S. vandalism in these settings was more than the entire budget of the state of Connecticut, without even taking into account the costs of physical and psychological injuries from vandalism, the inability to use facilities, the cost of alternative arrangements, and so on.

Surprisingly, relatively little research has been done on vandalism, though it has been found that certain *physical* and *social* conditions promote it. As discussed in Chapter 10, when the design of a setting allows residents little territorial control, vandalism becomes more common (Ley & Cybriwsky, 1974a; Newman, 1972). Thus, preventive strategies could focus on increasing territorial control (e.g., designing areas to promote defensible space). Aesthetic factors associated with an object's appearance (e.g., physical beauty) and the extent to which a site is "hardened" (made difficult to vandalize) also affect the level of vandalism. There is evidence that vandalism is lower when sites are hardened and when the aesthetic properties of a setting are high (Pablant & Baxter, 1975). Just as aesthetic variables affect how much we enjoy socially acceptable interactions with an object, they affect the pleasure we experience from vandalizing it. Objects that break in aesthetically interesting or pleasing ways may be more apt to be vandalized than those that break in dull, uninteresting ways (Allen & Greenberger, 1980; Greenberger & Allen, 1980). Designing objects (e.g., street lights) that will not break in a satisfying manner may be another way of decreasing vandalism (Figure 14–11).

Other factors have been implicated as causes of vandalism. Allen and Greenberger (1980) suggest that low perceived control (which can have many causes) will, under certain conditions, elicit vandalism as a means of reestablishing control. (For a discussion of perceived control, see Chapter 4.) When we come to believe we cannot control our outcomes

Figure 14–11 Vandalism constitutes an eyesore in many cities

(e.g., college students may not feel that they have enough control over policies in the dormitories), we sometimes resort to vandalism as a way of showing ourselves and others that we can control at least certain things (Warzecha, Fisher, & Baron, 1988). This would suggest that the greater people's overall control of a setting, the less vandalism. Also, it has been suggested that vandalism results when there is a "lack of fit" between the person and the environment (e.g., school vandalism may be due to poor congruence between personal characteristics of students and the social or physical environment of the school). Increasing the goodness of the fit through social and/or environmental means could help lower vandalism, according to this conceptualization. And work

by Richards (1979) has identified peer relationships (i.e., associations with antisocial peers) and adult–child conflict as major causes of vandalism by middle-class adolescents. Vandalism may also occur due to financial need, in the pursuit of social causes, due to nonmalicious play, or due to poor achievement (cf. Cohen, 1973; Sabatino et al., 1978).

A rather complete model of vandalism has been proposed (Baron & Fisher, 1984; Fisher & Baron, 1982). This model encompasses many of the reasons suggested above for why vandalism occurs, under the concept of **perceived inequity**. What is perceived inequity? Equity theories in social psychology imply that we are socialized to believe we should treat others fairly (or equitably), and should be treated equitably by others. When this does not occur (i.e., when we perceive we are being inequitably or unfairly treated), we become upset and try to restore equity. This can be done in several ways, but it typically involves our attempting to get more out of the relationship for what we put into it, or trying to ensure that the other gets less out of the relationship for what he or she puts in.

Fisher and Baron's model implies that vandalism may be one way of restoring equity in settings characterized by perceived inequity (or unfairness) between the parties. Vandalism can therefore be viewed as a way to restore equity by responding to one type of perceived rule breaking—unfairness in interpersonal relations—with another type (i.e., disregard for another's property rights). In effect, some types of vandalism say, "If I don't get any respect, I won't give you any either." What types of inequity are apt to promote vandalism? Inequity which can elicit vandalism may occur as a product of *ordinary economic exchange* (e.g., between a shopkeeper and a customer), from *discriminatory practices* and *inequitable rules and regulations* (e.g., between employer and employee; housing authority and resident), and

from *aspects of the physical environment in and of itself* (e.g., defective machines or facilities that cause an inequitable input/output ratio). Inflexible environmental settings (e.g., windows that will not open, thermostats we cannot adjust, dormitory furniture that will not move) may also make it difficult for us to receive a fair level of outcomes relative to our inputs, and may promote vandalism.

Will every instance of inequity result in vandalism? Obviously not. Fisher and Baron suggest that inequity will result in vandalism only when the person who feels inequitably treated has low perceived control—or little likelihood of influencing whether equity will be restored. When we have high perceived control we restore equity within the system (e.g., complain to the authorities), and when we have *very* low perceived control we become helpless, and simply accept our fate. But when we have moderate to low control, we are likely to opt for a way of restoring equity—like vandalism—which is an immediate, low effort, and certain means of paying society back. Fisher and Baron suggest that increasing perceptions of control, decreasing perceived inequity, or both, can be effective means of lowering vandalism.

CURBING ENVIRONMENTALLY DESTRUCTIVE ACTS: AN ASSESSMENT OF THE PRESENT AND THE FUTURE

How can we sum up the state of the art that deals with applying environmental psychology to moderate environmentally destructive behavior? It is probably fair to say that the techniques discussed in this chapter give us a good start toward improving many adverse environmental conditions, but that we still have a long way to go. Each of the methods we have presented has important strengths and weaknesses, and each

needs to be refined and improved by researchers in the future. (See box, page 507.) It is unfortunate that at present there is no overriding theory to help us conceptualize environmentally destructive behavior. Such a formulation would greatly enhance our efforts and could lead to a more focused approach by both researchers and practitioners. Finally, we should remember that the problems we face are multifaceted and

Encouraging Recycling Via the"Foot in the Door" Technique

In an attempt to provide detailed discussions of ways of dealing with some environmental problems, we have had to neglect others. One of those is recycling behavior. An interesting approach to encouraging recycling involves the "foot in the door" technique, which has been used in some classic studies in social psychology on gaining compliance. Like the salesperson who stands a better chance of making the sale if he can only get his "foot in the door," environmental psychologists may be more apt to get people to recycle (or engage in other proecological behavior) after eliciting a small commitment from them.

The standard **"foot in the door"** paradigm goes like this. The experimenter first makes a small request of the subject which very few are likely to refuse (e.g., sign a petition for a highly respectable proenvironmental cause). This is followed by progressively larger requests (e.g., recycle your soft drink containers). Because people who comply with the small initial request come to view themselves as interested in preserving the environment, they are more apt to agree to the second, larger request than are subjects who are never presented with the initial request.

Arbuthnot et al. (1976–1977) used this strategy to increase recycling behavior. Their initial smaller requests were to have people answer survey items favoring environmental protection, to save aluminum cans for a week, and to send in a postcard urging officials to expand a local recycling program. Did being confronted with these initial requests affect long-term use of a recycling center? The answer is yes: As long as 18 months after the initial request, subjects were more apt to use the center than those not exposed to the "foot in the door" strategy.

The above findings have some interesting implications. We might view responding to prompts, such as reminders to turn off lights, as analogous to initial requests in the foot in the door technique. This would suggest that responding to the multiple "small requests" being made of us to improve the environment these days may in some way "prime" us to comply with the larger, more important environmental demands we will face in the years ahead.

The study also suggests some potential problems with the use of reinforcement techniques, which we have discussed in this chapter, for encouraging proecological behavior. Self-perception theory in social psychology implies that often we infer our attitudes from observing our behavior and the circumstances under which it occurs (Bem, 1972). Arbuthnot et al. proposed that people in their study agreed to the larger requests because after complying with the initial request, they inferred from their behavior that they had proenvironmental attitudes. They had no incentives for their initial compliance, thus they must really care about the environment. This proecological self-perception may have been why long-term changes in recycling occurred in the foot in the door study. On the other hand, what would people infer about themselves from their behavior after recycling because they were offered a financial reward or reinforcement? Bem would say that instead of inferring that they care about the environment—a conclusion which could be associated with continued recycling—they might conclude they merely did it for the money. Such a self-perception could lead them to stop recycling as soon as the rewards for it were removed.

. . . .

complex and will certainly defy a simple solution. Therefore, we should not expect one.

Taking a broader scope, how would we evaluate the progress that environmental psychology as a *field* has made so far? While our current position vis-a-vis the environment is far from our ideal goal, it is in some ways quite encouraging. During its relatively short existence as a field, environmental psychology has been able to identify many of the positive and negative effects of the environment on behavior and to design some important conceptual frameworks for understanding them. It has also made some efforts to develop strategies for changing our destructive environmentally related behaviors and for facilitating those that have positive effects. This, added to the facts that at least some of us are becoming more acutely aware of our environment, and that behavioral technology is more advanced than ever before, should give us great hope. But in the end, all of us, individually and collectively, will decide our environmental future.

SUMMARY

Much environmentally destructive behavior can be conceptualized in terms of social traps. These are situations in which personal interests with a short-term focus conflict with societal needs with a long-term focus. For example, littering and purchasing nonreturnable bottles are forms of social traps. How can we escape from such traps? Research on the commons dilemma suggests dividing some common resources into territories helps to increase communication and trust and to alter reinforcements.

In this chapter, environmental education, use of environmentally relevant prompts, reinforcement-related techniques, and other methods are considered as potential means of altering environmentally destructive behavior. Each of these techniques has unique costs and benefits. Environmental education seems to be a relatively ineffective method at this time. However, future research may reveal situations in which it may lead to positive results. The use of environmentally related prompts is somewhat effective and relatively inexpensive. Finally, reinforcement techniques (positive reinforcement, negative reinforcement, punishment, and feedback) appear to be most effective, although they have several drawbacks. For example, reinforcement techniques may be quite expensive, and there is evidence that the effects often disappear when the reinforcement contingency is withdrawn. After reviewing the major techniques for dealing with environmentally destructive behavior, we considered specific strategies used to cope with littering, energy overconsumption, and vandalism. Some of these offer promise of significantly improving aspects of our environment.

SUGGESTED PROJECTS

1. Design an environmental education program that you feel would have an optimal chance of effectively changing behavior in an environmentally constructive direction. Use whatever media you like, focus on whatever population you desire, and choose a target behavior that corresponds to your area of major interest in environmental psychology.

2. Select an environmentally destructive target behavior on your university campus and design a prompt that would help alleviate the problem. If you can get the necessary permission from authorities, attempt to test the effectiveness of your technique.

3. Test Cialdini et al.'s hypothesis that a setting with a single violation of a norm serves as a more effective prompt than one with no evidence of norm violation. Some possible subjects for your investigation are the appropriate return of shopping carts at a local supermarket, graffiti in a restroom, or vandalism in a university building.

4. If you have lived in a college dormitory, design a program (using the techniques described in this chapter) to help alleviate noise. You may use the study we reported by Meyers and his colleagues as a jumping-off point, but try to use your own experience as a dormitory resident to form hypotheses and to structure your program.

GLOSSARY

acclimation–adaptation to one specific environmental stressor, such as temperature.

acclimatization–adaptation to multiple stresses in an environment, such as humidity, temperature, and wind.

accretion measure–an unobtrusive indication of behavior, involving traces of additions to the environment, such as litter or fingerprints.

action plan–a cognitive plan or strategy for moving from one place to another.

adaptation–weakening of a reaction (especially psychological) to a stimulus; becoming accustomed to a particular degree of a given type of stimulation; in Wohwill's ideas, a shift in optimal stimulation.

adaptation level (AL)–an ideal level of stimulation that leads to maximum performance or satisfaction.

adequately staffed–in ecological psychology, a condition in which the number of applicants is between maintenance minimum and capacity.

adjustment–Sonnenfeld's idea of technological change of a stimulus, as opposed to adaptation, which refers to change in the response to the stimulus.

adrenal–of the adrenal glands, endocrine glands which sit on top of the kidneys; catecholamine secretions from the adrenal glands are characteristic of stress reactions.

adventure playgrounds–playgrounds made up of "junk" materials that allow children to dig, build, and grow things under adult supervision.

aesthetics–the study of beauty and of psychological responses to it.

affect–feelings or emotional states.

affective appraisals–emotions directed toward some component of the environment.

affiliative behavior–interactions with others.

affordances–in Gibson's theory of ecological perception, the properties of an object or place that give it constant and automatically detectable functions.

aftereffects–consequences of a stimulus that occur after the stimulus has stopped; effects of a stressor on mood or behavior, often measured by task performance, that occur after termination of the stressor.

age-segregated–residential settings restricted to the elderly.

air ionization–condition in which molecules of air partially "split" into positively and negatively charged particles, or positive and negative ions.

air pollution–contamination of the air, especially by toxic substances such as carbon monoxide, oxides of nitrogen and sulfur, photochemical smog, and particulates.

air pollution syndrome (APS)–headache, fatigue, insomnia, irritability, depression and other symptoms occurring together and caused by combinations of air pollutants.

alarm reaction–a startle response to a stressor; the first stage of Selye's GAS.

alveolar walls–portion of the lung where oxygen and carbon dioxide are exchanged between the blood and the atmosphere.

Alzheimer's Disease–the most common progressive dementia, occurring primarily in the elderly, and accounting for half of all nursing home admissions.

ambient stressors–chronic, global stressors such as pollution, noise, or traffic congestion.

ambient temperature–surrounding or atmospheric temperature

amplitude–the amount of energy in a sound, as represented by the height of the sound wave, perceived psychologically as loudness.

analog representation–the theoretical case in which a cognitive map is stored in memory in a picture form that corresponds point for point to the physical environment.

annoyance–in noise, the irritating or bothersome aspect.

antecedent behavioral change techniques–behavioral change techniques that occur before the target behavior and that are designed to increase the likelihood of favorable acts.

anticipated crowding–when people expect to be crowded.

applicability gap–a two-way communications breakdown that occurs when scientists fail to ask questions with direct application to design problems or when designers neglect to employ those principles that have empirical support.

applicants–in ecological psychology, those who meet the membership requirements of a behavior setting and who are trying to become a part of it.

appraisal–cognitive assessment of a stressor along the dimensions of harm or loss, threat, and challenge.

approach prompts–prompts that supply an incentive for engaging in a particular behavior.

architectural determinism–a view that holds that the built environment directly causes or shapes the behavior of the people within it.

archival data–data which researchers may find in others' historical records, such as police crime reports, weather records, or hospital records.

arousal–a continuum of physiological or psychological activation ranging from sleep to excitement;

crowding, personal space intrusions, or other stressors can lead to overarousal.

assigned workspace–designating a particular machine or area to a particular worker in order to create a feeling of ownership.

attitude–a relatively stable tendency to evaluate a person, object, or idea in a positive or negative way; many definitions stress the interrelationship of feelings, cognitions, and behaviors.

attraction gradient–the likelihood that the design of an exhibit will attract museum visitors to view it.

augmentation–the addition of nonexistent features to a cognitive map based upon expectations of what "should" be there.

avoidance prompts–prompts that supply a disincentive for enacting a particular behavior.

axial landscape–landscapes in which parallel lines converge, directing the viewer's attention.

background stressors–persistent, repetitive stressors whose impact is relatively gradual, including daily hassles.

barometric pressure–atmospheric pressure, as read by a barometer.

Beaufort Scale–a scale of wind force developed by Admiral Sir Francis Beaufort in 1806.

behavior constraint–a model which emphasizes how the environment (e.g., urban life, personal space restrictions) may limit or interfere with activities, leading to loss of perceived control.

behavioral control–availability of a behavioral response which can change a threatening environmental event.

behavioral interference–the notion that under high density conditions, many negative effects are due to "getting in people's way" and similar mechanisms for blocking goals.

behavior mapping–a structured observational technique in which behaviors are observed, recorded, and located on a map of the setting being observed.

behavior setting–the basic unit of environment–

behavior relationships; in Barker's ecological psychology, an entity that encompasses the location of a large volume of behavior; consists of the interdependency between the standing patterns of behavior and the physical milieu.

behavioral sink– area in which the negative effects of high density are intensified.

bivariate theory– a theory which relates only two variables.

block organizations– neighborhood organizations formed to add social cohesiveness and overcome urban ills, which work for such improvements as better lighting, police protection, or street repairs.

blood pressure– the pressure of blood being pumped through blood vessels, determined by activity of the heart and the state of the blood vessels.

brightness– the psychological intensity of color.

capacity– in ecological psychology, the maximum number of inhabitants a behavior setting can hold; in overload notions, the limiting capability for processing information.

carbon monoxide– a common pollutant caused by incomplete burning of substances containing carbon.

carrying capacity– the amount of use a resource can support; with respect to recreation, the carrying capacity could be variously defined as the number of people who can fit in a given area, the number who can be accommodated without resource damage, or the number who can receive a satisfactory experience such as solitude.

cataclysmic events– sudden, powerful events that require a great deal of adaptation in order for people to recover, avoid, or cope with their effects, such as natural disasters.

catecholamines– epinephrine (adrenaline), norepinephrine, and dopamine— secretions which energize various systems in the body.

challenge appraisal– a cognitive appraisal component of the stress model which focuses on the possibility of overcoming the stressor.

chill factor–*see* wind chill.

chromatic aberration– the phenomenon in which refraction by the eye's cornea and lens causes short wavelengths (blues) to focus in front of the retina and longer wavelengths (reds) to converge behind the retina in a mid-range accommodated eye.

climate– average weather conditions or prevailing weather over a long period of time.

climatological determinism, possibilism, and probabilism–*see* geographical determinism, possibilism, and probabilism.

clockwise-for-increase principle– the population stereotype that says turning a knob clockwise will generally increase the controlled dimension such as sound, temperature, or pressure.

closed desk placement (or arrangement)– offices arranged so that the occupant's desk sits between him or her and visitors.

cognitive control– processing information about a threat in such a way as to appraise it as less threatening.

cognitive map– an internal representation of the spatial environment.

coherence– in landscape evaluations, the degree to which the elements in a scene are organized and seem to fit together.

collative stimulus properties– characteristics of a stimulus that create perceptual conflict and cause us to compare it to other stimuli to resolve the conflict.

commodity– the functional goal (intended use) of a design.

commons dilemma– Hardin's notion that depletion of scarce resources can happen because people sharing a resource harvest it with short-term self-interest in mind rather than long-term group interest.

compensatory behaviors– in personal space, behaviors such as increased eye contact that make up for inappropriately far distances, or such as leaning away from a person for inappropriately close distances.

complexity– with regard to landscape or architectural aesthetics, the variety and salience of elements in a scene.

complexity of spatial layout–the amount and difficulty of information that must be processed in order to move through the environment.

congruence–the "fit" between user needs or preferences and the physical features of a setting.

contemporary playgrounds–playgrounds designed with an eye to aesthetics and flexibility; typically, these feature abstract arrangements of multileveled wooden play structures with ramps, bridges, slides, and swings.

control–the perception that one's inputs and outcomes are linked (*see also* perceived control).

control models–environment–behavior models which emphasize consequences of loss of perceived control; the behavior constraint model is an example.

controls–knobs, levers, pedals, and so on which are used to adjust and control machines and systems.

coping–handling stressors; efforts to restore equilibrium after stressful events.

core temperature–the temperature inside the body.

correlational research–research that does not manipulate environmental occurrences or prescribe who should be involved as subjects; events occurring prior to the research and concurrent actions of other factors in the setting may interfere with the conclusions drawn.

corticosteroids–steroid compounds produced by the adrenal cortex; increased secretion is characteristic of alarm reactions.

crisis effect–phenomenon wherein disaster events attract a great deal of attention while they are occurring or shortly thereafter, but concern with them for future events decreases after that.

crowding–experiential state when the constraints of high density are salient to an individual.

cue utilization–the individual weights assigned by a person in making perceptual judgments based upon past experiences, personality, or other characteristics.

curvilinear relationship–a relationship between two variables that is not a straight line, such as a U-shaped or inverted-U function.

custodial care–a level of care for the elderly in which someone else must provide assistance with everyday activities of daily living, such as laundry, bathing, and dressing.

daily hassles–stable, low-intensity problems encountered as part of one's routine, such as commuting.

day-night reversal–a condition in dementia in which the patient becomes very active at night; also called "sundowning."

decibels (dB)–units of measure of loudness of sound, in the form of logarithmic representations of sound pressure.

decisional control–having a choice among several options.

decompression sickness–a condition caused by nitrogen bubbles forming in the blood when a person moves from high atmospheric pressure to low atmospheric pressure, as in "the bends."

deep body temperature–*see* core temperature.

defensible space–clearly bounded or semi-private areas that appear to belong to someone.

degree of visual access–the extent to which different parts of a setting can be seen from a number of vantage points; access facilitates the learning of a new environment.

deindividuation–according to Zimbardo, loss of individual identity (i.e., feeling of anonymity) which releases otherwise inhibited antisocial behavior.

delight–the aesthetic goal of design.

dementia–a medical term meaning loss of memory and confusion.

denial–ignoring or suppressing awareness of stressors and other problems.

density-intensity–Freedman's conceptualization that high density increases the intensity of behaviors and feelings that would have occurred anyway under lower density conditions.

dependent variable–in the experimental method,

the behavior of the subject that is measured by the experimenter.

descriptive landscape assessment—landscape assessment based upon the judgments of professionals trained to detect patterns, primarily based upon artistic judgment.

descriptive research—research that reports behavior or emotions or other characteristics that occur in a given setting or in response to a specific event.

design alternatives—the list of potential solutions to a design problem.

design cycle—a continuous cycle of information gathering, planning, and evaluation; the cyclical nature allows information gathered from one project to add to the knowledge for subsequent designs.

design spiral—the process of proposing, testing, refining, and retesting design alternatives until a final acceptable solution is encountered.

determinism—in a strict sense, a philosophical notion that circumstances have absolute causal relationships to events.

differentiation—distinctiveness; buildings or environments that are different or distinctive are more easily remembered.

diffusion of responsibility—an explanation for decreased helping behavior which posits that as the number of potential helpers increases, each one assumes less individual responsibility for helping.

disaster event—a powerful event that causes substantial disorganization, disruption, or destruction to an area, community, or series of communities.

discontinuity—the idea of changing a steady pattern in museum exhibits; breaking up the pattern helps relieve museum fatigue.

displays—dials, VDT screens, warning lights, and so on that allow the human operator to detect the status of a machine or system.

disruption—disturbance of individual, group, or organizational functioning and routine.

distortions—errors in cognitive maps based upon

inaccurate retrieval that leads us to put some things too close together, some too far apart, and to misalign others.

districts—large geographical areas which are identified in cognitive maps; typically, the places within a district have a common character and often are given names such as the French Quarter, Chinatown, or the East End.

diversity—in Berlyne's dimensions, change in stimulation.

diversive exploration—arousal seeking in response to understimulation.

dominance elements—line, form, color, and texture, from the descriptive approach to landscape assessment.

dominant Western world view—belief that human domination over infinite natural resources leads to inevitable progress.

double corridor design—hospital floorplan in which the nurses' station sits amid two (usually parallel) hallways.

ecological perception—the approach that emphasizes that perception is holistic and direct; according to this view, patterns of stimulation give the perceiver direct and immediate information about the environment with little effort or cognitive activity.

ecological psychology—Barker's behavior setting approach to studying the interaction between humans and their environment.

ecological validity—the objective usefulness of various environmental stimuli in making accurate perceptual judgments.

edges—elements in cognitive maps that limit or divide features such as paths or districts; edges may be elements such as walls, rail yards, or water features.

effective temperature—an adjustment in perceived temperature to account for humidity, similar to the Temperature–Humidity Index.

egocentric reference system—cognitive maps in which the image or stored information consists only of those elements in the environment that are of great personal significance.

electronic cottage–an in-the-home workplace connected to the parent organization by computers or other communication devices.

ELF–EMF–extremely low frequency electromagnetic fields associated with weather disturbances or power lines.

empirical–publicly observable.

empirical laws–statements of simple observable relationships between phenomena (often expressed in mathematical terms) that can be demonstrated time and time again.

encapsulation–in playground designs, enclosed, defensible spaces.

en masse behavior pattern–in Barker's ecological psychology, the behavior of a group.

environment–one's surroundings; the word is frequently used to refer to a specific part of one's surroundings, as in social environment (referring to the people and groups among whom one lives), physical environment (all of the non-animal elements of one's surroundings, such as cities, wilderness, or farmland), or built environment (referring specifically to that part of the environment built by humans).

environmental cognition–the ability or propensity to imagine and think about the spatial world.

environmental competence–*see* environmental press.

environmental education–making people aware of the scope and nature of environmental problems, and of behavioral alternatives to alleviate them.

Environmental Emotional Reaction Indices (EERI)–an assessment of the emotional reactions of humans to some component of environmental quality.

environmental load–a theoretical position based on overload of information from the environment.

environmental possibilism–views the environment as providing limits on behavior, but ascribing a larger function to individual choice and option than architectural determinism.

environmental press–a model which posits that the demands or press an environment places on its occupants as well as the competence of the occupants determine the consequences of interacting with the environment.

environmental probabilism–views the environment as providing enough structure to situations that even within the possible actions, some behaviors will be more probable than others.

environmental psychology–the study of the interrelationship between behavior and experience and the built and natural environment.

Environmental Quality Index (EQI)–objective measures of environmental quality—the chemical or physical properties of water or air, for example.

environmental spoiling hypothesis–the notion that perceived quality of the living environment is determined largely by the number of unpleasant contacts with others.

environmental stress model–a theoretical perspective which emphasizes how the environment can elicit stress and coping reactions when it is evaluated to be threatening.

epinephrine–adrenaline, a catecholamine that energizes physiological systems in response to stress.

equilibrium–a state of balance; the steady state to which stress reactions try to restore the organism.

ethological models–in personal space, formulations that assume when space is inadequate, fear and discomfort are experienced due to feelings of aggression or threat.

event duration–how long an event lasts.

exit gradient–how much a gallery exit attracts a museum visitor to use it.

expectancy-discrepancy models – in personal space, models which propose that there are learned expectancies about appropriate interaction distances, and that when these expectancies are disconfirmed (i.e., are discrepant with what actually occurs), compensation, reciprocation, or withdrawal occur to relieve the discomfort.

experience–with respect to recreation management, the group of short-term psychological outcomes obtained by participating in a particular activity.

experiential realism—the extent to which the experimental manipulation has impact on the subject and is representative of events that occur in the real world.

experimental method—a way of conducting research that allows inferences about what might cause a given effect; by varying two factors and studying effects of these factors under controlled conditions, one can observe specific causes for observed effects. (*See also* random assignment.)

external validity—the degree to which a research study's findings generalize to other contexts.

extra-individual behavior pattern—in Barker's ecological psychology, the behavior of large numbers of people.

extremely low frequency electromagnetic fields—*see* ELF–EMF.

extrinsic motivation—rewards that are administered by an outside agent and are satisfying independent of the events that produced them.

familiar stranger—someone you observe repeatedly for a long period of time, but never interact with.

feedback—a technique which provides information about whether one is attaining or failing to attain an environmental goal; as such, it is a means for changing environmentally destructive behavior.

field experiments—experiments that are done in field settings as opposed to laboratory settings.

field methods—techniques for studying behavior outside the laboratory.

firmness—the design goal of permanence and structural integrity.

fittingness—the harmony between built features and their environments.

folk design tradition—architecture based upon the day-to-day needs of people as they live, shop, and work.

foot in the door—a technique which increases compliance with a standard request by first asking for a small favor which the respondent is likely to agree to.

freedom of choice—with respect to recreation, an activity which is likely to be perceived as leisure if participation is voluntary.

free-rider—in the public goods problem, a person who fails to contribute to the common good but reaps the benefits of the contributions of the other participants.

frequency—the number of cycles per second in a sound wave; perceived psychologically as pitch.

friction-conformity model—Preiser's idea that pedestrians adjust their walking speed to barriers and to the flow of other pedestrian traffic.

frostbite—formation of ice crystals in the skin.

functional distance—a type of propinquity measured by the likelihood of two people coming into contact with each other, as in meeting at their mailboxes.

functionalism—a tradition within psychology that views behavior as a way of adapting or surviving the demands of the environment.

Gaia Hypothesis—the idea that heating and cooling of the earth (oceans, land and atmosphere) as well as associated operations of living things are part of a self-regulating system.

galvanic skin response (GSR)—a way of measuring arousal from the electrical conductance of the skin as it changes with sweating.

gaps—lapses in communication between designers, users, behavioral scientists, or clients that result in design errors or oversights.

general adaptation syndrome (GAS)—Selye's stress model, which consists of the alarm reaction, the stage of resistance, and the stage of exhaustion.

generalizability—a measurement of how well a finding, relationship, or theory applies from one setting to another.

gentrification—the emergence of middle- and upper-class areas in parts of the inner city that were formerly deteriorated.

geographical determinism—the idea that geography and climate forcefully cause a range of behaviors, such as hot climates causing crimes.

geographical possibilism—the idea that geography and climate set limits within which behavior may vary, such as modest winds permitting sailing but high winds restricting boating.

geographical probabilism–the idea that geography and climate influence the likelihood that some behaviors will occur and others will not.

Gestalt perception–an approach that argues for the analysis of perception as an integrated whole rather than as separable elements.

Gestalt psychology–*see* Gestalt perception.

Gouldian Maps–characteristics or qualities persons associate with different places within their familiar environment represented geographically on a base map.

grand design tradition–architecture such as monuments or impressive facades built to impress the populace, client, or other architects.

greenhouse effect–the excess heating of the earth due in part to carbon dioxide and other pollutants trapping too much heat close to the earth's surface.

habitability–the ability of a design to fit the needs of its inhabitants or users, especially in residential design.

habituation–the process (especially physiological) by which a person's responses to a particular stimulus become weaker over time.

harm or loss appraisal–a cognitive appraisal component of the stress model which focuses on damage already done.

Hawthorne effect–changes in behavior by virtue of observation alone rather than because of treatment effects.

hearing loss–permanent or temporary decrease in one's ability to hear caused by damage to the eardrum or to the tiny hair cells in the inner ear.

heat asthenia–fatigue and lethargy due to heat stress

heat exhaustion–moderate condition of faintness, nausea, headache, and restlessness due to heat stress.

heat stroke–severe and life-threatening condition of heat stress in which the sweating mechanism breaks down.

hedonic tone–the degree of pleasantness of an object or environment.

hertz (Hz)–cycles per second of a sound wave.

heuristics–simple principles that facilitate decision-making.

hierarchical memory–information storage based upon ordered categories.

high density–situations characterized by high social or spatial density.

hodometer–a device with sensors under a floor for measuring foot traffic.

homelessness–when a person does not have a fixed, regular, and adequate nighttime residence.

homeostatic–descriptive of automatic mechanisms which serve to maintain a state of balance, such as the sweating reaction to heat stress.

hue–color as it is experienced (e.g., red, yellow, or blue), primarily based on wavelength.

human factors–the discipline that concerns itself with the design and modification of equipment and workplaces to make them better adapted to the needs of humans.

human–machine system–a cycle of commands and feedback between human operators and machines.

humidity–the concentration of water vapor in the atmosphere.

hypertension–a form of cardiovascular disease characterized by sustained elevation of blood pressure.

hypothalamus–a primitive part of the brain responsible in part for regulating temperature, hunger, thirst, aggression, and the sex drive.

hypothermia–life-threatening decline in core temperature.

hypothesis–a scientific hunch or formal statement of an anticipated relationship between events.

hypoxia–reduced oxygen intake associated with low air pressure conditions such as high altitudes.

incongruity–in Berlyne's theory of aesthetics, the extent to which there is a mismatch between a component of the environment and its context.

independent variable–in the experimental method, the circumstances the experimenter manipulates in order to determine the impact on the dependent variable.

individual difference variables–variables which reflect differences in people in terms of background, personality, or other factors.

individual good–collective bad trap–a type of social trap in which a resource is depleted because short-term positive consequences of usage are experienced by the individual, but the long-term negative consequences are dispersed through the group.

individual personality traits–measurable personality factors such as internality–externality, authoritarianism, and so on.

inferential structuring–inclusion of elements in cognitive maps not because of direct experience with them, but because logic leads subjects to be expected.

information overload–a situation in which the demands on human attention exceed the ability to process them.

information processing–a theoretical approach that seeks to understand cognition in terms of how information is received, processed, stored, and retrieved.

informed consent–written permission from a subject agreeing to participate in a study after being informed of procedures, risks, and any circumstances which might alter the decision to participate.

inside density–population density indices using "inside" measures, such as number of people per residence or per room.

intensity–in Berlyne's dimensions, strength of stimulation.

intermediate care–a level of care for the elderly in which custodial care is emphasized.

internal validity–the rigor with which a research study is constructed so that one knows whether observed effects are due to variables of interest as opposed to such methodological artifacts as confounds or failure to control extraneous variables.

internality–externality – personality variable which taps whether people believe they, or outside forces, control their outcomes.

interpersonal distance – the distance between people.

intervening construct–an inferred phenomenon which mediates the relationship between other events or concepts.

intrinsic motivation–the degree to which an activity provides personal satisfaction and enjoyment.

invariant functional properties–in Gibson's theory of ecological perception, the properties of an object that do not change.

invasion of privacy–in research, access by the researcher into non-public activities of the research subject without the subject's permission.

laboratory methods–studying behavior (usually through systematic manipulation of variables) in a laboratory setting.

landmarks–structures or geographical entities that are distinctive; landmarks are usually visible from some distance, and include features such as tall buildings or monuments.

landscaped office–an open office; a large office area with few walls that is designed to be flexible and to facilitate the organizational processes that take place within it.

learned helplessness–Seligman's idea that once we believe we have lost control over the things that happen to us, we cease trying to change the situation; experienced state when people "learn" there is no contingency between their inputs and their outcomes.

legibility–the degree to which a scene is distinctive or memorable; in cognitive maps, the degree to which an area is easily learned or remembered.

lens model–the model of perception that emphasizes the active process by which humans make judgments based upon probablistic weighting of the variety of stimuli in the environment.

levee effect–the observation that once protective precautions are taken against a potential disaster, people tend to settle and live around these precautions, even though threats are still present.

linear relationship–straight-line (monotonic or rectilinear) relationship between two variables.

link analysis–the systematic investigation of the movements an operator makes to adjust controls or to read displays.

long, hot summer effect–the belief that heat wave conditions precipitate violence.

loose parts–in playgrounds, things that are not part of the playground structure itself, such as balls, games, or building materials.

loudness–the psychological perception of amplitude in a sound or noise.

low point–the point in a disaster at which victims perceive that the worst threat, harm, or adaptive demand has been reached; following this point, things gradually improve.

maintenance minimum–in ecological psychology, the minimum number of inhabitants needed to maintain a behavior setting.

masking–covering up or eliminating the distinct perception of a sound or noise by adding another sound or noise of similar frequency and similar or higher amplitude.

master plan–a long-range planning document; this often consists of a map showing locations for development or renovation.

mediating variable–a variable that operates in a sequence between other variables, such as arousal mediating the relationship between noise and aggression.

melatonin–a natural chemical associated with hibernation and possibly SAD.

missing hero situation–a type of social trap in which individuals fail to act for the benefit of the group because the penalty to the ''hero'' who does act seems inordinately large.

model–a relationship between concepts that is often based on analogies or metaphors.

modern design–the design tradition in industrialized societies; critics suggest that a premium is placed on originality and aesthetics at the expense of evolutionary development.

multidimensional scaling–a class of statistical procedures for displaying the relationships between concepts or places based upon their similarity on several dimensions of interest.

museum fatigue–Robinson's notion that museum visitors tire because they must pay attention to so much information in exhibits.

mystery–in landscape assessment, the degree to which hidden information creates intrigue and leads a viewer to further investigate a scene.

narrow band–a sound or noise with relatively few frequencies in it.

natural disaster–a disaster that is caused by natural (non-human) factors. (*see also* disaster event)

naturalness–scenes characterized by living things and either unmodified or landscaped views.

negative ions–*see* air ionization.

negative reinforcement–removing a noxious stimulus; increases desirable environmental behavior because people are motivated to avoid stimuli (e.g., fines) or to escape an ongoing noxious stimulus (e.g., high electric bills).

new ecological paradigm–belief that humans are interdependent with a fragile natural ecology with limited resources.

nodes–in cognitive maps, points where behavior is concentrated, such as at a place where major paths cross one another or intersect a landmark.

noise–sound that is undesirable or unwanted.

nonperformers–in ecological psychology, those who carry out secondary roles in a behavior setting.

norepinephrine–a catecholamine related to epinephrine; high concentrations can be indicative of stress.

normative theory–approaches to design based upon values and opinions rather than empirical facts.

novelty–the extent to which an environment contains new or previously unnoticed characteristics.

nuts game–a simulation of the commons dilemma developed by Edney.

object perception–the traditional approach to perception that investigates the patterns of sensations that allow us to identify distinct objects isolated from their context, especially in laboratory investigations.

objective physical distance–propinquity measured in terms of actual distance, or "as the crow flies."

observation–watching people behave and recording what is seen.

olfactory membrane–a membrane at the top of the nasal passage which detects chemical substances that the brain interprets as odors.

one atmosphere–atmospheric pressure at sea level, or 14.7 pounds per square inch.

one-person trap–another term for self-trap.

open classrooms–schools designed with few interior walls so that students and teachers are free to move about.

open desk arrangement (or placement)–offices arranged so that the desk does not form a barrier between the occupant and visitors.

open office–a large office area with few walls, which is designed to be flexible and to facilitate the organizational processes that take place within it.

operationally coordinated and hierarchically integrated reference system–a cognitive map type in which the environmental image is organized into a single spatial reference system.

organic growth–piecemeal changes in designs allowing gradual evolution of successful environments.

orientation–in general, the ability to determine one's place in the environment; design features which allow users to find their way about the environment; with respect to you-are-here maps, the ability to move or place the map so that it corresponds to the terrain.

outside density–population density indices using "outside" measures, such as number of persons, dwellings, or structures per acre.

overload–a condition in which the capacity for processing information is exceeded by the volume of incoming stimuli; the condition may be occasioned by urban life, crowding, noise, or other potential stressors.

overmanning–*see* overstaffed.

overstaffed–in ecological psychology, a condition of having too many participants, where the number of "participants" exceeds the capacity of the system.

overstimulation–*see* overload.

oxides of nitrogen and sulfur–substances such as sulfur dioxide and nitrogen oxide which are especially caused by burning of fossil fuels and which can be major pollutants.

ozone–a form of oxygen in which three atoms are molecularly combined (O_3).

ozone hole–atmospheric reduction in ozone around the polar regions due in part to chlorofluorocarbons.

palliative–emotion-focused (as opposed to direct-action focused) coping processes, such as denial, using drugs, or appraising the situation as nonthreatening.

palmar sweat index–a measure of arousal which uses a chemical to react with sweat on the palms.

partially coordinated reference system–a cognitive map type in which the subject can demonstrate an understanding of the relationship between elements within known clusters, but for which the clusters are not related to one another accurately.

participation–the degree to which users have opportunities to make substantive contributions to design.

particulates–air pollutants which can "settle out" of the atmosphere, often containing mercury, lead, and other toxic substances.

passive smoking–exposure to secondary cigarette smoke, that is, smoke produced by other people's smoking.

paths–shared travel corridors identified in cognitive maps such as streets, walkways, or riverways.

patterning–in Berlyne's dimensions, the degree to which a perception contains both structure and uncertainty.

pattern language–prescriptions for design problems presented in such a way that they can be used to allow user participation in design.

perceived control–belief that we can influence the things that are happening to us.

Perceived Environmental Quality Index (PEQI)–a subjective assessment of some characteristics of environmental quality as perceived by a human observer.

perceived inequity–the perception of being unfairly treated relative to another person.

perception–the process of extracting meaning from the complex stimuli we encounter in everyday life.

performers–in ecological psychology, those who carry out the primary tasks in a behavior setting.

peripheral vasoconstriction–constriction (narrowing) of blood vessels in the arms and legs, as in response to cold stress.

peripheral vasodilation–dilation (widening) of blood vessels in the arms and legs, as in response to heat stress.

permanent threshold shifts–hearing loss that is typically present a month or more after noise exposure ceases, characterized by increases in threshold below which sounds are inaudible.

personal space–a body buffer zone that people maintain between themselves and others.

personal stressors–stressful events that affect one person or only a few people at a time, such as loss of a loved one or loss of a job.

person–environment congruence–the notion that the setting promotes the behavior and goals within it; there is a good ''fit'' between people and their environment.

phon–a measure of loudness; the dB level of a 1000 Hz tone when it is judged to be of the same loudness as the sound being tested.

photochemical smog–air pollution resulting from sunlight combining a number of substances (including water vapor) which have been released into the atmosphere.

physical milieu–in Barker's ecological psychology, the physical component of the behavior setting.

physical-perceptual approach to landscape as- sessment–assessment strategies that emphasize the characteristics of the physical environment which can be statistically related to judgments of aesthetic quality.

piloerection–''goose bumps'' or the stiffening of hairs on the skin.

pitch–the psychological perception of the frequency of a sound.

place–the base spatial unit to which we attach information such as name, function, or affective quality.

policy capturing–a statistical procedure in which analysis shows the weights or relative importance an individual subject attaches to each of several predictor variables in making perceptual judgments.

population stereotypes–learned expectations about the relationship between controls, displays, and their movements.

positive ions–*see* air ionization.

positive reinforcement–when people are given positively valued stimuli for performing environmentally constructive acts.

positive theory–procedures or design components that are based upon empirical observations rather than opinions or values.

possibilism–the notion that the environmental context makes possible some activities but does not force them to occur, as in climatological, geographical, or architectural probabilism.

post-disaster groups–development of cohesive groups following disasters.

post-occupancy evaluation (POE)– a restrospective evaluation used to suggest modifications of the present structure, and to improve the available knowledge for future projects.

preindustrial vernacular design–the design of common buildings in nonindustrialized cultures; there is relatively little individual variation in style, but construction techniques often have evolved as good solutions to environmental demands.

primary appraisal–cognitive assessment of threat.

primary control–overt control over existing conditions.

primitive design–the architecture of so-called ''primitive'' societies; shelter is constructed according to standard techniques that have evolved over time; these are often quite sophisticated solutions to environmental demands.

privacy–an interpersonal boundary process by which people regulate interactions with others.

privacy gradient–different levels of privacy, as exemplified by different areas of the home.

privacy regulation model–Altman's model in which personal space, territoriality, and crowding are conceptualized as involving processes regulating privacy, or the desired degree of interaction with others.

probabilism–the notion that the environmental context makes some activities more probable than others, but does not absolutely determine which will occur, as in climatological, geographical, or architectural probabilism.

probabilistic functionalism–the model of perception that emphasizes the active process by which humans make judgments based upon probabilistic weighting of the variety of stimuli in the environment.

procedural theory–methods of gathering data and making decisions.

prompts–cues that convey a message.

propinquity–how close people are to each other in the places they occupy, in terms of objective physical, or functional, distance.

propositional storage–the theoretical position that the environment is stored not as a series of pictures, but as interconnected concepts or ideas connected to each other by a network of associations.

prosocial behavior–helping behavior or other activity to promote the welfare of others.

Pruitt-Igoe–a St. Louis housing project built to acclaim in the 1950's, but which because of poor design and unanticipated social factors became a classic case of what can go wrong in urban renewal, and was demolished in the 1970's.

psychological approach to landscape assessment–a theoretical approach that examines the psychological or cognitive processes that underlie aesthetic judgments.

psychological reactance–Brehm's notion that any time we feel our freedom of action being threatened, we act to restore that freedom.

psychological stress–the behavioral and emotional components of the stress model.

public goods problem–a situation where all participants need to contribute to a common asset; if too many people fail to contribute, the common good suffers.

punishment–administering a noxious or painful stimulus to those who engage in environmentally destructive behavior.

quasi-experimentation – experiments involving nonrandom assignment to conditions, but which attempt to infer causality to the extent possible.

radial ward design–hospital design in which hallways extend from a central nurses' station in the pattern of the spokes of a wheel.

radon–a colorless, odorless gas that comes from uranium deposits in the earth; it is naturally occurring, but is toxic.

random assignment–a critical element of the experimental method involving use of randomizing procedures (e.g., toss of a coin, use of a random number table) to determine which subjects will be in which conditions of the study.

reactance–*see* psychological reactance.

reciprocal response–in personal space, a similar response to that shown by the other person, such as moving closer when the other moves closer, or turning further away when the other turns away.

recognition tasks–tasks in which the subject needs only to report whether he or she is familiar with certain options, rather than having to recall them without cues.

refractory period–a time interval during which an organism recovers from a stressful event.

repression–sensitization–a continuum of ways of thinking about stressors: repressors tend to avoid and deny the existence of the stressor, sensitizers tend to approach and respond emotionally to the stressor.

residential care–a level of care for the elderly in which few if any medical services are needed on a routine basis; often termed "intermediate care."

residential preference–what people would most like to have in a home.

residential satisfaction–how pleased people feel about their place of residence.

REST–restricted environmental stimulation therapy (or technique), or a technique in which a level of sensory deprivation is used to modify behavior or relieve anxiety.

reticular formation–a part of the brain that regulates arousal.

retrospective control–perception of present control over a past aversive event.

Romanticism–a nineteenth-century artistic tradition that emphasized the sublime or picturesque.

saturation–the psychological or perceived purity of color.

scientific management–the management philosophy that believes that workers are primarily motivated by economic benefit, and that encourages the analysis of work activities to increase efficiency.

screening–ignoring extraneous stimuli, or prioritizing demands.

Seasonal Affective Disorder (SAD)–a psychiatric diagnosis in which a depressive state seems to come and go with seasonal changes.

secondary appraisal–cognitive appraisal of coping strategies.

secondary control–accommodating to existing reality and becoming satisfied with things the way they are.

self-report measures–measures of some feeling, belief, attitude, recollection, etc. that rely on a subject's report of how he or she feels, thinks, and so on; these may be oral reports, as in an interview, or they may be written, as on questionnaires.

self-trap–a type of "social trap" in which the momentary pleasures of the present have disastrous consequences in the long run, such as in addiction.

semantic network–information stored according to ordered categories interconnected by various associations.

sensation–the relatively straightforward activity of human sensory systems in reacting to simple stimuli such as an individual flash of light.

sensory deprivation–a condition in which environmental stimulation is kept to a minimum.

sequential maps–maps that are predominantly listings or drawings of the ordered places a person might come upon in traveling from one place to another.

setting–a discrete environment in which behavior occurs; within a particular environment, there are many settings (e.g., in a particular school building, there are many classrooms).

simulation or simulation methods–introduction of components of a real environment into an artificial laboratory setting in which control over assignment to conditions and experimental procedures can be maintained.

single corridor design–hospital design in which the nurses' station sits along one hallway.

situational conditions–the conditions that exist within a particular circumstance.

social comparison–comparing one's assets, values, or actions with those of another.

social density–manipulations that vary group size while keeping area consistent.

social dilemma–a situation where individual interests are pitted against group interests, such as in the commons dilemma.

social support–the feeling that one is cared about and valued by other people; the feeling that one belongs to a group.

social traps–Platt's notion that we get "trapped" into destructive behavior because we are motivated by short-term self-interest rather than long-term rewards (which may be shared by a group).

sociofugal–furniture arrangements, architectural designs, or social factors which discourage social interaction.

sociofugal seating–furniture arrangements that are closed and discourage social contact.

sociopetal–furniture arrangements, architectural designs, or social factors which encourage social interaction.

sociopetal seating–furniture arrangements that are open and welcome social contact.

solitude–the desire to be alone, especially to be away from the sights and sounds of unkown others.

sone–a measure of loudness; one sone is the perceived loudness of a 1000 Hz tone at 40 dB, two sones is the level of a sound perceived to be twice this standard, and so on.

sound–the perception of sound waves, which are caused by rapidly changing pressure of air molecules; these pressure changes are detectable by the eardrum.

spatial density–manipulations that vary area while keeping group size consistent.

spatial characteristics–direction, distance, and other spatial relationships reflected in cognitive maps.

spatial maps–cognitive maps in which the environment has become coded in an organized and flexible representation that resembles a ''bird's-eye'' view.

specific exploration–seeking to investigate an arousing stimulus to satisfy curiosity or to reduce uncertainty.

staffing theory–*see* theory of manning.

stage of exhaustion–depletion of coping reserves when coping skills are pushed to the limit; the third stage of Selye's GAS.

stage of resistance–reactions to stressors that seek to restore balance; the second stage of Selye's GAS.

standing patterns of behavior–in Barker's ecological psychology, the social component of the behavior setting, which is interdependent with the physical milieu.

stress–a formulation which predicts that certain environmental conditions lead to a stress reaction, which may have emotional, behavioral, and physiological components; *see* psychological stress.

structure matching–in you-are-here maps, the process of determining one's location by matching elements of the environment to those depicted in the map.

substantive theory–useful facts about the relationship between environmental variables such as construction techniques, color, or privacy and design goals.

surprisingness–the extent to which our expectations about an environment are disconfirmed.

survey knowledge–organization of a cognitive map spatially, or through a ''bird's-eye'' view.

symbolic barriers–physical features which are not actual barriers to other people but which signify that an area is someone's territory, such as name and address signs, hedges, or rock borders.

synomorphic–in Barker's ecological psychology, the similar structure of the physical milieu and the standing patterns of behavior.

systemic stress–from Selye, the physiological component of the stress model.

systems approach–with regard to perception, an approach that recognizes separate elements, but which emphasizes the need to study large units of behavior and complex patterns of mutual influence.

tactile discrimination–ability to distinguish stimuli through the sense of touch.

technological catastrophe–a disaster or emergency caused by human action or a mishap in human-made technology.

Temperature-Humidity Index (THI)–an index which attempts to allow for the contribution of both temperature and humidity in accounting for discomfort, similar to effective temperature.

temporary threshold shifts (TTS)–hearing loss that lasts for a day or less, characterized by increases in threshold below which sounds are inaudible.

terraforming–making an uninhabitable planet habitable.

territoriality–a set of behaviors and cognitions an organism or group exhibits, based on perceived ownership of physical space; claim to and defense of a geographic area.

territory–a set of behaviors and cognitions an organism or group exhibits, based on perceived ownership of physical space.

theory–a set of concepts and a set of relationships between the concepts.

theory of manning–in Barker's ecological psychology, the idea that performance and satisfaction are in part a function of the degree to which a behavior setting has too many or too few occupants.

thermoreceptors–nervous system sensory receptors which can detect changes in temperature.

threat appraisal–a cognitive appraisal component of the stress model that focuses on future dangers.

timbre–tonal quality; the purity of a sound, as determined by the number of frequencies in it.

tonal quality–timbre; the purity of a sound, as determined by the number of frequencies in it.

traditional playgrounds–playgrounds containing simple swings, monkey bars, seesaws, and so on, often geared primarily toward exercise.

transactional approach–a method of inquiry that concentrates on patterns of relationships rather than on specific causes; views the environment as an event in time whose components are so intermeshed that no part is understandable without the simultaneous inclusion of all of the other parts.

transient adaptation–changes in the sensitivity of the eyes when they are drawn momentarily to a bright light source, thus reducing their sensitivity to the primary task.

transition–the degree to which there is direct access from a building to a street; transition facilitates learning of a new environment.

uncertainty–arousal–according to Berlyne, increasing uncertainty in a situation leads to arousal and specific exploration aimed at reducing uncertainty.

understaffed–in ecological psychology, a condition of having too few participants.

understimulation–a condition of too few incoming stimuli, which leads to boredom.

unobtrusive measures–measures that can be collected without a subject's awareness.

urban homesteading–a program in which (usually poor) individuals are given abandoned urban property if they agree to rehabilitate it to meet existing housing codes and occupy it for a prescribed period of time.

urban renewal–a series of integrated steps taken to maintain and upgrade the environmental, economic, or social health of an urban area.

valuation–the process of rating or assigning value, as with assessments of environmental quality.

vandalism–willful or malicious destruction, injury, disfigurement, or defacement of any public or private property.

vernacular design–the traditional designs of the common, everyday buildings in a culture.

video display terminal (VDT)–a computer display device; depending upon the particular display, it may also be known as a Cathode Ray Tube (CRT).

visual air quality–the character of the atmosphere as perceived visually by a human observer.

Warrick's principle–a population stereotype that states that the pointer in a display will be expected to move in the same direction as that part of the control nearest the display.

wayfinding–the process of using stored spatial information to plan and carry out movement in the environment.

weather–relatively short-term changes in atmospheric conditions.

Weber-Fechner function–a psychophysical principle that says the higher the magnitude of a stimulus (e.g., loudness of a sound), the greater the difference in magnitude the next higher stimulus needs to be in order for it to be detected as different.

white noise–a very wide range of unpatterned sound frequencies, such as would be found when tuning a television to a channel with no station on it.

wide band–a sound or noise with many frequencies in it.

wilderness–with regard to recreation, refers to an environment that is dominated by nature and is relatively unmodified by humans.

wind chill–the effect of wind intensifying consequences of cold temperatures.

windowless classrooms–classroom learning environments without windows, designed to reduce distraction.

wind speed–straight-line velocity of wind, usually expressed in miles per hour or meters per second.

wind tunnel effect–a design phenomenon whereby building features, such as an open passageway below a tall structure, create high winds for pedestrians.

wind turbulence–gustiness and shifting directions of wind.

workflow–the movement of information or work materials between workstations.

workspace–the work environment.

workstation–the area of a factory or office assigned to an individual.

Yerkes-Dodson Law–states that performance is maximal at intermediate levels of arousal and declines as arousal increases or decreases from this point.

you-are-here maps–maps displayed in public locations as orientation devices.

REFERENCES

ABC New/Washington Post Survey. (1985, February 22) p. 44.

Abey-Wickrama, I., A'Brook, M. F., Gattoni, F. E. G., & Herridge, C. F. (1969). Mental hospital admissions and aircraft noise. *Lancet, 2,* 1275–1277.

Abramson, L. Y., Seligman, M. E. P., & Teasdale, J. D. (1978). Learned helplessness in humans: Critique and reformulation. *Journal of Abnormal Psychology, 87,* 49–74.

Acheson, J. M. (1975). The lobster fiefs: Economic and ecological effects of territoriality in the Maine lobster industry. *Human Ecology, 3,* 183–207.

Acking, D. A., & Kuller, R. (1972). The perception of an interior as a function of its color. *Ergonomics, 15,* 645–654.

Acredolo, L. P. (1976). Frames of reference used by children for orientation in unfamiliar spaces. In G. Moore & R. Golledge (Eds.), *Environmental knowing.* Stroudsburg, PA: Dowden, Hutchinson, & Ross.

Acredolo, L. P. (1977). Developmental changes in the ability to coordinate perspectives of a large-scale environment. *Developmental Psychology, 13,* 1–8.

Acton, W. I. (1970). Speech intelligibility in a background noise and noise-induced hearing loss. *Ergonomics, 13,* 546–554.

Adam, J. M. (1967). Military problems of air transport and tropical service. In C. N. Davies, P. R. Davis, & F. H. Tyrer (Eds.), *The effects of abnormal physical conditions at work* (pp. 74–80). London: E & S Livingstone.

Adams, J. R. (1973). Review of *Defensible space. Man–Environment Systems,* 267–268.

Adams, P. R., & Adams, G. R. (1984). Mount Saint Helens's ashfall: Evidence for a disaster stress reaction. *American Psychologist, 39,* 252–260.

Adler, A. (1943). Neuropsychiatric complications in victims of Boston's Cocoanut Grove disaster. *Journal of the American Medical Association, 17,* 1098–1101.

Ahrentzen, S., & Evans, G. (1984). Distraction, privacy, and classroom design. *Environment and Behavior, 16,* 437–454.

Ahrentzen, S., Jue, G. M., Skorpanich, M. A., & Evans, G. W. (1982). School environments and stress. In G.

W. Evans (Ed.), *Environmental stress* (pp. 224–255). New York: Cambridge University Press.

Aiello, J. R. (1977). A further look at equilibrium theory: Visual interaction as a function of interpersonal distance. *Environmental Psychology and Nonverbal Behavior, 1,* 122–140.

Aiello, J. R. (1987). Human spatial behavior. In D. Stokols & I. Altman (Eds.), *Handbook of Environmental Psychology,* (Vol. 1, pp. 505–531). New York: Wiley-Interscience.

Aiello, J. R., & Cooper, R. E. (1979). *Personal space and social affect: A developmental study.* Paper presented at the meeting of the Society for Research in Child Development, San Francisco.

Aiello, J. R., & Jones, S. E. (1971). Field study of the proxemic behavior of young school children in three subcultural groups. *Journal of Personality and Social Psychology, 19,* 351–356.

Aiello, J. R., Nicosia, G. J., & Thompson, D. E. (1979). Physiological, social, and behavioral consequences of crowding on children and adolescents. *Child Development, 50,* 195–202.

Aiello, J. R., & Thompson, D. E. (1980a). When compensation fails: Mediating effects of sex and locus of control at extended interaction distances. *Basic and Applied Social Psychology, 1,* 65–82.

Aiello, J. R., & Thompson, D. E. (1980b). Personal space, crowding, and spatial behavior in a cultural context. In I. Altman, J. F. Wohlwill, & A. Rapoport (Eds.), *Human behavior and environment.* (Vol. 4). New York: Plenum.

Aiello, J. R., Baum, A., & Gormley, F. B. (1981). Social determinants of residential crowding stress. *Personality and Social Psychology Bulletin, 7,* 643–649.

Aiello, J. R., DeRisi, D., Epstein, Y., & Karlin, R. (1977). Crowding and the role of interpersonal distance preference. *Sociometry, 40,* 271–282.

Aiello, J. R., Epstein, Y. M., & Karlin, R. A. (1975a). Effects of crowding on electrodermal activity. *Sociological Symposium, 14,* 43–57.

Aiello, J. R., Epstein, Y. M., & Karlin, R. A. (1975b). *Field experimental research in human crowding.* Paper presented at the meeting of the Eastern Psychological Association.

Aiello, J. R., Thompson, D. E., & Baum, A. (1981). The symbiotic relationship between social psychology and environmental psychology: Implications from crowding, personal space, and intimacy regulation research. In J. H. Harvey (Ed.), *Cognition and social behavior, and the environment*. Hillsdale, NJ: Erlbaum.

Aiello, J. R., Thompson, D. E., & Brodzinsky, D. M. (1983). How funny is crowding anyway? Effects of room size, group size, and the introduction of humor. *Basic and Applied Social Psychology, 4*, 193–207.

Aiello, J. R., Vautier, J. S., & Bernstein, M. D. (1983). *Crowding stress: Impact of social support, group formation, and control*. Paper presented at annual meeting of the American Psychological Association, Anaheim, CA.

Ajzen, I. (1985). From intentions to actions: A theory of planned behavior. In J. Kuhl & J. Beckman, (Eds.), *Action-control: From cognition to behavior* (pp. 11–39). Heidelberg: Springer.

Ajzen, I., & Madden, T. J. (1986). Prediction of goal-directed behavior: The role of intention, perceived control, and prior behavior. *Journal of Experimental Social Psychology, 22*, 453–474.

Albert, S., & Dabbs, J. M., Jr. (1970). Physical distance and persuasion. *Journal of Personality and Social Psychology, 15*, 265–270.

Aldwin, C. A., & Revenson, T. A. (1987). Does coping help? A reexamination of the relation between coping and mental health. *Journal of Personality and Social Psychology, 53*, 337–348.

Aldwin, C., & Stokols, D. (1988). The effects of environmental change on individuals and groups: Some neglected issues in stress research. *Journal of Environmental Psychology, 8*, 57–75.

Alexander, C. (1969). Major changes in environmental form required by social and psychological demands. *Ekistics, 28*, 78–85.

Alexander, C. (1979). *The timeless way of building*. New York: Oxford University Press.

Alexander, C., Ishikawa, S., & Silverstein, M. (1977). *A pattern language*. New York: Oxford University Press.

Alexander, C., Silverstein, M., Angel, S., Ishikawa, S., & Abrams, D. (1975). *The Oregon experiment*. New York: Oxford University Press.

Alland, A. (1972). *The human imperative*. New York: Columbia University.

Allen, G. H. (1972). How deep is environmental awareness? *Journal of Environmental Education, 3*, 1–3.

Allen, G. L., Siegel, A. W., & Rosinski, R. R. (1978). The role of perceptual context in structuring spatial knowledge. *Journal of Experimental Psychology: Human Learning and Memory, 4*, 617–630.

Allen, I. L. (1980). The ideology of dense neighborhood redevelopment: Cultural diversity and transcendent community experience. *Urban Affairs Quarterly, 15*, 409–428.

Allen, V. L., & Greenberger, D. B. (1980). Destruction and perceived control. In A. Baum & J. E. Singer (Eds.), *Advances in environmental psychology* (Vol. 2). Hillsdale, NJ: Erlbaum.

Allgeier, A. R., & Byrne, D. (1973). Attraction toward the opposite sex as a determinant of physical proximity. *Journal of Social Psychology, 90*, 213–219.

Alliance Housing Council. (1988). *Housing and homelessness*. Washington DC: National Alliance to End Homelessness.

Alloy, L. B., Peterson, C., Abramson, L. Y., & Seligman, M. E. P. (1984). Attributional style and the generality of learned helplessness. *Journal of Personality and Social Psychology, 46*, 681–687.

Allport, F. H. (1955). *Theories of perception and the concept of structure*. New York: Wiley.

Allport, G., & Pettigrew, T. (1957). Cultural influence on the perception of movement: The trapezoidal illusion among the Zulus. *Journal of Abnormal and Social Psychology, 55*, 104–113.

Altman, I. (1973). Some perspectives on the study of man–environment phenomena. *Representative Research in Social Psychology, 4*, 109–126.

Altman, I. (1975). *The environment and social behavior*. Monterey, CA: Brooks/Cole.

Altman, I. (1976a). Environmental psychology and social psychology. *Personality and Social Psychology Bulletin, 2*, 96–113.

Altman, I. (1976b). A response to Epstein, Proshansky, and Stokols. *Personality and Social Psychology Bulletin, 2*, 364–370.

Altman, I., & Chemers, M. (1980). *Culture and environment*. Monterey, Calif.: Brooks/Cole.

Altman, I., Lawton, M. P., & Wohlwill, J. F. (Eds.) (1984). *Elderly people and the environment*. New York: Plenum.

Altman, I., Nelson, P. A., & Lett, E. E. (1972, Spring). The ecology of home environments. *Catalog of Selected Documents in Psychology* (No. 150).

Altman, I., & Rogoff, B. (1987). World views in psychology: Trait, interactional, organismic, and transactional perspectives. In I. Altman & D. Stokols (Eds.), *Handbook of environmental psychology* (Vol. I, pp. 7–40). New York: Wiley-Interscience.

Altman, I., & Vinsel, A. M. (1977). Personal space: An analysis of E.T. Hall's proxemics framework. In I. Altman & J. F. Wohlwill (Eds.), *Human behavior and environment: Advances in theory and research* (Vol. 1). New York: Plenum.

Altman, I., & Wandersman, A. (Eds.) (1987). *Neighborhood and community environments*. New York: Plenum.

Altman, I., & Werner, C. M. (Eds.) (1985). *Home environments*. New York: Plenum.

Amato, P. R. (1981). The impact of the built environment on prosocial and affiliative behaviour: A field study of the Townsville city mall. *Australian Journal of Psychology, 33*, 297–303.

Amato, P. R. (1983). Helping behavior in urban and rural environments: Field studies based on taxonomic organization of helping episodes. *Journal of Personality and Social Psychology, 45*, 571–586.

American Public Transit Association. (1975, May 16). State funds flowing to R-GRTA. *Passenger Transport, 33*, 20(9).

Andersen, P. A., & Andersen, J. F. (1984). The exchange of nonverbal intimacy: A critical review of dyadic models. *Journal of Nonverbal Behavior, 8*, 327–349.

Anderson, B., Erwin, N., Flynn, D., Lewis, L., & Erwin, J. (1977). Effects of short-term crowding on aggression in captive groups of pigtail monkeys. *Aggressive Behavior, 3*, 33–46.

Anderson, C. A. (1987). Temperature and aggression: Effects on quarterly, yearly, and city rates of violent and nonviolent crime. *Journal of Personality and Social Psychology, 52*, 1161–1173.

Anderson, C. A. (in press). Temperature and aggression: The ubiquitous effects of heat on the occurrence of human violence. *Psychological Bulletin.*

Anderson, C. A., & Anderson, D. C. (1984). Ambient temperature and violent crime: Tests of the linear and curvilinear hypotheses. *Journal of Personality and Social Psychology, 46*, 91–97.

Anderson, D. H. & Brown, P. J. (1984). The displacement process in recreation. *Journal of Leisure Research, 16*, 61–73.

Anderson, E. N., Jr. (1972). Some Chinese methods in dealing with crowding. *Urban Anthropology, 1*, 141–150.

Anderson, T. W., Zube, E. H., & MacConnell (1976). Predicting scenic resource values. In E. H. Zube (Ed.), *Studies in landscape perception* (pp. 6–69). Publication No. R-76-1. Amherst, MA: Institute for Man and Environment, University of Massachusetts.

Ando Y., & Hattori, H. (1973). Statistical studies in the effects of intense noise during human fetal life. *Journal of Sound and Vibration, 27*, 101–110.

Antonovsky, A. (1979). *Health, stress, and coping*. San Francisco: Jossey-Bass.

Appleyard, D. (1969). Why buildings are known. *Environment and Behavior, 1*, 131–156.

Appleyard, D. (1970). Styles and methods of structuring a city. *Environment and Behavior*, 101–117.

Appleyard, D. (1976). *Planning a pluralistic city*. Cambridge, MA: M.I.T. Press.

Appleyard, D., & Lintell, M. (1972). The environmental quality of city streets: The residents' viewpoint.

Journal of the American Institute of Planners, 38, 84–101.

Aragones, J. I., & Arredondo, J. M. (1985). Structure of urban cognitive maps. *Journal of Environmental Psychology, 5*, 197–212.

Arbuthnot, J., Tedeschi, R., Wayner, M., Turner, J., Kressel, S., & Rush, R. (1976—1977). The induction of sustained recycling behavior through the foot-in-the-door technique. *Journal of Environmental Systems, 6*, 355–358.

Archer, J. (1970). Effects of population density on behavior in rodents. In J. H. Crook (Ed.), *Social behavior in birds and mammals*. New York: Academic Press.

Architectural Forum (1951, April). Slum surgery in St. Louis, pp. 128–136.

Ardrey, R. (1966). *The territorial imperative*. New York: Atheneum.

Argrist, S. S. (1974). Dimensions of well-being in public housing families. *Environment and Behavior, 6*, 495–517.

Argyle, M., & Dean, J. (1965). Eye-contact, distance and affiliation. *Sociometry, 28*, 289–304.

Arkkelin, D. (1978). *Effects of density, sex, and acquaintance level on reported pleasure, arousal, and dominance*. Doctoral dissertation, Bowling Green State University.

Arnstein, S. R. (1969). A ladder of citizen participation. *Journal of American Institute of Planners, 35*, 217.

Aronow, W. S., Harris, C. N., Isbell, M. W., Rokaw, M. D., & Imparato, B. (1972). Effect of freeway travel on angina pectoris. *Annals of Internal Medicine, 77*, 669–676.

Arreola, D. D. (1981). Fences as landscape taste: Tucson's barrios. *Journal of Cultural Geography, 2*, 96–105.

Asch, J., & Shore, B. M. (1975). Conservation behavior as the outcome to environmental education. *Journal of Environmental Education, 6*, 25–33.

Assael, M., Pfeifer, Y., & Sulman, F. G. (1974). Influence of artificial air ionization on the human electroencephalogram. *International Journal of Biometeorology, 18*, 306–312.

Atlas, R. (1984). Violence in prison: Environmental influences. *Environment and Behavior, 16*, 275–306.

Auble, D., & Britton, N. (1958). Anxiety as a factor influencing routine performance under auditory stimuli. *Journal of General Psychology, 58*, 111–114.

Auliciems, A. (1972). Some observed relationships between the atmospheric environment and mental work. *Environmental Research, 5*, 217–240.

Averill, J. R. (1973). Personal control over aversive stimuli and its relationship to stress. *Psychological Bulletin, 80*, 286–303.

Azuma, H. (1984). Secondary control as a heterogeneous category. *American Psychologist, 39*, 970–971.

Bacon-Prue, A., Blount, R., Pickering, D., & Drabman, R.

(1980). An evaluation of three litter control procedures—Trash receptacles, paid workers, and the marked item technique. *Journal of Applied Behavior Analysis, 13,* 165–170.

Baird, J. C. (1979). Studies of the cognitive representation of spatial relations: I. Overview. *Journal of Experimental Psychology: General, 108,* 90–91.

Baird, J. C., Merrill, A. A., & Tannenbaum, J. (1979). Studies of cognitive representations of spatial relations: II. A familiar environment. *Journal of Experimental Psychology: General, 108,* 92–98.

Baird, L. L. (1969). Big school, small school: A critical examination of the hypothesis. *Journal of Educational Psychology, 60,* 253–260.

Baker, G. W., & Chapman, D. W. (Eds.) (1962). *Man and society in disaster.* New York: Basic Books.

Balling, J. D., & Falk, J. H. (1982). Development of visual preference for natural environments. *Environment and Behavior, 14,* 5–28.

Baltes, M. M., & Hayward, S. C. (1976). Application and evaluation of strategies to reduce pollution: Behavioral control of littering in a football stadium. *Journal of Applied Psychology, 61,* 501–506.

Baltes, M. M., Kindermann, T., Reisenzein, R., & Schmid, U. (1987). Further observational data on the behavioral and social world of institutions for the aged. *Psychology and Aging, 2,* 390–403.

Bandura, A. (1969). *Principles of behavior modification.* New York: Holt, Rinehart and Winston.

Bandura, A. (1973). *Aggression: A social learning analysis.* Englewood Cliffs, NJ: Prentice-Hall.

Bandura, A. (1977). *Social learning theory.* Englewood Cliffs, NJ: Prentice-Hall.

Bandura, A., & Walters, R. H. (1967). *Social learning and personality development.* New York: Holt, Rinehart and Winston.

Banzinger, G., & Owens, K. (1978). Geophysical variables and behavior: II. Weather factors as predictors of local social indicators of maladaptation in two non-urban areas. *Psychological Reports, 43,* 427–434.

Barabasz, A., & Barabasz, M. (1985). Effects of restricted environmental stimulation: Skin conductance, EEG alpha, and temperature responses. *Environment and Behavior, 17,* 239–253.

Barabasz, A., & Barabasz, M. (1986). Antarctic isolation and inversion perception: Regression phenomena. *Environment and Behavior, 18,* 285–292.

Barash, D. P. (1973). Human ethology: Personal space reiterated. *Environment and Behavior, 5,* 67–73.

Barefoot, J. C., Hoople, H., & McClay, D. (1972). Avoidance of an act which would violate personal space. *Psychonomic Science, 28,* 205–206.

Barefoot, J., & Kleck, R. (1970). *The effects of race and physical proximity of a co-actor on the social facilitation of dominant responses.* Unpublished manuscript. Carleton University.

Barker, M. L. (1976). Planning for environmental indices: Observer appraisals of air quality. In K. H. Craik & E. H. Zube (Eds.), *Perceiving environmental quality: Research applications* (pp. 175–204). New York: Plenum.

Barker, R. G. (1960). Ecology and motivation. In M. R. Jones (Ed.), *Nebraska Symposium on Motivation* (Vol. 8, pp. 1–50). Lincoln: University of Nebraska Press.

Barker, R. G. (1968). *Ecological psychology: Concepts and methods for studying the environment of human behavior.* Stanford, CA: Stanford University Press.

Barker, R. G. (1979). Settings of a professional lifetime. *Journal of Personality and Social Psychology, 37,* 2137–2157.

Barker, R. G. (1987). Prospecting in environmental psychology: Oskaloosa revisited. In D. Stokols & I. Altman (Eds.), *Handbook of environmental psychology* (Vol. II, pp. 1413–1432). New York: Wiley-Interscience.

Barker, R. G., & Gump, P. V. (1964). *Big school, small school.* Stanford, CA: Stanford University Press.

Barker, R. G., & Schoggen, P. (1973). *Qualities of community life.* San Francisco: Jossey-Bass.

Barker, R. G., & Wright, H. F. (1951). *One boy's day.* New York: Row, Peterson.

Barker, R. G., & Wright, H. (1955). *Midwest and its children.* New York: Row, Peterson.

Barkow, B. (1974). *The psychology of car pooling.* Ontario, Canada: Ministry of Transportation and Communication.

Barnard, W. A., & Bell, P. A. (1982). An unobtrusive apparatus for measuring interpersonal distance. *Journal of General Psychology, 107,* 85–90.

Baron, R. A. (1972). Aggression as a function of ambient temperature and prior anger arousal. *Journal of Personality and Social Psychology, 21,* 183–189.

Baron, R. A. (1976). The reduction of human aggression: A field study of the influence of incompatible reactions. *Journal of Applied Social Psychology, 6,* 260–274.

Baron, R. A. (1987a). Effects of negative ions on cognitive performance. *Journal of Applied Psychology, 72,* 131–137.

Baron, R. A. (1987b). Effects of negative ions on interpersonal attraction: Evidence for intensification. *Journal of Personality and Social Psychology, 52,* 547–553.

Baron, R. A., & Bell, P. A. (1975). Aggression and heat: Mediating effects of prior provocation and exposure to an aggressive model. *Journal of Personality and Social Psychology, 31,* 825–832.

Baron, R. A., & Bell, P. A. (1976a). Aggression and heat: The influence of ambient temperature, negative affect, and a cooling drink on physical aggression. *Journal of Personality and Social Psychology, 33,* 245–255.

Baron, R. A., & Bell, P. A. (1976b). Physical distance and helping: Some unexpected benefits of "crowding in" on others. *Journal of Applied Social Psychology, 6*, 95–104.

Baron, R. A., & Lawton, S. F. (1972). Environmental influences on aggression: The facilitation of modeling effects by high ambient temperatures. *Psychonomic Science, 26*, 80–82.

Baron, R. A., & Ransberger, V. M. (1978). Ambient temperature and the occurrence of collective violence: The "long, hot summer" revisited. *Journal of Personality and Social Psychology, 36*, 351–360.

Baron, R. A., Russell, G. W., & Arms, R. L. (1985). Negative ions and behavior: Impact on mood, memory, and aggression among Type A and Type B persons. *Journal of Personality and Social Psychology, 48*, 746–754.

Baron, R. M., & Fisher, J. D. (1984). The equity-control model of vandalism: A refinement. In C. Levy-Leboyer (Ed.), *Vandalism: Behavior and Motivations*. Amsterdam: North Holland.

Baron, R. M., Mandel, D. R., Adams, C. A., & Griffen, L. M. (1976). Effects of social density in university residential environments. *Journal of Personality and Social Psychology, 34*, 434–446.

Baron, R. M., & Rodin, J. (1978). Personal control as a mediator of crowding. In A. Baum, J. E. Singer, & S. Valins (Eds.), *Advances in environmental psychology* (Vol. 1). Hillsdale, NJ: Erlbaum.

Barrios, B. A., Corbitt, L. C., Estes, J. P., & Topping, J. S. (1976). Effect of social stigma on interpersonal distance. *The Psychological Record, 26*, 343–348.

Bartley, S. H. (1958). *Principles of perception*. New York: Harper & Row.

Barton, A. (1969). *Communities in disaster*. Garden City, NY: Doubleday.

Barton, R. (1966). The patient's personal territory. *Hospital and Community Psychiatry, 17*, 336.

Bassuk, E., Rubin, L., & Lauriat, A. (1986). Characteristics of sheltered homeless families. *American Journal of Public Health, 76*, 1097–1101.

Baum, A. (1987). Toxins, technology, and natural disaster. In G. R. VandenBos & B. K. Bryant (Eds.), *Cataclysms, crises, and catastrophes: Psychology in action*. Washington, DC: American Psychological Association.

Baum, A., Aiello, J., & Calesnick, L. E. (1978). Crowding and personal control: Social density and the development of learned helplessness. *Journal of Personality and Social Psychology, 36*, 1000–1011.

Baum, A., Calesnick, L. E., Davis, G. E., & Gatchel, R. J. (1982). Individual differences in coping with crowding: Stimulus screening and social overload. *Journal of Personality and Social Psychology, 43*, 821–830.

Baum, A., & Davis, G. E. (1976). Spatial and social aspects of crowding perception. *Environment and Behavior, 8*, 527–545.

Baum, A., & Davis, G. E. (1980). Reducing the stress of high-density living: An architectural intervention. *Journal of Personality and Social Psychology, 38*, 471–481.

Baum, A., & Fisher, J. D. (1977). *Situation-related information as a mediator of responses to crowding*. Unpublished manuscript, Trinity College.

Baum, A., Fisher, J. D., & Singer, J. E. (1985). *Social psychology*. New York: Random House.

Baum, A., Fisher, J. D., & Solomon, S. (1981). Type of information, familiarity, and the reduction of crowding stress. *Journal of Personality and Social Psychology, 40*, 11–23.

Baum, A., Fleming, R., & Davidson, L. M. (1983). Natural disaster and technological catastrophe. *Environment and Behavior, 15*, 333–354.

Baum, A., & Gatchel, R. J. (1981). Cognitive determinants of response to uncontrollable events: Development of reactance and learned helplessness. *Journal of Personality and Social Psychology, 40*, 1078–1089.

Baum, A., Gatchel, R., Streufert, S., Baum, C. S., Fleming, R., & Singer, J. E. (1980). *Psychological stress for alternatives of decontamination of TMI-2 reactor building atmosphere*. U.S. Nuclear Regulatory Commission (NUREG/CR–1584).

Baum, A., & Greenberg, C. I. (1975). Waiting for a crowd: The behavioral and perceptual effects of anticipated crowding. *Journal of Personality and Social Psychology, 32*, 667–671.

Baum, A., Grunberg, N. E., & Singer, J. E. (1982). The use of physiological and neuroendocrinological measurements in the study of stress. *Health Psychology, 1*, 217–236.

Baum, A., & Koman, S. (1976). Differential response to anticipated crowding: Psychological effects of social and spatial density. *Journal of Personality and Social Psychology, 34*, 526–536.

Baum, A., & Paulus, P. B. (1987). Crowding. *Handbook of Environmental Psychology, 1*, 533–570.

Baum, A., Reiss, M., & O'Hara, J. (1974). Architectural variants of reaction to spatial invasion. *Environment and Behavior, 6*, 91–100.

Baum, A., Shapiro, A., Murray, D., & Wideman, M. (1979). Mediation of perceived crowding and control in residential dyads and triads. *Journal of Applied Social Psychology, 9*, 491–507.

Baum, A., Singer, J. E., & Baum, C. S. (1981). Stress and the environment. *Journal of Social Issues, 37*, 4–35.

Baum, A., & Valins, S. (1977). *Architecture and social behavior: Psychological studies of social density*. Hillsdale, NJ: Erlbaum.

Baum, A., & Valins, S. (1979). Architectural mediation of residential density and control: Crowding and the regulation of social contact. In L. Berkowitz (Ed.), *Advances in experimental social psychology*, (Vol. 12, pp. 131–175). New York: Academic Press.

Baumeister, R. F. (1985). The championship choke. *Psychology Today, 19*(4), 48–52.

Baumer, T. L., & Hunter, A. (1978). *Street traffic, social integration, and fear of crime.* Evanston, IL.: Center for Urban Affairs, Northwestern University.

Baxter, J. C., & Deanovich, B. S. (1970). Anxiety-arousing effects of inappropriate crowding. *Journal of Consulting and Clinical Psychology, 35,* 174–178.

Beal, J. B. (1974). Electrostatic fields, electromagnetic fields and ions—Mind/body/environment interrelationships. In J. G. Llaurado, A. Sances, & J. H. Battocletti (Eds.), *Biologic and clinical effects of low-frequency magnetic and electric fields* (pp. 5–20). Springfield, IL: Thomas.

Beard, R. & Grandstaff, N. (1970). Carbon monoxide exposure and cerebral function. *Annals of New York Academy of Sciences, 174,* 385–395.

Beard, R. R., & Wertheim, G. A. (1967). Behavioral impairment associated with small doses of carbon monoxide. *American Journal of Public Health, 57,* 2012–2022.

Beatty, V. L. (1974). *Highrise horticulture. American Horticulturist. 58,* 44–46.

Bechtel, R. B. (1970). Human movement and architecture. In H. M. Proshansky, W. H. Ittelson, & L. G. Rivlin (Eds.), *Environmental psychology: Man and his physical setting.* New York: Holt, Rinehart and Winston.

Bechtel, R. B. (1977). *Enclosing behavior.* Stroudsberg, PA: Dowden, Hutchinson, & Ross.

Beck, R. J. (1971). *Out shopping in the urban crowd.* Presented at the annual meeting of the American Psychological Association, Washington, D.C.:

Beck, R. J., & Wood, D. (1976). Cognitive transformation of information from urban geographic fields to mental maps. *Environment and Behavior, 8,* 199–238.

Becker, F. D. (1973). Study of spatial markers. *Journal of Personality and Social Psychology, 26,* 439–445.

Becker, F. D. (1981). *Workspace: Creating environments in organizations.* New York: CBS Educational and Professional Publishing.

Becker, F. D., & Coniglio, C. (1975). Environmental messages: Personalization and territory. *Humanitias, 11,* 55–74.

Becker, F. D., & Mayo, C. (1971). Delineating personal space and territoriality. *Environment and Behavior, 3,* 375–381.

Becker, F. D., Gield, B., Gaylin, K., & Sayer, S. (1983). Office design in a community college: Effect of work and communication patterns. *Environment and Behavior, 15,* 699–726.

Becker, F. D., Sommer, R., Bee, J., & Oxley, B. (1973). College classroom ecology. *Sociometry, 36,* 514–525.

Becker, L. J. (1978). The joint effect of feedback and goal setting on performance: A field study of residential energy conservation. *Journal of Applied Psychology, 63,* 228–233.

Becker, L., & Seligman, C. (1978). Reducing air-conditioning waste by signalling it is cool outside. *Personality and Social Psychology Bulletin, 4,* 412–415.

Beckey, T., & Nelson, L. W. (1981, January). Field test of energy savings with thermostat setback. *ASHRAE Journal, 67–70.*

Beckman, R. (1974, November). Getting up and getting out: Progressive patient care. *Progressive Architecture,* p. 64.

Beighton, P. (1971). Fluid balance in the Sahara. *Nature, 233,* 275–277.

Bell, C. R., Provins, K. A., & Hiorns, R. F. (1964). Visual and auditory vigilance during exposure to hot and humid conditions. *Ergonomics, 7,* 279–288.

Bell, P. A. (1978). Effects of heat and noise stress on primary and subsidiary task performance. *Human Factors, 20,* 749–752.

Bell, P. A. (1980). Effects of heat, noise stress, and provocation on retaliatory evaluative behavior. *Journal of Social Psychology, 40,* 97–100.

Bell, P. A. (1981). Physiological, comfort, performance, and social effects of heat stress. *Journal of Social Issues, 37,* 71–94.

Bell, P. A. (1982, August). *Theoretical interpretations of heat stress.* Paper presented at the meeting of the American Psychological Association, Washington, D.C.

Bell, P. A., & Barnard, S. W. (1977, May) *Sex differences in the effects of heat and noise stress on personal space permeability.* Paper presented at the meeting of the Rocky Mountain Psychological Association, Albuquerque.

Bell, P. A., & Baron, R. A. (1974). Environmental influences on attraction: Effects of heat, attitude similarity, and personal evaluations. *Bulletin of the Psychonomic Society, 4,* 479–481.

Bell, P. A., & Baron, R. A. (1976). Aggression and heat: The mediating role of negative affect. *Journal of Applied Social Psychology, 6,* 18–30.

Bell, P. A., & Baron, R. A. (1977). Aggression and ambient temperature: The facilitating and inhibiting effects of hot and cold environments. *Bulletin of the Psychonomic Society, 9,* 443–445.

Bell, P. A., & Baron, R. A. (1981). Ambient temperature and human violence. In P. F. Brain & D. Benton (Eds.), *A multidisciplinary approach to aggression research,* (pp. 421–430). Amsterdam: Elsevier/North-Holland Biomedical Press.

Bell, P. A., & Byrne, D. (1978). Repression-sensitization. In H. London & J. Exner (Eds.), *Dimensions of personality* (pp. 449–485). New York: Wiley.

Bell, P. A., & Doyle, D. P. (1983). Effects of heat and noise on helping behavior. *Psychological Reports, 53,* 955–959.

Bell, P. A., & Fusco, M. E. (1986). Linear and curvilinear relationships between temperature, affect, and violence:

Reply to Cotton. *Journal of Applied Social Psychology, 16,* 802–807.

Bell, P. A., & Fusco, M. E. (1989). Heat and violence in the Dallas field data: Linearity, curvilinearity, and heteroscedasticity. *Journal of Applied Social Psychology, 19,* 1479–1482.

Bell, P. A., Garnand, D. B., & Heath, D. (1984). Effects of ambient temperature and seating arrangement on personal and environmental evaluations. *Journal of General Psychology, 110,* 197–200.

Bell, P. A., & Greene, T. C. (1982). Thermal stress: Physiological, comfort, performance, and social effects of hot and cold environments. In G. W. Evans (Ed.), *Environmental stress,* (pp. 75–105). London: Cambridge University Press.

Bell, P. A., Kline, L. M., & Barnard, W. A. (1988). Friendship and freedom of movement as moderators of sex differences in interpersonal distancing. *Journal of Social Psychology, 128,* 305–310.

Bell, P. A., Loomis, R. J., & Cervone, J. C. (1982). Effects of heat, social facilitation, sex differences, and task difficulty on reaction time. *Human Factors, 24,* 19–24.

Bell, P. A., Peterson, T. R., & Hautaluoma, J. E. (1989). The effect of punishment probability on overconsumption and stealing in a simulated commons. *Journal of Applied Social Psychology, 19,* 1483–1495.

Bell, P. A., & Smith, J. M. (1989). *An empirical comparison of specialized Alzheimer's nursing home units.* Unpublished manuscript, Colorado State University, Ft. Collins, CO.

Bell, R. W., Miller, C. E., Ordy, J. M., & Rolsten, C. (1971). Effects of population density and living space upon neuroanatomy, neurochemistry and behavior in the C57B1 10 mouse. *Journal of Comparative and Physiological Psychology, 75,* 258–263.

Bellet, S., Roman, L., & Kastis, J. (1969). The effects of automobile driving on catecholamine and adrenocortical excretion. *The American Journal of Cardiology, 24,* 365–368.

Bem, D. (1971). *Beliefs, attitudes, and human affairs.* Belmont, CA: Brooks/Cole.

Bem, D. J. (1972). Self-perception theory. In L. Berkowitz (Ed.), *Advances in experimental social psychology* (Vol. 6). New York: Academic Press.

Benedak, T., (1952). *Psychosexual functions of women: Studies in psychosomatic medicine.* New York: Ronald Press.

Bennett, C. A., & Rey, P. (1972). What's so hot about red?. *Human Factors, 14,* 149–154.

Bennett, N., Andreae, J., Hegarty, P., & Wade, B. (1980). *Open plan schools.* Atlantic Highlands, NJ: Humanities.

Bennett, R., Rafferty, J. M., Canivez, G. L., & Smith, J. M. (1983, May). *The effects of cold temperature on altruism and aggression.* Paper presented at the meeting

of the Midwestern Psychological Association, Chicago, IL.

Benson, G. P., & Zieman, G. L. (1981). *The relationship of weather to children's behavior problems.* Unpublished manuscript, Colorado State University, Fort Collins.

Beranek, L. L. (1956). Criteria for office quieting based on questionnaire rating studies. *Journal of the Acoustical Society of America, 28,* 833–850.

Beranek, L. L. (1957). Revised criteria for noise in buildings. *Noise Control, 3,* 19–26.

Berglund, B., Berglund, U., & Lindvall, T. (1976). Psychological processing of odor mixtures. *Psychological Review, 83,* 432–441.

Bergman, B. A. (1971). *The effects of group size, personal space and success–failure on physiological arousal, test performance, and questionnaire responses.* Doctoral dissertation, Temple University.

Berk, L. E., & Goebel, B. L. (1987). High school size and extracurricular participation: A study of a small college environment. *Environment and Behavior, 19,* 53–76.

Berkowitz, L. (1970). The contagion of violence: An S–R mediational analysis of some effects of observed aggression. In W. J. Arnold & M. M. Page (Eds.), *Nebraska Symposium on Motivation* (Vol. 18, pp. 95–135). Lincoln: University of Nebraska Press.

Berlyne, D. E. (1960a). *Conflict, arousal, and curiosity.* New York: McGraw-Hill.

Berlyne, D. E. (1960b). Conflict and information-theory variables as determinants of human perceptual curiosity. *Journal of Experimental Psychology, 53,* 399–404.

Berlyne, D. E. (1972). *Aesthetics and psychobiology.* New York: Appleton-Century-Crofts.

Berlyne, D. E. (1974). *Studies in the new experimental aesthetics: Steps toward an objective psychology of aesthetic appreciation.* New York: Halsted Press.

Bernaldez, F. G., Gallardo, D., & Abello, R. P. (1987). Children's landscape preferences from rejection to attraction. *Journal of Environmental Psychology, 7,* 169–176.

Berry, P. C. (1961). Effects of coloured illumination upon perceived temperature. *Journal of Applied Psychology, 45,* 248–250.

Best, J. B. (1986). *Cognitive psychology.* St. Paul, MN: West Publishing Company.

Bickman, L. (1972). Environmental attitudes and actions. *Journal of Social Psychology, 87,* 323–324.

Bickman, L., Teger, A., Gabriele, T., McLaughlin, C., Berger, M., & Sunaday, E. (1973). Dormitory density and helping behavior. *Environment and Behavior, 5,* 465–490.

Biner, P. M., Butler, D. L., Fischer, A. R., & Westergren, A. J. (1989). An arousal optimization model of lighting level preferences: An interaction of social situation and task demands. *Environment and Behavior, 21,* 3–16.

Birren, F. (1969). *Light, color, and environment.* New York: Van Nostrand Rinhold.

Bishop, R. L., & Peterson, G. L. (1971). *A synthesis of environmental design recommendations from the visual preferences of children.* Chicago, IL: Northwestern University Department of Civil Engineering.

Bitgood, S., Patterson, D., & Benefield, A. (1988). Exhibit design and visitor behavior: Empirical relationships. *Environment and Behavior, 20,* 474–491.

Bitgood, S., Roper, J. T., Jr., & Benefield, A. (Eds.) (1988). *Visitor studies—1988: Theory, research, and practice.* Jacksonville, AL: Center for Social Design.

Black, J. C. (1968). *Uses made of spaces in owner-occupied houses.* Unpublished doctoral dissertation, University of Utah, Salt Lake City, UT.

Blackman, S., & Catalina, D. (1973). The moon and the emergency room. *Perceptual and Motor Skills, 37,* 624–626.

Blades, M. & Spencer, C. (1987). Young children's strategies when using maps with landmarks. *Journal of Environmental Psychology, 7,* 201 – 217.

Blaut, J., & Stea, D. (1971). Studies of geographical learning. *Annals of the Association of American Geographers, 61,* 387–393.

Blaut, J. M., & Stea, D. (1974). Mapping at the age of three. *Journal of Geography, 73,* 5–9.

Bleda, P. R., & Sandman, P. H. (1977). In smoke's way: Socioemotional reactions to another's smoking. *Journal of Applied Psychology, 62,* 452–458.

Bleda, P., & Bleda, S. (1978). Effects of sex and smoking on reactions to spatial invasion at a shopping mall. *Journal of Social Psychology, 104,* 311–312.

Block, J. (1971). *Lives Through Time.* Berkeley, CA: Bancroft.

Block, L. K., & Stokes, G. S. (1989). Performance and satisfaction in private versus nonprivate work settings. *Environment and Behavior, 21,* 277–297.

Bolin, R. (1985). Disaster characteristics and psychosocial impacts. In B. J. Sowder (Ed.), *Disasters and mental health: Selected contemporary perspectives* (pp. 3–28). Rockville, MD: U.S. Department of Health and Human Services.

Bolt, Beranek, & Newman, Inc. (1982). Occupational Noise: The subtle pollutant. In J. Ralof, *Science News, 121*(21), 347–350.

Bonio, S., Fonzi, A., & Saglione, G. (1978). Personal space and variations in the behaviour of ten-year-olds. *Italian Journal of Psychology, 10,* 15–25.

Bonnes, M., Giuliani, M. V., Amoni, F., & Bernard, Y. (1987). Cross-cultural rules for the optimization of the living room. *Environment and Behavior, 19,* 204 – 227.

Bonta, J. (1986). Prison crowding: Searching for the functional correlates. *American Psychologist, 41,* 99–101.

Booth, A. (1976). *Urban crowding and its consequences.* New York: Praeger.

Booth, W. (1988). Johnny Appleseed and the greenhouse. *Science, 242,* 19–20.

Booth-Kewly, S., & Friedman, H. S. (1987). Psychological predictors of heart disease: A quantitive review. *Psychological Bulletin, 101,* 343–362.

Borg, E. (1981). Noise, hearing, and hypertension (editorial). *Scandinavian Audiology, 10*(2), 125–126.

Bornstein, M. H. (1979). The pace of life revisited. *International Journal of Psychology, 14,* 83–90.

Borsky, P. N. (1969). Effects of noise on community behavior. In W. D. Ward & J. E. Fricke (Eds.), *Noise as a public health hazard.* Washington, DC: The American Speech and Hearing Association.

Borun, M. (1977). *Measuring the unmeasurable.* Washington, DC: Association for Science Technology Centers.

Boucher, M. L. (1972). Effect of seating distance on interpersonal attraction in an interview situation. *Journal of Consulting and Clinical Psychology, 38,* 15–19.

Bouska, M. L., & Beatty, P. A. (1978). Clothing as a symbol of status: Its effect on control of interaction territory. *Bulletin of the Psychonomic Society, 4,* 235–238.

Bovy, P. (1975). *Pedestrian planning and design: A bibliography.* (No. 918). Council of Planning Librarians Exchange Bibliography.

Bowman, U. (1964). Alaska earthquake. *American Journal of Psychology, 121,* 313–317.

Boyanowsky, E. O., Calvert, J., Young, J., & Brideau, L. (1981–82). Toward a thermoregulatory model of violence. *Journal of Environmental Systems, 11,* 81–87.

Boyce, P. (1981). *Human factors in lighting.* New York: Macmillan.

Boyer, R., & Savageau, D. (1985). Putting it all together: Finding the best places to live in America. In *Places Rated Almanac,* 415–442. Chicago: Rand McNally.

Brasted, W., Mann, M., & Geller, E. S. (1979, Summer). Behavioral interventions for litter control: A critical review. *Cornell Journal of Social Relations, 14,* 75–90.

Brechner, K. C. (1977). An experimental analysis of social traps. *Journal of Experimental Social Psychology, 13,* 552–564.

Brehm, J. W. (1966). *A theory of psychological reactance.* New York: Academic Press.

Brehm, S. S., & Brehm, J. W. (1981). *Psychological reactance: A theory of freedom and control.* New York: Academic Press.

Breisacher, P. (1971). Neuropsychological effects of air pollution. *American Behavioral Scientist, 14,* 837–864.

Brewer, M. B., & Kramer, R. M. (1986). Choice behavior in social dilemmas: Effects of social density, group size, and decision framing. *Journal of Personality and Social Psychology, 50,* 543–549.

Briere, J., Downes, A., & Spensley, J. (1983). Summer in

the city: Urban weather conditions and psychiatric-emergency room visits. *Journal of Abnormal Psychology, 92,* 77–80.

Broadbent, D. E. (1954). Some effects of noise on visual performance. *Quarterly Journal of Experimental Psychology, 6,* 1–5.

Broadbent, D. E. (1958). *Perception and communication.* Oxford: Pergamon.

Broadbent, D. E. (1963). Differences and interactions between stresses. *Quarterly Journal of Experimental Psychology, 15,* 205–211.

Broadbent, D. E. (1971). *Decision and stress.* New York: Academic Press.

Broadbent, D. E., & Little, E. (1960). Effects of noise reduction in a work situation. *Occupational Psychology, 34,* 133–140.

Broadbent, G. B. (1973). *Design in architecture.* New York: Wiley.

Brokemann, N. C., & Moller, A. T. (1973). Preferred seating position and distance in various situations. *Journal of Counseling Psychology, 20,* 504–508.

Bromet, E. (1980). *Preliminary report on the mental health of Three Mile Island residents.* Pittsburgh, Pa.: Western Psychiatric Institute, University of Pittsburgh.

Bromet, E., Ryan, C., and Parkinson, D. (1986). Psychosocial correlates of occupational lead exposure. In A. H. Lebovits, A. Baum, & J. Singer (Eds.), *Advances in Environmental Psychology* (Vol. 6, pp. 19–31). Hillsdale, NJ: Erlbaum.

Bronzaft, A. L. (1981). The effect of a noise abatement program on reading ability. *Journal of Environmental Psychology, 1,* 215–222.

Bronzaft, A. (1985–86). Combating the unsilent enemy—Noise, *Prevention in Human Services,* (Fall-Win) *4* (1–2), 179–192.

Bronzaft, A. L., & McCarthy, D. P. (1975). The effects of elevated train noise on reading ability. *Environment and Behavior, 7,* 517–527.

Brooks, M. J., & Kaplan, A. (1972). The office environment: Space planning and affective behavior. *Human Factors, 14,* 373–391.

Browder, A. A., Joselow, M. M., & Louria, D. B. (1973). The problem of lead poisoning. *Medicine, 52,* 121–139.

Brower, S., Dockett, K., & Taylor, R. (1983). Residents' perceptions of territorial features and perceived features and perceived local threat. *Environment and Behavior, 15,* 419–437.

Brown, B. (1987). Territoriality. In D. Stokols & I. Altman (Eds.), *Handbook of environmental psychology* (Vol. 1, pp. 505–531). New York: Wiley-Interscience.

Brown, B. B. (1979, Aug.). *Territoriality and residential burglary.* Paper presented at the meeting of the American Psychological Association, New York, NY.

Brown, B. B., & Altman, I. (1983). Territoriality, Defensible space, and residential burglary: An environment

analysis. *Journal of Environmental Psychology, 3,* 203–220.

Brown, B. B., & Werner, C. M. (1985). Social cohesiveness, territoriality, and holiday decorations: The influence of cul-de-sacs. *Environment and Behavior, 17,* 539–565.

Brown, C. E. (1981). Shared space invasion and race. *Personality and Social Psychology Bulletin, 7,* 103–108.

Brown, G. G., & Nixon, R. (1979). Exposure to polybrominated biphenyls: Some effects on personality and cognitive functioning. *Journal of the American Medical Association, 242,* 523–527.

Brown, G. I. (1964). The relationship between barometric pressure and relative humidity and classroom behavior. *Journal of Educational Research, 57,* 368–370.

Brown, I. D., & Poulton, E. C. (1961). Measuring the spare "mental capacity" of car drivers by a subsidiary task. *Ergonomics, 4,* 35–40.

Brown, J. G., & Burger, C. (1984). Playground design and preschool children's behaviors. *Environment and Behavior, 16,* 599–626.

Brown, T. C., & Daniel, T. C. (1987). Context effects in perceived environmental quality assessment. *Journal of Environmental Psychology, 7,* 233–250.

Brunetti, F. A. (1972). Noise, distraction and privacy in conventional and open school environments. In W. J. Mitchell (Ed.), *Environmental design: Research and practice* (pp. 12-2-1–12-2-6). Los Angeles: University of California.

Brunswik, E. (1956). *Perception and the representative design of psychological experiments.* Berkeley: University of California Press.

Brunswik, E. (1959). *The conceptual framework of psychology.* In O. Neurath, R. Camp, & C. Morris (Eds.), *Foundation of the unity of science: Toward an international encyclopedia of unified science.* Chicago: University of Chicago Press.

Bruvold, W. H. (1973). Belief and behavior as determinants of environmental attitudes. *Environment and Behavior, 5,* 202–218.

Bryan, M. E., & Tempest, W. (1973). Are our noise laws adequate? *Applied Acoustics, 6,* 219–232.

Bryant, K. J. (1982). Personality correlates of sense of direction and geographical orientation. *Journal of Personality and Social Psychology, 43,* 1318–1324.

Budd, G. M. (1973). Australian physiological research in the Antarctic and Subarctic, with special reference to thermal stress and acclimatization. In O. G. Edholm & E. K. E. Gunderson (Eds.), *Polar human biology.* London: Heineman, 1973.

Bull, A. J., Burbage, S. E., Crandall, J. E., Fletcher, C. I., Lloyd, J. T., Ravenberg, R. L., & Rockett, S. L. (1972). Effects of noise and intolerance of ambiguity upon attraction for similar and dissimilar others. *Journal of Social Psychology, 88,* 151–152.

Burdick, N. S. (1980). *The evolution of environmental consciousness in nineteenth-century America: An interdisciplinary study*. Unpublished doctoral dissertation: Case Western Reserve University.

Burrows, A. A., & Zamarin, D. M. (1972). Aircraft noise and the community: Some recent survey findings. *Aerospace Medicine, 43*, 27–33.

Bursill, A. E. (1958). The restriction of peripheral vision during exposure to hot and humid conditions. *Quarterly Journal of Experimental Psychology, 10*, 113–129.

Burton, I. (1962). *Types of Agriculture Occupance of Flood Plains of the United States*. Chicago: University of Chicago, Department of Geography.

Burton, I., & Kates, R. W. (1964). Perception of hazards in resource management. *Natural Resources Journal, 3*, 412–441.

Burton, I., Kates, R. W., & White, G. F. (1968). The human ecology of extreme geophysical events. *Natural Hazard Research Working Paper* No. 1, University of Toronto.

Butler, D. L., & Biner, P. M. (1987). Preferred lighting levels: Variability among settings, behaviors, and individuals. *Environment and Behavior, 19*, 695–721.

Butler, D. L., & Biner, P. M. (1989). Effects of setting on window preferences and factors associated with those preferences. *Environment and Behavior, 21*, 17–32.

Byrne, D. (1971). *The attraction paradigm*. New York: Academic Press.

Byrne, D., & Clore, G. L. (1970). A reinforcement model of evaluative responses. *Personality: An International Journal, 1*, 103–128.

Byrne, D., Baskett, G. D., & Hodges, L. (1971). Behavioral indicators of interpersonal attraction. *Journal of Applied Social Psychology, 1*, 137–149.

Byrne, D., Ervin, C. R., & Lamberth, J. (1970). Continuity between the experimental study of attraction and real life computer dating. *Journal of Personality and Social Psychology, 16*, 157–165.

Byrne, R. W. (1979). Memory for urban geography. *Quarterly Journal of Experimental Psychology, 31*, 147–154.

Cacioppo, J. T., & Petty, R. E. (1983). Foundations of social psychophysiology. In J. T. Cacioppo & R. E. Petty (Eds.), *Social psychophysiology: A sourcebook* (pp. 3–36). New York: Guilford.

Cahoon, R. L. (1972). Simple decision making at high altitude. *Ergonomics, 15*, 157–163.

Calhoun, J. B. (1962). Population density and social pathology. *Scientific American, 206*, 139–148.

Calhoun, J. B. (1964). The social use of space. In W. Mayer & R. Van Gelder (Eds.), *Physiological mammalogy*. New York: Academic Press.

Calhoun, J. B. (1967). Ecological factors in the development of behavioral anomalies. In J. Zubin & H. F. Hunt (Eds.), *Comparative psychopathology* (pp. 1–51). New York: Grune & Stratton.

Calhoun, J. B. (1970). Space and the strategy of life. *Ekistics, 29*, 425–437.

Calhoun, J. B. (1971). Space and the strategy of life. In A. H. Esser (Ed.), *Behavior and environment: The use of space by animals and men*. Bloomington: University of Indiana Press.

Calkins, M. P. (1987). *Designing for dementia*. Owings Mills, MD: National Health Publishing.

Cameron, P., Robertson, D., & Zaks, J. (1972). Sound pollution, noise pollution, and health: Community parameters. *Journal of Applied Psychology, 56*, 67–74.

Campbell, D. E. (1979). Interior office design and visitor response. *Journal of Applied Psychology, 64*, 648–653.

Campbell, D. E. (1982). Lunar-lunacy research: When enough is enough. *Environment and Behavior, 14*, 418–424.

Campbell, D. E., & Beets, J. L. (1977). Meteorological variables and behavior: An annotated bibliography. *JSAS Catalog of Selected Documents in Psychology, 7*, 1 (Ms. No. 1403).

Campbell, D. E., & Beets, J. L. (1978). Lunacy and the moon. *Psychological Bulletin, 85*, 1123–1129.

Campbell, D. E., & Beets, J. L. (1981). *Human response to naturally occurring weather phenomena: Effects of wind speed and direction*. Unpublished manuscript, Humboldt State University.

Campbell, D. E., & Campbell, T. A. (1988). A new look at informal communication: The role of the physical environment. *Environment and Behavior, 20*, 211–226.

Campbell, D. E., & Herren, K. (1978). Interior arrangement of the faculty office. *Psychological Reports, 43*, 234.

Campbell, D. E., & Shlechter, T. M. (1979). Library design influences on user behavior and satisfaction. *The Library Quarterly, 49*, 26–41.

Campbell, D. T., Kruskal, W. H., & Wallace, W. P. (1966). Seating aggregation as an index of attitude. *Sociometry, 29*, 1–15.

Campbell, J. (1983). Ambient stressors. *Environment and Behavior, 15*, 355–380.

Cannon, W. B. (1929). *Bodily changes in pain, hunger, fear, and rage*. Boston: Branford.

Cannon, W. B. (1931). Studies on the conditions of activity in the endocrine organs, XXVII. Evidence that the medulliadrenal secretion is not continuous. *American Journal of Physiology, 98*, 447–452.

Canter, D. (1972, September). Royal Hospital for Sick Children: A psychological analysis. *Architect's Journal*, 525–564.

Cappella, J. N., & Greene, J. O. (1982). A discrepancy-arousal explanation of mutual influence in expressive behavior in adult and infant–adult interaction. *Communication Monographs, 49,* 89–114.

Carlisle, S. G. (1982). French homes and French character. *Landscape, 26,* 13–23.

Carlsmith, J. M., & Anderson, C. A. (1979). Ambient temperature and the occurrence of collective violence: A new analysis. *Journal of Personality and Social Psychology, 37,* 337–344.

Carlsmith, J. M., Ellsworth, P. C., & Aronson, E. (1976). *Methods of research in social psychology.* Reading, Mass.: Addison-Wesley.

Carp, F. (1987). Environment and aging. In D. Stokols & I. Altman (Eds.), *Handbook of environmental psychology* (Vol. 1, pp. 329–360). New York: Wiley-Interscience.

Carp, F. M. (1976). Housing and living environments of older people. In R. H. Binstock & E. Shanas (Eds.), *Handbook of aging and the social sciences* (pp. 244–271). New York: Van Nostrand.

Carp, F. M., & Carp, A. (1982a). A role for technical environmental assessment in perceptions of environmental quality and well-being. *Journal of Environmental Psychology, 2,* 171–192.

Carp, F. M., & Carp, A. (1982b). Perceived environmental quality of neighborhoods: Development of assessment scales and their relation to age and gender. *Journal of Environmental Psychology, 2,* 295–312.

Carpenter, C. R. (1958). Territoriality: A review of concepts and problems. In A. Roe and G. G. Simpson (Eds.), *Behavior and evolution.* New Haven, CT: Yale University Press.

Carpman, J. R., Grant, M. A., & Simmons, D. A. (1983–84). Wayfinding in the hospital environment: The impact of various floor numbering alternatives. *Journal of Environmental systems, 13,* 353–364.

Carr, S. J., & Dabbs, J. M. (1974). The effects of lighting, distance, and intimacy on topic of verbal and visual behavior. *Sociometry, 37.*

Cass, R., & Edney, J. J. (1978). The commons dilemma: A simulation testing the effects of resource visibility and territorial division. *Human Ecology, 6,* 371–386.

Caudill, B. D., & Aiello, J. R. (1979). *Interpersonal equilibrium: A study of convergent and predictive validity.* Paper presented at the Eastern Psychological Association Convention, Philadelphia.

Cervone, J. C. (1977). *An environmental-social approach to an arousal-behavior relationship.* Unpublished master's thesis, Colorado State University, Ft. Collins, CO.

Chaiken, S., & Stangor, C. (1987). Attitudes and attitude change. *Annual Review of Psychology, 38,* 575–630.

Chapko, M. K., & Solomon, M. (1976). Air pollution and recreation behavior. *Journal of Social Psychology, 100,* 149–150.

Chapman, C., & Risley, T. R. (1974). Anti-litter proce-

dures in an urban high-density area. *Journal of Applied Behavior Analysis, 7,* 317–384.

Chapman. R., Masterpasqua, F., & Lore, R. (1976). The effects of crowding during pregnancy on offspring emotional and sexual behavior in rats. *Bulletin of the Psychonomic Society, 7,* 475–477.

Charry, J. M., & Hawkinshire, F. B. W. (1981). Effects of atmospheric electricity on some substrates of disordered social behavior. *Journal of Personality and Social Psychology, 41,* 185–197.

Cherek, D. R. (1985). Effect of acute exposure to increased levels of background industrial noise on cigarette smoking behavior. *International Archives of Occupational and Environmental Health, 56,* 23–30.

Cherulnik, P. D., & Wilderman, S. K. (1986). Symbols of status in urban neighborhoods: Contemporary perceptions of nineteenth-century Boston. *Environment and Behavior, 18,* 604–622.

Cheyne, J. A., & Efran, N. G. (1972). The effect of spatial and interpersonal variables on the invasion of group-controlled territories. *Sociometry, 35,* 477–489.

Chicago Tribune. (1974). Is it shameful to be poor? *Urban Problems Background Report.*

Choldin, H. M. (1978). *Annual Review of Sociology.* Palo Alto: Annual Reviews, Inc.

Chowns, R. H. (1970). Mental hospital admissions and aircraft noise. *Lancet, 1* (7644), 467.

Christensen, L. D. (1977). *Experimental methodology.* Boston: Allyn & Bacon.

Christensen, R. (1982). Alaskan winters: A mental health hazard? *Alaskan Medicine, 24,* 89.

Christensen, R. (1984). Cabin fever: A folk belief and the misdiagnosis of complaints. *Journal of Mental Health Administration, 11,* 2 – 3.

Christian, J. J. (1955). Effects of population size on the adrenal glands and reproductive organs of male mice in populations of fixed size. *The American Journal of Physiology, 182,* 292–300.

Christian, J. J. (1963). Pathology of overpopulation. *Military Medicine, 128,* 571–603.

Cialdini, R. (1977). *Littering as a function of extant litter.* Unpublished manuscript, Arizona State University.

Cialdini, R. B., & Kenrick, D. T. (1976). Altruism as hedonism: A social development perspective on the relationship of negative mood state and helping. *Journal of Personality and Social Psychology, 54,* 907–914.

Cialdini, R. B., Reno, R. R., & Kallgren, C. A. (1989). *Using a focus theory of normative conduct to reduce littering in public places.* Unpublished paper, Arizona State University.

Cicchetti, C. (1972). A review of the empirical analyses that have been based upon the national survey. *Journal of Leisure Research, 4,* 90–107.

Clark, R. E., & Flaherty, C. F. (1963). Contralateral effects of thermal stimuli on manual performance capability. *Journal of Applied Psychology, 18,* 769–771.

Clark, R. N., Hendee, J. C., & Burgess, R. L. (1972). The experimental control of littering. *Journal of Environmental Education, 4,* 22–28.

Clemente, F. & Kleiman, M. B. (1977). Fear of crime in the United States. *Social Forces, 51:* 176–531.

Clinard, M. B. (1964). Deviant behavior: Urban—rural contrasts. In L. E. Elias, Jr., J. Gillies, & S. Reimer (Eds.), *Metropolis: Values in conflict.* Belmont, CA.: Wadsworth.

Cobb, S. (1976). Social support as a moderator of life stress. *Psychosomatic Medicine, 38,* 300–314.

Cockerill, I. M., & Miller, B. P. (1983). Children's colour preferences and motor skill performance with variation in environmental color. *Perceptual and Motor Skills, 28,* 259–268.

Coffin, D., & Stokinger, H. (1977). Biological effects of air pollutants. In A. C. Stern (Ed.), *Air pollution* (3rd ed., Vol. 3). New York: Academic Press.

Cohen, H., Moss, S., & Zube, E. (1979). Pedestrians and wind in the urban environment. In A. D. Seidel & S. Danford (Eds.), *Environmental design: Research, theory, and application* (pp. 71–82). Washington, DC: Environmental Design Research Association.

Cohen, J. L., Sladen, B., & Bennett, B. (1975). The effects of situational variables on judgments of crowding. *Sociometry, 38,* 273–281.

Cohen, M. R. (1973). Environmental information vs. environmental attitudes. *Journal of Environmental Education, 5,* 5–8.

Cohen, R., Goodnight, J. A., Poag, C. K., Cohen, S., Nichol, G. T., & Worley, P. (1986). Easing the transition to kindergarten: The affective and cognitive effects of different spatial familiarization experiences. *Environment and Behavior, 18,* 330–345.

Cohen, S. (1978). Environmental load and the allocation of attention. In A. Baum, J. E. Singer, & S. Valins (Eds.), *Advances in environmental psychology* (Vol. 1, pp. 1–29). Hillsdale, NJ: Erlbaum, 1978.

Cohen, S. (1980). Aftereffects of stress on human performance and social behavior: A review of research and theory. *Psychological Bulletin, 87,* 578–604.

Cohen, S., Evans, G. W., Krantz, D. S., & Stokols, D. (1980). Physiological, motivational, and cognitive effects of aircraft noise on children: Moving from the laboratory to the field. *American Psychologist, 35,* 231–243.

Cohen, S., Evans, G. W., Krantz, D. S., Stokols, D., & Kelly, S. (1981). Aircraft noise and children: Longitudinal and cross-sectional evidence on adaptation to noise and the effectiveness of noise abatement. *Journal of Personality and Social Psychology, 40,* 331–345.

Cohen, S., Evans, G. W., Stokols, D., & Krantz, D. S. (1986). *Behavior, health and environmental stress.* New York: Plenum.

Cohen, S., Glass, D. C., & Phillips, S. (1977). Environment and health. In H. E. Freeman, S. Levine, & L. G. Reeder (Eds.), *Handbook of medical sociology.* Englewood Cliffs, NJ: Prentice-Hall.

Cohen, S., Glass, D. C., & Singer, J. E. (1973). Apartment noise, auditory discrimination, and reading ability in children. *Journal of Experimental Social Psychology, 9,* 407–422.

Cohen, S., Kamarck, T., & Mermelstein, R. (1983). A global measure of perceived stress. *Journal of Health and Social Behavior, 24,* 385–396.

Cohen, S., & Lezak, A. (1977). Noise and inattentiveness to social cues. *Environment and Behavior, 9,* 559–572

Cohen, S., & Spacapan, S. (1978). The aftereffects of stress: An attentional interpretation. *Environmental Psychology and Nonverbal Behavior, 3,* 43–57.

Cohen, S., & Spacapan, S. (1984). The social psychology of noise. In D. M. Jones & A. J. Chapman (Eds.), *Noise and society* (pp. 221–245). Chichester: Wiley.

Cohen, S., & Weinstein, N. D. (1982). Nonauditory effects of noise on behavior and health. In G. W. Evans (Ed.), *Environmental stress* (pp. 45–74). Cambridge: Cambridge University Press.

Cohen, S., & Wills, T. A. (1985). Stress, social support, and the buffering hypothesis. *Psychological Bulletin, 8,* 310–357.

Colligan, M. J., & Murphy, L. R. (1982). A review of mass psychogenic illness in work settings. In M. J. Colligan, J. W. Pennebaker, & L. R. Murphy (Eds.), *Mass psychogenic illness.* Hillsdale, NJ: Erlbaum.

Collins, A. M., & Loftus, E. F. (1975). A spreading activation theory of semantic processing. *Psychological Review, 82,* 407–428.

Collins, A. M., & Quillian, M. R. (1969). Retrieval time from semantic memory. *Journal of Verbal Learning and Verbal Behavior, 8,* 240–247.

Collins, B. L. (1975). *Windows and people: A literature survey. Psychological reaction to environments with and without windows.* NSB Building Science Series, 70, 88.

Collins, D. L., Baum, A., & Singer, J. (1983). Coping with chronic stress at Three Mile Island: Psychological and biochemical evidence. *Health Psychology, 2,* 149–166.

Committee for Health Care for Homeless People. (1988). *Homelessness, health and human needs.* Washington, DC: National Academy Press.

Commoner, B. (1963). *Science and survival.* New York: Viking.

Cone, J. D., & Hayes, S. C. (1978). Applied behavior analysis and the solutions of environmental problems. In J. F. Wohlwill & I. Altman (Eds.), *Human behavior and environment: Advances in theory and research* (Vol. 2). New York: Plenum.

Cone, J. D., & Hayes, S. C. (1980). *Environmental*

problems/behavioral solutions. Monterey, CA: Brooks/Cole.

Conroy, J., III, & Sundstrom, E. (1977). Territorial dominance in a dyadic conversation as a function of similarity of opinion. *Journal of Personality and Social Psychology, 35,* 570–576.

Cook, C. C. (1988). Components of neighborhood satisfaction: Responses from urban and suburban single-parent women. *Environment and Behavior, 20,* 115–149.

Cook, M. (1970). Experiments on orientation and proxemics. *Human Relations, 23,* 61–76.

Cook-Degan, R. M. (1987). *Losing a million minds: Confronting the tragedy of Alzheimer's Disease and other dementias*. Washington, DC: U.S. Government Printing Office.

Cooper, C. (1970). Adventure playground. *Landscape Architecture, 61,* 18–29; 88–91.

Cooper, C. (1972). The house as symbol. *Design and Environment, 14,* 178–182.

Cooper Marcus C., & Sarkissian, W. (1985). *Housing as if people mattered*. Berkeley, CA: University of California Press.

Corcoran, D. W. J. (1962). Noise and loss of sleep. *Quarterly Journal of Experimental Psychology, 14,* 178–182.

Cornell, E. H., & Hay, D. H. (1984). Children's acquisition of a route via different media. *Environment and Behavior, 16,* 627–642.

Cotton, J. L. (1986). Ambient temperature and violent crime. *Journal of Applied Social Psychology, 16,* 786–801.

Coughlin, R. E. (1976). The perception and valuation of water quality: A review of research method and findings. In K. H. Craik & E. H. Zube (Eds.), *Perceiving environmental quality: Research and applications*. New York: Plenum.

Coughlin, R. E., & Goldstein, K. A. (1970). *The extent of agreement among observers on environmental attractiveness*. Regional Science Research Institute Paper No. 37. Philadelphia: Regional Science Research Institute.

Cousins, J. H., Siegel, A. W., & Maxwell, S. E. (1983). Way finding and cognitive mapping in large scape environments: A test of a developmental model. *Journal of Experimental Child Psychology, 35,* 1–20.

Covington, J., & Taylor, R. (1989). Gentrification and crime: Robbery and larcency changes in appreciating Baltimore neighborhoods during the 1970's. *Urban Affairs Quarterly, 25,* 140–170.

Cox, V. C., Paulus, P. B., & McCain, G. (1984). Prison crowding research: The relevance for prison housing standards and a general approach regarding crowding phenomena. *American Psychologist, 39,* 1148–1160.

Cox, V. C., Paulus, P. B., McCain, G., & Karlovac, M. (1982). The relationship between crowding and health. In A. Baum & J. E. Singer (Eds.), *Advances in environmental psychology* (Vol. 4, pp. 271–294). Hillsdale, NJ: Erlbaum, 1982.

Craik, K. H. (1970a). A system of landscape dimensions: Appraisal of its objectivity and illustration of its scientific application. In *Report to Resources for the Future, Inc*. Berkley, CA, Institute of Personality Assessment and Research, University of California.

Craik, K. H. (1970b). The environmental dispositions of environmental decision makers. *Annals, 389,* 80–94.

Craik, K. H. (1971). The assessment of places. In P. McReynolds (Ed.), *Advances in Psychological Assessment* (Vol. 2, pp. 40–62). Palo Alto, CA: Science and Behavior Books.

Craik, K. H. (1983). *The psychology of the large-scale environment*. In N. R. Feimer & E. S. Geller (Eds.), *Environmental psychology: Directions and perspectives.* (pp. 67–105) New York: Praeger.

Craik, K. H., & Appleyard, D. (1980). Streets of San Francisco: Brunswik's lens model applied to urban inference and assessment. *Journal of Social Issues, 36,* 72–85.

Craik, K. H., & Feimer, N. R. (1987). Environmental assessment. In D. Stokols & I. Altman (Eds.), *Handbook of environmental psychology* (pp. 891–918). New York: Wiley-Interscience.

Craik, K. H., & Zube, E. H. (1976). *Perceiving environmental quality*. New York: Plenum.

Crawshaw, R. (1963). Reactions to a disaster. *Archives of General Psychiatry, 9,* 157–162.

Crew, F. A., & Mirskowa, L. (1931). Effects of density on adult mouse populations. *Biologia Generalis, 7,* 239–250.

Crockford, G. W. (1967). Heat problems and protective clothing in iron and steel works. In C. N. Davies, P. R. Davis, & F. H. Tyrer (Eds.), *The effects of abnormal physical conditions at work* (pp. 144–156). London: E & S Livingstone.

Crook, M. A., & Langdon, F. J. (1974). The effects of aircraft noise on schools in the vicinity of the London Airport. *Journal of Sound and Vibration, 34,* 241–248.

Crouch, A., & Nimran, U. (1989). Perceived facilitators and inhibitors of work performance in an office environment. *Environment and Behavior, 21,* 206–226.

Crowe, M. J. (1968). Toward a "definitional model" of public perceptions of air pollution. *Journal of the Air Pollution Control Association, 18,* 154–157.

Crump, S. L., Nunes, D. L., & Crossman, E. K. (1977). The effects of litter on littering behavior in a forest environment. *Environment and Behavior, 9,* 137–146.

Culver, R. Rotton, J., & Kelly, I. W. (1988). Geophysical variables and behavior: XLIX. Moon myths and mechanisms: A critical examination of purported explanations of lunar-lunacy relations. *Psychological Reports, 62,* 683–710.

Cunningham, M. R. (1979). Weather, mood, and helping behavior: Quasi experiments with the sunshine Samaritan. *Journal of Personality and Social Psychology, 37,* 1947–1956.

Cunningham, M. R., Steinberg, J., & Grev, R. (1980). Wanting to and having to help: Separate motivations for positive mood and guilt-induced helping. *Journal of Personality and Social Psychology, 38,* 181–192.

Cuthbertson, B. H., & Nigg, J. M. (1987). Technological disaster and the nontherapeutic community: A question of true victimization. *Environment and Behavior, 19,* 462–483.

Cyr, J. J., & Kaplan, R. A. (1987). Geophysical variables and behavior: XLVI. The lunar-lunacy relationship: A poorly evaluated hypothesis. *Psychological Reports, 61,* 391–400.

Cziffra, P., Graydon, E., Klath, N., & Wiggens, T. (1975). *Science and technology libraries space report.* Princeton, NJ: Princeton University Library.

D'Atri, D. A., Fitzgerald, E. F., Kasl, S. V., & Ostfeld, A. M. (1981). Crowding in prison: The relationship between changes in housing mode and blood pressure. *Psychosomatic Medicine, 43,* 95–105.

Dabbs, J. M. (1971). Physical closeness and negative feelings. *Psychonomic Science, 23,* 141–143.

Dabbs, J. M., Jr., & Stokes, N. A. (1975). Beauty is power: The use of space on the sidewalk. *Sociometry, 38,* 551–557.

Dabbs, J., Fuller, P., & Carr, S. (1973). *Personal space when cornered: College students and prison inmates.* Paper presented at the meeting of the American Psychological Association, Montreal, Canada.

Dahlof, L., Hard, E., & Larsson, K. (1977). Influence of maternal stress on offspring sexual behavior. *Animal Behavior, 25,* 958–963.

Damon, A. (1977). The residential environment, health, and behavior. Simple research opportunities, strategies, and some findings in the Solomon Islands and Boston, Massachusetts. In L. E. Hinckle, Jr., & W. C. Loring (Eds.), *The effect of the man-made environment on health and behavior.* Atlanta: Center for Disease Control, Public Health Service.

Daniel, T. C. & Boster, R. S. (1976). Measuring landscape aesthetics: The scenic beauty estimation method. In *Research Paper RM-167.* Ft. Collins, CO: U.S.D.A. Forest Service, Rocky Mountain Forest and Range Experiment Station.

Daniel, T. C. & Vining, J. (1983). Methodological issues in the assessment of landscape quality. In I. Altman & J. F. Wohlwill (Eds.), *Behavior and the natural environment* (pp. 39–84). New York: Plenum.

Daniel, T. C., & Schroeder, H. (1979). Scenic beauty estimation model: Predicting scenic beauty of forest landscapes. In G. H. Elsner & R. C. Smardon (Tech. Coods.), *Our National Landscape.* General Technical Rep. No. PSW-35, pp 524–531). Berkeley, CA: U.S. Department of Agriculture, Pacific Southwest Forest and Range Experiment Station.

Darley, J. M., & Latané, B. (1968). Bystander intervention in emergencies: Diffusion of responsibility. *Journal of Personality and Social Psychology, 8,* 377–383.

Dart, F. E., & Pradham, P. L. (1967). The cross cultural teaching of science. *Science, 155,* 649–656.

Daves, W. F., & Swaffer, P. W. (1971). Effect of room size on critical interpersonal distance. *Perceptual and Motor Skills, 33,* 926.

Davidson, L. M. & Baum, A. (1986). Chronic stress and post traumatic stress disorders. *Journal of Consulting & Clinical Psychology, 54,* 303–308.

Davidson, L. M., Baum, A., & Collins, D. L. (1982). Stress and control-related problems at Three Mile Island. *Journal of Applied Social Psychology, 12,* 349–359.

Davidson, L. M., Fleming, I., & Baum, A. (1986). Post-traumatic stress as a function of chronic stress and toxic exposures. In C. Figley (Ed.), *Trauma and its wake* (pp. 55–77). New York: Brunner Mazel.

Davidson, L. M., Fleming, R., & Baum, A. (1987). Chronic stress, catecholamines, and sleep disturbance at Three Mile Island. *Journal of Human Stress, 13,* 75–83.

Davis, B. (1989, January 5). Mars could become the place to live, but it needs work. *The Wall Street Journal,* pp. A1, A8.

Davis, G. E. (1977). *Crowding and helping: An empirical test of the social overload hypothesis.* Doctoral dissertation, State University of New York—Stony Brook.

Davis, G., & Ayers, V. (1975). Photographic recording of environmental behavior. In W. Michelson (Ed.), *Behavioral research methods in environmental design.* Stroudsburg, PA: Dowden, Hutchinson & Ross.

Davis, K. A. (1972). *World urbanization 1950–1970* (Vol. 2). Berkeley: Institute of International Studies.

Davis, K. A. (1973). Introduction. In K. Davis (Ed.), *Cities.* San Francisco: Freeman.

Dawes, R. M., McTavish, J., & Shaklee, H. (1977). Behavior, communication and assumptions about other people's behaviors in a commons dilemma situation. *Journal of Personality and Social Psychology, 35,* 1–11.

De Jonge, D. (1962). Images of urban areas. *Journal of American Institute of Planners, 28,* 266–276.

Dean, L. M., Willis, F. N., & Hewitt, J. (1975). Initial interaction distance among individuals equal and unequal in military rank. *Journal of Personality and Social Psychology, 32,* 294–299.

Dean, L., Pugh, W., & Gunderson, E. (1975). Spatial and perceptual components of crowding: Effects on health and satisfaction. *Environment and Behavior, 7,* 225–236.

Dean, L., Pugh, W., & Gunderson, E. (1978). The behavioral effects of crowding. *Environment and Behavior, 10,* 419–431.

DeFronzo, J. (1984). Climate and crime: Tests of an FBI assumption. *Environment and Behavior, 16,* 185–210.

DeGiovanni, F. F., & Paulson, N. A. (1984). Household diversity in revitalizing neighborhoods. *Urban Affairs Quarterly, 20*(2), 211–232.

DeGroot, I. (1967). Trends in public attitudes toward air pollution. *Journal of the Air Pollution Control Association, 17,* 679–681.

DeLong, A. J. (1973). Kinesic signals at utterance boundaries in preschool children. *Dissertation Abstracts, 33.*

Denison, D. M., Ledwith, F., & Poulton, E. C. (1966). Complex reaction times at simulated cabin altitudes of 5,000 ft. and 8,000 ft. *Aerospace Medicine, 37,* 1010.

Dennis, W. (1966). *Group values through children's drawings.* New York: McGraw-Hill.

Derogatis, L. R. (1977). *The SCL-90 Manual 1: Scoring, administration, and procedures for the SCL-90.* Baltimore: Johns Hopkins University School of Medicine, Clinical Psychometrics Unit.

DeSanctis, M., Halcomb, C. G., & Fedoravicius, A. S. (1981). *Meteorological determinants of human behavior: A holistic environmental perspective with special reference to air ionization and electrical field effects.* Unpublished manuscript, Texas Tech University, Lubbock, TX.

Deslauriers, B. C., & Everett, P. B. (1977). Effects of intermittent and continuous token reinforcement on bus ridership. *Journal of Applied Psychology, 62,* 360–375.

Desor, J. A. (1972). Toward a psychological theory of crowding. *Journal of Personality and Social Psychology, 21,* 79–83.

Deutsch, M., & Collins, M. E. (1951). *Interracial housing: A psychological evaluation of a social experiment.* Minneapolis: University of Minnesota Press.

Devlin, A. S. (1976). The small-town cognitive map: Adjusting to a new environment. In G. T. Moore & R. G. Golledge (Eds.), *Environmental knowing.* Stroudsburg, PA: Dowden, Hutchinson, & Ross.

Dexter, E. (1904). School deportment and weather. *Educational Review, 19,* 160–168.

Dickason, J. D. (1983). The origin of the playground: The role of the Boston women's clubs, 1885–1890. *Leisure Sciences, 6,* 83 – 98.

Dickson, D. (1987). Adjusting to an aging population. *Science, 236,* 772–773.

Dietrick, B. (1977, November). *The environment and burglary victimization in a metropolitan suburb.* Paper presented at the annual meeting of the American Society of Criminology, Atlanta, Georgia.

Digon, E., & Block, H. (1966). Suicides and climatology. *Archives of Environmental Health, 12,* 279–286.

Dill, C. A., Gilden, E. R., Hill, P. C., & Hanselka, L. L. (1982). Federal human subjects regulations: A methodological artifact? *Personality and Social Psychology Bulletin, 8,* 417–425.

Dillman, D., & Tremblay, K., Jr. (1977). The quality of life in rural America. *Annals of the American Academy of Political and Social Sciences, 429,* 115–129.

Ditton, R. B., & Goodale, T. L. (1974). Water quality perceptions and attitudes. *Journal of Environmental Education, 6,* 21.

Ditton, R. B., Fedler, A. J., & Graefe, A. R. (1982). Assessing recreational satisfaction among diverse participant groups. *Forest and river recreation: Research update.* St. Paul, MN: The University of Minnesota Agriculture Research Station.

Dohrenwend, B. P., Dohrenwend, B. S., Kasl, S. V., & Warheit, G. J. (1979). *Report of the Task Group on Behavioral Effects to the President's Commission on the accident at Three Mile Island.* Washington, DC.

Dohrenwend, B. S., & Dohrenwend, B. P. (1972). Psychiatric disorder in urban settings. In G. Caplan (Ed.), *American handbook of psychiatry* (Vol. 3), rev. ed. Warheit, NY: Basic Books. 1972.

Donnerstein, E., & Wilson, D. W. (1976). Effects of noise and perceived control on ongoing and subsequent aggressive behavior. *Journal of Personality and Social Psychology, 34,* 774–781.

Dooley, B. B. (1974). *Crowding stress: The effects of social density on men with "close" or "far" personal space.* Unpublished doctoral dissertation, University of California at Los Angeles.

Dooley, D., Rook, K., & Catalano, R. (1987). Job and non-job stressors and their moderators. *Journal of Occupational Psychology, 60,* 115–132.

Doring, H. J., Hauf, G., & Seiberling, M. (1980). Effects of high intensity sound on the contractile function of the isolated ileum of guinea pigs and rabbits. In *Noise as a public health problem, Proceedings of the Third International Congress* (ASHA Report No. 10). Rockville, MD: American Speech and Hearing Association.

Downs, R. M., & Stea, D. (1973). Cognitive maps and spatial behavior: Process and products. In R. M. Downs & D. Stea (Eds.), *Image and environment: Cognitive mapping and spatial behavior.* Chicago: Aldine.

Downs, R. M., & Stea, D. (1977). *Maps in minds: Reflections on cognitive mapping.* New York: Harper & Row.

Drabek, T., & Quarantelli, E. (1967). Scapegoats, villains, and disasters. *Trans-Action, 4,* 12–17.

Drabek, T., E., & Stephenson, J. S. (1971). When disaster strikes. *Journal of Applied Social Psychology, 1,* 187–203.

Draper, P. (1973). Crowding among hunter gatherers: The !Kung Bushman. *Science, 182,* 301–303.

Driver, B. L. (1972). Potential contributions of psychology to recreation resource management. In J. Wohlwill & D. H. Carson (Eds.), *Environment and the social sciences: Perspectives and applications.* Washington, DC: American Psychological Association.

Driver, B. L. (1975). Quantification of outdoor recreationists' preferences. In *Research camping and environmen-*

tal education (Pennsylvania State Series II). University Park, PA : Pennsylvania State University.

Driver, B. L. & Brown, P. J. (1983). Contributions of behavioral scientists to recreation resource management. In I. Altman & J. F. Wohlwill (Eds.), *Behavior and the environment*. New York: Plenum.

Driver, B. L., & Knopf, R. C. (1976). Temporary escape: One product of sport fisheries management. *Fisheries, 1,* 21–29.

Driver, B. L., & Knopf, R. C. (1977). Personality, outdoor recreation, and expected consequences. *Environment and Behavior, 9,* 169–193.

Driver, B. L., & Rosenthal, D. H. (1982). *Measuring and improving the effectiveness of public outdoor recreation programs.* Washington, DC: George Washington University Press.

Dubos, R. (1965). *Man adapting.* New Haven, CT: Yale University Press.

Duffy, M., Bailey, S., Beck, B., & Barker, D. G. (1986). Preferences in nursing home design: A comparison of residents, administrators, and designers. *Environment and Behavior, 18,* 246–257.

Duke, M. P., & Nowicki, S. (1972). A new measure and social learning model for interpersonal distance. *Journal of Experimental Research in Personality, 6,* 119–132.

Duke, M. P., & Wilson, J. (1973). The measurement of interpersonal distance in pre-school children. *Journal of Genetic Psychology, 123,* 361–362.

Duncan, J. Jr. (1973). Landscape taste as a symbol of group identity: A Westchester County village. *The Geographical Review, 63,* 334–355.

Duncan, J. S. (1985). The house as symbol of social structure: Notes on the language of objects among collectivistic groups. In I. Altman & C. M. Werner (Eds.), *Home environments* (pp. 133–151). New York: Plenum.

Dunlap, R. E. (Ed.) (1980, September/October). Ecology and the social sciences: An emerging paradigm. *American Behavioral Scientist, 24,* 1–149.

Dunlap, R. E., & Van Liere, K. D. (1978, Summer). The "New Environmental Paradigm": A proposed measuring instrument and preliminary results. *Journal of Environmental Education, 9,* 10–19.

Dunlap, R. E., & Van Liere, K. D. (1984). Commitment to the dominant social paradigm and concern for environmental quality. *Social Science Quarterly, 65,* 1013–1028.

Duvall, D., & Booth, A. (1978). The housing environment and women's health. *Journal of Health and Social Behavior, 19,* 410–417.

Easterbrook, J. A. (1959). The effects of emotion on cue-utilization and the organization of behavior. *Psychological Review, 66,* 183–201.

Ebbesen, E. B., Kjos, G. L., & Konecni, V. J. (1976). Spatial ecology: Its effects on the choice of friends and enemies. *Journal of Experimental Social Psychology, 12,* 505–518.

Eberts, E. H., & Lepper, M. R. (1975). Individual consistency in the proxemic behavior of pre-school children. *Journal of Personality and Social Psychology, 32,* 481–489.

Edney, J. J. (1972). Property, possession and permanence: A field study in human territoriality. *Journal of Applied Social Psychology, 2,* 275–282.

Edney, J. J. (1974). Human territoriality. *Psychological Bulletin, 81,* 959–975.

Edney, J. J. (1975). Territoriality and control: A field experiment. *Journal of Personality and Social Psychology, 31,* 1108–1115.

Edney, J. J. (1976). Human territories: Comment on functional properties. *Environment and Behavior, 8,* 31–48.

Edney, J. J. (1979). The nuts game: A concise commons dilemma analogue. *Environmental Psychology and Nonverbal Behavior, 3,* 252–254.

Edney, J. J. (1980). The commons problem: Alternative perspectives. *American Psychologist, 35,* 131–150.

Edney, J. J. (1981). Paradoxes on the commons: Scarcity and the problem of equality. *Journal of Community Psychology, 9,* 3–34.

Edney, J. J., & Bell, P. A. (1983). The commons dilemma: Comparing altruism, the Golden Rule, perfect equality of outcomes, and territoriality. *The Social Science Journal, 20,* 23–33.

Edney, J. J., & Bell, P. A. (1984). Sharing scarce resources: Group-outcome orientation, external disaster, and stealing in a simulated commons. *Small Group Behavior, 15,* 87–108.

Edney, J. J., & Bell, P. A. (1987). Freedom and equality in a simulated commons. *Political Psychology, 8,* 229–243.

Edney, J. J., & Harper, C. S. (1978a). Heroism in a resource crisis: A simulation study. *Environmental Management, 2,* 523–527.

Edney, J. J., & Harper, C. S. (1978b). The effects of information in a resource management problem: A social trap analog. *Human Ecology, 6,* 387–395.

Edney, J. J., Kline, L. K., Bell, P. A., Loomis, R. J., & Wolfe, D. (1985). Limitations on model house designs for trust, freedom, or control. *Perceptual and Motor Skills, 61,* 138.

Edney, J. J., & Uhlig, S. R. (1977). Individual and small group territories. *Small Group Behavior, 8,* 457–468.

Edwards, D. J. A. (1972). Approaching the unfamiliar: A study of human interaction distances. *Journal of Behavioral Sciences, 1,* 249–250.

Edwards, D. J. A. (1973). A cross-cultural study of social orientation and distance schemata by the method of doll placement. *Journal of Social Psychology, 89,* 165–173.

Efran, M. G., & Cheyne, J. A. (1973). Shared space: The

cooperative control of spatial areas by two interacting individuals. *Canadian Journal of Behavioural Science, 5*, 201–210.

Efran, M. G., & Cheyne, J. A. (1974). Affective concomitants of the invasion of shared space: Behavioral, physiological, and verbal indicators. *Journal of Personality and Social Psychology, 29*, 219–226.

Eggertsen, R., Svensson, A., Magnusson, M., & Andren, L. (1987). Hemodynamic effects of loud noise before and after central sympathetic nervous stimulation. *Acta Med Scand 221 (2)*, 159 – 164.

Ehrlich, P. (1968). *The population boom*. New York: Ballantine.

Eibl-Eibesfeldt, I. (1970). *Ethology: The biology of behavior*. New York: Holt, Rinehart and Winston.

Elgin, D., Thomas, T., & Logothetti, T. (1974). *City Size and the Quality of Life, 54*, 191, 287. Washington, DC: National Science Foundation (RANN).

Ellis, P., & Gashell, G. (1978). *A review of social research on the individual energy consumer*. Unpublished manuscript.

Ellsworth, P. C. (1977). *Some questions about the role of arousal in the interpretation of direct gaze*. Paper presented at the American Psychological Association Convention, San Francisco.

Engen, T. (1982). *The perception of odor*. Reading, MA: Addison-Wesley.

Environmental Protection Agency (EPA) (1972). *Report to the President and Congress on noise*. Washington, D.C.: U.S. Government Printing Office.

Eoyang, C. K. (1974). Effects of group size and privacy in residential crowding. *Journal of Personality and Social Psychology, 30*, 389–392.

Epstein, Y. M. (1982). Crowding stress and human behavior. In G. W. Evans (Ed.), *Environmental stress*. New York: Cambridge University Press.

Epstein, Y. M., & Karlin, R. A. (1975). Effects of acute experimental crowding. *Journal of Applied Social Psychology, 5*, 34–53.

Erikson, K. T. (1976). Loss of communality at Buffalo Creek. *American Journal of Psychiatry, 133*, 302–305.

Ernsting, J. (1963). The ideal relationship between inspired oxygen concentration and cabin altitude. *Aerospace Medicine, 34*, 991–997.

Ernsting, J. (1967). Physiological hazards of low pressure. In C. N. Davies, P. R. Davis, & F. H. Tyrer (Eds.), *The effects of abnormal physical conditions at work* (pp. 90–100). London: E & S Livingstone.

Esser, A. H. (1973). Cottage fourteen: Dominance and territoriality in a group of institutionalized boys. *Small Group Behavior, 4*, 131–146.

Esser, A. H. (1976). Discussion of papers presented in the symposium "Theoretical and empirical issues with regard to privacy, territoriality, personal space, and crowding." *Environment and Behavior, 8*, 117–125.

Esser, A. H. Chamberlain, A. S., Chapple, E. P., & Kline, N. S. (1965). Territoriality of patients on a research ward. In J. Wortis (Ed.), *Recent advances in biological psychiatry*. New York: Plenum.

Evans, G. W. (1975). *Behavioral and physiological consequences of crowding in humans*. Unpublished doctoral dissertation, University of Massachusetts, 1975.

Evans, G. W. (1978a). Crowding and the developmental process. In A. Baum & Y. Epstein (Eds.), *Human reponse to crowding*. Hillsdale, NJ: Erlbaum.

Evans, G. W. (1978b). Human spatial behavior: The arousal model. In A. Baum & Y. Epstein (Eds.), *Human response to crowding* (pp. 283–302). Hillsdale, NJ: Erlbaum.

Evans, G. W. (1979a). Behavioral and physiological consequences of crowding in humans. *Journal of Applied Social Psychology, 9*, 27–46.

Evans, G. W. (1979b). Design implications of spatial research. In J. Aiello & A. Baum (Eds.), *Residential crowding and design*. New York: Plenum.

Evans, G. W. (1980). Environmental cognition. *Psychological Bulletin, 88*, 259–287.

Evans, G. W., Brennan, P. L., Skorpanich, M. A., & Held, D. (1984). Cognitive mapping and elderly adults: Verbal and location memory for urban landmarks. *Journal of Gerontology, 39*, 452–457.

Evans, G. W., & Cohen, S. (1987). Environmental stress. In D. Stokols & I. Altman (Eds.), *Handbook of environmental psychology* (Vol. 1, pp. 571–610). New York: Wiley-Interscience.

Evans, G., Fellows, J., Zorn, M., & Doty, K. (1980). Cognitive mapping and architecture. *Journal of Applied Psychology, 65*, 474–478.

Evans, G. W., & Howard, H. R. B. (1972). A methodological investigation of personal space. In W. J. Mitchell (Ed.), *Environmental design: Research and practice, Proceedings of EDRA3/AR8 Conference*. Los Angeles: University of California.

Evans, G. W., & Howard, R. B. (1973). Personal space. *Psychological Bulletin, 80*, 334–344.

Evans, G. W., & Jacobs, S. V. (1981). Air pollution and human behavior. *Journal of Social Issues, 37*, 95–125.

Evans, G. W., & Jacobs, S. V. (1982). Air pollution and human behavior. In G. W. Evans (Ed.), *Environmental stress* (pp. 105–132). Cambridge: Cambridge University Press.

Evans, G. W., Jacobs, S. V., Dooley, D., & Catalano, R. (1987). The interaction of stressful life events and chronic strains on community mental health. *American Journal of Community Psychology, 15*, 23–34.

Evans, G. W., Jacobs, S., & Frager, N. (1979). *Human adaptation to photochemical smog*. Paper presented at the American Psychological Association meeting, New York.

Evans, G. W., Jacobs, S. V., & Frager, N. B. (1982). Behavioral responses to air pollution. In A. Baum & J.

Singer (Eds.), *Advances in environmental psychology* (pp. 237–270). Hillsdale, NJ: Erlbaum.

Evans, G. W., & Lovell, B. (1979). Design modification in an open-plan school. *Journal of Educational Psychology, 71,* 41–49.

Evans, G. W., Marrero, & Butler, P. A. (1981). Environmental learning and cognitive mapping. *Environment and Behavior, 13,* 83–104.

Evans, G., & Pezdek, K. (1980). Cognitive mapping: Knowledge of real-world distance and location information. *Journal of Experimental Psychology: Human Learning & Memory, 6,* 13–24.

Evans, G. W., Skorpanich, A., Garling, T., Bryant, K. J., & Bresolin B. (1984). The effects of pathway configuration, landmarks and stress on environmental cognition. *Journal of Environmental Psychology, 4,* 323–335.

Evans, G. W., Smith, C., & Pezdek, K. (1982). Cognitive maps and urban form. *American Planning Association Journal, 48,* 232–244.

Everett, P. B. (1973). The use of the reinforcement procedure to increase bus ridership. *Proceedings of the Eighty-First Annual Convention of the American Psychological Association, 8,* 891–892.

Everett, P. B. (1977). *A behavior science approach to transportation systems management.* Unpublished manuscript.

Everett, P. B., Deslauriers, B. C., Newson, T., & Anderson, V. B. (1978). The differential effects of two free ride dissemination procedures on bus ridership. *Transportation Research, 12,* 1–6.

Everett, P. B., Hayward, S. C., & Meyers, A. W. (1974). The effects of a token reinforcement procedure on bus ridership. *Journal of Applied Behavior Analysis, 7,* 1–9.

Fagan, G. & Aiello, J. R. (1982). Development of personal space among Puerto Ricans. *Journal of Non-Verbal Behavior, 7,* 59–68.

Fairchild, H. H., & Tucker, M. B. (1982). Black residential mobility: Trends and characteristics. *Journal of Social Issues, 38,* 51–74.

Fanger, P. O., Breun, N. O., & Jerking, E. (1977). Can colour and noise influence man's thermal comfort? *Ergonomics, 20,* 11–18.

Fazio, R. H., & Zanna, M. P. (1981). Direct experience and attitude–behavior consistency. *Advances in Experimental Social Psychology, 14,* 161–202.

Fazio, R. H., Sanbonmatsu, D. M., Powell, M. C., & Kardes, F. R. (1986). On the automatic activation of attitudes. *Journal of Personality and Social Psychology, 50,* 229–238.

Feather, N. T. (1961). The relationship of persistence at a task to expectation of success and achievement related motives. *Journal of Abnormal and Social Psychology, 63,* 552–561.

Federal Bureau of Investigation. (1979). *Uniform crime reports.* Washington, D.C.: U.S. Department of Justice.

Federal Bureau of Investigation (1981). *Uniform crime reports.* Washington, DC: U.S. Government Printing Office.

Federal Energy Administration. (1977). *Tips for energy savers.* Washington, DC: U.S. Government Printing Office.

Felipe, N. J., & Sommer, R. (1966). Invasions of personal space. *Social Problems, 14,* 206–214.

Feller, R. A. (1968). Effect of varying corridor illumination on noise level in a residence hall. *The Journal of College Personnel, 9,* 150–152.

Ferrari, N. A. (1960). *Institutionalization and attitude change in aged population: A field study in dissonance theory.* Unpublished doctoral dissertation, Western Reserve University.

Festinger, L. A. (1954). A theory of social comparison processes. *Human Relations, 7,* 117–140.

Festinger, L. A. (1957). *A theory on cognitive dissonance.* Stanford, CA: Stanford University Press.

Festinger, L. A., Schachter, S., & Back, K. (1950). *Social pressures in informal groups.* New York: Harper & Row.

Finckle, A. L., & Poppen, J. R. (1948). Clinical effects of noise and mechanical vibrations of a turbo-jet engine on man. *Journal of Applied Physiology, 1,* 183–204.

Fine, T. H., & Turner, J. W., Jr. (1982). The effect of brief restricted environmental stimulation therapy in the treatment of essential hypertension. *Behavior Research and Therapy, 20,* 567–570.

Fines, K. D. (1968). *Landscape evaluation: A research project in East Sussex.* Elmsford, NY: Pergamon.

Finnie, W. C. (1973). Field experiments in litter control. *Environment and Behavior, 5,* 123–144.

Firestone, I. J. (1977). Reconciling verbal and nonverbal models of dyadic communication. *Environmental Psychology and Nonverbal Behavior, 2,* 30–44.

Fischer, C. S. (1973). Urban malaise. *Social Forces, 52,* 221–235.

Fischer, C. S. (1976). *The urban experience.* New York: Harcourt Brace Jovanovich.

Fischer, C. S. (1978). Urban to rural diffusion of opinions in contemporary America. *American Journal of Sociology, 84,* 151–159.

Fischer, C. T. (1984). A phenomenological study of being criminally victimized: Contributions and constraints of qualitative research. *Journal of Social Issues, 40,* 161–178.

Fishbein, M., & Azjen, I. (1975). *Belief, attitude, intention, and behavior: An introduction to theory and research.* Reading, PA: Addison-Wesley.

Fisher, J. D. (1974). Situation-specific variables as determinants of perceived environmental aesthetic quality and perceived crowdedness. *Journal of Research in Personality, 8,* 177 – 188.

Fisher, J. D., & Baron, R. M. (1982). An equity-based model of vandalism. *Population and Environment, 5,* 182–200.

Fisher, J. D., & Baum, A. (1980). Situational and arousal-based messages and the reduction of crowding stress. *Journal of Applied Social Psychology, 10,* 191–201.

Fisher, J. D., & Byrne, D. (1975). Too close for comfort: Sex differences in response to invasions of personal space. *Journal of Personality and Social Psychology, 32,* 15–21.

Fleming, I. C. (1985). *The stress reducing functions of specific types of social support for victims of a technological catastrophe.* Unpublished doctoral dissertation, University of Maryland, College Park.

Fleming, I., Baum, A., & Weiss, L. (1987). Social density and perceived control as mediators or crowding stress in high-density residential neighborhoods. *Journal of Personality and Social Psychology, 52,* 899–906.

Fleming, R., Baum, A., Gisriel, M. M., & Gatchel, R. J. (1982). Mediation of stress at Three Mile Island by social support. *Journal of Human Stress, 8,* 14–22.

Flynn, C. B. (1979). Three Mile Island telephone survey. U.S. Nuclear Regulatory Commission (NUREG/CR-1093).

Fogarty, S. J., & Hemsley, D. R. (1983, March). Depression and the accessibility of memories: A longitudinal study. *British Journal of Psychiatry, 142,* 232–237.

Folk, G. E., Jr. (1974). *Textbook of environmental physiology.* Philadelphia: Lea & Febiger.

Folkman, S. (1984). Personal control and stress and coping processes: A theoretical analysis. *Journal of Personality and Social Psychology, 46,* 839–852.

Fontaine, A. (1982). *Loss of control in the institutionalized elderly.* Unpublished manuscript, University of Connecticut, Storrs.

Forbes, G., & Gromoll, H. (1971). The lost letter technique as a measure of social variables: Some exploratory findings. *Social Forces, 50,* 113–115.

Ford, A. B. (1976). *Urban health in America.* New York: Oxford University Press.

Ford, J. G., & Graves, J. R. (1977). Differences between Mexican-American and white children in interpersonal distance and social touching. *Perceptual and Motor Skills, 45,* 779–785.

Ford, W. S. (1973). Interracial public housing in a border city: Another look at the contact hypothesis. *American Journal of Sociology, 78,* 1426–1447.

Fortenberry, J. H., Maclean, J., Morris, P., & O'Connell, M. (1978). Mode of dress as a perceptual cue to deference. *Journal of Social Psychology, 104,* 139–140.

Fowler, F. J., McCall, M. E., & Mangione, T. W. (1979). *Reducing residential crime and fear: The Hartford neighborhood crime prevention program.* Washington, DC: U.S. Government Printing Office.

Fox, W. F. (1967). Human performance in the cold. *Human Factors, 9,* 203–220.

Foxx, R. M., & Hake, D. F. (1977). Gasoline conservation: A procedure for measuring and reducing the driving of college students. *Journal of Applied Behavior Analysis, 10,* 61–74.

Francescato, D., & Mebane, W. (1973). How citizens view two great cities: Milan and Rome. In R. M. Downs & D. Stea (Eds.), *Image and environment: Cognitive mapping and spatial behavior.* Chicago: Aldine.

Franck, K. A. (1984). Exorcising the ghost of physical determinism. *Environment and Behavior, 16,* 411–435.

Franck, K. D., Unseld, C. T., & Wentworth, W. E. (1974). *Adaptation of the newcomer: A process of construction.* Unpublished manuscript, City University of New York.

Frank, F. (1957). The causality of microtine cycles in Germany. *Journal of Wildlife Management, 21,* 113–121.

Franke, R. H., & Kaul, J. D. (1978). The Hawthorne experiments: First statistical interpretation. *American Sociological Review, 43,* 623–643.

Frankel, A. S., & Barrett, J. (1971). Variations in personal space as a function of authoritarianism, self-esteem, and racial characteristics of a stimulus situation. *Journal of Consulting and Clinical Psychology, 37,* 95–98.

Frankenhaeuser, M. (1971). Behavior and circulating catecholamines. *Brain Research, 31,* 241–262.

Frankenhaeuser, M. (1978). *Coping with stress: A psychobiological approach.* Reports from the Department of Psychology, University of Stockholm, 532.

Frankenhaeuser, M., & Lundberg, U. (1977). The influence of cognitive set on performance and arousal under different noise loads. *Motivation and Emotion, 1,* 139–149.

Frankenhaeuser, M., Jarpe, G., & Mattel, G. (1961). Effects of intravenous infusions of adrenaline and noradrenaline on certain psychological and physiological functions. *Acta Physiologica Scandinavia, 51,* 175–186.

Frazer, A., & Brown, R. (1987). Melatonin: A link between the environment and behavior. *Integrative Psychiatry, 5,* 3–10.

Freedman, J. L. (1975). *Crowding and behavior.* San Francisco: Freeman.

Freedman, J. L., & Perlick, D. (1979). Crowding, contagion, and laughter. *Journal of Experimental Social Psychology, 15,* 295–303.

Freedman, J. L., Birsky, J., & Cavoukiaı A. (1980). Environmental determinants of behavioral contagion:

Density and number. *Basic and Applied Social Psychology, 1,* 155–161.

Freedman, J. L., Klevansky, S., & Ehrlich, P. I., (1971). The effect of crowding on human task performance. *Journal of Applied Social Psychology, 1,* 7–26.

Freedman, J. L., Levy, A. S., Buchanan, R. W., & Price, J. (1972). Crowding and human aggressiveness. *Journal of Experimental Social Psychology, 8,* 528–548.

Freeman, H. (1978). Mental health and the environment. *British Journal of Psychiatry, 132,* 113–124.

Frey, J., Rotton, J., & Barry, T. (1979). The effects of the full moon on human behavior: Yet another failure to replicate. *Journal of Psychology, 103,* 159–162.

Fried, M. (1963). Grieving for a lost home. In L. J. Dohl (Ed.), *The urban condition.* New York: Basic Books.

Fried, M., & Gleicher, P. (1961). Some sources of residential satisfaction in an urban slum. *Journal of the American Institute of Planners, 27,* 305–315.

Frisancho, A. R. (1979). *Human adaptation.* St. Louis: Mosby.

Fritz, C. E. (1961). Disaster. In R. K. Merton & R. A. Nisbet (Eds.), *Contemporary social problems.* New York: Harcourt, Brace, & World.

Fritz, C. E., & Marks, E. S. (1954). The NORC Studies of Human Behavior in Disaster. *Journal of Social Issues, 10,* 26–41.

Frost, J. L., & Klein, B. L. (1979). *Children's play and playgrounds.* Boston : Allyn & Bacon.

Fry, A. M., & Willis, F. N. (1971). Invasion of personal space as a function of the age of the invader. *Psychological Record, 2,* 385–389.

Galle, O. R., & Gove, W. R. (1979). Crowding and behavior in Chicago, 1940–1970. In J. R. Aiello & A. Baum (Eds.), *Residential crowding and design.* New York: Plenum.

Galle, O. R., Gove, W. R., & McPherson, J. M. (1972). Population density and pathology: What are the relationships for man? *Science, 176,* 23–30.

Galloway, W. et al. (1974). In J. Ralof (Ed.) (1982), Occupational noise—the subtle pollutant. *Science News, 121*(21), 347–350.

Gallup Opinion Index. (1973). Princeton, NJ: American Institute of Public Opinion, No. 102.

Gallup Poll. (1978, March 2).

Gallup Poll. (1981, April 4).

Gallup Poll. (1981, April 19).

Galster, G., & Hesser, G. (1981). Residential satisfaction: Compositional and contextual correlates. *Environment and Behavior, 13,* 735–759.

Ganellen, R. J., & Blaney, P. H. (1984). Hardiness and social support as mediators of the effects of life stress. *Journal of Personality and Social Psychology, 47,* 156–163.

Gans, H. J. (1962). *The Organvillagers.* New York: The Free Press.

Gans, H. J. (1967). *The Levittowners: Ways of life in a new suburban community.* New York: Random House.

Garber, J., & Seligman, M. E. P. (Eds.) (1981). *Human helplessness: Theory and applications.* New York: Academic Press.

Garcia, K. D., & Wierwille, W. W. (1985). Effect of glare on performance of VDT reading-comprehension task. *Human Factors, 27,* 163–173.

Gardner, E. (1975). *Fundamentals of neurology.* Philadelphia: Saunders.

Gardner, G. T. (1978). Effects of federal human subjects regulations on data obtained in environmental stress research. *Journal of Personality and Social Psychology, 36,* 628–634.

Garfinkel, H. (1964). Studies of the routine grounds of everyday activities. *Social Problems, 11,* 225–250.

Garland, H., & Pearce, J. (1967). Neurological complications of carbon monoxide poisoning. *Quarterly Journal of Medicine, 36,* 445–455.

Gärling, T., Böök, A., & Ergezen, N. (1982). Memory for the spatial layout of the everyday physical environment. *Scandinavian Journal of Psychology, 23,* 23–35.

Gärling, T., Böök, A., & Lindberg, E. (1984). Cognitive mapping of large-scale environments: The interrelationship between action plans, acquisition, and orientation. *Environment and Behavior, 16,* 3–34.

Gärling, T., Böök, A., & Lindberg, E. (1986). Spatial orientation and wayfinding in the designed environment: A conceptual analysis and some suggestions for postoccupancy evaluation. *Journal of Architectural Planning Research, 3,* 55–64.

Gärling, T., Böök, A., Lindberg, E., & Nilsson, T. (1981). Memory for the spatial layout of the everyday physical environment: Factors affecting rate of acquisition. *Journal of Environmental Psychology, 1,* 263–277.

Gärling, T., Lindberg, E., Carreiras, M., & Book, A. (1986). Reference systems in cognitive maps. *Journal of Environmental Psychology, 6,* 1–18.

Garzino, S. J. (1982). Lunar effects on mental behavior: A defense of the empirical research. *Environment and Behavior, 4,* 395–417.

Gatchel, R. J., Schaeffer, M. A., & Baum, A. (1985). A psychological field study of stress at Three Mile Island. *Psychophysiology, 22,* 175–181.

Gaydos, H. F. (1958). Effect on complex manual performance of cooling the body while maintaining the hands at normal temperatures. *Journal of Applied Physiology, 12,* 373–376.

Gaydos, H. F., & Dusek, E. R. (1958). Effects of localized hand cooling versus total body cooling on manual performance. *Journal of Applied Physiology, 12,* 377–380.

Geen, R. G., & McGown, E. J. (1984). Effects of noise and attack on aggression and physiological arousal. *Motivation and Emotion, 8,* 231–241.

Geen, R. G., & O'Neal, E. C. (1969). Activation of cue-elicited aggression by general arousal. *Journal of Personality and Social Psychology, 11*, 289–292.

Geen, R. G., & O'Neal, E. C. (1976). *Prospectives on aggression.* New York: Academic Press.

Geller, D. M. (1980). Response to urban stimulation: A balanced approach. *Journal of Social Issues, 36*, 86–100.

Gelfand, D. M., Hartman, D. P., Walder, P., & Page, B. (1973). Who reports shoplifters? A field-experimental study. *Journal of Personality and Social Psychology, 25*, 276–285.

Geller, E. S. (1976). *Behavioral approaches to environmental problem solving: Littering and recycling.* Symposium presentation at the Association for the Advancement of Behavior Therapy meeting, New York.

Geller, E. S. (1980). Applications of behavioral analysis for litter control. In D. Glenwik & L. Jason (Eds.), *Behavioral community psychology: Progress and prospects.* New York: Praeger.

Geller, E. S. (1981). Evaluating energy conservation programs: Is verbal report enough? *Journal of Consumer Research, 8*, 331–335.

Geller, E. S. (1987). Applied behavior analysis and environmental psychology: From strange bedfellows to a productive marriage. In D. Stokols & I. Altman (Eds.). *Handbook of Environmental Psychology,* (Vol. 1, pp. 361–388). New York: Wiley-Interscience.

Geller, E. S., Chaffee, J. L., & Ingram, R. E. (1975). Promoting paper recycling on a university campus. *Journal of Environmental Systems, 5*, 39–57.

Geller, E. S., Mann, M., & Brasted, W. (1977). *Trash can design: A determinant of litter-related behavior.* Paper presented at the American Psychological Association meeting, San Francisco.

Geller, E. S., Winnett, R. A., & Everett, P. B. (1982). *Preserving the environment: New strategies for behavior change.* New York: Pergamon.

Geller, E. S., Witmer, J. F., & Orebaugh, A. L. (1976). Instructions as a determinant of paper disposal behaviors. *Environment and Behavior, 8*, 417–441.

Geller, E. S., Witmer, J. F., & Tuso, M. E. (1977). Environmental interventions for litter control. *Journal of Applied Psychology, 62*, 344–351.

George, J. R., & Bishop, L. K. (1971). Relationship of organizational structure and teacher personality characteristics to organizational climate. *Administrative Science Quarterly, 16*, 467–475.

Gergen, K. J., Gergen, M. K., & Barton, W. H. (1973). Deviance in the dark. *Psychology Today, 7*, 129–130.

Gerst, M., & Moos, R. H. (1972). The social ecology of university student residences. *Journal of Educational Psychology, 63*, 513–535.

Gibbs, J. P. (1971). Suicide. In R. K. Merton & R. A. Nisbet (Eds.), *Contemporary social problems* (3rd ed). New York: Harcourt Brace Jovanovich.

Gibbs, L. (1982). *Love Canal: My story.* Albany, NY: SUNY Press.

Gibbs, M. S. (1986). Psychopathological consequences of exposure to toxins in the water supply. In A. H. Lebovits, A. Baum, & J. Singer (Eds.), *Advances in environmental psychology* (pp. 47–70). Hillsdale, NJ: Erlbaum.

Gibson, J. J. (1950). *The perception of the visual world.* Boston: Houghton Mifflin.

Gibson, J. J. (1966). *The senses considered as perceptual systems.* Boston: Houghton Mifflin.

Gibson, J. J. (1979). *An ecological approach to visual perception.* Boston: Houghton Mifflin.

Giel, R., & Ormel, J. (1977). Crowding and subjective health in the Netherlands. *Social Psychiatry, 12*, 37–42.

Gifford, R. (1987). *Environmental psychology: Principles and practice.* Boston: Allyn & Bacon.

Gifford, R. (1988). Light, decor, arousal, comfort, and communication. *Journal of Environmental Psychology, 8*, 177–189.

Gifford, R., & Peacock, J. (1979). Crowding: More fearsome than crime-provoking? *Psychologia, 22*, 79–83.

Gimblett, R., Itami, R., & Fitzgibbon, J. (1985). Mystery in an information processing model of landscape preference. *Landscape Journal, 4*, 87–95.

Ginsberg, Y. (1975). *Jews in a changing neighborhood.* New York: Free Press.

Ginsburg, H., Pollman, V., Wauson, M., & Hope, M. (1977). Variation of aggressive interaction among male elementary school children as a function of changes in social density. *Environmental Psychology and Nonverbal Behavior, 2*, 67–75.

Glacken, C. J. (1967). *Traces on the Rhodian shore.* Berkeley, CA: University of California Press.

Glaser, D. (1964). *The effectiveness of a prison and parole system.* Indianapolis: Bobbs-Merrill.

Glass, D. C. (1976). *Behavior patterns, stress, and coronary disease.* Hillsdale, NJ: Erlbaum.

Glass, D. C., & Singer, J. E. (1972). *Urban stress.* New York: Academic Press.

Glass, D. C., Singer, J. E., & Friedman, L. W. (1969). Psychic cost of adaptation to an environmental stressor. *Journal of Personality and Social Psychology, 12*, 200–210.

Glass, D. C., Singer, J. E., Leonard, H. S., Krantz, D., Cohen, S., & Cummings, H. (1973). Perceived control of aversive stimulation and the reduction of stress responses. *Journal of Personality, 41*, 577–595.

Glenn, N., & Hill, L. (1977). Rural–urban differences in attitudes and behavior in the United States. *The Annals of the American Academy of Political and Social Science, 429*, 36–50.

Gleser, G., Green, B., & Winget, C. (1978). Quantifying interview data on psychic impairment of disaster survivors. *Journal of Nervous and Mental Disease, 166,* 209–216.

Gleser, G., Green, B., & Winget, C. (1981). *Prolonged psychosocial effects of disaster: A study of Buffalo Creek.* New York: Academic Press.

Gliner, J., Raven, P., Horvath, S., Drinkwater, B., & Sutton, J. (1975). Man's physiological response to long-term work during thermal and pollutant stress. *Journal of Applied Physiology, 39,* 628–632.

Glorig, A. (1971). Nonauditory effects of noise exposure. *Sounds and Vibration, 5,* 28–29.

Gobster, P. H. (1983). Judged appropriateness of residential structures in natural and developed shoreland settings. In D. Amedeo, J. B. Griffin, & J. J. Potter (Eds.), *EDRA 1983: Proceedings of the 14th International Conference of the Environmental Design Research Association* (pp. 105–112). Washington, DC: Environmental Design Research Association.

Goeckner, D., Greenough, W., & Maier, S. (1974). Escape learning deficit after overcrowded rearing in rats: Test of a helplessness hypothesis. *Bulletin of the Psychonomic Society, 3,* 54–57.

Gold, J. R. (1982). Territoriality and human spatial behavior. *Progress in Human Geography, 6,* 44–67.

Goldsmith, J. R. (1968). Effects of air pollution on human health. In A. C. Stern (Ed.), *Air pollution* (2nd ed). New York: Academic Press.

Goldsmith, J., & Friberg, L. (1977). Effects of air pollution on human health. In A. C. Stern (Ed.), *Air pollution* (3rd ed., Vol. 3). New York: Academic Press.

Goldstein, E. B. (1989). *Sensation and perception.* Belmont, CA: Wadsworth.

Golledge, R. G. (1987). Environmental cognition. In D. Stoklos & I. Altman (Eds.), *Handbook of environmental psychology.* (pp. 131 – 174). New York: Wiley.

Gonzales, M. H., Aronson, E. & Costanzo, M. A. (1988). Using social cognition to promote energy conservation: A quasi experiment. *Journal of Applied Social Psychology,* 1049–1066.

Goodrich, R. (1982). Seven office evaluations. *Environment and Behavior, 14,* 353–378.

Goranson, R. E., & King, D. (1970). *Rioting and daily temperature: Analysis of the U.S. riots in 1967.* York University, Toronto.

Gordon, M. S., Riger, S., Lebailly, R., & Heath, L. (1980). Crime, women, and the quality of urban life. *Signs, 5,* 144–160.

Gormley, F. P., & Aiello, J. R. (1982). Social density, interpersonal relationships, and residential crowding stress. *Journal of Applied Social Psychology, 12,* 222–336.

Gottfredson, S. D., Brower, S., & Taylor, R. B. (1979, September). *Design, social networks, and human territoriality: Predicting crime-related and social control outcomes.* Paper presented at the annual meeting of the American Psychological Association, New York.

Gottman, J. (1966). The growing city as a social and political process. *Transactions of the Bartlett Society, 5,* 9–46.

Gould, J. D., & Grischkowsky, N. (1984). Doing the same work with hard copy and with cathode-ray tube (CRT) computer terminals. *Human Factors, 26,* 323–337.

Gould, J. D., Alfaro, L., Finn, R., Haupt, B., & Minuto, A. (1987). Reading from CRT displays can be as fast as reading from paper. *Human Factors, 29,* 497–517.

Gould, P., & White, R. (1982). *Mental maps* (2nd ed.). Boston : Allen & Unwin.

Gove, W. R., & Hughes, M. (1983). *Crowding in the household.* New York: Academic Press.

Gramann, J. H., & Burdge, R. J. (1984). Crowding perception determinants at intensively developed outdoor recreation sites. *Leisure Sciences, 6,* 167–186.

Grandjean, E., Graf, P., Lauber, A., Meier, H. P., & Muller, R. (1973). A survey on aircraft noise in Switzerland. In W. D. Ward (Ed.), *Proceedings of the International Congress on Noise as a Public Health Problem. Washington, DC: U.S. Government Printing Office.*

Grandjean, E., Hunting, W., & Pidermann, M. (1983). VDT workstation design: Preferred settings and their effects. *Human Factors, 25,* 161–175.

Grandjean, P., Arnvig, E., & Beckmann, J. (1978). Psychological dysfunctions in lead-exposed workers. *Scandinavian Journal of Work, Environment and Health, 4,* 295–303.

Grant, D. P. (1970). Architect discovers the aged. *Gerontologist, 10,* 275–281.

Greenbaum, P. E., & Greenbaum, S. D. (1981). Territorial personalization: Group identity and social interaction in a Slavic-American neighborhood. *Environment and Behavior, 13,* 574–589.

Greenbaum, P., & Rosenfeld, H. M. (1978). Patterns of avoidance in response to interpersonal staring and proximity: Effects of bystanders on drivers at a traffic intersection. *Journal of Personality and Social Psychology, 36,* 575–587.

Greenberg, C. I. (1979). Toward an integration of ecological psychology and industrial psychology: Undermanning theory, organization size, and job enrichment. *Environmental Psychology and Nonverbal Behavior, 3,* 228–242.

Greenberg, C. I, & Baum, A. (1979). Compensatory response to anticipated densities. *Journal of Applied Social Psychology, 9,* 1–12.

Greenberg, C., & Firestone, I. (1977). Compensatory responses to crowding: Effects of personal space intrusion and privacy reduction. *Journal of Personality and Social Psychology, 35,* 637–644.

Greenberg, M. S. & Ruback, R. B. (1984). Criminal

victimization: Introduction and overview. *Journal of Social Issues, 40*(1), 1–8.

Greenberg, S. W., Williams, J. R., & Rohe, W. M. (1982). Safety in urban neighborhood: A comparison of physical characteristics and informal territorial control in high and low crime neighborhoods. *Population and Environment, 5,* 141–165.

Greenberger, D. B., & Allen, V. C. (1980). Destruction and complexity: An application of aesthetic theory. *Personality and Social Psychology Bulletin, 6,* 479–483.

Greene, L. R. (1977). Effects of verbal evaluation feedback and interpersonal distance on behavioral compliance. *Journal of Consulting Psychology, 24,* 10–14.

Greene, T. C., & Bell, P. A. (1980). Additional considerations concerning the effects of "warm" and "cool" wall colours on energy conservation. *Ergonomics, 23,* 949–954.

Greene, T. C., & Bell, P. A. (1986). Environmental stress. In M. A. Baker (Ed.), *Sex differences in human performance,* (pp. 81–106). London: Wiley.

Greene, T. C., & Connelly, C. M. (1988). Computer analysis of aesthetic districts In D. Lawrence, R. Habe, A. Hacker, & D. Sherrod (Eds.), *People's needs/Planet management: Paths to co-existence,* (pp. 333–335). Washington, D.C.: Environmental Design Research Association.

Greene, W. A. (1966). The psychosocial setting of development of leukemia and hypomania. *Annals of the New York Academy of Science, 125,* 794–801.

Griffiths, I. D. (1975). The thermal environment. In D. C. Canter (Ed.), *Environmental interaction: Psychological approaches to our physical surroundings* (pp. 21–52). New York: International Universities Press.

Griffiths, I. D., & Boyce, P. R. (1971). Performance and thermal comfort. *Ergonomics, 14,* 457–468.

Griffiths, I. D., & Raw, G. J. (1987). Community and individual response to changes in traffic noise exposure. In H. S. Koelega (Ed.), *Environmental annoyance: Characterization, measurement, and control* (pp. 333–343). Amsterdam: Elsevier Science Publishers.

Griffitt, W. (1970). Environmental effects on interpersonal affective behavior: Ambient effective temperature and attraction. *Journal of Personality and Social Psychology, 15,* 240–244.

Griffitt, W., & Veitch, R. (1971). Hot and crowded: Influences of population density and temperature on interpersonal affective behavior. *Journal of Personality and Social Psychology, 17,* 92–98.

Grossman, L. M. (1987, June 17). City pedestrian malls fail to fulfill promise of revitalizing downtown. *Wall Street Journal,* p. 27.

Gubrium, J. F. (1974). Victimization in old age: Available evidence and three hypotheses. *Crime and Delinquency, 20:* 245–250.

Guenther, R. (1982, Aug. 4) Ways are found to minimize pollutants in airtight houses. *Wall Street Journal,* p. 25.

Gulliver, F. P. (1908). Orientation of maps. *Journal of Geography, 7,* 55–58.

Gump, P. V. (1974, August). Operating environments in schools of open and traditional design. *School Review, 84,* 574–593.

Gump, P. V. (1984). School environments. In I. Altman & J. F. Wohlwill (Eds.), *Children and the environment* (pp. 131–174). New York: Plenum.

Gump, P. V. (1987). School and classroom environments. In D. Stokols & I. Altman (Eds.), *Handbook of environmental psychology* (Vol. 1, pp. 691–732). New York: Wiley-Interscience.

Gunderson, E. K. E. (1968). Mental health problems in Antarctica. *Archives of Environmental Health, 17,* 558–564.

Gunter, B. G. (1979). Some properties of leisure. In H. Ibrahim & R. Crandall (Eds.), *Leisure: A psychological approach.* Los Alamitos, CA: Hwong.

Gunter, B. G. (1987). The leisure experience: Selected properties. *Journal of Leisure Research, 19,* 115–130.

Gutman, G. M. (1978). Issues and findings relating to multilevel accommodation for seniors. *Journal of Gerontology, 33,* 592–600.

Haase, R. S., & Pepper, D. T. (1972). Nonverbal components of empathic communication. *Journal of Counseling Psychology, 19,* 417–424.

Haber, G. M. (1976). *The organization of space in the college classroom.* Doctoral dissertation, New York University.

Haber, G. M. (1980). Territorial invasion in the classroom: Invadee response. *Environment and Behavior, 12,* 17–31.

Hackett, T. P., & Weisman, A. D. (1964). Reactions to the imminence of death. In G. H. Grosser, H. Weschler, & M. Greenblatt (Eds.), *The threat of impending disaster* (pp. 300–311). Cambridge, MA: M.I.T. Press.

Hackney, J., Linn, W., Karuza, S., Buckley, R., Law, D., Bates, D., Hazucha, M., Pengelly, L., & Silverman, F. (1977). Effects of ozone exposure in Canadians and Southern Californians. *Archives of Environmental Health, 32,* 110–116.

Hake, D. F., & Foxx, R. M. (1978). Promoting gasoline conservation: The effects of reinforcement schedules, a leader and self-recording. *Behavior Modification, 2,* 339–369.

Hall, E. T. (1959). *The silent language.* New York: Doubleday.

Hall, E. T. (1963). A system for the notation of proxemic behavior. *American Anthropologist, 65,* 1003–1026.

Hall, E. T. (1966). *The hidden dimension.* New York: Doubleday.

Hall, E. T. (1968). Proxemics. *Current Anthropology, 9,* 83–107.

Halpin, A. W., & Crofts, D. B. (1963). The organizational climate of schools. *Administrators Notebook, 11,* 1–4.

Hambrick-Dixon, Priscilla J. (1986). Effects of experimentally imposed noise on task performance of Black children attending day care centers near elevated subway trains. *Developmental Psychology, 22,* 259–264.

Hamilton, D. L., & Bishop, G. D. (1976). Attitudinal and behavioral effects of initial integration of white suburban neighborhoods. *Journal of Social Issues, 32,* 47–68.

Hammen, C., & Mayol, A. (1982). Depression and cognitive characteristics of stressful life events. *Journal of Abnormal Psychology, 91,* 165–174.

Hammitt, W. E. (1982). Cognitive dimensions of wilderness solitude. *Environment and Behavior, 14,* 478–493.

Hancock, J. (1980). The apartment house in urban America. In A. D. King (Ed.), *Building and society: Essays on the social development of the built environment* (pp. 151–189). London: Routledge & Kegan Paul.

Hancock, P. A. (1986). Sustained attention under thermal stress. *Psychological Bulletin, 99,* 263–281.

Haney, W. G., & Knowles, E. S. (1978). Perception of neighborhoods by city and suburban residents. *Human Ecology, 6,* 201–214.

Hannson, R. O., & Slade, K. M. (1977). Altruism toward a deviant in city and small town. *Journal of Applied Social Psychology, 7,* 272–279.

Hansen, W. B., & Altman, I. (1976). Decorating personal places: A descriptive analysis. *Environment and Behavior, 8,* 491–505.

Hanson, S., Vitek, J. D., & Hanson, P. O. (1979). Natural disaster: Long-range impact on human response to future disaster threats. *Environment and Behavior, 11,* 268–284.

Hansson, R. O., Noulles, D., & Bellovich, S. J. (1982). Social comparison and urban-environmental stress. *Personality and Social Psychology Bulletin, 8,* 68–73.

Harburg, E., Erfrut, J. C., Chape, C., Hauenstein, L. S., Schull, W. J., & Schork, M. A. (1973). Socioecological stressor areas and black–white blood pressure. *Journal of Chronic Diseases, 26,* 595–611.

Hardin, G. (1968). The tragedy of the commons. *Science, 162,* 1243–1248.

Hargreaves, A. G. (1980, April). Coping with disaster. *American Journal of Nursing,* p. 683.

Harries, K. D., & Stadler, S. J. (1983). Determinism revisited: Assault and heat stress in Dallas, 1980. *Environment and Behavior, 15,* 235–256.

Harries, K. D., & Stadler, S. J. (1985–86). Aggravated assault and the urban system: Dallas, 1980–81. *Journal of Environmental Systems, 15,* 243–253.

Harries, K. D., & Stadler, S. J. (1988). Heat and violence: New findings from Dallas field data, 1980–1981. *Journal of Applied Social Psychology, 18,* 129–138.

Harries, K. D., & Stadler, S. J., & Zdrokowski, R. T. (1984). Seasonality and assault: Explorations in interneighborhood variation, Dallas, 1980. *Annals of the Association of American Geographers, 74,* 590–604.

Harris, H., Lipman, A., & Slater, R. (1977). Architectural design: The spatial location and interactions of old people. *Gerontology, 23,* 390–400.

Hart, R. A., & Moore, G. T. (1973). The development of spatial cognition: A review. In R. M. Downs and D. Stea (Eds.), *Image and environment: Cognitive mapping and spatial behavior* (pp. 246–288). Chicago: Aldine.

Hart, R. H. (1970). The concept of APS: Air Pollution Syndrome(s). *Journal of the South Carolina Medical Association, 66,* 71–73.

The Hartford Courant. (1979, November 25). Town pointing way in saving energy, p. 18.

Hartsough, D. M., & Savitsky, J. C. (1984). Three Mile Island: Psychology and environmental policy at a crossroads. *American Psychologist, 39,* 1113–1122.

Hawkins, L. H., & Barker, T. (1978). Air ions and human performance. *Ergonomics, 21,* 273–278.

Hay, D. G., & Wantman, M. J. (1969). Selected chronic diseases: Estimates of prevalence and of physician's service. New York: Center for Social Research, Graduate Center, City University of New York.

Hayduk, L. A. (1978). Personal space: An evaluative and orienting overview. *Psychological Bulletin, 85,* 117–134.

Hayduk, L. A. (1981). The permeability of personal space. *Canadian Journal of Behavioral Science, 13,* 274–287.

Hayduk, L. A. (1983). Personal space: Where we now stand. *Psychological Bulletin, 94,* 293–335.

Hayduk, L. A. (1985). Personal space: The conceptual and measurement implications of structural equation models. *Canadian Journal of Behavioral Science, 17,* 140–149.

Hayes, S. C., & Cone, J. D. (1977a). Decelerating environmentally destructive lawn-walking behavior. *Environment and Behavior, 9,* 511–534.

Hayes, S. C., & Cone, J. D. (1977b). Reducing residential electrical energy use: Payments, information and feedback. *Journal of Applied Behavior Analysis, 10,* 425–435.

Hayes, S. C., & Cone, J. D. (1981). Reduction of residential consumption of electricity through simple monthly feedback. *Journal of Applied Behavior Analysis, 14,* 81–88.

Hayes, S. C., Johnson, V. S., & Cone, J. D. (1975). The marked item technique: A practical procedure for litter control. *Journal of Applied Behavior Analysis, 8,* 381–386.

Hayward, D. G., Rothenberg, M., & Beasley, R. R.

(1976). Children's play and urban playground environments: A comparison of traditional, contemporary, and adventure playground types. In H. M. Proshansky, W. H. Ittelson, & L. Rivlin (Eds.), *Environmental psychology* (2nd. ed.). New York: Holt, Rinehart, and Winston.

Heath, D., & Williams, D. R. (1977). *Man at high altitude: The patho-physiology of acclimatization and adaptation.* Edinburgh: Churchill Livingstone, 1977.

Hebb, D. O. (1972). *Textbook of psychology* (3rd ed.). Philadelphia: Saunders.

Heberlein, T. A. (1975). Conservation information: The energy crisis and electricity consumption in an apartment complex. *Energy Systems and Policy, 1,* 105–117.

Heberlein, T. A. (1976). Some observations on alternative mechanisms for public involvement: The hearing, the public opinion poll, and the quasi-experiment. *Natural Resources Journal, 16,* 197–212.

Hecht, M. E. (1975). The decline of the grass lawn tradition in Tucson. *Landscape, 19,* 3–10.

Hediger, H. (1950). *Wild animals in captivity.* London: Butterworth.

Heerwagen, J. H., & Orians, G. H. (1986). Adaptations to windowlessness: A study of the use of visual decor in windowed and windowless offices. *Environment and Behavior, 18,* 623–639.

Heft, H. (1979a). The role of environmental features in route-learning: Two exploratory studies of wayfinding. *Environmental Psychology and Nonverbal Behavior, 3,* 172–185.

Heft, H. (1979b). Background and focal environmental conditions of the home and attention in young children. *Journal of Applied Social Psychology, 9,* 47–69.

Heft, H. (1981). An examination of constructivist and Gibsonian approaches to environmental psychology. *Population and Environment, 4,* 227–245.

Heft, H. (1983). Wayfinding as the perception of information over time. *Population and Environment, 6,* 133–150.

Heft, H., & Wohlwill, J. F. (1987). Environmental cognition in children. In D. Stokols & I. Altman (eds.), *Handbook of Environmental Psychology,* New York: John Wiley & Sons.

Heimstra, N. W., & McFarling, L. H. (1974). *Environmental Psychology.* Belmont, CA: Wadsworth.

Heimstra, N. W., & McFarling, L. H. (1978). *Environmental psychology* (2nd ed.) Monterey, Calif.: Brooks/Cole.

Heller, J., Groff, B., & Solomon, S. (1977). Toward an understanding of crowding: The role of physical interaction. *Journal of Personality and Social Psychology, 35,* 183–190.

Helson, H. (1964). *Adaptation level theory.* New York: Harper & Row.

Hemphill, K. K. (1956). *Group dimensions: A manual for their measurement.* Columbus, OH: Ohio State University.

Henderson, L. F., & Jenkins, D. M. (1974). Response of pedestrians to traffic challenge. *Transportation Research, 8,* 71–74.

Henderson, S. & Bostock, T. (1977). Coping Behavior after shipwreck. *British Journal of Psychiatry, 131,* 15–20.

Hendrick, C., Wells, K. S., & Faletti, M. V. (1982). Social and emotional effects of geographical relocation on elderly retirees. *Journal of Personality and Social Psychology, 42,* 951–962.

Henig, J. R. (1981). Gentrification and displacement of the elderly. *The Gerontologist, 21,* 67–75.

Henig, J. R. (1982). Neighborhood response to gentrification: Conditions to mobilization. *Urban Affairs Quarterly, 17,* 343–358.

Hensley, W. E. (1982). Professor poxemics: Personality and job demands as factors of faculty office arrangement. *Environment and Behavior, 14,* 581–591.

Herridge, C. F. (1974). Aircraft noise and mental health. *Journal of Psychosomatic Research, 18,* 239–243.

Herridge, C. F., & Low-Beer, L. (1973). Observations of the effects of aircraft noise near Heathrow Airport on mental health. In W. D. Ward (Ed.), *Proceedings of the International Congress on Noise as a Public Health Problem.* Washington, DC: U.S. Government Printing Office.

Herzberg, F. (1966). *Work and the nature of man.* Cleveland, OH: World Publishing.

Herzberg, F., Mausner, B., & Snyderman, B. (1959). *The motivation to work.* New York: Wiley.

Herzog, T. R. (1984). A cognitive analysis of preference for field-and-forest environments. *Landscape Research, 9,* 10–16.

Herzog, T. R. (1987). A cognitive analysis of preference for natural environments: mountains, canyons, deserts. *Landscape Journal, 6,* 140–152.

Herzog, T. R., & Smith, G. A. (1988). Danger, mystery, and environmental preference. *Environment and Behavior, 20,* 320–344.

Heshka, S., & Nelson, Y. (1972). Interpersonal speaking distance as a function of age, sex, and relationship. *Sociometry, 35,* 491–498.

Heshka, S., & Pylypuk, A. (1975, June). *Human crowding and adrenocortical activity.* Paper presented at the meeting of the Canadian Psychological Association. Quebec.

Hicks, P. E. (1977). *Introduction to industrial engineering and management science.* New York: McGraw-Hill.

Hill, J. W. (1967). Applied problems of hot work in the glass industry. In C. N. Davies, P. R. Davis, & F. H. Tyrer (Eds.), *The effects of abnormal physical condi-*

tions at work (pp. 130–143). London: E & S Livingstone.

Hinshaw, M., & Allott, K. (1972). Environmental preferences of future housing consumers. *Journal of the American Institute of Planners, 38,* 102–107.

Hiroto, D. S. (1974). Locus of control and learned helplessness. *Journal of Experimental Psychology, 102,* 187–193.

Hirst, E. (1976). Transportation energy conservation policies. *Science, 192,* 15–20.

Hoch, I. (1972). Urban scale and environmental quality. In P. Ridker (Ed.), *Population resources and the environment* (Vol. 3). Washington, DC: U.S. Government Printing Office.

Holahan, C. J. (1972). Seating patterns and patient behavior in an experimental dayroom. *Journal of Abnormal Psychology, 80,* 115–124.

Holahan, C. J. (1976a). Environmental change in a psychiatric setting: A social systems analysis. *Human Relations, 29,* 153–166.

Holahan, C. J. (1976b). Environmental effects on outdoor social behavior in a low income urban neighborhood: A naturalistic investigation. *Journal of Applied Social Psychology, 6,* 48–63.

Holahan, C. J. (1978). *Environment and behavior.* New York: Plenum.

Holahan, C. J. (1982). *Environmental psychology.* New York: Random House.

Holahan, C. J., & Dobrowolny, M. B. (1978). Cognitive and behavioral correlates of the spatial environment: An interactional analysis. *Environment and Behavior, 10,* 317–334.

Holahan, C. J., & Moos, R. H. (1981). Social support and psychological distress: A longitudinal analysis. *Journal of Abnormal Psychology, 49,* 365–370.

Holahan, C. J., & Saegert, S. (1973). Behavioral and attitudinal effects of large-scale variation in the physical environment of psychiatric wards. *Journal of Abnormal Psychology, 83,* 454–462.

Hollander, J. & Yeostros, S. (1963). The effect of simultaneous variations of humidity and barometric pressure on arthritis. *Bulletin of the American Meteorological Society, 44,* 489–494.

Hollingshead, A. B., & Rogler, L. H. (1963). Attitudes toward slums and public housing in Puerto Rico. In L. J. Duhl (Ed.), *The urban condition.* New York: Simon & Schuster.

Hollister, F. D. (1968). *Greater London Council: A report on the problems of windowless environments.* London: Hobbs.

Horowitz, M. J., Duff, D. F., & Stratton, L. O. (1964). Body-buffer zone. *Archives of General Psychiatry, 11,* 651–656.

Horvath, S. M., Dahms, T. E., & O'Hanlon, J. F. (1971).

Carbon monoxide and human vigilance: A deleterious effect of present urban concentrations. *Archives of Environmental Health, 23,* 343–347.

Hourihan, K. (1984). Context-dependent models of residential satisfaction: An analysis of housing groups in Cork, Ireland. *Environment and Behavior, 16,* 369–393.

House, J. S., & Wolf, S. (1978). Effects of urban residence on interpersonal trust and helping behavior. *Journal of Personality and Social Psychology, 36,* 1029–1043.

Houts, P. S., Miller, R. W., Tokuhata, G. K., & Ham, K. S. (1980, April 8). *Health-related behavioral impact of the Three Mile Island nuclear incident.* Report submitted to the TMI Advisory Panel on Health Research Studies of the Pennsylvania Department of Health, Part I.

Howell, D. L., & Warmbrod, J. R. (1974). Developing student attitudes toward environmental protection. *Journal of Environmental Education, 5,* 29–30.

Hubel, D. H., & Wiesel, T. N. (1979). Brain mechanisms of behavior. *Scientific American, 241,* 150–162.

Hughes, J., & Goldman, M. (1978). Eye contact, facial expression, sex, and the violation of personal space. *Perceptual and Motor Skills, 46,* 579–584.

Hummel, C. F. (1977). *Effects of induced cognitive sets in viewing air pollution scenes.* Unpublished doctoral dissertation, Colorado State University.

Hummel, C. F., Levitt, L., & Loomis, R. J. (1973). *Research strategies for measuring attitudes toward pollution.* Unpublished manuscript, Colorado State University.

Hummel, C. F., Loomis, R. J., & Hebert, J. A. (1975). *Effects of city labels and cue utilization on air pollution judgments (Working Papers in Environmental-Social Psychology,* No. 1). Unpublished manuscript, Colorado State University.

Hundert, A. J., & Greenfield, N. (1969). Physical space and organizational behavior: A study of an office landscape. *Proceedings of the 77th Annual Convention of the American Psychological Association, 4,* 601–602.

Hunt, J. (1975). Fundamental studies of wind flow near buildings: Models and systems in architecture and building. *LUBFS Conference Proceedings* (2). Lancaster, England: Construction Press.

Hunt, M. E. (1984). Environmental learning without being there. *Environment and Behavior, 16,* 307–334.

Hunt, T. J., & May, P. I. (1968). *A preliminary investigation into a psychological assessment of driving stress.* London: Metropolitan Police Accident Research Unit.

Hunter, A. (1978). Persistence of local sentiments in mass society. In D. Street (Ed.), *Handbook of contemporary urban life.* San Francisco: Jossey-Bass.

Huntington, E. (1915). *Civilization and climate*. New Haven: Yale University Press.

Huntington, E. (1945). *Mainsprings of civilization*. New York: Wiley.

Hurt, H. (1975). The hottest place in the whole U.S.A. *Texas Monthly, 3,* 50–52, 84, 89–93.

Hutt, C., & Vaizey, M. S. (1966). Differential effects of group density on social behavior. *Nature, 209,* 1371–1372.

Hynson, L. M. (1975). Rural–urban difference in satisfaction among the elderly. *Rural Sociology, 46,* 64–66.

Ickes, W., Patterson, M. L., Rajecki, D. W., & Tanford, S. (1982). Behavioral and cognitive consequences of reciprocal versus compensatory responses to pre-interaction expectancies. *Social Cognition, 1,* 160–190.

Im, S. (1984). Visual preferences in enclosed urban spaces: An exploration of a scientific approach to environmental design. *Environment and Behavior, 16,* 235–262.

Imamoglu, V. (1973). The effect of furniture density on the subjective evaluation of spaciousness and estimation of size in rooms. In R. Kuller (Ed.), *Architectural psychology: Proceedings of the Lund Conference.* Stroudsburg, PA: Dowden, Hutchinson, & Ross.

Ingram, R. E., & Geller, E. S. (1975). A community integrated behavior modification approach to facilitating paper recycling. *JSAS Catalog of Selected Documents in Psychology, 5,* 327 (Ms. No. 1097).

Isen, A. M. (1970). Success, failure, attention, and reaction to others: The warm glow of success. *Journal of Personality and Social Psychology, 15,* 294–301.

Isen, A. M., Shalker, T. E., Clark, M. & Karp, L. (1978). Affect, accessibility of material in memory, and behavior: A cognitive loop? *Journal of Personality & Social Psychology, 36,* 1–12

Ising, H., & Melchert, H. U. (1980). Endocrine and cardiovascular effects of noise. In *Noise as a public health problem: Proceedings of the Third International Congress.* (ASHA Report No. 10). Rockville, MD: American Speech and Hearing Association.

Iso-Ahola, S. E. (1986). A theory of substitutability of leisure behavior. *Leisure Science, 8,* 367–389.

Ittelson, W. H. (1970). Perception of the large-scale environment. *Transactions of the New York Academy of Sciences, 32,* 807–815.

Ittelson, W. H. (1973a). *Environment and cognition*. New York: Seminar Press.

Ittelson, W. H. (1973b). Environmental perception and contemporary perceptual theory. In: W. H. Ittelson (Ed.), *Environment and cognition* (pp. 1–19). New York: Seminar Press.

Ittelson, W. H. (1976). Some issues facing a theory of environment and behavior. In H. M. Proshansky, W. H. Itelson, & L. Rivlin (Eds.), *Environmental psychology: people and their physical settings.* New York: Holt, Rinehart and Winston.

Ittelson, W. H. (1978). Environmental perception and urban experience. *Environment and Behavior, 10,* 193–213.

Ittelson, W. H., Proshansky, H. M., & Rivlin, L. G. (1970). A study of bedroom use on two psychiatric wards. *Hospital and Community Psychology, 21,* 25–28.

Ittelson, W. H., Proshansky, H. M., & Rivlin, L. G. (1972). Bedroom size and social interaction of the psychiatric ward. In J. Wohlwill & D. Carson (Eds.), *Environment and the social sciences* Washington, DC: American Psychological Association. (Reports based on the same data appeared in: Ittelson, W. H., Proshansky, H. M., & Rivlin, L. G. (1970). A study of bedroom use on two psychiatric wards. *Hospital and Community Psychology, 21*(6), 25–28; and Ittelson, W. H., Proshansky, H. M. Ittelson, W. H., Proshansky, H. M., Rivlin, L. G., & Winkel, G. H. (1974). *An introduction to environmental psychology.* New York: Holt, Rinehart and Winston.

Ittelson, W. H., Rivlin, L. G., & Proshansky, H. M. (1976). The use of behavioral maps in environmental psychology. In H. M. Proshansky, W. H. Ittelson, & L. G. Rivlin (Eds.), *Environmental psychology: People and their physical settings.* New York: Holt, Rinehart and Winston.

Jackson, E. L. (1981). Responses to earthquake hazard: The west coast of America. *Environment and Behavior, 3,* 387–416.

Jackson, J. B. (1975). The historic American landscape. In E. H. Zube, R. O. Brush, & J. G. Fabos (Eds.), *Landscape assessment: Values, perceptions, and resources* (pp. 4–9). Stroudsburg, PA: Dowden, Hutchinson, & Ross.

Jackson, K. (1985). *Crabgrass frontier*. London: Oxford University Press.

Jackson, S. W. (1986). *Melancholia and depression from Hippocratic times to modern times*. New Haven: Yale University Press.

Jacobs, H., Fairbanks, D., Doche, C., & Bailey, J. S. (1982). Behavioral community psychology: Multiple incentives in encouraging carpool formation on a university campus. *Journal of Applied Behavior Analysis, 15,* 141–149.

Jacobs, J. (1961). *The death and life of great American cities*. New York: Random House.

Jain, U. (1978). Competition tolerance in high- and low-density urban and rural areas. *Journal of Social Psychology, 105,* 297–298.

James, B. (1984). A few words about the home field advantage. In B. James (Ed.), *The Bill James baseball abstract 1984*. New York: Ballantine.

James, W. (1979). The dilemma of determinism. In F. H. Burkhardt, F. Bowers, & I. K. Skrupkelis (Eds.), *Will to believe* (pp. 114–140). Cambridge, MA: Harvard.

Janis, I. L. (1958). *Psychological stress: Psychoanalytic and behavioral studies of surgical patients.* New York: Wiley.

Jansen, G. (1973). Non-auditory effects of noise—Physiological and psychological reactions in man. *Proceedings of the International Congress on Noise as a Public Health Problem.* Dubrovnik, Yugoslavia, May 13–18. Washington, DC: U.S. Environmental Protection Agency.

Jason, L. A., Zolik, E. S., & Matese, F. (1979). Prompting dog owners to pick up dog droppings. *American Journal of Community Psychology, 7,* 339–351.

Jerdee, T. H., & Rosen, B. (1974). The effects of opportunity to communicate and visibility of individual decisions on behavior in the common interest. *Journal of Applied Psychology, 59,* 712–716.

Johnson, J. E. (1973). Effects of accurate expectations about sensations on the sensory and distress components of pain. *Journal of Personality and Social Psychology, 27,* 261–275.

Johnson, J. E., & Leventhal, H. (1974). Effects of accurate expectations and behavioral instructions on reactions during a noxious medical examination. *Journal of Personality and Social Psychology, 29,* 710–718.

Johnson, R., & Richards, B. (1988, November 2). The buyer of Sears Tower will face rather shattering problem: Windows. *The Wall Street Journal,* p. A8.

Joiner, D. (1971). Office territory. *New Society, 7,* 660–663.

Jones, J. W. (1978). Adverse emotional reactions of nonsmokers to secondary cigarette smoke. *Environmental Psychology and Nonverbal Behavior, 3,* 125–127.

Jones, J. W., & Bogat, G. A. (1978). Air pollution and human aggression. *Psychological Reports, 43,* 721–722.

Jones, S. E., & Aiello, J. R. (1979). A test of the validity of projective and quasi-projective measures of interpersonal distance. *The Western Journal of Speech Communication, 43,* 143–152.

Jorgenson, D. O. (1981). Locus of control and perceived causal influence of the lunar cycle. *Perceptual and Motor Skills, 52,* 864.

Jorgenson, D. O., & Dukes, F. O. (1976). Deindividuation as a function of density and group membership. *Journal of Personality and Social Psychology, 34,* 24–39.

Jorgenson, D. O., & Papciak, A. S. (1981). The effects of communication, resource feedback and identifiability on behavior in a simulated commons. *Journal of Experimental Social Psychology, 17,* 373–385.

Jourard, S. M., & Rubin, J. E. (1968). Self-disclosure and touching: A study of two modes of interpersonal

encounter and their interrelation. *Journal of Humanistic Psychology, 8,* 39–48.

Joy, V. D., & Lehmann, N. (1975). *The cost of crowding: Responses and adaptations.* Unpublished manuscript, New York State Department of Mental Hygiene.

Jung, J. (1984). Social support and its relation to health: A critical examination. *Basic and Applied Social Psychology, 5,* 143–149.

Kahneman, D. (1973). *Attention and effort.* Englewood Cliffs, NJ: Prentice-Hall.

Kammann, R., Thompson, R., & Irwin, R. (1979). Unhelpful behavior in the street: City size or immediate pedestrian density? *Environment and Behavior, 11,* 245–250.

Kaplan, R. (1975). Some methods and strategies in the prediction of preference. In E. H. Zube, J. G. Fabos, & R. O. Brush (Eds.), *Landscape assessment: Values, perceptions, and resources.* (pp. 118–129) Stroudsburg, PA.: Dowden, Hutchinson & Ross.

Kaplan, R. (1983). The role of nature in the urban context. In I Altman & J. F. Wohlwill (Eds.). *Behavior and the natural environment* (pp. 127–162). New York: Plenum.

Kaplan, R. (1984). Wilderness perception and psychological benefits: An analysis of a continuing program. *Leisure Sciences, 6,* 271–290.

Kaplan, R. (1985). Nature at the doorstep: Residential satisfaction and the nearby environment. *Journal of Architectural Planning Research, 2,* 115–127.

Kaplan, R. (1987). Validity in environment/behavior research. *Environment and Behavior, 19,* 495–500.

Kaplan, R., & Kaplan, S. (1987). The garden as a restorative experience. In M. Francis & R. T. Hester, Jr. (Eds.), *Meanings of the garden* (pp. 334–341). Davis, CA: University of California, Davis.

Kaplan, S. (1973). Cognitive maps in perception and thought. In R. Downs & D. Stea (Eds.), *Image and the Environment.* Chicago: Aldine.

Kaplan, S. (1975). An informal model for the prediction of preference. In E. H. Zube, J. G. Fahos, & R. O. Brush (Eds.), *Landscape assessment: Values perceptions, and resources* (pp. 92–101). Stroudsburg, PA: Dowden, Hutchinson, & Ross.

Kaplan, S. (1976). Adaptation, structure, and knowledge. In G. Moore & R. Golledge (Eds.), *Environmental knowing* (pp. 32–45). Stroudsburg, PA: Dowden, Hutchinson, & Ross.

Kaplan, S. (1987). Aesthetics, affect, and cognition. *Environment and Behavior, 19,* 3–32.

Kaplan, S., & Kaplan, R. (1982). *Cognition and the environment: Functioning in an uncertain world.* New York: Praeger.

Kaplan, S., Kaplan, R., & Wendt, J. S. (1972). Rated preference and complexity for natural and urban visual material. *Perception and Psychophysics, 12,* 354–356.

Karabenick, S. A., & Meisels, M. (1972). Effects of performance evaluation on interpersonal distance. *Journal of Personality, 40,* 275–286.

Kardiner, A., Linton, R., Du Bois, C., & West, J. (1945). *The psychological frontiers of society.* New York: Columbia University Press.

Karlin, R. A., Epstein, Y., & Aiello, J. (1978). Strategies for the investigation of crowding. In A. Esser & B. Greenbie (Eds.), *Design for communality and privacy.* New York: Plenum.

Karlin, R. A., McFarland, D., Aiello, J. R., & Epstein, Y. M. (1976). Normative mediation of reactions to crowding. *Environmental Psychology and Nonverbal Behavior, 1,* 30–40.

Karlin, R. A., Rosen, L., & Epstein, Y. (1979). Three into two doesn't go: A follow-up of the effects of overcrowded dormitory rooms. *Personality and Social Psychology Bulletin, 5,* 391–395.

Karmel, L. J. (1965). Effects of windowless classroom environment on high school students. *Perceptual and Motor Skills, 20,* 277–278.

Kasl, S. V. (1976). Effects of housing on mental and physical health. In *U. S. Department of Housing and Urban Development, Housing in the seventies* (working papers 1). Washington, DC: Government Printing Office.

Kasl, S. V., & Cobb, S. (1970). Blood pressure changes in men undergoing job stress: A preliminary report. *Psychosomatic Medicine, 32,* 19–38.

Kasl, S. V. & Harburg, E. (1972). Perceptions of the neighborhood and the desire to move out. *Journal of the American Institute of Planners, 38,* 318 – 324.

Kasmar, J. V. (1970). The development of a usable lexicon of environmental descriptors. *Environment and Behavior, 2,* 153–169.

Kastka, J. (1980) *Noise annoyance reduction in residential areas by traffic control technics.* 10th International Congress on Acoustics, Sydney.

Kates, R. W. (1976). Experiencing the environment as hazard. In H. M. Proshansky, W. H. Ittelson, & L. G. Rivlin (Eds.), *Environmental psychology: People and their physical settings* (2nd ed.). New York: Holt, Rinehart and Winston.

Kates, R. W., Haas, J. E., Amaral, D. J., Olson, R. A., Ramos, R., & Olson, R. (1973). Human impact of the Managua earthquake: Transitional societies are peculiarly vulnerable to natural disasters. *Science, 182,* 981–989.

Katovich, M. (1986). Ceremonial openings in bureaucratic encounters: From shuffling feet to shuffling papers. In N. K. Denzin (Ed.), *Studies in symbolic interaction* (Vol. 6). Greenwich, CT: JAI Press.

Katz, P. (1937). *Animals and men.* New York: Longmans, Green.

Kaufman, J., & Christensen, J. (Eds.) (1984). *IES lighting handbook.* New York: Illuminating Engineering Society of North America.

Keating, J., & Snowball, H. (1977). Effects of crowding and depersonalization on perception of group atmosphere. *Perceptual and Motor Skills, 44,* 431–435.

Keeley, R. M., & Edney, J. J. (1983). Model house designs for privacy, security, and social interaction. *Journal of Social Psychology, 119,* 219–228.

Kelley, H., & Arrowwood, A. (1960). Coalitions in the triad: Critique and experiment. *Sociometry, 23,* 231–244.

Kelly, I. W., Rotton, J., & Culver, R. (1985–86). The moon was full and nothing happened. *Skeptical Inquirer, 10,* 129–143.

Kelly, J. R. (1983). *Leisure identities and interactions.* London: George Allen & Unwin.

Kelly, J. T. (1985). Trauma: With the example of San Francisco's shelter programs. In P. W. Brickner, L. K. Scharer, B. Conanan, A. Elvy, & M. Savarese (Eds.), *Health care of homeless people* (pp. 77–91). New York: Springer-Verlag.

Kenrick, D. T., & Johnson, G. A. (1979). Interpersonal attraction in aversive environments. A problem for the classical conditioning paradigm. *Journal of Personality and Social Psychology, 87,* 572–579.

Kenrick, D. T., & MacFarlane, S. W. (1986). Ambient temperature and horn honking: A field study of the heat/aggression relationship. *Environment and Behavior, 18,* 179–191.

Kent, S. J., von Gierke H. E., Tolan G. D. (1986). Analysis of the potential association between noise-induced hearing loss and cardiovascular disease in USAF aircrew members. *Aviation Space Environmental Medicine, 4,* 348–61.

Kerr, R. A. (1988a). Is the greenhouse here? *Science, 239,* 559–561.

Kerr, R. A. (1988b). Ozone hole bodes ill for the globe. *Science, 241,* 785–786.

Kerr, R. A. (1988c). Indoor radon: The deadliest pollutant. *Science, 240,* 606–608.

Kessler, R. C., House, S. J., & Turner, J. B. (1987). Unemployment and health in a community sample. *Journal of Health and Social Behavior, 28,* 51–59.

Kevan, S. M. (1980). Perspectives on season of suicide: A review. *Social Science and Medicine, 14,* 369–378.

Key, W. (1968). Rural–urban social participation. In S. Fava, (Ed.), *Urbanism in world perspective.* New York: Crowell.

Kilijanek, T. S., & Drabek, T. E. (1979). Assessing long-term impacts of a natural disaster: A focus on the elderly. *Gerontologist, 19:* 555–566.

Killian, E. (1970). Effects of geriatric transfers on mortality rates. *Social Work, 15,* 19–26.

Kinarthy, E. L. (1975). *The effect of seating position on*

performance and personality in a college classroom. Doctoral dissertation, University of Southern California.

Kinzel, A. S. (1970). Body buffer zone in violent prisoners. *American Journal of Psychiatry, 127,* 59–64.

Kira, A. (1976). *The bathroom.* New York: Viking.

Kirkpatrick, D. (1988). How safe are video terminals?. *Fortune,* 66–68.

Kirmeyer, S. L. (1978). Urban density and pathology. *Environment and Behavior, 10,* 247–270.

Kleeman, W. B. (1982). The future of the office. *Environment and Behavior, 14,* 593–610.

Klein, K., & Beith, B. (1985). Re-examination of residual arousal as an explanation of aftereffects: Frustration tolerance versus response speed. *Journal of Applied Psychology, 70,* 642–650.

Klein, K., & Harris, B. (1979). Disruptive effects of disconfirmed expectancies about crowding. *Journal of Personality and Social Psychology, 37,* 769–777.

Kline, L. M., Bell, P. A., & Babcock, A. M. (1984). Field dependence and interpersonal distance. *Bulletin of the Psychonomic Society, 22,* 421–422.

Kline, L. M., Harrison, A., Bell, P. A., Edney, J. J., & Hill, E. (1984). Verbal reinforcement and feedback as solutions to a simulated commons dilemma. *Psychological Documents, 14,* 24. (ms. No. 2648).

Klopfer, P. H. (1968). From Ardrey to altruism: A discourse on the biological basis of human behavior. *Behavioral Science, 13,* 399–401.

Kmiecik, C., Mausar, P., & Banziger, G. (1979). Attractiveness and interpersonal space. *Journal of Social Psychology, 108,* 227–278.

Knipschild, P. G. (1980). Aircraft noise and hypertension. In J. V. Tobias, G. Jansen, & W. D. Ward (Eds.), *Noise as a public health problem: Proceedings of the Third International Congress* (ASHA Report No. 10). Rockville, MD: American Speech and Hearing Association.

Knowles, E. S. (1972). Boundaries around social space: Dyadic responses to an invader. *Environment and Behavior, 4,* 437–447.

Knowles, E. S. (1973). Boundaries around group interaction: The effect of group and member status on boundary permeability. *Journal of Personality and Social Psychology, 26,* 327–331.

Knowles, E. S. (1977). *Affective and cognitive mediators of spatial behavior.* Paper presented at the American Psychological Association Convention, San Francisco.

Knowles, E. S. (1978). The gravity of crowding: Application of social physics to the effects of others. In A. Baum & Y. Epstein (Eds.), *Human response to crowding.* Hillsdale, NJ: Erlbaum.

Knowles, E. S. (1980a). An affiliative conflict theory of personal and group spatial behavior. In P. B. Paulus (Ed.), *Psychology of group influence* (pp. 133–188). Hillsdale, NJ: Erlbaum.

Knowles, E. S. (1980b). Convergent validity of personal space measures: Consistent results with low intercorrelations. *Journal of Nonverbal Behavior, 4,* 240–248.

Knowles, E. S. (1983). Social physics and the effects of others: Tests of the effects of audience size and distance on social judgements and behavior. *Journal of Personality and Social Psychology, 45,* 1263–1279.

Knowles, E. S., & Bassett, R. I. (1976). Groups and crowds as social entities: Effects of activity, size and member similarity on nonmembers. *Journal of Personality and Social Psychology, 34,* 837–845.

Knowles, E. S., & Brickner, M. A. (1981). Social cohesion effects on spatial cohesion. *Personality and Social Psychology Bulletin, 7,* 309–313.

Knowles, E. S., & Johnson, P. K. (1974). Intrapersonal consistency and interpersonal distance. *JSAS Catalog of Selected Documents in Psychology, 4,* 124.

Knowles, E. S., Kreuser, B., Haas, S., Hyde, M., & Schuchart, G. E. (1976). Group size and the extension of social space boundaries. *Journal of Personality and Social Psychology, 33,* 647–654.

Koelega, H. S., Brinkman, J. A. (1986). Noise and vigilance: An evaluative review. *Human Factors, 28,* 465–481.

Kohlenberg, R., & Phillips, T. (1973). Reinforcement and rate of litter depositing. *Journal of Applied Behavior Analysis, 6,* 391–396.

Kohlenberg, R., Phillips, T., & Proctor, W. (1976). A behavioral analysis of peaking in residential electrical energy consumers. *Journal of Applied Behavior Analysis, 9,* 13–18.

Kojima, H. (1984). A significant stride toward the comparative study of control. *American Psychologist, 39,* 972–973.

Komorita, S. S. (1987). Cooperative choice in decomposed social dilemmas. *Personality and Social Psychology Bulletin, 13,* 53–63.

Konar, E., Sundstrom, E., Brady, C., Mandel, D., & Rice R. (1982). Status markers in the office. *Environment and Behavior, 14,* 561–580.

Konecni, V. J., Libuser, L., Morton, H., & Ebbesen, E. B. (1975). Effects of a violation of personal space on escape and helping responses. *Journal of Experimental Social Psychology, 11,* 288–299.

Koneya, M. (1976). Location and interaction in row-and-column seating arrangements. *Environment and Behavior, 8,* 265–283.

Konzett, H. (1975). Jahre osterreichischle Pharmakologie. *Wien Med Wochenscher, 125* (1–2 suppl), 1–6.

Konzett, H., Hortnagel, H., Hortnagel, L., & Winkler, H. (1971). On the urinary output of vasopressin, epinephrine and norepinephrine during different stress situations. *Psychopharmacologia, 21,* 247–256.

Koocher, G. P. (1977). Bathroom behavior and human dignity. *Journal of Personality and Social Psychology, 35,* 120–121.

Koop, C. E. (1986). The health consequences of involuntary smoking: A report of the Surgeon General. Rockville, MD: U.S. Department of Health and Human Services, Public Health Service, Centers for Disease Control, Center for Health Promotion and Education, Office on Smoking and Health.

Korte, C. (1980). Urban–nonurban differences in social behavior and social psychological models of urban impact. *Journal of Social Issues, 36,* 29–51.

Korte, C., & Kerr, N. (1975). Responses to altruistic opportunities under urban and rural conditions. *Journal of Social Psychology, 95,* 183–184.

Korte, C., Ypma, I., & Toppen, A. (1975). Helpfulness in Dutch society as a function of urbanization and environmental input level. *Journal of Personality and Social Psychology, 32,* 996–1003.

Kosslyn, S. M. (1975). Information representation in visual images. *Cognitive Psychology, 7,* 341–370.

Kosslyn, S. M. (1980). *Image and mind.* Cambridge, MA: Harvard University Press.

Kosslyn, S. M. (1983). *Ghosts in the mind's machine: Creating images in the brain.* New York: W. W. Norton & Company.

Kosslyn, S. M., & Pomerantz, J. P. (1977). Imagery, propositions, and the form of internal representations. *Cognitive Psychology, 9,* 52–76.

Kosslyn, S. M., Ball, T. M., & Reiser, B. J. (1978). Visual images preserve metric spatial information: Evidence from studies of image scanning. *Journal of Experimental Psychology: Human Perception and Performance, 4,* 47–60.

Kostof, S. (1987). *America by design.* New York: Oxford University Press.

Kovach, E. J., Jr., Surrette, M. A., & Aamodt, M. G. (1988). Following informal street maps: Effects of map design. *Environment and Behavior, 20,* 683 – 699.

Kovrigin, S. D., & Mikheyev, A. P. (1965). *The effect of noise level on working efficiency.* Rept. N65-28297. Washington, DC: Joint Publications Research Service.

Kozlowski, L. T., & Bryant, K. (1977). Sense of direction, spatial orientation, and cognitive maps. *Journal of Experimental Psychology: Human perception and Performance, 3,* 590–598.

Kramer, R. M., & Brewer, M. B. (1984). Effects of group identity on resource use in a simulated commons dilemma. *Journal of Personality and Social Psychology, 46,* 1044–1057.

Krauss, R. M., Freedman, J. L., & Whitcup, M. (1978). Field and laboratory studies of littering. *Journal of Experimental Social Psychology, 14,* 109–122.

Krebs, C. J. (1972). *Ecology: The experimental distribution and abundance.* New York: Harper & Row.

Kristeller, J. L., Schwartz, G. E., & Black, H. (1982). The use of restricted environmental stimulation therapy (REST) in the treatment of essential hypertension: Two case studies. *Behavior Research and Therapy, 20,* 561–566.

Kroling, P. (1985). Natural and artificial air ions—a biologically relevant climatic factor? *International Journal of Biometeorology, 29,* 233–242.

Krupat, E. (1982). *People in cities.* Unpublished manuscript, Massachusetts College of Pharmacy and Allied Health Sciences.

Krupat, E. (1985). *People in cities: The urban environment and its effects.* New York: Cambridge University Press.

Krupat, E., Guild, W., & Miller, M. (1977). *Characteristics of large and medium sized cities, and small towns.* Unpublished manuscript, Boston College.

Kryter, K. D. (1970). *The effects of noise on man.* New York: Academic Press.

Lacey, J. I. (1967). Somatic response patterning and stress: Some revisions of activation theory. In W. H. Appley & R. Trumball (Eds.), *Psychological stress* (pp. 14–37). New York: Appleton-Century-Crofts.

Ladd, F. C. (1972). Black youths view their environments. *Journal of the American Institute of Planners, 38,* 108–115.

La Hart, D., & Bailey, J. S. (1975). Reducing children's littering on a nature trail. *Journal of Environmental Education, 7,* 37–45.

Lakota, R. A. (1975). *The National Museum of History as a behavioral environment. Part I: An environmental analysis of behavioral performance.* Washington, D.C.: Office of Museum Programs, The Smithsonian Institution.

Landesberger, H. A. (1958). *Hawthorne revisited.* Ithaca, NY: Cornell University Press.

Landy, F. J. (1989). *Psychology of work behavior.* Pacific Grove, CA: Brooks/Cole.

Lang, J. (1987). *Creating architectural theory: The role of the behavioral sciences in environmental design.* New York: Van Nostrand Reinhold.

Lang, J. (1988). Understanding normative theories of architecture. *Environment and Behavior, 20,* 601–632.

Lang, J., Burnette, C., Moiesk, W., & Vachon, D. (1974). *Designing for human behavior: Architecture and the behavioral sciences.* Stroudsburg, PA: Dowden, Hutchinson, & Ross.

Langdon, P. (1984). The legacy of Kevin Lynch. *Planning,* 12 – 16.

Langer, E. J., & Rodin, J. (1976). The effects of choice and enhanced personal responsibility for the aged: A field experiment in an institutional setting. *Journal of Personality and Social Psychology, 34,* 191–198.

Langer, E., & Saegert, S. (1977). Crowding and cognitive control. *Journal of Personality and Social Psychology, 35,* 175–182.

Lassen, C. L. (1973). Effects of proximity on anxiety and communication in the initial psychiatric interview. *Journal of Abnormal Psychology, 81,* 226–232.

Latané, B., & Darley, J. M. (1970). *The unresponsive bystander: Why doesn't he help?* New York: Appleton-Century-Crofts.

Latta, R. M. (1978). Relation of status incongruence to personal space. *Personality and Social Psychology Bulletin, 4,* 143–146.

Laumann, E. O., & House, J. S. (1972). Living room styles and social attributes: The patterning of material artifacts in a modern urban community. In E. O. Laumann, P. M. Sigel, & R. W. Hodges (Eds.), *The logic of social hierarchies* (pp. 189–203). Chicago: Markham.

Lauridsen, P. K. (1977). *Decreasing gasoline consumption in fleet-owned automobiles through feedback, and feedback plus lottery.* Unpublished master's thesis, Drake University.

Lave, L. B., & Seskin, E. P. (1973). *Air pollution and human health.* Baltimore: Johns Hopkins Press.

LaVerne, A. A. (1970). Nonspecific Air Pollution Syndrome (NAPS): Preliminary report. *Behavioral Neuropsychiatry, 2,* 19–21.

Lavrakas, P. J. (1982). Fear of crime and behavior restriction in urban and suburban neighborhoods. *Population and Environment, 5,* 242–264.

Lawson, B. R., & Walters, D. (1974). The effects of a new motorway on an established residential area. In D. Canter & T. Lee (Eds.), *Psychology and the built environment.* New York: Wiley.

Lawton, M. P. (1975). Competence, environmental press, and the adaptation of older people. In P. G. Windley & G. Ernst (Eds.), *Theory development in environment and aging* (pp. 13–83). Washington, DC: Gerontological Society.

Lawton, M. P. (1979). Therapeutic environments for the aged. In D. Canter & S. Canter (Eds.), *Designing for therapeutic environments: A review of research* (pp. 233–276). Chichester, England: Wiley.

Lawton, M. P., & Cohen, J. (1974). Environment and the well-being of elderly inner city residents. *Environment and Behavior, 6,* 194–211.

Lawton, M. P., Fulcomer, M., & Kleban, M. H. (1984). Architecture for the mentally impaired elderly. *Environment and Behavior, 16,* 730–757.

Lawton, M. P., & Nahemow, L. (1973). Ecology and the aging process. In C. Eisdorfer & M. P. Lawton (Eds.), *The psychology of adult development and aging* (pp. 619–674). Washington, DC: American Psychological Association.

Lawton, M. P., Nahemow, L., & Yeh, T. M. (1980). Neighborhood environment and the well-being of older tenants in planned housing. *Journal of Aging and Human Development, 11,* 211–227.

Lazarus, R. (1966). *Psychological stress and the coping process.* New York: McGraw-Hill.

Lazarus, R. S., & Cohen, J. B. (1977). Environmental stress. In I. Altman & J. F. Wohlwill (Eds.), *Human behavior and the environment: Current theory and research* (Vol. 2, pp. 89–127). New York: Plenum.

Lazarus, R. S., DeLongis, A., Folkman, S., & Gruen, R. (1985). Stress and adaptational outcomes: The problem of confounded measures. *American Psychologist, 40,* 770–779.

Lazarus, R. S., & Folkman, S. (1984). *Stress, appraisal, and coping.* New York: Springer.

Lazarus, R. S., & Launier, R. (1978). Stress-related transactions between person and environment. In L. A. Pervin & M. Lewis (Eds.), *Perspectives in interactional psychology* (pp. 287–327). New York: Plenum.

LeBlanc, J. (1956). Impairment of manual dexterity in the cold. *Journal of Applied Physiology, 9,* 62–64.

LeBlanc, J. (1962). Local adaptation to cold of Gaspé fisherman. *Journal of Applied Physiology, 17,* 950–952.

LeBlanc, J. (1975). *Man in the cold.* Springfield, IL: Thomas.

Lebo, C. P., & Oliphant, K. P. (1968). Music as a source of acoustical trauma. *Laryngoscope, 78,* 1211–1218.

Lebovits, A., Byrne, M., & Strain, J. (1986). The case of asbestos-exposed workers: A psychological evaluation. In A. Lebovits, A. Baum, & J. Singer (Eds.), *Advances in environmental psychology* (Vol. 6, pp. 3–17). Hillsdale, NJ: Erlbaum, 1986.

Lee, D. H. K. (1964). Terrestrial animals in dry heat: Man in the desert. In D. B. Dill, E. G. Adolph, & C. G. Wilbur (Eds.), *Handbook of physiology* (pp. 551–582). Washington, DC: The American Physiological Society.

Lee, T. R. (1970). Perceived distance as a function of direction in the city. *Environment and Behavior, 2,* 39–51.

Leff, H. L. (1974). *Experience, environment, and human potentials.* New York: Oxford University Press.

Lehman, D. R., Wortman, C. B., & Williams, A. F. (1987). Long-term effects of losing a spouse or child in a motor vehicle crash. *Journal of Personality and Social Psychology, 52,* 218–231.

Leithead, C. S., & Lind, A. R. (1964). *Heat stress and heat disorders.* London: Cassell.

Lemke, S., & Moos, R. H. (1986). Quality of residential settings for elderly adults. *Journal of Gerontology, 41,* 268–276.

Lemke, S., & Moos, R. H. (1987). Measuring the social climate of congregate residences for older people: Sheltered Care Environmental Scale. *Psychology and Aging, 2,* 20–29.

Leopold, R. L., & Dillon, H. (1963). Psychoanatomy of a disaster: A long term study of post-traumatic neurosis in survivors of a marine explosion. *American Journal of Psychiatry, 119,* 913–921.

Lerner, R. N., Iwawaki, S., & Chihara, T. (1976). Development of personal space schemata among Japanese children. *Developmental Psychology, 12,* 466–467.

Lester, D. (1979). Temporal variation in suicide and homicide. *American Journal of Epidemiology, 109,* 517–520.

Lester, D., Brockopp, G. W., & Priebe, K. (1969). Association between a full moon and completed suicide. *Psychological Reports, 25,* 598.

Levine, A. G. (1982). *Love Canal: Science, politics and people.* Lexington, MA: Lexington Books, D.C. Heath.

Levine, A., & Stone, R. (1986). Threats to people and what they value. Residents' perceptions of the hazards of Love Canal. In A. H. Lebovits, A. Baum, & J. Singer (Eds.), *Advances in environmental psychology* (Vol. 6, pp. 109–130). Hillsdale, NJ: Erlbaum.

Levine, M. (1982). You-are-here maps: Psychological considerations. *Environment and Behavior, 14,* 221–237.

Levine, M., Marchon, I., & Hanley, G. (1984). The placement and misplacement of you-are-here maps. *Environment and Behavior, 16,* 139–157.

Levine, R. (1988, November). City stress index: 25 best, 25 worst. *Psychology Today, 22,* 53–58.

Levine, R. V., Lynch, K., Miyake, K., & Lucia, M. (1988). *The Type A city: Coronary heart disease and the pace of life.* Unpublished manuscript, California State University: Fresno.

Levine, R. V., Miyake, K., & Lee, M. (1988). *Places rated revisited: Psycho-social pathology in metropolitan areas.* Unpublished manuscript, California State University, Fresno.

Levitt, L., & Leventhal, G. (1984, August). *Litter reduction: How effective is the New York State bottle bill?* Paper presented at the meeting of the American Psychological Association, Toronto, Canada.

Levy, L., & Herzog, A. N. (1974). Effects of population density and crowding on health and social adaptation in the Netherlands. *Journal of Health and Social Behavior, 15,* 228–240.

Lewin, K. (1951). Formalization and progress in psychology. In D. Cartwright (Ed.), *Field theory in social science.* New York: Harper.

Lewis, C. A. (1973). People–plant interaction: A new horticultural perspective. *American Horticulturist, 52,* 18–25.

Lewis, D. A. & Maxfield, M. G. (1980). Fear in the neighborhoods: An investigation of the impact of crime. *Journal of Research in Crime and Delinquency, 17,* 160–169.

Lewis, J., Baddeley, A. D., Bonham, K. G., & Lovett, D. (1970). Traffic pollution and mental efficiency. *Nature, 225,* 95–97.

Ley, D., & Cybriwsky, R. (1974a). The spatial ecology of stripped cars. *Environment and Behavior, 6,* 53–68.

Ley, D., & Cybriwsky, R. (1974b). Urban graffiti as territorial markers. *Annals of the Association of American Geographers, 64,* 491–505.

Lieber, A. L., & Sherin, C. R. (1972). Homicides and the lunar cycle: Toward a theory of lunar influence on human emotional disturbance. *American Journal of Psychiatry, 129,* 101–106.

Lifton, R. J., & Olson, E. (1976). The human meaning of total disaster. The Buffalo Creek experience. *Psychiatry, 39,* 1–18.

Lindberg, E., & Gärling, T. (1983). Acquisition of different types of locational information in cognitive maps: Automatic or effortful processing? *Psychological Research, 45,* 19–38.

Lindsay, J. J., & Ogle, R. A. (1972). Socioeconomic patterns of outdoor recreation use near urban areas. *Journal of Leisure Research, 4,* 19–24.

Lingwood, D. A. (1971). Environmental education through information-seeking: The case of an environmental teach-in. *Environment and Behavior, 3,* 220–262.

Link, J. M., & Pepler, R. D. (1970). Associated fluctuations in daily temperature, productivity and absenteeism. *ASHRAE Transactions, 76* (Pt. 2), 326–337.

Lipetz, B. (1970). *User requirements in identifying desired works in a large library.* New Haven: Yale University Library.

Lipman, A. (1967). Chairs as territory. *New Society, 20,* 564–566.

Lipman, A., & Slater, R. (1979). Homes for old people: Toward a positive environment. In D. Canter & S. Canter (Eds.), *Designing for therapeutic environments: A review of research* (pp. 277–308). Chichester, England: Wiley.

Lippert, S. (1971). Travel in nursing units. *Human Factors, 13,* 269–282.

Lipsey, M. W. (1977). Attitudes toward the environment and pollution. In S. Oskamp (Ed.), *Attitudes and opinions.* Englewood Cliffs, NJ: Prentice-Hall.

Lipton, S. G. (1977). Evidence of central city revival. *American Planning Association Journal, 45,* 136–147.

Little, K. B. (1965). Personal space. *Journal of Experimental Social Psychology, 1,* 237–247.

Little, K. B. (1968). Cultural variations in social schemata. *Journal of Personality and Social Psychology, 10,* 1–7.

Litton, R. B., Jr. (1972). Aesthetic dimensions on the landscape. In J. Z. Krutilla (Ed.), *Natural environments: Studies in theoretical and applied analysis* (pp. 262–291). Baltimore: Johns Hopkins University Press.

Lloyd, A. J., & Shurley, J. T. (1976). The effects of sensory perceptual isolation on single motor unit conditioning. *Psychophysiology, 13,* 340–361.

Lloyd, R., & Steinke, T. (1986). The identification of regional boundaries in cognitive maps. *Professional Geographer, 38,* 149–159.

Lockhard, J. S., McVittie, R. I., & Isaac, L. M. (1977). Functional significance of the affiliative smile. *Bulletin of the Psychonomic Society, 9,* 367–370.

Lofland, J. (1973). *Analyzing social settings.* New York: Belmont Books.

Loftus, G. R. (1985). Say it ain't Pittsburgh. *Psychology Today.*

Logan, J., & Berger, E. (1961). Measurement of visual information cues. *Illuminating Engineering, 56,* 393–403.

Logue, J. N., Hansen, F., & Struening, E. (1979). Emotional and physical distress following Hurricane Agnes in the Wyoming Valley of Pennsylvania. *Public Health Reports, 94,* 495–502.

Lomranz, J., Shapira, A., Choresh, N., & Gilat, Y. (1975). Children's personal space as a function of age and sex. *Developmental Psychology, 11,* 541–545.

London, B., Lee, B., & Lipton, S. G. (1986). The determinants of gentrification in the United States: A city level analysis. *Urban Affairs Quarterly, 21,* 369–387.

Long, G. T., Selby, J. W., & Calhoun, L. G. (1980). Effects of situational stress and sex on interpersonal distance preference. *Journal of Psychology, 105,* 231–237.

Loo, C. (1972). The effects of spatial density on the social behavior of children. *Journal of Applied Social Psychology, 4,* 372–381.

Loo, C. (1973). Important issues in researching the effects of crowding on humans. *Representative Research in Social Psychology, 4,* 219–226.

Loo, C. (1978). Density, crowding, and preschool children. In A. Baum & Y. Epstein (Eds.), *Human response to crowding.* Hillsdale, NJ: Erlbaum.

Loo, C. M., & Ong, P. (1984). Crowding perceptions, attitudes, and consequences of crowding among the Chinese. *Environment and Behavior, 16,* 55–67.

Loo, C., & Kennelly, D. (1979). Social density: Its effects on behaviors and perceptions of preschoolers. *Environmental Psychology and Nonverbal Behavior, 3,* 131–146.

Loo, C., & Smetana, J. (1978). The effects of crowding on the behavior and perception of 10-year-old boys. *Environmental Psychology and Nonverbal Behavior, 2,* 226–249.

Loomis, R. J. (1987). *Museum visitor evaluation: New tool for management.* Nashville, TN: American Association for State and Local History.

Lorenz, K. (1966). *On aggression.* New York: Harcourt Brace Jovanovich.

Lott, B. S., & Sommer, R. (1967). Seating arrangements and status. *Journal of Personality and Social Psychology, 7,* 90–95.

Love, K. D., & Aiello, J. R. (1980). Using projective techniques to measure interaction distance: A methodological note. *Personality and Social Psychology Bulletin, 6,* 102–104.

Lovelock, J. (1988). *The ages of Gaia.* New York: W.W. Norton.

Lozar, G. C. (1974). Methods and measures. In D. Carson, (Ed.), *Man–environment interactions: Evaluations and applications* (Part 2). Stroudsburg, PA.: Dowden, Hutchinson & Ross.

Lublin, J. S. (1985, June 20). The suburban life: Trees, grass plus noise, traffic and pollution. *The Wall Street Journal,* p. 29.

Lucas, R. C. (1964). *The recreational capacity of the Quetico–Superior area* (Research Paper No. LS-15). St. Paul, MN: U.S. Department of Agriculture, Lake States Forest Experiment Station.

Lukas, J. S. (1975). Noise and sleep: A literature review and a proposed criterion for assessing effect. *Journal of the Acoustical Society of America, 58b,* 1232–1242.

Lundberg, U. (1976). Urban commuting: Crowdedness and catecholamine excretion. *Journal of Human Stress, 2,* 26–32.

Luquette, A. J., Landiss, C. W., & Merki, D. J. (1970). Some immediate effects of a smoking environment on children of elementary school age. *Journal of School Health, 40,* 533–536.

Luxenberg, S. (1977, July 17). Crime pays: A prison boom. *The New York Times,* pp. 1–5.

Luyben, P. D. (1980). Effects of informational prompts on energy conservation in college classrooms. *Journal of Applied Behavior Analysis, 13,* 611–617.

Luyben, P. D., & Bailey, J. S. (1975, March). *Newspaper recycling behaviors: The effects of reinforcement versus proximity of containers.* Paper presented at the meeting of the Midwestern Association for Behavior Analysis, Chicago.

Lynch, K. (1960). *The image of the city.* Cambridge, MA: The M.I.T. Press.

Lyons, E. (1983). Demographic correlates of landscape preference. *Environment and Behavior, 15,* 487–511.

McBride, G., King, M. G., & James, J. W. (1965). Social proximity effects on galvanic skin responses in human adults. *Journal of Psychology, 61,* 153–157.

McCain, G., Cox, V. C., & Paulus, P. B. (1976). The relationship between illness complaints and degree of crowding in a prison environment. *Environment and Behavior, 8,* 283–290.

McCallum, R., Rusbult, C., Hong, G., Walden, T., & Schopler, J. (1979). Effect of resource availability and importance of behavior on the experience of crowding. *Journal of Personality and Social Psychology, 37,* 1304–1313.

McCarthy, D. P., & Saegert, S. (1979). Residential density, social overload, and social withdrawal. In J. R. Aiello & A. Baum (Eds.), *Residential crowding and design.* New York: Plenum.

McCauley, C., & Taylor, J. (1976). Is there overload of acquaintances in the city? *Environmental Psychology and Nonverbal Behavior, 1,* 41–55.

McCauley, C., Coleman, G., & DeFusco, P. (1977).

Commuters' eye contact with strangers in city and suburban train stations: Evidence of short-term adaptation to interpersonal overload in the city. *Environmental Psychology and Nonverbal Behavior, 2,* 215–225.

McCaull, J. (1977). Discriminatory air pollution. If poor, don't breathe. *Environment, 18,* 26–31.

McChesney, K. Y. (1986). New findings on homeless families. *Family Professional, 1*(2).

McClelland, L. A. (1974). *Crowding and social stress.* Unpublished doctoral dissertation, University of Michigan.

Maccoby, E. (Ed.) (1966). *The development of sex differences.* Stanford, CA: Stanford University Press.

Maccoby, E., & Jacklin, C. (1974). *The psychology of sex.* Stanford, CA: Stanford University Press.

MacDougall, James M. et al. (1983, September). Selective cardiovascular effects of stress and cigarette smoking. *Journal of Human Stress, 9,* 13–21.

McElroy, J. C., Morrow, P. C., & Wall, L. C. (1983). Generalizing impact of object language to other audiences: Peer response to office design. *Psychological Reports, 53,* 315–322.

McFarland, R. A. (1972). Psychophysiological implications of life at high altitude and including the role of oxygen in the process of aging. In M. K. Yousef, S. M. Horvath, & R. W. Bullard (Eds.), *Physiological adaptations: Desert and mountain* (pp. 157–181). New York: Academic Press.

McGrath, J. E. (1970). *Social and psychological factors in stress.* New York: Holt, Rinehart and Winston.

McGuiness, D., & Sparks, J. (1979). Cognitive style and cognitive maps: Sex differences in representations of familiar terrain. *Journal of Mental Imagery, 7,* 101–118.

McGuire, W. J. (1985). Attitudes and attitude change. In: G. Lindsey & E. Aronson, *The handbook of social psychology* (pp. 223–346). New York: Random House.

McGuire, W. J., & Gaes, G. G. (1982). *The effects of crowding versus age composition in aggregated prison assault rates.* Unpublished manuscript, Office of Research, Federal Prison System, Washington, DC.

Mack, R. (1954). Ecological patterns in an industrial shop. *Social Forces, 32,* 118–138.

McKechnie, G. E. (1977). Simulation techniques in environmental psychology. In D. Stokols (Ed.), *Perspectives on environment and behavior.* New York: Plenum.

MacKenzie, S. T. (1975). *Noise and office work: Employee and employer concerns.* Ithaca: New York State School of Industrial and Labor Relations, Cornell University.

McLean, E. K., & Tarnopolsky, A. (1977). Noise, distress, and mental health. *Psychological Medicine, 7,* 19–62.

McMillan, R. (1974). *Analysis of multiple events in a ghetto household.* Doctoral dissertation, Columbia University Teachers College.

McNamara, T. P. (1986). Mental representations of spatial relations. *Cognitive psychology, 18,* 87–121.

Mandal, M. K. & Maitra, S. (1985). Perception of facial affect and physical proximity. *Perceptual and Motor Skills, 60,* 782.

Mandel, D. R., Baron, R. M., & Fisher, J. D. (1980). Room utilization and dimensions of density. *Environment and Behavior, 12,* 308–319.

Mann, P. H. (1964). *An approach to urban sociology.* London: Routledge & Kegan Paul, 1964.

Mannell, R. C. (1980). Social psychological techniques and strategies for studying the leisure experience. In S. E. Iso-Ahola (Ed.), *Social psychological perspectives on leisure and recreation.* Springfield, IL: Thomas.

Mannell, R. C., & Bradley, W. (1986). Does greater freedom always lead to greater leisure? Testing a person X environment model of freedom and leisure. *Journal of Leisure Research, 18,* 215–230.

Manning, R. E. (1985). Crowding norms in backcountry settings: A review and synthesis. *Journal of Leisure Research, 17,* 75–89.

Marans, R. W. (1972). Outdoor recreation behavior in residential environments. In J. F. Wohlwill & D. H. Carson, (Eds.), *Environment and the social sciences: Perspectives and applications.* Washington, DC: The American Psychological Association.

Marans, R. W., & Rodgers, W. (1975). Toward an understanding of community satisfaction. In A. Hawley & V. Rock (Eds.), *Metropolitan America in contemporary perspective.* New York: Halsted Press.

Marans, R. W., & Spreckelmeyer, K. F. (1981). *Evaluating built environments.* Ann Arbor: Institute for Social research, The University of Michigan.

Marans, R. W., & Spreckelmeyer, K. F. (1982). Evaluating open and conventional office design. *Environment and Behavior, 14,* 333–351.

Marine, G. (1966). I've got nothing against the colored, understand. *Ramparts, 5,* 13–18.

Markham, S. (1947). *Climate and the energy of nations.* New York: Oxford.

Markowitz, J. S., & Gutterman, E. M. (1986). Predictors of psychological distress in the community following two toxic chemical incidents. In A. H. Lebovits, A. Baum, & J. E. Singer (Eds.) *Advances in environmental psychology,* (vol. 6, pp. 89–107). Hillsdale, NJ: Erlbaum.

Marsden, H. M. (1972). Crowding and animal behavior. In J. F. Wohlwill & D. H. Carson (Eds.), *Environment and the social sciences: Perspectives and applications.* Washington, DC: American Psychological Association.

Marshall, E. (1985). Space junk grows with weapons tests. *Science, 230,* 424–425.

Marshall, M. (1972). Privacy and environment. *Human Ecology, 1,* 93–110.

Martin, R. A., Kuiper, N. A., Olinger, L. J., & Dobbin, J.

(1987). Is stress always bad? Telic versus paratelic dominance as a stress-moderating variable. *Journal of Personality and Social Psychology, 53,* 970–982.

Martin, R. A., & Lefcourt, H. M. (1983). The sense of humor as a moderator of the relationship between stressors and moods. *Journal of Personality and Social Psychology, 45,* 1313–1324.

Martindale, D. A. (1971). Territorial dominance behavior in dyadic verbal interactions. *Proceedings of the Annual Convention of the American Psychological Association, 6,* 305–306.

Marwell, G., & Ames, R. E. (1979). Experiments on the provisions of public goods. *American Journal of Sociology, 84,* 1335–1360.

Maslow, A. H., & Mintz, N. C. (1956). Effects of esthetic surrounding: I. Initial effects of three esthetic conditions upon perceiving "energy" and "well-being" in faces. *Journal of Psychology, 41,* 247–254.

Mathews, K. E., & Canon, L. K. (1975). Environmental noise level as a determinant of helping behavior. *Journal of Personality and Social Psychology, 32,* 571–577.

Mathews, K. E., Canon, L. K., & Alexander, K. (1974). The influence of level of empathy and ambient noise on the body buffer zone. *Proceedings of the American Psychological Association Division of Personality and Social Psychology, 1,* 367–370.

Matus, V. (1988). *Design for northern climates: Cold-climate planning and environmental design.* New York: Van Nostrand Reinhold.

Maurer, R. & Baxter, J. (1972). Images of neighborhood among black, Anglo, and Mexican-American children. *Environment and Behavior, 4,* 351–388.

Mawby, R. I. (1977). Defensible space: A theoretical and empirical appraisal. *Urban Studies, 14,* 169–179.

Maxfield, M. G. (1984). The limits of vulnerability in explaining fear of crime: A comparative neighborhood analysis. *Research in Crime and Delinquency, 21,* 233–249.

Medalia, N. Z. (1964). Air pollution as a socio-environmental health problem: A survey report. *Journal of Health and Human Behavior, 5,* 154–165.

Meer, J. (1986, May). The strife of the bath. *Psychology Today, 20*(5), 6.

Mehrabian, A. (1968). Relationships of attitude to seated posture, orientation, and distance. *Journal of Personality and Social Psychology, 10,* 26–30.

Mehrabian, A. (1976). *Public places and private spaces.* New York: Basic Books.

Mehrabian, A. (1976–77). A questionnaire measure of individual differences in stimulus screening and associated differences in arousability. *Environmental Psychology and Nonverbal Behavior, 1,* 89–103.

Mehrabian, A., & Diamond, S. G. (1971a). Effects of furniture arrangement, props, and personality on social interaction. *Journal of Personality and Social Psychology, 20,* 18–30.

Mehrabian, A., & Diamond, S. G. (1971b). Seating arrangement and conversation. *Sociometry, 34,* 281–289.

Mehrabian, A., & Russell, J. A. (1974). *An approach to environmental psychology.* Cambridge, MA: M.I.T. Press.

Meisels, M., & Dosey, M. A. (1971). Personal space, anger arousal, and psychological defense. *Journal of Personality, 39,* 333–334.

Meisels, M., & Guardo, C. J. (1969). Development of personal space schemata. *Child Development, 49,* 1167–1178.

Melton, A. W. (1933). Studies of installation at the Pennsylvania Museum of Art. *Museum News, 10,* 5–8.

Melton, A. W. (1936). Distribution of attention in galleries in a museum of science and industry. *Museum News, 14,* 5–8.

Melton, A. W. (1972). Visitor behavior in museums: Some early research in environmental design. *Human Factors, 14,* 393–403.

Mendelsohn, R., & Orcutt, G. (1979). An empirical analysis of air pollution dose-response curves. *Journal of Environmental Economics and Management, 6,* 85–106.

Menninger, W. C. (1952). Psychological reactions in an emergency (flood). *American Journal of Psychiatry, 109,* 128–130.

Mercer, G. W., & Benjamin, M. L. (1980). Spatial behavior of university undergraduates in double-occupancy residence rooms: An inventory of effects. *Journal of Applied Social Psychology, 10,* 32–44.

Mercer, S., & Kane, R. A. (1979). Helplessness and hopelessness among the institutionalized aged: An experiment. *Health and Social Work, 4,* 90–116.

Merrill, A., & Baird, J. C. (1979). Studies of the cognitive representation of spatial relations: III. Hypothetical environment. *Journal of Experimental Psychology: General, 108,* 99–106.

Merry, S. E. (1981) Defensible space undefended: Social factors in crime control through environmental design. *Urban Affairs Quarterly, 16,* 397–422.

Merry, S. E. (1987). Crowding, conflict, and neighborhood regulation. In I. Altman & A. Wandersman (Eds.), *Neighborhood and community environments* (pp. 35–68). New York: Plenum.

Messick, D. M., Wilke, H., Brewer, M. B., Kramer, R. M., Zemke, P. E., & Lui, L. (1983). Individual adaptations and structural change as solutions to social dilemmas. *Journal of Personality and Social Psychology, 44,* 294–309.

Meyers, A. W., Artz, L. M., & Craighead, W. E. (1976). The effects of instructions, incentives and feedback on a community problem: Dormitory noise. *Journal of Applied Behavior Analysis, 9,* 445–457.

Michelini, R. L., Passalacqua, R., & Cusimano, J. (1976). Effects of seating arrangement on group participation. *Journal of Social Psychology, 99,* 179–186.

Michelson, W. (1968). Most people don't want what architects want. *Trans-Action, 5,* 37–43.

Michelson, W. (1970). *Man and his urban environment: A sociological approach.* Reading, MA: Addison-Wesley.

Michelson, W. (1977a). *Environmental choice, human behavior, and residential satisfaction.* New York: Oxford University Press.

Michelson, W. (1977b). From congruence to antecedent conditions: A search for the basis of environmental improvement. In D. Stokols (Ed.), *Perspective in environment and behavior: Theory, research, and applications.* New York: Plenum.

Middlemist, R. D., Knowles, E. S., & Matter, C. F. (1976). Personal space invasions in the lavatory: Suggestive evidence for arousal. *Journal of Personality and Social Psychology, 33,* 541–546.

Miles, S. (1967). The medical hazards of diving. In C. N. Davies, P. R. Davis, & F. H. Tyrer (Eds.), *The effects of abnormal physical conditions at work* (pp. 111–120). London: E & S Livingstone.

Milgram, S. (1970). The experience of living in cities. *Science, 167,* 1461–1468.

Milgram, S. (1977). *The individual in a social world.* Reading, MA: Addison-Wesley.

Milgram, S., & Jodelet, D. (1976). Psychological maps of Paris. In H. R. Proshansky, W. Ittelson, & L. Rivlin (Eds.), *Environmental psychology: people and their physical settings.* New York: Holt, Rinehart, and Winston.

Miller, I. W., III, & Norman, W. H. (1979). Learned helplessness in humans: A review and attribution theory model. *Psychological Bulletin, 86,* 93–118.

Miller, J. D. (1974). Effects of noise on people. *Journal of the Acoustical Society of America. 56,* 729–764.

Miller, J. F. (1978). *The effects of four proxemic zones on the performance of selected sixth-, seventh-, and eighth-grade students.* Doctoral dissertation, East Tennessee State University.

Miller, M. (1982). Cited in J. Raloff, Occupational noise—the subtle pollutant. *Science News, 121,* 347–350.

Miller, M., Albert, M., Bostick, D., & Geller, E. S. (1976). *Can the design of a trash can influence litter-related behavior?* Paper presented at Southeastern Psychological Association meeting. New Orleans.

Miller, S., & Nardini, R. M. (1977). Individual differences in the perception of crowding. *Environmental Psychology and Nonverbal Behavior, 2,* 3–13.

Miller, S., Rossbach, J., & Munson, R. (1981). Social density and affiliative tendency as determinants of dormitory residential outcomes. *Journal of Applied Social Psychology, 11,* 356–365.

Mills, C. (1934). *Living with the weather.* Cincinnati: Caxton Press.

Milne, G. (1977). Cyclone Tracey: 1. Some consequences of the evacuation for adult victims. *Australian Psychologist, 12,* 39–54.

Minckley, B. (1968). A study of noise and its relationship to patient discomfort in the recovery room. *Nursing Research, 17,* 247–250.

Miransky, J., & Langer, E. J. (1978). Burglary (non)prevention: An instance of relinquishing control. *Personality and Social Psychology Bulletin, 4,* 399–405.

Mitchell, H. (1974). Professional and client: An emerging collaborative relationship. In J. Lang (Ed.), *Designing for human behavior: Architecture and the behavioral sciences* (pp. 15–22). Stroudsburg, PA: Dowden, Hutchinson, & Ross.

Moeser, S. D. (1988). Cognitive Mapping in a complex building. *Environment and Behavior, 20,* 3–20.

Montagu, A. (1971). *Touching: The human significance of the skin.* New York: Columbia University Press.

Montano, D., & Adamopoulous, J. (1984). The perception of crowding in interpersonal situations: Affective and behaviorial responses. *Environment and Behavior, 16,* 643–667.

Moore, B. C. (1982). *An introduction to the psychology of hearing* (2nd ed.). New York: Academic Press.

Moore, G. (1987). Environment and behavior research in North America: History, developments, and unresolved issues. In D. Stokols & I. Altman (Eds.), *Handbook of environmental psychology* (Vol. 2, pp. 1359–1410).

Moore, G. T. (1979). Knowing about environmental knowing: The current state of theory and research about environmental cognition. *Environment and Behavior, 11,* 33–70.

Moore, H. E. (1958). Some emotional concomitants of disaster. *Mental Hygiene, 42,* 45–50.

Moore, R. C. (1973). Childhood city. In W. F. E. Preiser (Ed.), *Environmental design research, Vol 2: Symposia and workshops.* Stroudsburg, PA: Dowden, Hutchinson, & Ross.

Moore, S. F., Shaffer, L. S., Pollak, E. L., & Taylor-Lemke, P. (1987). The effects of interpersonal trust and prior common problem experience on commons management. *Journal of Social Psychology, 127,* 19–29.

Moos, R. H. (1975). Assessment and impact of social climates. In P. McReynolds (Ed.), *Advances in psychological assessment* (Vol. 3). San Francisco, CA: Jossey-Bass.

Moos, R. H. (1976). *The human context: Environmental determinants of behavior.* New York: Wiley.

Moos, R. H. (1980). *The environmental quality of residen-*

tial care settings. Paper presented at the annual conference of the Environmental Design Research Association, Charleston, SC.

Moos, R. H., & Gerst, M. S. (1974). *University Residence Environment Scale*. Palo Alto, CA: Consulting Psychologists Press.

Moos, W. S. (1964). The effects of ''Foehn'' weather on accident rates in the city of Zurich (Switzerland). *Aerospace Medicine, 35*, 643–645.

Morasch, B., Groner, N., & Keating, J. (1979). Type of activity and failure as mediators of perceived crowding. *Personality and Social Psychology Bulletin, 5*, 223–226.

Moreland, R. L., & Zajonc, R. B. (1982). Exposure effects in person perception: Familiarity, similarity, and attraction. *Journal of Experimental Social Psychology, 18*, 395–415.

Morris, E. W. (1987). Comment on ''Castles in the Sky.'' *Environment and Behavior, 19*, 115–119.

Morrow, P. C., & McElroy, J. C. (1981). Interior office design and visitor response. *Journal of Applied Psychology, 66*, 646–630.

Moser, G., & Levy-Leboyer, C. (1985). Inadequate environment and situation control: Is a malfunctioning phone always an occasion for aggression? *Environment and Behavior, 17*, 520–533.

Muecher, H., & Ungeheuer, H. (1961). Meteorological influences on reaction time, flicker fusion frequency, job accidents, and use of medical treatment. *Perceptual and Motor Skills, 12*, 163–168.

Mullins, P., & Robb, J. (1977). Residents assessment of a New Zealand public-housing scheme. *Environment and Behavior, 9*, 573–625.

Munrowe, R. L., & Munrowe, R. H. (1972). Population density and affective relationships in three East African societies. *Journal of Social Psychology, 88*, 15–20.

Murphy-Berman, V., & Berman, J. (1978). Importance of choice and sex invasions of personal space. *Personality and Social Psychology Bulletin, 4*, 424–428.

Myers, K., Hale, C. S., Mykytowycs, R., & Hughes, R. L. (1971). Density, space, sociality and health. In A. H. Esser (Ed.), *Behavior and environment*. New York: Plenum.

Myers, P. (1978). Neighborhood conservation and the elderly. Washington, DC: Conservation Foundation.

Nahemow, L., & Lawton, M. P. (1973). Toward an ecological theory of adaptation and aging. In W. F. E. Preisser (Ed.), *Environmental design research* (Vol. 1, pp. 24–32). Stroudsberg, PA: Dowden, Hutchinson, & Ross.

Nahemow, L., & Lawton, M. P. (1975). Similarity and propinquity in friendship formation. *Journal of Personality and Social Psychology, 32*, 205–213.

Nakshian, J. S. (1964). The effects of red and green surroundings on behavior. *Journal of General Psychology, 70*, 143–161.

Nasar, J. L., & Min, M. S. (1984). *Modifiers of perceived spaciousness and crowding: A cross cultural study*. Paper presented at the annual meeting of the American Psychological Association. Toronto: Canada.

Nash, R. (1982). *Wilderness and the American mind* (3rd. ed.). New Haven, CT: Yale University Press.

National Academy of Sciences. (1977). *Medical and biological effects of environmental pollutants*. Washington, DC: National Academy of Sciences.

National Academy of Sciences. (1981). *The effect on human health from long-term exposure to noise* (Report of Working Group 81). Washington, DC: National Academy Press.

National Opinion Research Center. (1987, July). *General Social Survey*.

Neal, A. (1969). *Help! For the small museum*. Boulder, CO: Pruett Press.

Neisser, U. (1976). *Cognitive psychology*. New York: Appleton-Century-Crofts

Nelson, P. D. (1976, September). Psychologists in habitability research. Paper presented at the meeting of the American Psychological Association: Washington, DC.

Nemecek, J., & Grandjean, E. (1973). Results of an ergometric investigation of large space offices. *Human Factors, 15*, 111–124.

Nero, A. V., Schwehr, M. B., Nazaroff, W. W., & Revzan, K. L. (1986). Distribution of airborne radon-222 concentrations in U.S. homes. *Science, 234*, 992–997.

Neulinger, J. (1981). *To leisure: An introduction*. Boston: Allyn & Bacon.

Newhall, S. M. (1941). Warmth and coolness of colors. *The Psychological Record, 4*, 198–212.

Newman, C. J. (1976). Children of disaster. Clinical observations at Buffalo Creek. *American Journal of Psychiatry, 133*, 306–309.

Newman, J., & McCauley, C. (1977). Eye contact with strangers in city, suburb, and small town. *Environment and Behavior, 9*, 547–558.

Newman, O. (1972). *Defensible space*. New York: Macmillan.

Newman, O. (1975). Reactions to the defensible space study and some further findings. *International Journal of Mental Health, 4*, 48–70.

Newman, O. & Franck, K. (1981a). The effects of building size on personal crime and fear of crime. Presented at the 76th annual meeting of the American Sociological Association, Toronto, Ontario, Canada.

Newman, O., & Franck, K. (1981b). *Factors influencing crime and instability in urban housing developments. Draft Executive Summary*. New York: Institute for Community Analysis.

Newman, O. & Franck, K. (1982). The effects of building size on personal crime and fear of crime. *Population and Environment, 5,* 203–220.

Ng, L. K. Y., Marsden, H. M., Colburn, R. W., & Thoa, N. B. (1973). Population density and social pathology in mice. Differences in catecholamine metabolism associated with differences in behavior. *Brain Research, 59,* 323–330.

Nicholson, M. (1970). *The environmental revolution.* London: Hodder & Stoughton.

Nicosia, G. J., Hyman, D., Karlin, R. A., Epstein, Y. M., & Aiello, J. R. (1979). Effects of bodily contact on reactions to crowding. *Journal of Applied Social Psychology, 9,* 508–523.

Noble, A., & Dixon, R. (1977). *Ward evaluation: St. Thomas Hospital.* London: Medical Architecture Research Unit, The Polytechnic of North London.

Norman, D. A. (1988). *The psychology of everyday things.* New York: Basic Books.

Normoyle, J. B., & Foley, J. M. (1988). The defensible space model of fear and elderly public housing residents. *Environment and Behavior, 20,* 50–74.

Normoyle, J., & Lavrakas, P. J. (1984). Fear of crime in elderly women: Perceptions of control, predictability, and territoriality. *Personality and Social Psychology Bulletin, 10,* 191–202.

Novaco, R. W., Stokols, D., Campbell, J., & Stokols, J. (1979). Transportation stress and community psychology. *American Journal of Community Psychology, 4,* 361–380.

O'Donnel, R., Mikulka, P., Heinig, P., & Theodore, J. (1971). Low level carbon monoxide exposure and human psychomotor performance. *Journal of Applied Toxicology and Pharmacology, 18,* 593–602.

O'Donnell, C. R., & Lydgate, T. (1980). The relationship of crimes to physical resources. *Environment and Behavior, 12,* 207–230.

O'Hare, M. (1974). The public's use of art: Visitor behavior in an art museum. *Curator, 17,* 309–320.

Ohta, R. J., & Ohta, B. M. (1988). Special units for Alzheimer's Disease patients: A critical look. *The Gerontologist, 28,* 803–808.

Okabe, A., Aoki, K., & Hamamoto, W. (1986). Distance and direction judgment in a large-scale natural environment: Effects of a slope and a winding trail. *Environment and Behavior, 18,* 755–772.

Oldham, G. (1988). Effects of changes in workspace partitions and spatial density on employee reactions: A quasi-experiment. *Journal of Applied Psychology. 73,* 253–258.

Oldham, G. R., & Brass, D. J. (1979). Employee reactions to an open-plan office: A naturally occurring quasi-experiment. *Administrative Science Quarterly, 24,* 267–284.

Olsen, M. E. (1981). Consumers' attitudes toward energy conservation. *Journal of Social Issues,* 1981, *37,* 108–131.

Olsen, R. (1978). *The effect of the hospital environment.* Unpublished doctoral dissertation, City University of New York.

Olszewski, D. A., Rotton, J., & Soler, E. A. (1976, May). *Conversation, conglomerate noise, and behavioral after-effects.* Paper presented at the meeting of the Midwestern Psychological Association, Chicago.

O'Neal, E. C., Brunault, M. A., Carifio, M. S., Troutwine, R., & Epstein, J. (1980). Effects of insult upon personal space preferences. *Journal of Nonverbal Behavior, 5,* 56–62.

O'Neal, E. C., Brunault, M. A., Marquis, J. F., & Carifio, M. (1979). Anger and the body-buffer zone. *Journal of Social Psychology, 108,* 135–136.

O'Neal, E. C., Caldwell, C., & Gallup, G. (1975). *Territorial invasion and aggression in young children.* Unpublished manuscript. Tulane University.

O'Neal, E. C., & McDonald, P. J. (1976). The environmental psychology of aggression. In R. G. Geen & E. C. O'Neal (Eds.), *Perspectives on aggression.* New York: Academic Press.

O'Neill, G. W., Blanck, L. S., & Joyner, M. A. (1980). The use of stimulus control over littering in a natural setting. *Journal of Applied Behavior Analysis, 13,* 379–381.

O'Neill, S. M., & Paluck, B. J. (1973). Altering territoriality through reinforcement. *Proceedings of the 81st Annual Convention of the American Psychological Association,* Montreal, Canada, *8,* 901–902.

O'Riordan, T. (1976). Attitudes, behavior, and environmental policy issues. In I. Altman & J. F. Wohlwill (Eds.), *Human behavior and environment: Advances in theory and research* (Vol. 1). New York: Plenum.

Orleans, P. (1973). Differential cognition on urban residents: Effects of social scale on mapping. In R. M. Downs & D. Stea (Eds.), *Image and environment: Cognitive mapping and spatial behavior* (pp. 115–130). Chicago: Aldine.

Orleans, P. & Schmidt, S. (1972). Mapping the city: Environmental cognition of urban residents. In W. Mitchell (Ed.), *EDRA 3* (pp. 1-4-1–1-4-9). Los Angeles : University of California.

Osborne, J. G., & Powers, R. B. (1980). Controlling the litter problem. In G. L. Martin & J. G. Osborne, (Eds.), *Helping the community: Behavioral applications.* New York: Plenum.

Osmond, H. (1957). Function as the basis of psychiatric ward design. *Mental Hospitals* (Architectural Supplement), *8,* 23–29.

Owens, P. L. (1985). Conflict as a social interaction process in environment and behavior research: The example of leisure and recreation research. *Journal of Environmental Psychology, 5,* 243–259.

Owens, R. D., & Sever, H. L. (1977). *The 3M commute-a-van program (progress report).* St. Paul, MN: 3M Company.

Oxley, D., & Barrera, M., Jr. (1984). Undermanning theory and the workplace: Implications of setting size for job satisfaction and social support. *Environment and Behavior, 16,* 211–234.

Oxley, D., Haggard, L. M., Werner, C. M., & Altman, I. (1986). Transactional qualities of neighborhood social networks: A case study of "Christmas Street." *Environment and Behavior, 18,* 640–677.

Oxman, R., & Carmon, N. (1986). Responsive public housing: An alternative for low-income families. *Environment and Behavior, 18,* 258–284.

Pablant, P., & Baxter, J. C. (1975, July). Environmental correlates of school vandalism. *Journal of the American Institute of Planners,* 270–279.

Page, R. A. (1977). Noise and helping behavior. *Environment and Behavior, 9,* 559–572.

Page, R. A. (1978, May). *Environmental influences on prosocial behavior: The effect of temperature.* Paper presented at the meeting of the Midwestern Psychological Association, Chicago, IL.

Palamarek, D. L., & Rule, B. G. (1979). The effects of temperature and insult on the motivation to retaliate or escape. *Motivation and Emotion, 3,* 83–92.

Pallack, M. S., Cook, D. A., & Sullivan, J. J. (1980). Commitment and energy conservation. In L. Bickman (Ed.), *Applied Social Psychology Annual, 1,* 235–253.

Palmer, J. F., & Zube, E. H. (1976). Numerical and perceptual landscape classification. In E. H. Zube (Ed.), *Studies in landscape perception* (Publication No. R-76-1) (pp. 43–57). Amherst: Institute for Man and Environment, University of Massachusetts.

Palmer, M. H., Lloyd, M. E., & Lloyd, K. D. (1978). An experimental analysis of electricity conservation procedures. *Journal of Applied Behavior Analysis, 10,* 665–672.

Parker, G. (1977). Cyclone Tracy and Darwin evacuees. On the restoration of the species. *British Journal of Psychiatry, 130,* 548–555.

Parkes, C. M. (1972). *Bereavement: Studies of grief in adult life.* New York: International Universities Press.

Parr, A. E. (1966). Psychological aspects of urbanology. *Journal of Social Issues, 22,* 39–45.

Parsons, H. M. (1972). The bedroom. *Human Factors, 14,* 421–450.

Parsons, H. M. (1978). What caused the Hawthorne effect? A scientific detective story. *Administration & Society, 10,* 259–283.

Parsons, P., & Loomis, R. J. (1973). *Patterns of museum visitor exploration: Then and now.* Washington, D.C.: The Smithsonian Institution.

Passini, R. (1984). Spatial representations, a wayfinding perspective. *Journal of Environmental Psychology, 4,* 153–164.

Pastalan, L. (1976). *Report on Pennsylvania nursing home relocation program: Interim research findings.* Ann Arbor: Institute of Gerontology, University of Michigan.

Patterson, A. H. (1977). Methodological developments in environment–behavioral research. In D. Stokols (Ed.), *Perspectives on environment and behavior.* New York: Plenum.

Patterson, M. L. (1974, September). *Factors affecting interpersonal spatial proximity.* Paper presented at the annual meeting of the American Psychological Association, New Orleans, LA.

Patterson, M. L. (1975). Personal space: Time to burst the bubble? *Man–Environment Systems, 5,* 67.

Patterson, M. L. (1976). An arousal model of interpersonal intimacy. *Psychological Review, 83,* 235–245.

Patterson, M. L. (1977). Interpersonal distance, affect, and equilibrium theory. *Journal of Social Psychology, 101,* 205–214.

Patterson, M. L. (1978). Arousal change and the cognitive labeling: Pursuing the mediators of intimacy exchange. *Environmental Psychology and Nonverbal Behavior, 3,* 17–22.

Patterson, M. L. (1982). A sequential functional model of nonverbal exchange. *Psychological Review, 89,* 231–249.

Patterson, M. L., & Holmes, D. S. (1966). Social interaction correlates of MMPI extraversion–introversion scale. *American Psychologist, 21,* 724–725.

Patterson, M. L., & Sechrest, L. B. (1970). Interpersonal distance and impression formation. *Journal of Personality, 38,* 161–166.

Patterson, M. L., Kelly, C. E., Kondracki, B. A., & Wulf, L. J. (1979). Effects of seating arrangement on small-group behavior. *Social Psychology Quarterly, 42,* 180–185.

Patterson, M. L., Mullens, S., & Romano, J. (1971). Compensatory reactions to spatial intrusion. *Sociometry, 34,* 114–121.

Paulhus, D. (1983). Sphere-specific measures of perceived control. *Journal of Personality and Social Psychology, 44,* 1253–1265.

Paulus, P. B. (1977). *Crowding in the laboratory and its relation to social facilitation.* Paper presented at the meeting of the Midwestern Psychological Association, Chicago.

Paulus, P. B. (1980). Crowding. In P. B. Paulus (Ed.), *Psychology of group influence* (pp. 245–290). Hillsdale, NJ: Erlbaum.

Paulus, P. (1988). *Prison crowding: A psychological perspective.* NY: Springer-Verlag.

Paulus, P. B., Annis, A. B., Seta, J. J., Schkode, J. K., & Matthews, R. W. (1976). Crowding does affect task performance. *Journal of Personality and Social Psychology, 34,* 248–253.

Paulus, P., Cox, V., McCain, G., & Chandler, J. (1975). Some effects of crowding in a prison environment. *Journal of Applied Social Psychology, 5,* 86–91.

Paulus, P., & Matthews, R. (1980). Crowding, attribution, and task performance. *Basic and Applied Social Psychology, 1,* 3–13.

Paulus, P., McCain, G., & Cox, V. (1978). Death rates, psychiatric commitments, blood pressure and perceived crowding as a function of institutional crowding. *Environmental Psychology and Nonverbal Behavior, 3,* 107–116.

Paulus, P. B., McCain, G., & Cox, V. (1981). Prison standards: Some pertinent data on crowding. *Federal Probation, 15,* 48–54.

Pawson, I. G., & Jest, C. (1978). The high-altitude areas of the world and their cultures. In P. T. Baker (Ed.), *The biology of high altitude peoples* (pp. 17–45). New York: Cambridge.

Payne, R. J., & Pigram, J. J. (1981). Changing evaluations of floodplain hazard: The Hunter Valley, Australia. *Environment and Behavior, 13,* 461–480.

Pearce, P. L. (1977). Mental souvenirs: A study of tourists and their city maps. *Australian Journal of Psychology, 29,* 203–210.

Pearson, O. P. (1966). The prey of carnivores during one cycle of mouse abundance. *Journal of Animal Ecology, 35,* 217–233.

Pearson, O. P. (1971). Additional measurements of the impact of carnivores on California voles (Microtus Californicus). *Journal of Mammalogy, 52,* 41—49.

Pellegrini, R. J., & Empey, J. (1970). Interpersonal spatial orientation in dyads. *Journal of Psychology, 76,* 67–70.

Pempus, E., Sawaya, C., & Cooper, R. E. (1975). *"Don't fence me in": Personal space depends on architectural enclosure.* Paper presented at the meeting of the American Psychological Association, Chicago.

Penick, E. C., Powell, B. J., & Sieck, W. A. (1976). Mental health problems and natural disaster: Tornado victims. *Journal of Community Psychology, 4,* 64–67.

Pennebaker, J. W., & Newtson, D. (1983). Observation of a unique event: The psychological impact of the Mount Saint Helens volcano. In H. T. Reiss (Ed.), *Naturalistic approaches to studying social interaction. New directions for methodology of social and behavioral science* (No. 15, pp. 93–109). San Francisco: Jossey-Bass.

Penwarden, A. D. (1973). Acceptable wind speeds in towns. *Building Science, 8,* 259–267.

Pepler, R. D. (1963). Performance and well-being in heat. In J. Hardy (Ed.), *Temperature: Its measurement and control in science and industry* (Vol. 3, pp. 319–336). New York: Van Nostrand Reinhold.

Pepler, R. D. (1972). The thermal comfort of students in climate controlled and non-climate controlled schools. *ASHRAE Transactions, 78,* 97–109.

Perry, J. D., & Simpson, M. E. (1987). Violent crimes in a city: Environmental determinants. *Environment and Behavior, 19,* 77–90.

Persinger, M. A., Ludwig, H. W., & Ossenkopf, K. P. (1973). Psychophysiological effects of extremely low frequency electromagnetic fields: A review. *Perceptual and Motor Skills, 26,* 1131–1159.

Peterka, J. A., & Cermak, J. E. (1973). *Wind engineering study of Mountain Bell Denver Service Center* (Tech. Rep. CER73-74JAP-JEC14). Fort Collins, CO: Colorado State University Fluid Mechanics Program.

Peterka, J. A., & Cermak, J. E. (1975). *Wind engineering study of Merchant's Plaza, Indianapolis, IN* (Tech. Rep. CER74-75JAP-JEC47). Fort Collins, CO: Colorado State University Fluid Mechanics Program.

Peterka, J. A., & Cermak, J. E. (1977). *Wind tunnel study of phase I building, Block 141, Denver* (Tech. Rep. CER76-77JAP-JEC36). Fort Collins, CO: Colorado State University Fluid Mechanics Program.

Peterson, C., & Seligman, M. E. P. (1984). Causal explanations as a risk factor for depression: Theory and evidence. *Psychological Review, 91,* 347–374.

Peterson, R. L. (1975). *Air pollution and attendance in recreation behavior settings in the Los Angeles basin.* Paper presented at the American Psychological Association meeting, Chicago.

Petty, R. E. & Cacioppo, J. T. (1981). *Attitudes and persuasion: Classic and contemporary approaches.* Dubuque, IA: Wm. C. Brown.

Pheysey, D. C. & Payne, R. L. (1970). The Hemphill Group Dimensions Descriptive Questionnaire: A British industrial application. *Human Relations, 23,* 473–497.

Piaget, J., & Inhelder, B. (1967). *The child's conception of space.* New York: Norton.

Pile, J. F. (1978). *Open office planning.* New York: Whitney Library of Design.

Pill, R. (1967). Space and social structure in two children's wards. *Sociological Review, 15,* 179–192.

Pirages, D. C., & Ehrlich, P. R. (1974). *Ark II: Social response to environmental imperatives.* San Francisco: Freeman.

Pitelka, F. A. (1957). Some aspects of population structure in the short-term cycle of the brown lemming in northern Alaska. *Cold Spring Harbor Symposia on Quantitative Biology, 22,* 237–251.

Pitt, D. G. (1976). Physical dimensions of scenic quality in streams. In E. H. Zube (Ed.), *Studies in landscape perception.* (Publication No. R-76-1). Amherst: Institute for Man and Environment, University of Massachusetts.

Pitt, D. G., & Zube, E. H. (1979). The Q-sort method: Use in landscape assessment research and in resource planning. In *Proceedings of our national landscape: A* conference on applied techniques for analysis and management of the visual resource. (USDA Forest Service General Technical Report PSW-35.) Berkeley, CA: Pacific Southwest Forest and Range Experiment Station.

Pitt, D., & Zube, E. (1987). Management of natural environments. In D. Stokols & I. Altman (Eds.), *Handbook of environmental psychology* (pp. 1009—1042). New York: John Wiley & Sons.

Platt, J. (1973). Social traps. *American Psychologist, 28,* 641–651.

Ploeger, A. (1972). A 10-year follow-up of miners trapped for 2 weeks under threatening circumstances. In C. D. Spielberger & I. G. Sarason (Eds.), *Stress and anxiety* (Vol. 4). Washington, DC: Hemisphere.

Plotkin, W. B. (1978). Long-term eyes-closed alpha-enhancement training: Effects on alpha amplitudes and on experimental state. *Psychophysiology, 15,* 40–52.

Pokorny, A., Davis, F., & Haberson, W. (1963). Suicide, suicide attempts, and weather. *American Journal of Psychiatry, 120,* 377–381.

Pollack, L. M., & Patterson, A. H. (1980). Territoriality and fear of crime in elderly and nonelderly homeowners. *Journal of Social Psychology, 111,* 119–129.

Pollet, D. (1976, February). You can get there from here. *Wilson Library Bulletin, 50,* 456–462.

Pollett, D., & Haskell, P. C. (1979). *Sign systems for libraries.* New York: Bowker.

Porteous, C. W. (1972). *Learning as a function of molar environmental complexity.* Unpublished master's thesis, University of Victoria, British Columbia.

Porteous, J. D. (1985). Smellscape. *Progress in Human Geography, 9,* 358–378.

Porteus, J. (1977). *Environment and behavior.* Reading, MA: Addison-Wesley.

Poulton, E. C. (1970). *The environment and human efficiency.* Springfield, IL: Thomas.

Poulton, E. C. (1976). Arousing environmental stress can improve performance, whatever people say. *Aviation Space and Environmental Medicine, 47,* 1193–1204.

Poulton, E. C., Hunt, J. C. R., Mumford, J. C., & Poulton, J. (1975). Mechanical disturbance produced by steady and gusty winds of moderate strength: Skilled performance and semantic assessments. *Ergonomics, 18,* 651–673.

Poulton, E. C., & Kerslake, D. McK. (1965). Initial stimulating effect of warmth upon perceptual efficiency. *Aerospace Medicine, 36,* 29–32.

Powers, R. B., Osborne, J. G., & Anderson, E. G. (1973). Positive reinforcement of litter removal in the natural environment. *Journal of Applied Behavior Analysis, 6,* 579—586.

Pratsch, L. (1977, April). *Vanpooling discussion paper.* Washington, DC: Federal Highway Administration, unpublished manuscript.

Preiser, W. F. E. (1972). Application of unobtrusive

observation techniques in building performance appraisal. In B. E. Foster (Ed.), *Performance concept in buildings.* (Special Publication No. 361, Vol. 1). Washington, DC: National Bureau of Standards.

Preiser, W. F. E. (1973). An analysis of unobtrusive observations of pedestrian movement and stationary behavior in a shopping mall. In R. Kuller (Ed.), *Architectural psychology* (pp. 287–300). Stroudsburg, PA: Dowden, Hutchinson & Ross.

Prerost, F. J. (1982). The development of the mood inhibiting effects of crowding during adolescence. *Journal of Psychology, 110,* 197–202.

Prerost, F. J., & Brewer, R. K. (1980). The appreciation of humor by males and females during conditions of crowding experimentally induced. *Psychology, A Journal of Human Behavior, 17,* 15–17.

Price, J. L. (1971). *The effects of crowding on the social behavior of children.* Unpublished doctoral dissertation, Columbia University.

Pritchard, D. (1964). Industrial lighting in windowless factories. *Light and Lighting, 57,* 265.

Proshansky, H. M. (1972). Methodology in environmental psychology: Problems and issues. *Human Factors, 14,* 451–460.

Proshansky, H. M. (1973). Theoretical issues in ''environmental psychology.'' *Representative Research in Social Psychology, 4,* 93–107.

Proshansky, H. M. (1976a, September). *City and self-identity.* Paper presented at the annual meeting of the American Psychological Association, Washington, DC.

Proshansky, H. M. (1976b). Comment on environmental and social psychology. *Personality and Social Psychology Bulletin, 2,* 359–363.

Proshansky, H. M. (1976c). Environmental psychology and the real world. *American Psychologist, 31,* 303–310.

Proshansky, H. M., Ittelson, W. H., & Rivlin, L. G. (Eds.) (1970). *Environmental psychology: Man and his physical setting.* New York: Holt, Rinehart and Winston.

Provins, K. A. (1958). Environmental conditions and driving efficiency: A review. *Ergonomics, 2,* 63–88.

Provins, K. A. (1966). Environmental heat, body temperature, and behavior: An hypothesis. *Australian Journal of Psychology, 18,* 118–129.

Provins, K. A., & Bell, C. R. (1970). Effects of heat stress on the performance of two tasks running concurrently. *Journal of Experimental Psychology, 85,* 40–44.

Provins, K. A., & Clarke, R. S. J. (1960). The effect of cold on manual performance. *Journal of Occupational Medicine, 2,* 169–176.

Pugh, D. S., Hickson, D. J., & Hinings (1969). An empirical taxonomy of work organization structures. *Administrative Science Quarterly, 14,* 115–126.

Purcell, A. T. (1986). Environmental perception and affect: A schema discrepancy model. *Environment and Behavior, 18,* 3–30.

Putz, J., (1979). The affects of carbon monoxide on dual-task performance. *Human Factors, 21,* 13–24.

Pylyshyn, Z. W. (1973). What the mind's eye tells the mind's brain: A critique of mental imagery. *Psychological Bulletin, 80,* 1–24.

Quarantelli, E. L. (Ed.) (1978). *Disasters: Theory and research.* Beverly Hills, CA: Sage.

Quarantelli, E. L. (1985). Realities and mythologies in disaster films. *Communications, 11,* 31–44.

Quarantelli, E. L., & Dynes, R. R. (1972). When disaster strikes. *Psychology Today, 5*(9), 66–70.

Quick, A. D., & Crano, W. D. (1973). *Effects of sex, distance, and conversation in the invasion of personal space.* Paper presented at the Midwestern Psychological Association convention.

Rainwater, L. (1966). Fear and the house as haven in the lower class. *Journal of the American Institute of Planners, 32,* 23–31.

Raloff, J. (1982). Occupational noise—The subtle pollutant. *Science News, 121,* 347–350.

Ramsey, J. (1970). Oxygen reduction and reaction time in hypoxic and normal drivers. *Archives of Environmental Health, 20,* 597–601.

Rangell, L. (1976). Discussion of the Buffalo Creek disaster: The course of psychic trauma. *American Journal of Psychiatry, 133,* 313–316.

Rankin, R. E. (1969). Air pollution control and public apathy. *Journal of the Air Pollution Control Association, 19,* 565–569.

Rankin, R. E., A prescription for world survival, *Time Magazine,* June 13, 1977, pg. 59. (A summary of United Nations State of the Environment report).

Rapoport, A. (1969). *House form and culture.* Englewood Cliffs, NJ: Prentice-Hall.

Rapoport, A. (1975). Toward a redefinition of density. *Environment and Behavior, 7,* 133–158.

Raw, G. J., & Griffiths, I. D. (1985). The effect of changes in aircraft noise exposure (letter to the editor). *Journal of Sound and Vibration, 101,* 273–275.

Rawls, J. R., Trego, R. E., McGaffey, C. N., & Rawls, D. J. (1972). Personal space as a predictor of performance under close working conditions. *Journal of Social Psychology, 86,* 261–267.

Reddy, D. M., Baum, A., Fleming, R., & Aiello, J. R. (1981). Mediation of social density by coalition formation. *Journal of Applied Social Psychology, 11,* 529–537.

Reich, J. W., & Robertson, J. L. (1979). Reactance and normal appeal in antilittering messages. *Journal of Applied Social Psychology, 9,* 91–101.

Reichel, D. A., & Geller, E. S. (1980). *Group versus individual contingencies to conserve transportation energy.* Paper presented at the Southeastern Psychological Association meeting, Washington, DC.

Reichner, R. (1979). Differential responses to being ignored: The effects of architectural design and social density on interpersonal behavior. *Journal of Applied Social Psychology, 9,* 13–26.

Reifman, A. S., Larrick, R., & Fein, S. (1988, August). *The heat–aggression relationship in major-league baseball.* Paper presented at the meeting of the American Psychological Association, Atlanta, GA.

Reisenzein, R. (1983). The Schachter theory of emotion: Two decades later. *Psychological Bulletin, 94,* 239–264.

Reiter, R. (1985). Frequency distribution of positive and negative small ions, based on many years' recordings at two mountain stations located at 740 and 1780 m ASL. *International Journal of Biometeorology, 29,* 223–231.

Reiter, S. M., & Samuel, W. (1980). Littering as a function of prior litter and the presence or absence of prohibitive signs. *Journal of Applied Social Psychology, 10,* 45–55.

Reizenstein, J. E. (1976). *Social research and design: Cambridge hospital social service offices.* Springfield, VA: National Technical Information Service.

Reizenstein, J. E. (1982). Hospital design and human behavior: A review of the recent literature. In A. Baum & J. E. Singer (Eds.), *Advances in environmental psychology* (Vol. 4, pp. 137–170). Hillsdale, NJ: Erlbaum.

Rent, G. S., & Rent, C. S. (1978). Low income housing factors related to residential satisfaction. *Environment and Behavior, 10,* 459–488.

Reppetto, T. A. (1976). Crime prevention through environmental policy. *American Behavioral Scientist, 20,* 275–288.

Reusch, J., & Kees, W. (1956). *Nonverbal communication: Notes on the visual perception of human relations.* Berkeley, CA: University of California Press.

Rhodes, F., & Houser, G. (1986, May). Provider initiatives: Caring is the heart of the matter at ARA. *Provider,* pp. 28–32.

Richards, P. (1979). Middle class vandalism and the age-status conflict. *Social Problems, 26,* 482–497.

Riess, M., Kalle, R. J., & Tedeschi, J. T. (1981). Bogus pipeline attitude assessment, impression management, and misattribution in induced compliance settings. *Journal of Social Psychology, 115,* 247–258.

Rim, Y. (1975). Psychological test performance during climatic heat stress from desert winds. *International Journal of Biometeorology, 19,* 37–40.

Risk, P. H. (1976). *Effects of an experimental wilderness survival experience on self-concept, personality, and values.* Unpublished doctoral dissertation: Michigan State University.

Rivlin, L. G., & Rothenberg, M. (1976). The use of space in open classrooms. In H. M. Proshansky, W. H. Ittelson, & L. G. Rivlin (Eds.), *Environmental psychology: People and their physical settings* (pp. 479–489). New York: Holt, Rinehart and Winston.

Rivlin, L. G., & Wolfe, M. (1972). The early history of a psychiatric hospital for children: Expectations and reality. *Environment and Behavior, 4,* 33–72.

Rivlin, L. G., & Wolfe, M. (1985). *Institutional settings in children's lives.* New York: Wiley-Interscience.

Rivlin, L. G., Wolfe, M., & Beyda, M. (1973). Age-related differences in the use of space. In W. F. E. Preiser (Ed.), *Environmental design research* (Vol. 1, pp. 191–203). Stroudsberg, PA: Dowden, Hutchinson, & Ross.

Roberts, C. (1977). Stressful experiences in urban places: Some implications for design. *EDRA 8 Conference Proceedings.*

Roberts, L. (1988). Is there life after climate change? *Science, 242,* 1010–1012.

Robillard, D. A. (1984). *Public space design in museums* (R84-7). Milwaukee, WI: School of Architecture & Urban Planning, University of Wisconsin at Milwaukee.

Robinson, E. S. (1928). *The behavior of the museum visitor. (No. 5 in Publications of the American Association of Museums New Series.)* Washington, DC: American Association of Museums.

Rodin, J. (1976). Crowding, perceived choice and response to controllable and uncontrollable outcomes. *Journal of Experimental Social Psychology, 12,* 564–578.

Rodin, J. (1986). Aging and health: Effects of the sense of control. *Science, 233,* 1271–1276.

Rodin, J., & Baum, A. (1978). Crowding and helplessness: Potential consequences of density and loss of control. In A. Baum & Y. Epstein (Eds.), *Human response to crowding* (pp. 389–401). Hillsdale, NJ: Erlbaum.

Rodin, J., & Langer, E. J. (1977). Long-term effects of a control-relevant intervention with the institutionalized aged. *Journal of Personality and Social Psychology, 35,* 897–902.

Rodin, J., Solomon, S., & Metcalf, J. (1978). Role of control in mediating perceptions of density. *Journal of Personality and Social Psychology, 36,* 989–999.

Roethlisberger, F. J., & Dickson, W. J. (1939). *Management and the worker.* Cambridge, MA: Harvard University Press.

Roger, D. B., & Schalekamp, E. E. (1976). Body-buffer zone and violence: A cross-cultural study. *Journal of Social Psychology, 98,* 153–158.

Rohe, W. M. (1982). The response to density in residential settings: The mediating effects of social and personal variables. *Journal of Applied Social Psychology, 12,* 292–303.

Rohe, W., & Patterson, A. H. (1974). *The effects of varied levels of resources and density on behavior in a day care center.* Paper presented to Environmental Design Research Association, Milwaukee.

Rohles, F. H. (1974). The modal comfort envelope and its use in current standards. *Human Factors, 16,* 314–322.

Ronco, P. (1972). Human factors applied to hospital patient care. *Human Factors, 14,* 461–470.

Rook, K. S. (1987). Social support versus companionship: Effects of life stress, loneliness, and evaluations by others. *Journal of Personality and Social Psychology, 52,* 1132—1147.

Rose, E. F., & Rose, M. (1971). Carbon monoxide: A challenge to the physician. *Clinical Medicine, 78,* 12–18.

Rose, H. S., & Hinds, D. H. (1976). South Dixie Highway contraflow bus and car pool lane demonstration project. *Transportation Research Record, 606,* 18–22.

Rose, L. (1987). Workplace video display terminals and visual fatigue. *Journal of Occupational Medicine, 29,* 321–324.

Rosen, S. (1979). *Weathering: How the atmosphere conditions your body, your mind, your moods—and your health.* New York: Evans.

Rosen, S., Bergman, M., Plestor, D., El-Mofty, A., & Satti, M. (1962). Presbycosis study of a relatively noise-free population in the Sudan. *Annals of Otology, Rhinology, and Laryngology, 71,* 727–743.

Rosenfeld, H. M. (1965). Effect of an approval-seeking induction on interpersonal proximity. *Psychological Reports, 17,* 120–122.

Rosenfeld, H. M., Breck, R. E., Smith, S. E., & Kehoe, S. (1984). Intimacy-mediators of the proximity-gaze compensation effect: Movement, controversial role, acquaintance, and gender. *Journal of Nonverbal Behavior, 8,* 235–249.

Rosenman, R. H. (1985). Health consequences of anger and implications for treatment. In M. A. Chesney & R. H. Rosenman (Eds.), *Anger and hostility in cardiovascular and behavioral disorders* (pp. 103–125). New York: Hemisphere.

Rosenthal, N. E., Sack, D. A., Gillen, J. C., Lewy, A. J., Goodwin, F. K., Davenport, Y., Mueller, P. S., Newsome, D. A., & Wehr, T. A. (1984). Seasonal affective disorder: A description of the syndrome and preliminary findings with light therapy. *Archives of General Psychiatry, 41,* 72–80.

Rosenzweig, M. R. (1966). Environmental complexity, cerebral change and behavior. *American Psychologist, 21,* 321–322.

Ross, M., Layton, B., Erickson, B., & Schopler, J. (1973). Affect, facial regard, and reactions to crowding. *Journal of Personality and Social Psychology, 28,* 69–76.

Ross, P., Bluestone, H., & Hines, F. (1979). *Indicators of social well-being in U.S. counties.* Washington, DC: U.S. Department of Agriculture.

Ross, R. T. (1938). Studies in the psychology of the theater. *Psychological Record, 2,* 127–190.

Roth, S., & Cohen, L. J. (1986). Approach, avoidance, and coping with stress. *American Psychologist, 41,* 813–819.

Rothbaum, F., Weisz, J. R., & Snyder, S. S. (1982). Changing the world and changing the self: A two-process model of perceived control. *Journal of Personality and Social Psychology, 42,* 5–37.

Rothenberg, M., & Rivlin, L. (1975). *An ecological approach to the study of open classrooms.* Paper presented at a conference on ecological factors in human development, University of Surrey, England.

Rotter, J. (1966). Generalized expectancies for internal vs. external control of reinforcement. *Psychological Monographs, 80* (Whole No. 609).

Rotton, J. (1978). *Air pollution is no choke.* Unpublished manuscript. University of Dayton.

Rotton, J. (1983). Affective and cognitive consequences of malodorous pollution. *Basic and Applied Social Psychology, 4,* 171–191.

Rotton, J. (1985, August). *Pedestrian movement in warm and cool settings: Three quasi-experiments.* Paper presented at the meeting of the American Psychological Association, Los Angeles, CA.

Rotton, J. (1986). Determinism *redux:* Climate and cultural correlates of violence. *Environment and Behavior, 18,* 346–368.

Rotton, J. (1987a). Clearing the air about ions. *Skeptical Inquirer, 11,* 305–306.

Rotton, J. (1987b). Hemmed in and hating it: Effects of shape of room on tolerance for crowding. *Perceptual and Motor Skills, 64,* 285–286.

Rotton, J. (in press). Individuals under stress. In C. E. Kimble (Ed.), Social psychology: Living with people. New York: W. C. Brown.

Rotton, J., Barry, T., Frey, J., & Soler, E. (1978). Air pollution and interpersonal attraction. *Journal of Applied Social Psychology, 8,* 57–71.

Rotton, J., Barry, T., & Kimble, C. A. (1985, August). *Climate and crime: Coping with multicolinearity.* Paper presented at the meeting of the American Psychological Association, Los Angeles, CA.

Rotton, J., & Frey, J. (1985). Air pollution, weather, and violent crimes: Concomitant time-series analysis of archival data. *Journal of Personality and Social Psychology, 49,* 1207–1220.

Rotton, J., Frey, J., Barry, T., Milligan, M., & Fitzpatrick, M. (1979). The air pollution experience and interpersonal aggression. *Journal of Applied Social Psychology, 9,* 397–412.

Rotton, J., & Kelly, I. W. (1985a). A scale for assessing belief in lunar effects: Reliability and concurrent validity. *Psychological Reports, 57,* 239–245.

Rotton, J., & Kelly, I. W. (1985b). Much ado about the full moon: A meta-analysis of lunar-lunacy research. *Psychological Bulletin, 97,* 286–306.

Rotton, J., & Kelly, I. W. (1987). Comment on ''The lunar-lunacy relationship'': More ado about the full moon. *Psychological Reports, 61,* 733–734.

Rotton, J., Kelly, I. W., & Elortegui, P. (1986). Assessing belief in lunar effects: Known-groups validation. *Psychological Reports, 59,* 171–174.

Rotton, J., Oszewski, D., Charleton, M., & Soler, E. (1978). Loud speech, conglomerate noise, and behavior after-effects. *Journal of Applied Psychology, 63,* 360–365.

Rotton, J., Yoshikawa, J., Francis, J., & Hoyler, R. (1978). *Urban atmosphere: Evaluative effects of malodorous air pollution.* Paper presented at the Southeastern Psychological Association meeting, Atlanta, GA.

Rowe, J. W., & Kahn, R. L. (1987). Human aging: Usual and successful. *Science, 237,* 143–149.

Ruback, R. B. & Innes, C. A. (1988). The relevance and irrelevance of psychological research: The example of prison crowding. *American Psychologist, 43,* 683–693.

Ruback, R. B., & Carr, T. S. (1984). Crowding in a women's prison: Attitudinal and behavioral effects. *Journal of Applied Social Psychology, 14,* 57–68.

Ruback, R. B., Carr, T. S., & Hopper, C. H. (1986). Perceived control in prison: Its relation to reported crowding, stress, and symptoms. *Journal of Applied Social Psychology, 16,* 375–386.

Rubin, A. I., & Elder, J. (1980). *Building for people.* Washington, DC: U.S. Government Printing Office Special Publication 474.

Rullo, G. (1987). People and home interiors: A bibliography of recent psychological research. *Environment and Behavior, 19,* 250–259.

Rummo, N., & Sarlanis, K. (1974). The effect of carbon monoxide on several measures of vigilance in a simulated driving task. *Journal of Safety Research, 6,* 126–130.

Rumsey, N., Bull, R., & Gahagan, D. (1982). The effects of facial disfigurement on the proxemic behavior of the general public. *Journal of Applied Social Psychology, 12,* 137–150.

Runnion, A., Watson, J. D., & McWhorter, J. (1978). Energy savings in interstate transportation through feedback and reinforcement. *Journal of Organizational Behavior Management, 1,* 180–191.

Russell, J. A. & Lanius, U. F. (1984). Adaptation level and the affective appraisal of environments. *Journal of Environmental Psychology. 4,* 119–135.

Russell, J. A., & Mehrabian, A. (1978). Environmental task, and temperamental effects on work performance. *Humanitas, 14,* 75–95.

Russell, J. A., & Pratt, G. (1980). A description of the affective quality attributed to environments. *Journal of Personality and Social Psychology, 38,* 311–322.

Russell, J. A., & Snodgrass, J. (1987). Emotion and the environment. In D. Stokols & I. Altman (Eds.), *Handbook of environmental psychology* (Vol. 1, pp. 245–280). New York: Wiley-Interscience.

Russell, J. A., & Ward, L. M. (1982). *Environmental*

psychology. Annual Review of Psychology, 33, 651–688.

Russell, J. A., Ward, L. M., & Pratt, G. (1981). Affective quality attributed to environments: A factor analytic study. *Environment and Behavior, 13,* 259–288.

Russell, M. B., & Bernal, M. E. (1977). Temporal and climatic variables in naturalistic observation. *Journal of Applied Behavior Analysis, 10,* 399–405.

Russell, M., Cole, P., & Brown, E. (1973). Absorption by non-smokers of carbon monoxide from room air polluted by tobacco smoke. *Lancet, 1,* 576–579.

Ruys, T. (1970). Windowless offices. *Man–Environment Systems, 1,* 49.

Saal, F. E., & Knight, P. A. (1988). *Industrial/organizational psychology: Science and practice.* Pacific Grove, CA: Brooks/Cole.

Saarinen, T. F. (1969). *Perception of environment* (Resource Paper No. 5). Washington, DC: Association of American Geographers, Commission on College Geography.

Sabatino, D. A., Meald, J. E., Rothman, S. G., & Miller, T. L. (1978). Destructive norm-violating social behavior among adolescents. A review of protective efforts. *Adolescence, 13,* 675–680.

Sadalla, E. K., Burroughs, J., & Quaid, M. (1980). House form and social identity. In R. Stough (Ed.), *Proceedings of the 11th International Meeting of the Environmental Design Research Association, 11,* 201–206.

Sadalla, E. K., & Magel, S. G. (1980). The perception of traversed distance. *Environment and Behavior, 12,* 65–79.

Sadalla, E. K., & Staplin, L. J. (1980a). An information storage model for distance cognition. *Environment and behavior, 12,* 183–193.

Sadalla, E. K., & Staplin, L. J. (1980b). The perception of traversed distance: Interactions. *Environment and Behavior, 12,* 167–182.

Siegel, A. W., & White, S. (1975). The development of spatial representations of large-scale environments. In H. W. Reese (Ed.), *Advances in child development and behavior* (pp. 9–55). New York: Academic Press.

Saegert, S. (1974). *Effects of spatial and social density on arousal, mood, and social orientation.* Unpublished doctoral dissertation, University of Michigan.

Saegert, S. (1982). Environment and children's mental health: Residential density and low income children. In A. Baum & J. E. Singer (Eds.), *Handbook of psychology and health* (Vol. 2). Hillsdale, NJ: Erlbaum.

Saegert, S., MacIntosh, E., & West, S. (1975). Two studies of crowding in urban public spaces. *Environment and Behavior, 1,* 159–184.

Saegert, S., Swap, W., & Zajonc, R. B. (1973). Exposure, context, and interpersonal attraction. *Journal of Personality and Social Psychology, 25,* 234–242.

Sagawa, S., Shiraki, K., Yousef, M. K., & Miki, K.

(1988). Sweating and cardiovascular responses of aged men to heat exposure. *Journal of Gerontology: Medical Sciences, 43,* M1–8.

Samuelson, C. D., & Messick, D. M. (1986). Inequities in access to and use of shared resources in social dilemmas. *Journal of Personality and Social Psychology, 51,* 960–967.

Samuelson, C. D., Messick, D. M., Rutte, C. G., & Wilke, H. (1984). Individual and structural solutions to resource dilemmas in two cultures. *Journal of Personality and Social Psychology, 47,* 94–104.

Samuelson, D. J., & Lindauer, M. S. (1976). Perception, evaluation, and performance in a neat and messy room by high and low sensation seekers. *Environment and Behavior, 8,* 291–306.

Sanborn, D. E., Casey, T. M., & Niswander, G. D. (1970). Suicide: Seasonal patterns and related variables. *Diseases of the Nervous System, 31,* 702–704.

Sanders, J. L. (1978). Relation of personal space to the human menstrual cycle. *Journal of Psychology, 100,* 275–278.

Sanders, M. S., & McCormick, E. J. (1987). *Human factors in engineering and design* (6th ed.). New York: McGraw-Hill.

Sandman, P. M., Weinstein, N. D., & Klotz, M. L. (1987). Public response to the risk from geological radon. *Journal of Communication, 37,* 93–108.

Santrock, J. W. (1976). Affect and facilitative self-control: Influence of ecological setting, cognition, and social agent. *Journal of Educational Psychology, 68,* 529–535.

Saunders, M., Gustanski, J., & Lawton, M. (1974). Effect of ambient illumination on noise levels of groups. *Journal of Applied Psychology, 59,* 527–528.

Savinar, J. (1975). The effect of ceiling height on personal space. *Man–Environment Systems, 5,* 321–324.

Savitz, D. A., & Calle, E. E. (1987). Leukemia and occupational exposure to electromagnetic fields: Review of epidemiologic surveys. *Journal of Occupational Medicine, 29,* 47–51.

Savitz, D. A., Wachtel, H., Barnes, F. A., John, E. M., & Tvrdik, J. G. (1988). Case-control study of childhood cancer and exposure to 60-Hz magnetic fields. *American Journal of Epidemiology, 128,* 21–38.

Schachter, S. (1959). *The psychology of affiliation.* Stanford, CA: Stanford University Press.

Schachter, S., & Singer, J. E. (1962). Cognitive, social, and physiological determinants of emotional states. *Psychological Review, 69,* 379–399.

Schaeffer, G. H., & Patterson, M. L. (1980). Intimacy, arousal, and small group crowding. *Journal of Personality and Social Psychology, 38,* 283–290.

Schaeffer, M. A., Baum, A., Paulus, P. B., & Gaes, G. G. (1988). Architecturally mediated effects of social density in prison. *Environment and Behavior, 20,* 3–19.

Schavio, S. (1975). *Factors mediating responses of invasions of personal space*. Paper presented at the annual meeting of the Rocky Mountain Psychological Association.

Scheflen, A. E. (1971). Living space in an urban ghetto. *Family Process, 10,* 429–450.

Scheier, M. F., Carver, C. S., & Gibbons, F. X. (1979). Self-directed attention, awareness of bodily states, and suggestibility. *Journal of Personality and Social Psychology, 37,* 1576–1588.

Scherer, S. E. (1974). Proxemic behavior of primary school children as a function of their socioeconomic class and subculture. *Journal of Personality and Social Psychology, 29,* 800–805.

Schettino, A. P., & Borden, R. J. (1976). Group size versus group density: Where is the affect? *Personality and Social Psychology Bulletin, 2,* 67–70.

Schiffenbauer, A. I. (1979). Designing for high-density living. In J. R. Aiello & A. Baum (Eds.), *Residential crowding and design.* New York: Plenum.

Schiffenbauer, A., & Schiavo, R. S. (1975). *Physical distance and attraction: An intensification effect.* Unpublished manuscript. Virginia Polytechnic Institute and State University.

Schindler, D. W. (1988). Effects of acid rain on freshwater ecosystems. *Science, 239,* 149–157.

Schkade, J. (1977). *The effects of expectancy set and crowding on task performance.* Doctoral dissertation, University of Texas at Arlington.

Schmidt, C. W., & Ulrich, R. E. (1969). Effects of group contingent events upon classroom noise. *Journal of Applied Behavior Analysis, 2,* 171–179.

Schmidt, D. E., & Keating, J. P. (1979). Human crowding and personal control: An integration of the research. *Psychological Bulletin, 86,* 680–700.

Schmidt, J. R. (1976). *Territorial invasion and aggression.* Doctoral dissertation, Louisiana State University and Agricultural and Mechanical College.

Schneider, F. W., Lesko, W. A., & Garrett, W. A. (1980). Helping behavior in hot, comfortable, and cold temperatures. *Environment and Behavior, 12,* 231–240.

Schneiderman, N. (1982). Animal behavior models of coronary heart disease. In D. S. Krantz, A. Baum, & J. E. Singer (Eds.), *Handbook of psychology and health* (Vol. 3, pp. 19–56). Hillsdale, NJ: Erlbaum.

Schnelle, J. F., Gendrich, J. G., Beegle, G. P., Thomas, M. M., & McNess, M. P. (1980). Mass media techniques for prompting behavior change in the community. *Environment and Behavior, 12,* 157–166.

Schopler, J., McCallum, R., & Rusbult, C. (1978). *Behavioral interference and internality–externality as determinants of subject crowding.* Unpublished manuscript, University of North Carolina.

Schopler, J., & Stockdale, J. (1977). An interference analysis of crowding. *Environmental Psychology and Nonverbal Behavior, 1,* 81–88.

Schopler, J., & Walton, M. (1974). *The effects of structure, expected enjoyment, and participant's internality–externality upon feelings of being crowded.* Unpublished manuscript. University of North Carolina.

Schreyer, R., & Roggenbuck, J. W. (1978). The influence of experience expectations on crowding perceptions and social psychological carrying capacities. *Leisure Sciences, 1,* 373–394.

Schulte, J. H. (1963). Effects of mild carbon monoxide intoxication. *Archives of Environmental Health, 7,* 524–530.

Schultz, D. B. (1965). *Sensory restriction.* New York: Academic Press.

Schulz, R. (1976). Effects of control and predictability on the physical and psychological well-being of the institutionalized aged. *Journal of Personality and Social Psychology, 33,* 563–573.

Schulz, R., & Brenner, G. (1977). Relocation of the aged: A review and theoretical analysis. *Journal of Gerontology, 32,* 323–333.

Schulz, R., & Hanusa, B. H. (1978). Long-term effects of control and predictability-enhancing interventions: Findings and ethical issues. *Journal of Personality and Social Psychology, 36,* 1194–1201.

Schuman, H., & Johnson, M. P. (1976). Attitudes and behavior. *Annual Review of Sociology, 2,* 161–207.

Schussheim, M. J. (1974). *A modest commitment to cities.* Lexington. MA: Lexington Books.

Schwartz, B., & Barsky, S. P. (1977). The home advantage. *Social Forces, 55,* 641–661.

Schwartz, D. C. (1968). On the ecology of political violence: "The long hot summer" as a hypothesis. *American Behavioral Scientist,* July–August, 24–28.

Schwartz H., & Werbik, H. (1971). Eine experimentelle Untersuchung uber den Einfluss der syntaktischen Information der Anordnung von Baukörpern entlang einer Strasse auf Stimmungen des Betrachters. *Zeitschrift fur experimentelle und angewandte Psychologie, 18,* 499–511.

Schwebel, A. I., & Cherlin, D. L. (1972). Physical and social distancing in teacher–pupil relationships. *Journal of Educational Psychology, 63,* 543–550.

Sears, D. O., Peplau, L. A., Freedman, J. L., & Taylor, S. E. (1988). *Social psychology* (6th ed.). Englewood, Cliffs, NJ: Prentice-Hall.

Sebba, R., & Churchman, A. (1983). Territories and territoriality in the home. *Environment and Behavior, 15,* 191–210.

Segal, M. W. (1974). Alphabet and attraction: An unobtrusive measure of the effect of propinquity in a field setting. *Journal of Personality and Social Psychology, 30,* 655–657.

Segall, M. H., Campbell, D. T., & Herskovits, M. J. (1966). *The influence of culture on visual perception.* Indianapolis: Bobbs-Merrill.

Seidel, A. D. (1985). What is success in E&B research utilization? *Environment and Behavior, 17.* 47–70.

Seidel, A. D. (1988). Political behavior and office designs: An introduction. *Environment and Behavior, 20,* 531–536.

Seligman, C., & Darley, J. M. (1977). Feedback as a means of decreasing residential energy consumption. *Journal of Applied Psychology, 62,* 363–368.

Seligman, C., Kriss, M., Darley, J. M., Fazio, R. H., Becker, L. J., & Pryor, J. B. (1979). Predicting summer energy consumption from homeowners' attitudes. *Journal of Applied Social Psychology, 9,* 70–90.

Seligman, M. E. P. (1975). *Helplessness.* San Francisco: Freeman.

Sell, R. (1976). *Cooperation and competition as a function of residential environment, consequences of game strategy choices, and perceived control.* Doctoral dissertation, State University of New York—Stony Brook.

Sells, S. B., & Will, D. P. (1971). *Accidents, police incidents, and weather: A further study of the city of Fort Worth, Texas, 1968.* Technical Report No. 15, Fort Worth Group Psychology Branch, Office of Naval Research and Institute of Behavioral Research, Texas Christian University, Fort Worth.

Selye, H. (1956). *The stress of life.* New York: McGraw-Hill.

Seta, J. J., Paulus, P. B., & Schkade, J. K. (1976). Effects of group size and proximity under cooperative and competitive conditions. *Journal of Personality and Social Psychology, 34,* 47–53.

Shafer, E. L. (1969). Perceptions of natural environments. *Environment and Behavior, 1,* 71–89.

Shafer, E., Jr., Hamilton, J. F., & Schmidt, E. A. (1969). Natural landscape preferences: A predictive model. *Journal of Leisure Research, 1,* 1–19.

Shaffer, D. R., & Sadowski, C. (1975). This table is mine: Respect for marked barroom tables as a function of gender of spatial marker and desirability of locale. *Sociometry, 38,* 408–419.

Sharpe, G. W. (1976). *Interpreting the environment.* New York: Wiley.

Shaw, L. G. (1987). Designing playgrounds for able and disabled children. In C. S. Weinstein & T. G. David (Eds.), *Spaces for children.* pp. 187–213. New York: Plenum.

Shaw, S. M. (1985). The meaning of leisure in everyday life. *Leisure Sciences, 7,* 1–24.

Sheflen, A. E. (1976). *Human territories: How we behave in space-time.* Englewood Cliffs, NJ: Prentice-Hall.

Shepard, R. N. (1975). Form, formation, and transformation of internal representation. In R. L. Solso (Ed.) *Information processing and cognition: The Loyola Symposium.* Hillsdale, NJ: Erlbaum.

Sherrod, D. R. (1974). Crowding, perceived control and behavioral aftereffects. *Journal of Applied Social Psychology, 4,* 171–186.

Sherrod, D. R., Armstrong, D., Hewitt, J., Madonia, B., Speno, S., & Fenyd, D. (1977). Environmental attention, affect and altruism. *Journal of Applied Social Psychology, 7,* 359–371.

Sherrod, D. R., & Cohen, S. (1979). Density, personal control, and design. In J. Aiello & A. Baum (Eds.), *Residential crowding and design.* New York: Plenum.

Sherrod, D. R., & Downs, R. (1974). Environmental determinants of altruism: The effects of stimulus overload and perceived control on helping. *Journal of Experimental Social Psychology, 10,* 468–479.

Shippee, G. E. (1978). *Leadership, group participation, and avoiding the tragedy of the commons.* Unpublished doctoral dissertation, Arizona State University, Tempe, AZ.

Shippee, G. E., Burroughs, J., & Wakefield, S. (1980). Dissonance theory revisited: Perception of environmental hazards in residential areas. *Environment and Behavior, 12,* 35–51.

Shlay, A. B. (1985). Castles in the sky: Measuring housing and neighborhood ideology. *Environment and Behavior, 17,* 593–626.

Shlay, A. B. (1987). Who governs housing preferences: Comment on Morris. *Environment and Behavior, 19,* 121–136.

Shumaker, S. A., & Stokols, D. (1982). Residential mobility as a social issue and research topic. *Journal of Social Issues, 38,* 1–19.

Shute, S. J., & Starr, S. J. (1984). Effects of adjustable furniture on VDT users. *Human Factors, 26,* 157–170.

Siegel, A. W., & White, S. (1975). The development of spatial representations of large scale environments. In H. W. Reese (Ed.), Advances in child development and behavior (pp. 9–55). NY: Academic Press.

Siegel, J. M., & Steele, C. M. (1980). Environmental distraction and interpersonal judgments. *British Journal of Social and Clinical Psychology, 19,* 23–32.

Sime, J. D. (1986). Creating places or designing spaces? *Journal of Environmental Psychology, 6,* 49–63.

Simmel, G. (1957). The metropolis and mental life. In K. H. Wolff (Ed. & Trans.), *The sociology of Georg Simmel* (pp. 409–424). London: The Free Press of Glencoe.

Simpson-Housley, P., Moore, R. J., Larrain, P., & Blair, D. (1982). Repression-sensitization and flood hazard appraisal in Carman, Manitoba. *Psychological Reports, 50,* 839–842.

Sims, J. H., & Baumann, D. D. (1972). The tornado threat: Coping styles of the North and South. *Science, 176,* 1386–1391.

Singer, J. E., Lundberg, U., & Frankenhaeuser, M. (1978). Stress on the train: A study of urban commuting. In A. Baum, J. E. Singer, & S. Valins (Eds.), *Advances in environmental psychology* (Vol. 1, pp. 41–56). Hillsdale, NJ: Erlbaum.

Skeen, D. R. (1976). Influence of interpersonal distance in serial learning. *Psychological Reports, 39,* 579–582.

Skinner, B. F. (1971). *Beyond freedom and dignity.* New York: Knopf.

Skogan, W., & Maxfield, M. (1981). *Coping with crime.* Beverly Hills, CA: Sage.

Skolnick, P., Frasier, L., & Hadar, I. (1977). Do you speak to strangers? A study of invasions of personal space. *European Journal of Social Psychology, 7,* 375–381.

Skotko, V. P., & Langmeyer, D. (1977). The effects of interaction distance and gender on self-disclosure in the dyad. *Sociometry, 40,* 178–182.

Slaven, R. E., Wodarksi, J. S., & Blackburn, B. L. (1981). A group contingency for electricity conservation in master-metered apartments. *Journal of Applied Behavior Analysis, 14,* 357–363.

Sloan, A. W. (1979). *Man in extreme environments.* Springfield, IL: Thomas.

Slote, L. (1961). An experimental evaluation of man's reaction to an ionized air environment. *Proceedings of the International Conference on Ionization of the Air, 2,* 1–22.

Slotsky, R. J. (1973). *Wilderness experience: A therapeutic modality.* San Francisco, CA: California School of Professional Psychology.

Slovic, P., Fischhoff, B., & Lichtenstein, S. (1981). Perceived risk: Psychological factors and social implications. *Proceedings of the Royal Society of London, A 376,* 17–34.

Smith, A. P. & Stansfeld, S. (1986). Aircraft noise exposure, noise sensitivity, and everyday errors. *Environment & Behavior, 18,* 214–226.

Smith, C. D. (1984). The relationship between the pleasingness of landmarks and the judgment of distance in cognitive maps. *Journal of Environmental Psychology, 4,* 229–234.

Smith, E. E., Shoben, E. J., & Rips, L. J. (1974). Structure and process in semantic memory: A featural model for semantic decisions. *Psychological Review, 81,* 214–241.

Smith, J. M., Bell, P. A., & Fusco, M. E. (1988). The influence of attraction on a simulated commons dilemma. *Journal of General Psychology, 115,* 277–283.

Smith, P., & Connolly, K. (1977). Social and aggressive behavior in preschool children as a function of crowding. *Social Science Information, 16,* 601–620.

Smith, R. J., & Knowles, E. S. (1979). Affective and cognitive mediators of reactions to spatial invasions. *Journal of Experimental Social Psychology, 15,* 437–452.

Smither, R. D. (1988). *The psychology of work and human performance.* New York: Harper & Row.

Snyder, L. H., & Ostrander, E. R. (1972, June). *Spatial and physical considerations in the nursing home environment: An interim report of findings.* Paper presented at the Cornell University Conference on Nursing Homes, Ithaca, NY.

Snyder, R. L. (1966). Fertility and reproductive performance of grouped male mice. In K. Benirschke (Ed.), *Symposium on comparative aspects of reproductive behavior.* Berlin: Springer Press.

Socolow, R. H. (1978). *Saving energy in the home.* Cambridge, MA: Ballinger.

Sommer, R. (1959). Studies in personal space. *Sociometry, 22,* 247–260.

Sommer, R. (1965). Further studies of small group ecology. *Sociometry, 28,* 337–348.

Sommer, R. (1969). *Personal space.* Englewood Cliffs, NJ: Prentice-Hall.

Sommer, R. (1972). *Design awareness.* San Francisco: Rinehart Press.

Sommer, R. (1974). *Tight spaces: Hard architecture and how to humanize it.* Englewood Cliffs, NJ: Prentice-Hall.

Sommer, R., & Olsen, H. (1980). The soft classroom. *Environment and Behavior, 12,* 3–16.

Sommer, R., & Ross, H. (1958). Social interaction on a geriatrics ward. *International Journal of Social Psychiatry, 4,* 128–133.

Sommers, P., & Moos, R., (1976). The weather and human behavior. In R. H. Moos, *The human context: Environmental determinants of behavior* (pp. 73–107). New York: Wiley.

Sonnenfeld, J. (1966). Variable values in space and landscape: An inquiry into the nature of environmental necessity. *Journal of Social Issues, 22,* 71–82.

Southwick, C. H. (1955). The population dynamics of confined mice supplied with unlimited food. *Ecology, 36,* 212–225.

Southwick, C. H. (1967). An experimental study of intragroup agonistic behavior in rhesus monkeys (Macaca mulatta). *Behavior, 28,* 182–209.

Spivey, G. H., Brown, C. P., Baloh, R. W., Campion, D. S., Valentine, J. L., Massey, F. J., Jr., Browdy, B. L., & Culver, B. D. (1979). Subclinical effects of chronic increased lead absorption—A prospective study. I. Study design and analysis of symptoms. *Journal of Occupational Medicine, 21,* 423–429.

Srivastava, R. K. (1974). Undermanning theory in the context of mental health care environments. In D. H. Carson (Ed.), *Man–environment interactions* (Part 2, pp. 245–258). Stroudsberg, PA: Dowden, Hutchinson & Ross.

Srole, L. (1972). Urbanization and mental health: Some reformulations. *American Scientist, 60,* 576–583.

Srole, L. (1976). The city vs. the country: New evidence on an ancient bias. In L. Srole & A. Fischer (Eds.), *Mental health in the metropolis* (2nd ed.). New York: Harper & Row.

Stadler, S. J., & Harries, K. D. (1985). Assault and deviations from mean temperatures: An inter-year comparison in Dallas. *Proceedings of the 8th Annual Applied Geography Conference, 8,* 207–215.

Stainbrook, E. (1966). Architects not only design hospitals: They also design patient behavior. *Modern Hospital, 106,* 100.

Stankey, G. H. (1973). Visitor perception of wilderness recreation carrying capacity. (Research Paper NO. INT-142, p. 62). Ogden, UT: U.S. Department of Agriculture, Intermountain Forest and Range Experiment Station.

Starr, S. J., Thompson, C. R., & Shute, S. J. (1982). Effects of video display terminals on telephone operators. *Human Factors, 24,* 699–711.

Stea, D., & Blaut, J. M. (1973). Some preliminary observations on spatial learning in school children. In R. Downs & D. Stea, *Image and the Environment.* Chicago: Aldine.

Stea, D., & Blaut, J. M. (1987). Clark remembered. *Journal of Environmental Psychology, 7,* 379–388.

Steblay, N. M. (1987). Helping behavior in rural and urban environments: A meta analysis. *Psychological Bulletin, 102,* 346–356.

Steidl, R. E. (1972). Difficult factors in homemaking tasks: Implications for environmental design. *Human Factors, 14,* 471–482.

Steinitz, C. (1968). Meaning and congruence of urban form and activity. *Journal of the American Institute of Planners, 34,* 233–248.

Steinzor, B. (1950). The spatial factor in face-to-face discussion groups. *Journal of Abnormal and Social Psychology, 45,* 552–555.

Stephan, W. (1978). School desegregation: An evaluation of predictions made in Brown vs. the Board of Education. *Psychological Bulletin, 85,* 217–238.

Sterling, E. (1979). The impact of air pollution on residential design. In A. D. Seidel & S. Danford (Eds.), *Environmental design: Research, theory, and application.* Washington, DC: Environmental Design Research Association.

Stern, G. G. (1963). *Scoring Instructions and College Norms: Activities Index and College Characteristics Index.* Syracuse, NY: Syracuse University, Psychological Research Center.

Stern, P. C. (1976). Effect of incentives and education on resource conservation decisions in a simulated commons dilemma. *Journal of Personality and Social Psychology, 25,* 1285–1292.

Stern, P. C. & Aronson, E. (Eds.) (1984). *Energy use: The human dimension.* New York: Freeman.

Stern, P. C., & Gardner, G. T. (1981). Psychological research and energy policy. *American Psychologist, 4,* 329–342.

Stern, P. C. & Oskamp, S. (1987). Managing scarce environmental resources. In D. Stokols & I. Altman (Eds.), *Handbook of environmental psychology, 2,* 1043–1088. New York: Wiley.

Stevens, A., & Coupe, P. (1978). Distortions in judged spatial relations. *Cognitive Psychology, 10,* 422–437.

Stevens, S. S. (1955). The measurement of loudness. *Journal of the Acoustical Society of America, 27,* 815–829.

Stevens, W., Kushler, M., Jeppesen, J., & Leedom, N. (1979). *Youth energy education strategies: A statistical evaluation.* Lansing, MI: Energy Extension Service, Department of Commerce.

Stewart, T. R. (1987). Developing an observer-based measure of environmental annoyance. In H.S. Koelega (Ed.), *Environmental annoyance: Characterization, measurement, and control* (pp. 213–222). New York: Elsevier.

Stewart, T. R., Dennis, R. L., & Ely, D. W. (1984). Citizen participation and judgment of policy analysis: A case study in urban air quality policy. *Policy Sciences, 17,* 67–87.

Stewart, T. R., Middleton, P., & Ely, D. (1983). Urban visual air quality judgments: Reliability and validity. *Journal of Environmental Psychology, 1,* 129–145.

Stires, L. (1980). Classroom seating location, student grades and attitudes: Environment or selection? *Environment and Behavior, 12,* 241–254.

Stobaugh, R., & Yergin, D. (1979). *Energy future: Report of the energy project of the Harvard Business School.* New York: Random House.

Stokols, D. (1972). On the distinction between density and crowding: Some implications for future research. *Psychological Review, 79,* 275–278.

Stokols, D. (1976). The experience of crowding in primary and secondary environments. *Environment and Behavior, 8,* 49–86.

Stokols, D. (1978). A typology of crowding experiences. In A. Baum & Y. Epstein (Eds.), *Human response to crowding* (pp. 219–255). Hillsdale, NJ: Erlbaum.

Stokols, D. (1979). A congruence analysis of human stress. In I. G. Sarason & C. D. Spielberger (Eds.), *Stress and anxiety* (Vol. 6, pp. 27–53). New York: Wiley.

Stokols, D. (1983). Editor's introduction: Theoretical directions of environment and behavior research. *Environment and Behavior, 15,* 259–272.

Stokols, D., & Altman, I. (Eds.) (1987). *Handbook of environmental psychology* (Vol. 1, pp. xi-xii). New York: Wiley.

Stokols, D. & Novaco, R. W. (1981). Transportation and well-being: An ecological perspective. In I. Altman, J. F. Wohlwill, & P. B. Everett (Eds.), *Transportation and behavior.* New York: Plenum.

Stokols, D., & Ohlig, W. (1975). *The experience of crowding under different social climates.* Paper presented at the meeting of the American Psychological Association, Chicago.

Stokols, D., Ohlig, W., & Resnick, S. (1979). Perception of residential crowding, classroom experiences, and student health. In J. R. Aiello & A. Baum (Eds.), *Residential crowding and design*. New York: Plenum.

Stokols, D., Rall, M., Pinner, B., & Schopler, J. (1973). Physical, social and personal determinants of the perception of crowding. *Environment and Behavior, 5,* 87–117.

Stolper, J. H. (1977). Color induced physiological response. *Man–Environment Systems, 7,* 101–108.

Stone, G. L., & Morden, C. J. (1976). Effect of distance on verbal productivity. *Journal of Counseling Psychology, 23,* 486–488.

Stone, J., Breidenbach, S., & Heimstra, N. (1979). Annoyance response of nonsmokers to cigarette smoke. *Perceptual and Motor Skills, 49,* 907–916.

Storms, M. D., & Thomas, G. C. (1977). Reactions to physical closeness. *Journal of Personality and Social Psychology, 35,* 412–418.

Strahilevitz, N., Strahilevitz, A., & Miller, J. E. (1979). Air pollution and the admission rate of psychiatric patients. *American Journal of Psychiatry, 136,* 206–207.

Strakhov, A. B. (1966). *Some questions of the mechanism of the action of noise on an organism* (Report N67-11646). Washington, D.C.: Joint Publication Research Service.

Strodtbeck, F., & Hook, H. (1961). The social dimensions of a 12-man jury table. *Sociometry, 24,* 397–415.

Strube, M. J., & Werner, C. (1984). Psychological reactance and the relinquishment of control. *Personality and Social Psychology Bulletin, 10,* 225–234.

Studer, R. (1970). The organization of spatial stimuli. In L. Pastlan & D. Caron (Eds.), *The spatial behavior of older people*. Ann Arbor: University of Michigan Press.

Suedfeld, P. (1975). The benefits of boredom: Sensory deprivation reconsidered. *American Scientist, 63,* 60–69.

Suedfeld, P. (1980). *Restricted environmental stimulation: Research and clinical applications*. New York: Wiley.

Suedfeld, P., & Baker-Brown, G. (1986). Restricted environmental therapy and aversive conditioning in smoking cessation: Active and placebo effects. *Behavior Research and Therapy, 24,* 421–428.

Suedfeld, P., & Mocellin, J. S. P. (1987). The ''sensed presence'' in unusual environments. *Environment and Behavior, 19,* 33–52.

Suedfeld, P., Roy, C. & Landon, P. B. (1982). Restricted environmental stimulation therapy in the treatment of essential hypertension. *Behavior Research and Therapy, 20,* 553–559.

Suedfeld, P., Schwartz, G., & Arnold, W. (1980). Study of restricted environmental stimulation therapy (REST) as

a treatment for autistic children. *Journal of Autism and Developmental Disorders, 10,* 337–378.

Sulman, F. G., Danon, A., Pfeifer, Y., Tal, E., & Weller, C. P. (1970). Urinalysis of patients suffering from climatic heat stress (Sharav). *International Journal of Biometeorology, 14,* 45–53.

Sun, M. (1988). Radon's health risks. *Science, 239,* 250.

Sundeen, R. A., & Mathieu, J. T. (1976). Fear of crime and its consequences among elderly in three urban communities. *The Gerontologist, 16,* 211–219.

Sundet, J. M. (1978). Effects of colour on perceived depth: Review of experiments and evaluation of theories. *Scandinavian Journal of Psychology, 19,* 133–143.

Sundstrom, E. (1975). An experimental study of crowding: Effects of room size, intrusion, and goal-blocking on nonverbal behaviors, self-disclosure, and self-reported stress. *Journal of Personality and Social Psychology, 32,* 645–654.

Sundstrom, E. (1976). Interpersonal behavior and the physical environment. In L. S. Wrightsman (Ed.), *Social psychology* (2nd ed). Monterey, CA: Brooks/Cole.

Sundstrom, E. (1978). Crowding as a sequential process: Review of research on the effects of population density on humans. In A. Baum & Y. M. Epstein (Eds.), *Human response to crowding*, Hillsdale, NJ: Erlbaum.

Sundstrom, E. (1986). *Work places: The psychology of the physical environment in offices and factories*. New York: Cambridge.

Sundstrom, E. (1987). Work environments: Offices and factories. In D. Stokols & I. Altman (Eds.), *Handbook of environmental psychology*. New York: Wiley.

Sundstrom, E., & Altman, I. (1976). Personal space and interpersonal relationships: Research review and theoretical model. *Human Ecology, 4,* 47–67.

Sundstrom, E., Herbert, R. K., & Brown, D. W. (1982). Privacy and communication in an open plan office. *Environment and Behavior, 14,* 379–392.

Sundstrom, E., & Sundstrom, M. G. (1977). Personal space invasions: What happens when the invader asks permission? *Environmental Psychology and Nonverbal Behavior, 2,* 76–82.

Suter, T. W., Buzzi, R., Woodson, P. P., & Bättig, K. (1983, December). Psychophysiological correlates of conflict solving and cigarette smoking. *Activitas Nervosa Superior, 25,* 261–272.

Suttles, G. D. (1968). *The social order of the slum: Ethnicity and territory in the inner city*. Chicago: University of Chicago Press.

Swan, J. A. (1970). Response to air pollution: A study of attitudes and coping strategies of high school youths. *Environment and Behavior, 2,* 127–152.

Swanson, C. P. (1973). *The natural history of man*. Englewood Cliffs, NJ: Prentice-Hall.

Swap, W. C. (1977). Interpersonal attraction and repeated

exposure to rewarders and punishers. *Personality and Social Psychology Bulletin, 3,* 248–251.

Sweeney, P. D., Anderson, K., & Bailey, S. (1986). Attributional style in depression: A meta-analytic review. *Journal of Personality and Social Psychology, 50,* 974–991.

Szilagyi, A. D., & Holland, W. E. (1980). Changes in social density: Relationships with functional interaction and perceptions of job characteristics, role stress, and work satisfaction. *Journal of Applied Psychology, 65,* 28–33.

Taggart, P., Gibbons, D., & Sommerville, W. (1969). Some effects of motor-car driving on the normal and abnormal heart. *British Medical Journal, 4,* 130–134.

Talbot, J. F., & Kaplan, S. (1986). Perspectives on wilderness: Re-examining the value of extended wilderness experiences. *Journal of Environmental Psychology, 6,* 177–188.

Tasso, J., & Miller, E. (1976). The effects of the full moon on human behavior. *Journal of Psychology, 93,* 81–83.

Taylor, D. (1974). Should we integrate organizations? In H. Fromkin & J. Sherwood (Eds.), *Integrating the organization* (pp. 340–361). New York: Free Press.

Taylor, F. W. (1911). *The principles of scientific management.* New York: Harper and Brothers.

Taylor, H. R., West, S. K., Rosenthal, F. S., Munoz, B., Newland, H. S., Abbey, H., & Emmett, E. A. (1988). Effect of ultraviolet radiation on cataract formation. *New England Journal of Medicine, 319,* 1429–1433.

Taylor, R. B. (1978). Human territoriality: A review and a model for future research. *Cornell Journal of Social Relations, 13,* 125–151.

Taylor, R. B., & Brooks, D. K. (1980). Temporary territories: Responses to intrusions in a public setting. *Population and Environment, 3,* 135–145.

Taylor, R. B., & Brower, S. (1985). Home and near-home territories. In I. Altman & C. Werner (Eds.), *Human behavior and environment: Current theory and research, 8, Home environments.* New York: Plenum.

Taylor, R. B., & Covington, J. (1988). Neighborhood changes. *Ecology and Violent Criminology, 26,* 553–591.

Taylor, R. B., & Ferguson, G. (1978). *Solitude and intimacy: Privacy experiences and the role of territoriality.* Paper presented at the annual meeting of the American Psychological Association, Toronto.

Taylor, R. B., Gottfredson, S. D., & Brower, S. (1980). The defensibility of defensible space: A critical review and a synthetic framework for future research. In T. Hirshi & M. Gottfredson (Eds.), *Understanding crime.* Beverly Hills, CA: Sage.

Taylor, R. B., Gottfredson, S. D., & Brower, S. (1981). Territorial cognitions and social climate in urban neighborhoods. *Basic and Applied Social Psychology, 2,* 289–303.

Taylor, R. B., Gottfredson, S., & Brower, S. (1984). Understanding block crime and fear. *Journal of Research in Crime and Delinquency, 21,* 303–331.

Taylor, R. B., & Hale, M. (1986). Testing alternative models of fear of crime. *The Journal of Law and Criminology, 77,* 151–189.

Taylor, R. B., & Lanni, J. C. (1981). Territorial dominance: The influence of the resident advantage in triadic decision making. *Journal of Personality and Social Psychology, 41,* 909–915.

Taylor, R. B., & Stough, R. R. (1978). Territorial cognition: Assessing Altman's typology. *Journal of Personality and Social Psychology, 36,* 418–423.

Taylor, S. (1979). Hospital patient behavior: Reactance, helplessness, or control? *Journal of Social Issues, 35,* 156–184.

Taylor, V., & Quarantelli, E. (1976). *Some needed cross-cultural studies of disaster behavior.* Columbus, OH: Disaster Research Center.

Tennen, H., & Eller, S. J. (1977). Attributional components of learned helplessness and facilitation. *Journal of Personality and Social Psychology, 35,* 265–271.

Tennis, G. H., & Dabbs, J. M. (1975). Sex, setting and personal space: First grade through college. *Sociometry, 38,* 385–394.

Terry, R. L., & Lower, M. (1979). Perceptual withdrawal from an invasion of personal space. *Personality and Social Psychology Bulletin, 5,* 396–397.

Thalhofer, N. N. (1980). Violation of a spacing norm in high social density. *Journal of Applied Social Psychology, 10,* 175–183.

Thomas, W. A. (1972). *Indicators of Environmental Quality.* New York: Plenum.

Thompson, S. C. (1981). Will it hurt less if I can control it? A complex answer to a simple question. *Psychological Bulletin, 90,* 89–101.

Thompson, W. R., & Heron, W. (1954). The effects of restricting early experience on the problem-solving capacity of dogs. *Canadian Journal of Psychology, 8,* 17–31.

Thomson, G. (1986). *The museum environment* (2nd ed.). Stoneham, MA: Butterworth.

Thorndyke, P. W., & Hayes-Roth, B. (1982). Differences in spatial knowledge acquired from maps and navigation. *Cognitive psychology, 14,* 560–589.

Thorne, R., Hall, R., & Munro-Clark, M. (1982). Attitudes toward detached houses, terraces and apartments: Some current pressures towards less preferred but more accessible alternatives. In P. Bart, A. Chen, & G. Francescato (Eds.), *Knowledge for design: Proceedings of the 13th Environmental Design Research Association Conference* (pp. 435–448). Washington, DC: Environmental Design Research Association.

Tien, J. M., O'Donnell, V. F., Barnett, A., & Mirchandini, P. B. (1979). *Street lighting projects*. Washington, DC: Department of Justice.

Timasheff, N. S. (1967). *Sociological theory: Its nature and growth* (3rd ed.). New York: Random House.

Tinsley, H. E. A., Kass, R. A., & Driver, B. L. (1981). Reliability and concurrent validity of the recreation experience preference scales. *Educational and Psychological Measurement, 41,* 897–907.

Tinsley, H. E., & Johnson, T. L. (1984). A preliminary taxonomy of leisure activities. *Journal of Leisure Research, 16,* 234–244.

Tinsley, H. E., & Tinsley, D. J. (1986). A theory of the attributes, benefits, and causes of leisure experience. *Leisure Sciences, 8,* 1–45.

Titchener, J., & Kapp, F. I. (1976). Family and character change at Buffalo Creek. *American Journal of Psychiatry, 133,* 295–299.

Toffler, A. (1980). *The third wave*. New York: Bantam Books.

Tognoli, J. (1980). Differences in women's and men's responses to domestic space. *Sex Roles, 6,* 833–842.

Tognoli, J. (1987). Residential environments. In D. Stokols & I. Altman (Eds.), *Handbook of environmental psychology* (Vol. 1, pp. 655–690). New York: Wiley-Interscience.

Tolman, E. C. (1948). Cognitive maps in rats and men. *Psychological Review, 55,* 189–208.

Tolman, E. C., Ritchie, B. F., & Kalish, D. (1946). Studies in spatial learning I. Orientation and the short-cut. *Journal of Experimental Psychology, 36,* 13–24.

Towler, J., & Swan, J. E. (1972). What do people really know about pollution? *Journal of Environmental Education, 4,* 54–57.

Traub, R. E., & Weiss, J. (1974). Studying openness in education: An Ontario example. *Journal of Research and Development in Education, 8,* 47–59.

Trice, H. M. (1966). *Alcoholism in America*. New York: McGraw-Hill.

Trites, D., Galbraith, F. D., Sturdavent, M., & Leckwart, J. F. (1970). Influence of nursing unit design on the activities and subjective feelings of nursing personnel. *Environment and Behavior, 2,* 303–334.

Tromp, S. W. (1980). *Biometeorology: The impact of weather and climate on humans and their environment*. Philadelphia: Heyden.

Trotter, D. (1982). *The lighting of underground mines*. Clausthal-Zellerfeld, Germany: Trans Tech Publications.

Trowbridge, C. C. (1913). On fundamental methods of orientation and ''imaginary maps.'' *Science, 88,* 888–896.

Truscott, J. C., Parmelle, P., & Werner, C. (1977). Plate touching in restaurants—Preliminary observations of a food-related marking behavior in humans. *Jour-nal of Personality and Social Psychology, 3,* 425–428.

Turk, A., Johnston, J. W., & Moulton, D. G. (Eds.) (1974). *Human responses to environmental odors*. New York: Academic Press.

Turk, A., Turk, J., Wittes, J. T., & Wittes, R. (1974). *Environmental science*. Philadelphia: Saunders.

Turner, F. J. (1920). *The frontier in American history*. New York: Holt, Rinehart and Winston.

Tversky, B. (1981). Distortions in memory for maps. *Cognitive Psychology, 13,* 407–433.

Tyler, T. R. (1981). Perceived control and behavioral reactions to crime. *Personality and Social Psychology Bulletin, 7,* 212–217.

U.S. Conference of Mayors. (1987). Status report on homeless families in America's cities: A 29-city survey. Washington DC: U. S. Conference of Mayors.

U.S. Department of Commerce, Bureau of the Census (1985). *U.S. Bureau of the Census world population profile*. Washington, DC: U.S. Government Printing Office.

U.S. Department of Interior: Heritage Conservation and Recreation Service (1979). *The third nationwide outdoor recreation plan*. Washington, DC: U.S. Government Printing Office.

U.S. Environmental Protection Agency (1974). *Information on levels of environmental noise requisite to protect public health and welfare with an adequate margin for safety*. Washington, DC: U.S. Government Printing Office.

U.S. Riot Commission (1968). *Report of the National Advisory Commission on Civil Disorders*. New York: Bantam Books.

Ugwuegbu, D. C., & Anusiem, A. U. (1982). Effects of stress on interpersonal distance in a simulated interview situation. *Journal of Social Psychology, 116,* 3–7.

Ulrich, R. S. (1977). Visual landscape preference: A model and applications. *Man–Environment Systems, 7,* 279–292.

Ulrich, R. S. (1979). Visual landscapes and psychological well-being. *Landscape Research, 4,* 17–23.

Ulrich, R. S. (1984). View through a window may influence recovery from surgery. *Science, 224,* 420–421.

Ulrich, R. S. (1986). Human responses to vegetation and landscapes. *Landscape and Urban Planning, 13,* 29–44.

Unger, D., & Wandersman, A. (1983). Neighboring and its role in block organizations: An exploratory report. *American Journal of Community Psychology, 11,* 291–300.

Uniform Crime Reporting Handbook. (1978). Federal Bureau of Investigation. Washington, DC, U. S. Government Printing Office.

Ury, H. K., Perkins, N. M., & Goldsmith, J. R. (1972).

Motor vehicle accidents and vehicular pollution in Los Angeles. *Archives of Environmental Health, 25,* 314–322.

Vallet, M. (1987). The effects of non-acoustic factors on annoyance due to traffic noise. In H. S. Koelega (Ed.), *Environmental annoyance: Characterization, measurement, and control (pp. 371–382). Amsterdam: Elsevier Science Publishers.*

van der Pligt, J. (1985). Public attitudes to nuclear energy: Salience and anxiety. *Journal of Environmental Psychology, 5,* 87–97.

Van Valkenburgh, M. (1978). The design implications of grade school children's use of and attitudes about two-way play areas in Carle Park, Urbana, Illinois. In W. Rogers & W. Ittelson (Eds.), *New dimensions in environmental design.* Washington, DC: Environmental Design Research Association.

van Vliet, W. (1981). Neighborhood evaluations by city and suburban children. *Journal of the American Planning Association, 47,* 458–466.

van Vliet, W. (1983). Families in apartment buildings: Sad stories for children? *Environment and Behavior, 15,* 211–234.

Vanetti, E. J., & Allen, G. L. (1988). Communicating environmental knowledge: The impact of verbal and spatial abilities on the production and comprehension of route directions. *Environment and Behavior, 20,* 667–682.

Veitch, J. A., & Kaye, S. M. (1988). Illumination effects on conversational sound levels and job candidate evaluations. *Journal of Environmental Psychology, 8,* 223–233.

Venturi, R. (1966). *Complexity and contradiction in architecture.* New York: Museum of Modern Art.

Verderber (1986). Dimensions of person–window transactions in the hospital environment. *Environment and Behavior, 18,* 450–466.

Vernon, J., & McGill, T. E. (1957). The effect of sensory deprivation upon rote learning. *American Journal of Psychology, 70,* 637–639.

Vining, T., Daniel, T. C., & Schroeder, H. W. (1984). Predicting scenic values in forested residential landscapes. *Journal of Leisure Research, 16,* 124–135.

Vinsel, A., Brown, B., Altman, I., & Foss, C. (1980). Privacy regulation, territorial displays, and effectiveness of individual functioning. *Journal of Personality and Social Psychology, 39,* 1104–1115.

Volkman, N. (1981). User perceptions of underground houses and implications for site planning. In A. E. Osterberg, C. P. Tiernan, & R. A. Findlay (Eds.), *Design Research interactions: Proceedings of the 12th Environmental Design Research Association Conference (pp. 277–281). Washington, DC: Environmental Design Research Association.*

Wack, J., & Rodin, J. (1978). Nursing homes for the aged: The human consequences of legislation-shaped environments. *Journal of Social Issues, 34,* 6–21.

Walden, T. A., Nelson, P. A., & Smith, D. E. (1981). Crowding, privacy, and coping. *Environment and Behavior, 13,* 205–224.

Walder, D. N. (1967). Decompression sickness in tunnel workers. In C. N. Davies, P. R. Davis, & F. H. Tyrer (Eds.), *The effects of abnormal physical conditions at work (pp. 101–110). London: E & S Livingstone.*

Waldrop, M. M. (1988). Taking back the night. *Science, 241,* 1288–1289.

Walker, J. M. (1979). Energy demand behavior in a master-meter apartment complex: An experimental analysis. *Journal of Applied Psychology, 64,* 190–196.

Wallace, L., Bromberg, S., Pellizzari, E., Hartwell, T., Zelon, H., & Sheldon, L. (1984). Plan and preliminary results of U.S. EPA's indoor air monitoring program. In B. Berglund, T. Lindvall, & J. Sundell, (Eds.). *Indoor air: Vol 1. Recent advances in the health sciences and technology.* Stockholm: Swedish Council for Building Research.

Wandersman, A., & Florin, P. (1981). A cognitive social learning approach to the crossroads of cognitive social behavior and the environment. In J. Harvey (Ed.), *Cognitive social behavior and environment.* Hillsdale, NJ: Erlbaum.

Ward, L. M., & Russell, J. A. (1981a). Cognitive set and the perception of place. *Environment and Behavior, 13,* 610–632.

Ward, L. M., & Russell, J. A. (1981b). The psychological representation of molar physical environments. *Journal of Experimental Psychology: General, 110,* 121–152.

Ward, L. M., & Suedfeld, P. (1973). Human responses to highway noise. *Environmental Research, 6,* 306–326.

Ward, L. M., Snodgrass, J., Chew, B., & Russell, J. A. (1988). The role of plans in cognitive and affective responses to places. *Journal of Environmental Psychology, 8,* 1–8.

Ward, P. (1975). Deadly throwaways: Plastic six-pack binders and metal pull-tabs doom wildlife. *Defenders.*

Ward, S. L., Newcombe, N., & Overton, W. F. (1986). Turn left at the church or three miles north: A study of direction giving and sex differences. *Environment and Behavior, 18,* 192–213.

Warner, S. B., Jr. (1978). *Streetcar suburbs: The process of growth in Boston, 1870–1900* (2nd ed.). Cambridge, MA: Harvard University Press.

Warzecha, S., Fisher, J. D. & Baron, R. M. (1988). The equity-control model as a predictor of vandalism among college students. *Journal of Applied Social Psychology, 18,* 80–91.

Watson, O. M., & Graves, T. D. (1966). Quantitative research in proxemic behavior. *American Anthropologist, 68,* 971–985.

Wayne, W., Wehrle, P., & Carroll, R. (1967). Oxidant air

pollution and athletic performance. *Journal of the American Medical Association, 199,* 901–904.

Webb, E. J., Campbell, D. T., Schwartz, R. D., & Sechrest, L. (1966). *Unobtrusive measures: Non-reactive research in the social sciences.* Chicago: Rand McNally.

Webb, E. J., Campbell, D. T., Schwartz, R. D., Sechrest, L., & Grove, J. B. (1981). *Nonreactive measures in social sciences* (2nd ed.). Dallas: Houghton Mifflin.

Webber, M. M. (1963). Order in diversity: Community without propinquity. In L. Wingo, Jr. (Ed.), *Cities and space: The future use of urban land* (pp. 23–54). Baltimore: The Johns Hopkins Press.

Weber, M. (1981). Model of habitability parameters utilized in study of earth sheltered housing. In A. E. Osterberg, C. P. Tiernan, & R. A. Findlay (Eds.), *Design research interactions: Proceedings of the 12th Environmental Design Research Association Conference* (pp. 272–276). Washington, DC: Environmental Design Research Association.

Wehr, T. A., Jacobsen, F. M., Sack, D. A., Arendt, J., Tamarkin, L., & Rosenthal, N. E. (1986). Phototherapy of seasonal affective disorder. *Archives of General Psychiatry, 43,* 870–875.

Wehr, T. A., Sack, D. A., & Rosenthal, N. E. (1987). Seasonal affective disorder with summer depression and winter hypomania. *American Journal of Psychiatry, 144,* 1602–1603.

Weidemann, S., & Anderson, J. R. (1982). Residents' perceptions of satisfaction and safety: A basis for change in multifamily housing. *Environment and Behavior, 14,* 695–724.

Weidemann, S., & Anderson, J. R., (1985). A conceptual framework for residential satisfaction. In I. Altman & C. M. Werner (eds.), *Home Environments* (pp. 153–182). New York: Plenum.

Weigel, R. H., & Newman, L. S. (1976). Increasing attitude–behavior correspondence by broadening the scope of the behavioral measure. *Journal of Personality and Social Psychology, 33,* 793–802.

Weil, R. J., & Dunsworth, F. A. (1958). Psychiatric aspects of disaster—a case history. Some experiences during the Springhill, Nova Scotia, mining disaster. *Canadian Psychiatric Association Journal, 3,* 11–17.

Weiner, F. H. (1976). Altruism, ambiance, and action: The effects of rural and urban rearing on helping behavior. *Journal of Personality and Social Psychology, 34,* 112–124.

Weinstein, L. (1965). Social schemata of emotionally disturbed boys. *Journal of Abnormal Psychology, 76,* 457–461.

Weinstein, M. S. (1980). *Health in the city: Environmental and behavioral influences.* New York: Pergamon.

Weinstein, N. D. (1974). Effect of noise on intellectual performance. *Journal of Applied Psychology, 59,* 548–554.

Weinstein, N. D. (1976). The statistical prediction of environmental preferences. *Environment and Behavior, 8,* 611–626.

Weisman, G. D. (1983). Environmental programing and action research. *Environment and Behavior, 15,* 381–408.

Weisman, J. (1981). Wayfinding and the built environment. *Environment and Behavior, 13,* 189–204.

Weisner, T., & Weibel, J. (1981). Home environments and family lifestyles in California. *Environment and Behavior, 13,* 417–460.

Weiss, B. (1983). Behavioral toxicology and environmental health science. *American Psychologist, 38,* 1174–1187.

Weisz, J. R., Rothbaum, F. M., & Blackburn, T. C. (1984). Standing out and standing in: The psychology of control in America and Japan. *American Psychologist, 39,* 955–969.

Wellens, A. R., & Goldberg, M. L. (1978). The effects of interpersonal distance and orientation upon the perception of social relationships. *Journal of Psychology, 99,* 39–47.

Wellman, B., & Leighton, B. (1979). Networks, neighborhoods, and communities: Approaches to the study of the community question. *Urban Affairs Quarterly, 14,* 363–390.

Wellman, J. D., & Buhyoff, G. J. (1980). Effects of regional familiarity on landscape preferences. *Journal of Environmental Management, 11,* 105–110.

Wener, R. (1977). Non-density factors in the perception of crowding. *Dissertation Abstracts International, 37D,* 3569–3570.

Wener, R., Frazier, F. W., & Farbstein, J. (1985). Three generations of evaluation and design of correctional facilities. *Environment and Behavior, 17,* 71–95.

Wener, R., Frazier, W., & Farbstein, J. (1987, June). Building better jails. *Psychology Today, 21,* 40–44, 48–49.

Wener, R., & Kaminoff, R. D. (1983). Improving environmental information: Effects of signs on perceived crowding and behavior. *Environment and Behavior, 15,* 3–20.

Wener, R., & Keys, C. (1988). The effects of changes in jail population densities on crowding, sick call, and spatial behavior. *Journal of Applied Social Psychology, 18,* 852—866.

Werner, C. M. (1987). Home interiors: A time and place for interpersonal relationships. *Environment and Behavior, 19,* 169–179.

Werner, C. M., Altman, I., & Oxley, D. (1985). Temporal aspects of homes: A transactional perspective. In I. Altman & C. M. Werner (Eds.), *Home environments* (pp. 1–32). New York: Plenum.

Werner, C. M., Brown, B. B., & Damron, G. (1981). Territorial marking in the game arcade. *Journal of Personality and Social Psychology, 41,* 1094–1104.

Werner, R., & Szigeti, F. (Eds.) (1987). *Cumulative index to the EDRA proceedings: Volumes 1–18.* Washington, DC: Environmental Design Research Association.

West, P. C. (1982). Effects of user behavior on the perception of crowding in backcountry forest recreation. *Forest Science, 28,* 95–105.

Westover, T. N. (1989). Perceived crowding in recreational settings: An environment-behavior model. *Environment and Behavior, 21,* 258–276.

Weyant, J. M. (1978). Effects of mood states, costs, and benefits on helping. *Journal of Personality and Social Psychology, 36,* 1169–1176.

Wheeldon, P. D. (1969). The operation of voluntary associations and personal networks in the political processes of an interethnic community. In J. C. Mitchell (Ed.), *Social networks in urban situations.* Manchester NH: University of Manchester Press.

White, M. (1975). Interpersonal distance as affected by room size, status, and sex. *Journal of Social Psychology, 95,* 241–249.

White, M., Kasl, S. V., Zahner, G. E. P., & Will, J. C. (1987). Perceived crime in the neighborhood and mental health of women and children. *Environment and Behavior, 19,* 588–613.

Whyte, W. H. (1974). The best street life in the world. *New York Magazine, 15,* 26–33.

Whyte, W. H. (1980). *The social life of small urban spaces.* New York: The Conservation Foundation.

Wicker, A. W. (1969a). Attitudes versus actions: The relationship of verbal and overt behavioral responses to attitude objects. *Journal of Social Issues, 24,* 41–78.

Wicker, A. W. (1969b). Size of church membership and members' support of church behavior settings. *Journal of Personality and Social Psychology, 13,* 278–288.

Wicker, A. W. (1973). Undermanning theory and research: Implications for the study of psychological and behavioral effects of excess populations. *Representative Research in Social Psychology, 4,* 185–206.

Wicker, A. W. (1979). *An introduction to ecological psychology.* Monterey, CA: Brooks/Cole.

Wicker, A. W. (1987). Behavior settings reconsidered: Temporal stages, resources, internal dynamics, context. In D. Stokols & I. Altman (Eds.), *Handbook of environmental psychology* (Vol. II, pp. 613–653). New York: Wiley-Interscience.

Wicker, A. W., & Kauma, C. (1974). Effects of a merger of a small and a large organization on members' behaviors and experiences. *Journal of Applied Psychology, 59,* 24–30.

Wicker, A. W., & Kirmeyer, S. (1976). From church to laboratory to national park: A program of research on excess and insufficient populations in behavior settings. In S. Wapner, S. B. Cohen, & B. Kaplan (Eds.), *Experiencing the environment* (pp. 157–185). New York: Plenum.

Wicker, A. W., Kirmeyer, S. L., Hanson, L., & Alexander, D. (1976). Effects of manning levels on subjective experiences, performance, and verbal interaction in groups. *Organizational Behavior and Human Performance, 17,* 251–274.

Wicker, A. W., McGrath, J. E., & Armstrong, G. E. (1972). Organization size and behavior setting capacity as determinants of member participation. *Behavioral Science, 17,* 499–513.

Wicker, A. W., & Mehler, A. (1971). Assimilation of new members in a large and a small church. *Journal of Applied Psychology, 55,* 151–156.

Wilkinson, R. T. (1974). Individual differences in response to the environment. *Ergonomics, 17,* 745–756.

Wilkinson, R. T., Fox, R. H., Goldsmith, R., Hampton, I. F. G., & Lewis, H. E. (1964). Psychological and physiological responses to raised body temperature. *Journal of Applied Physiology, 19,* 287–291.

Will, D. P., & Sells, S. B. (1969). *Prediction of police incidents and accidents by meteorological variables.* Technical Report No. 14, Group Psychology Branch, Office of Naval Research and Institute of Behavioral Research, Texas Christian University, Fort Worth.

Willis, F. N. (1966). Initial speaking distance as a function of the speakers' relationship. *Psychonomic Science, 5,* 221–222.

Willis, F. N., Carlson, R., & Reeves, D. (1979). The development of personal space in primary school children. *Environmental Psychology and Nonverbal Behavior, 3,* 195–204.

Willner, Paul & Neiva, Judith. (1986, May). Brief exposure to uncontrollable but not to controllable noise biases the retrieval of information from memory. *British Journal of Clinical Psychology, 25,* 93–100.

Wills, T. A. (1981). Downward comparison principles in social psychology. *Psychological Bulletin, 90,* 245–271.

Wilner, D., Walkley, T., Pinkerton, T., & Tayback, M. (1962). *The housing environment and family life.* Baltimore, MD: Johns Hopkins Press.

Wilson, C. W., & Hopkins, B. L. (1973). The effects of contingent music on the intensity of noise in junior high home economics classes. *Journal of Applied Behavior Analysis, 6,* 269–275.

Wilson E. O. (1975). *Sociobiology.* Cambridge, MA: Harvard University Press.

Wilson, G. D. (1966). Arousal properties of red versus green. *Perceptual and Motor Skills, 23,* 947–949.

Wilson, S. (1972). Intensive care delirium. *Archives of Internal Medicine, 130,* 225.

Wineman, J. D. (1982). Office design and evaluation: An overview. *Environment and Behavior, 14,* 271–298.

Winkel, G. H. (1987). Implications of environmental context for validity assessments. In D. Stokols & I. Altman (Eds.), *Handbook of environmental psychology* (Vol. I, pp. 71–98). New York: Wiley-Interscience.

Winkel, G., Olsen, R., Wheeler, F., & Cohen, M. (1976). *The museum visitor and orientational media: An experimental comparison of different approaches in the Smithsonian Institution and National Museum of History and Technology*. New York: City University of New York Center for Environment and Behavior.

Winkler, R. C., & Winnett, R. A. (1982). Behavioral interventions in resource management. *American Psychologist, 37,* 421–435.

Winneke, G., & Kastka, J. (1987). Comparison of odour-annoyance data from different industrial sources: Problems and implications. In H. S. Koelega (Ed.), *Environmental annoyance: Characterization, measurement, and control* (pp. 129–138). Amsterdam: Elsevier Science Publishers.

Winnett, R. A., Hatcher, J., Leckliter, I., Ford, T. R., Fishback, J. F., Riley, A. W., & Love, S. (1981). *The effects of videotape modeling and feedback on residential comfort, the thermal environment and electricity consumption: Winter and summer studies*. Unpublished manuscript. Department of Psychology, Virginia Polytechnic Institute and State University.

Winnett, R. A., Kagel, J. H., Battalio, R. C., & Winkler, R. C. (1978). Effects of monetary rebates, feedback and information on residential energy conservation. *Journal of Applied Psychology, 63,* 73–78.

Winnett, R. A., Neale, M. S., & Grier, H. C. (1979). The effects of self-monitoring and feedback on residential electricity consumption. *Journal of Applied Behavior Analysis, 12,* 173–184.

Winnett, R. A., Neale, M. S., Williams, K. R., Yokley, J., & Kauder, H. (1979). The effects of individual and group feedback on residential electricity consumption: Three replications. *Journal of Environmental Systems, 8,* 217–233.

Winnett, R. A., & Nietzel, M. T. (1975). Behavioral ecology: Contingency management of consumer energy use. *American Journal of Community Psychology, 3,* 123–133.

Winston, B. J. (1974). The relationship of awareness to concern for environmental quality among selected high school students. *Dissertation Abstracts International, 35A,* 3412.

Wirth, I. (1938). Urbanism as a way of life. *American Journal of Sociology, 44,* 1–24.

Wofford, J. C. (1966). Negative ionization: An investigation of behavioral effects. *Journal of Experimental Psychology, 71,* 608–611.

Wohlwill, J. F. (1966). The physical environment: A problem for a psychology of stimulation. *Journal of Social Issues, 22,* 29–38.

Wohlwill, J. F. (1973). The environment is not in the head. In W. F. E. Prieser (Ed.), *Environmental design research: Vol 2. Symposia and workshops*. Proceedings of the Fourth International Environmental Design Research Association Conference. Stroudsburg, PA: Dowden, Hutchinson, & Ross.

Wohlwill, J. F. (1974). Human response to levels of environmental stimulation. *Human Ecology, 2,* 127–147.

Wohlwill, J. F. (1976a). Environmental aesthetics: The environment as a source of affect. In I. Altman & J. F. Wohlwill (Eds.), *Human behavior and environment: Advances in theory and research* (Vol. 1). New York: Plenum.

Wohlwill, J. F. (1976b). Environmental aesthetics: The emerging discipline of environmental psychology. *American Psychologist, 25,* 303–312.

Wohlwill, J. F. (1976c). Searching for the environment in environmental cognition research: A commentary on research strategy. In G. W. Moore & R. G. Golledge (eds.), *Environmental knowing*. Stroudsburg, PA: Dowden, Hutchinson, & Ross.

Wohlwill, J. F. (1983). The concept of nature: A psychologist's view. In I. Altman & J. F. Wohlwill (Eds.), *Behavior and the natural environment*. New York: Plenum.

Wohlwill, J. F., & Harris, G. (1980). Response to congruity or contrast for man-made features in natural-recreation settings. *Leisure Sciences, 3,* 349–365.

Wohlwill, J., & Kohn, I. (1973). The environment as experienced by the migrant: An adaptation level view. *Representative Research in Social Psychology, 4,* 135–164.

Wolfe, M. (1975). Room size and density: Behavior patterns in a children's psychiatric facility. *Environment and Behavior, 7,* 199–225.

Womble, P., & Studebaker, S. (1981). Crowding in a national park campground: Katmai National Monument in Alaska. *Environment and Behavior, 13,* 557–573.

Woodhead, M. M. (1964). Visual searching in intermittent noise. *Journal of Sound Vibration, 1,* 157–161.

Woodson, P. P., Buzzi, R., Nil, R., & Battig, K. (1986). Effects of smoking on vegetative reactivity to noise in women. *Psychophysiology, 23,* 272–282.

Woodward, N. J., & Wallston, B. S. (1987). Age and health care beliefs: Self-efficacy as a mediator of low desire for control. *Psychology and Aging, 2,* 3–8.

Worchel, S., & Brown, E. H. (1984). The role of plausibility in influencing environmental attributions. *Journal of Experimental Social Psychology, 20,* 86–96.

Worchel, S., & Teddlie, C. (1976). The experience of crowding: A two-factor theory. *Journal of Personality and Social Psychology, 34,* 36–40.

World Development Report. (1987). Published for World Bank, Washington, DC (Table 33, 266–277). Oxford University Press.

Wormith, J. S. (1984). Personal space of incarcerated offenders. *Journal of Clinical Psychology, 40*, 815–827.

Wortman, C. B., & Brehm, J. W. (1975). Responses to uncontrollable outcomes: An integration of reactance theory and the learned helplessness model. In L. Berkowitz (Ed.), *Advances in experimental social psychology* (Vol. 8, pp. 277–336). New York: Academic Press.

Wright, B., & Rainwater, L. (1962). The meaning of color. *Journal of General Psychology, 67*, 89–99.

Wright, R. A. (1984). Motivation, anxiety, and the difficulty of avoidant control. *Journal of Personality and Social Psychology, 46*, 1376–1388.

Wyndham, C. H. (1970). Adaptation to heat and cold. In D. H. K. Lee & D. Minard (Eds.), *Physiology, environment, and man* (pp. 177–204). New York: Academic Press.

Wynne-Edwards, V. C. (1962). *Animal dispersion in relation to social behavior.* Edinburgh: Oliver & Boyd.

Yamagishi, T. (1986). The provision of a sanctioning system as a public good. *Journal of Personality and Social Psychology, 51*, 110–116.

Yancey, W. L. (1972). Architecture, interaction, and social control: The case of a large scale housing project. In J. F. Wohlwill & D. H. Carson (Eds.), *Environment and the social sciences: Perspectives and applications.* Washington, DC: American Psychological Association.

Yinon, Y., & Bizman, A. (1980). Noise, success, and failure as determinants of helping behavior. *Personality and Social Psychology Bulletin, 6*, 125–130.

Young, M., & Willmott, P. (1957). *Family and kinship in East London.* Baltimore: Penguin.

Zajonc, R. B. (1968). Attitudinal effects of mere exposure. *Journal of Personality and Social Psychology, 8*, 1–29.

Zeisel, J. (1975). *Sociology and architectural design. Social science frontiers* (6). New York: Russell Sage Foundation.

Zeisel (1981). *Inquiry by design: Tools for environment-behavior research.* Monterey, CA: Brooks/Cole.

Zeisel, J., & Griffin, M. (1975). *Charlesview housing: A diagnostic evaluation.* Cambridge, MA: Harvard University Graduate School of Design.

Zika, S., & Chamberlain, K. (1987). Relation of hassles and personality to subjective well-being. *Journal of Personality and Social Psychology, 53*, 155–162.

Zillmann, D. (1979). *Hostility and aggression.* Hillsdale, NJ: Erlbaum.

Zillmann, D. (1983). Arousal and aggression. In R. G. Geen & E. Donnerstein (Eds.), *Aggression: Theoretical and empirical reviews* (Vol. 1, pp. 75–101). New York: Academic Press.

Zillmann, D., Baron, R. A., & Tamborini, R. (1981).

Social costs of smoking: Effects of tobacco smoke on hostile behavior. *Journal of Applied Social Psychology, 11*, 548–561.

Zimbardo, P. G. (1969). The human choices: Individuation, reason, and order versus deindividuation, impulse, and chaos. In W. J. Arnold & D. Levine (Eds.), *Nebraska Symposium on Motivation.* Lincoln: University of Nebraska Press.

Zimring, C. M. (1981). Post-occupancy evaluation: An overview. *Environment and Behavior, 12*, 429–451.

Zimring, C., Carpman, J. R., & Michelson, W. (1987). Design for special populations: Mentally retarded persons, children, hospital visitors. In D. Stokols & I. Altman (Eds.), *Handbook of environmental psychology* (Vol. 2, pp. 919–949). New York: Wiley-Interscience.

Zimring, C. M., & Reizenstein, J. E. (1981). Post-occupancy evaluation: An overview. *Environment and Behavior, 12*, 429–451.

Zlutnick, S., & Altman, I. (1972). Crowding and human behavior. In J. Wohlwill & D. Carson (Eds.), *Environment and the social sciences: Perspectives and applications* (pp. 44–58). Washington, DC: American Psychological Association.

Zube, E. H. (1973). Rating everyday rural landscapes for the Northeastern U.S. *Landscape Architecture, 63*, 92–97.

Zube, E. H., & Mills, L. V., Jr. (1976). Cross-cultural explorations in landscape perception. In E. H. Zube (Ed.), *Studies in landscape perception* (Publication No. R-76-1). Amherst: Institute for Man and Environment, University of Massachusetts.

Zube, E. H., Pitt, D. G., & Anderson, T. W. (1974). *Perception and measurements of scenic resources in the southern Connecticut River Valley.* Amherst: Institute for Man and Environment, University of Massachusetts.

Zube, E. H., Pitt, D. G., & Evans, G. W. (1983). A lifespan developmental study of landscape assessment. *Journal of Environmental Psychology, 3*, 115–128.

Zube, E. H., Sell, J. L., & Taylor, J. G (1982). Landscape perception: Research, application and theory. *Landscape Planning, 9*, 1–33.

Zube, E. H., Vining, J., Law, C. S., & Bechtel, R. B. (1985). Perceived urban residential quality: A cross-cultural bimodal study. *Environment and Behavior, 17*, 327–350.

Zubek, J. P. (Ed.) (1969). *Sensory deprivation: Fifteen years of research.* New York: Appleton-Century-Crofts.

Zuckerman, M. (1979). *Sensation seeking: Beyond the optimal level of arousal.* Hillsdale, NJ: Erlbaum.

Zweig, J., & Csank, J. (1975). Effects of relocation on chronically ill geriatric patients of a medical unit: Mortality rates. *Journal of the American Geriatrics Society, 23*, 132–136.

Zweigenhaft, R. (1976). Personal space in the faculty office: Desk placement and the student. *Journal of Applied Psychology, 61*, 529–532.

ACKNOWLEDGMENTS OF PERMISSION

Excerpt on pages 318–319 reprinted by permission of the Putnam Publishing Group from Son of the Great Society by Art Buchwald. Copyright © 1966 by Art Buchwald.

Excerpt on page 351 from Jacobs, J. *The Death of Great American Cities*. New York: Random House, 1961.

Figure on page 18 from Srivastava, R. and Peel, T. Human movement as a function of color stimulation, Environmental Research and Development Foundation, 1968. Fig. 4, p. 25.

Figure on page 28 adapted from Goldstein, B. *Sensation and Perception*, Third Edition, © 1989 by Wadsworth, Inc. Adapted by permission of the publisher.

Figure on page 32 adapted from Brunswik, E. (1956). *Perception and the Representative Design of Psychological Experiments*. Berkeley: University of California Press.

Figure on page 40 from Russell, J. A. and Lanius, U. F. (1984). Adaptation level and the affective appraisal of environments. *Journal of Environmental Psychology*, vol. 4.

Figure on page 63 adapted from Appleyard, D. (1970). Styles and methods of structuring a city. *Environment and Behavior*, vol. 2, pp. 100–118. Reprinted by permission of Sage Publications, Inc.

Figure on page 67 adapted from Abler, Adams, & Gould (1971). *Spatial Organization*. Englewood Cliffs, NJ: Prentice-Hall. Reprinted by permission.

Figure on page 70 from Downs, R. M. and Stea, D. (1977). *Maps in Minds: Reflections on Cognitive Mapping*. Reprinted by permission of Harper and Row.

Figure on page 82 adapted from Levine, M. (1982). You are here maps: Psychological considerations. *Environment and Behavior*, vol. 14, pp. 221–237. Reprinted by permission of Sage Publications.

Figure on page 83 adapted from Levine, M. (1982). You are here maps: Psychological considerations. *Environment and Behavior*, vol. 14, pp. 221–237. Reprinted by permission of Sage Publications.

Figure on page 93 from Wicker, A. W., and Kirmeyer, S. (1976). From church to laboratory to national park. In W. Wapner, B. Kaplan, and S. Cohen (Eds.), *Experiencing the Environment*. Reprinted by permission of Plenum Publishing.

Figures on page 129 from Gardner, E. (1975). *Fundamentals of Neurology*, Sixth Edition, © 1975 by Saunders College Publishing, a division of Holt, Rinehart and Winston, Inc., reprinted by permission of the publisher.

Figure on page 130 from Turk, A., Turk, J., and Wittes, J. T. (1978). *Environmental Science*, Third Edition, copyright © 1978 by Saunders College Publishing, a division of Holt, Rinehart and Winston, Inc., reprinted by permission of the author.

Figures on page 137 adapted from Cherek, D. R. (1985). Effects of acute exposure to increased levels of background industrial noise on cigarette smoking behavior. *International Archives of Occupational and Environmental Health*, vol. 56, pp. 23–30. Reprinted by permission of Springer-Verlag.

space invasions in the lavoratory: Suggestive evidence from arousal. *Journal of Personality and Social Psychology*, vol. 33, pp. 541–546. Copyright 1976 by the American Psychological Association. Reprinted by permission of the author and publisher.

Table on page 256 based on Altman, I. (1975). *The Environment and Social Behavior*. Monterey, CA: Brooks/Cole.

Table on page 258 based on Taylor, R. B. (1978). Human territoriality: A review and a model for future research. *Cornell Journal of Social Relations*, vol. 13, pp. 125–151.

Table on page 266 reprinted from Schwartz, B., and Barsky, S. P. (1977). The home advantage. *Social Forces*, vol. 55, 1975. Copyright © the University of North Carolina Press.

Figures on page 269 from Brown and Altman, 1983; Brown, B. B., (1985). Residential Territories Cues to Burglary. *Journal of Architectural Planning Research*, 2, 231–243.

Figure on page 270 courtesy of Jury Analysts Inc., 315 S. Allen, No. 225, State College, PA.

Figure on page 272 from Duke, M. P. and Nowicki, S. (1972). A new measure and social learning model for interpersonal distance. *Journal of Experimental Research in Personality*, vol. 6, pp. 119–132. Used by permission of Academic Press.

Figure on page 277 from "Population Density and Social Pathology" by John B. Calhoun. Copyright © 1962 by Scientific American Inc. All rights reserved.

Figure on page 286 from Ross, M., Layton, B., Erickson, B., and Schloper, J. (1973). Affect, racial regard, and reactions to crowding. *Journal of Personality and Social Psychology*, vol. 28, pp. 69–76.

Figure on page 288 based on Paulus, P. B., McCain, G. and Cox, V. (1978). Death rates, psychiatric commitments, blood pressure and perceived crowding as a function of institutional crowding. *Environmental Psychology and Nonverbal Behavior*, vol. 36, pp. 997–999.

Table on page 289 based on Baron, R., Mandel, D., Adams, C., and Griffin, L. (1976). Effects of social density in university residential environments. *Journal of Personality and Social Psychology*, vol. 34, pp. 434–446.

Table on page 290 based on Epstein, Y., and Karlin, R. (1975). Effects of acute experimental crowding. *Journal of Applied Social Psychology*, vol. 5, pp. 34–53.

Figures on page 291 from Baum, A. and Valins, S. (1977). *Architecture and Social Behavior: Psychological Studies of Social Density*. Hillsdale, N.J.: Erlbaum. Published with permission of Lawrence Erlbaum Associates.

Table on page 294 based on Paulus, P., Annis, A., Setta, M., Schade, J., and Matthews, R. (1976). Crowding does affect task performance. *Journal of Personality and Social Psychology*, vol. 34, pp. 248–253.

Figure on page 295 based on Heller, J., Groff, B., and Solomon, S. (1977). Toward an understanding of crowding: The role of physical interaction. *Journal of Personality and Social Psychology*, vol. 35, pp. 83–190.

Table on page 297 from *Newsweek*, Aug. 29, 1988. Copyright © 1988, Newsweek, Inc. All rights reserved. Reprinted by permission.

Table on page 323 from Boyer, R. and Savageau, D. (1985). Putting it all together: Finding the best places to live in America, *Places Rated Almanac*, 2e, Chicago: Rand McNally.

Table on page 324 based on Loftus, G. R. (1985). Twenty original places rated, *Psychology Today*, vol. 24, p. 10.

Table on page 329 from Berstein, M. H. (1979). The pace of life: Revisited. *International Journal of Psychology*, vol. 14, p. 84.

Table on page 333 from Newman, J., and McCauley, C. (1977). Eye contact with strangers in city, suburb, and small town. *Environment and Behavior*, vol. 9, pp. 547–557. Reprinted by permission of Sage Publications, Inc.

Table on page 337 from *Uniform Crime Reports*, 1979.

Table on page 344 adapted from Haney, W., and Knowles, E. (1978). Perception of neighborhoods by city and suburban residents. *Human Ecology,* vol. 6, pp. 201–214. Reprinted by permission of Plenum Publishing.

Figure on page 366 adapted from Lang, J. (1987). *Creating Architectural Theory: The Role of the Behavioral Sciences in Environmental Design.* New York: Van Nostrad Reinhold Co.

Figure on page 372 from Zeisel, J. (1975). The design cycle. *Sociology and Architectural Design.* Social Science Frontiers, No. 6. New York: Russell Sage Foundation. © 1975 Russell Sage Foundation. Used by permission.

Figure on page 375 adapted from Zeisel J. (1981). *Inquiry by Design.* Pacific Grove, CA: Brooks/Cole.

Figures on page 409 from *Help! For the Small Museum.* Boulder, CO: Pruett Press, 1969.

Figure on page 410 reprinted, with permission, from *Museum News,* January 15, 1933, the American Association of Museums. All rights reserved.

Figure on page 417 from Trites et al. (1970). *Environment and Behavior,* vol. 2, pp. 303– 334. Reprinted by permission of Sage Publications, Inc.

Figure on page 438 from Chapanis, A. (1976). Engineering psychology. In M. Dunnette (Ed.). *Handbook of Industrial and Organizational Psychology.* Chicago: Rand McNally. Reprinted by permission of John Wiley and Sons.

Figure on page 452 reprinted courtesy of the Haggin Museum.

Figure on page 453 adapted from Driver, B. and Brown, P. (1983). Contributions of behavioral scientists to recreation resource management. In I. Altman and J. F. Wohwill, (Eds.), *Behavior in the Natural Environment.* New York: Plenum Press.

Figure on page 485 from Clark, R., Hendee, J., and Burgess, R. (1972). The experimental control of littering. *Journal of Environmental Education,* vol. 4, pp. 22–28.

Figure on page 488 from Cialdini, R. (1977). Unpublished manuscript, Arizona State University.

Table on page 493 from Geller, E., Winnett, R. and Everett, P. (1982). *Preserving the Environment: New Strategies for Behavior Change.* NY: Pergamon.

PHOTO CREDITS

Figures: 1–2, Marc Schaeffer; 1–3, John Rundell; 5–1, Joel Gordon, 1981; 5–7, Sheldon Cohen; 6–9, Courtesy of the Sunbox Co.; 7–1A, Benyas-Kaufman/Black Star, 1984; 7–1B, Ed Lirkle/Black Star, 1981; 7–2A, Leo Touchet/Black Star, 1969; 7–2B, Owen Franken/Stock Boston; 7–3, Courtesy of the Anchorage Museum; 7–4, AP/Wide World Photos; 7–5, UPI; 7–6, Marc Schaeffer; 7–7, Rene Burri/Magnum; 7–8, Environmental Protection Agency; 8–1, Marc Antman/Stock Boston; 8–5, Joel Gordon, 1978; 8–9A&B, Eric Knowles; 8–12, Raymond Depardon/Magnum; 9–1, Owen Franken/ Stock Boston; 9–4, Bruno Barbey/Magnum; 9–1, Bruno Barbey/Magnum; 9–5, A. Meyerson/Image Bank; 9–6, Jake Rajs/Image Bank; 9–11, Patrick Zachmann/Magnum; 9–12, G. Brimacombe/Image Bank; 10–1B, Marc Romanelli/Image Bank; 10–2, Wide World Photos; 10–4A, Alfred Gescheidt/ Image Bank; 10–4B, M. Beebe/Image Bank; 10–8, Billy E. Barnes/Black Star; 10–9, UPI; 10–10, Joel Gordon, 1978; 11–2, Derek Lepper/Black Star; 11–3, Steffens-Colmer/Black Star; 12–2, Ken Tremblay; 12–6, From A. Neal, *Help! For the Small Museum.* Pruett Publishing, 1969; 13–5A&B, John Rundell; 13–8, The Haggin Collection, The Haggin Museum, Stockton, California.

AUTHOR INDEX

SUBJECT INDEX